THE GUINNESS WHO'S WHO OF

FIFTIES MUSIC

General Editor: Colin Larkin

Introduction by John Martland

GUINNESS PUBLISHING

Dedicated to Guy Mitchell, who started all this.

First published in 1993 by
GUINNESS PUBLISHING LTD
33 London Road, Enfield, Middlesex EN2 6DJ, England

GUINNESS is a registered trademark of Guinness Publishing Ltd

British Library Cataloguing-in-Publication data
A catalogue record for this book is available from the British Library

ISBN 0-85112-732-0

Conceived, designed, edited and produced by
SQUARE ONE BOOKS LTD
Iron Bridge House, 3 Bridge Approach, Chalk Farm, London NW1 8BD
Editor and Designer: Colin Larkin
Picture Editors: Colin Larkin and John Martland
Editorial and production assistant: Susan Pipe
Logo concept: Darren Perry

Image set by L & S Communications Ltd

Printed and bound in Great Britain by The Bath Press

EDITORS NOTE

The Guinness Who's Who Of Fifties Music forms a part of the multi-volume *Guinness Encyclopedia Of Popular Music*. A further 16 specialist single volumes are planned in the near future.

Already available:
The Guinness Who's Who Of Indie And New Wave Music.
The Guinness Who's Who Of Heavy Metal.
The Guinness Who's Who Of Sixties Music.
The Guinness Who's Who Of Seventies Music.
The Guinness Who's Who Of Jazz.
The Guinness Who's Who Of Country Music.
The Guinness Who's Who Of Blues.
The Guinness Who's Who Of Folk.
The Guinness Who's Who Of Soul.

The glorious fifties were the years of cosy post-war euphoria, the years of actually having spare cash to indulge in record players or a 'stereogram''. This pivotal era before Beatlemania has often been unfairly overshadowed by subsequent musical decades. Casual observers will note that it was the age of the Wurlitzer juke box, beautiful convertable cars, smart suits, Brylcreme and pretty frocks. It was also the decade of rock 'n' roll: Bill Haley, Chuck Berry, Little Richard, the Platters, Fats Domino, the Everly Brothers, Buddy Holly and the greatest musical icon of the 20th century, Elvis Presley. Of vital importance to the shaping of 50s pop are vocalists such as Perry Como, Guy Mitchell, Frankie Laine, Johnnie Ray, Dean Martin and the great female stars Doris Day, Peggy Lee, Rosemary Clooney, Kay Starr and Teresa Brewer. The single most influential artist of 50s popular music was Frank Sinatra, who in turn spawned a host of imitators both good and bad. While Britain had to wait until the 60s to assert itself as a major force, it did produce Tommy Steele, Marty Wilde, Cliff Richard, Dickie Valentine, Dennis Lotis, Ted Heath, Ronnie Hilton, Lonnie Donegan, Petula Clark, Ruby Murray, Lita Roza, Joan Regan and the highly underrated Alma Cogan. Stage Musicals were having a golden age with *The Pajama Game*, *The King And I*, *My fair Lady* and *West Side Story* all producing memorable hits. We have attempted to include artists that convey the flavour of the fifties, and through their inclusion show just how important these years became in positioning 'pop' for the decade that was to follow. In selecting entries for this single volume we have attempted to include as many artists as space would allow. Further suggestions and additions for the next edition will be considered by writing to the Editor.

In the preparation of this work contributions were received from Bruce Crowther, Peter Doggett, Brian Hogg, Colin Larkin, Spencer Leigh, John Martland, Johnny Rogan, Jeff Tamarkin, Hugh T. Wilson, Tony Burke, Rick Christian, Alan Clayson, John Eley, Dave Laing, Graham Lock, Dave MacAleer, Alex Ogg, Robert Pruter and Steve Smith.

Photographic acknowledgements: To Tony Gale of Pictorial Press, who has an amazing photographic archive of many original items. He supplied every picture inside this book.

Thanks to John Martland who joined us at a

very difficult time and took to the task with care, enthusiasm and good humour. His specialist knowledge of the 50s enabled us to obtain up-to-date information on many artists who have had a low profile for many years. John Martland's following introduction captures the decade perfectly. To Susan Pipe for her continuing super-calm efficiency in putting it all together at the end, especially now that she has begun to master Quark XPress. To Sue Craig, Jo Ford and Oscar O'Connor of Interskill who I am still talking to. To Chris Stoker and Andy Reid of Macawmac for solving countless Apple problems. To June McLachlan and John Burton for still sending in cuttings and obituarys. Messrs Brian Hogg, Dave Laing, Fred Dellar, Neil Slaven, Alex Ogg and Peter Doggett for usually coming up with the right answers. To everybody at Carlin Music for making us so welcome and to Kip Trevor, Jane Nesbitt, Amos Biegun and Dave Carroll for their additional help. To my family, who no longer believe me when I tell them this is the last book (for a while).

Colin Larkin, July 1993

INTRODUCTION

They're often called 'The Fabulous 50s' - the years that led from post-war austerity into the emancipated 60s; when 'popular music' went 'pop', and was transformed beyond recognition; and when any youngster who could play a few guitar chords and wiggle their hips at the same time - could hit the big time - in no time at all. No wonder that, by 1957, when prime minister Harold Macmillan was telling the people of Britain: 'You've never had it so good!'; musically, at least, many of the nation's teenagers were beginning to believe he might be right.

Yet, in England, immediately following the dawn of the decade, things seemed much the same as before: the national football team lost in the World Cup (to the USA!), petrol (de-rationed) was three shillings a gallon, Burgess and MacLean (along with a lot of the UK's top secret information) had re-located to Russia; and Billy Cotton was *still* insisting: 'I've Got A Lovely Bunch Of Coconuts'.

In the USA, however, the signs of change were beginning to emerge, even if they were small, and not all that obvious. Looking back, one of the first significant pointers came in 1949, when *Billboard* magazine, which had been charting the progress of the best-selling records and sheet music for some years, began listing the most popular 'Rhythm & Blues' records, reflecting the growing influence of black music, which, in a more sanitised form, would, in the not too distant future, become known as 'rockabilly' and 'rock 'n' roll'. Those terms meant nothing in Britain in the

days of yore long before satellite communications and MTV. In fact, if a young couple enjoying a night out at their local Palais de Danse, had requested the bandleader to 'give us some rock', the odds are that they would have ended up with a long, cylindrical (usually pink) piece of confectionery with the name of a seaside town printed through the middle. Of course, that would only apply after 1953, when war-time sweet rationing came to an end. Nothing similar to *Billboard*'s barometers existed in the UK until November 1952, when the *New Musical Express* announced its first 'Record Hit Parade', but since that contained artists and material such as Al Martino ('Here In My Heart') and Max Bygraves ('Cowpuncher's Cantata'), it gave no clues as the radical musical changes that were soon to take place. Even Vera Lynn, the 'Forces Sweetheart', and still enormously popular now that the 'boys' were back home, was on that first UK chart with 'Forget-Me-Not' and 'Auf Wiedersehen Sweetheart'. The latter record became the first by a female British artist to reach the number one spot in the USA - and it had the nerve to stay there for nine weeks!

In 1950, Frank Sinatra, another wartime idol who had been the bobby-soxers' blue-eyed boy for most of the 40s, came under the influence of the US A&R producer Mitch Miller. This liaison eventually lead to Sinatra making a recording of 'Mama Will Bark', on which he was joined by a woman and a man pretending to be a dog. Hardly surprising then, that when he appeared at the London Palladium in July, his career was sinking faster than the Oxford crew did in the University Boat Race of 1951. The kids had stopped swooning, and the English critics were very unkind: 'It is like being force-fed with treacle', wrote one. Like Sinatra himself, they would change their tune before long - his comeback, sparked off by an Academy Award-winning performance in *From Here To Eternity*, was only three years away, and would continue on and off for a good 40 years after that.

In 1953, whilst that particular Frankie was earning his Oscar, another Frankie - Laine - was riding high in the USA on the strength of early 50s hits such as 'The Cry Of The Wild Goose', 'Jezebel', 'Jealousy' and 'High Noon (Do Not Forsake Me)'. Far more 'hairy-chested' in style than the other, 'bony baritone', Laine also spent a record total of 27 weeks at the top of the UK Hit Parade, with a pop version of Boudleaux Bryant's country-styled 'Hey Joe', along with heart-rending ballads such as 'I Believe' and 'Answer Me'. In June of that year, Edmund Hillary and Sherpa Tensing climbed even higher than that - to the roof of the world: Mount Everest was conquered at last. The news of their triumph was released on the morning of the Coronation of Queen Elizabeth II. Billy Cotton, 'coconuts' thankfully discarded, captured the affectionate mood of the nation with his recording of 'In A Golden Coach (There's A Heart Of Gold)'. The USA had its own 'coronation' in 1953, when Dwight D. Eisenhower, ('Ike' to his friends), took sufficient time off from the golf course to be inaugurated as his country's 34th President. In September, his eventual successor, John Fitzgerald Kennedy, married Miss Jacqueline Lee Bouvier, thereby beginning a process that would result, in the words of Alan Jay Lerner, in 'one, brief, shining moment, that was known as 'Camelot''.

Kennedy's rise to political power during the 50s coincided with the staggering technological developments that were taking place in the USA, especially in the race with the Soviet Union to put a man in space. More down to earth were the technical changes in domestic entertainment: on both sides of the Atlantic self-contained record playing equipment, with light-weight 'pickups', was taking the place of ancient phonographs and gramophones. Plastic records of seven, 10, and 12 inches in diameter, spinning at a bewildering 45 and 33 revolutions per minute, were replacing the old fashioned shellac 78s. Many of those were already broken anyway, having been dropped from a great height on primitive 'auto-change' equipment. How appropriate it seems that all this happened well before Jack Kennedy became the US President in 1960. It's difficult, if not impossible, to imagine him having to put a 78 rpm record on the White House turntable!

Frank Sinatra, a favourite of the Kennedys, was one of the first major artists to take advantage of the new, exciting formats. In the early 50s he broke free from the confines of the three minute 'single', and then, in 1956, sang 15 songs on his exhilarating 'long playing' record (LP), *Songs For Swingin' Lovers!* It became a number 2 album in the USA, entered the *singles* charts in Britain, and has remained in the Capitol catalogue ever since. Naturally, it was recorded in 'Hi-Fi' sound, the then currently fashionable phrase which apparently had something to do with 'flutter on your top, and wow on your bottom'. In layman's terms it simply meant an almost complete absence of the background crackle and hiss that used to sound as if a member of the band was cooking the singer's breakfast for him. Superior audio reproduction was, however, accompanied by food for thought - especially for the likes of Sinatra, Slim Whitman, Doris Day, Rosemary Clooney, Jimmy Young, Dickie Valentine, and the other chart-toppers of the early 50s. By 1956, rock 'n' roll was here - and to stay. Leading the onslaught (because that's what it amounted to) was Bill Haley, complete with kiss-curl and Comets.

Haley's breakthrough came in 1955, when his

'Rock Around The Clock' spent eight weeks at the top of the US chart after being played over the opening credits of the controversial and hard-hitting drama, *Blackboard Jungle*. A year later it lent its title to a second-feature film which generated a sensational response in the USA and many other countries around the world. When it was released in the conservative UK, the film 'caused riots in cinemas all around the country, as 'Teddy Boys', decked out in draped jackets with velvet collars, bootlace ties, and 'D.A.' haircuts, jived in the aisles' before being ejected into the arms of the startled constabulary. Banished to the pavements, they missed some of the movie's other highspots, such as the Platters' 'Only You' and 'The Great Pretender', several other numbers by Haley including 'See You Later, Alligator' and 'Razzle Dazzle', Freddie Bell And The Bellboys' 'Giddy Up A Ding Dong', and an appearance by the fast-talking Alan Freed. Freed, a US disc jockey, is generally credited (especially by himself) with coining the phrase 'rock 'n' roll' in an effort to camouflage the black rhythm and blues music he played on his *Moondog's Rock 'N' Roll Party* radio programme in the early 50s.

Right behind Haley in the first wave of the musical invasion, were senior lieutenants, Little Richard with his 'Tutti-Fruitti', 'Long Tall Sally' and 'Rip It Up'; Chuck Berry, armed with 'Maybellene', 'School Day'. 'Rock & Roll Music', 'Sweet Little Sixteen', and 'Johnny B. Goode'; Jerry Lee Lewis, with 'Great Balls Of Fire', 'Breathless', and 'Whole Lotta Shakin' Going On'; and Fats Domino, bringing up the rear, with his 'Ain't That A Shame', 'I'm In Love Again' and 'Blueberry Hill' Reinforcements included Gene Vincent, Eddie Cochran, Buddy Holly, the Everly Brothers, Ricky Nelson, Duane Eddy, Carl Perkins, Conway Twitty, and many more. The five-star General in charge of the advancing forces was, of course, Elvis Presley.

Early on in the campaign it became obvious that the General was exposing too much of himself to the opposition (ie parents of young girls). This became a subject of national concern 1956, when, after storming the heights of the US and UK charts with 'Heartbreak Hotel' and 'Blue Suede Shoes', he appeared on Ed Sullivan's top-rated US television show, performing 'Hound Dog' and 'Love Me Tender' 'as if he was sneering with his legs'. For some time afterwards he was only televised from the waist up. That still proved far too much for a great many US citizens, especially when they realised to their horror that 'Elvis' rhymed with 'pelvis'. Up until that time, their idea of a 'good mover' had always been Fred Astaire. From an early stage in his career, Elvis's off-stage movements were master-minded by one Colonel Parker, who, for mysterious personal reasons allegedly known only to the US immigration authorities (if Parker left the country, would Parker get back in again?), was reluctant to allow his client to appear outside of the USA. In response to one UK impresario's offer of £250,000, he wired: 'That's OK for me - now, how about my boy?'.

Presley apart, the American stars flocked to the UK during the 50s, so much so that the London Palladium was christened 'the 49th state of the Union'. Johnnie Ray sobbed there, Billy Daniels weaved 'That Old Black Magic', and others such as Lena Horne, Nat 'King' Cole, Judy Garland, Dean Martin and Jerry Lewis, Danny Kaye, and Guy Mitchell, delighted audiences with their sheer professionalism. Mitchell in particular, one of the decade's most popular and likeable singing stars, captivated the British public with a string of hits that included 'Pretty Black Eyed Susie', 'Look At That Girl', 'Cloud Lucky Seven', 'Chicka Boom', Rock-A-Billy', and 'Heartaches By The Number'. However, early in 1957, his records of 'Singing The Blues' and 'Knee Deep In The Blues' met with stern opposition, and vied for the UK top spot with cover versions by a local boy, a typical 'cockney sparrer', named Tommy Steele.

Steele, a 20-year-old ex-merchant seaman with a seemingly permanent grin, was the product of the 50s 'frothy-coffee' scene, the focus of which was the 2I's coffee bar in London's Soho district. The venue was a hot-bed of young musical talent which harboured Adam ('What Do You Want?') Faith; several future Shadows, such as Jet Harris, Tony Meehan, and Hank Marvin, who, led by Wally Whyton, formed the Vipers skiffle group around 1956 B.C. (Before Cliff). Another regular 2I's caffeine consumer, Lionel Bart, provided Steele with his first hit, 'Rock With The Caveman' and several of the singer's other chart entries, including 'Butterfingers', 'Handful Of Songs', 'Water Water', and 'Little White Bull' (1959). Shortly afterwards, Steele (*Half A Sixpence*), and Bart (*Fings Ain't What They Used T'Be* and *Oliver!*), swapped East End pop for West End musicals, but not before Bart had given Cliff Richard's career a kick-start with his 'Living Doll', which became Richard's first UK number 1.

Steele's name is often linked with skiffle, but it really was only the first rung of a musical ladder he was destined to climb (or descend - depending on your point of view) on the way to a comfortable existence as an 'all-round entertainer'. The latter occupation was the declared aim of many a young rocker in those days - along with the ambition (if he was ever able to prise the money away from his manager) to buy his old mum and dad a retirement bungalow by the sea.

In the UK during the late 50s, skiffle and the embryonic 'trad jazz' existed side by side. Lonnie Donegan, a former sideman with traditionalists Ken Colyer and Chris Barber, was the undisputed leader of the skiffle brigade: his ebullient 'Rock Island Line' is supposed to have been the catalyst that begat the boom in washboard and tea chest sales. It was closely followed by 'Cumberland Gap', 'Gamblin' Man', 'Puttin' On the Style', 'The Battle Of New Orleans', and many others. Shrewdly, he broadened his image by including several comedy items in his act,

such as 'Does Your Chewing Gum Lose It's Flavour' and 'My Old Man's A Dustman'. Donegan was one of the first guests on *Six-Five Special*, which began its journey in February 1957. Introduced by Pete Murray and Josephine Douglas, it was BBC Television's first attempt to deal with 'this new-fangled music'. The BBC's radio arm was not so flexible, sticking with safe, old fashioned record programmes left over from the 40s, such as *Family Favourites* and *Housewives Choice*. In the USA, the myriad of radio stations easily accommodated the musical maelstrom of the late 50s and early 60s, but it was to be 1967, and the enforced birth of Radio 1 following the success of the North Sea pirate stations, before BBC radio reluctantly embraced contemporary pop - and even then, it was a shotgun wedding.

In 1958, that scenario probably never even crossed the minds of millions of parents as they breathed collective sighs of relief when Elvis Presley lost his freedom (and his sideburns), and joined the US Army in March 1958. Instead of driving their daughters wild, Elvis drove tanks in German for two years, relying on stock-piled material to keep the fans happy, and to retain a blue-suede foothold in the upper reaches of the charts. With supreme irony, his first public performance following demobilization in 1960 was on a Frank Sinatra television special. There they were, the two dominant musical personalities of the 50s, each representing tastes and ideas that could hardly be further apart, reluctantly rubbing shoulders for the sake of the ratings. Elvis suggested they sing one of each other's songs: Frank agreed: 'OK, you do 'Witchcraft', and I'll do . . . one of the other ones!'. That turned out to be an uneasy up-tempo version of 'Love Me Tender', one of Presley's five number 1's of 1956 - and the divide widened even further.

Another of Elvis's 'big five' of 1956, 'Hound Dog', was written by Jerry Leiber and Mike Stoller, the top rock 'n' roll writers and record producers of the 50s. As well as concocting numerous hits such as 'Yakety Yak', 'Charlie Brown', and 'Poison Ivy' for the Coasters and others, the team also contributed the title songs to *Jailhouse Rock* and *King Creole*, two of Presley's best films, made shortly before Colonel Parker decided that 'his boy' should waste his talent (while making millions of dollars) parading his pectorals in a series of beach movies. Presley himself is credited as the co-composer of some of his biggest hits, but generally speaking the 50s was still a time of demarcation - songwriters wrote the songs, and singers sang them. The last few years of the decade saw a significant transformation of this rather antiquated system: Paul Anka registered strongly with his own compositions, including 'Diana', 'I Love You Baby', 'You Are My Destiny', 'Lonely Boy' and 'Put Your Head On My Shoulder'; Neil Sedaka began his long career as a performer and writer with 'I Go Ape' and 'Oh! Carol'; and some of the other significant 60s singer-songwriters such as Lennon and McCartney, Mick Jagger and Keith Richard, Jimmy Webb, Carole King, Roy Orbison, and the rest, were already scribbling away in their old school notebooks.

On the subject of songs, as in any other decade the 50s had its fair share of pedestrian novelty items, and one of the market leaders in that area was Bob Merrill. Now it can be told that Merrill, who later wrote the sophisticated lyrics for Broadway shows such as *Carnival!* and *Funny Girl*, amongst others, was the 'guilty guy' responsible, not only for the words and music to '(How Much Is) That Doggie In The Window', a chart-topper for Patti Page in the USA, and for Lita Roza in the UK, but for several other equally meaningless meanderings such as 'Feet Up (Pat Him On The Po-Po)' and 'She Wears Red Feathers' for Guy Mitchell; and 'Mambo Italiano', which was successful for Rosemary Clooney. The most bizarre song title of the whole decade, 'Gilly Gilly Ossenfeffer Katzenellen Bogen By The Sea', was cooked up by Al Hoffman and Dick Manning for the Four Lads in the USA, and Max Bygraves in

Britain. Hoffman and Manning also boosted Patti Page and Alma Cogan's record sales with the terpsichorean teaser, 'I Can't Tell A Waltz From A Tango', and provided Perry Como with several of his less than romantic chart entries, including 'Papa Loves Mambo' and 'Hot Diggity'.

Como's position as one of the 50s leading recording artists was due in no small part to his weekly hour-long musical variety show. It made its debut on the infant US television network in 1955, when its affable host was already a venerable (in pop music terms) 43 years old. Relaxed and religious as the old boy was, his image was nowhere near as squeaky clean as another of the decade's superstars, Pat Boone. His huge hits included 'I'll Be Home', 'Friendly Persuasion', 'Love Letters In The Sand', and 'April Love', and he was roughly the same age as Presley, but, in the public's perception the two were worlds apart. Boone's refusal to 'smoke, cuss, drink, or kiss women in his films', prompted Dean Martin (who has been known to take the occasional drink) to remark: 'I shook hands with Pat Boone once, and my whole right side sobered up!'. His overly 'goody-goody' attitude may well have been one of the reasons why Boone never made it in films. Mario Lanza, one of Hollywood's biggest stars in the 50s, whose celluloid extravaganzas included *The Toast Of New Orleans* (1950) and *The Great Caruso* (1951), was certainly not renowned for his monastic habits. Neither was the charismatic James Dean, the cult film actor of the decade. On the other hand, Lanza died in 1959 at the age of 38, and Dean expired even earlier when he was only 24, so perhaps Boone wasn't so naive after all.

Those two Lanza movies heralded what was to prove a vintage period for the Hollywood musical. In the space of just 10 years from 1950, the screen was blessed with productions such as *Annie Get Your Gun, Show Boat, An American In Paris* (six Oscars), *Singin' In The Rain, Hans Christian Andersen, Road To Bali, Call Me Madam, The Band Wagon, Kiss Me*

Kate, The Glenn Miller Story, Seven Brides For Seven Brothers, A Star Is Born (with Garland, not Streisand), *Brigadoon, White Christmas, It's Always Fair Weather, Guys And Dolls, Oklahoma!, Carousel, High Society, The King And I, Funny Face, Silk Stockings, Pal Joey, The Joker Is Wild, Gigi, South Pacific,* and *Damn Yankees,* amongst others. The 'others', included vehicles for two of the big screen's favourite leading ladies, Doris Day and Marilyn Monroe. Day, the perennial 'girl next door', starred in a series of musicals which included *The Pajama Game* and *Young At Heart,* and sang the Oscar-winning songs, 'Secret Love' in *Calamity Jane,* and 'Que Sera, Sera (Whatever Will Be, Will Be)', from *The Man Who Knew Too Much.* According to the stories that circulated after Marilyn Monroe's untimely death in 1962, either of those songs could have appropriately described her unhappy private life. On the big screen, though, she proved to be a delightful comedienne and singer in films such as *Gentlemen Prefer Blondes, How To Marry A Millionaire, There's No Business Like Show Business, The Seven Year Itch,* and the best of the lot, *Some Like It Hot.*

Broadway musicals, too, flourished in the 50s. High class, conventional Broadway productions of *Bells Are Ringing, The Boy Friend, The Most Happy Fella, Flower Drum Song, The Music Man, Gypsy, The Sound Of Music,* and *My Fair Lady,* contrasted sharply with the gritty *West Side Story,* complete with Leonard Bernstein's exciting, jazzy music. Bernstein's influence was also felt on America's west coast, when he wrote the score for *On The Waterfront,* at a time when Marlon Brando was slim, and you could understand what he was saying. Elmer Bernstein (no relation) brought the same brand of thrilling music to *The Man With The Golden Arm,* one of the decade's foremost hard-edged films.

Important as instrumental music was in the 50s, it was also a time for conventional solo singers - the balladeers - who came into their own having broken free from the big bands in

the late 40s. However, their joy was to be short-lived. In the UK, a few of them, such as Shirley Bassey and Petula Clark, were destined for long-term international stardom, but they were in the minority. Inevitably, in the face of the musical revolution that had taken place all around them in the 50s, many of the decade's much-loved artists 'went to the wall' as the 60s dawned, or soon afterwards - in terms of record sales at least. Things would never be the same again for Russ Conway, Gary Miller, Eddie Calvert, David Whitfield, Winifred Atwell, Joe 'Mr. Piano' Henderson, Jimmy Young, Dickie Valentine, Dennis Lotis, Alma Cogan, Tony Brent, the Beverley Sisters, Michael Holliday, and Britain's premier female recording star of the 50s, Ruby Murray. In the USA, the writing was on that same wall for Eddie Fisher, Vic Damone, Tennessee Ernie Ford, Don Cornell, Tommy Edwards, Teresa Brewer, Al Martino, Tony Martin, Tab Hunter, Jimmie Rodgers, and Guy Mitchell; vocal groups such as the Four Aces, the McGuire Sisters, the Four Lads, and the Ames Brothers; and the three top girl singers of the 50s, Patti Page, Rosemary Clooney, and Jo Stafford. Of course they all continued to perform and give their fans enormous pleasure - some of them for many years - but, by the 60s, they were considered to be out of date - the (hit) parade had passed them by.

The survivors weathered the storm in different ways: Nat 'King' Cole annoyed many of his fans by recording 'unsuitably commercial' material such as 'Ramblin' Rose', prior to his death in 1965; Dean Martin adopted a kind of alcoholic C&W approach - Kay Starr, too, went down the country music road; Perry Como and Johnny Mathis were absent from the charts for nearly 10 years before getting their second wind in the early 70s; Andy Williams took over Como's television mantle - and even encouraged the Osmond Brothers; Bobby Darin, who began as a rocker, changed to a supper-club vocalist, and ended up as a folkie. Connie Francis thrived until serious personal problems cut short her career; Doris Day moved into frothy film comedies; Peggy Lee, Tony Bennett, Lena Horne, Dinah Shore, Judy Garland, Bing Crosby, and the rest, continued to record classy albums whenever they could find companies willing to issue them. Frank Sinatra did, too - but then *he* had his own record company.

It all happened a long time ago, and as far as most of today's generation are concerned, it might as well not have happened at all. In 1993, celebrations are under way marking 30 years of popular music - in other words it all started with the Beatles. Not to those who lived through the 50s, it didn't. Equally, many of those who were part of that mixed-up, thrilling, decade, refuse to accept that anything musically worthwhile has happened *since* then; and that's a pity, too, because they're missing out on a such lot.

Some of the icons of the times died young, or relatively so, but others, like Frankie Laine and Perry Como, now both octogenarians, and Frank Sinatra too, are still very much around. Between the following pages, you'll find they're all back together again, young and old - frozen in time - and just as they were in those sometimes frightening, but definitely 'Fabulous Fifties'.

John Martland

A

Adler, Larry

b. Lawrence Cecil Adler, 10 February 1914, Baltimore, Maryland, USA. A mouth-organist - that's how he likes be known - and arguably the most accomplished and celebrated exponent of the instrument there has ever been. His orthodox Judaism gave him the opportunity to train in religious music, and he became a cantor at the age of 10. He sang, and learned to play the piano and mouth-organ by ear from listening to phonograph records, and didn't bother to learn to read to music until 1941. After being expelled from the Peabody Conservatory of Music, he won the Maryland Harmonica Championship in 1927. Shortly afterwards, he ran away to New York and joined one of the Paramount units, playing in movie theatres, between features. He was also presented as a 'ragged urchin' ('just in from the street, folks!') in vaudeville, and in Lew Leslie's revue, Clowns In Clover (1928). He also served as Eddie Cantor's stooge for a time, and accompanied Fred Astaire in Florenz Ziegfeld's Smiles. His life-long affection and appreciation of George Gershwin began when he was introduced to him by Paul Whiteman, and his interpretations of the composer's works, especially Porgy And Bess and the 'Rhapsody In Blue' are definitive. Many years later, in 1981, Adler's haunting version of Gershwin's 'Summertime' played a significant role in the success of the enormously popular UK ice dancers, Torvill and Dean. In 1934, after further minor roles, on stage in Flying Colours, and on film in Paramount's Many Happy Returns, in which he was backed by Duke Ellington's Orchestra, Adler was spotted at New York's Palace Theatre by the English producer C.B. Cochran, who engaged him for the London revue, Streamline. Shortly after the show opened, sales of mouth-organs in the UK went up by several thousand per cent, and fan clubs proliferated. Adler played the top nightclubs, and in 1937, the revue Tune Inn was built round him. After marrying top mannequin Eileen Walser, he toured South Africa and Australia before returning to the US in 1939, where he gained national recognition in the classical field when he appeared as a soloist with the Chicago Women's Symphony Orchestra. During the 40s, Adler appeared at Carnegie Hall with the dancer, Paul Draper, and toured with him extensively in the US, Africa and the Middle East, entertaining troops, and insisting on a non-segregation policy between whites and Negroes at concerts. Adler also entertained in the South Pacific with artists such Carol Landis, Martha Tilton and comedian Jack Benny, and worked consistently for the war effort and the Allied forces. He was 'on duty' again in 1951 during the Korean conflict. By then, as a high-profile liberal, he had been included on McCarthy's 'communist' blacklist, and moved to live and work in England, only for the 'red spectre' to follow him even there. In 1954, he was forced by the Rank film organization to give up his billing rights on US prints of the highly popular comedy film, Genevieve, for which he had written the gentle, but highly distinctive score. Sure enough, the music was nominated for an Academy Award, and an embarrassed Rank were only able to offer orchestra conductor Muir Mathieson's name as composer. Fortunately for them it did not win the Oscar - voters preferred Dimitri Tiomkin's music for The High And The Mighty - and Adler had to wait until 1986 for the Academy's official recognition of his work. In 1952, Adler experienced 'the highlight of his musical life', at a Royal Albert Hall Promenade Concert, when he was 'forced' to encore Ralph Vaughan Williams' 'Romance For Mouth-Organ, Piano And Strings', a piece which had been written especially for him. In the 50s, although domiciled in the UK, Adler made frequent trips to the US, where life was made difficult for him, and worked in many other countries of the world with major symphony orchestras. In 1963, as a soloist at the Edinburgh Festival, Adler gave the first performance of 'Lullaby Time', a string quartet written by George Gershwin in 1921, and presented to Adler by Ira Gershwin. That piece, and several other unpublished works by such as Cole Porter, Harold Arlen and Richard Rodgers, were included on his RCA album, Discovery. His own most familiar composition is, of course, the music for Genevieve, but he has composed for other films, such as The Hellions, King And Country, High Wind In Jamaica and The Great Chase; for television programmes and plays, including Midnight Men; and has written concert pieces such as 'Theme And Variations'. Works have been specially composed for him by Malcolm Arnold, Darius Milhaud, Arthur Benjamin, Gordon Jacobs and others. In 1965, Adler was back at the Edinburgh Festival, with his one man show, Hand To Mouth, and in 1967 and

Larry Adler (centre)

1973, gave his services to Israel in aid of those affected by the Six Day and Yom Kippur wars. In 1988, as busy as ever, he appeared at New York's Ballroom club with Harold Nicholas, one half of the legendary dance team, the Nicholas Brothers, who were so popular in the old film musicals. To many, the engagement brought back memories of Adler's tours in the 40s with his friend, tap-dancer Paul Draper. As usual on these occasions Adler skilfully blended classical selections with a 'honky-tonk jazz' approach to numbers written by the 'great' popular writers. In the following year he was in concert at London's Royal Albert Hall, marking his 75th birthday, accompanied by pianist John Ogden, and the Wren Orchestra conducted by Stanley Black. During the early 90s he played regularly at the Pizza on the Park, sometimes accompanied by 'The Hot Club Of London', and reached back through the years for life-long specialities, such as 'Ravel's Bolero'. As a musician and a journalist, Adler seems to have met and worked with almost everyone who is (or has been) anyone in show business, politics and other walks of life. A tennis fanatic, he once played in a doubles match with Charles Chaplin, Greta Garbo and Salvador Dali, and is always prepared to talk about it.

Further reading: All titles by Larry Adler *How I Play. Larry Adler's Own Arrangements. Jokes And How To Tell Them. It Ain't Necessarily So: His Autobiography.*

Ainsworth, Alyn

b. 24 August 1924, Bolton, Lancashire, England, d. 4 October 1990, London, England. Ainsworth was a highly-respected musical director and arranger for records, television and the West End stage. He studied guitar from the age of seven, and left school at 14 to join Herman Darewski's Orchestra as a boy soprano, and sang at the London Palladium. When his voice broke, he returned to Bolton and became an assistant golf professional, and played guitar in his own band, the Falcons, while also studying musical arranging. In the late 40s, he worked as a staff arranger for Oscar Rabin, and then Geraldo, one of the top UK dance bands. In 1951, he began to arrange for the newly-formed BBC Northern Variety Orchestra, and, when its conductor, Vilem Tausky, moved on to the Northern Symphony Orchestra, Ainsworth was offered the job of resident conductor with NVA. In December 1952, BBC Television launched *The Good Old Days* from the City Variety Theatre in Leeds - this music-hall show ran for over 30 years -

Ainsworth and the Northern Variety Orchestra provided the appropriate musical setting. Economics, it is said, persuaded the BBC to prune the orchestra, removing all the members of the string section, bar one, and renaming it the Northern Dance Orchestra. With accompanists such as trumpeter Syd Lawrence. Ainsworth welded the NDO into one of the finest units of its kind in the world. Based in Manchester for a decade Ainsworth and the NDO appeared on numerous radio and television programmes, accompanying singers such as Frankie Vaughan, Ronnie Hilton, and David Whitfield, and, together with singer Sheila Buxton and laid-back announcer Roger Moffat, they had their own highly-acclaimed late-night television show, *Make Way For Music.* In 1961 Ainsworth moved from Manchester to London to serve as musical director for the imported American musical, *Bye Bye Birdie,* which starred Chita Rivera and UK pop star Marty Wilde. He was a recording artist for Parlophone Records in the mid-50s. Between 1958-65 the Alyn Ainsworth Orchestra recorded a number of orchestral pieces for George Martin. During the 60s Ainsworth became a leading conductor and arranger for West End shows such as *Gentlemen Prefer Blondes, Hello Dolly!, A Funny Thing Happened On The Way To The Forum, She Loves Me* and *Sweet Charity.* He also orchestrated Bricusse and Newley's *The Roar Of The Greasepaint, The Smell Of The Crowd.* The 60s also saw the start of his long and successful collaboration with singer Shirley Bassey, acting as musical director for her many cabaret seasons in the UK and abroad. In the UK, his television credits included Val Parnell's *Sunday Night At The London Palladium, International Cabaret From the Talk Of The Town, The David Nixon Show, Dee Time, The Cannon And Ball Show, Search For A Star, Night Of Hundred Stars, The BAFTA Awards, Live From Her Majesty's, Bruce's Big Night Out,* more than 10 *Royal Command Performances*; and many 'specials' featuring artists such as Cilla Black, Russ Abbott and Stanley Baxter, Vera Lynn and Lulu. He also composed the theme music for several of the shows. His other compositions included 'Bedtime For Drums', 'Italian Sunset', 'Mi Amor', 'Pete's Party' and 'If I Were A Buddy Rich Man'. Ainsworth was also associated the Brotherhood Of Man and conducted them for the Eurovision Song contest which they won in 1976 with 'Save Your Kisses For Me'. He conducted, and sometimes arranged, for hit recordings by artists such as Des O'Connor, Frankie Vaughan, and Shirley Bassey, and worked

with visiting Americans, including Johnny Mathis, Neil Sedaka and Barry Manilow. Ainsworth also worked with the Beverley Sisters on titles such as 'Triplets', and was engaged for a time to one of the twins, Teddy. His own records included a rare excursion into rock 'n' roll with '18th Century Rock', credited to 'Alyn Ainsworth with The Rock-A-fellas', and the more typically smooth, *Themes And Dreams* and *True Love*. The ultimate professional, Ainsworth would often conduct the first house of one West End show, and the second house of another, after rehearsing for television during the day. He was capable of producing his best work under extreme pressure, while also motivating others, and was the man whom producers could rely on for the big occasion.
Selected albums: *Themes And Dreams* (1982), *True Love* (1982).

Allyn, David

b. 19 July 1923, Hartford, Connecticut, USA. From a musical family, his mother was a singer and his father a French horn player, Allyn became a semi-pro vocalist by the time he was 17, before joining Jack Teagarden's short-lived big band of the early 40s. After service in World War II, during which he was awarded the Purple Heart, he worked for leaders such as Van Alexander and Henry Jerome before joining the Boyd Raeburn orchestra where his musical skills were tested by the demanding work of several forward-looking arrangers, including George Handy. In the 40s, apart from his work with Raeburn, Allyn also recorded with such jazzmen as Lucky Thompson. When the Raeburn band split up, Allyn moved to the west coast and became solo act. His Dick Haymes-like vocals gained him regular club work and a recording contract with Discovery, and later, World Pacific. During the 50s he recorded some highly regarded albums with arrangements by Johnny Mandel and Bill Holman and with accompanists of the calibre of Jimmy Rowles, Frank Rosolino and Barry Harris. In the late 60s and early 70s Allyn worked infrequently in music, spending time actively involved in social work including the rehabilitation of drug users. Allyn's good pitch and diction, allied to his intense feeling for jazz and consummate musical skill, made him one of the best male singers of jazz and standard songs of his time, albeit one little known to the popular or even fringe jazz audience. In 1986, on the basis of an 'up-from-the-ashes' life story and generous recommendations from some major singers, Allyn was again receiving favourable

reviews for his 'smoky instrument that he uses to glide through songs with effortless power', at clubs such as George's in Chicago. (On some recordings Allyn's name is spelled Allen).
Albums: *Sure Thing* (1957), *Yours Sincerely* (1958), *I Only Have Eyes For You* (1959), with Jimmy Rowles, Frank Rosolino *In The Blue Of The Evening* (1966), with Barry Harris *Don't Look Back* (1975), *Soft As Spring* (1976). Compilations: *Boyd Raeburn On The Air Vol. 2* (1945-48 recordings), *Boyd Raeburn On The Air Vol. 1* (1946), *Boyd Raeburn* (1946-47 recordings).

Ames Brothers

This family group from Malden, Massachusetts, USA featured Joe Ulrick (b. 3 May 1924), Gene Ulrick (b. 13 February 1925), Vic Ulrick (b. 20 May 1926, d. 23 January 1978) and Ed Ulrick (b. 9 July 1927). The group were consistently popular from the late 40s, through the 50s. The brothers started singing together in high school and won several amateur contests in their home town. They first sang professionally in Boston, and later in clubs and theatres in New York, Chicago and Hollywood. After recording 'A Tree In A Meadow', with Monica Lewis, for the independent Signature label, they signed for Coral, later switching to RCA Victor. After minor success with 'You, You, You Are The One' and 'Cruising Down The River', they had two number 1 hits in 1950 with the novelty, 'Rag Mop' (a million-seller), and 'Sentimental Me'. During the 50s they were extremely popular in stage shows and on US television, with their skilful blend of comedy and an uncomplicated singing style on bouncy numbers and ballads. They also had four more million-selling records: 'Undecided' (backed by Les Brown and his orchestra), 'You, You You', 'The Naughty Lady Of Shady Lane' and 'Melodie D'Amour'. Their other US Top 20 hits were 'Can Anyone Explain? (No No No)', 'Put Another Nickel In (Music! Music! Music!)', 'Stars Are The Windows Of Heaven', 'Oh Babe!', 'Wang Wang Blues', 'I Wanna Love You', 'Auf Wiederseh'n Sweetheart', 'String Along', 'My Favorite Song', 'The Man With The Banjo', 'My Bonnie Lassie', 'It Only Hurts For A Little While', 'Tammy', 'A Very Precious Love' and 'Pussy Cat'. Around 1960, the group disbanded, but Ed continued as a solo act, appearing frequently on US television. He also had hit singles in 1967 with 'My Cup Runneth Over' and 'Who Will Answer?', plus several 60s US chart albums. In the 70s he was still popular on television and the nightclub circuit. His brother Vic died in

1978 in a car crash in Nashville, Tennessee.
Selected albums: Ames Brothers *There'll Always Be A Christmas* (1957), *With Roy Smeck Serenaders* (1958), *Destination Moon* (1958), *Smoochin' Time* (1959), *Words & Music* (1959), *Sing Famous Hits Of Famous Quartets* (1959), *Concert* (c.50s), *Love's Old Sweet Song* (c.50s), *Our Golden Favorites* (c.50s) *Sing The Best In Country* (1960), *Sing The Best Of The Bands* (1960), *Blend & The Beat* (1960), *Hello Amigos* (1960), *Sweet & Swing* (1960), *Knees Up!* (1963), *With Ed Ames* (1968). Ed Ames *The Ed Ames Album* (1964), *My Kind Of Songs* (1965), *It's A Man's World* (1966), *More I Cannot Wish You* (1966), *My Cup Runneth Over* (1967), *Time, Time* (1967), Selected compilation: *Best Of The Ames Brothers* (1958).

Anderson, Ernestine

b. 11 November 1928, Houston, Texas, USA. Raised in Seattle, Anderson has been singing professionally since her mid-teens. She worked extensively with R&B bands in the 40s, including those led by Russell Jacquet and Johnny Otis. A year with Lionel Hampton in the early 50s and a Scandinavian tour with bop trumpeter Rolf Ericson broadened her repertoire, but she remained well-rooted in the blues. In later years Anderson developed her technique and range, her rich, molten sound being especially effective on the better contemporary pop songs. Despite spending long periods overseas (including several years' residence in England from 1965), her international appeal remained limited. Indeed, the spell in Europe adversely affected her career in her homeland; even a national magazine profile, which described her as the 'new Sarah Vaughan and Ella Fitzgerald', did not help. A chance appearance at the 1976 Concord Summer Jazz Festival deservedly brought her to the attention of a new and wider audience, and since then she has performed and recorded extensively, although she is now based chiefly on the west coast.
Albums: *Ernestine Anderson With The Gigi Gryce Orchestra And Quartet* (1955), with Rolf Ericson *Hot Cargo* (1956), *Ernestine Anderson i* (1958), *Ernestine Anderson ii* (1959), *Ernestine Anderson iii* (1960), *Ernestine Anderson iv* (1960), *Moanin', Moanin', Moanin'* (1960), *Ernestine Anderson v* (1963-64), *Hello Like Before* (1976), *Live From Concord To London* (1976-77), *Sunshine* (1979), *Never Make Your Move Too Soon* (c.1980), *Big City* (1983), *When The Sun Goes Down* (1984), *Be Mine Tonight* (1986), with Capp-Pierce Juggernaut *Live At The Alleycat* (1987), with George Shearing *A Perfect Match* (1988), *Live At The Concord Festival: The Third Set* (1990).

Andrews, Julie

b. Julia Wells, 1 October 1935, Walton-On-Thames, Surrey, England. After singing lessons with Madam Lillian Stiles-Allan, which formed her precise vocal style and typically English delivery, she made her professional debut in her parent's variety act at the age of 10. Two years later she performed at the London Hippodrome in the Pat Kirkwood musical, *Starlight Roof*, and the following year appeared in the Royal Command Performance. On BBC radio, she was Archie Andrew's playmate in *Educating Archie*, while appearing on stage in the title role of *Humpty Dumpty* at the London Casino at the age of 13. Her big break came in 1954 when she played Polly Brown in the Broadway production of Sandy Wilson's *The Boy Friend*. Having insisted on only a one-year contract for the latter, she was available to star with Rex Harrison in one of Broadway's major musicals, Lerner & Loewe's *My Fair Lady*, later repeating her performance in London before returning to Broadway as Queen Guinevere, with Richard Burton as King Arthur, in *Camelot*. To her chagrin, she was not required for the movie versions of the last two shows but, instead, gained an Oscar for her performance as the 'flying nanny' in the title role of Disney's *Mary Poppins* in 1964. Since then, her career in film musicals has taken her from the blockbuster heights of *The Sound Of Music* to the critical depths of the Gertrude Lawrence bio-pic *Star*, with *Thoroughly Modern Millie*, and a transvestite role in *Victor/Victoria*, in-between. The latter film, and her straight roles in movies such as *10* and *S.O.B.*, directed by her second husband Blake Edwards, have sometimes seemed a direct effort to counter her life-long cosy, old fashioned image. Nevertheless, she has been a major film star for over 25 years, and in 1989 was awarded BAFTA's Silver Mask in recognition of her outstanding contribution to the medium. She was not so successful on the small screen, and her 1992 ABC comedy series, *Julie*, received poor reviews. In the same year, she sang the role of Anna in a CD recording of *The King And I*, amid general amazement that had never played the part on the stage; British actor, Ben Kinsgsley, was her regal partner in the studio. In 1993, Andrews was set to return to the New York stage for the first time since *Camelot* (1960), in the Off-Broadway Sondheim revue, *Putting It Together*.
Albums: *My Fair Lady* (1956, Broadway Cast)

Camelot (1961, Broadway Cast), with Carol Burnett *Julie And Carol At Carnegie Hall* (1962), *Mary Poppins* (1964, film soundtrack), *The Sound Of Music* (1965, film soundtrack), *A Christmas Treasure* (1968), *Love Me Tender* (1983), *The Secret Of Christmas* (1977), *Broadway's Fair* (1984), *The Sound Of Christmas* (1987), *Julie Andrews And Carol Burnett At The Lincoln Center* (1989), *Love Julie* (1989), *The King And I* (1992, studio cast).

Anka, Paul

b. 30 July 1941, Ottawa, Ontario, Canada. A prolific songwriter and child prodigy, Anka was one of the major teen idols of the 50s. He burst on the scene in 1957 with the self-written 'Diana', an intense ballad detailing the frustration and unrequited love of a young teenager for a slightly older female. With its distinctive rhythm pattern, the song was powerfully evocative and stayed top of the UK charts for a lengthy nine weeks as well as reaching number 1 in the USA. It sold a reported 10 million copies world-wide. Anka followed up with a series of hits such as 'You Are My Destiny', 'Lonely Boy', 'Put Your Head On My Shoulder' and 'Puppy Love'. Pubescent worries and the desire to be taken seriously by condescending parents were familiar themes in those songs and contributed strongly to his success. As the 50s wound to a close he wisely moved away from teen ballads and planned for a long term future as a songwriter and cabaret artist. His moving 'It Doesn't Matter Anymore' was a posthumous UK number 1 for Buddy Holly in 1959 and during the same year Anka starred in his first film, *Girls' Town*. This prepared him for the more serious *The Longest Day* three years later. During the 60s the former teen star was a regular at New York's Copacabana and Los Angeles' Coconut Grove, and was in-demand on the night club circuit. Additionally he tried acting, making an appearance in *The Longest Day*. For much of the decade however he was earning large sums of money appearing at Las Vegas hotels The success of Donny Osmond, meanwhile, who took 'Puppy Love' to the top in Britain kept Anka's early material alive for a new generation. Songwriting success continued, most notably with Frank Sinatra's reading of his lyric to 'My Way' and Tom Jones's million-selling 'She's A Lady'. In the 70s, Anka himself returned to number 1 in the USA courtesy of a risque duet with his protegee Odia Coates with the song, '(You're) Having My Baby'. A spree of hits followed punctuated by regular supper club appearances. As late as 1983,

the former 50s teen star was back in the charts with 'Hold Me Till The Mornin' Comes'. He continued to play luctrative seasons in Las Vegas, and Atlantic City, and toured the UK in 1992 for the first time in 25 years. In the following year he threatened to sue Dulux, a UK house-paint manufacturer, when their television commercial portrayed a sheepdog apparently singing a parody of 'My Way'.

Albums: *Paul Anka* (1958), *My Heart Sings* (1959), *Paul Anka Swings For Young Lovers* (1960), *Anka At The Copa* (1960), *It's Christmas Everywhere* (1960), *Strictly Instrumental* (1961), *Diana* (1962), *Young, Alive And In Love!* (1962), *Let's Sit This One Out!* (1962), *Our Man Around The World* (1963), *Songs I Wished I'd Written* (1963), *Excitement On Park Avenue* (1964), *Strictly Nashville* (1966), *Paul Anka Alive* (1967), *Goodnight My Love* (1969), *Life Goes On* (1969), *Paul Anka* (1971), *Jubilation* (1972), *Anka* (1974), *Feelings* (1975), *The Painter* (1976), *The Music Man* (1977), *Listen To Your Heart* (1978), *Both Sides Of Love* (1981), *Walk A Fine Line* (1983), *Italiano* (1987 - 10-inch album). Selected compilations: *Paul Anka Sings His Big 15* (1960), *Paul Anka Sings His Big 15, Volume 2* (1961), *Paul Anka Sings His Big 15, Volume 3* (1961), *Paul Anka's 21 Golden Hits* (1963), *Paul Anka Gold* (1974), *Times Of Your Life* (1975), *Essential Paul Anka* (1976), *Vintage Years, 1957-61* (1977), *Paul Anka - His Best* (1980), *Gypsy Ways* (1988), *The Ultimate Collection* (1992).

Anthony, Ray

b. Raymond Antonini, 20 January 1922, Bentleyville, Pennsylvania, USA. After playing in local bands in Cleveland, Anthony spent brief spells in the trumpet sections of the Al Donahue, Glenn Miller and Jimmy Dorsey orchestras. Following a four-year period in the US Navy, where he led a services orchestra, Anthony formed his own band in 1946 and signed with Capitol Records. The band became one of the top attractions of the 50s, touring colleges and universities, producing hit singles such as 'At Last', 'Harbour Lights', the television themes from *Dragnet* and *Peter Gunn*, plus novelty dance numbers, such as 'The Bunny Hop' and 'I Can't Tell A Waltz From A Tango'. From the start, the band had always had a Millerish reed sound, so when the Miller 'revival' happened they participated more successfully than most. Anthony appeared with his band in two movies, Fred Astaire's *Daddy Long Legs* and *This Could Be The Night*. He appeared on his own in the Jayne Mansfield/Tom Ewell rock 'n' roll spoof, *The Girl*

Paul Anka

Can't Help It, and in an eerie piece of Hollywood casting, featured as saxophone-playing Jimmy Dorsey in the Red Nichols biopic, *The Five Pennies*. In the 60s, with a limited market for 16-piece bands, Anthony formed a sextet, with a female vocal duo, playing clubs and lounges throughout the USA. Recently he has been active in providing and preserving big band music for schools and radio stations.

Albums: *Golden Horn* (1955), *Dream Dancing* (1956), *Young Ideas* (1957), *The Dream Girl* (1958), *Worried Mind* (1962), *More Dream Dancing* (1983), *Plays For Dream Dancing* (1984), *Swingin' On Campus* (1985), *Dream Dancing Melody* (1985), *Dancing Alone Together* (1986), in 1986 the Aerospace label re-launched a series of Ray Anthony titles: *Arthur Murray Dance Party*, *Big Band Jazz*, *Dream Dancing Around The World*, *Dancing In The Dark*, *Touch Dancing*, *Big Band Singer*, *Brass Galore*, *Let's Go Dancing*, *Swinging At The Tower*, *Swing*, *Dancer's Choice*, *Let's Dance Again*, *Music Of Your Memories*, *Sweet And Swingin' 1949-53* (1987), *Hooked On Big Bands - Live On Radio* (1988 - Aerospace label), *For Dancers Only* (1988), *House Party Hop* (1988), *Glenn Miller - Then And Now* (1988), *I Get The Blues When It Rains* (1989), *Dancers In Love* (1989). Compilations: all on Aerospace *The Sampler* (1986), *The Hits Of Ray Anthony* (1986), *Show And Dance And Party* (1986).

Arnaz, Desi

b. Desiderio Alberto Arnez y de Acha III, 2 March 1917, Santiago, Cuba, d. 2 December 1986, Del Mar, California, USA. Arnaz came to the USA in the early 20s and began singing and playing bongo and conga drums with Xaviar Cugat and others before forming his own band. Arnaz achieved sufficient popularity to be offered musical spots in films. While working on one of these, *Dance, Girl, Dance* (1940), he met and subsequently married Lucille Ball. In the late 40s Ball appeared on radio in a popular series, *My Favourite Husband*, in which she co-starred with film actor Richard Denning. In the early 50s Ball decided to adapt the show for television with her real life husband as producer, and she also decided that Arnaz should play her television husband – two decisions frowned upon by executives at CBS and Philip Morris (cigarette makers and potential sponsors for the show). Their reluctance stemmed from the fact that as a producer Arnaz was an unknown quantity and as an actor he was a potential liability because of his pronounced Cuban accent. In the event, Ball and Arnaz prevailed but had to make concessions.

These included taking a salary reduction, though as compensation CBS made the multi-million-dollar blunder of allowing the couple to retain 100% residuals. The new show, *I Love Lucy*, was a runaway success and made a fortune for Desilu, the company Ball and Arnaz had formed to produce the show. *I Love Lucy* ran until 1959 and the following year the couple were divorced although they continued as business partners. After *I Love Lucy*, Ball starred in *The Lucy Show* which was produced by Arnaz. In 1962 Ball bought out Arnaz's share of their company and for a while ran Desilu on her own, producing such popular television shows as *Star Trek* and *Mission: Impossible*. Arnaz made a few film appearances in the mid-50s, including the popular *The Long, Long Trailer* with Ball, but then drifted into retirement. Later, he returned for occasional cameo roles, produced the NBC television series, *The Mothers-In-Law* (1967), which starred Eve Arden and Kaye Ballard, and published his autobiography. His daughter, Lucie Arnaz, was gaining favourable reviews for her singing in New York clubs in the early 90s. In 1993, she, and her husband, Laurence Luckinbill, were the executive producers of *Lucy And Desi: A Home Movie*, 'their own version of Lucy and Desi's entwined careers', which was shown in the USA on NBC Television.

Further reading: *The Book*, Desi Arnaz. *Desilu: The Story Of Lucille Ball And Desi Arnaz*, Coyne Steven Sanders and Tom Gilbert.

Arnold, Malcolm

b. 21 October 1921, Northampton, England. A composer, conductor, arranger and trumpet player. Arnold became aware of music at the age of four, and taught himself to play trumpet – his inspiration was Louis Armstrong. He began his career in 1941 as an instrumentalist with the London Philharmonic Orchestra, and returned to the orchestra in 1946 after brief service in World War II, and a spell with the BBC Symphony Orchestra. During these times he was also composing; one of his best known pieces, 'Sea Shanties', was written in 1943. He became a full time composer in the early 50s, and soon won much critical acclaim as 'one of the great hopes of British music'. His work schedule was exhausting; from 1951-56 he is said to have written the music for over 70 films; as well as three operas, ballet music, concertos and other classical and light works. One of his more unusual compositions was the 'Grand Overture' for a Gerald Hoffnung concert, in which the more conventional instruments of the orchestra were

augmented by three vacuum cleaners and an electric polisher. His film scores, many of which complemented classic British productions, including *The Sound Barrier* (1952), *The Holly And The Ivy*, *The Captain's Paradise*, *Hobson's Choice*, *Prize Of Gold*, *I Am A Camera*, *Trapeze*, *Tiger In The Smoke*, *The Deep Blue Sea*, *Island In The Sun*, *The Bridge On The River Kwai* (one of the film's six Oscars went to Arnold), *Blue Murder At St. Trinians*, *The Inn Of The Sixth Happiness* (the film theme won an Ivor Novello Award in 1959), *The Key*, *The Root Of Heaven*, *Dunkirk*, *Tunes Of Glory*, *The Angry Silence*, *No Love For Johnnie*, *The Inspector*, *Whistle Down The Wind*, *The Lion*, *Nine Hours To Rama*, *The Chalk Garden*, *The Heroes Of Telemark*, *The Thin Red Line*, *Sky West And Crooked*, and *The Reckoning* (1969). During the 60s the whole thing went sour. Arnold was ignored, even reviled, by the critics and sections of the concert and broadcasting establishment. He was called 'a clown', and his work was regarded as 'out of phase' with the current trends in music. There were alcohol problems, he suffered several nervous breakdowns, and attempted suicide more than once. He continued to write, when he was able, and was particularly interested in brass band music, but his work generally went unappreciated. His ninth and final symphony, written in 1986, still had not received a proper premiere by 1991, when low-key celebrations for his 70th birthday involved a concert at London's Queen Elizabeth Hall, which included his double violin concerto, commissioned by Yehudi Menuhin in 1962. In 1993, Malcolm Arnold received a knighthood in the Queen's New Year honours list.
Further reading: *Malcolm Arnold: A Catalogue Of His Music*, A. Poulton.

Atkins, Chet

b. Chester Burton Atkins, 20 June 1924, Luttrell, Tennessee, USA. Atkins is one of the most influential and prolific guitarists of the 20th century, as well as an important producer and an RCA Records executive. The son of a music teacher and brother of guitarist Jim Atkins (who played with Les Paul), Atkins began as a fiddler in the early 40s, with the Dixieland Swingers in Knoxville, Tennessee. He also played with artists including Bill Carlisle and Shorty Thompson. He moved to Cincinnati, Ohio in 1946 and his first recording session took place that year, for Jim Bullet, and in 1947 Atkins was signed to RCA, recording 16 tracks on August 11, including a number of vocals. Atkins first performed at the *Grand Ole Opry* in Nashville in 1948, working with a band that included satirists Homer And Jethro. He toured with Maybelle Carter in 1949 and recorded as an accompanist with the Carter Family the following year. At that time he made a decision to concentrate on session work, encouraged and often hired by music publisher Fred Rose. Atkins recorded largely with MGM Records artists, such as Red Sovine and the Louvin Brothers, during this period, and most notably on 24 of Hank Williams' tracks for the label. He also recorded on several of the Everly Brothers' Cadence Records hits later in the 50s. In 1952 RCA executive Steve Sholes, who had signed Atkins for session work, gave him authority to build up the label's roster, and Atkins began a second career as a talent scout. By the mid-50s he was recording his own albums and producing 30 artists a year for RCA. Atkins' first album, *Chet Atkins' Gallopin' Guitar*, was issued in 1953, his discography eventually reaching to over 100 albums under his own name. Among the other artists with whom he worked at RCA were Elvis Presley, Jim Reeves, Don Gibson, Charley Pride, Waylon Jennings, Hank Snow, Jerry Reed, Perry Como and many others. He is generally regarded as the chief architect of the 'Nashville Sound'. His trademark guitar was a Grestch, which was later manufactured as the 'Chet Atkins Country Gentleman'. George Harrison endorsed this instrument, and this led to a huge increase in sales for the company during the 60s. During this decade Chet recorded the first of a series of guitar duet albums; including works with Snow, Reed, Merle Travis, Les Paul and Doc Watson. Atkins was named an RCA vice president in 1968 and remained in that position until 1979. In the early 80s he left RCA for Columbia Records and continued to record for that company into the 90s. He has won several Grammy awards and was elected to the Country Music Hall of Fame in 1973.
Selected albums: *Chet Atkins' Gallopin' Guitar* (1953), *Chet Atkins In Three Dimensions* (1956), *Finger Style Guitar* (1958), *Mister Guitar* (1959), *Teensville* (1959), *Chet Atkins' Workshop* (1960), *Down Home* (1961), *The Best Of Chet Atkins* (1963), with Hank Snow *Reminiscing* (1964), *Chet Atkins Picks On The Beatles* (1965), with Jerry Reed *Me And Jerry* (1970), with Merle Travis *The Atkins-Travis Traveling Show* (1974), with Les Paul *Chester And Lester* (1975), with Floyd Cramer and Danny Davis *Chet, Floyd And Danny* (1977), *Me And My Guitar* (1977), with Les Paul *Guitar Monsters* (1978),

The First Nashville Guitar Quartet (1979), The Best Of Chet On The Road...Live (1980), with Doc Watson Reflections (1980), with Lenny Breau Standard Brands (1981), Work It Out With Chet Atkins 1983), Stay Tuned (1985), Sails (1987), Chet Atkins, C.G.P. (1988), with Mark Knopfler Neck & Neck (1992), with Jerry Reed Sneakin' Around (1992). Compilations: Solid Gold Guitar (1982), Guitar Pickin' Man (1983), 20 Of The Best (1986), Best Of Chet Atkins And Friends (1987), The RCA Years (1992, 2-CD box set).

Atlantic Records

The Atlantic label was founded in 1947 by Herb Abrahamson, a dentistry student, and Ahmet Ertegun, the son of a Turkish ambassador. The New York-based company's early releases included R&B and jazz but by the early 50s it became established as a leading outlet for all facets of black music. Ruth Brown, Joe Turner, the Clovers and the Drifters were among its most successful acts during this period. Jerry Wexler, a former journalist with Billboard magazine, joined the flourishing label in 1953, as a producer and, later, director. Abrahamson meanwhile, was drafted and although he returned to the company in 1955, events within Atlantic had overtaken him. Ahmet's brother Nesuhi was involved in building a formidable jazz catalogue while Abrahamson became responsible for the newly-formed Atco subsidiary. His wife Miriam also became a key member of the board, looking after the fast growing accounts department. He grew increasingly unhappy with his role and sold his share to the company's three executives. Atlantic's success continued unabated throughout the 50s with hits by the Coasters, Bobby Darin and, crucially, Ray Charles. This gifted performer provided the natural stepping-stone between the R&B prevalent during the decade and the soul of the next, by which time the label had grown into a major concern. As such it began lucrative distribution deals with independent outlets, one of which was Stax. This Memphis-based label/studio was instrumental in shaping Atlantic's 60s identity through hits for Otis Redding, Sam And Dave, Wilson Pickett and Carla Thomas. However, unrest between its owner, Jim Stewart, and Wexler, latterly soured the relationship, and the two sides split in 1968. In the meantime Wexler had entered another fruitful partnership with the Alabama-based Fame studio following success with Percy Sledge. It was here that Aretha Franklin recorded her first major smash, 'I Never Loved A Man (The Way I Love You)', which began a long, critically and commercially rewarding relationship between the singer and outlet.

Despite continuing its work with black music, Atlantic was increasingly drawn towards white rock. The Rascals, a blue-eyed soul quartet, and Sonny And Cher were successful singles' acts but the floodgates to the album market were opened when the label secured with their Atco subsidiary the American rights for Cream's releases. New groups, including Vanilla Fudge, Iron Butterfly (whose second album, In A Gadda Da Vida was, for many years, the label's biggest selling album) and Crosby, Stills, Nash And Young, furthered a process culminating in Atlantic's commercial triumphs with British acts Led Zeppelin and Yes. This period was also marked by a lucrative marketing deal with the newly-inaugurated Rolling Stones' label. Atlantic retained its black heritage during the 70s with the Detroit Spinners, Roberta Flack and Blue Magic, but its autonomous position had been undermined following its acquisition by Warner Brothers. The newly-inaugurated WEA group was itself taken over by the Kinney Corporation in 1969. Although the label continues to forge success on several musical fronts, Atlantic no longer boasts the individuality which made it such a potent force during its first 25 years. Ertegun, however, remains one of the most important ever figures in popular music.

Selected compilations: This Is Soul (1968), Atlantic R&B (1986), Atlantic Blues (1987 - four double-album box-set), Atlantic Jazz (1987 - 15 album box-set), Atlantic Soul Classics (1987), Atlantic Soul Ballads (1988), Great Moments In Jazz (1988 - three album box-set), Classic Rock 1966-1988 (1988).

Further reading: Making Tracks - The History of Atlantic Records, Charlie Gillett.

Atwell, Winifred

b. 1914, Tunapuna, Trinidad, d. February 1983, Sydney, Australia. Atwell began playing piano at the age of four, gave classical recitals when six and played concerts at the Services Club, Trinidad. She went to New York and studied with Alexander Borovsky before moving to London for tuition with Harold Craxton. Supplementing her income from classical music by playing boogie-woogie gained her a contract with Decca Records and throughout the 50s she had great success with a series of 'knees up', sing-along medleys and 'rags', mostly on her old honky-tonk, 'other' piano. The first of these, 'Black And White Rag' was later selected as the signature tune for Pot Black, BBC

Winifred Atwell

Frankie Avalon

Television's first regular snooker programme. Other 50s Top 10 hits were 'Britannia Rag', 'Coronation Rag', 'Flirtation Waltz', 'Let's Have A Party', 'Let's Have A Ding Dong', 'Make It A Party', 'Let's Have A Ball', 'Piano Party', and two chart-toppers, 'Poor People Of Paris' and 'Let's Have Another Party'. Atwell's dubbing of John Mills' piano playing in the 1956 movie *It's Great To Be Young*, included a jumping version of 'The Original Dixieland One Step'. In the middle of all the pop there was the 'back to her roots' single, 'Rachmaninov's 18th Variation On A Theme By Paganini' which went to number 9 in the UK chart. Thereafter, she continued to combine the two musical forms. At her peak she was a huge UK star, but in the 60s her career declined and in the 70s she went to live in Australia, where she died in 1983.
Selected albums: *Around The World Of Winifred Atwell* (1972), *Seven Rags, Seven Boogies* (1975), *It's Ragtime* (1982), *Winifred Atwell Plays 50 All-Time Greats* (1983), *Winifred Atwell, Piano Party* (1984), *Winifred Atwell's Piano Party* (1985).

Avalon, Frankie

b. Francis Avallone, 18 September 1939, Philadelphia, USA. The photogenic 50s teen idol started as a trumpet-playing child prodigy. His first recordings in 1954 were the instrumentals 'Trumpet Sorrento' and 'Trumpet Tarantella' on X-Vik Records (an RCA Records subsidiary). In the mid-50s, he appeared on many television and radio shows including those of Paul Whiteman, Jackie Gleason and Ray Anthony. He joined Rocco & The Saints and was seen singing with them in the 1957 film *Jamboree* (*Disc Jockey Jamboree* in the UK). Avalon signed to Chancellor Records and in 1958 his third single for them 'Dede Dinah' reached the US Top 10. It was the first of his 25 US chart entries, many of which were written by his hard-working manager, Bob Marucci.
Despite the fact that he had a weak voice, he quickly became one of the top stars in the US and managed two chart toppers in 1959 'Venus' and 'Why', which were his only UK Top 20 entries. He had to wait until his 21st birthday in 1961 to receive the $100,000 he had earned to date and by that time he had passed his peak as a singer and turned his attention to acting. His acting career was also successful, with appearances in many films including a string of beach movies, alongside fellow 50s pop star Annette. He also appeared in the very successful 1978 film, *Grease*. He later recorded with little success on United Artists, Reprise, Metromedia, Regalia, Delite, Amos and Bobcat. Apart from his film and occasional television appearances, Avalon still performs on the supper-club circuit. Alongside his fellow Chancellor Records artist Fabian, he is often put down by rock critics, yet remains one of the American public's best loved 50s teen idols.
Selected albums: *Frankie Avalon* (1958), *The Young Frankie Avalon* (1959), *Swingin' On A Rainbow* (1959), *Young And In Love* (1960), *Summer Scene* (1960), *And Now About Mr. Avalon* (1961), *Italiano* (1962), *You Are Mine* (1962), *Frankie Avalon Christmas Album* (1962), *Muscle Beach Party* (1964, film soundtrack), *I'll Take Sweden* (1965, film soundtrack), *I Want You Near Me* (1970), *Bobby Sox To Stockings* (1984), *Frankie Avalon* (1987). Selected compilations: *A Whole Lotta Frankie* (1961), *15 Greatest Hits* (1964), *Best Of Frankie Avalon* (1984).

Bailey, Pearl

b. 29 March 1918, Newport News, Virginia, USA, d. 17 August 1990, Philadelphia, Pennsylvania, USA. Pearlie Mae, as she was known, was an uninhibited performer, who mumbled her way through some songs and filled others with outrageous asides and sly innuendoes. She entered the world of entertainment as a dancer but later sang in vaudeville, graduating to the New York nightclub circuit in the early 40s. After working with the Noble Sissle Orchestra, she became band-vocalist with Cootie Williams with whom she recorded 'Tessa's Torch Song' previously sung by Dinah Shore in the movie *Up In Arms*. Bailey received strong critical acclaim after substituting for Rosetta Tharpe in a show, and was subsequently signed to star in the 1946 Harold Arlen/Johnny Mercer Broadway musical *St. Louis Woman*. A year later her slurred version of 'Tired' was the highlight of the movie *Variety Girl*. Subsequently her best films were *Carmen Jones* (1954), *St. Louis Blues* (1958) and *Porgy And Bess* (1959). During her stay with Columbia Records (1945-50) Bailey

4818

Pearl Bailey

recorded a series of duets with Frank Sinatra, trumpeter Oran 'Hot Lips' Page and comedienne Moms Mabley. She also recorded some solo tracks with outstanding arrangers/conductors, Gil Evans and Tadd Dameron. Upon joining the Coral label in 1951, she employed Don Redman as her regular musical director, the association lasting for 10 years. In 1952, she had her biggest hit record 'Takes Two To Tango'. In that same year she married drummer Louie Bellson and he took over from Redman as her musical director in 1961. Although few of her records have sold in vast quantities, Bailey had always been a crowd-pulling, on-stage performer and, following her early stage triumph in *St. Louis Woman*, was later cast in other shows including *The House Of Flowers*, *Bless You All*, *Arms And The Girl* and an all-black cast version of *Hello, Dolly!*. She has also starred in several US television specials, playing down the double-entendre that caused one of her albums, *For Adults Only*, to be 'restricted from air-play'.

Selected albums: *Pearl Bailey A-Broad* (1957), *Gems* (1958), *For Adults Only* (1958), *Sings!* (1959), *St. Louis Blues* (1959), *Porgy & Bess & Others* (1959), *More Songs For Adults* (1960), *Songs Of Bad Old Days* (1960), *Naughty But Nice* (1961), *Songs She Loves By Arlen* (1962), *Come On Let's Play With Pearlie Mae* (1962), *Intoxicating* (1964), *Songs By Jimmy Van Heusen* (1964), *For Women Only* (1965), *Birth Of The Blues* (c.60s), *Cultered Pearl* (c.60s), *The Definitive* (c.60s), *For Adult Listening* (c.60s), *About Good Girls & Bad Boys* (c.60s), *C'est La Vie* (c.60s), *Risque World* (c.60s). Selected compilations: *The Best Of - The Roulette Years* (1991).

Further reading: *The Raw Pearl*, Pearl Bailey.

Baker, Chet

b. Chesney H. Baker, 23 December 1929, Yale, Oklahoma, USA, d. 13 May 1988. One of the more lyrical of the early post-war trumpeters, Baker's fragile sound epitomized the so-called 'cool' school of west coast musicians who dominated the American jazz scene of the 50s. Baker studied music while in the army and soon after his discharge, in 1951, he was playing with Charlie Parker. He gained international prominence as a member of Gerry Mulligan's pianoless quartet and in late 1953, after another short stint with Parker, formed his own group, which proved to be extremely popular. Baker kept this band together for the next three years, but he was not cut out for the life of a bandleader, nor was he able to withstand the pressures and temptations which fame brought him. He

succumbed to drug addiction and the rest of his life was a battle against dependency. Inevitably, his music frequently fell by the wayside. In the 80s, in control of his life, although not fully over his addiction, he was once again a regular visitor to international jazz venues and also made a few incursions into the pop world, guesting, for example, on Elvis Costello's 'Shipbuilding'. Probably his best work from this later period comes on a series of records he made for the Danish Steeplechase label with a trio that comprised Doug Raney and Niels-Henning Ørsted Pedersen. By this time his clean-cut boyish good looks had vanished beneath a mass of lines and wrinkles - fellow trumpeter Jack Sheldon, told by Baker that they were laugh-lines remarked, 'Nothing's that funny!'. In his brief prime, Baker's silvery filigrees of sound, albeit severely restricted in tonal and emotional range, brought an unmistakable touch to many fine records; however, his lack of self-esteem rarely allowed him to assert himself or to break through the stylistic bounds imposed by exemplars such as Miles Davis. A film, *Let's Get Lost* (1989), charts the closing years of the erratic life of this largely unfulfilled musician, who died - falling or possibly jumping from an Amsterdam hotel window - on 13 May 1988.

Albums: *Mulligan-Baker* (1952), *The Complete Pacific Jazz Recordings Of The Chet Baker Quartet* (1953-56), *Chet Baker Quartet* (1955), *The Newport Years* (1955-56), with Art Pepper *Playboys* (1956), *Exitus: Live In Europe Vol. 1* (1956), *Cool Blues: Live In Europe Vol. 2* (1956), *It Could Happen To You* (1958), *Italian Movies* (1958-62), *Chet In New York* (1959), *Chet* (1959), *Chet Baker In Milano* (1959), *Chet Baket With Strings* (1959), *Chet Is Back* (1962), *The Italian Sessions* (1962), *Chet Baker Sings & Plays Billie Holiday* (1965), *Boppin' With The Chet Baker Quintet* (1965), *Groovin' With The Chet Baker Quintet* (1965), *Smokin' With The Chet Baker Quintet* (1965), *Comin' On With The Chet Baker Quintet* (1965), *Cool Burnin' With The Chet Baker Quintet* (1965), *Chet Baker With The Carmel Strings* (60s), *In The Mood* (60s), *Blood, Chet And Tears* (70s), *You Can't Go Home Again* (1973), *She Was Too Good To Me* (1974), *Chet Baker In Concert* (1974), *Once Upon A Summer Time* (1977), *Flic Ou Voyou* (1977), *The Incredible Chet Baker Plays And Sings* (1977), *Broken Wing* (1978), *Two A Day* (1978), *Chet Baker In Paris* (1978), *Live At Nick's* (1978), with Wolfgang Lackerschmid *Ballads For Two* (1979), *The Touch Of Your Lips* (1979), *Rendez-vous* (1979), *All Blues* (1979), *No Problem* (1979), *Daybreak* (1979), *This Is Always* (1979),

Chet Baker/Wolfgang Lackerschmid (1979), *Someday My Prince Will Come* (1979), *Deep In A Dream Of You* (1980), *Un/Deux* (1980), *In Your Own Sweet Way* (1980), *Tune Up* (1980), *Night Bird* (1980), *Salsamba* (1980), *Soft Journey* (1980), *Leaving* (80s), *Seven Faces Of My Funny Valentine* (1980-87), *My Funny Valentine* (1981), *Once Upon A Summertime* (1981), *Chet Baker Live: 'Round Midnight* (1981), *Peace* (1982), *Studio Trieste* (1982), *Les Landis D'Hortense* (1983), *Chet Baker Live In Sweden* (1983), *The Improviser* (1983), *Chet Baker At Capolinea* (1983), *Blues For A Reason* (1984), *The Chet Baker Trio* (1985), *Chet's Choice* (1985), *My Foolish Heart* (1985), *Misty* (1985), *Time After Time* (1985), *Live From The Moonlight* (1985), *Candy* (1985), *Naima* (1985-87), *As Time Goes By* (1986), *Night Bird* (1986), *Live At Rosenheimer* (1988), *Let's Get Lost* (1989, film soundtrack), *Live In Brussells 1964* (1993).

Baker, Kenny

b. 1 March 1921, Withernsea, Yorkshire, England. After taking up the trumpet and playing in brass bands, Baker moved to London, in the late 30s, to become a professional musician. During the next few years he established himself as an outstanding technician capable of playing in any jazz or dance band. In the early 40s, he played in the bands of Lew Stone and George Chisholm before joining Ted Heath in 1944. He remained with Heath until 1949, and was featured on many recording sessions and countless concerts. In the early 50s he was regularly on the radio, leading his own band, the Baker's Dozen, on a weekly late-night show which lasted throughout the decade. In the 60s he led his own groups and recorded film soundtracks, all the while building his reputation as one of the best trumpet players in the world even though he played only rarely outside the UK. At the end of the decade he was featured in Benny Goodman's British band. Baker's career continued throughout the 70s, with appearances as co-leader of the Best of British Jazz touring package, and with Ted Heath recreations and the bands led by Don Lusher and other former colleagues. In the early 80s, Baker turned down an invitation to take over leadership of the Harry James band after the latter's death. He could still be regularly heard playing concerts and club dates and was also on television, usually off-camera, playing soundtracks for Alan Plater's popular UK television series *The Beiderbecke Affair* and *The Beiderbecke Tapes*. In 1989, he took part in a major recording undertaking which set out to recreate the classic recordings of Louis Armstrong using modern recording techniques. Baker took the Armstrong role, comfortably confounding the date on his birth certificate with his masterful playing. A fiery soloist with a remarkable technical capacity which he never uses simply for effect, Baker is one of the UK's greatest contributions to the international jazz scene.

Albums: *Kenny Baker's Half-Dozen* (1957), *Date With The Dozen* (1957), *Baker Plays McHugh* (1958), *The Phase 4 World Of Kenny Baker* (1977), with Benny Goodman *London Date* (1969), *George Chisholm* (1973), *The Very Best Of British Jazz* (1983), with Don Lusher *The Big Band Sound Of Ted Heath* (1986), *The Louis Armstrong Connection Vols 1-7* (1989), *Tribute To The Great Trumpeters* (1993).

Baker, LaVern

b. Delores Williams, 11 November 1928, Chicago, Illinois, USA. LaVern Baker was discovered in a Chicago nightclub by bandleader Fletcher Henderson. Although still in her teens, the singer won a recording deal with the influential OKeh Records, where she was nicknamed 'Little Miss Sharecropper' and 'Bea Baker'. Having toured extensively with the Todd Rhodes Orchestra, Baker secured a prestigious contract with Atlantic Records, with whom she enjoyed a fruitful relationship. 'Tweedle Dee' reached both the US R&B and pop charts in 1955, selling in excess of one million copies, and the artist was awarded a second gold disc two years later for 'Jim Dandy'. In 1959, she enjoyed a number 6 pop hit with 'I Cried A Tear' and throughout the decade Baker remained one of black music's leading performers. Although eclipsed by newer acts during the 60s, the singer scored further success with 'Saved', written and produced by Leiber And Stoller, and 'See See Rider', both of which inspired subsequent versions, notably by the Band and the Animals. Baker's final chart entry came with 'Think Twice' a 1966 duet with Jackie Wilson as her 'classic' R&B intonation grew increasingly out of step with the prevalent soul/Motown boom. After leaving Atlantic, Baker is probably best known for 'One Monkey Don't Stop The Show'. In the late 60s, while entertaining US troops in Vietnam, she became ill, and went to the Philippines to recuperate. She stayed there in self-imposed exile for 22 years, reviving her career in 1991 at New York's Village Gate club. During 1992 she undertook a short UK tour, but audience numbers were disappointing for the only woman, along with Aretha Franklin, who had, at that time, been

elected to the US Rock 'n' Roll Hall Of Fame.
Albums: *LaVern* (1956), *LaVern Baker* (1957), *LaVern Baker Sings Bessie Smith* (1958), *Blues Ballads* (1959), *Precious Memories* (1959), *Saved* (1961), *See See Rider* (1963), *I'm Gonna Get You* (1966). Compilations: *The Best Of LaVern Baker* (1963), *Real Gone Gal* (1984).

Barber, Chris

b. 17 April 1930, Welwyn Garden City, Hertfordshire, England. In the 40s Barber studied trombone and bass at the Guildhall School of Music, eventually settling on the former as his principal instrument (although he occasionally played bass in later years). In the late 40s he formed his first band which, unusually, was formed as a cooperative. Also in the band were Monty Sunshine, Ron Bowden and Lonnie Donegan. By the early 50s the band had gained a considerable following but it was nevertheless decided to invite Ken Colyer to join. The move was musically promising but proved to be unsuccessful when the personalities involved clashed repeatedly. Eventually, Colyer left and was replaced by Pat Halcox. With a remarkably consistent personnel the Barber band was soon one of the UK's leading traditional groups and well placed to take advantage of the surge of interest in this form of jazz in the late 50s and early 60s. The decline of popularity in 'trad', which came on the heels of the rock explosion, had a dramatic effect on many British jazz bands but Barber's fared much better than most. In part this was due to his astute business sense and in part thanks to his keen awareness of musical trends and a willingness to accommodate other forms without compromising his high musical standards. In the 60s Barber changed the name of the band to the Chris Barber Blues and Jazz Band. Into the traditional elements of the band's book he incorporated ragtime but also worked with such modern musicians as Joe Harriott. Amongst his most important activities at this time was his active promotion of R&B and the blues, which he underlined by bringing major American artists to the UK, often at his own expense. Through such philanthropy he brought to the attention of British audiences the likes of Sister Rosetta Tharpe, Brownie McGhee, Louis Jordan and Muddy Waters. Not content with performing the older blues styles, Barber also acknowledged the contemporary interest in blues evinced by rock musicians and audiences and hired such players as John Slaughter and Pete York (ex-Spencer Davis Group), who worked happily beside long-serving

sidemen Halcox, Ian Wheeler, Vic Pitt and others. In the 70s, Barber focused more on mainstream music, showing a special affinity for small Duke Ellington-styled bands, and now toured with visitors like Russell Procope, Wild Bill Davis, Trummy Young and John Lewis. He also maintained his contact with his jazz roots and, simultaneously, the contemporary blues scene by touring widely with his *Take Me Back To New Orleans* show, which featured Mac 'Dr John' Rebenneck. As a trombone player, Barber's work is enhanced by his rich sound and flowing solo style. It is, however, as bandleader and trendspotter that he has made his greatest contribution to the jazz scene, both internationally and, especially, in the UK. In the early 90s he was happily entering his fifth decade as a bandleader with no discernible flagging of his interest, enthusiasm, skill or, indeed, of his audience. In 1991 he was awarded the OBE. Selected albums: *Ragtime* (1960), *Chris Barber At The London Palladium* (1961), *Getting Around* (1963), *Battersea Rain Dance* (1967-68), *Live In East Berlin* (1968), *Get Rolling!* (1969-71), *Sideways* (1974), *Echoes Of Ellington* (1976), *Take Me Back To New Orleans* (1980), *Mardi Gras At The Marquee* (1983), *Concert For The BBC* (1986), *Classics Concerts In Berlin* (1988, rec. 1959), *Stardust* (1988). Compilations: *Can't We Get It Together? (1954-84)* (1986), *The Best Of Chris Barber (1959-62)* (1988).

Bart, Lionel

b. Lionel Begleiter, 1 August 1930, London, England. The comparative inactivity of Bart for many years has tended to cloud the fact that he is one of the major songwriters of 20th-century popular song. The former silk-screen printer was at the very hub of the rock 'n' roll and skiffle generation that came out of London's Soho in the mid-50s. As a member of the Cavemen with Tommy Steele he later became Steele's main source of non-American song material. In addition to writing the pioneering 'Rock With The Cavemen' he composed a series of glorious singalong numbers including 'A Handful Of Songs', 'Water Water' and the trite but delightfully innocent 'Little White Bull'. Much of Bart's work was steeped in the English music-hall tradition with a strong working class pride and it was no surprise that he soon graduated into writing songs for full-length stage shows. *Lock Up Your Daughters* and *Fings Ain't Wot They Used To Be* were two of his early successes, both appearing during 1959, the same year he wrote the classic 'Living Doll' for Cliff Richard. Bart was one of the first writers to

Lionel Bart

introduce mild politics into his lyrics; beautifully transcribed with topical yet humourously ironic innocence, for example: 'They've changed our local Palais into a bowling alley and fings ain't wot they used to be.' As the 60s dawned Bart unconsciously embarked on a decade that saw him reach dizzy heights of success and made him one of the musical personalities of the decade. During the first quarter of the year he topped the charts with 'Do You Mind' for Anthony Newley; a brilliantly simple and catchy song complete with Bart's own finger-snapped accompaniment. The best was yet to come when that year he launched *Oliver!*, a musical based on Dickens' *Oliver Twist*. This became a phenomenal triumph, and remains one of the most successful musicals of all time. Bart's knack of simple melody combined with unforgettable lyrics produced a plethora of classics including the pleading 'Who Will Buy', the rousing 'Food Glorious Food' and the poignant 'As Long As He Needs Me' (also a major hit for Shirley Bassey, although she reputedly never liked the song). Bart was a pivotal figure throughout the swinging London scene of the 60s, although he maintains that the party actually started in the 50s. Lionel befriended Brian Epstein, the Beatles, the Rolling Stones, became an international star following *Oliver!'s* success as a film (winning six Oscars) and was romantically linked with Judy Garland and Alma Cogan. Following continued,

although lesser success, with *Blitz!* and *Maggie May*, Lionel came down to reality when the London critics damned his 1965 musical *Twang*, based upon the life of Robin Hood. Bart's philanthropic nature made him a prime target for business sharks and he was wrested of much of his fortune by trusting too many people. By the end of the 60s the cracks were beginning to show; his dependence on drugs and alcohol increased and he watched many of his close friends die in tragic circumstances; Cogan with cancer, Garland through drink and drugs and Epstein's supposed suicide. In 1969, *La Strada* only had a short run in New York before Lionel retreated into himself, and for many years kept a relatively low-profile, watching the 70s and 80s pass almost as a blur, only making contributions to *The Londoners* and *Costa Packet*. During this time the gutter press were eager for a kiss-and-tell story, but Bart remained silent, a credible action considering the sums of money he was offered. During the late 80s Lionel finally beat his battle with booze and ended the decade a saner, wiser and healthier man. His renaissance started in 1989 when he was commissioned by a UK building society to write a television jingle. The composition became part of an award-winning advertisement, featuring a number of angelic children singing with Bart, filmed in pristine monochrome. The song 'Happy Endings' was a justifiable exhumation of a man who remains an immensely talented figure and whose work ranks with some of the greatest of the American 'musical comedy' songwriters. In the early 90s, his profile continued to be high, with revivals, by the talented National Youth Theatre, of *Oliver!*, *Maggie May* and *Blitz!;* the latter production commemorating the 50th anniversary of the real thing.

Bartholomew, Dave

b. 24 December 1940, Edgard, Louisiana, USA. Dave Bartholomew was one of the most important shapers of New Orleans R&B and rock 'n' roll during the 50s. A producer, arranger, songwriter, bandleader and artist, Bartholomew produced and co-wrote most of Fats Domino's major hits for Imperial Records. Bartholomew started playing the trumpet as a child, encouraged by his father, a dixieland jazz tuba player. He performed in marching bands throughout the 30s and then on a Mississippi riverboat led by Fats Pichon beginning in 1939, and learned songwriting basics during a spell in the US Army. Upon his return to New Orleans in the late 40s he formed his first band, which became one of the city's most popular. He also backed Little Richard on some early recordings. Bartholomew worked for several labels, including Specialty, Aladdin and De Luxe, for whom he had a big hit in 1949 with 'Country Boy'. In the same year he started a long-term association with Imperial as a producer and arranger. The previous year Bartholomew had discovered Domino in New Orleans's Hideaway Club and he introduced him to Imperial. They collaborated on 'The Fat Man', which, in 1950, became the first of over a dozen hits co-authored by the pair and produced by Bartholomew. Others included 'Blue Monday', 'Walking To New Orleans', 'Let The Four Winds Blow', 'I'm In Love Again', 'Whole Lotta Loving', 'My Girl Josephine' and 'I'm Walkin'', the latter also becoming a hit for Ricky Nelson. Bartholomew's other credits included Smiley Lewis's 'I Hear You Knocking' (later a hit for Dave Edmunds) and 'One Night' (later a hit for Elvis Presley, with its lyrics tamed), Lloyd Price's 'Lawdy Miss Clawdy', and records for Shirley And Lee, Earl King, Roy Brown, Huey 'Piano' Smith, Bobby Mitchell, Chris Kenner, Robert Parker, Frankie Ford and Snooks Eaglin. In 1963, Imperial was sold to Liberty Records, and Bartholomew declined an invitation to move to their Hollywood base, preferring to stay in New Orleans. In 1972, Chuck Berry reworked 'My Ding-A-Ling', a song Bartholomew had penned in 1952, into his only USA number 1 single.

Although Bartholomew, who claims to have written over 4,000 songs, recorded under his own name, his contribution was primarily as a behind-the-scenes figure. He recorded a dixieland album in 1981 and in the early 90s was still leading a big band at occasional special events such as the New Orleans Jazz & Heritage Festival.

Albums: *Jump Children* (1984), *The Monkey* (1985), *Heritage* (1986), *Graciously* (1987). Compilation: *The Best Of Dave Bartholomew: The Classic New Orleans R&B Band Sound* (1989).

Basie, Count

b. William Basie, 21 August 1904, Red Bank, New Jersey, USA, d. 26 April 1984. Bandleader and pianist Basie grew up in Red Bank, just across the Hudson River from New York City. His mother gave him his first lessons at the piano, and he used every opportunity to hear the celebrated kings of New York keyboard - James P. Johnson, Willie 'The Lion' Smith and especially Fats Waller. Ragtime was all the rage, and these keyboard professors ransacked the European tradition to achieve ever more spectacular improvisations. The young Basie listened to Fats Waller playing the organ in Harlem's Lincoln Theater and received tuition from him. Pianists were in demand to accompany vaudeville acts, and Waller recommended Basie as his successor in the Katie Crippen And Her Kids troupe, and with them he toured black venues throughout America (often referred to as the 'chitlin' circuit'). Stranded in Kansas City after the Gonzel White tour collapsed, Basie found it 'wide-open'. Owing to the *laissez-faire* administration of Democrat leader Tom Pendergast, musicians could easily find work, and jazz blossomed alongside gambling and prostitution (many people trace the origins of modern jazz to these circumstances - see Kansas City Jazz). Basie played to silent movies for a while, then in 1928 joined Walter Page's Blue Devils, starting a 20-year-long association with the bassist. When the Blue Devils broke up, Basie joined Bennie Moten, then, in 1935 started his own band at the Reno Club and quickly lured Moten's best musicians into its ranks. Unfettered drinking hours, regular broadcasts on local radio and Basie's feel for swing honed the band into quite simply the most classy and propulsive unit in the history of music. Duke Ellington's band may have been more ambitious, but for sheer unstoppable *swing* Basie could not be beaten. Impresario John Hammond recognised as much when he heard them on their local broadcast: in January 1937 an augmented Basie band made its recording debut for Decca. By this time the classic rhythm section - Freddie Green (guitar), Walter Page (bass) and Jo Jones (drums) - had been established. The horns - which included Lester Young (tenor saxophone) and Buck Clayton (trumpet) - sounded magnificent buoyed by this team and the goadings of Basie's deceptively simple piano. Basie frequently called himself a 'non-pianist': actually, his incisive minimalism had great power and influence - not least on Thelonious Monk, one of bebop's principal architects.

In 1938, the band recorded the classic track 'Jumpin' At The Woodside', a Basie composition featuring solos by Earl Warren (alto saxophone) and Herschel Evans (clarinet), as well as Young and Clayton. The track could be taken as a definition of swing. Basie's residency at the Famous Door club on New York's West 52nd Street from July 1938 to January 1939 was a great success, CBS broadcasting the band over its radio network (transcriptions of these broadcasts have recently been made available - although hardly hi-fi, they are fascinating documents, with Lester Young playing clarinet as well as tenor). This booking was followed by a six-month residency in Chicago. It is this kind of regular work - spontaneity balanced with regular application - that explains why the recorded sides of the period are some of the great music of the century. In 1939 Basie left Decca for Columbia, with whom he stayed until 1946. Throughout the 40s the Count Basie band provided dancers with conducive rhythms and jazz fans with astonishing solos: both appreciated his characteristic contrast of brass and reeds. Outstanding tenors emerged: Don Byas, Buddy Tate, Lucky Thompson, Illinois Jacquet, Paul Gonsalves, as well as trumpeters (Al Killian and Joe Newman) and trombonists (Vic Dickenson and J.J. Johnson). On vocals Basie used Jimmy Rushing for the blues material and Helen Humes for pop and novelty numbers. Economic necessity pared down the Basie band to seven members at the start of the 50s, but otherwise Basie maintained a big band right through to his death in 1984. In 1954 he made his first tour of Europe, using arrangements by Ernie Wilkins and Neal Hefti. In June 1957 Basie broke the colour bar at New York's Waldorf-Astoria Hotel; his was the first black band to play there, and they stayed for a four month engagement. The 1957 *The Atomic Mr Basie* set Hefti's arrangements in glorious stereo sound and was acknowledged as a classic. Even the cover made its mark: in the 70s Blondie adapted its

period nuclear-chic to frame singer Debbie Harry.

In 1960, Jimmy Rushing left the band, depriving it of a popular frontman, but the European tours continued - a groundbreaking tour of Japan in 1963 was also a great success. Count Basie was embraced by the American entertainment industry and appeared in the films *Sex And The Single Girl* and *Made In Paris*. He became a regular television guest alongside the likes of Frank Sinatra, Fred Astaire, Sammy Davis Jnr. and Tony Bennett. Arranging for Basie was a significant step in the career of Quincy Jones (now famous as Michael Jackson's producer). The onslaught of the Beatles and rock music in the 60s was giving jazz a hard time: Basie responded by giving current pop tunes the big band treatment. Jones arranged *Hits Of The 50s And 60s*. Its resounding commercial success led to a string of similar albums arranged by Bill Byers: the brass adopted the stridency of John Barry's James Bond scores and, unlike the work of the previous decades, these records now sound dated. In 1965, Basie signed to Sinatra's Reprise label, and made several recordings and appearances with him. By 1969 most of Basie's original sidemen had left the band, though Freddie Green was still with him. Eddie 'Lockjaw' Davis (tenor) was now his most distinguished soloist. The arranger Sammy Nestico provided some interesting compositions, and 1979 saw the release of *Afrique*, an intriguing and unconventional album arranged by Oliver Nelson with tunes by *avant garde* saxophonists such as Albert Ayler and Pharoah Sanders. In 1975, after recording for a slew of different labels, Basie found a home on Pablo Records (owned by Norman Granz, organizer of the Jazz At The Philharmonic showcases). This produced a late flowering, as, unlike previous producers, Granz let Basie do what he does best - swing the blues - rather than collaborate with popular singers. In 1983, the death of his wife Catherine, whom he had married 40 years before while he was with the Bennie Moten band, struck a heavy blow and he himself died the following year. The later compromises should not cloud Basie's achievements: during the 30s he integrated the bounce of the blues into sophisticated ensemble playing. His piano work showed that rhythm and space were more important than technical virtuosity: his composing gave many eminent soloists their finest moments. Without the Count Basie Orchestra's sublimely aerated versions of 'Cherokee' it is unlikely that Charlie Parker could have ever created 'Koko'. Modern jazz stands indubitably in Basie's debt.

Selected albums: *Jumpin' At The Woodside* (1938

recordings), *Count Basie And His Orchestra* (1944 recordings), *At The Blue Note* (1955-56 recordings), *The Atomic Mr Basie* (1957), *Count Basie and the Kansas City Seven* (1962), *At The Montreux Jazz Festival* (1975), with Dizzy Gillespie *The Gifted Ones* (1977), *Afrique* (1979), *Basic Basie* (1974), *Live In Japan '78* (1985), *Birdland Era, Vols. 1 & 2* (1986). Numerous compilations are always available.

Bassey, Shirley

b. 8 January 1937, Tiger Bay, Cardiff, Wales. Her early jobs included work in a factory's wrapping and packing department, while playing working men's clubs at weekends. After touring the UK in revues and Variety, Lancashire comedian Al Read included her in his 1955 Christmas Show at London's Adelphi Theatre, and his revue, *Such Is Life*, which ran for a year. Her first hit, in 1957, was the calypso-styled 'Banana Boat Song', followed by 'Kiss Me Honey Honey, Kiss Me' nearly two years later. With her powerful voice (she was sometimes called 'Bassey the Belter'), the unique Bassey style and phrasing started to emerge in 1959 with 'As I Love You' which topped the UK chart, and continued through to the mid-70s via such heart rending ballads as Lionel Bart's 'As Long As He Needs Me' (Nancy's big song from *Oliver*), 'You'll Never Know', 'I'll Get By', 'Reach For The Stars'/'Climb Every Mountain', 'What Now My Love', '(I) Who Have Nothing', George Harrison's, 'Something', 'For All We Know', and an Italian hit with a new lyric by Norman Newell, 'Never, Never, Never'. Her singles sales were such that, even into the 80s, her records had spent more weeks in the UK chart than those of any other female performer. Hit albums included *Shirley, Something, Something Else, Never Never Never, The Shirley Bassey Singles Album* and *25th Anniversary Album*. In 1962, she was accompanied on *Let's Face The Music* by top USA arranger/conductor Nelson Riddle. In live performances her rise to the top was swift and by the early 60s she was headlining in New York and Las Vegas. In 1964 Bassey had a big hit in the USA with 'Goldfinger', one of three songs she sang on the title sequences of James Bond movies. The others were 'Diamonds Are Forever' and 'Moonraker'. In 1969, she moved her base to Switzerland but continued to play major concert halls throughout the world. The American Guild Of Variety Artists voted her 'Best Female Entertainer' for 1976, and in the same year she celebrated 20 years as a recording artist with a 22-date British tour. In 1977, she received a Britannia Award for the 'Best Female Solo Singer In The Last 50 Years'.

In 1981, Bassey withdrew to her Swiss home and announced her semi-retirement, but continued to emerge occasionally throughout the 80s for television specials, concert tours, and a few albums including *Love Songs* and *I Am What I Am*. In one of pop's more unlikely collaborations, she was teamed with Yello in 1987 for the single, 'The Rhythm Divine'. In the 90s, with her provocative body language, ever more lavish gowns, and specialities such as 'Big Spender', 'Nobody Does It Like Me', 'Tonight' and 'What Kind Of Fool Am I', together with more contemporary material, the 'Tigress Of Tiger Bay' has shown herself to be a powerful and exciting performer. Her 1993 UK concert tour attracted favourable reviews, even from some hardened rock critics, and, in the same year, a new cabaret club was opened in Cardiff - named 'Bassey's'

Albums: *The Bewitching Miss Bassey* (1959), *Fabulous Shirley Bassey* (1960), *Shirley* (1961), *Shirley Bassey* (1962), *Let's Face The Music* (1962), *Shirley Bassey At The Pigalle* (1965), *Shirley Bassey Belts The Best!* (1965), *I've Got A Song For You* (1966), *Twelve Of Those Songs* (1968), *Live At The Talk Of The Town* (1970), *Something* (1970), *Something Else* (1971), *Big Spender* (1971), *It's Magic* (1971), *What Now My Love* (1971), *I Capricorn* (1972), *And I Love You So* (1972), *Never, Never, Never* (1973), *Live At Carnegie Hall* (1973), *Broadway, Bassey's Way* (1973), *Nobody Does It Like Me* (1974), *Good, Bad But Beautiful* (1975), *Love, Life And Feelings* (1976), *Thoughts Of Love* (1976), *You Take My Heart Away* (1977), *The Magic Is You* (1979), *As Long As He Needs Me* (1980), *As Time Goes By* (1980), *I'm In The Mood For Love* (1981), *Love Songs* (1982), *All By Myself* (1984), *I Am What I Am* (1984), *Playing Solitaire* (1985), *I've Got You Under My Skin* (1985), *Sings The Songs From The Shows* (1986), *Born To Sing The Blues* (1987), *Let Me Sing And I'm Happy* (1988), *Her Favourite Songs* (1988), *Keep The Music Playing* (1991). Compilations: *Golden Hits Of Shirley Bassey* (1968), *The Shirley Bassey Collection* (1972), *The Shirley Bassey Singles Album* (1975), *25th Anniversary Album* (1978), *21 Hit Singles* (1979), *Tonight* (1984), *Diamonds - The Best Of Shirley Bassey* (1988), *The Bond Collection - 30th Anniversary* (1993).

Baxter, Les

b. 14 March 1922, Mexia, Texas, USA. Baxter studied piano at Detroit Conservatory then moved to Los Angeles for further studies at Pepperdine

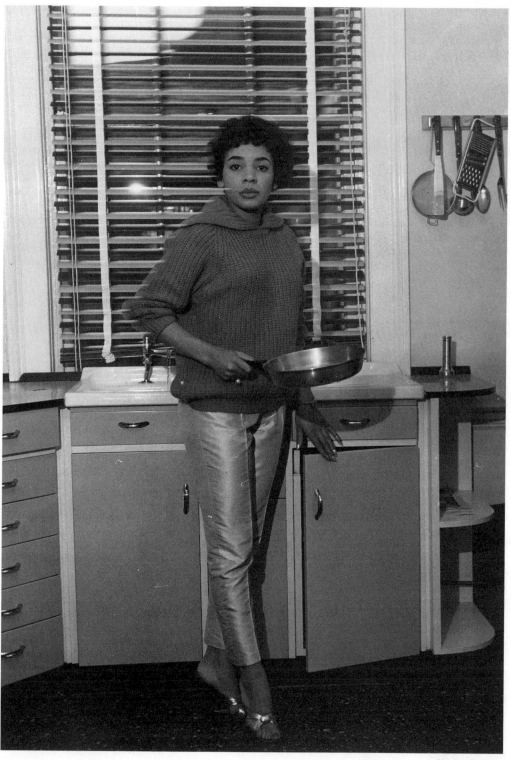

Shirley Bassey

College. Abandoning a concert career as a pianist he went into popular music as a singer, and at the age of 23 he joined Mel Tormé's Mel-Tones, providing vocals on Artie Shaw records like 'What Is This Thing Called Love'. He then turned to arranging and conducting for Capitol Records in 1950 and was responsible for early Nat 'King' Cole hits 'Mona Lisa' and 'Too Young'. With his own orchestra he released a number of hits including 'April In Portugal', 'Ruby' (1953), 'Unchained Melody' (1955), and 'Poor People Of Paris' (1956). He also did well with concept albums of his own orchestral suites *Le Sacre Du Sauvage*, *Festival Of The Gnomes*, *Ports Of Pleasure*, *Brazil Now*, the first three on Capital the latter on Gene Norman's Crescendo label. Baxter obviously had a penchant for writing Latin music for strings, but he did not restrict his activities to recording. He operated in radio as musical director of *Halls Of Ivy* and the Bob Hope and Abbott & Costello shows; worked on films and later composed and conducted scores for Roger Corman's Edgar Allan Poe films and other horror stories and teenage musicals, including *Comedy Of Terrors* (1963), *Muscle Beach Party* (1964), *The Dunwich Horror* (1970) and *Frogs* (1972).

Selected albums: *Le Sacre Du Sauvage* (1952), *Music Of Prince Di Candriano* (1953), *Festival Of the Gnomes* (1953), *Thinking Of You* (1954), *Arthur Murray Modern Waltzes* (1955), *Ports Of Pleasure* (1958), *Love Is A Fabulous Thing* (1958), *Wild Guitars* (1959), *African Jazz* (1959), *South Pacific* (1959), *Young Pops* (1960), *Teen Drums* (1960), *Broadway '61* (1961), *Jewels Of The Sea* (1961), *Sensational!* (1962), *Brazil Now!* (1967).

Becaud, Gilbert

b. Francois Silly, 24 October 1927, Toulon, France. A popular singer-songwriter in France in the 50s and 60s, rivalling Charles Trenet and Charles Aznavour, Becaud studied music in Nice and started writing songs around 1946. His first collaborator was lyricist Pierre Delanoe in 1946. One of their first successes was 'Je T'ai Dans La Peau' for Edith Piaf in 1950. He served as an accompanist for Piaf, and other artists such as Jacques Pills. Later he sang in cabaret, and made his first stage appearance in 1952 at Versailles. Two years later a dramatic performance at the Olympia Music Hall gained him the title of 'Monsieur 1000 Volts', and elevated him to national stardom. In the early 50s he had hit records with 'Les Croix', 'Quand Tu Danses' and 'Mes Mains'. Later successes included 'Dimanche A Orly', 'Le Jour Ou La Pluie Viendra', 'Couventine', 'Heureusement, Y'a Les Copains', 'Viens Danser' and 'Tu Le Regretteras'. In 1958, his 'The Day The Rains Came', written with Delanoe and Carl Sigman, became a UK number 1 for Jane Morgan, and in 1962, Morgan also recorded their 'What Now My Love', although it was Shirley Bassey's dramatic version which had the most chart impact. The song was revived by Sonny And Cher in 1966 and was later covered by many other artists including Frank Sinatra. In the following year, Vikki Carr's emotive rendering of 'It Must Be Him' ('Seul Sur Son Etoile'), written with lyricist Mack David, made both the US and UK Top 5. Becaud himself had a UK hit in 1975 with 'A Little Love And Understanding', written with Marcel Stellman. His other collaborators included Louis Amade Maurice Vidalin, and the English librettist and lyricist, Julian More, with whom he worked on *Roza*, the 1987 Broadway musical based on Romain Gary's novel, *La Vie Devant Soi'*. The show closed after 12 performances.

Selected albums: *Et Maintenant...Gilbert Becaud* (1964), *Gilbert Becaud* (1968), *Becaud Olympia '70* (1970). Compilations: *Collection* (1983), *Disque D'or, Volumes 1 & 2* (1983).

Belafonte, Harry

b. Harold George Belafonte, 1 March 1927, New York, USA. In recent years, the former 'King Of Calypso' has become better known for his work with UNICEF and his enterprise with USA For Africa. Prior to that, Belafonte had an extraordinarily varied life. His early career was spent as an actor, until he had time to demonstrate his silky smooth and gently relaxing singing voice. He appeared as Joe in Oscar Hammerstein's *Carmen Jones*; an adaptation of *Carmen* by Bizet, and in 1956 he was snapped up by RCA Victor. Belafonte was then at the forefront of the calypso craze which was a perfect vehicle for his happy-go-lucky folk songs. Early hits included 'Jamaica Farewell', 'Mary's Boy Child' and the classic transatlantic hit 'Banana Boat Song' with its unforgettable refrain; 'Day-oh, dayyo, daylight come and me wanna go home'. *Calypso* became the first ever album to sell a million copies, and spent 31 weeks at the top of the US charts. Belafonte continued throughout the 50s with incredible success. He was able to cross over into many markets appealing to pop, folk, jazz as well as the with ethnic population with whom he became closely associated, particularly during the civil rights movement. He appeared in many films

Harry Belafonte

including *Island In The Sun*, singing the title song and *Odds Against Tomorrow*. His success as an album artist was considerable; between 1956 and 1962 he was hardly ever absent from the album chart. *Belafonte At Carnegie Hall* spent over three years in the charts, and similar success befell *Belafonte Returns To Carnegie Hall*, featuring Miriam Makeba, the Chad Mitchell Trio and Odetta with the memorable recording of 'There's A Hole In My Bucket'. Throughout the 60s Belafonte was an ambassador of human rights and a most articulate speaker at rallies and on television. His appeal as a concert hall attraction was immense, no less than seven of his albums were recorded in concert. Although his appearances in the best-sellers had stopped by the 70s he remained an active performer, recording artist and continued to appear on film, although in lightweight movies like *Buck And The Preacher* and *Uptown Saturday Night*. In the mid-80s he was a leading light in the USA For Africa appeal and sang on 'We Are The World'. His sterling work continued into the 90s with UNICEF. Belafonte was one of the few black artists who broke down barriers of class and race and should be counted with Martin Luther King as a major figure in achieving equal rights for blacks in America, although he did it through popular music in a less obvious way.
Albums: *Mark Twain And Other Folk Favorites* (1955), *Belafonte* (1956), *Calypso* (1956), *An Evening With Belafonte* (1957), *Belafonte Sings Of The Caribbean* (1957), *Belafonte Sings The Blues* (1958), *Love Is A Gentle Thing* (1959), *Porgy And Bess* (1959), *Belafonte At Carnegie Hall* (1959), *My Lord What A Mornin'* (1960), *Belafonte Returns To Carnegie Hall* (1960), *Jump Up Calypso* (1961), *The Midnight Special* (1962), *The Many Moods Of Belafonte* (1962), *To Wish You A Merry Christmas* (1962), *Streets I Have Walked* (1963), *Belafonte At The Greek Theatre* (1964), *Ballads Blues And Boasters* (1964), *An Evening With Belafonte/Makeba* (1965), *An Evening With Belafonte/Mouskouri* (1966), *In My Quiet Room* (1966), *Calypso In Brass* (1967), *Belafonte On Campus* (1967), *Homeward Bound* (1970), *Turn The World Around* (1977), *Loving You Is Where I Belong* (1981), *Paradise In Gazankulu* (1988). Compilations: *Collection - Castle Collector Series* (1987), *Banana Boat Song* (1988), *All Time Greatest Hits* (1989), *The Very Best Of* (1992).

Bell, Freddie, And The Bellboys

This early US rock 'n' roll six-piece outfit was led by singer Freddie Bell. Their slightly 'big band' style of rock 'n' roll included a version of Willie Mae Thornton's 'Hound Dog' for the Teen label in 1955. Elvis Presley saw them performing the song live in April 1956 and recorded his own version in July. The Bellboys achieved another landmark by appearing in the first rock 'n' roll movie- *Rock Around The Clock* in 1956. They were also the first US rock act to tour the UK, supporting Tommy Steele in 1956. Their best-known number was also released that year, 'Giddy Up A Ding Dong' and became a number 4 hit in the UK. Other singles included 'The Hucklebuck', 'Teach You To Rock' and 'Rockin' Is My Business'. Another film appearance awaited in the 1964 pop exploitation movie *The Swingin' Set* (*Get Yourself A College Girl* In The US), where Roberta Linn sang with them. The Animals, the Dave Clark Five and the Standells also featured.
Albums: *Rock 'n' Roll All Flavours* (1958), *Bells Are Swinging* (1964).

Bells Are Ringing

Despite its unlikely setting, a telephone answering service, the stage musical *Bells Are Ringing* benefited from a strong and original book, by Betty Comden and Adolph Green (they also wrote the lyrics) and some delightful tunes by Jule Styne. The show was created by Comden and Green for Judy Holliday with whom they had worked in the past. Holliday played the role of Ella Peterson, an employee of Susanswerphone, who becomes romantically involved with one of her unseen clients and also solves the problems of others. Amongst the show's songs were two which have become standards, 'The Party's Over' and 'Just In Time'. *Bells Are Ringing* opened on Broadway on 29 November 1956 and ran for 924 performances. The 1960 screen version also starred Holliday but the magic of the stage show was somehow mislaid in the transition.

Belmonts

The Belmonts were one of the leading American doo-wop groups of the late 50s comprising, Angelo D'Aleo (b. 3 February 1940, Bronx, New York, USA), Carlo Mastrangelo (b. 5 October 1938, Bronx, New York, USA), and Freddie Milano (b. 22 August 1939, Bronx, New York, USA). Their leader was Dion DiMucci, who left for a solo career in 1960. The band soldiered on for three more years after being signed to a new record label Sabina. They had enough fans to give them six further hits including a smooth version of the Ink Spots hit 'Don't Get Around Much Anymore'. They reformed briefly with Dion in

1967, 1972 and 1973. Their most memorable work remains in the 50s with Dion.
Compilation: *The Belmont's Carnival Of Hits* (1962).

Bennett, Tony

b. Anthony Dominick Benedetto, 13 August 1926, Astoria, New York, USA. The son of an Italian father and American mother, Bennett studied music and painting at the High School of Industrial Arts. He later became a talented artist, exhibiting under his real name in New York, Paris and London. Originally possessing a tenor voice which would deepen over the years, Bennett sang during service with the US Army's entertainment unit late in World War II. Upon his discharge he worked in clubs before joining a Pearl Bailey revue in Greenwich Village as singer and master of ceremonies under the name of Joe Bari, where he was spotted by Bob Hope who engaged him to sing in his Paramount show and changed his name to Tony Bennett. In 1950 he successfully auditioned for Columbia Records' producer Mitch Miller, singing 'Boulevard Of Broken Dreams', and a year later topped the US chart with 'Because Of You' and 'Cold, Cold Heart'. Other 50s hits, mostly backed by the Percy Faith Orchestra, included 'Rags To Riches', 'Just In Time', 'Stranger In Paradise' (from *Kismet*), 'There'll Be No Teardrops Tonight', 'Cinnamon Sinner', 'Can You Find It In Your Heart' and 'In The Middle Of An Island'. In 1958, his album *Basie Swings-Bennett Sings* was a precursor to later jazz-based work. That same year 'Firefly', by the new songwriting team of Cy Coleman and Carolyn Leigh, was Bennett's last US Top 40 entry until 1962, when he made a major comeback with 'I Left My Heart In San Francisco' and a sell-out Carnegie Hall concert, which was recorded and released on a double-album set. This period also marked the start of a long association with pianist/arranger Ralph Sharon, and frequently featured cornet soloist, Bobby Hackett. Often quoted as being unable to find suitable new material, Bennett nevertheless made the 60s singles charts with contemporary songs such as 'I Wanna Be Around', 'The Good Life', 'Who Can I Turn To' and 'If I Ruled The World'. Even so, the future lay with concerts and his prolific album output which included US Top 40 albums such as *I Wanna Be Around*, *The Many Moods Of Tony*, *The Movie Song Album*, and four albums with Canadian composer/conductor Robert Farnon. In the 70s Bennett left Columbia and recorded for various labels including his own, and made albums with jazz-musicians Ruby Braff and Bill Evans. His return to Columbia in the mid-80s produced *The Art Of Excellence*, which included a duet with Ray Charles, and *Bennett/Berlin* accompanied by the Ralph Sharon Trio, a celebration of America's premier songwriter. He continued to gain excellent reviews at venues such as the Desert Inn, Las Vegas, and, in 1991, celebrated 40 years in the business with a concert at London's Prince Edward Theatre. In 1993, he was awarded a Grammy for 'Best Traditional Pop Performance' for his album, *Perfectly Frank*.

Albums: *Treasure Chest Of Songs* (1955), *Cloud Seven* (1955), *Tony* (1957), *The Best Of My Heart* (1957), *Long Ago And Far Away* (1958), *Basie Swings-Bennett Sings* (1958), *Blue Velvet* (1959), *If I Ruled The World* (1959), *Alone At Last With Tony Bennett* (1959), *Because Of You* (1959), with Count Basie *Tony Bennett In Person* (1959), *Hometown, My Hometown* (1959), *To My Wonderful One* (1960), *Tony Sings For Two* (1960), *Alone Together* (1960), *A String Of Harold Arlen* (1960), *My Heart Sings* (1961), *Bennett And Basie Strike Up The Band* (1961), *Mr. Broadway* (1962), *I Left My Heart In San Francisco* (1962), *Tony Bennett At Carnegie Hall* (1962), *I Wanna Be Around* (1963), *This Is All I Ask* (1963), *The Many Moods Of Tony* (1964), *When Lights Are Low* (1964), *Who Can I Turn To* (1964), *If I Ruled The World - Songs For The Jet Set* (1965), *The Movie Song Album* (1966), *A Time For Love* (1966), *Tony Makes It Happen!* (1967), *For Once In My Life* (1967), *Snowfall/The Tony Bennett Christmas Album* (1968), *I've Gotta Be Me* (1969), *Tony Sings The Great Hits Of Today!* (1970), *Tony Bennett's 'Something'* (1970), *Love Story* (1971), *Get Happy With The London Philharmonic Orchestra* (1971), *Summer Of '42* (1972), *With Love* (1972), *The Good Things In Life* (1972), *Rodgers And Hart Songbook* (1973), *Chicago* (1984), *Anything Goes* (1985), *The Art Of Excellence* (1986), *Bennett/Berlin* (1987), *Jazz* (1987), *Astoria: Portrait Of The Artist* (1990), *Perfectly Frank* (1992). Compilations: *Tony's Greatest Hits* (1958), *More Tony's Greatest Hits* (1960), *Tony's Greatest Hits, Volume III* (1965), *A String Of Tony's Hits* (1966), *Tony Bennett's Greatest Hits, Volume IV* (1969), *Tony Bennett's All-Time Greatest Hits* (1972), *The Very Best Of Tony Bennett - 20 Greatest Hits* (1977), *Forty Years Of The Artistry Of Tony* (1991).

Bernstein, Elmer

b. 4 April 1922, New York, USA. An important and prolific arranger-conductor, and composer of over 100 films scores, including biblical epics, westerns, comedies, thrillers and social dramas. Bernstein was hailed as a 'musical genius' in the classical field at the age of 12. Despite being a talented actor, dancer and painter, he devoted himself to becoming a concert pianist and toured nationally while still in his teens. His education at New York University was interrupted when he joined the United States Air Force during World War II. Throughout his four years service he composed and conducted music for propaganda programmes, and produced musical therapy projects for operationally fatigued personnel. After the war he attended the Juilliard School of Music and studied composition with the distinguished composer, Roger Sessions. Bernstein moved to Hollywood and started writing film scores in 1950 and, two years later, wrote the background music for *Sudden Fear*, a suspense thriller starring Joan Crawford and Jack Palance. Agent and producer Ingo Preminger, impressed by the Bernstein music, recommended him to his brother Otto, for the latter's 1955 film project, *The Man With The Golden Arm*. A tense, controversial movie, its theme of drug addiction, accompanied by the Berstein modern jazz score, played by top instrumentalists such as Shelly Manne, Shorty Rogers, Pete Candoli and Milt Bernhart, caused distribution problems in some American states. The film won Oscar nominations for Frank Sinatra in the role of Frankie Machin, the junkie and would-be drummer, and for Bernstein's powerful, exciting music score. Bernstein made the US Top 20 with his record of the film's 'Main Title', and Billy May entered the UK Top 10 with his version. In 1956, Bernstein wrote the score for Cecil B. De Mille's epic *The Ten Commandments*, starring Charlton Heston. Thereafter, he provided the background music for an impressive array of movies with varied styles and subjects, including *Fear Strikes Out* (1957), *Sweet Smell Of Success* (1957), *God's Little Acre* (1958), *Some Came Running* (1958), *The Rat Race* (1960), *The Birdman Of Alcatraz* (1962), *The Great Escape* (1963), *A Walk In The Spring Rain* (1970), *The Shootist* (1976), *National Lampoon's Animal House* (1978), *An American Werewolf In London* (1981), *Ghostbusters* (1984), *!Three Amigos!* (1986), *Amazing Grace And Chuck* (1987), *Slipstream* (1988), *DA* (1988), (*My Left Foot* (1989), *The Grifters* (1990), *The Field* (1990), *Rambling Rose* (1991), *Oscar* (1991) *A Rage In Harlem* (1991) and *The Babe* (1992). In 1991, Bernstein was the musical director, and arranger (or re-arranger) of Bernard Herrman's original score for the 1962 classic, *Cape Fear*. He received Academy Award nominations for his work on the highly-acclaimed western, *The Magnificent Seven* (1960), *Summer And Smoke* (1961), the title song for *Walk On The Wild Side* (1961), with a lyric by Mack David; *To Kill A Mockingbird* (1962), said to be Bernstein's favourite of his own scores; the scores for *Return Of The Seven* (1966), and *Hawaii* (1966) (and a song from *Hawaii*, 'Wishing Doll', lyric by Mack David); the title song from *True Grit* (1969), lyric by Don Black; a song from *Gold* (1974), 'Wherever Love Takes Me', lyric by Don Black; and *Trading Places* (1983). Bernstein won an Oscar for his original music score for the 20's spoof, *Thoroughly Modern Millie* (1967), in which Beatrice Lillie contrived to steal the picture from Julie Andrews. Coincidentally, Bernstein was the musical arranger and conductor at the Academy Awards ceremony when his award was announced, so he had to relinquish the baton before going on stage to receive his Oscar. Apart from films, Bernstein worked extensively in television. In 1958 he signed for US Revue Productions to provide background music for television dramas. One of his most notable scores was for *Staccato* (1959) (later re-titled *Johnny Staccato*), a series about a jazz musician turned private eye, starring John Cassavetes. The shows were a big hit in the UK, where Bernstein's recording of 'Staccato's Theme' rose to Number 4 in the singles chart in 1959, and re-entered the following year.

Selected albums: *What Is Jazz?* (1958), *Desire Under The Elms* (1959), *God's Little Acre* (1959), *King Go Forth* (1959), *Some Came Running* (1960), *Walk On the Wild Side* (1962), *To Kill A Mocking Bird* (1962), *Movie And TV Themes* (1963), *The Great Escape* (1963), *The Carpetbaggers* (1964), *Hallelujah Trail* (1965), *The Sons Of Katie Elder* (1965), *The Ten Commandements* (1966).

Bernstein, Leonard

b. Louis Bernstein, 25 August 1918, Lawrence, Massachusetts, USA, d. 14 October 1990, New York, USA. Bernstein was a major and charismatic figure in modern classical music, and the Broadway musical theatre. He was also a conductor, composer, pianist, author and lecturer. A son of immigrant Russian Jews, Bernstein started to play the piano at the age of 10. In his teens he showed an early interest in the theatre by organizing productions such as *The Mikado*, and an unconventional adaptation of *Carmen*, in which he played the title role. Determined to make a career in music, despite his father's insistence that 'music just keeps people awake at night', Bernstein eschewed the family beauty parlour business. He went on to study firstly with Walter Piston and Edward Burlingaunt Hill at Harvard, then with Fritz Reiner, Isabella Vengerova and Randall Thompson at the Curtis Institute in Philadephia, and finally with Serge Koussevitzky at the Berkshire Music Institute at Tanglewood. Bernstein had gone to Harvard regarding himself as a pianist but became influenced by Dimitri Mitropoulos and Aaron Copland. They inspired him to write his first symphony, *Jeremiah*. By 1943 he was chosen by Artur Rodzinski to work as his assistant at the New York Philharmonic. On 14 November 1943, Bernstein deputized at the last minute for the ailing Bruno Walter, and conducted the New York Philharmonic in a concert which was broadcast live on network radio. The next day, for what would not be the last time, he made the front pages and became a celebrity over-night. In the same year he wrote the music for *Fancy Free*, a ballet, choreographed by Jerome Robbins, about three young sailors on 24 hours shore leave in New York City. It was so successful that they expanded it into a Broadway musical, with libretto and lyrics by Betty Comden and Adolph Green. Retitled *On The Town* and directed by George Abbott, it opened in 1944, with a youthful, vibrant score which included the anthem 'New York, New York', 'Lonely Town', 'I Get Carried Away' and 'Lucky To Be Me'. The 1949 film version, starring Frank Sinatra and Gene Kelly, and directed by Kelly and Stanley Donen, is often regarded as innovatory in its use of real New York locations, although Bernstein's score was somewhat truncated in the transfer. In 1950 Bernstein wrote both music and lyrics for a musical version of J. M. Barrie's *Peter Pan*, starring Jean Arthur and Boris Karloff. His next Broadway project, *Wonderful Town* (1953), adapted from the play, *My Sister Eileen*, by Joseph Fields and Jerome Chodorov, again had lyrics by Comden and Green, and starred Rosalind Russell, returning to Broadway after a distinguished career in Hollywood. Bernstein's spirited, contemporary score for which he won a Tony Award, included 'Conversation Piece', 'Conga', 'Swing', 'What A Waste', 'Ohio', 'A Quiet Girl' and 'A Little Bit Of Love'. The show had a successful revival in London in 1986, with Maureen Lipman in the starring role. *Candide* (1956) was one of Bernstein's most controversial works. Lillian Hellman's adaptation of the Voltaire classic, sometimes termed a 'comic operetta', ran for only 73 performances on Broadway. Bernstein's

score was much admired though, and one of the most attractive numbers, 'Glitter And Be Gay', was sung with great effect by Barbara Cook, one year before her Broadway triumph in Meredith Willson's *The Music Man*. *Candide* has been revived continually since 1956, at least twice by producer Hal Prince. It was his greatly revised production, including additional lyrics by Stephen Sondheim and John Latouche, to the originals by Richard Wilbur, which ran for 740 performances on Broadway in 1974. The Scottish Opera's production, directed by Jonathan Miller in 1988, is said to have met with the composer's approval, and Bernstein conducted a concert version of the score at London's Barbican Theatre in 1989, which proved his last appearance in the UK.

Bernstein's greatest triumph in the popular field came with *West Side Story* in 1957. This brilliant musical adaptation of Shakespeare's *Romeo And Juliet* was set in the New York streets and highlighted the violence of the rival gangs, the Jets and the Sharks. With a book by Arthur Laurents, lyrics by Sondheim in his first Broadway production, and directed by Jerome Robbins, Bernstein created one of the most dynamic and exciting shows in the history of the musical theatre. The songs included 'Jet Song', 'Something's Coming', 'Maria', 'Tonight', 'America', 'Cool', 'I Feel Pretty', 'Somewhere' and 'Gee, Officer Krupke!'. In 1961, the film version gained 10 Oscars, including 'Best Picture'. Bernstein's music was not eligible because it had not been written for the screen. In 1984, he conducted the complete score of *West Side Story* for the first time, in a recording for Deutsche Grammophon, with a cast of opera singers including Kiri Te Kanawa, José Carreras, Tatania Troyanos and Kurt Allman. Bernstein's last Broadway show, *1600 Pennsylvania Avenue* (1976) was an anti-climax. A story about American presidents, with book and lyrics by Alan Jay Lerner, it closed after only seven performances. Among Bernstein's many other works was the score for the Marlon Brando film, *On The Waterfront* (1954), for which he was nominated for an Oscar; a jazz piece, 'Prelude, Fugue And Riffs', premiered on US television by Benny Goodman in 1955; and 'My Twelve Tone Melody' written for Irving Berlin's 100th birthday in 1988. In his classical career, which ran parallel to his work in the popular field, he was highly accomplished, composing three symphonies, a full length opera, and several choral works. He was music director of the New York Philharmonic from 1958-69, conducted most of the world's premier orchestras, and recorded many of the major classical works. In the first week of October 1990, he announced his retirement from conducting because of ill health, and expressed an intention to concentrate on composing. He died one week later on 14 October 1990.

Further reading: *The Joy Of Music*, Leonard Bernstein. *Leonard Bernstein*, John Briggs. *Leonard Bernstein*, Peter Gadenwitz. *Leonard Bernstein*, Joan Peyser.

Berry, Chuck

b. Charles Edward Anderson Berry, 18 October 1926, St. Louis, Missouri, USA. A seminal figure in rock's evolution, Chuck Berry's influence as songwriter and guitarist is incalculable. His cogent songs captured adolescent life, yet the artist was 30 years old when he commenced recording. Introduced to music as a child, Berry learned guitar while in his teens, but this period was blighted by a three-year spell in Algoa Reformatory following a conviction for armed robbery. On his release Berry undertook several blue-collar jobs while pursuing part-time spots in St. Louis bar bands. Inspired by Carl Hogan, guitarist in Louis Jordan's Timpani Five, and Charlie Christian, he continued to hone his craft and in 1951 purchased a tape recorder to capture ideas for compositions. The following year Berry joined Johnnie Johnson (piano) and Ebby Hardy (drums) in the houseband at the Cosmopolitan Club. Over the ensuing months the trio became a popular attraction, playing a mixture of R&B, country/hillbilly songs and standards, particularly those of Nat 'King' Cole, on whom Berry modelled his cool vocal style. The guitarist also fronted his own group, the Chuck Berry Combo, at the rival Crank Club, altering his name to spare his father's embarrassment at such worldly pursuits.

In 1955, during a chance visit to Chicago, Berry met bluesman Muddy Waters, who advised the young singer to approach the Chess label. Chuck's demo of an original song, 'Ida Mae', was sufficient to win a recording deal and the composition, retitled 'Maybellene', duly became his debut single. This ebullient performance was a runaway success, topping the R&B chart and reaching number 5 on the US pop listings. Its lustre was partially clouded by a conspiratorial publishing credit which required Berry to share the rights with Russ Fratto and disc jockey Alan Freed, in deference to his repeated airplay. This situation remained unresolved until 1986.

Berry enjoyed further hits with 'Thirty Days' and 'No Money Down', but it was his third recording session which proved highly productive, producing a stream of classics, 'Roll Over Beethoven', 'Too Much Monkey Business' and 'Brown-Eyed Handsome Man'. The artist's subsequent releases read like a lexicon of pop history - 'School Days' (a second R&B number 1), 'Reelin' And Rockin'', 'Rock 'N' Roll Music' (all 1957), Sweet Little Sixteen', 'Johnny B. Goode' (1958), 'Back In The USA', 'Let It Rock' (1959), 'Bye Bye Johnny' (1960) are but a handful of the peerless songs written and recorded during this prolific period. In common with contemporary artists, Berry drew from both country and R&B music, but his sharp, often piquant lyrics, clarified by the singer's clear diction, introduced a new discipline to the genre. Such incomparable performances not only defined rock 'n' roll, they provided a crucial template for successive generations. Both the Beatles and Rolling Stones acknowledged their debt to Berry. The former recorded two of his compositions, taking one, 'Roll Over Beethoven', into the US charts, while the latter drew from his empirical catalogue on many occasions. This included 'Come On', their debut single, 'Little Queenie', 'You Can't Catch Me' and 'Around And Around', as well as non-Berry songs which nonetheless aped his approach. The Stones' readings of 'Route 66', 'Down The Road Apiece' and 'Confessin' The Blues' were indebted to their mentor's versions while Keith Richards's rhythmic, propulsive guitar figures drew from Berry's style. Elsewhere, the Beach Boys re-wrote 'Sweet Little Sixteen' as 'Surfin' USA' to score their first million-seller while countless other groups scrambled to record his songs which somehow combined immediacy with longevity.

Between 1955-60, Berry seemed unassailable. He enjoyed a run of 17 R&B Top 20 entries, appeared in the films *Go Johnny Go*, *Rock, Rock, Rock* and *Jazz On A Summer's Day*, the last of which documented the artist's performance at the 1958 *Newport Jazz Festival*, where he demonstrated the famed 'duckwalk' to a bemused audience. However, personal impropriety undermined Berry's personal and professional life when, on 28 October 1961, he was convicted under the Mann Act of 'transporting an under-age girl across state lines for immoral purposes'. Berry served 20 months in prison, emerging in October 1963 just as 'Memphis Tennessee', recorded in 1958, was providing him with his first UK Top 10 hit. He wrote several stellar compositions during his incarceration, including 'Nadine', 'No Particular

Place To Go', 'You Never Can Tell' and 'Promised Land', each of which reached the UK Top 30. Such chart success soon waned as the immediate R&B bubble burst and in 1966 Berry sought to regenerate his career by moving from Chess to Mercury. However, an ill-advised *Golden Hits* set merely featured re-recordings of old material, while attempts to secure a contemporary image on *Live At The Fillmore Auditorium* (recorded with the Steve Miller Band) and *Concerto In B. Goode* proved equally unsatisfactory. He returned to Chess in 1969 and immediately re-established his craft with the powerful 'Tulane'. *Back Home* and *San Francisco Dues* were cohesive selections and in-concert appearances showed a renewed purpose. Indeed, a UK performance at the 1972 Manchester Arts Festival not only provided half of Berry's *London Sessions* album, but also his biggest-ever hit. 'My Ding-A-Ling', a mildly ribald *double entendre* first recorded by Dave Bartholomew, topped both the US and UK charts, a paradox in the light of his own far superior compositions which achieved lesser commercial plaudits. It was his last major hit, and despite several new recordings, including *Rock It*, a much-touted release on Atco, Berry became increasingly confined to the revival circuit. He gained an uncomfortable reputation as a hard, shrewd businessman and disinterested performer, backed by pick-up bands with which he refused to rehearse. Tales abound within the rock fraternity of Berry's refusal to tell the band which song he was about to launch into. Pauses and changes would come about by the musicians watching Berry closely for an often disguised signal. Berry has insisted for years upon pre-payment of his fee, usually in cash, and he will only perform an encore after a further negotiation for extra payment. Berry's continued legal entanglements resurfaced in 1979 when he was sentenced to a third term of imprisonment following a conviction for income tax evasion. Upon release he embarked on a punishing world tour, but the subsequent decade proved largely unproductive musically and no new recordings were undertaken. In 1986, the artist celebrated his 60th birthday with gala performances in St. Louis and New York. Keith Richard appeared at the former, although relations between the two men were strained, as evinced in the resultant documentary, *Hail! Hail! Rock 'N' Roll*, which provided an overview of Berry's entire career. Sadly, the 90s began with further controversy and allegations of indecent behaviour at the singer's Berry Park centre. Although these serve to undermine the individual, his stature as an essential figure in the evolution of popular music cannot be underestimated.

Albums: *After School Session* (1958), *One Dozen Berrys* (1958), *Chuck Berry Is On Top* (1959), *Rockin' At The Hops* (1960), *New Juke Box Hits* (1961), *Chuck Berry Twist* (1962), *More Chuck Berry* (1963), *Chuck Berry On Stage* (1963), *The Latest And Greatest* (1964), *St. Louis To Liverpool* (1964), with Bo Diddley *Two Great Guitars* (1964), *Chuck Berry In London* (1965), *Fresh Berrys* (1965), *Golden Hits* (1967, new recordings), *Chuck Berry In Memphis* (1967), *Live At The Fillmore Auditorium* (1967), *From St. Louis To Frisco* (1968), *Concerto In B. Goode* (1969), *Back Home* (1970), *San Francisco Dues* (1971), *The London Chuck Berry Sessions* (1972), *Bio* (1973), *Chuck Berry* (1975), *Live In Concert* (1978), *Rock It* (1979), *Rock! Rock! Rock 'N' Roll!* (1980), *Hail, Hail Rock 'N' Roll* (1988, film soundtrack). Compilations: *Chuck Berry's Greatest Hits* (1964), *Chuck Berry's Golden Decade* (1967), *Golden Decade, Volume 2* (1973), *Golden Decade, Volume 3* (1974), *Motorvatin'* (1977), *Spotlight On Chuck Berry* (1980), *Chess Masters* (1983), *Reelin' And Rockin' (Live)* (1984), *Rock 'N' Roll Rarities* (1986), *More Rock 'N' Roll Rarities* (1986), *Chicago Golden Years* (1988), *Decade '55 To '65* (1988), *The Great Twenty-Eight* (1990).

Further reading: *Chuck Berry - The Autobiography*, Chuck Berry.

Beverley Sisters

This close harmony UK vocal group consisting of three sisters: Joy Beverley (b. 1929) and twins Teddie and Babs (b. 1932) were all born in London, England, daughters of the singing-comedy duo Coram And Mills. The girls discovered they could sing harmony on school hymns; Teddie, singing the low parts, ('down in her boots', as she puts it). They started recording in the early 50s with songs such as 'Ferry Boat Inn', 'My Heart Cries For You', and 'Teasin'', and later had hits with 'I Saw Mommy Kissing Santa Claus', 'Little Drummer Boy' and 'Little Donkey'. During 1953 they performed in the USA, appeared in a record-breaking theatre season in Blackpool, played at the London Palladium with Bob Hope and presented their own television series, *Three Little Girls In View*. Their act was particularly suited to cabaret because of its risque element ('sassy, but classy', according to Ed Sullivan). Songs such as 'We Like To Do Things Like That', 'It's Illegal, It's Immoral Or It Makes You Fat' and 'He Like It, She Like It', inevitably led to one entitled 'We Have To Be So Careful All The Time'. They wore identical

outfits, on and off stage, and once bought the house next door in which to store them. Enormously popular in the UK during the 50s, they were still a top act into the 60s, until they retired in 1967 to raise children. Joy, who was married to ex-England football captain, Billy Wright, had two daughters, Vicky and Babette and Teddie had one girl, Sasha. In the 80s, the three young girls formed a pop group, the Little Foxes. In 1985, while watching their daughters perform at Peter Stringfellow's Hippodrome nightspot in London, the Beverley Sisters themselves were booked to appear there on Mondays, the 'Gay Night'. They received extraordinary receptions, with the audience singing along on the old specialities such as 'Sisters' and 'Together'. Personal appearances and cabaret dates followed; a new album, *Sparkle*, was issued and some of their stage outfits were exhibited at the Victoria & Albert museum in London. The comeback endured into the 90s.
Selected albums: *The World Of The Beverley Sisters* (1971), *Together* (1985), *Sparkle* (1985).

Big Bopper

b. Jape Perry Richardson, 24 October 1930, Sabine Pass, Texas, USA, d. 2 February 1959. After working as a disc jockey in Beaumont, Richardson won a recording contract with Mercury, releasing two unsuccessful singles in 1957. The following year, under his radio moniker 'The Big Bopper', he recorded the ebullient 'Chantilly Lace', a rock 'n' roll classic, complete with blaring saxophone and an insistent guitar run. Backed with the satiric 'The Purple People Eater Meets The Witch Doctor', the disc was a transatlantic hit. The follow up, 'Big Bopper's Wedding' underlined the singer's love of novelty and proved popular enough to win him a place on a tour with Buddy Holly and Ritchie Valens. On 2 February 1959, a plane carrying the three stars crashed, leaving no survivors. Few of Richardson's recordings were left for posterity, though there was enough for a posthumous album, *Chantilly Lace*, which included the rocking 'White Lightning'. In 1960, Johnny Preston provided the ultimate valediction by taking the Big Bopper's composition 'Running Bear' to number 1 on both sides of the Atlantic.
Album: *Chantilly Lace* (1959). Compilation: *Hellooo Baby* (1989).

Big Maybelle

b. Mabel Louise Smith, 1 May c.1920, Jackson, Tennessee, USA, d. 23 January 1972. Maybelle was discovered singing in church by Memphis bandleader Dave Clark in 1935. When Clark disbanded his orchestra to concentrate on record promotion, Smith moved to Christine Chatman's orchestra with whom she first recorded for Decca in 1944. Three years later, Smith made solo records for King and in 1952 she recorded as Big Maybelle when producer Fred Mendelsohn signed her to OKeh, a subsidiary of CBS. Her blues shouting style (a female counterpart to Big Joe Turner) brought an R&B hit the next year with 'Gabbin' Blues' (a cleaned-up version of the 'dirty dozens' on which she was partnered by songwriter Rose Marie McCoy). 'Way Back Home' and 'My Country Man' were also best sellers. In 1955, she made the first recording of 'Whole Lotta Shakin' Goin' On', which later became a major hit for Jerry Lee Lewis. Big Maybelle was also a star attraction on the chitlin' circuit of black clubs, with an act that included risque comedy as well as emotive ballads and brisk boogies. Leaving OKeh, she next recorded for Savoy where 'Candy' (1956) brought more success and in 1958, she appeared in *Jazz On A Summer's Day*, the film of that year's Newport Jazz Festival. Despite her acknowledged influence on the soul styles of the 60s, later records for Brunswick, Scepter and Chess made little impact until she signed to the Rojac label in 1966. There she was persuaded to cut some recent pop hits by the Beatles and Donovan and had some minor chart success of her own with versions of 'Don't Pass Me By' and '96 Tears'. The latter was composed by Rudy Martinez who also recorded it with his band ? & the Mysterians. Maybelle's career was marred by frequent drug problems which contributed to her early death in Cleveland Ohio in January 1972.
Albums: *Big Maybelle Sings* (1958), *Blues, Candy And Big Maybelle* (1958), *What More Can A Woman Do?* (1962), *The Soul Of Big Maybelle* (1964), *Great Soul Hits* (1964), *Got A Brand New Bag* (1967), *The Gospel Soul Of Big Maybelle* (1968), *The Last Of* (1973). Compilations: *The OKeh Sessions* (1983), *Roots Of R&R And Early Soul* (1985).

Blackwell, Otis

b. 1931, Brooklyn, New York, USA. The author of 'Great Balls Of Fire', 'Fever' and 'All Shook Up', Blackwell was one of the greatest songwriters of the rock 'n' roll era. He learned piano as a child and grew up listening to both R&B and country music. Victory in a talent contest at Harlem's Apollo Theatre led to a recording contract with the Joe Davis label. His first release was his own composition 'Daddy Rolling Stone' which became a favourite in Jamaica where it was recorded by Derek Martin. The song later became part of the Who's 'Mod' repertoire.

During the mid-50s, Blackwell also recorded in a rock 'n' roll vein for RCA and Groove before turning to writing songs for other artists. His first successes came in 1956 when Little Willie John's R&B hit with the sultry 'Fever' was an even bigger pop success for Peggy Lee. Then, 'All Shook Up' (first recorded by David Hill on Aladdin) began a highly profitable association with Elvis Presley, who was credited as co-writer. The rhythmic tension of the song perfectly fitted Elvis's stage persona and it became his first UK number 1. It was followed by 'Don't Be Cruel' (1956), 'Paralysed' (1957), and the more mellow 'Return To Sender' (1962) and 'One Broken Heart For Sale'. There was a distinct similarity between Blackwell's vocal style and Presley's, which has led to speculation that Elvis adopted some of his songwriter's mannerisms.

The prolific Blackwell (who wrote hundreds of songs) also provided hits for Jerry Lee Lewis ('Breathless' and his most famous recording 'Great Balls Of Fire', 1958), Dee Clark ('Hey Little Girl' and 'Just Keep It Up', 1959), Jimmy Jones ('Handy Man', 1960) and Cliff Richard ('Nine Times Out Of Ten', 1960). As the tide of rock 'n' roll receded, Blackwell returned to recording R&B material for numerous labels including Atlantic, MGM and Epic. In later years he was in semi-retirement, making only occasional live appearances.

Album: *These Are My Songs* (1978).

Blackwell, Robert 'Bumps'

b. Robert A. Blackwell, 23 May 1918, Seattle, Washington, USA (of mixed French, Negro and Indian descent), d. 9 March 1985. An arranger and studio band leader with Specialty Records, Blackwell had led a band in Seattle. After arriving in California in 1949 he studied classical composition at the University of California at Los Angeles, and within a few years was arranging and producing gospel and R&B singles for the likes of Lloyd Price and Guitar Slim. Previously he had written a series of stage revues - *Blackwell Portraits* - very much in the same vein as the *Siegfield Follies*. His Bumps Blackwell Jnr. Orchestra featured, at various times, Ray Charles and Quincy Jones. He also worked with Lou Adler and Herb Alpert before taking over the A&R department at Specialty Records where he first came into contact

with Little Richard. His boss, Art Rupe, sent him to New Orleans in 1955 where he recorded 'Tutti Frutti' and established a new base for rock 'n' roll. Blackwell was a key producer and songwriter in the early days of rock 'n' roll, particularly with Little Richard. He was responsible for tracking down Little Richard and buying his recording contract from Peacock in 1955. Blackwell helped to rewrite 'Tutti Frutti' in a cleaned-up version more appropriate to white audiences. which he recorded at Richard's first Specialty session in New Orleans. As well as being involved with the writing of some of Richard's hits, he also produced some of his early work, and became his personal manager. Along with John Marascalco he wrote 'Ready Teddy', 'Rip It Up', and, with Enotris Johnson and Richard Penniman (Little Richard) 'Long Tall Sally'. He also helped launch the secular careers of former gospel singers Sam Cooke and Wynona Carr. After leaving Specialty, he was involved in setting up Keen Records which furthered the careers of Sam Cooke and Johnny 'Guitar' Watson among others. In 1981 he co-produced the title track of Bob Dylan's *Shot Of Love*, before his death from pneumonia in 1985.

Bleyer, Archie

b. 12 June 1909, Corona, New York, USA, d. 20 March 1989, Sheboygan, Wisconsin, USA. Bandleader, musical arranger, and founder of Cadence Records, Bleyer began playing the piano at the age of seven. He enlisted at Columbia College in 1927, intending to become an electrical engineer, but switched to music in his second year, then left to become a musical arranger. After organizing a local band, he went to New York in the late 30s and conducted for several Broadway shows. He also composed the jazz piece, 'Business In Q', which was performed by various 'hot' bands in the 30s, and became one of the best-known writers of stock arrangements for music publishers. In the 40s Bleyer joined CBS radio as a musical conductor, and worked extensively on the *Arthur Godfrey Show*, and stayed with it when it transferred to television in the 50s. He left the show in 1953, and formed Cadence Records. He had immediate success with artists such as Julius LaRosa ('Eh Cumpari'), the Chordettes ('Mr Sandman', number 1), several chart-toppers for the Everly Brothers and Andy Williams ('Canadian Sunset', 'Butterfly' and 'Are You Sincere'). He also provided the orchestral backing for several of his artists, including Janette Davis, Marion Marlowe, Alfred Drake, and Arthur Godfrey, whose husky baritone can be heard on the album *Arthur Godfrey's TV Calendar Show*. Bleyer also had Top 20 hits with his own orchestra, including 'Hernando's Hideaway' (from *The Pajama Game*); and the novelty number, 'The Naughty Lady Of Shady Lane'. He continued to work into the early 60s, but retired from show business in the late 60s, and dissolved the Cadence label. He died in March 1989.

Bobbettes

The first all-female R&B group to have a major pop hit record was not the Chantels, as is popularly believed, but the Bobbettes. Their 'Mr. Lee' beat the Chantel's 'He's Gone' to the charts by one month and out-ranked it in the US pop charts. The Bobbettes formed in 1955 in Harlem, New York City, USA, at PS 109, where they attended school. Consisting of Emma Pought, her sister Jannie, Laura Webb, Helen Gathers and Heather Dixon, the group was originally called the Harlem Queens. The girls were aged between 11 and 13 years old at the time of their formation. In 1957 they appeared on a local television programme, which led to an audition for Atlantic Records. 'Mr. Lee' was a song the girls had written in honour of their fifth-grade teacher, although the lyrics were not as kind in their original version. (In fact, their second chart single was titled 'I Shot Mr. Lee'.) The infectious 'Mr. Lee' was released in the summer of 1957 and ascended to number 6 in the US chart. Follow-up singles on Atlantic did not chart; the Bobbettes' subsequent singles were issued on the Triple-X, Gone, Jubilee, Diamond and RCA Records labels. Although their last chart success was in 1961, four of the original members were still performing together in the late 80s. They never recorded an album.

Boone, Pat

b. Charles Eugene Boone, 1 June 1934, Jacksonville, Florida, USA. Boone sold more records during the late 50s than any other artist except Elvis Presley. To date, only four artists (Presley, the Beatles, James Brown and Stevie Wonder) are ranked above him in terms of total singles sales and their relative chart positions. Boone had a total of 60 hits in the US singles charts during his career, six of which reached number 1. A bona fide 'teen idol', Boone was, however, a personality quite unlike Presley. Where Elvis represented the outcast or rebel, Boone was a clean-cut conformist. He was a religious, married family man who at one point turned down a film role with Marilyn Monroe rather than having to kiss a woman who was not his wife. While Elvis wore long sideburns and greasy hair, Boone was recognised by his 'white buck' shoes and ever-present smile. Boone even attended college during the height of his career. Accordingly, Boone's music, although considered to be rock 'n' roll during his first few years of popularity, was considerably less manic than that being made by Presley and the early black rockers. Boone, in fact, built his career on 'cover' records, tame, cleaned-up versions of R&B songs originally recorded by black artists like Fats Domino, Little Richard, Ivory Joe Hunter, the Flamingos and the El Dorados.

Boone grew up in the Nashville, Tennessee, area, where he began singing in public at the age of 10. He appeared on the national *Ted Mack Amateur Hour* and *Arthur Godfrey's Talent Scouts* television programmes in the early 50s, and had his own radio programme on Nashville's WSIX. In 1953, he married Shirley Foley, daughter of country star Red Foley. The following year, Boone recorded his first of four singles for the small Republic label in Nashville, all of which failed.

That year the Boones moved to Denton, Texas, and began raising a family of four daughters, the third of whom, Debby Boone, would, in 1977, score a smash hit with the ballad 'You Light Up My Life'. Pat signed to Dot Records and recorded his first single for the company, 'Two Hearts' (originally by R&B group Otis Williams And The Charms) in February 1955. Admittedly unfamiliar with the genre, Boone quickly adapted the raw music to his own crooning style. His second single, Domino's 'Ain't That A Shame', went to number 1, and was followed by a non-stop procession of hits. Boone stayed with the R&B covers until 1957. Even today it is a controversial question whether Boone's cover records helped open the door to the black originators or shut them out of the white marketplace. By 1957, when Presley had established himself as the reigning white rocker, Boone had given up rock and switched to ballads. Among the biggest sellers were 'Friendly Persuasion', 'Don't Forbid Me', 'Love Letters In The Sand' and 'April Love'. Some of Boone's recordings by this time were taken from films in which he starred. He also appeared often on television, toured the country, and was the subject of magazine articles praising his positive image and outlook. Boone even wrote several books giving advice to teenagers.

From 1957-60, Boone hosted his own television show, *The Pat Boone-Chevy Showroom*. Although

Pat Boone

still popular, by the dawn of the 60s, his place at the top had slipped somewhat. 'Moody River' in 1961, and 'Speedy Gonzales', a novelty rock number of the following year, were his last major pop hits. By 1966 Boone's contract with Dot ended. He drifted from one label to the next, trying his hand at country music and, primarily, gospel. Although he had started recording Christian music as early as 1957, his concentration on that form was near-total by the late 70s; he recorded over a dozen Christian albums during that decade, several with his wife and children as the Boone Family Singers. He continued to make live appearances into the 90s, and became an outspoken supporter of politically conservative and religious causes. By 1991 he had begun discussing the possibility of singing rock music again. In 1993 Boone joined another 50s legend, Kay Starr, on 'The April Love Tour' of the UK.

Selected albums: *Pat Boone* (1956), *Howdy!* (1956), *'Pat'* (1957), *Hymns We Love* (1957), *Stardust* (1958), *Yes Indeed!* (1958), *Pat Boone Sings Irving Berlin* (1958), *Tenderly* (1959), *Moonglow* (1960), *He Leadeth Me* (1960), *This And That* (1960), *Moody River* (1961), *White Christmas* (1961), *My God And I* (1961), *I'll See You In My Dreams* (1962), *Pat Boone Reads From The Holy Bible* (1962), *State Fair* (1962, film soundtrack), *Pat Boone Sings Guess Who?* (1963), *The Star Spangled Banner* (1963), *My Tenth Anniversary With Dot Records* (1964), *Wish You Were Here Buddy* (1966), *Departure* (1969), *The Pat Boone Family In The Holy Land* (1972), *The New Songs Of The Jesus People* (1972), *The Family Who Prays* (1973), *All In The Boone Family* (1973), *The Country Side Of Pat Boone* (1977), *Whispering Hope* (1982), *Golden Hymns* (1984). Compilations: *Pat's Great Hits* (1957), *Pat's Great Hits, Volume 2* (1960), *20 Best Loved Gospel Songs* (70s), *16 Golden Classics* (1987), *Golden Greats* (1993).

Bostic, Earl

b. Eugene Earl Bostic, 25 April 1913, Tulsa, Oklahoma, USA, d. 28 October 1965. The romantic and smooth sound of Bostic's band, usually featuring the vibes of Gene Redd, piano of Fletcher Smith, bass of Margo Gibson, drums of Charles Walton, guitar of Alan Seltzer, and the marvellous alto saxophone of Bostic was one of the great and distinctive sounds of both R&B and pop music, and his records became perennials on the juke boxes during the 50s. Bostic was best known for his alto saxophone sound but he also played tenor saxophone, flute and clarinet on his records. Bostic was formally trained in music, having

received a degree in music theory at Xavier University. He moved to New York City and formed a jazz combo in 1938. In the early 40s he was playing in the Lionel Hampton band. He left Hampton in 1945 to form a combo, recording tracks for Majestic, but did not make much of an impression until he signed with New York-based Gotham in 1948. He immediately hit with 'Temptation' (US R&B number 10). During the 50s he recorded prolifically for Cincinnati-based King Records, and had two big singles, 'Sleep' (US R&B number 6) and 'Flamingo' (US R&B number 1) in 1951. The smooth but perky performance on the latter became his signature tune and made him something of a Beach Music artist in the Carolinas.

Albums: *The Best Of Bostic* (1956), *For You* (1956), *Alto-Tude* (1957), *Dancetime* (1957), *Let's Dance* (1957), *Invitation To Dance* (1957), *C'mon & Dance* (1957), *Bostic Rocks-Hits From The Swing Age* (1958), *Bostic Showcase Of Swinging Dance Hits* (1958), *Alto Magic In Hi-Fi* (1958), *Sweet Tunes Of The Fantastic 50's* (1958), *Sweet Tunes Of The Roaring 20's* (1959), *Sweet Tunes Of the Swinging 30's* (1959), *Sweet Tunes Of The Sentimental 40's* (1959), *Musical Pearls* (1960), *Hit Tunes Of The Big Broadway Shows* (1961), *By Popular Demand* (1962), *Bossa Nova* (1963), *Jazz I Feel It* (1963), *The Best Of Earl Bostic Vol. 2* (1964), *The Great Hits Of 1964* (1964), *Harlem Nocturne* (1969), *Sax 'O Woogie* (1984), *Blows A Fuse* (1985), *That's Earl, Brother* (1985), *Dance Music From The Bostic Workshop* (1992), *Let's Dance* (1993).

Boswell, Eve

b. 11 May 1924, Budapest, Hungary. A singer with a vivacious style, who was especially popular in the UK during the 50s. She is also an accomplished pianist and ballet dancer, and speaks four languages fluently. Educated in Lausanne, Switzerland, Boswell later studied music at the Budapest Academy. She came from a vaudeville family with whom she appeared as a teenager in an act known as the Three Hugos. After working in South Africa in Boswell's Circus, and marrying the owner, she went to the UK in 1949 and replaced Doreen Lundy as the star vocalist in Geraldo's Orchestra. After featuring on several of the orchestra's records, including 'Again', 'Best Of All' and, somewhat curiously, 'Confidentially' (the composition and theme song of comedian, Reg Dixon), she left Geraldo in 1951, and toured the UK with George & Alfred Black's revue, *Happy-Go-Lucky*, and was their leading lady in the musical, *The Show Of*

Earl Bostic

Shows, at the Opera House, Blackpool. She also toured Korea and the Far East, entertaining British Forces, appearing regularly in the UK on the radio, television and variety circuit, and at the 1953 Royal Command Performance. Signed to the Parlophone label in 1950, her first record, 'Bewitched', was followed by several other successful titles, including 'Beloved Be Faithful', 'The Little Shoemaker' and 'Ready, Willing And Able'. Her biggest hits were two up-tempo South African songs, 'Sugarbush' in 1952, and 'Pickin' A Chicken', which entered the UK chart in 1955, and re-surfaced twice during the following year. Her album, *Sentimental Eve*, revealed that she could also handle a ballad effectively, with such tracks as 'A Little On The Lonely Side', 'I'll Buy That Dream' and 'You'll Never Know'. She remained active in the UK during the 50s and into the 60s, then faded from the scene. Her album *Sugar Bush 75*, featured arrangements by Roland Shaw.
Albums: *Sentimental Eve* (1958), *Sugar Bush 75* (1976). Compilations: *Sentimental Journey* (1988), *The EMI Years* (1989).

Boy Friend, The

Despite a quiet opening, at London's Players' Theatre, Sandy Wilson's stage musical *The Boy Friend* became a huge popular success upon transferring to Wyndham's nine months after its early-1953 opening. At Wyndham's the show ran for more than 2,000 performances and was revived in 1983. An affectionate pastiche of the musical theatre of 20s, *The Boy Friend* starred Anne Rogers, who came in 48 hours before the show was due to open, and included several delightful songs of which the most lasting are 'Never Too Late To Fall In Love' and the wistful 'Room In Bloomsbury'. Julie Andrews played the lead in the New York production, while the disastrous 1971 film version starred Twiggy and future Broadway star, Tommy Tune.

Brent, Tony

b. 26 August 1927, Bombay, India. A popular singer in the UK during the 50s, Brent's first big career move came in the 40s, when he travelled from India to the USA, and sang with former Glenn Miller accompanist, Tex Beneke, and his band. In 1950, he moved to the UK, and won a talent contest at the Kingston Regal Theatre, which led to work with Ambrose, and Cyril Stapleton's BBC Showband. In 1952, he made his chart debut with a cover of one Sammy Kaye's last hits, 'Walkin' To Missouri', and began to tour the Variety circuit and appear on television. His other chart entries, through until 1959, included 'Make It Soon', 'Got You On My Mind', 'Cindy, Oh Cindy', 'Dark Moon', 'The Clouds Will Soon Roll By', 'Girl Of My Dreams' and 'Why Should I Be Lonely?' on which Brent was joined by the vivacious Billie Anthony. Brent also released two sets of standards, *Off Stage* and *Tony Takes Five*. His EPs included *Time For Tony*, and *Tony Calls The Tune*. He was subsequently overwhelmed by the 60s beat group scene and retreated to the clubs. Eventually, he resumed his travels, and left the UK for Australia, where he was reported to be living and working in the early 90s.

Brewer, Teresa

b. Theresa Breuer, 7 May 1931, Toledo, Ohio, USA. A child prodigy, Brewer first appeared on radio at the age of two and sang on the *Major Bowes Amateur Hour* between 1938 and 1943. She was a veteran radio and club performer by the time she joined London Records in 1949. The attractive and strong-voiced teenager topped the US chart in 1950 with her debut hit 'Music Music Music' on which she was backed by the Dixieland All Stars. She joined Coral Records in 1952 and continued hitting the US Top 10 with records like 'Ricochet', 'Jilted' and the number 1 'Till I Waltz Again With You'. In 1953 she made her film debut in *Those Redheads From Seattle* with Guy Mitchell. Her first transatlantic Top 10 hit was her version of 'Let Me Go Lover' in 1955, which she followed with two more in 1956; 'A Tear Fell' and 'Sweet Old-Fashioned Girl'. As rock 'n' roll took over, Brewer's sales declined and like many other MOR pop stars of the time she reverted to covering R&B hits for the white record-buying public. In this vein she had some success with tracks like 'Pledging My Love', 'Tweedle Dee' and 'You Send Me'.
Brewer had a brief flirtation with country-styled material in the early 60s and then joined the lucrative night-club and Las Vegas circuit. She later recorded for Philips, Signature, Project Three and Amsterdam, the latter label being owned by her producer husband Bob Thiele. In all, Brewer accumulated 38 US chart hits but by the late 50s, when rock was firmly established, there was no place in the charts for this sweet, old-fashioned girl.
Albums: *Teresa Brewer* (50s), *A Bopuquet Of Hits* (1954), *Till I Waltz Again With You* (1954), *Music, Music, Music* (1958), *Teresa* (1958), *For Teenagers In Love* (1958), *Teresa Brewer At Christmas Time* (1958), *Miss Music* (1958), *Time For Teresa* (1958),

Teresa Brewer

Teresa Brewer And The Dixieland Band (1959), *When Your Love Has Gone* (1959), *Heavenly Lover* (1959), *Ridin' High* (1960), *Naughty, Naughty, Naughty* (1960), *My Golden Favorites* (1960), *Songs Everybody Knows* (1961), *Aloha From Teresa* (1961), *Don't Mess With Tess* (1962), *Terrific Teresa* (1963), *Moments To Remember* (1964), *Golden Hits Of 1964* (1964), *Goldfinger And Other Great Movie Songs* (1965), *Songs For Our Fighting Men* (1966), *Gold Country* (1966), *Texas Leather And Mexican Lace* (1967), *I Dig Big Band Singers* (1983), *Good News* (1984), *On The Road Again* (1984), *Teresa Brewer* (1984), *Teresa Brewer In London* (1984), *When Your Lover Has Gone* (1984), *Live At Carnegie Hall & Montreux* (1985). Compilations: *The Best Of Teresa Brewer* (1981), *Golden Greats* (1985), *Golden Hits* (1989).

Bricusse, Leslie

b. 29 January 1931, London, England. A composer, lyricist, librettist and screenwriter, Bricusse was influenced by the MGM musicals of the 40s, paricularly *Words And Music*, the Richard Rodgers and Lorenz Hart biopic. He originally intended to be a journalist, but, while studying at Cambridge University, started to write, direct and appear in the Cambridge footlights revues. In 1953, he wrote the music and lyrics (with Robin Beaumont) for *Lady At the Wheel*, a musical with the Monte Carlo rally as its setting, which included songs such as 'The Early Birdie', 'Pete Y'Know', 'Love Is' and a comedy tango, 'Siesta'. It was presented at the local Arts Theatre, and, five years later, had a limited run in the West End. Well before that, in 1954/5, Bricusse had appeared on the London stage himself, and with a theatrical legend, in *An Evening With Beatrice Lillie*. For a while during the 50s, he was under contract as a writer at Pinewood Film Studios, and, in 1954, wrote the screenplay, and the songs (with Beaumont), for *Charley Moon*, which starred Max Bygraves. The popular singer/comedian took one of the numbers, 'Out Of Town', into the UK Top 20, and it gained Bricusse his first Ivor Novello Award: he won several others, including one for 'My Kind Of Girl' (words and music by Bricusse), which was a UK Top 5 hit for Matt Monro in 1961. Bricusse also wrote a good deal of special material for Bygraves, including one of his 'catch-phrase' songs, 'A Good Idea - Son!'. Early in 1961, Bricusse went to New York to write for another Beatrice Lillie revue, taking Anthony Newley with him to develop ideas for a show of their own. The result, *Stop The World - I Want To Get Off*, written in around three weeks, opened in London's West End in July of that year, and stayed there until November 1962. It later ran for over 500 performances on Broadway, and was filmed in 1966. Book, music and lyrics were jointly credited to Bricusse and Newley - the latter starred as the central character, Littlechap, in London and New York. The score included several hit songs, including 'What Kind Of Fool Am I?', 'Once In A Lifetime' and 'Gonna Build A Mountain', as well as other, more specialized numbers, such as 'Lumbered', 'Typically English' and 'Someone Nice Like You'. While Newley went off to appear in the off-beat, parochial movie, *The World Of Sammy Lee*, Bricusse collaborated with Cyril Ornadel on the score for the musical, *Pickwick* (1963), which starred the 'Goon with the golden voice', Harry Secombe, in the title role. His recording of the show's big ballad, 'If I Ruled The World', was a Top 20 hit in the UK, and, later, after the Broadway production had flopped, it became part of Tony Bennett's repertoire. Reunited in 1964, Bricusse and Newley's next major stage project, *The Roar Of The Greasepaint - The Smell Of The Crowd* (1965), was regarded as similar to their previous effort, a moral tale of a downtrodden little man, bucking the system. It toured (Bricusse: 'We managed to empty every provincial theatre in England'), but did not play the West End. Bricusse, and others, felt that comedian, Norman Wisdom, was miscast in the central role, and Newley took over for the Broadway run of 232 performances. Once again, though, the hit songs were there - in this case, 'Who Can I Turn To?' and 'A Wonderful Day Like Today', plus other items such as 'This Dream', 'The Beautiful Land', 'The Joker', 'Where Would You Be Without Me?', 'Nothing Can Stop Me Now' and 'Feeling Good'. The latter number was popularized in the USA by Joe Sherman, and received an impressive, extended treatment from Steve Winwood's UK rock group, Traffic, on their live *Last Exit* (1969). In 1964, Bricusse and Newley turned their attention to the big screen, providing the lyric to John Barry's music for the title song to the James Bond movie, *Goldfinger* (1964), which Shirley Bassey sang over the titles. Bricusse and Barry later wrote another Bond theme for *You Only Live Twice* (1968), popularized by Nancy Sinatra. In 1967, Bricusse wrote the screenplay and the complete song score for *Doctor Dolittle*, which starred Newley, along with Rex Harrison, who sang the Oscar-winning 'Talk To The Animals'. Considered an 'expensive dud', there was no mention of a *Doctor Dolittle II*. Far more to the public's taste was Roald Dahl's *Willy Wonka And The Chocolate Factory* (1971). Bricusse and Newley's score contained 'The Candy Man', a song which gave Sammy Davis Jnr. a US number 1 in the following year. Davis was one of the songwriting team's favourite people - Bricusse estimates that he recorded at least 60 of his songs, including a complete album of *Doctor Dolittle*. Davis also starred in a revival of *Stop The World - I Want To Get Off* during the 1978-79 Broadway season.

After writing several numbers for a 1971 US television adaptation of *Peter Pan*, which starred Danny Kaye and Mia Farrow, Bricusse and Newley returned to the stage with *The Good Old Bad Old Days*. Newley directed and starred in the show, which ran for 10 months in London, and included the jolly title song and several other appealing numbers, such as 'I Do Not Love You', 'It's A Musical World', 'The People Tree' and 'The Good Things In Life'. Since then, their back catalogue has been re-packaged in productions such as *The Travelling Music Show* (1978), with Bruce Forsyth; and *Once Upon A Song*, in which Newley occasionally appears when he is not singing for big dollars in Las Vegas. Also in 1978, Bricusse collaborated with composer Armando Trovajoli on *Beyond the Rainbow*, an English language version of the Italian musical *Aggiungi Una Posta Alla Tavola*, which ran for six months in London - a good deal longer than his own *Kings And Clowns*. He also wrote some new songs for a Chichester Festival Theatre production of his film score for *Goodbye, Mr Chips* (1982). By then, he was generally wearing his Hollywood hat, and had received Oscar nominations for his work on *Goodbye, Mr Chips* (1969, original song score, with John Willams), *Scrooge* (1970, original song score with Ian Fraser and Herbert W. Spencer, and his own song, 'Thank You Very Much'), *That's Life* (1986, 'Life In a Looking Glass', with Henry Mancin), *Home Alone* (1990, 'Somewhere In My Memory', with John Williams), and *Hook* (1991, 'When You're Alone', with John Williams). He won his second Academy Award in 1982, in collaboration with Henry Mancini, for the original song score to *Victor/Victoria*. Bricusse and Newley were inducted into the Songwriters' Hall Of Fame in 1989, a year that otherwise proved something of a disappointment for partners: an updated version of *Stop The World*, directed by, and starring Newley, staggered along for five weeks in London, and Bricusse's *Sherlock Holmes*, with Ron Moody and Liz Robertson, opened there as well, to disappointing reviews. The latter show re-surfaced

in 1993, and toured the UK with Robert Powell in the title role, shortly after *Scrooge*, Bricusse's stage adaptation of his film score, had enjoyed a limited run at the Alexandra Theatre in Birmingham, England, with Newley in the title role. Also in 1993, Harry Secombe was set to recreate his orginal role in *Pickwick*, at Chichester, and Broadway was buzzing with talk of possible stage productions of *Victor/Victoria*, and *Jekyll & Hyde*, a show that Bricusse wrote with Frank Wildhorn, and released on CD in 1990.

Brown, Ruth

b. 30 January 1928, Portsmouth, Virginia, USA. In 1948 Brown was singing with a band led by her husband Jimmy in Washington, DC, when Willis Conover (from the radio show *Voice Of America*) recommended her to Ahmet Ertegen of the newly-formed Atlantic Records. Ertegun signed her, despite competition from Capitol, but on the way up to New York for an appearance at the Apollo Theatre, she was involved in a car crash. Hospitalized for nine months, her medical bills were paid by Atlantic and she rewarded them handsomely with her first big hit, 'Teardrops From My Eyes', in 1950. More hits followed with '5-10-15 Hours' (1952) and 'Mama, He Treats Your Daughter Mean' (1953). Atlantic's first real star, Brown became a major figure in 50s R&B, forming a strong link between that music and early rock 'n' roll. Her records were characterized by her rich and expressive singing voice (not unlike that of Dinah Washington) and accompaniment by breathy saxophone solos (initially by Budd Johnson, later by Willie Jackson). Brown's concentration upon R&B has not kept her from associations with the jazz world; very early in her career she sang briefly with the Lucky Millinder band, and has recorded with Jerome Richardson and the Thad Jones-Mel Lewis big band. She also brought a distinctively soulful treatment to varied material such as 'Yes, Sir, That's My Baby', 'Sonny Boy', 'Black Coffee' and 'I Can Dream, Can't I?'. In 1989 she won a Tony Award for her performance in the Broadway show, *Black And Blue*, and was receiving enthusiastic reviews for her nightclub act in New York, at Michael's Pub and the Blue Note, into the 90s.

Albums: *Ruth Brown Sings* (1956), *Ruth Brown* (1957), *Late Date With Ruth Brown* (1959), *Miss Rhythm* (1959), *Along Comes Ruth* (1962), *Gospel Time* (1962), *Ruth Brown '65* (1964), *Black Is Brown And Brown Is Beautiful* (1969), *The Real Ruth Brown* (70s), *You Don't Know Me* (70s), *Touch Me In The*

Ruth Brown

Morning (70s), *Sugar Babe* (1977), *Takin' Care Of Business* (1980), *The Soul Survives* (1982), *Brown Sugar* (1986), *Sweet Baby Of Mine* (1987), *Blues On Broadway* (1989), with Linda Hopkins and Carrie Smith *Black And Blue* (1989), *Fine And Mellow* (1992). Compilation: *The Best Of Ruth Brown* (1963), *Rockin' With Ruth* (1984, 1950-60 recordings).

Browns

Ella Maxine Brown (b. 27 April 1932, Sampti, Louisiana, USA), Jim Edward Brown (b. 1 April 1934, Sparkman, Arkansas, USA) and Bonnie Brown (b. 31 July 1937, Sparkman, Arkansas, USA). In 1953, greatly influenced by WSM broadcasts of the *Grand Ole Opry*, Maxine and her brother began singing as a duo. They first featured on *Barnyard Hayride* on KLRA Little Rock, before being signed to the *Louisiana Hayride* on KWKH Shreveport. They recorded some duet tracks for Fabor and in 1954 registered a Top 10 US country hit with their own song 'Looking Back To See'. (Jim Reeves actually played rhythm guitar on the recording.) In 1955, after being joined by sister Bonnie, they became a featured act on Red Foley's *Ozark Jubilee* and their recording of 'Here Today And Gone Tomorrow' became their first country hit as a trio. In 1956, with help from Jim Reeves, they moved to RCA, where they immediately had a US country number 2 hit with their recording of the Louvin's 'I Take The Chance'. The following year they had major success with 'I Heard The Bluebirds Sing', but it was in 1959 that they scored their biggest hit with their million-selling recording of 'The Three Bells'. Based on a song called 'While The Angelus Was Ringing' and sometimes known as 'The Jimmy Brown Song' or 'Les Trois Cloches', the song was popularized in Europe by both Les Compagnons de la Chanson and Edith Piaf. The Browns recording topped both the US country and pop charts and even reached number 6 on the UK pop charts. Between 1959 and 1967, 12 further hits followed including 'Scarlet Ribbons', 'The Old Lamplighter', 'Then I'll Stop Loving You' and 'I'd Just Be Fool Enough'. In the early 60s, they appeared on all major television shows and toured extensively including trips to Europe and Japan, as well as running their own club in Pine Bluff, Arkansas. They joined the *Opry* in 1963 but, in 1967, with Maxine and Bonnie wishing to spend more time with their families, they disbanded. In 1968, Maxine had a minor hit as a solo artist on the Chart label with 'Sugar Cane County' while Jim Ed continued his career as a solo artist with RCA.

Albums: *Jim Edward, Maxine & Bonnie Brown* (1957), *Sweet Sounds By The Browns* (1959), *Town & Country* (1960), *The Browns Sing Their Hits* (1960), *Our Favorite Folk Songs* (1961), *Songs From The Little Brown Church Hymnal* (1961), *Grand Ole Opry Favorites* (1964), *This Young Land* (1964), *I Heard The Bluebirds Sing* (1965), *Our Kind Of Country* (1966), *The Big Ones From The Country* (1967), *The Old Country Church* (1967), *A Harvest Of Country Songs* (1968). Maxine Brown solo: *Sugar Cane County* (1969).

Brubeck, Dave

b. David Warren Brubeck, 6 December 1920, Concord, California, USA. Initially taught piano by his mother, Brubeck showed an immediate flair for the instrument, and was performing with professional jazz groups at the age of 13. Enrolling at the College of the Pacific in Stockton, California, he continued his involvement in jazz by establishing a 12-piece band, but most of his time was spent in the study of theory and composition under Darius Milhaud. After he graduated from the Pacific, Brubeck decided to continue his formal classical training. However, his time at Mills College, studying under Schoenberg, was interrupted by military service in World War II. Returning from Europe in 1946, he went back to Milhaud, and about this time formed his first serious jazz group - the Jazz Workshop Ensemble, an eight-piece unit which recorded three years later as the Dave Brubeck Octet. He began a more consistent professional involvement in the jazz scene in 1949, with the creation of his first trio, with Cal Tjader and Norman Bates (who was soon replaced by Ron Crotty), but it was with the addition of alto saxophonist Paul Desmond in 1951, that Brubeck's group achieved major critical acclaim. Replacing Tjader and Crotty with Gene Wright and Joe Morello towards the end of the 50s, Brubeck led this celebrated and prolific quartet as a unit until 1967, when Desmond left the group. After replacing him for a short time with Gerry Mulligan, Brubeck began using a new group in 1972 involving his three sons and, apart from a brief classic quartet reunion in 1976, most of his now rare concert appearances have since been in this setting. Brubeck's musical relationship with Desmond was central to his success. The group's 1959 classic 'Take Five' was composed by Desmond, and it was the saxophonist's extraordinary gift for melodic improvisation that gave the group much of its musical strength.

Browns

Dave Brubeck (right)

Always seeing himself primarily as a composer rather than a pianist, Brubeck, in his own solos, tended to rely too much on his ability to work in complex time-signatures (often two at once). His work in the field of composition has produced, several jazz standards, two ballets, a musical, a mass, works for television and film, an oratorio and two cantatas. However, Brubeck will always be primarily associated with his quartet recordings with Paul Desmond, and 'Take Five' in particular. His band has been a central attraction at almost all the major international jazz festivals, and during the 50s and 60s, frequently won both *Downbeat* and *Metronome* polls. As early as 1954, Brubeck appeared on the cover of *Time* magazine, and 10 years later was invited to play at the White House (which he repeated in 1981). He remains a household name, and perhaps the most popular figure in modern jazz. He was still working on projects such as the Take Five UK Jazz Tour, in 1992.

Selected albums: *Dave Brubeck Octet* (1949), *Jazz At Oberlin* (1953), *Dave Brubeck At Storyville: 1954* (1955), *Brubeck Time* (1955), *Jazz: Red Hot And Cool* (1955), *Jazz Impressions Of The USA* (1957), *Jazz Goes To Junior College* (1957), *Solo Piano* (1957), *Time Out Featuring 'Take Five'* (1959), with the New York Philharmonic Orchestra *Bernstein Plays Brubeck Plays Bernstein* (1960), *Time Further Out* (1961), *Countdown - Time In Outer Space* (1962), *Bossa Nova USA* (1963), *At Carnegie Hall* (1963), *Brandenburg Gate: Revisited* (1963), *Time Changes* (1964), *Jazz Impressions Of Japan* (1964), *Jazz Impressions Of New York* (1965), *Angel Eyes* (1965), *My Favorite Things* (1966), with Gerry Mulligan *Compadres* (1968), *Adventures In Time* (1972), with Paul Desmond *Duets* (1975), *The Dave Brubeck Quartet 25th Anniversary Reunion* (1976), *Concord On A Summer Night* (1982), *When I Was Very Young* (1992). Compilations: *Dave Brubeck's Greatest Hits* (1966), *Collection* (1985), *The Essential Dave Brubeck* (1992).

Bryant, Boudleaux

b. Diadorius Boudleaux Bryant, 13 February 1920, Shellman, Georgia, USA, d. 30 June 1987. With his wife Felice Bryant, he formed one of the greatest songwriting teams in country music and pop history. From a musical family Boudleaux learned classical violin and piano from the age of five. During the early 30s his father organized a family band with Boudleaux and his four sisters and brothers, playing at county fairs in the mid-west. In 1937 Boudleaux moved to Atlanta, playing with the Atlanta Symphony Orchestra as well as jazz and country music groups. For several years he went on the road, playing in radio station bands in Detroit and Memphis before joining Hank Penny's Radio Cowboys which performed over the airwaves of WSB Atlanta.

In 1945 he met and married Felice Scudato and the pair began composing together. The earliest recordings of Bryant songs included the Three Sons 'Give Me Some Sugar, Sugar Baby, And I'll Be Your Sweetie Pie' but the first break came when they sent 'Country Boy' to Nashville publisher Fred Rose of Acuff-Rose. When this became a hit for Jimmy Dickens, the duo moved to Nashville as staff writers for Acuff-Rose. Among their numerous successes in the 50s were 'Have A Good Time' (a pop success for Tony Bennett in 1952), 'Hey Joe' (recorded by Carl Smith and Frankie Laine in 1953) and the Eddy Arnold hits 'I've Been Thinking' and 'The Richest Man' (1955).

In 1957, Fred's son Wesley Rose commissioned the Bryants to switch to teenage material for the Everly Brothers. Beginning with 'Bye Bye Love', they supplied a stream of songs which were melodramatic vignettes of teen life. Several of them were composed by Boudleaux alone. These included the wistful 'All I Have To Do Is Dream', the tough and vengeful 'Bird Dog', 'Devoted To You' and 'Like Strangers'. At this time he wrote what has become his most-recorded song, 'Love Hurts'. This sorrowful, almost self-pitying ballad has been a favourite with the country-rock fraternity, through notable versions by Roy Orbison and Gram Parsons. There have also been less orthodox rock treatments by Jim Capaldi and Nazareth. From the early 60s, the Bryants returned to the country sphere, composing the country standard 'Rocky Top' as well as providing occasional hits for artists such as Sonny James ('Baltimore' 1964) and Roy Clark ('Come Live With Me' 1978). Shortly before Boudleaux's death in June 1987, the Bryants were inducted into the Songwriters' Hall Of Fame.

Albums: *A Touch Of Bryant* (1978), *Surfin' On A New Wave* (1979).

Bryant, Felice

b. Felice Scaduto, 7 August 1925, Milwaukee, Wisconsin, USA. The lyricist of some of the Everly Brothers' biggest hits, Felice Bryant was a member of one of the most famous husband-and-wife songwriting teams in pop and country music. Recordings of their 750 published songs have sold over 300 million copies in versions by over 400 artists as diverse as Bob Dylan and Lawrence Welk. Of Italian extraction, Felice was already writing lyrics when she met Boudleaux Bryant while working as an elevator attendant in a Milwaukee hotel. A violinist with Hank Penny's band, Boudleaux had composed instrumental pieces and after their marriage in 1945 the duo began to write together. The success of 'Country Boy' for Jimmy Dickens led them to Nashville where they were the first full-time songwriters and pluggers. During the 50s, the Bryants' country hits were often covered by pop artists such as Al Martino, Frankie Laine and Tony Bennett. Then, in 1957, they switched to composing teenage pop material for the Everly Brothers. Felice and Boudleaux proved to have a sharp eye for the details of teen life and among the hits they supplied to the close-harmony duo were 'Bye Bye Love', 'Wake Up Little Susie', 'Problems', 'Poor Jenny' and 'Take A Message To Mary'. They also composed 'Raining In My Heart' (for Buddy Holly) and the witty 'Let's Think About Livin'' (Bob Luman).

After the rock 'n' roll era had subsided, the Bryants returned to the country scene, composing prolifically throughout the 60s and 70s in such genres as bluegrass and American Indian folk material. Their most enduring song from this period has been 'Rocky Top', a hymn of praise to the state of Tennessee. First recorded by the Osborne Brothers in 1969, it was adopted as a theme song by the University of Tennessee. In the late 70s, Felice and Boudleaux recorded their own compositions for the first time.

Albums: *A Touch Of Bryant* (1977), *Surfin' On A New Wave* (1979).

Burnette, Dorsey

b. 28 December 1932, Memphis, Tennessee, USA, d. 19 August 1979. He was a member of a classic 50s rock 'n' roll act, a hit soloist act in the 60s and a country star in the 70s. He helped form the highly respected Johnny Burnette Trio, with younger brother Johnny in 1953. After appearing in the film *Rock, Rock, Rock* in 1956, Dorsey left the trio. He recorded with Johnny as The Texans (on Infinity and Jox) and wrote big hits for Ricky Nelson including, 'It's Late' and 'Waitin' In School'. As a soloist, he recorded for Abbott, Cee-Jam, and then Era, where he had his two biggest solo hits 'Tall Oak Tree' and 'Hey Little One' in 1960, both classics of their kind and both showcasing his deep rich country style voice. He then recorded without luck on Lama, Dot, Imperial, Reprise, Mel-O-Day, Condor, Liberty, Merri, Happy Tiger, Music Factory, Smash (where he re-recorded 'Tall Oak Tree'), Mercury and Hickory. In the 70s he had 15 Top 100 country hits (none making the Top 20) on Capitol, Melodyland, Calliope and Elektra, with whom he had only recently signed when he died of a heart attack on 19 August 1979. His son Billy Burnette is also a recording artist.

Selected album: *Great Shakin' Fever* (1992).

Burnette, Johnny

b. 28 March 1934, Memphis, Tennessee, USA, d. 1 August 1964, Clear Lake, California, USA. Having attended the same high school as Elvis Presley, Johnny moved into the rockabilly genre by forming a trio with his brother Dorsey Burnette on string bass and school friend Paul Burlison on guitar. Allegedly, rejected by Sun Records' supremo Sam Phillips, the group recorded 'Go Mule Go' for Von Records in New York and were subsequently signed to Coral, where they enjoyed a minor hit with 'Tear It Up'. After touring with Carl Perkins and Gene Vincent, the trio underwent a change of personnel in November 1956 with the recruitment of drummer Tony Austin. That same month, the trio were featured in Alan Freed's movie *Rock, Rock, Rock*. During this period, they issued a number of singles, including 'Honey Hush', 'The Train Kept A-Rollin'', 'Lonesome Train', 'Eager Beaver Baby', 'Drinkin' Wine', 'Spo-Dee-O-Dee' and 'If You Want It Enough', but despite the quality of the songs their work was unheralded. By the autumn of 1957, the trio had split and the Burnette brothers moved on to enjoy considerable success as songwriters. Writing as a team, they provided Ricky Nelson with the hits 'It's Late', 'Believe What You Say' and 'Just A Little Too Much'. After briefly working as a duo, the brothers parted for solo careers. Johnny proved an adept interpreter of teen ballads, whose lyrics conjured up innocent dreams of wish-fulfilment. Both 'Dreamin'' and 'You're Sixteen' were transatlantic Top 10 hits, perfectly suited to Burnette's light but expressive vocal. A series of lesser successes followed with 'Little Boy Sad', 'Big Big World', 'Girls' and 'God, Country And My Baby'. With his recording career in decline, Burnette formed his own label Magic Lamp in 1964. In August that year, he accidentally fell from his boat during a fishing trip in Clear Lake, California and drowned. Among the family

he left behind was his son Rocky Burnette, who would subsequently achieve recording success at the end of the 70s.

Albums: as the Johnny Burnette Trio *Rock 'N' Roll Trio* (1957), *The Legendary Rock 'N' Roll Trio* (1984); Solo *Dreamin'* (1961), *You're Sixteen* (1961), *Johnny Burnette* (1961), *Johnny Burnette Sings* (1961), *Burnette's Hits And Other Favourites* (1962), *Roses Are Red* (1962). Compilations: *The Johnny Burnette Story* (1964), *Tenth Anniversary Album* (1974), *We're Having A Party* (1988), *The Best Of Johnny Burnette* (1989).

Burns, Ray

A popular singer in the UK in the 50s, Burns entered showbusiness straight after demobilization from the RAF in 1945. In the early days he was encouraged by Issy Bonn, and then, while performing at the Blue Lagoon club, he was spotted by Ambrose, and recorded with the Ambrose Orchestra in 1949. After singing with Jack Nathan's band at the Coconut Grove and other night spots such as Selby's and the Stork Club, he spent some time with Dave Shand's Orchestra, before signing for Columbia Records in 1953. His early sides included 'Mother Nature And Father Time' and 'Lonely Nightingale'. He had two chart entries in 1955, 'Mobile' (written by US songwriters Bob Wells and David Holt) and 'That's How A Love Song Was Born' (composed by the British team of record producer Norman Newell and Philip Green). His other releases during the 50s included 'Begorrah', 'Rags To Riches', 'I Can't Tell A Waltz From A Tango', 'Why?', 'A Smile Is Worth A Million Tears', 'Blue Star', 'Wonderful! Wonderful!', 'Meanwhile, Back In My Arms' and 'Condemned For Life (With A Rock And Roll Wife)'.

Busch, Lou

b. 18 July 1910, Louisville, Kentucky, USA, d. 19 September 1979. After playing with the George Olsen and Hal Kemp bands in the 30s, Lou Busch became the in-house producer for Capitol Records. In the early 50s his orchestra was prominent on hits by Margaret Whiting, whom he later married, and Kay Starr. He occasionally recorded under the name of Joe 'Fingers' Carr (with the Carr-Hopps), and enjoyed US chart success with 'Down Yonder' and 'Portuguese Washerwoman', both featuring his honky tonk-style piano playing. His most famous record, 'Zambesi', a UK Top 3 hit in early 1956 was covered by UK group the Piranhas in late 1982.

Max Bygraves with son Anthony

Bygraves, Max

b. Walter Bygraves, 16 October 1922, London, England. Performing as a soloist in his school choir and employing Max Miller impressions in the RAF, with music hall dates in the late 40s, led Bygraves quickly to his recording debut and first Royal Command Performance in 1950. His debut record, with the Carrol Gibbons Band, contained impressions of Al Jolson, and was followed by a string of novelty hits through the 50s such as, 'Cowpuncher's Cantata', 'Heart Of My Heart', 'Gilly Gilly Ossenfeffer Katzenellen Bogen By The Sea', 'Meet Me On The Corner', 'You Need Hands'/'Tulips From Amsterdam', 'Jingle Bell Rock' and 'Fings Ain't Wot They Used To Be'. On the popular BBC radio show, *Educating Archie*, scripted by comedian Eric Sykes, he gave a receptive nation catch phrases like, 'a good idea son!' and 'bighead!'. Bygraves became enormously popular on stage and television with his clever mix of song and patter, defying the dramatic changes in music and entertainment taking place in the 60s. In the early 70s with Pye Records musical director Cyril Stapleton and the Tony Mansell Singers, Bygraves recorded an album of standard songs in medley form, called *Sing Along With Max*. It was the first of an amazingly successful series for which he has now won over 30 Gold Discs. Surprisingly, he has never adapted his 'song and dance' image to films, although he has played several, mainly dramatic, roles to substantial critical acclaim, including *A Cry From The Streets* and *Spare The Rod*. As early as the late 50s he formed his own music publishing company, Lakeview Music. It was intended to publish his own songs, like 'You Need Hands', however he bought the publishing rights to a 16 song show score for £350 because he liked one of the numbers. The show was Lionel Bart's *Oliver*, and in the 80s he sold the rights to Essex Music for a quarter of a million pounds. In 1982 he received the OBE, and, 10 years later, celebrated his 70th birthday by attending a lunch given in his honour by the Variety Club, and including in his theatre act a cheeky parody of the old number, 'They're Changing Guard At Buckingham Palace', entitled 'They're Changing *Wives* At Buckingham Palace'.

Selected albums: *Sing Along With Max* (1972), *Sing Along With Max, Vol. 2* (1972), *Singalongamax, Vol. 3* (1973), *Singalongamax, Vol. 4* (1973), *Singalongapartysong* (1973), *You Make Me Feel Like Singing A Song* (1974), *Singalongaxmas* (1974), *Golden Greats Of The 30s* (1977), *Golden Greats Of The 40s* (1977), *Golden Greats Of 50s* (1977), *Lingalongamax* (1978), *Song And Dance Men* (1978), *Discolongamax* (1979), *Maximemories* (1981), *You're My Everything* (1982), *Happy Hits* (1983), *Max Sings While Ted Swings* (1983), *Together: Max Bygraves And Victor Silvester* (1985), *Singalong A Christmas* (1988), *Singalongawaryears* (1989), *Singalongawaryears, Vol. 2* (1989). Compilations: *100 Golden Greats* (1976), *The Singalong Collection* (1987), *An Hour With Max Bygraves* (1988), *Tulips From Amsterdam* (1990).

Further reading: *I Wanna Tell You A Story*, Max Bygraves. *I Wanna Tell You A Funny Story*, Max Bygraves.

Byrnes, Edd

b. Edward Breitenberger, 30 July 1933, New York City, New York, USA. Byrnes gained fame as the character Gerald Lloyd Kookson III on the US television series *77 Sunset Strip* during the late 50s and early 60s. Sporting a large pompadour hairstyle, the character, known as 'Kookie', could often be seen combing his hair. Byrnes, who became popular among teenage girls, took that nickname in his off-screen career as well. In 1959 he recorded a novelty single, 'Kookie, Kookie, Lend Me Your Comb', on Warner Brothers Records, a duet with actress-singer Connie Stevens, it reached number 4 in the US. Only one follow-up single, 'Like I Love You', with Joanie Sommers charted; two further singles did not do very well and Byrnes returned to acting without repeating his early success.

Album: *Kookie* (1959).

C

Cahn, Sammy

b. Samuel Cohen, 18 June 1913, New York, USA, d. 15 January 1993, Los Angeles, California, USA. The son of Jewish immigrant parents from Galicia, Poland, Cahn grew up on Manhatten's Lower East Side. Encouraged by his mother, he learned to play the violin, joined a small orchestra that played at bar mitzvahs and other functions, and later worked as a violinist in Bowery burlesque houses. At the age of 16 he wrote his first lyric, 'Like Niagrara Falls, I'm Falling For You', and persuaded a fellow member of the orchestra, Saul Chaplin, to join him in a songwriting partnership. Their first published effort was 'Shake Your Head From Side To Side', and in the early 30s they wrote special material for vaudeville acts and bands. In 1935 they had their first big hit when the Jimmy Lunceford orchestra recorded their 'Rhythm Is Our Business'. The following year Andy Kirk topped the US Hit Parade with the duo's 'Until The Real Thing Comes Along', and Louis Armstrong featured their 'Shoe Shine Boy' in the Cotton Club Revue. In 1937 Cahn and Chaplin had their biggest success to date when they adapted the Yiddish folk song, 'Beir Mir Bist Du Schöen'. It became the top novelty song of the year and gave the Andrews Sisters their first million-seller. The team followed with 'Please Be Kind', a major seller for Bob Crosby, Red Norvo and Benny Goodman. During this time Cahn and Chaplin were also under contract to Warner Brothers, and soon after that commitment ended they decided to part company. In 1942, Cahn began his very productive partnership with Jule Styne, with their first chart success, 'I've Heard That Song Before'. Just as significant was Cahn's renewed association with Frank Sinatra, whom he had known when the singer was with Tommy Dorsey. Cahn and Styne wrote the score for the Sinatra films *Step Lively* (1944), ('Come Out Wherever You Are' and 'As Long As There's Music'); *Anchors Aweigh* (1945), ('I Fall In Love Too Easily', 'The Charm Of You', and 'What Makes The Sunset?') and *It Happened In Brooklyn* (1947), ('Time After Time', 'It's The Same Old Dream' and 'It's Gotta Come From The Heart'). Sinatra also popularized several other 40s Cahn/Styne songs, including 'I'll Walk Alone', 'Saturday Night Is The Loneliest Night In The Week', 'The Things We Did Last Summer', 'Five Minutes More', and the bleak, 'Guess I'll Hang My Tears Out To Dry', which appeared on his 1958 album, *Only The Lonely*. Some of their other hits included 'It's Been A Long, Long Time', associated with Harry James and his vocalist Kitty Kallen, 'Let It Snow! Let It Snow! Let It Snow!' (Vaughan Monroe), and 'There Goes That Song Again' (Kay Kyser and Russ Morgan). Cahn and Styne wrote the score for several other films including *Tonight And Every Night* (1945), two Danny Kaye vehicles, *Wonder Man* (1945) and *The Kid From Brooklyn* (1946), and *West Point Story* (1950). They also provided the songs for *Romance On The High Seas*

(1948), the film in which Doris Day shot to international stardom, singing 'It's Magic' and 'Put 'Em In A Box, Tie 'Em With A Ribbon'. The two songwriters also wrote the Broadway show, *High Button Shoes* (1947), starring Phil Silvers (later Sgt. Bilko) and Nanette Fabray, which ran for 727 performances and introduced songs such as 'I Still Get Jealous', 'You're My Girl' and 'Papa, Won't You Dance With Me'. After *High Button Shoes* Cahn went to California, while Styne stayed in New York. Cahn collaborated with Nicholas Brodsky for a while in the early 50s, writing movie songs for Mario Lanza, including 'Be My Love', 'Wonder Why', 'Because You're Mine', 'Serenade' and 'My Destiny'. The collaboration also composed 'I'll Never Stop Loving You' for the Doris Day film, *Love Me Or Leave Me* (1955). Cahn and Styne re-united briefly in 1954, ostensibly to write the score for the film, *Pink Tights*, to star Sinatra and Marilyn Monroe, but the project was shelved. Soon afterwards Cahn and Styne were asked to write the title song for the film, *Three Coins In The Fountain*. The result, a big hit for Sinatra and for the Four Aces, gained Cahn his first Academy Award. Cahn and Styne eventually worked with Monroe when they wrote the score for the comedy, *The Seven Year Itch* (1955). In the same year Cahn started his last major collaboration - with Jimmy Van Heusen and, some would say, with Frank Sinatra as well. They had immediate success with the title song of the Sinatra movie, *The Tender Trap* (1955), and won Academy Awards for songs in two of his movies, 'All The Way', from *The Joker Is Wild* (1957) and 'High Hopes', from *A Hole In The Head* (1959). A parody of 'High Hopes' was used as John F. Kennedy's presidential campaign song in 1960. Among the many other songs written especially for Sinatra were 'My Kind Of Town' (from *Robin And The Seven Hoods*)(1964) and the title songs for his best-selling albums, *Come Fly With Me*, *Only The Lonely*, *Come Dance With Me!*, *No One Cares*, *Ring-A-Ding-Ding!* and *September Of My Years*. Cahn and Van Heusen also produced his successful Timex television series during 1959-60. In the movies they won another Oscar for the song 'Call Me Irresponsible', (from *Papa's Delicate Condition*, 1963), Cahn's fourth Oscar from over 30 nominations, and contributed to many other films including 'The Second Time Around' (from *High Time*) and the title songs from *A Pocketful Of Miracles*, *Where Love Has Gone*, *Thoroughly Modern Millie* and *Star*. The songwriters also supplied the score for a television musical version of Thorton

Wilder's play, *Our Town*, which introduced the songs, 'Love And Marriage' and 'The Impatient Years'. They also received critical approval for their score of the Broadway musical *Skyscraper* (1965), which included the songs, 'Everybody Has The Right To Be Wrong' and 'I'll Only Miss Her When I Think Of Her'. They also provided music and lyrics for the British musical *Walking Happy*, which opened on Broadway in 1966. In 1969 Cahn dissolved his partnership with Van Heusen and collaborated once more with Jule Styne on the Broadway musical, *Look To The Lilies*. His other collaborators included Axel Stordahl and Paul Weston ('Day By Day' and 'I Should Care'), Gene DePaul ('Teach Me Tonight'), Arthur Schwartz ('Relax-Ay-Voo'), George Barrie ('All That Love To Waste'), and Vernon Duke ('That's What Makes Paris Paree', and 'I'm Gonna Ring The Bell Tonight'). In 1972 Cahn was inducted into the Songwriters Hall Of Fame after claiming throughout his lifetime that he only wrote songs so that he could demonstrate them. In the same year he mounted his 'one man show', *Words and Music*, on Broadway, and despite his voice being described by a New York critic as that of 'a vain duck with a hangover', the nostalgic mixture of his songs, sprinkled with amusing anecdotes of the way they came about, won rave notices and the Outer Circle Critics Award for the best new talent on Broadway. He repeated his triumph in England two years later, and then re-mounted the whole thing all over again in 1987. After over six decades of 'putting *that* word to *that* note', as he termed it, he died in January 1993. His books include a songbook, *Words and Music* and *The Songwriter's Rhyming Dictionary*.
Album: *I've Heard That Song Before* (1977).
Further reading: *I Should Care - The Sammy Cahn Story*, Sammy Cahn.

Call Me Madam

With pre-opening ticket sales exceeding $1,000,000, the stage musical *Call Me Madam* was a guaranteed hit. With music and lyrics by Irving Berlin, the book by Russell Crouse and Howard Lindsay was based loosely upon the life and career of Perle Mesta, a famous Washington, D.C. hostess who became the US Ambassador to Luxembourg. As Sally Adams, the Mesta character, the show starred Ethel Merman. Amongst the songs were 'The Best Thing For You', 'It's A Lovely Day Today', 'Can You Use Any Money Today?, 'Marrying For Love', 'The Hostess With The Mostes' On The Ball', 'They Like Ike' (about US Army General Dwight D. Eisenhower, who attended the opening night), and 'You're Just In Love', an engaging contrapuntal song with two melodies and two sets of lyrics, and sung in the show by Merman and Russell Nype. The show opened in October 1950 and ran for almost 650 performances. It was made into a film in 1953, with Merman, George Sanders and Donald O'Connor.

Calvert, Eddie

b. 15 March 1922, Preston, Lancashire, England, d. 7 August 1978. Calvert's father taught him to play the trumpet and, at the age of 11, he joined the Preston Town Silver Band. In the 40s he played with Billy Ternent and Geraldo before forming his own group for night club engagements. By the early 50s he was touring the British variety circuit, and became known as 'The Man With The Golden Trumpet'. In 1953 he recorded a Swiss tune 'O Mein Papa' which went to number 1 in the UK and made the Top 10 in the USA. Two years later he topped the UK charts again with a cover of the Perez Prado hit 'Cherry Pink And Apple Blossom White', and in the late 50s had more success with 'Zambesi', 'Mandy' and the theme from the Peter Sellers' movie *John And Julie*. Calvert had enormous success in theatres and clubs in the UK, including the London Palladium and major regional venues, until he moved to South Africa in 1968, where he was appointed liaison officer between the Government and the Bantu tribe. He died from a heart attack on 7 August 1978 in Johannesburg, South Africa.
Selected albums: *Latin Carnival* (1960), *All In The Summer Evening (And Other Songs Of Faith)* (1965), *Eddie Calvert Salutes The Trumpet Greats* (1967). Compilations: *20 Golden Trumpet Greats* (1979), *The Man With The Golden Trumpet* (1978).

Cameo Records (see Cameo-Parkway Records)

Cameo-Parkway Records

Founded in Philadelphia, Pennsylvania, USA, 1957 by songwriter Bernie Lowe, Cameo Records and its Parkway subsidiary were the home of most of the major hits by such artists as Chubby Checker, the Dovells, Dee Dee Sharp, the Orlons, Bobby Rydell and the Tymes. Lowe was soon joined in his endeavour by fellow songwriters Kal Mann and Dave Appell. The first Cameo hit was rockabilly singer Charlie Gracie's 'Butterfly', a number 1 single in 1957. The Rays' doo-wop classic 'Silhouettes' was next, in 1957. White teen idol

Eddie Calvert

Rydell gave the label a steady string of pop hits beginning in 1959, including 'We Got Love', 'Wild One' and 'Swingin' School'. The Parkway label was launched in 1958 but had no real success until 1960, when former chicken plucker Ernest Evans was rechristened Chubby Checker and scored a major dance sensation with 'The Twist'. Checker continued to have hits throughout the early 60s. Other Cameo-Parkway hits included Sharp's 'Mashed Potato Time', Big Dee Irwin's duet with Little Eva 'Swing On A Star', the Orlons' 'South Street' and 'Don't Hang Up', and the Tymes' 'So Much In Love'. Cameo-Parkway were unable to weather the transition in musical climate signalled by the arrival of the British groups, despite having released the Kinks' first single, 'Long Tall Sally', in the USA. The label's last major hit was ? And The Mysterians' '96 Tears' in 1966. In 1968 the Cameo-Parkway catalogue was sold to entrepreneur Allen Klein, who continues to own it today.

Compilation: *All The Hits By All The Stars* (1962).

Can-Can

For *Can-Can*, his penultimate Broadway stage musical, Cole Porter chose the setting of turn-of-the-century Paris. Centring upon the flimsiest of plots, an attempt by the authorities to close down a Montmartre nightclub that features the outrageous can-can dance, it is essentially a love story. As Judge Aristide Forestier, who investigates allegations of impropriety, and La Mome Pistache, who operates the nightclub, the show starred Peter Cookson and Lilo. However, the real show-stopping star was Gwen Verdon as Claudine, a dancer. With splendid choreography by Michael Kidd, *Can-Can* was a great success following its opening in May 1953, and ran for almost 900 performances. Despite fine performances and great dancing, however, *Can-Can*'s greatest strengths lay in Porter's music and lyrics. The songs included 'It's All Right With Me', 'Allez-Vous-En', 'Come Along With Me', 'Maidens Typical of France', 'I Am In Love' and two major hits, 'C'est Magnifique' and Porter's eloquent hymn to the city he adored, 'I Love Paris'. The 1960 film version starred Frank Sinatra, Shirley MacLaine and Maurice Chevalier.

Capitol Records

The Capitol label was founded in Hollywood, USA in 1942 by songwriter Johnny Mercer, record store magnate Glenn Wallichs and Paramount Pictures executive Buddy de Sylva. Initially incorporated as 'Liberty Records', the company was given its above name at the directors' first formal meeting. Despite astringent war-time restrictions, Capitol quickly established itself as a leading outlet. Its early roster included Nat 'King' Cole and Peggy Lee, but success was also derived from jazz arranger/composer Stan Kenton ('Tampico' and 'Artistry In Rhythm') and country singer Tex Williams ('Smoke, Smoke, Smoke That Cigarette'). During the early 50s the venture was considerably strengthened by the addition of Dean Martin, Al Martino and Frank Sinatra, the last of whom embraced the nascent album market with a series of seminal period-piece recordings, notably *Songs For Swinging Lovers* (1956) and *Come Fly With Me* (1958). Jo Stafford and Les Paul And Mary Ford also enjoyed best-sellers, while the label expanded its C&W division with Tex Ritter and Tennessee Ernie Ford. In 1955 EMI took a controlling interest in Capitol. This not only gave the British company a share of the lucrative US market - between 1948 and 1955 Decca had distributed Capitol product in the UK.- but established an outlet for home-recorded material. Capitol nonetheless retained its autonomy, but despite signing Gene Vincent, interest in the emergent rock 'n' roll phenomenon was negligible. The label did become involved in teenage mores until it signed the Beach Boys, who quickly outstripped the transitory surfing craze to become one of the 60s most enduring and biggest-selling acts. Having initially viewed the Beatles as 'too English', Capitol quickly rescinded and enjoyed unparalleled success throughout the decade, and beyond with this remarkable group. In 1964 the label revived Tower as a wholly-owned subsidiary to encompass material either drawn from independent producers or deemed unsuitable for the parent company. Its diverse catalogue included Freddie And The Dreamers (whose 'I'm Telling You Now' was Tower's solo chart-topper), the Standells and Pink Floyd, but the outlet was also known for R&B releases. Capitol itself was noticeably weak within the soul market, preferring to opt for the sophisticated approach of Lou Rawls or Nancy Wilson. Its leading position within the country market was enhanced by Buck Owens, Sonny James and Merle Haggard and although late in exploiting the 'west coast' scene in nearby San Francisco, captured two of the genre's finest exponents in the Quicksilver Messenger Service and the Steve Miller Band. By the end of the decade Capitol's MOR division enjoyed success with Glen Campbell and Anne Murray, while its

Pearl Carr (left) with Eve Boswell

rock counterpart had acquired the Band and Grand Funk Railroad. The label's progress throughout the ensuing decade was equally impressive. Dr. Hook, Bob Seger and Kraftwerk represented the now-divergent AOR market, while the acquisition of established 'stars' Paul McCartney (USA only), Diana Ross and Neil Diamond added prestige to its roster. Tavares, Maze and Natalie Cole brought a consistent profile in the R&B charts, although EMI instilled a sense of internal competition by founding EMI-America and (later) EMI-Manhattan. In 1979 the UK company took full control of Capitol which during the 80s continued strengthening its ties with black music with releases by Peabo Bryson and Melba Moore. A once-premier place now taken by other outlets, Capitol nonetheless remains one of the most important post-war record labels, and celebrated its silver anniversary in 1992 with several special releases under the title of *Capitol Sings*.

Selected albums: *Sings Johnny Mercer: Too Marvellous For Words* (1991), *Sings Cole Porter: Anything Goes* (1991), *Sings Jerome Kern: The Song Is You* (1992), *Sings Rodgers And Hart: Isn't It Romantic?* (1992).

Carr, Pearl, And Teddy Johnson

Both were popular solo vocalists before they married in 1955. Carr (b. 2 November 1923, Exmouth, Devon, England) worked with several name bands and was lead singer with the Keynotes, the resident vocal group on BBC radio's *Take It From Here*. She also appeared on radio as comedienne and singer on *Breakfast* (and *Bedtime*) *With Braden* and had her own series, *In The Blue Of The Evening*. Johnson (b. 1920) led his own five-piece amateur band at the age of 14 and sang and played drums professionally at the age of 17. He recorded extensively for Columbia in the early 50s, and also worked as a disc jockey for Radio Luxembourg. Their professional liaison proved to be extremely successful, especially during the late 50s when they became known as Britain's Mr and Mrs Music. In 1959 they made the UK Top 20 chart with 'Sing Little Birdie', a song which they had taken to second place in the *Eurovision Song Contest*. They had another hit in 1961 with the Italian 'Aneme e Core (How Wonderful To Know)'. More recently they have been involved in biographical stage presentations which they have devised and appeared in, such as *The Bing Crosby Story* and *London To Hollywood*. In 1987 they were contemplating retirement when they accepted an offer to appear as two aging vaudeville stars in Stephen Sondheim's *Follies*, their first London West End musical.

Carroll, Ronnie

b. Ronald Cleghorn, 18 August 1934, Belfast, Northern Ireland. A singer with a high baritone voice and known as 'The Minstrel'. Carroll has been a baker, plumber, greengrocer, milkman, car mechanic and auctioneer's assistant. He began his career in shows promoted by Ruby Murray's father, then joined Eddie Lee's *Hollywood Doubles Show*, blacking up to provide Nat 'King' Cole impressions. Cole attended his performance in Liverpool and asked, 'What are you trying to do, cripple me?' Carroll toured the UK Variety circuit with the show, adding Billy Eckstine material to his repertoire. After BBC producer Albert Stevenson gave him his television debut, he met singer/actress Millicent Martin on a show and they were married in 1959. Carroll was signed to Philips by A&R manager Johnny Franz who had seen him at the London Metropolitan, Edgware Road. In the late 50s he had UK hits with 'Walk Hand In Hand' (1956) and 'The Wisdom Of A Fool' (1957), and in the early 60's with 'Footsteps' (1960), 'Roses Are Red' (1962 - a number 3 hit), 'If Only Tomorrow' (1962) and two songs with which he won the British heats of the *Eurovision Song Contest*, 'Ring-A-Ding Girl' (1962) and 'Say Wonderful Things' (1963 - Top 10). He was still working in the 80s, but the recession in the UK northern club business forced him to seek work in holiday camps and in Singapore and Kuala Lumpur hotels. In 1989, Carroll was discharged from bankruptcy with reported debts of many thousands of pounds.

Selected albums: *Lucky Thirteen* (1959), *Sometimes I'm Happy, Sometimes I'm Blue* (1963), *Carroll Calling* (1965).

Carson, Mindy

b. 16 July 1927, New York City, New York, USA. After singing on bandleader Paul Whiteman's 40s radio show, female pop vocalist Mindy Carson first hit the US Top 20 in 1946 in a duet with Harry Cool, with a version of Frankie Carle's number 1 'Rumors Are Flying'. She continued to have chart successes until the mid-50s - including two with Guy Mitchell - by covering the big hits of the day, including Dean Martin's 1956 UK and US chart-topper 'Memories Are Made Of This' and R&B singer Ivory Joe Hunter's 'Since I Met You Baby' She also hosted her own radio and television programmes.

Chacksfield, Frank

b. 9 May 1914, Battle, Sussex, England. After early training on the piano and organ, Chacksfield led

Ronnie Carroll

small groups in the late 30s before becoming arranger for the *Stars In Battledress* entertainment unit in World War II. His first radio broadcast was *Original Songs At The Piano* from Glasgow, and during the late 40s he worked with comedian Charlie Chester's *Stand Easy* making his recording debut accompanying Chester's resident singer, Frederick Ferrari. He also conducted for the Henry Hall and Geraldo orchestras before forming his own band the Tunesmiths in 1953 and, with composer Jack Jordan on the clavioline, had a hit with the novelty, 'Little Red Monkey'. Later that year, with a 40-piece orchestra featuring a large string section, he made the Top 10 in the UK and US charts with Charles Chaplin's 'Terry's Theme From *Limelight*', repeating the process in 1954 with his version of 'Ebb Tide'. Both records became million-sellers. He had further success in the 50s with 'In Old Lisbon', 'Donkey Cart', 'Flirtation Waltz', 'Memories Of You', and another Chaplin theme, 'Smile'. Since then he has broadcast regularly, recorded many albums reflecting music from all over the world, interpreting many composers and styles and has been musical director on several films.

Albums: *The Ebb Tide* (1960), *The New Ebb Tide* (1964), *New Limelight* (1965), *Beyond The Sea* (1965), *Great Country And Western Hits* (1966), *Film Festival* (1968), *South Sea Island Magic* (1969), *Tango* (1970), *New York* (1970), *Plays The Beatles Songbook* (1970), *Plays Simon And Garfunkel/Jim Webb* (1971), *Mediterranean Moonlight* (1971), *Bacharach* (1972), *The World Of Immortal Classics* (1972), *Music Of Cole Porter* (1973), *Opera's Golden Moments* (1973), *Music For Christmas* (1973), *The World Of Immortal Serenades* (1973), *Music Of Nöel Coward* (1974), *Romantic Europe* (1974), *The Glory That Was Gershwin* (1974), *The Incomparable Jerome Kern* (1975), *Plays Rodgers And Hart* (1975), *The World Of Immortal Strauss Waltzes* (1975), *The World Of Operatic Melodies* (1976), *Plays Lerner And Loewe* (1976), *Plays Irving Berlin* (1976), *Vintage '52* (1977), *Plays Hoagy Carmichael* (1977), *Hawaii* (1979), *Could I Have This Dance?* (1981), *Chariots Of Fire* (1984), *Love Is In The Air* (1984), *Nice 'N' Easy* (1984), *A Little More Love* (1987). Compilations: *The World Of Frank Chacksfield* (1969), *The World Of Frank Chacksfield, Volume Two* (1971), *Focus On Frank Chacksfield* (1977), *Stardust* (1981), *Limelight And Other Favourites* (1985).

Champs

Best known for the classic 1958 rock 'n' roll near-instrumental 'Tequila', a US number 1 song, the Champs were formed in Los Angeles, California, USA in December 1957. The five musicians initially comprising the group were Dave Burgess (rhythm guitar), Danny Flores (saxophone/piano), Cliff Hills (bass), Buddy Bruce (lead guitar) and Gene Alden (drums). The musicians were united by Joe Johnson, co-owner of Challenge Records, for the purpose of providing backing for the Kuf-Linx vocal group. With time left after that session, the musicians recorded three instrumentals written by Burgess. Flores, who also went under the name Chuck Rio as he was already contracted to the RPM label, taught the others 'Tequila' from a riff he had worked on to play at club dates in Los Angeles. The recording was considered a 'throwaway' by the musicians, who did not even stay to hear the final playback. Issued in January 1958 under the name Champs (in honour of Champion, a horse owned by Challenge founder Gene Autry), 'Tequila' was planned as the b-side to 'Train To Nowhere'. Radio stations preferred 'Tequila' and the Champs' version battled for chart positions with a cover of the song by Eddie Platt; the latter's version reached number 20 in the US charts while the Champs' made number 1. With the song a success there was a need for them to tour, so a new line-up was formed including Flores, Burgess, Alden and new members Dale Norris (guitar) and Joe Burnas (bass). Flores and Alden left in late 1958 and were replaced by Jim Seals (saxophone), Dash Crofts (drums) and Dean Beard (piano). Seals And Crofts remained with the group until its termination, before forming the Dawnbreakers and then re-emerging in the late 60s as a popular acoustic music duo. The Champs placed a further seven singles in the charts through 1962, none of which came close to matching the debut's success. Further personnel changes occurred throughout their history, most notably the replacement of Burgess by young guitarist Glen Campbell in 1960. The Champs disbanded in 1964.

Albums: *Go Champs Go* (1958), *Everybody's Rockin' With The Champs* (1959), *Great Dance Hits Of Today* (1962), *All American Music With The Champs* (1962).

Chantels

Regarded as the first true 'girl group', this New York vocal quintet - Arlene Smith (b. 5 October

1941, New York, USA), Sonia Goring, Rene Minus, Lois Harris and Jackie Landry - were all members of a high school choir when they auditioned for producer Richie Barrett in 1957. The group made its recording debut with 'He's Gone' following two months of rehearsal, and this plaintive offering set the tone for the Chantels' subsequent work. Their impassioned style culminated with 'Maybe', wherein Arlene Smith's heart-wrenching plea carried an inordinate passion. Barely 16 years-old on its release, the singer's emotional delivery belies her youth. The single reputedly sold in excess of one million copies, but pirated pressings were prevalent in many American states, undermining the group's potential. Subsequent releases failed to match its quality and the Chantels grew disenchanted with their management and label. Lois Harris had already dropped out of the line-up and Arlene Smith embarked on a solo career under the tutelage of Phil Spector, while Barrett continued to produce the remaining trio but with different singers in place of the former vocalist. The Chantels enjoyed two US Top 30 hits with 'Look In My Eyes' and 'Well I Told You', but they lacked the distinctiveness of the earlier releases.

Albums: *The Chantels* aka *We Are The Chantels* (1958), *The Chantels On Tour* (1961), *There's Our Song Again* (1962). Compilations: *Arlene Smith And The Chantels* (1987), *The Best Of The Chantels* (1990).

Charles, Bobby

b. Robert Charles Guidry, 1938, Abbeville, Louisiana, USA. Charles became well-known in the 50s when three of his songs - 'See You Later Alligator', 'Walkin' To New Orleans' and 'But I Do' - were successfully covered by Bill Haley, Fats Domino and Clarence 'Frogman' Henry. The composer also recorded in his own right for Chicago's Chess label, but returned to the south the following decade for a series of low-key, largely unsuccessful, releases. The singer's career was relaunched in 1972 upon signing with Albert Grossman's Bearsville label. *Bobby Charles* featured support from several members of the Band, and this excellent album combined the artist's R&B and cajun roots to create a warm, mature collection. The set offered several excellent compositions, the highlight of which was the much-covered 'Small Town Talk'. Charles then guested on both of the albums by Paul Butterfield's Better Days, but he has since maintained a relatively low profile. However a new recording, *Clean Water*, was

released in Europe in 1987.

Albums: *Bobby Charles* (1972, later reissued as *Small Town Talk* in 1988), *Clean Water* (1987). Compilations of Chess recordings: *Bobby Charles* (1983), *Chess Masters* (1986).

Charles, Ray

b. Ray Charles Robinson, 23 September 1930, Albany, Georgia, USA. Few epithets sit less comfortably than that of genius; Ray Charles has borne this title for over thirty years. As a singer, composer, arranger and pianist, his prolific work deserves no other praise. Born in extreme poverty, Ray was slowly blinded by glaucoma until, by the age of seven, he had lost his sight completely. He learned to read and write music in braille and was accomplished on several instruments by the time he left school. Orphaned at age 15, Charles drifted around the Florida circuit, picking up work where he could, before moving across the country to Seattle. Here he continued his itinerant career, playing piano at several nightclubs in a style reminiscent of Nat 'King' Cole.

Ray began recording in 1949 and this early, imitative approach was captured on several sessions. Three years later Atlantic Records acquired his contract, but initially the singer continued his 'cool' direction, baring only an occasional hint of the passions later unleashed. 'It Should've Been Me', 'Mess Around' and 'Losing Hand' best represent this early R&B era, but Ray's individual style emerged as a result of his work with Guitar Slim. This impassioned, almost crude blues performer sang with a gospel-based fervour that greatly influenced Charles' thinking. He arranged Slim's million-selling single, 'Things That I Used To Do', of which the riffing horns and unrestrained voice set the tone for Ray's own subsequent direction. This effect was fully realized in 'I Got A Woman' (1954), a song soaked in the fervour of the Baptist Church, but rendered salacious by the singer's abandoned, unrefined delivery. Its extraordinary success, commercially and artistically, inspired similarly compulsive recordings including 'This Little Girl Of Mine' (1955), 'Talkin' 'Bout You' (1957) and the lush and evocative 'Don't Let The Sun Catch You Crying' (1959), a style culminating in the thrilling call and response of 'What'd I Say' (1959). This acknowledged classic is one of the all-time great encore numbers to be found being performed by countless singers and bands in stadiums, clubs and bars all over the world. However, Charles was equally adept at slow ballads, as his heartbreaking interpretations of 'Drown In My Own Tears' and 'I Believe To My Soul' (both 1959) clearly show. Proficient in numerous styles, Ray's recordings embraced blues, jazz, standards and even country, as his muscular reading of 'I'm Movin' On' attested.

In November 1959, Charles left the Atlantic label for ABC Records, where he secured both musical and financial freedom. Commentators often note this as the point at which the singer lost his fire, but early releases for this new outlet simply continued his groundbreaking style. 'Georgia On My Mind' (1960) and 'Hit The Road Jack' (1961) were, respectively, poignant and ebullient, and established the artist as an international name. This stature was enhanced further in 1962 with the release of the massive selling album, *Modern Sounds In Country And Western*, a landmark collection which produced the million-selling single 'I Can't Stop Loving You'. Its success defined the pattern for Ray's later career; the edges were blunted, the vibrancy was stilled as Charles' repertoire grew increasingly inoffensive. There were still moments of inspiration, 'Let's Go Get Stoned' and 'I Don't Need No Doctor' brought a glimpse of a passion now too often muted, while *Crying Time*, Ray's first album since kicking his heroin habit, compared favourably with any Atlantic release. This respite was, however, temporary and as the 60s progressed so the singer's work became less compulsive and increasingly MOR. Like most artists, he attempted cover versions of Beatles' songs and had substantial hits with versions of 'Yesterday' and 'Eleanor Rigby'. Two 70s' releases, *A Message From The People* and *Renaissance*, did include contemporary material in Stevie Wonder's 'Living In The City' and Randy Newman's 'Sail Away', but subsequent releases reneged on this promise. Charles' 80s' work included more country-flavoured collections and a cameo appearance in the film *The Blues Brothers*, but the period is better marked by the singer's powerful appearance on the USA For Africa release, 'We Are The World' (1985). It brought to mind a talent too often dormant, a performer whose marriage of gospel and R&B prepared the basis for soul music. His influence is inestimable, his talent widely acknowledged and imitated by formidable white artists such as Steve Winwood, Joe Cocker, Van Morrison and Eric Burdon. Charles has been honoured with countless awards during his career including the Lifetime Achievement Award. He has performed rock, jazz, blues and country with spectacular ease but it is as 'father of soul music'

that remains his greatest title, so it was fitting that, in 1992, an acclaimed documentary, *Ray Charles: The Genius Of Soul*, was broadcast by PBS television.

Selected albums: *Hallelujah, I Love Her So* aka *Ray Charles* (1957), *The Great Ray Charles* (1957), with Milt Jackson *Soul Meeting* (1958), *Ray Charles At Newport* (1958), *Yes Indeed* (1958), *What'd I Say* (1959), *The Genius Of Ray Charles* (1959), *Ray Charles In Person* (1960), *Genius Hits The Road* (1960), *The Genius After Hours* (1961), *The Genius Sings The Blues* (1961), *Dedicated To You* (1961), *Genius + Soul = Jazz* (1961), with Betty Carter *Ray Charles And Betty Carter* (1961), *Modern Sounds In Country And Western Music* (1962), *Modern Sounds In Country And Western Music, Volume 2* (1962), *Ingredients In A Recipe For Soul* (1963), *Sweet And Sour Tears* (1964), *Have A Smile With Me* (1964), *Live In Concert* (1965), *Country And Western Meets Rhythm And Blues* aka *Together Again* (1965), *Crying Time* (1966), *Ray's Moods* (1966), *Ray Charles Invites You To Listen* (1967), *A Portrait Of Ray* (1968), *I'm All Yours, Baby!* (1969), *Doing His Thing* (1969), *My Kind Of Jazz* (1970), *Love Country Style* (1970), *Volcanic Action Of My Soul* (1971), *A Message From The People* (1972), *Through The Eyes Of Love* (1972), *Come Live With me* (1974), *Renaissance* (1975), *Live In Japan* (1975), with Cleo Laine *Porgy And Bess* (1976), *True To Life* (1977), *Love And Peace* (1978), *Ain't It So* (1979), *Brother Ray Is At It Again* (1980), *Wish You Were Here Tonight* (1983), *Do I Ever Cross Your Mind* (1984), *Friendship* (1985), *Just Between Us* (1988), *My World* (1993). Compilations: *The Ray Charles Story* (1962), *A Man And His Soul* (1967), *25th Anniversary In Show Business Salute To Ray Charles* (1971), *The Right Time* (1987), *The Collection* (1990 - ABC recordings), *The Living Legend* (1993). In addition to these releases Charles' big band recorded the following: *My Kind Of Jazz* (1970), *Jazz Number II* (1973), *My Kind Of Jazz, Part 3* (1975).

Further reading: *Brother Ray*, Ray Charles and David Ritz.

Cherry, Don

b. 11 January 1924, Wichita, Texas, USA. Cherry sang briefly with the post-war orchestras of Jan Garber, Victor Young and Tommy Dorsey. His first solo hits for Decca Records in 1950/51 were 'Thinking Of You' from the Fred Astaire/Vera Ellen movie *Three Little Words*, 'Vanity' and 'Belle, Belle, My Liberty Belle', the latter beaten to the upper reaches of the US chart by Guy Mitchell's version. Switching to Columbia, Cherry had a massive seller in 1955 with the Bob Musel and Jack Taylor ballad, 'Band Of Gold' (not to be confused with another song with the same title which was a hit in 1970 for Freda Payne). The unusual choral backing on the Cherry record signified trombonist/arranger Ray Conniff's first arrangement for Columbia. After further US success in 1956 with 'Wild Cherry', 'Ghost Town' and 'Namely You', Cherry, always a keen amateur golfer, launched an assault on the USA professional circuit, but was still recording occasionally on the Monument label well into the 60s. In the mid-80s, he was still putting the golf stories inbetween songs such as 'Wind Beneath My Wings' and 'Band Of Gold', in his Las Vegas nightclub act.

Selected albums: with Ray Conniff And His Orchestra *Swingin' For Two* (1956), *Don Cherry* (1967).

Chipmunks

A fictional group, the Chipmunks were three cartoon characters, Alvin, Theodore and Simon, who were created by Ross Bagdasarian (b. 27 January 1919, Fresno, California, USA), a multi-faceted performer, who had earlier had an international hit as David Seville, with 'Witch Doctor', in early 1958. On that hit, Bagdasarian had manipulated a tape recorder so that normally sung vocals played back at a faster speed. Using the same technique, he experimented with the sound of three voices harmonizing at that faster speed and it reminded him of the chattering of chipmunks. Bagdasarian had recorded 'Witch Doctor' for Liberty Records (the three Chipmunks were named after Liberty executives) which released 'The Chipmunk Song' for the Christmas 1958 season. It reached number 1 in the US and was quickly followed by 'Alvin's Harmonica' which climbed to number 3. In all, the Chipmunks placed 15 songs on the US charts between 1958 and 1962, spawning a hit television programme. They continued well into the 60s, recording an album of Beatles songs. Bagdasarian died in January 1972 but the Chipmunks were revived in 1980 by his son, Ross Bagdasarian Jnr., and his partner Janice Karmen, this time recording albums of punk, country and current rock!

Albums: *Let's All Sing With The Chipmunks* (1959), *Sing Again With The Chipmunks* (1960), *Christmas With The Chipmunks* (1962), *Christmas With The Chipmunks - Volume Two* (1963), *The Chipmunks Sing The Beatles Hits* (1964), *The Chipmunks Sing With Children* (1965), *Chipmunk Punk* (1980), *Urban Chipmunk* (1981), *A Chipmunk Christmas* (1981), *Chipmunk Rock* (1982), *Merry Christmas Fun With The Merry Chipmunks* (1984). Compilation: *Twenty All-Time Greatest Hits* (1982).

Chordettes

Formed in 1946 in Sheboygan, Wisconsin, USA, the Chordettes were a female singing group whose career extended into the rock era. Initially envisioning themselves as a female barbershop quartet the members were Dorothy Schwartz (lead), Janet Ertel (bass), Carol Buschman (baritone) and Jinny Lockard (tenor). In 1949 the group came to the attention of Arthur Godfrey, whose national *Talent Scouts* radio programme was a popular means for acts to break through to a wider audience. Godfrey offered the Chordettes a permanent spot on the show and they were signed to Columbia Records, for which they recorded a series of 10-inch EPs. In 1953 the group left Godfrey and signed to Cadence Records, operated by Godfrey's musical director, Archie Bleyer. Their first recording for Cadence, 'Mr. Sandman', in 1954, became a million seller, logging seven weeks at number 1 in the US charts. It featured Lynn Evans, who had replaced Schwartz, as lead singer, and Margie Needham, who had replaced Lockard. The Chordettes remained with Cadence until the early 60s, scoring three other Top 10 hits: 'Born To Be With You' (1956), 'Just Between You And Me' (1957) and 'Lollipop' (1958). Ertel married Bleyer in 1954; the group disbanded in the mid-60s. Janet Bleyer, died at the age of 75 on 4 November 1988, in Black River, Wisconsin, USA.

Albums: *Harmony Time* (1950), *Harmony Time* (1951), *Harmony Encores* (1953), *Your Requests* (1953), *Listen* (1954), *The Chordettes* (1955), *The Chordettes* (1957), *Close Harmony* (1957), *Never On Sunday* (1962). Compilations: *The Chordettes* (1982), *The Best Of The Chordettes* (1985).

Chords

The original members were brothers Carl (lead tenor) and Claude Feaster (baritone), Jimmy Keyes (tenor), Floyd McRae (tenor), William Edwards (bass) and pianist Rupert Branker; all school friends from the Bronx, New York, USA. The Chords, who evolved out of three other groups, the Tunetoppers, the Keynotes and the Four Notes, were one of the first acts signed to the Atlantic subsidiary label, Cat. Their debut disc was a doo-wop version of the then current Patti Page hit 'Cross Over The Bridge'. On the b-side of this 1954 release Cat begrudgingly put one of the group's own songs 'Sh-Boom' which became a milestone in rock 'n' roll music. This fun piece of nonsense took the USA by storm and featured the joyous but contentious lyric, 'Ah, life could be a dream, sh-boom, sh-boom!'. Some claim that this was rock 'n' roll's first 'drug song'. It shot into the Top 10, a unique occurrence in those days for an R&B record, while a watered-down cover version by Canada's Crew Cuts had the honour of being America's first number 1 rock 'n' roll hit. The song created such a furore that even ace satirist Stan Freberg's cruel take-off of the Chords' record also made the Top 20. Since a group on Gem Records was already using the same name the group quickly became the Chordcats. They tried to follow the monster novelty hit with other similar tracks, like the follow-up 'Zippety-Zum', but with no success. Some personnel changes and another new name, the inevitable Sh-Booms, also failed to return them to the charts. The Chords, who were probably the first R&B group to appear on USA television nationwide, also recorded on Vik, Roulette (under the name Lionel Thorpe), Atlantic and Baron amongst others. They occasionally reunited to play 'oldies' shows until lead singer Carl died in January 1981.

Christy, June

b. Shirley Luster, 20 November 1925, Springfield, Illinois, USA, d. 21 June 1990. Christy first came to prominence with the bands of Boyd Raeburn and Stan Kenton, although her chirpy singing style somtimes sat oddly with the earnestly progressive experiments with her employers. Her bright, bubbling personality glowed through her performances and she was especially effective on up-tempo swingers. Yet she was also adept on reflective ballads and was never afraid to have fun with a song. With Kenton she had successes in all of these areas. One of her first recordings with the band was 'Tampico', which became a million-seller; another was 'How High The Moon'. During the late 40s she was one of the band's main attractions. Kenton and his chief arranger, Pete Rugolo, responded by providing effective settings for her voice which, while of limited range, was engaging and her performances were always highly professional. During this same period she married Kenton tenor saxophonist Bob Cooper, with whom she made some fine recordings backed by his small group. After leaving Kenton in 1948 Christy worked as a solo artist, making many successful recordings for Capitol Records, including three US Top 20 albums, Something Cool

(imaginatively arranged for her by Rugolo), The Misty Miss Christy and June - Fair And Warmer!. After many years in retirement, she died in June 1990.

Albums: Shorty Rogers Plus Kenton And Christy (1950), Something Cool (1954), with Stan Kenton Duet (1955), The Misty Miss Christy (1956), June - Fair And Warmer! (1957), Gone For The Day (1957), June's Got Rhythm (1958), The Song Is June! (1959), with Kenton The Road Show, Volumes 1 & 2 (1959), June Christy Recalls Those Kenton Days (1959), Ballads For Night People (1959), The Cool School (1960), Off Beat (1961), Do-Re-Mi (1961, film soundtrack), That Time Of Year (1961), Big Band Specials (1962), The Intimate June Christy (1962), Something Broadway, Something Latin (1965), Impromptu (1977), Willow Weep For Me (c.1979), Interlude (1985). Compilations: This Is June Christy (1956), The Best Of June Christy (1962), The Capitol Years (1989), A Lovely Way To Spend An Evening (1989).

Clark, Dee

b. Delecta Clark, 7 November 1938, Blytheville, Arkansas, USA, d. 7 December 1990. Clark had a wonderfully impassioned tenor voice and enjoyed a spate of rock 'n' roll hits in the late 50s and a lesser body of soul work in the 60s. Clark's entertainment career began in 1952 as a member of the Hambone Kids, who, with band leader Red Saunders, recorded a novelty number in which Clark's group patted a rhythm known as the Hambone. Clark later joined a vocal group, the Goldentones, who won first prize in a talent show at Chicago's Roberts Show Lounge. Noted disc jockey Herb 'Kool Gent' Kent then took the group to VeeJay Records, where they recorded as the Kool Gents. Clark's distinctive stylings soon engendered a solo contract and in 1958 he scored a hit with 'Nobody But You' (R&B number 3 and pop Top 30). 'Just Keep It Up' (R&B number 9 and pop Top 20) and 'Hey Little Girl' (R&B number 2 and pop Top 20) proved equally popular the following year. The artist's major success came in 1962 with 'Raindrops' (R&B number 3 and pop number 2). This plaintive offering, co-written by Clark and Phil Upchurch, eventually sold in excess of 1 million copies. Sadly, Clark was unable to repeat this feat, but continued on Chicago-based Constellation with a spate of moderate R&B hits, namely 'Crossfire Time' (1963), 'Heartbreak' (1964), and 'TCB' (1965). His career faded after Constellation went out of business in 1966. In the UK he had a sizable hit in 1975 with 'Ride A Wild

Horse'; in the US the record failed to chart. Clark died of a heart attack in 1990.

Albums: *Dee Clark* (1959), *How About That* (1960), *You're Looking Good* (1960), *Hold On, It's Dee Clark* (1961), *Raindrops* (1982), *Hey Little Girl* (1982). Compilations: *The Best Of Dee Clark* (1964), *Keep It Up* (1980), *The Delectable Sound Of Dee Clark* (1986), *Raindrops* (1987).

Clark, Dick

b. Richard Wagstaff Clark, 30 November 1929, Mount Vernon, New York, USA. Dick Clark became a showbusiness giant via the USA television dance programme *American Bandstand*, the longest-running variety show in television history. As its host for over 30 years, Clark brought rock 'n' roll music and dancing into millions of American homes. He has been nicknamed 'America's Oldest Living Teenager'. Clark's career began in 1947, upon his graduation from high school. After working at minor jobs at his uncle's radio station, WRUN (Utica, New York), Clark debuted on the air at WAER, the radio station at Syracuse University, which he attended. Further radio jobs followed, until Clark took his first television job, as a newscaster, in 1951. He returned to radio upon moving to Philadelphia's WFIL, but by 1956 WFIL's television outlet needed a replacement host for its *Bandstand* show. Clark was offered the position and started his new job on 9 July 1956.

Bandstand's format was simple: play current hit records and invite local teenagers to come in and dance to them. The programme was a surprise success and a year later the ABC network decided to broadcast it nationally, changing the name to *American Bandstand* on 5 August 1957. Clark continued to host, bringing in guest artists - particularly top rock 'n' roll artists of the day - and the programme became a national phenomenon. Record promoters coveted airplay on *Bandstand* as its power to 'break' records was unparalleled, and managers clamoured to land their artists on the programme to 'lip-sync' their latest hit. Many artists, particularly such Philadelphia-based singers as Fabian, Bobby Rydell, Chubby Checker and Frankie Avalon, largely owed their success to *Bandstand* exposure. Bobby Darin, Paul Anka and Connie Francis were also regulars.

By this time Clark's own power within the music industry had grown, and when the US government cracked down on so-called 'payola', the practice of disc jockeys accepting money or gifts in exchange for airplay, and in 1959-60 Clark was called to

Washington to testify. He claimed innocence and was cleared with his reputation intact, although he divested himself of some $8 million in music business-related investments. Clark had formed a production company early in his career, and in the mid-60s began producing other music television programmes, such as *Where The Action Is* and *Happening*. He also produced television game shows and films (including *Psych-Out* and *Because They're Young*). Clark's later creations include the *American Music Awards*, the *Country Music Awards* and television films about the Beatles and Elvis Presley - ironically, the only two major pop artists never to appear on *American Bandstand*. Clark also arranged tours called the Caravan of Stars, which took top musical stars of the day on series of one-night-stand concerts throughout the USA in the early 60s.

In 1964 *Bandstand* moved to Los Angeles from Philadelphia, and eventually it was scaled down from a daily to a weekly show. It continued until the late 80s, featuring contemporary artists such as Madonna, Prince and Cyndi Lauper. Clark remained an enormously powerful and influential figure in the entertainment industry into the 90s.

Clark, Petula

b. 15 November 1932, Epsom, Surrey, England. Her Welsh mother, a soprano, taught Petula to sing, which enabled her to commence a stage career at the age of seven and in broadcasting two years later. Her youthful image and crystal-clear enunciation were ideal for radio and by 1943, she had her own programme with the accent on wartime, morale-building songs. She made her first film, *Medal For The General*, in 1944 and then signed for the J. Arthur Rank Organization appearing in over 20 feature films, including the *Huggett* series, alongside other young hopefuls such as Anthony Newley and Alec Guinness. By 1949 she was recording, and throughout the 50s had several hits including 'The Little Shoemaker', 'Suddenly There's A Valley' 'With All My Heart' and 'Alone'. Around this period, Petula's success in France led to many concert appearances in Paris and recording, in French, for the Vogue label. Eventually, in 1959, at the age of 27 and unhappy with the British audiences' reluctance to see her as anything but a sweet adolescent, she moved to France, where she married Vogue's PR representative, Cluade Wolff. At the Olympia Theatre, Paris in 1960 she introduced her new sound, retaining the ultra-clear vocals, but adding to them electronic effects and a hefty beat. Almost immediately her career took off. She had a massive hit with 'Ya-Ya Twist', for which she received the Grand Prix du Disque, and by 1962 was France's favourite female vocalist, ahead even of the legendary Edith Piaf. Meanwhile, in Britain, Petula's versions of 'Romeo', 'My Friend The Sea' and 'Sailor', were chasing Elvis Presley up the charts. Her international breakthrough began in 1964 when songwriter/arranger Tony Hatch presented Petula with 'Downtown'. It became a big hit in western Europe, and a year later climbed to the top of the US charts, clinching her popularity in a country where she was previously unknown. The record sold over three million copies worldwide and gained a Grammy Award in the USA as the best rock 'n' roll single. Petula's subsequent recordings of other Hatch songs, written sometimes with his lyricist wife, Jackie Trent, such as 'Don't Sleep In The Subway', 'The Other Man's Grass', 'I Couldn't Live Without Your Love', 'My Love', and 'I Know A Place' all made the US Top 10. Her recording of 'This Is My Song', written by Charles Chaplin for the Marlon Brando/Sophia Loren epic, *A Countess From Hong Kong* (1967) reached number 1 in the UK charts. Tours of the USA and television guest shots followed. As well as hosting her own BBC television series, she was given her own US NBC television special *Petula*, in 1968. This was marred by the programme sponsor's request that a sequence in which she touched the arm of black guest Harry Belafonte, should be removed in deference to the southern States. The show was eventually transmitted complete. That same year Petula revived her film career when she appeared as Sharon, the 'Glocca Morra' girl in 'Yip' Harburg and Burton Lane's *Finian's Rainbow*, co-starring with Fred Astaire and Tommy Steele. While the film was generally regarded as too old fashioned for 60s audiences, Petula's performance, with just a touch of the blarney, was well received, as was her partnership with Peter O'Toole in MGM's 1969 re-make of *Goodbye, Mr. Chips*, marking her 30 years in show business. She was, by now, not only a major recording star, but an international personality, able to play all over the world, in cabaret and concerts. Between 1981 and 1982 she played the part of Maria in the London revival of Richard Rodgers/Oscar Hammerstein II's *The Sound Of Music*. It ran for 14 months, and was a great personal success. In 1989 PYS Records issued a 'radically remixed' version of her 60s hit, 'Downtown', with the original vocal accompanied by 'acid house' backing. It went to number 10 in

the UK chart. To date she has sold over 30 million records worldwide and has been awarded more gold discs than any other British female singer. From early in her career she has written songs, sometimes under the pseudonym of Al Grant. So it was especially pleasing for Clark, in 1990, to write the music, and appear in the London West End musical, *Someone Like You*. The show opened in March to mixed reviews, and had only a brief run. In 1992, Clark made her first concert tour of the UK for 10 years.

Albums: *Petula Clark Sings* (1956), *A Date With Pet* (1956), *You Are My Lucky Star* (1957), *Pet Clark* (1959), *Petula Clark In Hollywood* (1959), *In Other Words* (1962), *Petula* (1962), *Les James Dean* (1962), *Downtown* (1964), *I Know A Place* (1965), *The World's Greatest International Hits!* (1965), *The New Petula Clark Album* (1965), *Uptown With Petula Clark* (1965), *In Love* (1965), *Petula '65* (1965), *My Love* (1966), *Petula '66* (1966), *My Love* (1966), *Hello Paris, Vol. I* (1966), *Hello Paris, Vol. II* (1966), *Petula Clark Sings For Everybody* (1966), *I Couldn't Live Without Your Love* (1966), *Hit Parade* (1967), *Colour My World/Who Am I?* (1967), *These Are My Songs* (1967), *The Other Man's Grass Is Always Greener* (1968), *Petula* (1968), *Portrait Of Petula* (1969), *Just Pet* (1969), *Memphis* (1970), *The Song Of My Life* (1971), *Wonderland Of Sound* (1971), *Today* (1971), *Petula '71* (1971), *Warm And Tender* (1971), *Live At The Royal Albert Hall* (1972), *Now* (1972), *Live In London* (1974), *Come On Home* (1974), *C'est Le Befrain De Ma Vie* (1975), *La Chanson De Marie-Madeloine* (1975), *I'm The Woman You Need* (1975), *Just Petula* (1975), *Noel* (1975), *Beautiful Sounds* (1976), *Destiny* (1978), *An Hour In Concert With Petula Clark* (1983). Compilations: *Petula's Greatest Hits, Volume 1* (1968), *Petula Clark's 20 All Time Greatest* (1977), *Spotlight On Petula Clark* (1980), *100 Minutes Of Petula Clark* (1982), *Early Years* (1986), *The Hit Singles Collection* (1987), *My Greatest* (1989), *Downtown* (1989), *Treasures Vol. 1* (1992), *Jumble Sale: Rarities And Obscurities 1959-64*, 2 CD-set (1992).

Cleftones

This R&B vocal group from Queens, New York, USA, consisted of Herb Cox (b. 6 May 1939, Cincinnati, Ohio, USA; lead), Charlie James (b. 1940; first tenor), Berman Patterson (b. 1938; second tenor), William McClain (b. 1938; baritone), and Warren Corbin (b. 1939; bass). The group came together at Jamaica High School in 1955. After joining George Goldner's Gee label,

the group launched their recording career with 'You Baby You', a regional hit in late 1955. The record with Cox's dry lead, Warren Corbin's effective bassfills, and session musician Jimmy Wright's frantic saxophone blowing set the tenor of the group's subsequent records. With their second record, 'Little Girl Of Mine', another peppy number, the group became nationally known as the record went to number 8 R&B and number 57 pop in 1956. Two excellent follow-ups the same year, 'Can't We Be Sweethearts' and 'String Around My Heart', were superbly representative of the Cleftones exuberant style, but both remained regional hits. A turn to a ballad in 1957, the outstanding 'See You Next Year', did not restore the Cleftones to national prominence. In 1959 Gene Pearson (from the Rivileers) replaced McClain, and the following year Patricia Spann was added to the group. The addition of the female to the group also signalled a slight change in style: the leads began to take greater prominence over the ensemble sound as doo-wop was giving beginning to fade. 'Heart And Soul', a rock 'n' roll remake of an evergreen, typified the new approach and proved to be the group's biggest hit, going to number 10 R&B and number 18 pop in 1961. Other important tracks from this era included the album cut, 'Please Say You Want Me' (featuring Pat Spann in a beautiful remake of the Schoolboys' hit) and another evergreen remake, 'For Sentimental Reasons'. The Cleftones recording career came to an end in 1964.
Albums: *Heart And Soul* (1961), *For Sentimental Reasons* (1962). Compilation: *The Best Of The Cleftones* (1991).

Clooney, Rosemary

b. 23 May 1928, Maysville, Kentucky, USA. While very young, Rosemary and her sister Betty sang at political rallies in support of their paternal grandfather. When Rosemary was 13 the Clooney children moved to Cincinnati, Ohio and appeared on radio station WLW. In 1945 they auditioned successfully for tenor saxophonist Tony Pastor and joined his band as featured vocalists, travelling the country doing mainly one-night stands. Rosemary made her first solo record in 1946 with 'I'm Sorry I Didn't Say I'm Sorry When I Made You Cry Last Night'. After about three years of touring Betty quit, and Rosemary stayed on as a soloist with the band. She signed for Columbia Records in 1950 and had some success with children's songs such as 'Me And My Teddy Bear' and 'Little Johnny Chickadee' before coming under the influence of

A&R manager Mitch Miller who had a penchant for folksy, novelty dialect songs. In 1951 Clooney's warm, husky melodious voice registered well on minor hits, 'You're Just In Love', a duet with Guy Mitchell, and 'Beautiful Brown Eyes'. Later that year she topped the US chart with 'Come On-My House', from the off-Broadway musical, 'The Son', with a catchy harpsichord accompaniment by Stan Freeman. During the next four years Clooney had a string of US hits including 'Tenderly', which became her theme tune, 'Half As Much' (number 1), 'Botcha-Me', 'Too Old To Cut The Mustard' (a duet with Marlene Dietrich), 'The Night Before Christmas Song' (with Gene Autrey), 'Hey There' and 'This Ole House' (both number 1 hits), and 'Mambo Italiano'. UK hits included 'Man', with the b-side, 'Woman', sung by her husband, actor/producer/director Jose Ferrer, and the novelty, 'Where Will The Dimple Be'. Her last singles hit was 'Mangos', in 1957. Her own US television series regularly featured close harmony vocal group the Hi-Lo's, leading to their communal album *Ring Around Rosie*. Clooney's film career started in 1953 with *The Stars Are Singing* and was followed by three films the next year, *Here Come The Girls* with Bob Hope, *Red Garters* (1954) with Guy Mitchell and the Sigmund Romberg bio-pic, *Deep In My Heart* in which she sang 'Mr And Mrs' with Jose Ferrer. In the same year she teamed with Bing Crosby in *White Christmas*. Highly compatible, with friendly, easy-going styles, their professional association was to last until Crosby died, and included, in 1958, the highly regarded album *Fancy Meeting You Here*, a musical travelogue with special material by Sammy Cahn and James Van Heusen, arranged and conducted by Billy May. Semi-retired in the 60s, her psychiatric problems were chronicled in her autobiography, *This For Remembrance*, later dramatized on television as *Escape From Madness*. Her more recent work has been jazz-based, including a series of tributes to the 'great' songwriters such as Harold Arlen, Cole Porter and Duke Ellington, released on the Concorde Jazz label. In 1991 Clooney gave an 'assured performance' in concert at Carnegie Hall, and duetted with her guest artist, Linda Ronstadt. Two years later she was still playing clubs in New York.
Albums: *Deep In My Heart* (1954, film soundtrack), *Hollywood's Best* (1955), *Blue Rose* (1956), *Clooney Times* (1957), with the Hi-Lo's *Ring A Round Rosie* (1957), *Swing Around Rosie* (1958), with Bing Crosby *Fancy Meeting You Here* (1958), *The Ferrers At Home* (1958), *Hymns From The Heart* (1959),

Rosemary Clooney

Rosemary Clooney Swings Softly (1960), A Touch Of Tobasco (1960), Clap Hands, Here Comes Rosie (1960), Rosie Solves The Swingin' Riddle (1961), Country Hits From The Past (1963), Love (1963), Thanks For Nothing (1964), with Crosby That Travelin' Two Beat (1965), Look My Way (1976), Nice To Be Around (1977), Here's To My Lady (1979), Rosemary Clooney Sings The Music Of Cole Porter (1982), Rosemary Clooney Sings Harold Arlen (1983), My Buddy (1983), Rosemary Clooney Sings The Music Of Irving Berlin (1984), Sings Ballads (1985), Our Favourite Things (1986), Mixed Emotions (1986), Rosemary Clooney Sings The Lyrics Of Johnny Mercer (1987), Rosemary Clooney Sings The Music Of Jimmy Van Heusen (1987), Show Tunes (1989), Everything's Coming Up Rosie (1989), Girl Singer (1992). Compilations: Rosie's Greatest Hits (1957), Rosemary Clooney Showcase Of Hits (1959), Greatest Hits (1983), The Best Of Rosemary Clooney (1984), The Rosemary Clooney Songbook (1984).
Further reading: This For Remembrance, Rosemary Clooney.

Clovers

This US R&B vocal ensemble formed in Washington, DC in 1946. The Clovers who built a career recording smooth ballads and bluesy jumps for New York independent Atlantic Records were one of the biggest vocal groups of the 50s. By the time the group first got on record for Rainbow Records in early 1950, they consisted of John 'Buddy' Bailey (b. 1930, Washington, DC, USA; lead), Matthew McQuater (tenor), Harold Lucas (baritone), Harold Winley (bass), with instrumental accompaniment from Bill Harris (b. 14 April 1925, Nashville, Tennessee, USA; guitar). Later in the year the Clovers joined the fledgling Atlantic label. In 1952 Charles White (b. 1930, Washington DC, USA), who had earlier experience in the Dominoes and the Checkers, became the Clovers new lead replacing Buddy Bailey who was drafted into the US Army. In late 1953 Billy Mitchell took over from White. Bailey rejoined the group in 1954 but Mitchell remained and the two alternated the leads. Whoever was the lead, from 1951 to 1956 the Clovers achieved a consistent sound and remarkably consistent success. They had three number 1 R&B hits with 'Don't You Know I Love You', 'Fool, Fool, Fool' (both 1951) and 'Ting-A-Ling' (1952), plus four number 2 R&B hits with 'One Mint Julep', 'Hey, Miss Fannie' (both 1952), 'Good Lovin'' (1953) and 'Lovey Dovey' (1954). The best-known of the remaining 11 other Top 10 hits for Atlantic was 'Devil Or

Angel', a song frequently covered, most notably by Bobby Vee. The Clovers only made the US pop charts with 'Love Love Love' (number 30, 1956) and 'Love Potion No. 9' (number 23, 1959). The latter, one of Leiber And Stoller's best songs, was recorded for United Artists, the only label other than Atlantic that got the Clovers on the charts. In 1961 the Clovers split into rival groups led respectively by Buddy Bailey and Harold Lucas, and the hits dried up. Various permutations of the Clovers continued to record and perform for years afterwards, particularly in the Carolinas where their brand of music was popular as 'beach music'. Bill Harris died 6 December 1988.
Albums: The Clovers (1956), Dance Party (1959), In Clover (1959), Love Potion Number Nine (1959), Clovers Live At CT's (1989). Compilations: The Original Love Potion Number Nine (1964), All Righty Oh Sweetie (1990), Love Potion Number Nine (1991), Down In The Alley (1991).

Coasters

This R&B vocal group hailed from Los Angeles, USA. The illustrious career of the Coasters, the pre-eminent vocal group of the early rock 'n' roll era, was built on a remarkable body of cleverly comic R&B songs of their producers, Leiber And Stoller. Under their direction, the Coasters eschewed the crooning of ballads favoured by most groups of the era for robust and full-throated R&B shouting. The group came together in 1955 from remnants of the Robins, who had a dispute with their producers/songwriters, Leiber and Stoller. The original Coasters consisted of two ex-Robins, Carl Gardner (b. 29 April 1928, Tyler, Texas, USA; lead) and Bobby Nunn (b. 1925, Birmingham, Alabama, USA; bass), plus Leon Hughes (b. 1938; tenor), Billy Guy (b. 20 June 1936, Itasca, Texas, USA; lead and baritone) and Adolph Jacobs (b. Oakland, California, USA; guitar). Hughes was replaced in 1956 by Young Jessie who in turn was replaced by ex-Flairs Cornell Gunther (b. 14 November 1936, Los Angeles, California, USA). Nunn in 1958 was replaced by ex-Cadets Will 'Dub' Jones (b. 1939, Los Angeles, California, USA). Ex-Cadillacs Earl Carroll (b. Gregory Carroll, 2 November 1937, New York, New York, USA) replaced Gunther in 1961.
The Coasters first charted with 'Down In Mexico' (US R&B Top 10) in 1956, but the double-sided hit from 1957, 'Searchin'' (US R&B number 1 and pop number 3) and 'Young Blood' (US R&B number 2 and pop Top 10) established the group

Clovers

as major rock 'n' roll stars. (In the UK 'Searchin'' reached number 30). Three more giant hits sustained the Coasters' career, namely 'Yakety Yak' (US R&B and pop number 1 in 1958), 'Charlie Brown' (US R&B and pop number 2 in 1959), and 'Poison Ivy' (US R&B number 1 and pop Top 10 in 1959). In the UK 'Yakety Yak' went to number 12, 'Charlie Brown' to number 6, and 'Poison Ivy' to number 15, the group's last chart record in the UK. By this time, they were generally regarded as one of the wittiest exponents of teenage growing problems to emerge from the rock 'n' roll era. By the early 60s the lustre had worn off, as the hits increasingly emphasized the comic lyrics to the detriment of the music. The group continued for decades as an oldies act, and fractured into two different groups playing the oldies circuit. Bobby Nunn died on 5 November 1986; Cornell Gunther on 26 February 1990.

Albums: *The Coasters* (1958), *One By One* (1960), *Coast Along With The Coasters* (1962), *On Broadway* (1974). Compilations: *The Coasters' Greatest Hits* (1959), *Their Greatest Recordings: The Early Years* (1971), *What Is The Secret Of Your Success?* (1980), *Thumbin' A Ride* (1985), *The Ultimate Coasters* (1986), *Let's Go To The Dance* (1988), *Poison Ivy* (1991).

Cochran, Eddie

b. Edward Cochrane, 3 October 1938, Albert Lea, Minnesota, City, USA, d. 17 April 1960, Wiltshire, England. Although Cochran's career was brief, during which time he topped the charts only once, he is now regarded as one of the finest ever rock 'n' roll artists. Originally one half of the Cochran Brothers (with non-relative Hank) he started as a country singer, and demonstrated an early prowess as an outstanding rockabilly guitarist with his trademark Gretsch guitar. In 1956 his cameo performance of 'Twenty Flight Rock' in the film *The Girl Can't Help It* gave this handsome James Dean lookalike the career boost he needed and he was signed by Liberty Records. Strangely, his new record company decided to release a ballad, 'Sittin' In The Balcony', which became a US Top 20 hit. The following year the first of his classic anthems was released. The song 'Summertime Blues' has been recorded and performed by dozens of artists, and is now one of the most famous rock songs of all time. This lyric of teenage angst is timeless and contains many perceptive lines of frustration, for example; 'Well my ma and papa told me son, you gotta make some money, if you wanna use the car to go a-riding next Sunday'. The repeated chorus 'Sometimes I wonder what I'm a gonna do, but there ain't no cure for the Summertime Blues' perfectly summed up an American teenager's attitude. Additionally, the infectious riff has been copied down the ages, as the simple chord progression EABE sounds *great* to every guitar novice. The Who's lengthy and gutsy version is probably the most famous other than Cochran's. The following year another timeless classic appeared, 'C'mon Everybody', with a similarly infectious riff; this time Cochran brilliantly conveyed the relief of finishing a hard day's work and of going for a night out; 'Well c'mon everybody and lets get together tonight, I've got some money in my jeans and I'm really gonna spend it right', and then the repeated and long anticipated chorus 'Whooah c'mon everybody'. This gem of a record ably showed how 50s rock 'n' roll could be uplifting, musically brilliant and yet contain such simple, honest and everlasting lyrics. The following year during a package tour in Britain, Cochran was killed in a hit and run car crash. Gene Vincent was a badly injured passenger, as was Sharon Sheeley, co-writer of his posthumous hit 'Something Else', which became a major hit for the Sex Pistols in 1979. His biggest record was the inappropriately titled 'Three Steps To Heaven' which topped the UK chart shortly after his untimely death. 'Weekend' was the last of his classics, another tale of simple youthful enthusiasm for life; 'Friday night and everything's right for the weekend, boy its great for staying out late at the weekend'. In 1963 ex-Tornados' bassist, Heinz launched his solo career with the Joe Meek produced tribute 'Just Like Eddie'. Heinz was just one of the many artists who have been influenced by Cochran. His reputation continues to grow as his slim catalogue of recordings is constantly repackaged to a perennial audience wanting to hear one of the greatest exponents of 'progressive' rock 'n' roll.

Albums: *Singing To My Baby* (1958), *The Eddie Cochran Memorial Album* (1960), *Cherished Memories* (1962), *My Way* (1964), *On The Air* (1972), *The Many Sides Of Eddie Cochran* (1975), *The Young Eddie Cochran* (1982), *Words And Music* (1985), *Portrait Of A Legend* (1985), *The Many Styles Of Eddie Cochran* (1985), *The Hollywood Sessions* (1985). Compilations: *The Very Best Of Eddie Cochran* (1970), *The 25th Anniversary Album* (1985), *The Early Years* (1988), *C'mon Everybody* (1988), *The Eddie Cochran Box Set* (1988), *The EP Collection* (1991).

Eddie Cochran

Cogan, Alma

b. 19 May 1932, London, England, d. 26 October 1966. After appearing in the stage revues of *Sauce Tartare* and *High Button Shoes*, Cogan was spotted by A&R representative Wally Ridley and signed to HMV Records. Although she began her career as a balladeer, her breakthrough came with the novelty hit 'Bell Bottom Blues', which reached the Top 5 in the UK in 1954. A cover of Kitty Kallen's 'Little Things Mean A Lot' followed quickly and during that same year Cogan turned up with Frankie Vaughan on a couple of unsuccessful singles. Her lone UK number 1 occurred in the spring of 1955 with 'Dreamboat' and the following Christmas she was back with the novelty 'Never Do A Tango With An Eskimo'. A duet with Ronnie Hilton appeared on the b-side of his chart-topper 'No Other Love' and throughout this period Cogan earnestly covered a string of US hits including Jewel Akens' 'The Birds And The Bees' and Frankie Lymon And The Teenagers' 'Why Do Fools Fall In Love?'. By the end of the 50s, she had notched up 18 chart entries, more than any female singer of her era. Meanwhile, she was succeeding as a top variety star and enjoyed the luxury of her own television programme. Another duet, this time with Ocher Nebbish, appeared on one of her b-sides. Nebbish was, in fact, famed composer Lionel Bart, who not only cast Alma in *Oliver!*, but planned to marry her, much to the astonishment of the showbiz community. The unlikely nuptials never occurred, and by the end of the 60s, Alma was no longer a chart regular. Always a candidate for the cover version game, she cut the bouncy 'Tell Him' but lost out to Billie Davis. Paul McCartney made a surprise appearance playing tambourine on the b-side of one of her singles and she repaid the compliment by cutting 'Eight Days A Week', a belated shot at chart fame that narrowly missed. In March 1966, doctors discovered that the singer had cancer. During a period of convalescence she wrote a number of songs under the pseudonym Al Western, including Ronnie Carroll's 'Wait For Me' and Joe Dolan's 'I Only Dream Of You'. At the peak of the *Man From UNCLE* television series, she cut the tribute disc to its star David McCallum. 'Love Ya Illya' by the pseudonymous Angela And The Fans received extensive airplay and barely missed the charts in 1966. That autumn, while working in Sweden, Alma collapsed and was sent home. On 26 October 1966, she lost her fight against cancer and died at London's Middlesex Hospital. In 1992, she was the subject of a 30 minute documentary as part of BBC Television's *The Lime Grove Story*.
Albums: *I Love To Sing* (1958), *With You In Mind* (1961), *Alma Sings With You In Mind* (1961), *How About Love* (1962). Compilations: *The Alma Cogan Collection* (1977), *The Second Collection* (1978), *The Very Best Of Alma Cogan* (1984), *Celebration* (1987). Further reading: *Alma Cogan* (a novel), Gordon Burn. *Alma Cogan: The Girl With The Laugh In Her Voice*, Sandra Caron (Alma Cogan's sister).

Cole, Nat 'King'

b. Nathaniel Adams Cole, 17 March c.1916, Montgomery, Alabama, USA, d. 15 February 1965. Cole was born into a family that held a key position in the black community: his father was pastor of the First Baptist Church. In 1921 the family migrated to Chicago, part of the mass exodus of black people seeking a better life in the booming industrial towns of the north. He learned piano by ear from his mother, who was choir director in the church, from the age of four. When he was 12 years old he took lessons in classical piano, 'everything from Bach to Rachmaninoff'. Jazz was everywhere in Chicago, and Cole's school was a musical hotbed, producing musicians of the stature of Ray Nance, Eddie South and Milt Hinton. His first professional break came touring with the show *Shuffle Along*, a revival of the first all-black show to make it to Broadway, which he joined with his bass-playing brother, Eddie. Stranded in Los Angeles when the show folded, Cole looked for club work and found it at the Century Club on Santa Monica Boulevard. It was a hangout for musicians and the young pianist made a splash: 'All the musicians dug him,' said Bumps Blackwell, 'that cat could play! He was unique.'. In 1939 Cole formed an innovative trio with Oscar Moore on guitar and Wesley Prince on bass, eschewing the noise of drums. Like Fats Waller in the previous generation, Cole managed to combine pleasing and humorous ditties with piano stylings that were state-of-the-art. Times had moved on, and Cole had a suave sophistication that expressed the new aspirations of the black community. In 1943 he cut his 'Straighten Up And Fly Right' for Capitol - it was an instant hit. Cole's future as a pop success was assured. In 1946 'The Christmas Song' added strings, starting a process that would lead to Nat Cole emerging as a middle-of-the-road singer, accompanied by such leading arrangers and conductors as Nelson Riddle, Gordon Jenkins, Ralph Carmichael, Pete Rugolo, Billy May and others. Before that happened, in the 40s Cole made several memorable sides with the Trio, including 'Sweet Lorraine', 'It's Only A Paper Moon', '(Get Your Kicks) On Route 66' and '(I Love You) For Sentimental Reasons'. By 1948, and 'Nature Boy' (a US number 1), on which Cole was accompanied by Frank DeVol's Orchestra, the move away from small group jazz, towards his eventual position as one of the most popular vocalists of the day, was well under way. Absolute confirmation came in 1950, when Cole, with Les Baxter conducting Nelson Riddle's lush arrangement of 'Mona Lisa', spent eight weeks at the top of the US chart with what was to become one of his most celebrated recordings. Throughout the 50s the singles hits continued to flow, mostly with ballads such as 'Too Young', 'Faith Can Move Mountains', 'Because You're Mine', 'Unforgettable', 'Somewhere Along The Way', 'Funny (Not Much)', 'Pretend', 'Can't I?', 'Answer Me, My Love', 'Smile', 'Darling Je Vous Aime Beaucoup', 'The Sand And The Sea', 'A Blossom Fell', 'When I Fall In Love' and 'Stardust' (said to be composer Hoagy Carmichael's favourite version of his song). No doubt because of his jazz grounding, Cole was equally at home with the more up-tempo 'Orange Coloured Sky', backed by Stan Kenton And His Orchestra, 'Walkin' My Baby Back Home', 'Night

Lights' and 'Ballerina'. In the same period, his best-selling albums included *After Midnight* (with the Trio), *Love Is The Thing*, which was at the top of the US chart for eight weeks, *Just One Of Those Things*, *Cole Espanol* and *The Very Thought Of You*. During the 50s he was urged to make films, but his appearances were few and far between - character parts in such as *Blue Gardenia*, *China Gate* and *Night Of The Quarter Moon*. Cole's most effective movie role came in 1958 when he played W.C. Handy in *St. Louis Blues*. He also appeared on screen with Stubby Kaye, singing the linking ballads in the spoof western, *Cat Ballou* (1965), but it was clear that his enormous appeal lay in concerts and records. One of his lesser-known albums, *Welcome To The Club*, featured the Basie Orchestra, apart from the Count himself (for contractual reasons), and included Cole's superior readings of 'She's Funny That Way', 'Avalon' and 'Look Out For Love'. The title track was composed by Noel Sherman, who, with his brother Joe, wrote 'Mr Cole Won't Rock And Roll', an amusing piece performed by the singer in his concert show, 'Sights And Sounds', which played over 100 cities in the early 60s. It wasn't so much rock 'n' roll that concerned Cole's purist fans around that time: they had acute reservations about another of the

Nat 'King' Cole with Errol Flynn

Sherman Brothers' numbers, 'Ramblin' Rose' (1962), the singer's first big hit in four years, which came complete with a 'twangy C&W feeling'. They also objected to 'Those Lazy Hazy Crazy Days Of Summer' ('unabashed corn'), which also made the Top 10 in the following year. Cole himself felt that he was 'just adjusting to the market: as soon as you start to make money in the popular field, they scream about how good you were in the old days, and what a bum you are now'. As part of his most agreeable musical association during the early 60s, *Nat King Cole Sings/George Shearing Plays*, Cole went back to 1940 for Ian Grant and Lionel Rand's 'Let There Be Love'. His version became a hit single in many parts of the world, and remains a particularly fondly remembered performance. In a way, he was back to where he started out at around the time the song was written: singing with a small jazz group - albeit this time with Shearing's polite piano and the inevitable 'String Choir'. During the years of Cole's enormous popularity in the 'easy listening' field, jazz fans had to turn out to see him in the clubs to hear his glorious piano - an extension of the Earl Hines style that had many features of the new, hip sounds of bebop. If Cole had not had such an effective singing voice he might have well been one of bebop's cohorts. Bebop was an expression of black pride, but so was Cole's career, creating opportunities for all kinds of 'sepia Sinatras' (Charles Brown, Sammy Davis Jnr., etc) who proved that whites had no monopoly on sophistication. Cole bore the brunt of racism, meeting objections when he bought a house in fashionable Beverly Hills, being the first black television presenter (he abandoned the role in 1957, protesting that the agencies would not find him a national sponsor). Though his position entailed compromises that gained him the hostility of civil rights activists in the early 60s, he was a brave and decent figure in a period when race prejudice was at its most demeaning. Before his death from lung cancer in 1965, he was planning a production of James Baldwin's play *Amen Corner*, showing an interest in radical black literature at odds with his image as a sentimental crooner. Nat Cole's voice, which floats butter-won't-melt vowel sounds in an easy, dark drawl, is one of the great moments of black music, and no matter how sugary the arrangements he always managed to sing as if it mattered. In 1991 his daughter Natalie Cole revived his 'Unforgettable', singing a duet with his recorded vocal. Despite the questionable taste of duets-beyond-the-grave, Cole's piano intro was a startling reminder of the extraordinary harmonic creativity he brought to the pop music of his time. Perhaps, like Louis Armstrong, the most moving aspect of his legacy is the way his music cuts across the usual boundaries - chart watchers and jazz heads, rock 'n' rollers and MOR fans can all have a good time with his music.

Albums: *The King Cole Trio* (1950), *Penthouse Serenade* (1953), *Unforgettable* (1953), *Nat 'King' Cole Sings For Two In Love* (1954), *Tenth Anniversary Album* (1954), *Vocal Classics* (1955), *Instrumental Classics* (1955), *The Piano Style of Nat King Cole* (1956), *Ballads Of The Day* (1956), *After Midnight* (1957), *Love Is The Thing* (1957), *This Is Nat 'King' Cole* (1957), *Just One Of Those Things* (1957), *St. Louis Blues* (1958, film soundtrack), *Cole Espanol* (1958), *The Very Thought Of You* (1958), *Welcome To The Club* (1959), *To Whom It May Concern* (1959), *Tell Me All About Yourself* (1960), *Wild Is Love* (1960), *The Touch Of Your Lips* (1961), *String Along With Nat 'King' Cole* (1961), *Nat 'King' Cole Sings/George Shearing Plays* (1962), *Ramblin' Rose* (1962), *Dear Lonely Hearts* (1962), *Where Did Everyone Go?* (1963), *Those Lazy-Hazy-Crazy Days Of Summer* (1963), *The Christmas Song* (1963), *I Don't Want To Be Hurt Anymore* (1964), *My Fair Lady* (1964), *L-O-V-E* (1965), *Songs From 'Cat Ballou' And Other Motion Pictures* (1965), *Looking Back* (1965), *Nat 'King' Cole At The Sands* (1966), *The Great Songs!* (1966, recorded in 1957), *Close-Up* (1969), with Dean Martin *White Christmas* (1971), *Christmas With Nat 'King' Cole* (1988). Selected compilations: *20 Golden Greats* (1978), *Greatest Love Songs* (1982), *Trio Days* (1984), *The Capitol Years* (1990, 20-disc boxed set), *The Unforgettable Nat 'King' Cole* (1991), *The Nat King Cole Gold Collection* (1993).

Further reading: *Nat King Cole, The Man And His Music*, James Haskins with Kathleen Benson. *Unforgettable - The Life And Mystique Of Nat King Cole*, Leslie Gourse.

Colyer, Ken

b. 18 April 1928, Great Yarmouth, Norfolk, England, d. 8 March 1988, France. Of all the musicians involved in the British Revivalist movement of the late 40s and early 50s, trumpeter Colyer was the only one to achieve the status of an jazz legend. He achieved through a gritty determination to stick to what he believed to be the true spirit of jazz. Colyer first demonstrated his obsession with the great traditions of New Orleans jazz in the early 50s. He joined the Merchant Navy in order to visit the USA, where he promptly jumped ship and headed for the Crescent City. In New Orleans he sat in with local grand masters, including George Lewis and Emile Barnes, before the authorities caught up with him and he was deported. Before his visit to the USA Colyer had already worked with the Crane River Jazz Band and the Christie Brothers Stompers, but his American exploits had made him a big name in the UK and he was invited to front the co-operative band formed a little earlier by Chris Barber and Monty Sunshine. Although this unit was working regularly and building a reputation, Barber and Sunshine felt that Colyer's fame would be an asset. For a while this assumption proved correct but personality clashes developed, particularly when Colyer appeared to lose sight of the fact that the band he was leading was not his own but was a collective venture. In 1954 Barber took over the reins and Colyer formed his own band, which, with various personnel changes, he continued to lead for the next 30 years. Among the many musicians who worked under Colyer's leadership were Acker Bilk, Diz Disley, Ian Wheeler and Sammy Rimington. Conceding that his technique was limited, Colyer overcame any deficiencies in style through an unflinching determination not to be swayed by changing public tastes or commercial considerations, although he did play guitar and sing in a skiffle group in the mid-50s. In 1957 he returned to the US and joined the George Lewis band, and arranged their trips to Europe. His last significant work was as part of the touring jazz show *New Orleans Mardi Gras*. Colyer defeated cancer, and the temporary retirement this necessitated, playing on into the 80s. He died in the south of France in 1988. A year later, a commemorative blue plaque was placed on the wall of the 100 Club in London, and many of his former colleagues took part in a concert organized by the Ken Colyer Trust.

Selected albums: *Ken Colyer In New Orleans* (1953), *New Orleans To London* (1953), *In The Beginning...* (1954), *A Very Good Year* (1957), *When I Leave The World Behind* (1963), *Out Of Nowhere* (1965), *Live At The Dancing Slipper* (1969), *Ken Colyer And His Handpicked Jazzmen* (1972), *Spirituals, Vols. 1 & 2* (both 1974), *Swinging And Singing* (1975), *Painting The Clouds With Sunshine* (1979), *Ken Colyer With John Petters' New Orleans Allstars* (1985), with Max Collie, Cy Laurie *New Orleans Mardi Gras* (1985), with Acker Bilk *It Looks Like A Big Time Tonight* (1985), *Too Busy* (1985). Compilations: *The Decca Years, Vol. 1 (1955-1959)* (1985), *The Decca Years, Vol. 2 (1955-1959)* (1986), *The Decca Skiffle Sessions (1954-57)* (1987), *The Decca Years, Vol. 3 (1955-1959)* (1987), *The Guv'nor (1959-61)* (1989).

Further Reading: *When Dreams Are In The Dust (The Path Of A Jazzman)*, Ken Colyer.

Como, Perry

b. Pierino Como, 18 May 1912, Canonsburg, Pennsylvania, USA. An accomplished popular singer with a warm baritone voice, whose repertoire has included ballads, novelty numbers and singalongs. Como left his hometown barber shop in 1933 and toured with the local band of Freddie Carlone. His big break came in 1936 when he joined trombonist Ted Weems' band and featured on their *Beat The Band* radio show. He left the band when it broke up in 1942, and the following year signed for RCA Records. After minor hits with 'Long Ago And Far Away', 'I'm Gonna Love That Gal' and 'If I Loved You', he topped the US charts in 1945 with 'Till The End Of Time', based on Chopin's 'Polonaise In A-Flat Major'. A comparatively late starter in hit parade terms, he made up for lost time in the late 40s with a string of US hits including 'Did You Ever Get That Feeling In The Moonlight?', 'Dig You Later (A Hubba-Hubba-Hubba)', 'I'm Always Chasing Rainbows' (adapted from another Chopin theme), 'You Won't Be Satisfied (Until You Break My Heart)', 'Prisoner Of Love' (number 1), 'All Through The Day', 'They Say It's Wonderful', 'Surrender' (number 1), 'Chi-Baba, Chi-Baba, (My Baby Go To Sleep)' (number 1), 'When You Were Sweet Sixteen', 'I Wonder Who's Kissing Her Now' (a 1939 recording when Como was with Ted Weems), 'Because' (a 1902 song, originally sung by Enrico Caruso), 'Far Away Places', 'Forever And Ever', 'A-You're Adorable' (a number 1, with the Fontane Sisters), 'Some Enchanted Evening' (number 1) and 'A Dreamer's Holiday'. He also featured regularly on radio programmes, such as his own *Supper Club* series, and made four films, *Something for The Boys* (1944), loosely based on the Cole Porter Broadway show, *Doll Face, If I'm Lucky* (1946), and the star-studded Richard Rodgers/Lorenz Hart bio-pic, *Words And Music* (1948). The 50s were even more fruitful years for Como, mainly because of the apparent ease with which he adapted to television. His easy, relaxed singing style coupled with an engaging sense of humour proved ideal for the relatively new medium, and his weekly *Music Hall*, with its theme, 'Dream Along With Me', ran from 1955-63 and is still regarded as the best of its kind. It also

Perry Como (right) with Dave King

inspired the albums *We Get Letters* and *Dear Perry*. In the early 50s, despite the onset on rock 'n' roll, the hits continued with 'Hoop-Dee-Doo' (number 1) and 'You're Just In Love' (both with the Fontane Sisters), 'Patricia', 'A Bushel And A Peck', 'If', 'Maybe' (with Eddie Fisher), 'Don't Let The Stars Get In Your Eyes' (number 1 in the US and UK), 'Wild Horses' (adapted From Robert Schumann's 'Wild Horseman'), 'Say You're Mine Again', 'No Other Love' (based on the theme from the 1954 documentary *Victory At Sea*), 'You Alone', 'Wanted' (number 1), and 'Papa Loves Mambo'. During the latter half of the 50s, with the advantage of the television showcase, he still registered strongly in the USA with 'Ko Ko Mo (I Love You So)', 'Tina Marie', 'Hot Diggity (Dog Ziggitty Boom)' (number 1), 'Juke Box Baby', 'More', 'Glendora', 'Round And Round' (number 1), 'Catch A Falling Star' (number 1), 'Magic Moments' (UK number 1 - an early Burt Bacharach and Hal David song) and 'Kewpie Doll'. He also made the UK Top 10 with 'Love Makes The World Go Round', 'Tomboy' and 'Delaware'. Semi-retired during the 60s, he emerged in 1970 to play 'live' for the first time for over 20 years, an event celebrated by the album *Live At The International Hotel Las Vegas*. He then, somewhat surprisingly, embarked on a series of world tours, and had his first hit singles for over a decade with the Mexican song 'It's Impossible', composed by Armando Manzanero, with a new lyric by Sid Wayne, 'And I Love You So' and 'For The Good Times'. At this time Como's records sales were estimated at over 60 million, including twenty gold discs. To many, Como's laid-back approach and many popular television specials, particularly at Christmas, bordered on parody, and yet his immense commercial success is undeniable, and is perhaps one of the reasons when male song stylists are discussed, that he is too often underrated. In the late 80s he was still performing occasionally in Las Vegas, and received generous media tributes two years later on the occasion of his 80th birthday. .

Albums: *I Believe* (1954), *So Smooth* (1955), *Relaxing With Perry Como* (1955), *A Sentimental Date With Perry Como* (1955), *Hits From Broadway Shows* (1956), *We Get Letters* (1957), *Merry Christmas Music* (1957), *Dream Along With Me* (1957), *Saturday Night With Mr. C.* (1958), *Dear Perry* (1958), *When You Come To The End Of The Day* (1958), *Como Swings* (1959), *Season's Greetings* (1959), *Sing To Me Mr. C.* (1961), *For The Young At Heart* (1961), *By Request* (1962), *The Best Of Irving Berlin's Songs From 'Mr. President'* (1962), *The Songs I Love* (1963), *The Scene Changes* (1965), *Lightly Latin* (1966), *Perry Como In Italy* (1966), *Seattle* (1969), *It's Impossible* (1970), *I Think Of You* (1971), *And I Love You So* (1973), *Perry* (1974), *Just Out Of Reach* (1975), *Best Of British* (1977), *Something Special* (1978), *Especially For You* (1980), *Perry Como* (1980), *Live On Tour* (1981), *So It Goes* (1983), *Perry Como Today* (1987). Compilations: *Como's Golden Records* (1958), *Memories Are Made Of Hits* (1975), *40 Greatest Hits* (1975), *A Legendary Performer* (1976), *The Perry Como Christmas Collection* (1979), *For The Good Times* (1983), *16 Million Hits* (1983), with the Ted Weems Orchestra *The Young Perry Como (1936-41)* (1984), *The Best Of Times* (1986), *Jukebox Baby* (1988), *Collection* (1988), *The Living Legend* (1992).

Conniff, Ray

b. 6 November 1916, Attelboro, Massachusetts, USA. Taught to play the trombone by his father, Conniff studied arranging with the aid of a mail-order course while still at college. In 1934, after graduation, he worked with small bands in Boston before joining Bunny Berigan as trombonist/arranger in 1936. After a spell with Bob Crosby's Bobcats, Conniff spent four years with Artie Shaw and featured on several successful records including 'Concerto For Clarinet', 'Dancing In The Dark' and 'St James Infirmary'. During this period he was also studying at the New York Juilliard School of Music. After army service in World War II Conniff spent some time as an arranger with Harry James, then freelanced, while searching for a successful formula for making hit records. He joined Columbia Records in 1954, and worked with several of their artists including Johnny Ray, Rosemary Clooney, Guy Mitchell and Marty Robbins. In 1954 he provided the arrangement for Don Cherry's million-seller, 'Band Of Gold', and in 1956 was given the chance, by Columbia producer Mitch Miller, to make an album featuring his 'new sound'. The successful result, *'S Wonderful*, was a set of familiar songs with an orchestra, and a cleverly blended mixed chorus of wordless voices, sometimes used as extra instruments within the songs' arrangements. *'S Wonderful* was followed, naturally, by *'S Marvellous* and *'S Awful Nice*, all in the same vein. *It's The Talk Of The Town*, in 1960, featured a larger chorus, and for the first time they sang - words. From 1957-68 Conniff had 28 albums in the US Top 40, including, *Say It With Music (A Touch Of Latin)*, *Memories Are Made Of This*, and in 1966, the million-seller, *Somewhere My Love*. The album's title track, 'Lara's Theme' from the film *Doctor Zhivago* (1965), also made the US Top 10 singles chart. In 1969 he topped the UK album charts with *His Orchestra, His Chorus, His Singers, His Sound*, and in 1974 became the first American popular musician to record in Russia, where he made *Ray Conniff In Moscow*, using a local chorus. More recent albums have included three Spanish sets, *Amor, Amor, Exclusivamente Latino* and *Fantastico*, and *The Nashville Collection* with country guest stars including Barbara Mandrell, George Jones and Charly McClain who featured on songs as diverse as 'Oh, Lonesome Me' and 'Smoke Gets In Your Eyes'.

Albums: with Don Cherry *Swingin' For Two* (1956), *'S Wonderful!* (1957), *'S Marvelous* (1957), *'S Awful Nice* (1958), *Concert In Rhythm* (1958), *Broadway In Rhythm* (1959), *Hollywood In Rhythm* (1959), with Billy Butterfield *Conniff Meets Butterfield* (1959), *Christmas With Conniff* (1959), *It's The Talk Of The Town* (1960), *Concert In Rhythm - Volume II* (1960), *Young At Heart* (1960), *Hi-fi Companion Album* (1960), *Say It With Music (A Touch Of Latin)* (1960), *Memories Are Made Of This* (1961), *Somebody Loves Me* (1961), *So Much In Love* (1962), *'S Continental* (1962), *Rhapsody In Rhythm* (1962), *We Wish You A Merry Christmas* (1962), *The Happy Beat* (1963), with Butterfield *Just Kiddin' Around* (1963), *You Make Me Feel So Young* (1964), *Speak To Me About Love* (1964), *Invisible Tears* (1964), *Friendly Persuasion* (1965), *Music From Mary Poppins, The Sound Of Music, My Fair Lady & Other Great Movie Themes* (1965), *Love Affair* (1965), *Happiness Is* (1966), *Somewhere My Love* (1966), *Ray Conniff's World Of Hits* (1967), *En Espanol!* (1967), *This Is My Song* (1967), *Hawaiian Album* (1967), *It Must Be Him* (1968), *Honey* (1968), *Turn Around Look At Me* (1968), *I Love How You Love Me* (1969), *Jean* (1969), *Bridge Over Troubled Water* (1970), *Concert In Stereo/Live At The Sahara/Tahoe* (1970), *We've Only Just Begun* (1970), *Love Story* (1971), *Great Contemporary Instrumental Hits* (1971), *I'd Like To Teach The World To Sing* (1972), *Love Theme From The 'Godfather'* (1972), *Alone Again (Naturally)* (1972), *I Can See Clearly Now* (1973), *You Are The Sunshine Of My Life* (1973), *Harmony* (1973), *Evergreens* (1973), *Love Will Keep Us Together* (1975), *Plays The Carpenters* (1975), *Laughter In The Rain* (1975), *Send In The Clowns* (1976), *I Write The Songs* (1976), *Smoke Gets In Your Eyes* (1977), *If You Leave Me Now* (1977), *Sentimental Journey* (1978), *I Will Survive* (1979), *The Perfect Ten Classics* (1981), *The Nashville Connection* (1982), *Amor, Amor* (1984), *Exclusivamente Latino* (1984), *Fantastico* (1984), *Smoke Gets In Your Eyes* (1984), *Always In My Heart* (1988). Compilations: *'S Wonderful's 'S Marvellous* (1962), *Ray Conniff's Greatest Hits* (1969), *His Orchestra, His Chorus, His Singers, His Sound* (1969), *Happy Beat Of Ray Conniff* (1975), *The Ray Conniff Songbook* (1984), *16 Most Requested Songs* (1993).

Connor, Chris

b. 8 November 1927, Kansas City, Missouri, USA. After singing publicly while still at school, Connor worked with the bands of Claude Thornhill, where she was a member of the vocal group, the Snowflakes, and Herbie Fields in the late 40s and early 50s. Audibly influenced by Anita O'Day, Connor quickly developed her own recognizable style and built a localized reputation. Having sung in high school with a Kenton-style band it was especially appropriate when June Christy, in 1953, recommended Chris to Stan Kenton as her replacement, after this period her career was much enhanced. She continued singing for the next 30-plus years, working mostly as a soloist and usually with jazz musicians in her backing group. In the late 80s she was to be heard singing in Europe showing a few signs of deterioration in her voice while, stylistically, she was as good as ever. In 1990 she was a featured artist at London's Soho Jazz Festival.

Selected albums: with Stan Kenton *Some Women I've Known* (1953), *Chris Connor With Ellis Larkins/Lullabies Of Birdland* (1954), *Chris Connor Sings Lullabies For Lovers* (1954), *This Is Chris* (1955), *Chris* (1955), *Cocktails At Dusk* (1955), *Out Of This World* (1956), *Songs* (1956), *A Jazz Date With Chris Connor* (1956), *Chris Connor i* (1957), *Chris Craft* (1958), *Ballads Of The Sad Cafe* (1959), *Chris In Person* (1959), *Witchcraft* (1959), *Chris Connor ii* (1959), *Portrait Of Chris* (1960), *Double Exposure* (1960), *Chris Connor iii* (1962), *Live At The Village Gate* (1963), *Chris Connor iv* (c.60s), *Chris Connor v* (1965), *Chris Connor vi* (c.60s), *Sketches* (1972), *Chris Moves* (1976), *Sweet And Swinging* (1978), *Alone Together* (1978), *Chris Connor Live* (1981), *Love Being Here With You* (1983), *As Time Goes By* (1992).

Conrad, Jess

b. 1935, Brixton, London, England. Christened Jesse James, Conrad began his career as a repertory actor and film extra before being cast as a pop singer in a television play, *Rock-A-Bye Barney*. Initially, his singing voice was overdubbed by that

of Gary Mills, but before long life imitated art and Conrad was transformed into a pop adonis. Championed by television producer Jack Good, he appeared in *Oh Boy!*, *Wham!* and *Boy Meets Girl*, which led to a recording contract with Decca Records and some minor early 60s hits with 'Cherry Pie', 'Mystery Girl' and 'Pretty Jenny'. When his recording career waned, he continued acting in low budget movies and pantomime, and in the 70's appeared in the musicals *Joseph And His Amazing Technicolour Dreamcoat* and *Godspell* as well as taking a cameo part in the Sex Pistols' celluloid excursion, *The Great Rock 'N' Roll Swindle*. One of Conrad's early singles, 'This Pullover' was belatedly named the worst single ever made in a novelty compilation of pop atrocities. Conrad continued to work throughout the 80s, and, in 1993, shed his 'squeaky-clean' image when he appeared as Prince Charming, with comedians Charlie Drake and Jim Davidson, in Davidson's 'blue' pantomime, *Sinderella*.
Album: *Jess For You* (1961).

Conway, Russ

b. Trevor Stanford, 2 September 1927, Bristol, Avon, England. Conway not only played the piano as a young boy, but won a scholarship to join the choir at the Bristol Cathedral School. He was conscripted into the Royal Navy in 1942 and, during a varied career, was awarded the DSM for service during campaigns in the Mediterranean and Aegean sea and lost part of a finger while using a bread slicer. In 1955, following spells in the post-war Merchant Navy, Conway played piano in nightclubs, worked as rehearsal pianist for choreographer Irving Davies and audition pianist for Columbia (UK) record producer Norman Newell. He later served as accompanist for star singers such as Dennis Lotis, Gracie Fields and Joan Regan. Signed to Columbia, his first hit, 'Party Pops' in 1957, was an instrumental medley of standard songs. It was the first of 20 UK chart entries featuring his catchy piano playing, through to 1963, including two number 1 singles, 'Side Saddle' and 'Roulette', and Top 10 entries 'China Tea' and 'Snowcoach', all of which were his own compositions. He headlined several times at the London Palladium, had his own television show and regularly guested on others, including the Billy Cotton Band Show on BBC television where his cross-talk and vocal duets with the host revealed a genuine flair for comedy and an acceptable light baritone voice. During the 60s his career was marred by ill health, a nervous breakdown while

Russ Conway

on stage and a mild stroke which prevented him from working during 1968-1971. Since then, still an anachronism, his combination of lively tunes, light classical themes and shy smile have consistently proved a big draw abroad, and in the UK where he promotes his own nostalgia package shows and charity concerts.

Albums: *Pack Up Your Troubles* (1958), *Songs To Sing In Your Bath* (1958), *Family Favourites* (1959), *Time To Celebrate* (1959), *My Concerto For You* (1960), *Party Time* (1960), *At The Theatre* (1961), *At The Cinema* (1961), *Happy Days* (1961), *Concerto For Dreamers* (1962), *Russ Conway's Trad Party* (1962), *Something For Mum* (1963), *Enjoy Yourself* (1964), *Concerto For Lovers* (1964), *Once More It's Party Time* (1965), *Pop-A-Conway* (1966), *Concerto For Memories* (1966), *Russ Hour* (1966), *New Side Of Russ Conway* (1971), *Songs From Stage And Screen* (1974), *The One And Only* (1979), *Always You And Me* (1981), *A Long Time Ago* (1986). Compilations: *The Very Best Of Russ Conway* (1976), *24 Piano Greats* (1977), *Russ Conway Playing Great Piano Hits* (1980), *The Two Sides Of Russ Conway* (1986), *Greatest Hits* (1986), *The Magic Of Russ Conway* (1988), *The EMI Years: The Best Of Russ Conway* (1989).

Cooke, Sam

b. Sam Cook, 22 January 1931, Clarksdale, Mississippi, USA, d. 11 December 1964, Los Angeles, California, USA. Cooke first performed publicly with his brother and two sisters in their Baptist quartet, the Soul Children. As a teenager he joined the Highway QCs, before replacing Robert 'R.H.' Harris in the Soul Stirrers. Between 1951 and 1956 Cooke sang lead with this innovative gospel group. His distinctive florid vocal style was soon obvious on 'Touch The Hem Of His Garment' and 'Nearer To Thee'. The Soul Stirrers recorded for the Specialty label where the singer's popularity encouraged producer 'Bumps' Blackwell to provide Sam with pop material. 'Loveable'/'Forever' was issued as a single, disguised under the pseudonym 'Dale Cook' to avoid offending the gospel audience. Initially content, the label's owner, Art Rupe, then objected to the sweetening choir on a follow-up recording, 'You Send Me', and offered Cooke a release from his contract in return for outstanding royalties. The song was then passed to the Keen label, where it sold in excess of 2 million copies. Further hits, including 'Only Sixteen' and 'Wonderful World', followed. The latter was latter used extensively in a television jeans commercial

and in 1986 the re-issue reached number 2 in the UK charts. Sam left the label for RCA where 'Chain Gang' (1960), 'Cupid' (1961) and 'Twistin' The Night Away' (1962), displayed a pop craft later offset by such grittier offerings as 'Bring It On Home To Me' and 'Little Red Rooster'. Cooke also founded the Sar and Derby labels on which the Simms Twins' 'Soothe Me' and the Valentinos' 'It's All Over Now' were issued. Cooke's own career remained in the ascendant with '(Ain't That) Good News' and 'Good Times' but the purity of such music made his tawdry fate all the more perplexing. On 11 December 1964, following an altercation with a girl he had picked up, the singer was fatally shot by the manageress of a Los Angeles motel. The ebullient 'Shake' became a posthumous hit, but its serene coupling, 'A Change Is Gonna Come', was a more melancholic epitaph. Arguably his finest composition, its title suggested a metaphor for the concurrent Civil Rights movement. Cooke's legacy continued through his various disciples - Johnnie Taylor, who had replaced Cooke in the Soul Stirrers, bore an obvious debt, as did Bobby Womack of the Valentinos. Sam's songs were interpreted by acts as diverse as Rod Stewart, the Animals and Cat Stevens, while the Rolling Stones' version of 'Little Red Rooster' echoed Cooke's reading rather than that of Howlin' Wolf. Otis Redding, Aretha Franklin, Smokey Robinson - the list of those acknowledging Cooke's skill is a testimony in itself. A seminal influence on soul music and R&B his effortless and smooth delivery has rarely been bettered. *Sam Cooke: A Man And His Music* provides an overview of the singer's whole career.

Albums: *Sam Cooke* (1958), *Sam Cooke Encore* (1959), *Tribute To The Lady* (1959), *Hit Kit* (1960), *I Thank God* (1960), *Wonderful World Of Sam Cooke* (1960), *Cooke's Tour* (1960), *Hits Of The 50s* (1960), *Swing Low* (1961), *My Kind Of Blues* (1961), *Twisting The Night Away* (1962), *Mr. Soul* (1963), *Night Beat* (1963), *Ain't That Good News* (1964), *Sam Cooke At The Copa* (1964), *Shake* (1965), *Try A Little Love* (1965), *Sam Cooke Sings Billie Holiday* (1976), *Live At Harlem Square Club* (1986). Compilations: *The Best Of Sam Cooke, Volume 1* (1962), *The Best Of Sam Cooke, Volume 2* (1965), *The Late And Great* (1969), *The Two Sides Of Sam Cooke* (1971), *This Is Sam Cooke* (1971), *The Golden Age Of Sam Cooke* (1976), *The Man And His Music* (1986).

Cornell, Don

b. 1924, New York City, New York, USA.

During the late 30s Cornell sang and played guitar with several bands including Lennie Hayton, Red Nichols, and Mickey Alpert, before joining Sammy Kaye, mainly as a guitar player, in 1942. He stayed with Kaye until 1950, with a break for military service, and sang on several of the band's hits including 'I Left My Heart At The Stage Door Canteen', 'Tell Me A Story' and 'It Isn't Fair', (a million-seller) all for RCA Victor. His first solo success, 'I Need You So', was also on that label, but his move to Coral in 1951 produced several winners including 'I'll Walk Alone', 'I', (the shortest song title ever charted), 'Heart Of My Heart', accompanied by Alan Dale and ex-Glenn Miller vocalist Johnny Desmond, and two more gold discs with 'I'm Yours' and 'Hold My Hand'. The latter song was featured in the 1954 movie *Susan Slept Here*, starring Dick Powell and Debbie Reynolds, and was nominated for an Academy Award, only to be beaten by 'Three Coins In The Fountain'. Later in the 50s Cornell had several US Top 30 entries including 'Stranger In Paradise', 'Most Of All', 'The Bible Tells Me So', 'Love Is A Many Splendoured Thing' and 'Young Abe Lincoln'. After that the hits dried up, but Cornell's seemingly effortless high baritone voice remained in demand for club and theatre work.

Selected albums: *Don Cornell* (1959), *I Wish You Love* (1966). Compilation: *Don's Great Hits* (1959).

Cotton, Billy

b. 6 May 1899, Westminster, London, England, d. 25 March 1969, London, England. The youngest of 10 children, Cotton sang solo treble in the choir of St. Margaret's Church, Westminster. In 1914 he joined the army as a bugler-drummer and served in the Dardanelles Campaign in Gallipoli before returning to the UK and spending the rest of World War I in the Royal Flying Corps. After the war he drove London buses, played for Brentford Football Club as an amateur (and later, for the then Athenian league club, Wimbledon), and raced motorcycles and cars. In the early 20s he played drums for various groups, including the Laurie Johnson Band at the 1924 British Empire Exhibition at Wembley and then formed his own London Savannah Band. Cotton gave up the drumstool to front the band in 1925 when Clem Bernard joined the organization as pianist/arranger and stayed for over 40 years as the musical brain behind the Cotton band. Initially they played the big dancehalls, including the Astoria in London's Charing Cross Road, and top nightclubs such as Ciro's, in both London and Paris. During the 30s

they switched, via cine-variety, to become a theatre showband, introducing lewd visual humour and saucy songs. Their records reflected the change with such songs as 'Bessie Couldn't Help It', 'She Was Only Somebody's Daughter' and 'They All Start Whistling At Mary', besides the 'hotter' numbers, 'New Tiger Rag', 'Truckin'' and 'Shine', which featured Nat Gonella, Teddy Foster and the American trombonist and skilful tap-dancer Ellis Jackson. Sixteen examples of Cotton's 30s style can be found on *The Golden Age Of Billy Cotton*. During World War II, Cotton toured France with ENSA and was put in charge of Air Training Corps entertainment, besides touring the music halls. After the war he boosted his declining variety theatre bookings with *Wakey Wakey!!* a Sunday lunchtime BBC radio programme which became a national institution and ran for over 20 years. The material was much the same as ever, 'Oh, Oh, Oh, Oh, What A Referee', 'Oh, Nicholas, Don't Be So Ridiculous', 'Forty Fousand Fevvers On A Frush', ' The Dambusters March', 'The Sunshine Of Your Smile' 'Fall In And Follow Me', 'Maybe It's Because I'm A Londoner', heralded by his theme, 'Somebody Stole My Gal'. All these tunes were played and sung by regulars, Doreen Stevens, Johnny Johnson, Rita Williams And The Highlights, Kathy Kaye, trumpeter Grisha Farfel and vocalist/general all-rounder Alan Breeze, ever-present with Cotton since the early 30s. During the 50s he had chart hits with 'In A Golden Coach' (to celebrate the 1953 Coronation), 'I Saw Mommy Kissing Santa Claus', 'Friends And Neighbours' and 'Puttin' On The Style'. In 1957, following an unsatisfactory flirtation with commercial television, *The Billy Cotton Band Show* came to BBC television. At 60 years of age and substantially built, Cotton danced with the Silhouettes, a line of dancing girls; sung with and insulted his favourite guest stars, Russ Conway, Alma Cogan and Max Bygraves; conducted the band, and joined in throwing cotton wool balls into the audience during one of their favourite numbers, 'I've Got A Lovely Bunch Of Coconuts'. By now he was one of the most popular figures in UK light entertainment. Some of the shows were produced by Cotton's son, Bill Jnr., who later became Controller of BBC television. In 1962 Cotton Snr. was voted 'Show Business Personality Of The Year'. He also suffered a stroke which slowed him down, though he did work again during the 60s until his untimely death whilst watching a boxing match at Wembley Arena in March 1969. He was buried at St. Margaret's Church where he had once been a choirboy.

Compilations: *The World Of Billy Cotton* (1969), *The World Of Billy Cotton, Volume Two* (1971), *Billy Cotton* (1971), *That Rhythm Man 1928-31* (1982), *Rock Your Cares Away* (1983), *Let's All Join In* (1983), *Sing A New Song 1930-32* (1983), *The Golden Age Of Billy Cotton* (1984), *Wakee Wakee* (1985), *Somebody Stole My Gal* (1986), *Crazy Weather* (1986), *Nobody's Sweetheart* (1987), *Wakey Wakey!!* (1988).

Further reading: *I Did It My Way*, Billy Cotton.

Crew-Cuts

Formed in Toronto, Ontario, Canada in 1952, the Crew-Cuts were a white vocal quartet which had success in the early 50s by covering black R&B songs. Their version of 'Sh-Boom', originally a number 2 R&B hit for the Chords in 1954, became a simultaneous number 1 pop hit for the Crew-Cuts, staying in that position for nine weeks and helping to usher in the rock 'n' roll era. The group was comprised of Rudi Maugeri (b. 21 January 1931; baritone), Pat Barrett (b. 15 September 1931; tenor), John Perkins (b. 28 August 1931; lead) and his brother Ray Perkins (b. 28 November 1932; bass), all born in Toronto. The group met at Toronto's Cathedral School, where they all sang in the choir, and decided to form a barber shop-style group. Initially called the Canadaires, the group received its first break in Cleveland, Ohio, USA, where they appeared on Gene Carroll's television programme. After that show they were introduced to the influential local disc jockey Bill Randle, who suggested the name change (after a popular short-cropped hairstyle). Randle introduced the group to Mercury Records, which signed them. Their first recording, an original composition called 'Crazy 'Bout Ya Baby', made the Top 10 in the US charts. Mercury suggested covering 'Sh-Boom' and its massive success led to further covers of R&B records by the group, including the Penguins' 'Earth Angel', Nappy Brown's 'Don't Be Angry' and the Nutmegs' 'A Story Untold'. The success of the Crew-Cuts and other white cover artists helped pave the way for recognition and acceptance of the black originators. In addition to 'Sh-Boom', other Top 10 placings were 'Earth Angel' (1955), 'Ko Ko Mo (I Love You So)' (1955) and 'Gum Drop' (1955). The Crew-Cuts placed 14 singles in the charts throughout 1957 moving to RCA Records in 1958 and disbanded in 1963.

Albums: *The Crew-Cuts Go Longhair* (1954), *The Crew-Cuts On The Campus* (1954), *Crew-Cut Capers* (1954), *Music Ala Carte* (1955), *Rock And Roll Bash* (1955), *Surprise Package* (1958), *The Crew-Cuts Sing!* (1959), *You Must Have Been A Beautiful Baby* (1960), *The Crew-Cuts Sing Folk* (early 60s).

Crickets

Despite being formed essentially to back Buddy Holly and to record his 'vocal group' songs, the Crickets have continued occasionally to record and tour as a unit ever since Holly's death in 1959. In addition to Holly, the original long-serving members were drummer Jerry Allison (b. 31 August 1939, Hillsboro, Texas, USA), bassist Joe B. Mauldin and guitarist Nicky Sullivan. When they were signed to Decca in 1957, it was decided that the tracks produced by Norman Petty should be released under two names, as Holly solo items (on Decca) and as the Crickets (on Coral). It was 'That'll Be The Day', credited to the Crickets which was the first number 1 hit. Other Crickets' successes with Holly on lead vocals included 'Oh Boy', 'Maybe Baby' and 'Think It Over'. However, by the end of 1958, Holly had moved to New York to concentrate on his solo career and the Crickets did not accompany him on his final tour. Petty and Jerry Allison had already begun recording independently of Holly, issuing 'Love's Made A Fool Of You' with Earl Sinks on lead vocals. On the later singles 'Peggy Sue Got Married' and 'More Than I Can Say' Sinks was replaced by Sonny Curtis (b. 9 May 1937, Meadow, Texas, USA; guitar/vocals who was an early Texas associate of Holly and Allison. Written by Curtis and Allison, 'More Than I Can Say' was a hit for Bobby Vee and in 1961 the Crickets moved to Vee's label, Liberty and recorded an album of Holly numbers with the singer the following year. Glen D. Hardin (b. 18 April 1939, Wellington, Texas, USA; piano) joined at this point. The group also released a series of singles between 1962 and 1965. These made little impact in the USA but 'Please Don't Ever Change' (a Carole King/Gerry Goffin number) and 'My Little Girl' were Top 20 hits in Britain, where the group continued to tour.

There followed a five-year hiatus in the group's career as Curtis and Allison worked as songwriters and session musicians. They were persuaded to re-form the Crickets in 1970, to record a rock revival album for the Barnaby label. This led to a contract with Mercury and two albums containing mostly original country-rock style songs, such as Allison's powerfully nostalgic 'My Rockin' Days'. The producer was Bob Montgomery who had been

Buddy Holly's earliest songwriting partner. The group now included singer/writer Steve Krikorian and two English musicians: guitarist Albert Lee and ex-Family and Blind Faith bassist Ric Grech.

The most recent phase of the Crickets' career was stimulated by the purchase from Paul McCartney's publishing company of Norman Petty's share of the Holly/Allison song catalogue. During the 80s, Allison led the band for revival tours and he returned to recording in 1987 with original bassist Mauldin and newcomer Gordon Payne on guitar and vocals. They released *Three-Piece* on Allison's own Rollercoaster label, which became *T-Shirt* on CBS with the addition of the title track, the winner of a UK songwriting competition organized by McCartney's company.

Selected albums: *In Style With The Crickets* (1961), *Bobby Vee Meets The Crickets* (1962), *Something Old, Something New, Something Borrowed, Something Else* (1963), *California Sun* (1964), *Rockin' 50s Rock 'N' Roll* (1970), *Bubblegum, Bop, Ballads And Boogies* (1973), *A Long Way From Lubbock* (1975), *Three-Piece* (1988), *T-Shirt* (1989).

Crombie, Tony

b. 27 August 1925, London, England. Active among the eager young British beboppers of the early 40s, Crombie, a self-taught drummer, broadened his musical knowledge by securing work on post-war transatlantic liners. The main objective by many British musicians, like Crombie, who obtained such employment, was not to play dance music for the passengers but to get to New York where he could hear American bebop artists in person. In the late 40s and early 50s he was still playing in London clubs and also working as an accompanist to visiting American stars, including singers Lena Horne and Carmen McRae. In the 50s he worked regularly with Ronnie Scott and Victor Feldman and was much in demand to accompany jazz solo musicians touring the UK. Anything but narrow in his musical tastes, in 1956 Crombie formed a rock 'n' roll band, the Rockets (a name he also used, confusingly, for a 1958 band which featured many of the outstanding British jazzmen of the period, including Scott and Tubby Hayes). Crombie's roots were in jazz, however, and he was a member of the resident rhythm section at Ronnie Scott's club. In the late 50s and throughout the 60s, he turned more and more to writing: he wrote scores for films and television and also composed tunes recorded by a wide range of artists including Miles Davis, who featured 'So Near, So Far' on *Seven Steps To Heaven*. A duo he

formed with organist Alan Haven had considerable popular success. In the 70s and 80s he continued to write but also played frequently at clubs and in concert, often with Scott but also with the popular jazz-loving singer/organist Georgie Fame. A highly versatile musician, Crombie also plays piano and vibraphone. His piano playing, especially on his own compositions, has a sombre beauty which reflects his love and admiration for the music of Duke Ellington.

Selected albums: *At The Royal Festival Hall With The Ronnie Scott Orchestra And Tony Crombie* (1956), *Atmosphere* (1958), *Relaunch* (1958), *Man From Interpol* (1960), *Tony Crombie* i (1960), *Tony Crombie* ii (1960), *Sweet, Wild And Blue* (1960), with Alan Haven *Through Till Two* (1966), with Mike Carr *Hammond Under Pressure* (1968), *Tony Crombie And Friends* (1989).

Crosby, Bing

b. Harry Lillis Crosby, 3 May 1903, Tacoma, Washington, USA, d. 14 October 1977. Crosby picked up his nickname through a childhood addiction to a strip cartoon character in a local newspaper. After first singing with a jazz band at high school, he sang at university with a friend, Al Rinker. The duo decided to take a chance on showbiz success, quit school and called on Rinker's sister, Mildred Bailey, in the hope that she could help them find work. Their hopes were fulfilled and they were soon hired by Paul Whiteman. With the addition of Harry Barris they formed the singing trio, the Rhythm Boys, and quickly became one of the major attractions of the Whiteman entertainment package. The popularity of the trio on such recordings as 'Mississippi Mud' and 'I'm Coming Virginia' and an appearance in the film, *The King Of Jazz* (1930), gave Crosby an edge when he chose to begin a solo career. The late 20s saw a great increase in the use of microphones in public auditoriums and the widespread use of more sophisticated microphones in recording studios. This allowed singers to adopt a more confidential singing style, which became known as 'crooning'. Of all the new breed of crooners, Crosby was by far the most popular and successful. Although never a jazz singer, Crosby worked with many jazzmen, especially during his stint with Whiteman, when his accompanists might include Jimmy and Tommy Dorsey, Joe Venuti and Bix Beiderbecke. This early experience, and a sharp awareness of the rhythmic advances of Louis Armstrong, brought Crosby to the forefront of popular American singers in an era when jazz styles were beginning to reshape popular music. Also contributing to his rise was the fact that the new singing style was very well suited to radio, which currently dominated the entertainment industry. He made numerous film appearances and many hundreds of records, several of them massive hits. Indeed, sales of his records eclipsed every recording artist who had gone before and by the 40s these had helped build Crosby into the world's biggest singing star. In contrast, his films were usually frothy affairs and he displayed only limited acting ability. However, in the early 40s his film career took an upswing with a series of comedies in which he co-starred with Bob Hope and Dorothy Lamour, while some good light dramatic roles advanced his career still further. Throughout the 50s Crosby continued to work in radio and television, and made regular concert appearances and still more records. During his radio and television career Crosby often worked with other leading entertainers, among them Al Jolson, Connee Boswell, Dinah Shore, Judy Garland, Armstrong, Hope and his brother, Bob Crosby. By the mid-60s he was content to take things a little easier, although he still made records and personal appearances. Despite his carefree public persona, Crosby was a complex man, difficult to know and understand. As a singer, his seemingly lazy intonation often gave the impression that anyone could sing the way he did, itself a possible factor in his popularity. Nevertheless, his distinctive phrasing was achieved by a good ear, selective taste in building his repertoire, and an acute awareness of what the public wanted. Although his countless fans may well regard it as heresy, Crosby's way with a song was not always what songwriters might have wanted. Indeed, some of Crosby's recordings indicate scant regard for the meaning of lyrics and unlike, say, Frank Sinatra, he was never a major interpreter of songs. Despite this casual disregard for the niceties of music and lyrics, many of Crosby's best-known recordings remain definitive by virtue of the highly personal stylistic stamp he placed upon them. Songs such as 'Pennies From Heaven', 'Blue Skies', 'White Christmas', 'The Bells Of St Mary's', 'Moonlight Becomes You', 'Love In Bloom', 'How Deep Is The Ocean', 'The Blue Of The Night' and 'Temptation' became his. Although Sinatra is the major male song-stylist of American popular music, and also the one who most influenced other singers, every vocalist who followed Crosby owes him a debt for the manner in which his casual, relaxed approach completely altered audience perceptions of how a singer should behave. Towards the end of his life Crosby's star had waned but he was still capable of pulling in sell-out crowds for his occasional public appearances, even though he preferred to spend as much time as he could on the golf course. It was while playing golf in Spain that he collapsed and died.

Selected albums: (10-inch releases) *White Christmas* (1945), *Jerry Kern Songs* (1949), *Foster* (1950), *El Bingo* (1950), *Christmas Greetings* (1950), *St. Patrick's Day* (1950), *St. Valentine's Day* (1950), *Blue Skies* (1950), *The Bell's Of St. Mary's* (1950, film soundtrack), *Don't Fence Me In* (1950), *Bing Sings Cole Porter* (1950), *Bing Sings George Gershwin* (1950), *Holiday Inn* (1950, film soundtrack), *Blue Of The Night* (1950), *Cowboy Songs* (1950), *Drifting And Dreaming* (1950), *Stardust* (1950), *Cowboy Songs, Volume 2* (1950), *Bing Sings Hits* (1950), *Top O' The Morning* (1950, film soundtrack), *Mr. Music* (1950, film soundtrack), *Hits From Broadway Shows* (1951), *Favorite Hawaiian Songs* (1951), *Go West, Young Man* (1951), *Way Back Home* (1951), *Bing And The Dixieland Bands* (1951), *Yours Is My Heart Alone* (1951), *Country Style* (1951), *Down Memory Lane* (1951), *Down Memory Lane, Volume 2* (1951), *Bing And Connee Boswell* (1951), *When Irish Eyes Are Smiling* (1952), *The Road To Bali* (1952, film soundtrack), *Country Girl* (1953), *Song Hits Of Paris* (1954), *The Small One* (1955), *Ichabod Crane* (1955), *Two For Tonight* (1956, film soundtrack), *Rhythm Of The Range* (1956, film soundtrack), *Waikiki Wedding* (1956, film soundtrack), *The Road To Singapore* (1956), *The Star Maker* (1956, film soundtrack); (12-inch releases) *A Man Without A Country* (1956), White Christmas (1956, film soundtrack), *Lullabye Time* (1956), *A Christmas Sing With Bing Around The World* (1956), *Shillelaghs And Shamrocks* (1956), *Home On The Range* (1956), *Blue Hawaii* (1956), *High Tor* (1956, film soundtrack), *High Society* (1956, film soundtrack), *Bing With A Beat* (1957), *Songs I Wish I Had Sung* (1958), *Twilight On The Trail* (1958), *Some Fine Old Chestnuts* (1958), *New Tricks* (1958), *Around The World* (1958), *Bing In Paris* (1958), with Rosemary Clooney *Fancy Meeting You Here* (1958), with Clooney *That Travellin' Two Beat* (1958), *That Christmas Feeling* (1958), *Paris Holiday* (1958, film soundtrack), *In A Little Spanish Town* (1959), *High Time* (1960, film soundtrack), *Bing And Satchmo* (1960), *Senor Bing* (1960), *Join Bing And Sing Along* (1960), *101 Gang Songs* (1961), *On The Happy Side* (1962), *I Wish You A Merry Christmas* (1962), *Easy To Remember* (1962), *Pennies From Heaven* (1962), *Pocketful Of Dreams* (1962), *East Side Of Heaven*

(1962), *The Road Begins* (1962), *Only Forever* (1962), *Swinging On A Star* (1962), *Accentuate The Positive* (1962), *But Beautiful* (1962), *Sunshine Cake* (1962), *Cool Of The Evening* (1962), *Zing A Little Zong* (1962), *Anything Goes* (1962), *Holiday In Europe* (1962), *The Small One* (1962), *Songs Everybody Knows* (1964), *Return To Paradise Islands* (1964), with Frank Sinatra and Fred Waring *America, I Hear You Singing* (1964), *Bing In Hollywood* (1967), *Hey Jude/Hey Bing!* (1969), *That's What Life Is All About* (1975), *Live At The London Palladium* (1977), *Seasons* (1977), *Songs Of A Lifetime* (1979, previously unreleased recordings). Compilations: *The Best Of Bing* (1977, MCA label), *Bing In The Thirties Volumes. 1-8* (1984-88, Spokane label), *The Radio Years Volumes 1-4* (1985-87/GNP Cresendo label), *10th Anniversary Album* (1987, Warwick label), *Bing Crosby 1929-34, Classic Years Volume 1* (1987, BBC label), *Chronological Bing Crosby Vols 1-10* (1985-88, Jonzo label), *The Jazzin' Bing Crosby* (1992, Charly label), *The Quintessential Bing Crosby* (1993), *The EP Collection* (1993), *Bing Crosby And Friends* (1993).

D

Dale, Alan

b. Aldo Sigismondi, 9 July 1926, Brooklyn, New York, USA. Formerly with Carmen Cavallaro, Alan Dale first graced the US charts when his rich baritone vocal style provided Ray Bloch And His Orchestra with the 'swing' hit 'Kate (Have I Come Too Early Too Late)' in 1947. In the following year he duetted with Connie Haines on 'At The Darktown Strutters' Ball'. In 1951 he hosted his own US television series, which led to more success, most notably with 'Heart Of My Heart' (with Johnny Desmond and Don Cornell), and 'East Side, West Side' (with Desmond and Buddy Greco). In 1955 he again made the US Top 20 with 'Cherry Pink (And Apple Blossom White)' and an adaptation of a Cuban mambo-cha-cha 'Me Lo Dijo Adela', entitled 'Sweet And Gentle'.

Dale, Jim

b. Jim Smith, 15 August 1935, Kettering, Northamptonshire, England. Dale, a failed impressionist, who wanted to be an all-round entertainer, had a two-year gig with Carrol Levis' touring show as part of a comedy tumbling act. He then became a solo comedian and only turned to singing when he found people preferred his finale song to his tame comedy. He joined the BBC television series, *6.5 Special* in April 1957 and shortly after signed to Parlophone Records, where he was produced by George Martin. His only Top 20 hit came with his second single, a cover of Johnny Madara's 'Be My Girl', which reached number 2 in late 1957. He had three more UK Top 40 entries, the last being a version of the McGuire Sisters' US hit 'Sugartime' in 1958. In the 60s Dale pursued his acting career, and appeared in a string of successful *Carry On* films, and others, such as *Lock Up Your Daughters*. He made his West End debut in a musical, *The Wayward Way*, and appeared at the Edinburgh Festival in a pop version of *The Winter's Tale*. He also co-wrote the Seekers' smash hit, 'Georgy Girl', for which he was nominated for an Academy Award, and contributed to the music for movies such as *Shalako* and *Lola*. In the late 60s and early 70s, as member of the National Theatre Company, he appeared in several productions at the Old Vic and the Young Vic. He also made more films, including *Adolph Hitler - My Part In His Downfall* and *Digby, The Biggest Dog In The World*. In 1973, Dale played for six months at the Queen's Theatre, London in the musical, *The Card*, and around the same time, hosted the popular television show, *Sunday Night At The London Palladium*. In 1974 he went to the US with the National Theatre Company and created a stir with his performance as an 'ingratiating scamp' in the Moliére farce, *Scapino*, which brought him Drama Desk and Outer Critics Circle Awards, and a Tony nomination. During the late 70s, by now domiciled in the US, he appeared in stage productions of *Comedians* and *Privates On Parade*, as well as making several other movies, three of them for the Disney Studio. In 1980 Dale found the ideal property for his talents in *Barnum*, a musical about the life of the US showman, which involved juggling, trampoline, and tightrope walking, among other skills. He stayed with the show for over a year, following ecstatic opening reviews. In the 80s he made more films, and appeared on the New York stage in productions as diverse as Peter Nichol's *Joe Egg* (1985), *Me And My Girl* (1987), and a revival of *Privates On Parade* (1989). In 1992

Jim Dale (right) with Don Lang

he returned to the UK, and his 60s roots, to play the title role in the film, *Carry On Columbus*. Selected album: *Jim!* (1958).

Damn Yankees

Combining the improbable ingredients of a Faustian plot with a baseball setting, itself a notoriously jinx-ridden subject, the stage musical *Damn Yankees* was an unexpected hit following its opening on 5 May 1955. With music and lyrics by Jerry Ross and Richard Adler, the show starred the remarkable Gwen Verdon. The storyline of *Damn Yankees* follows hapless Senator Joe Boyd, a middle-aged baseball fan, who announces that he would willingly sell his soul to the Devil if only the team he supports could win the pennant. The Devil promptly appears and grants his wish although Joe believes he can outsmart 'Old Nick' if he can remain faithful to his wife. Rejuvenated, the Senator becomes Joe Hardy, a handsome young ballplayer, and is amorously entangled with Lola, the Devil's glamorous recreation of an ugly old hag. The Devil fails to make Joe unfaithful to his wife and eventually, after his team has won the pennant, Joe returns to plump middle-age and his dull and ordinary wife, while Lola reverts to being

a hag. In addition to Verdon as Lola, the show starred Stephen Douglass as Joe and Ray Walston as 'Mr Applegate', the name by which the Devil was known for his earthly manifestations. Thanks to a powerful and sexy performance from Verdon and some of the music, notably 'Whatever Lola Wants', 'Two Lost Souls', and 'Heart', (which became a big hit in the US for Eddie Fisher and the Four Aces, and in the UK for Max Bygraves), the show was a great success, running for over 1,000 performances. The 1958 film teamed Verdon with pop heart-throb, Tab Hunter - and Walston, who, as usual, stole the show from everyone.

Damone, Vic

b. Vito Farinola, 12 June 1928, Brooklyn, New York, USA. A romantic balladeer with a strong, smooth baritone voice, Damone took singing lessons while working as an usher and an elevator operator at New York's Paramount Theater. After appearing with *Arthur Godfrey's Talent Scouts*, he sang at La Martinique Club, a venue known as a nursery for young vocalists. When he started recording for Mercury Records in 1947 his first chart successes included 'I Have But One Heart', 'You Do', and 'Say Something Sweet To Your

Vic Damone

Sweetheart' (with Patti Page). In 1949 he had two million-sellers: 'Again', from the Ida Lupino film, *Roadhouse*; and 'You're Breaking My Heart'. In the late 40s Damone also had his own CBS radio show, *Saturday Night Serenade*. His film career started in 1951 when he featured in *Rich, Young And Pretty*, the first in a series of musicals with soprano Jane Powell. These included *Athena* (1954), the Sigmund Romberg bio-pic, *Deep In My Heart* (1954) and *Hit The Deck* (1955). Damone also appeared in *The Strip* (1951), a musical mystery melodrama, which featured Mickey Rooney, and jazz stars Jack Teagarden, Louis Armstrong, Earl 'Fatha' Hines and Barney Bigard; and a screen adaptation of the stage musical *Kismet* (1955), co-starring with Howard Keel, Anne Blyth and Dolores Gray.

His many record hits during the 50s included 'Tzena, Tzena, Tzena' (adapted from an Israeli song), 'Cincinnati Dancing Pig', 'My Heart Cries For You', 'My Truly, Truly Fair', 'Here In My Heart' (a UK number 1 for Al Martino), 'April In Portugal', 'Eternally' (the theme from Charlie Chaplin's film, *Limelight*), 'Ebb Tide', 'On The Street Where You Live' (Damone's third million-seller) and 'An Affair To Remember' (one of prolific film composer Harry Warren's last songs). He was also in the album charts with *That Towering Feeling*, and had his own television series in 1956-57. Like many other singers of his kind, Damone suffered from the changing musical climate of the 60s and 70s, although he did make some well-regarded albums such as *Linger Awhile* and *On the South Side*, and had a US Top 30 single in 1965 with 'You Were Only Fooling (While I Was Falling In Love)'. He made a remarkable comeback in the UK in the early 80s, chiefly because of the plugging of his back catalogue by BBC Radio 2 presenter, David Jacobs. Suddenly he was in fashion again. Most of his old albums were reissued, and many of his hit singles, and others, were repackaged on *Vic Damone Sings The Great Songs*. Throughout the 80s he recorded several new albums including *Now, Make Someone Happy* and *Now And Forever*, promoting them in the UK through regular concert tours.

Albums: *Athena* (1954, film soundtrack), *Rich, Young And Pretty* (1955, film soundtrack), *The Voice Of Vic Damone* (1956), *That Towering Feeling!* (1956), *The Stingiest Man In The World* (1956, film soundtrack), *The Gift Of Love* (1958, film soundtrack), *Closer Than A Kiss* (1959), *Angela Mia* (1959), *This Game Of Love* (1959), *On The Swingin' Side* (1961), *Linger Awhile With Vic Damone* (1962), *Strange Enchantment* (1962), *The Lively Ones* (1962), *My Baby Loves To Swing* (1963), *The Liveliest* (1963), *On The Street Where You Live* (1964), *You Were Only Fooling* (1965), *Stay With Me* (1976), *Damone's Feeling 1978* (1979), *Now* (1981), *Make Someone Happy* (1981), *Now And Forever* (1982), *Vic Damone Sings The Great Songs* (1983), *On The South Side Of Chicago* (1984), *The Damone Type Of Thing* (1984), *Christmas With Vic Damone* (1984), *The Best Of Vic Damone, Live* (1989). Compilations: *Vic Damone's Best* (1980), *Twenty Golden Pieces* (1982), *16 Golden Classics* (1986), *Didn't We?* (1986), *The Capitol Years* (1989), *16 Most Requested Songs* (1992).

Daniels, Billy

b. 12 September 1915, Jacksonville, Florida, USA, d. 7 October 1988. Daniels began his career as a singing waiter before working with dance bands and in vaudeville. In the late 30s he became popular in clubs and on radio. In 1943, during a club appearance, he performed 'That Old Black Magic', giving the song a highly dramatic, visually exciting treatment it had never had before, and from that time onwards the singer and the song were inseparable. At his best in a cabaret setting, Daniels was a natural for television and from 1950, in partnership with pianist Bennie Payne, appeared regularly in the USA and UK. He made a few film appearances and was also in the television production of *Night Of The Quarter Moon*. P.J. Proby used much of Daniels' vocal technique with his epic ballads during the 60s. In 1975 he worked with Pearl Bailey in *Hello, Dolly!* and two years later starred in London in the UK version of *Bubbling Brown Sugar*. He also appeared with Sammy Davis Jnr. in the revival of *Golden Boy*. Offstage, Daniels frequently associated with underworld characters. He was stabbed in one incident and was once charged with a shooting. Late in his life he suffered ill-health and twice underwent heart by-pass surgery. He died in October 1988.

Selected albums: *Around That Time* (c.50s), *At The Stardust Las Vegas* (c.50s), *Love Songs For A Fool* (c.50s), *You Go to My Head* (1957), *The Masculine Touch* (1958), *At the Crescendo* (1959), *Dance To The Magic* (1959), *Bubbling Black Magic* (1978). Compilation: *The Magic Of Billy Daniels* (c.1976).

Dankworth, John

b. 20 September 1927, London, England. Dankworth started playing clarinet as a child and in the early 40s was a member of a traditional jazz band. In the mid-40s he studied at the Royal Academy of Music and extended his knowledge of jazz by taking work on transatlantic liners, so that he could hear leading jazzmen in New York. Among his influences at this time was Charlie Parker and Dankworth now concentrated on alto saxophone. He was an active participant in the London bebop scene of the late 40s and early 50s, often playing at the Club 11. In 1950 he formed his own band, the Johnny Dankworth Seven, which included Jimmy Deuchar and Don Rendell. Three years later he formed a big band, playing his own, sometimes innovative, arrangements. The band's singer was Cleo Laine whom Dankworth married in 1958. For his big band Dankworth drew upon the best available modern jazzmen; at one time or another artists such as Dick Hawdon, Kenny Wheeler, Rendell, Danny Moss, Peter King, Dudley Moore and Kenny Clare were in its ranks. Dankworth's writing, especially for the big band, demonstrated his considerable arranging skills, although for many fans it is performances by the Seven that linger longest in fond memory. In the 60s Dankworth was in demand for film work, which together with the growing popularity of Laine led to a shift in policy. In the early 70s Dankworth became Laine's musical director, touring extensively with her and making many records. Dankworth's musical interests extend beyond jazz and he has composed in the classical form, including a nine-movement work, 'Fair Oak Fusions', written for cellist Julian Lloyd Webber. He has also experimented with third-stream music. His deep interest in music education led in 1969 to the founding of the Wavendon Allmusic Plan, which has continued to attract performers, students and audiences from around the world to concerts, classes, courses and lectures. Although a reliable performer on alto, it is as an arranger and tireless promoter of music that Dankworth has made his greatest contributions to the international jazz scene. In 1974, in recognition of his work, he became a Companion of the British Empire.

Albums: *What The Dickens!* (1963), *Zodiac Variations* (1964), *Shakespeare - And All That Jazz* (1964), *The $1,000,000 Collection* (1970), *Full Circle* (1972), *Lifeline* (1973), *Movies 'N' Me* (1974), *Sepia* (c.1979), *Fair Oak Fusions* (c.1982), *Symphonic Fusions* (c.1985), *Innovations* (c.1987). Compilations: with others *Bop At Club 11* (1949 recordings), *Johnny Dankworth Seven And Orchestra* (1953-57 recordings), *Featuring Cleo Laine* (1953-58 recordings).

Danny And The Juniors

This Philadelphia-based, Italian-American vocal quartet comprised lead vocalist Danny Rapp (b. 10 May 1941); first tenor Dave White; second tenor Frank Mattei and baritone Joe Terranova. Formed in 1955 as the Juvenairs, their song 'Do The Bop' came to the attention of Dick Clark who suggested it be changed to 'At The Hop'. They took his advice and released the song in 1957, initially with few sales. However, after they sang it on Clark's television show *Bandstand*, it was picked up by ABC-Paramount and shot to the top of the US chart for five weeks. Despite comments from the British music press that the group was amateur and imitative, it made the UK Top 3 and sold over two million copies worldwide. They followed it with their only other US Top 20 hit, the similar sounding and prophetically titled 'Rock 'n' Roll Is Here To Stay'. In 1960 they signed to Dick Clark's Swan Records where they scored their fourth and last US Top 40 hit 'Twistin' USA' (they re-recorded it unsuccessfully for the UK as 'Twistin' England'). They recorded songs about dance crazes such as the Mashed Potato, Pony, Cha Cha, Fish, Continental Walk and Limbo, but could not repeat their earlier success, even when they released 'Back To The Hop' in 1961. Later in the 60s they also appeared on Guyden, Mercury and Capitol, where they re-recorded 'Rock 'n' Roll Is Here To Stay' in 1968. Dave White left the group in the early 60s to concentrate on writing and production and composed a number of hits like 'You Don't Own Me' for Lesley Gore and '1-2-3' and 'Like A Baby' for Len Barry, before recording a solo album on Bell in 1971. In the 70s they played the 'oldies' circuit with a line-up that included Fabian's ex-backing singer Jimmy Testa. In 1976 a re-issue of their classic 'At The Hop' returned them to the UK Top 40. After a few quiet years, leader Rapp was found dead in Arizona in 1983 - he had apparently committed suicide.

Darin, Bobby

b. Walden Robert Cassotto, 14 May 1936, New York, USA, d. 20 December 1973. Darin's entry to the music business occurred during the mid-50s following a period playing in New York coffee houses. His friendship with co-writer/entrepreneur Don Kirshner resulted in his first single, 'My First Love'. A meeting with Connie Francis' manager George Scheck led to a prestigious television appearance on the Tommy Dorsey television show and a contract with Decca. An unsuccessful attempt

Danny And The Juniors

Bobby Darin with Connie Francis

to score a hit with a cover of Lonnie Donegan's 'Rock Island Line' was followed by a move towards pop novelty with 'Splish Splash'. Darin's quirky vocal ensured that his song was a worldwide hit, although he was outsold in Britain by a rival version from comedian Charlie Drake. During this period, Darin also recorded in a group called the Ding Dongs, which prompted a dispute between Atco and Brunswick Records, culminating in the creation of a new group, the Rinky Dinks who were credited as the backing artists on his next single, 'Early In The Morning'. Neither that, nor its successor, 'Mighty Mighty', proved commercially viable, but the intervening Darin solo release, 'Queen Of The Hop', sold a million. The period charm of 'Plain Jane' presaged one of Darin's finest moments - the exceptional 'Dream Lover'. An enticing vocal performance allied to strong production took the song to number 1 in the UK and number 2 in the USA.

Already assured of considerable status as a pop artist, Darin dramatically changed direction with his next recording and emerged as a finger-clicking master of the supper club circuit. 'Mack The Knife', composed by Bertolt Brecht and Kurt Weill for the celebrated *Threepenny Opera*, proved a million-seller and effectively raised Darin to new status as a 'serious singer' - he even compared himself favourably with Frank Sinatra, in what was a classic example of pop hubris. Darin's hit treatments of 'La Mer (Beyond The Sea)', 'Clementine', 'Won't You Come Home Bill Bailey?' and 'You Must Have Been A Beautiful Baby' revealed his ability to tackle variety material and transform it to his own ends.

In 1960, Darin adeptly moved into film and was highly praised for his roles in *Come September* (whose star Sandra Dee he later married), *State Fair*, *Too Late Blues*, *If A Man Answers*, *Pressure Point*, *Hell Is For Heroes* and *Captain Newman MD*. He returned to form as a pop performer with the lyrically witty 'Multiplication' and the equally clever 'Things'. In the meantime, he had recorded an album of Ray Charles' songs, including the standard 'What'd I Say'. During the beat boom era Darin briefly reverted to show tunes such as 'Baby Face' and 'Hello Dolly', but a further change of style beckoned with the folk-rock boom of 1965. Suddenly, Darin was a protest singer, summing up the woes of a generation with the surly 'We Didn't Ask To Be Brought Here'. Successful readings of Tim Hardin songs, including 'If I Were A Carpenter' and 'The Lady Came From Baltimore', and John Sebastian's 'Lovin' You' and 'Darling Be

Home Soon' demonstrate his potential as a cover artist of seemingly limitless range. A more contemporary poet/political direction was evident on the album *Born Walden Robert Cassotto*, and its serious follow-up *Commitment*. As the 60s ended Darin was more actively involved in related business interests, although he still appeared regularly on television. One of the great vocal chameleons of pop music, Darin suffered from a weak heart and after several operations time finally caught up with the singer at Hollywood's Cedars of Lebanon Hospital in December 1973.

Albums: *Bobby Darin* (1959), *That's All* (1959), *This Is Darin* (1960), *Darin At The Copa* (1960), *For Teenagers Only* (1960), with Johnny Mercer *Two Of A Kind* (1961), *Love Swings* (1961), *Twist With Bobby Darin* (1962), *Darin Sings Ray Charles* (1962), *It's You Or No-One* (1962), *Oh Look At Me Now* (1962), *Earthy* (1962), *You're The Reason I'm Leaving* (1963), *Eighteen Yellow Roses* (1963), *From Hello Dolly To Goodbye Charlie* (1964), *Venice Blues* (1965), *In A Broadway Bag (Mame)* (1966), *If I Were A Carpenter* (1967), *Bobby Darin Something Special* (1967), *Born Walden Robert Cassotto* (1968), *Commitment* (1969). Compilations: *The Bobby Darin Story* (1961), *Things And Other Things* (1962), *The Versatile Bobby Darin* (1985), *The Legend Of Bobby Darin* (1985), *His Greatest Hits* (1985).

Davis, Sammy, Jnr.

b. 8 December 1925, Harlem, New York, USA, d. 16 May 1990, Los Angeles, California, USA. A dynamic and versatile all-round entertainer - a trouper in the old-fashioned tradition. The only son of two dancers in a black vaudeville troupe, called Will Mastin's Holiday in Dixieland, Davis Jnr. made his professional debut with the group at the age of three, as 'Silent Sam, The Dancing Midget'. While still young he was coached by the legendary tap-dancer, Bill 'Bojangles' Robinson. Davis left the group in 1943 to serve in the US Army, where he encountered severe racial prejudice for the first, but not the last, time. After the war he rejoined his father and adopted uncle in the Will Mastin Trio. By 1950 the Trio were headlining at venues such as the Capitol in New York and Ciro's in Hollywood with stars such as Jack Benny and Bob Hope, but it was Davis who was receiving the standing ovations for his singing, dancing, drumming, comedy and apparently inexhaustible energy. In 1954 he signed for Decca Records, and released two albums, *Starring Sammy Davis Jr* (number 1 in the US chart), featuring his impressions of stars such as Dean Martin and Jerry

Sammy Davis Jnr. with Shirley Bassey

Lewis, Johnnie Ray and Jimmy Durante; and *Just For Lovers*. He also made the US singles chart with 'Hey There', from *The Pajama Game* and in the same year he lost his left eye in a road accident. When he returned to performing in January 1955 wearing an eyepatch he was greeted even more enthusiastically than before. During that year he continued to reach the US Top 20 with 'Something's Gotta Give', 'Love Me Or Leave Me' and 'That Old Black Magic'. In 1956 he made his Broadway debut in the musical *Mr Wonderful*, music and lyrics by Jerry Bock, Larry Holofiener and George Weiss. Also in the show were the rest of the Will Mastin Trio, Sammy's uncle and Davis Snr. The show ran for nearly 400 performances and produced two hits, 'Too Close For Comfort', and the title song, which was very successful for Peggy Lee. Although generally regarded as the first popular American black performer to become acceptable to both black and white audiences, Davis attracted heavy criticism in 1956 over his conversion to Judaism, and later for his marriage to Swedish actress Mai Britt. He described himself as a 'one-eyed Jewish nigger'. Apart from a few brief appearances when he was very young, Davis started his film career in 1958 with *Anna Lucasta*, and was critically acclaimed in the following year for his performance as Sporting Life in *Porgy And Bess*. By this time Davis was a leading member of Frank Sinatra's 'inner circle', called variously, the 'Clan', or the 'Rat Pack'. He appeared with Sinatra in three movies, *Ocean's Eleven* (1960), *Sergeants 3* (1962), and *Robin And The Seven Hoods* (1964), but made, perhaps, a greater impact when he co-starred with another member of the 'Clan', Shirley MacLaine, in the Cy Coleman and Dorothy Fields' film musical, *Sweet Charity*. The 60s were good times for Davis, who was enormously popular on records and television, but especially 'live', at Las Vegas and in concert. In 1962 he made the US chart with the Anthony Newley/Leslie Bricusse number, 'What Kind Of Fool Am I?', and thereafter featured several of the their songs in his act. He sang Bricusse's nominated song, 'Talk To The Animals', at the 1967 Academy Awards ceremony, and collected the Oscar, on behalf of the songwriter, when it won. And in 1972, he had a million-selling hit record with the Newley/Bricusse song, 'The Candy Man', from the film, *Willy Wonka And The Chocolate Factory*. He appeared again on Broadway in 1964 in *Golden Boy*, Charles Strouse and Lee Adams' musical adaptation of Clifford Odet's 1937 drama of a young man torn between the boxing ring and his violin. Also in the cast was Billy Daniels. The show ran for 569 performances in New York, and went to London in 1968. During the 70s he worked less, suffering, it is said, as a result of previous alcohol and drug abuse. He entertained US troops in the Lebanon in 1983, and five years later undertook an arduous comeback tour of the USA and Canada with Sinatra and Dean Martin. In 1989 he travelled further, touring Europe with the show, *The Ultimate Event*, along with Liza Minnelli and Sinatra. While he was giving everything to career favourites such as 'Birth Of The Blues', 'Mr Bojangles' and 'Old Black Magic' he was already ill, although he did not let it show. After his death in 1990 it was revealed that his esate was almost worthless. In 1992, an all-star tribute, led by Liza Minnelli, was mounted at the Royal Albert Hall in London, the city which had always welcomed him. Proceeds from the concert went to the Royal Marsden Cancer Appeal.

Selected albums: *Starring Sammy Davis Jr* (1955), *Just For Lovers* (1955), *Mr. Wonderful* (1956, film soundtrack), *Here's Looking At You* (late 50s), with Carmen McRae *Boy Meets Girl* (late 50s), *It's All Over But The Swingin'* (late 50s), *Mood To Be Wooed* (late 50s), *All The Way And Then Some* (late 50s), *Sammy Davis Jr. At Town Hall* (1959), *Porgy And Bess* (1959), *Sammy Awards* (1960), *I Got A Right To Swing* (1960), *What Kind Of Fool Am I And Other Show-Stoppers* (1962), *Sammy Davis Jr. At The Cocoanut Grove* (1963), *As Long As She Needs Me* (1963), *Sammy Davis Jr. Salutes The Stars Of The London Palladium* (1964), *The Shelter Of Your Arms* (1964), with Count Basie *Our Shining Hour* (1965), *Sammy's Back On Broadway* (1965), *I've Gotta Be Me* (1969), *Sammy Davis Jr. Now* (1972), *Portrait Of Sammy Davis Jr.* (1972), *It's A Musical World* (1976), *The Song And Dance Man* (1977), *Sammy Davis Jr. In Person 1977* (1983), *Closest Of Friends* (1984). Compilations: *The Best Of Sammy Davis Jr.* (1982), *Collection* (1989), *The Great Sammy Davis Jr.* (1989), *Sammy Davis Jr Capitol Collectors Series* (1990).

Further reading: *Yes I Can*, Sammy Davis Jnr. *Why Me?*, Sammy Davis Jnr.

Day, Dennis

b. Eugene McNulty, 21 May 1917, New York City, New York, USA, d. 22 June 1988, Brentwood, California, USA. Day was a popular singer, from the late 30s to the 60s, whose distinctive Irish tenor voice and flair for comedy gained him a prestigious spot on the top rated Jack Benny radio show. Day graduated from St. Patrick's Cathedral High School, and attended Manhattan College, planning to study law. He first appeared on Benny's show in 1939, replacing another tenor, Kenny Baker. After military service during World War II, Lewis became the comedian's regular foil, and moved with him to television in the 50s, and until the show ended in the mid-60s. He would continually frustrate Benny with his clowning, and favourite line: 'Oh, Mr. Benny'; to which the comedian would invariably reply: 'Oh, for heaven's sake. Sing Dennis!'. He also had his own show for a while on NBC, and appeared frequently on other programmes such as *Max Leiberman Presents*, *Hour Glass*, *All Star Review* and Milton Berle's *Texaco Star Theatre*. In the late 40s and early 50s Day had hits with 'Mamselle', 'Clancy Lowered The Boom', 'Dear Hearts And Gentle People', 'Goodnight, Irene', 'Mona Lisa', 'All My Love' and 'Mister And Mrs Mississippi'. He was also well known for his renditions of Irish favourites such as 'Peg O' My Heart', 'Too-Ra-Loo-Ra-Loo-Ral', 'McNamara's Band' and 'Danny Boy'. Day's film appearances included *Buck Benny Rides Again* (1940, with Jack Benny), *The Powers Girl* (1942), *I'll Get By* (1950), *Golden Girl* (1951) and *The Girl Next Door* (1953). He also provided the voice of 'Johnny Appleseed' for the cartoon *Melody Time*, along with Frances Langford, Ethel Smith and the Andrews Sisters. By the late 60s he had more or less retired from show business, but continued to perform occasionally at conventions and fairs. He was a zealous supporter, and vice president of the Muscular Dystrophy Association. Critically injured in a fall at his home in March 1988, he died there, in June 1988.

Compilation: *America's Favorite Irish Tenor* (1989).

Day, Doris

b. Doris Von Kappelhoff, 3 April 1924, Cincinnati, Ohio, USA. One of popular music's premier post-war vocalists and biggest names, Kappelhoff originally trained as a dancer, before turning to singing at the age of 16. After changing her surname to Day, she became the featured singer with the Bob Crosby Band. A similarly successful period with the Les Brown Band saw her record her single for Columbia, 'Sentimental Journey', which sold in excess of a million copies. Already an accomplished businesswoman, it was rumoured that she held a substantial shareholding in her record company. After securing the female lead in the 1948 film, *Romance On The High Sea*, in which she introduced Sammy Cahn and Jule Styne's 'It's Magic', she enjoyed a stupendous movie career.

Doris Day

Her striking looks, crystal clear singing voice and willingness to play tomboy heroines, as well as romantic figures, brought her a huge following. In common with other female singers of the period, she was occasionally teamed with the stars of the day and enjoyed collaborative hits with Frankie Laine ('Sugarbush') and Johnnie Ray ('Let's Walk That A-Way'). She appeared in nearly 40 movies over two decades, which included *It's A Great Feeling* (1949), *Young Man With A Horn* (1950), *Tea For Two* (1950), *West Point Story* (1950), *Lullaby Of Broadway* (1951), *On Moonlight Bay* (1951), *Starlift* (1951), *I'll See You In My Dreams* (1951), *April In Paris* (1952), *By The Light Of The Silvery Moon* (1953), *Calamity Jane* (1953), *Young At Heart* (1954), *Love Me Or Leave Me* (1955), *The Man Who Knew Too Much* (1956), *The Pyjama Game, Pillow Talk* (1959) and *Jumbo* (1962). These films featured some of her most well-known hits. Her finest performance undoubtedly occurred in the uproarious romantic western, *Calamity Jane*, which featured her enduringly vivacious versions of 'The Deadwood Stage' and 'Black Hills Of Dakota'. The movie also gave her a US/UK number 1 single with the yearningly sensual 'Secret Love' (later a lesser hit for Kathy Kirby). Day enjoyed a further UK chart topper with the romantically uplifting 'Whatever Will Be Will Be (Que Sera, Sera)'. After a gap of nearly six years, she returned to the charts with the sexually inviting movie theme 'Move Over Darling', co-written by her producer son Terry Melcher. Her Hollywood career ended in the late 60s and thereafter she was known for her reclusiveness. After more than 20 years away from the public's gaze, she emerged into the limelight in 1993 for a charity screening of *Calamity Jane* in her home town of Carmel, California. History has made her an icon, whose fresh-faced looks, sensual innocence and strikingly pure vocal style effectively summed up an era of American music.

Albums: *Young At Heart* (1955), *Love Me Or Leave Me* (1955), *Day By Day* (1957), *Day By Night* (1957), *Hooray For Hollywood* (1958), *Cuttin' Capers* (1959), *Show Time* (1960), *What Every Girl Should Know* (1960), *Listen To Day* (1960), *Bright & Shiny* (1961), *I Have Dreamed* (1961), with Andre Previn *Duet* (1962), *Love Him* (1964) *Sentimental Journey* (1965), *Latin For Lovers* (1965), *It's Magic* 6-CD set (1993). Various soundtrack albums and compilations have also been issued.

Further reading: *Doris Day: Her Own Story*, Doris Day and A.E. Hotcher. *Doris Day*, Eric Braun.

Day, Jill

b. Yvonne Page, 5 December 1930, Brighton, Sussex, England, d. 16 November 1990, Kingston, Surrey, England. Originally a band singer, Day became main vocalist in the Geraldo orchestra. By 1954, she had topped the bill at the London Palladium and co-starred in the West End production of *The Talk Of The Town*. Screen appearances followed in *Always The Bride* and *All For Mary*. Although she registered no chart hits, her name became synonymous with a number of ballads including 'I'm Old Fashioned', 'Mangoes', 'A Holiday Affair' and 'I've Got My Love To Keep Me Warm'. Diminutive but tough, she was known for her fierce temper, made worse by her inexorable slide into alcoholism. Although various comebacks were mooted, including a prestigious part in the musical *Follies*, her singing career declined during the 60s. In 1963, she made the headlines when she emptied a tureen of peas over a waiter, at the Pigalle theatre restaurant, complaining that he clattered plates and cutlery during her act. Later, she owned racehorses, and her business ventures included a theatrical agency and a baby clothes company. She died of cancer in 1990.

De Castro Sisters

Peggy De Castro (b. Dominican Republic), Babette De Castro (b. Havana, Cuba) and Cherie De Castro (b. New York, USA). The sisters were a close-harmony vocal trio extremely popular in the USA during the 50s, on record, with a mixture of ballads and novelty numbers, and with their flamboyant (some say flashy), nightclub act. The sisters were raised in Cuba, on their father's sugar plantation, and began singing as a group when they moved to New York. Signed to the small Abbott label, they had a smash hit in 1954 with 'Teach Me Tonight', written by Sammy Cahn and Gene de Paul, which sold over five million copies. In 1955 they made the US charts again, with 'Boom Boom Boomerang'. Other important 50s titles included 'Too Late Now', 'Snowbound For Christmas', 'It's Yours', 'Who Are They To Say', 'Cuckoo In The Clock', 'Give Me Time' and 'Cowboys Don't Cry'. In 1959, they re-recorded their original hit as 'Teach Me Tonight Cha Cha', perhaps a sign that their appeal, at least on records, was fading. Despite the rapidly changing musical climate, they released *Sing* and *Rockin' Beat* in the early 60s. More than 25 years later, in 1988, the De Castro Sisters hit the comeback trail at Vegas World, Las Vegas. Reliving 50s joys while also strutting to later anthems such as 'New York, New York', they made up for tired vocal chords with an abundance of showbiz flair.

Selected albums: *The DeCastro Sisters* (1960), *The Rockin' Beat* (1961), *At The Stardust* (c.60s).

Delaney, Eric

b. 22 May 1924, London, England. Delaney came from a musical family and played the piano at school. He started playing drums at the age of 10, and studied tympani at the Guildhall School of Music in London during 1946-47. After playing in other bands, including Geraldo's, Delaney formed his own unit in 1954, built around his 'Siamese twin drum kit', revolving stage, and a distinctive percussion sound. The record catalogues of the day listed him as a 'swing drummer'. His novel recording of 'Oranges And Lemons' helped the band take off, and it toured the UK Variety circuit in 1955, and in the following year played in the Royal Command Performance at the London Palladium, besides visiting the USA. Typical of the band's repertoire were 'Roamin' In The Gloamin'', 'Hornpipe Boogie', 'Cockles And Muscles', 'Say Si Si', 'Fanfare Jump' and the album *Cha-Cha-Cha Delaney*, all of which appeared on the UK Pye label. In 1960 Delaney switched to Parlophone Records and made an album *Swingin'*

Thro' The Shows, produced by George Martin. In the 80s he was still touring with a small group, predominantly in the north of England. In 1991, sporting a 'Yul Brynner' haircut, Delaney announced his return to work following a three month lay-off brought about by a condition he described as 'Lumbar Sacral Spondylosis'.

Selected albums: *Cha-Cha-Cha Delaney* (late 50s), *Swingin' Thro' The Shows* (1960).

Dell-Vikings

The original group bearing this name was formed in 1955 at the Air Force Serviceman's Club in Pittsburg, Ohio, USA. This racially integrated group, consisting of Corinthian 'Kripp' Johnson, Donald 'Gus' Backus, Norman Wright, David Lerchey and Clarence Quick, scored a gold disc in 1957 with the Quick-penned 'Come Go With Me', but the promise of this buoyant performance was undermined by internal conflict. Backus left to found a rival act - dubbed the Del Vikings - which scored a pop and US R&B Top 20 hit with 'Cool Shake'. Johnson meanwhile established another line-up, which included Chuck Jackson, and as the Dell-Vikings, recorded a haunting version of 'Whispering Bells', a Top 10 entry in both US listings. Although Backus' version later took the ascendancy, the confusion hampered both groups' progress. Jackson meanwhile enjoyed considerable

Dell-Vikings

success as a solo artist during the 60s.

Albums: *Come Go With The Del Vikings* (1957), *They Sing - They Swing* (1957), *A Swinging, Singing Record Session* (1958), *Newies And Oldies* (late 50s), *The Del Vikings And The Sonnets* (1963), *Come Go With Me* (1966). Compilations: *Del Vikings* (1988), *Cool Shake* (1988).

Delmark Records

Formed 1953 in St. Louis, Missouri, USA as Delmar Records, by Bob Koester. Delmark became a key blues label and was still in operation in the 90s. It was among the first record companies to record entire albums as opposed to the dominant singles of the 50s. After releasing dixieland jazz records, Delmark delved into the blues in 1956 with an album by pianist Rufus Perryman. Big Joe Williams' *Piney Woods Blues* was an early release and helped establish the label. Moving to Chicago in 1958, Koester added modern jazz to his roster, while recording albums by bluesmen, including Sleepy John Estes and Roosevelt Sykes. In 1965, *Hoodoo Man Blues* by Junior Wells was a big seller for the company. In the 70s the label concentrated on Chicago blues by such artists as Magic Sam, Otis Rush and J.B. Hutto. During that decade Delmark also purchased reissue rights for the United and States labels and released classic 50s material by Memphis Slim, Robert Nighthawk and others. More recently they have expanded to record new artists in addition to acquiring Apollo Records.

Dene, Terry

b. Terence Williams, 20 December 1938, London, England. Dene was discovered singing in the famous Soho coffee bar the 2 I's. His big break came when he appeared on the *6.5 Special* BBC television show in April 1957. After being rejected by EMI, he was signed by Decca A&R man Dick Rowe and his version of Marty Robbins' 'A White Sport Coat' became the first of his three UK Top 20s between in 1957 and 1958. His other big hits were 'Start Movin'', a cover of the Sal Mineo original and another Marty Robbins' song 'The Stairway Of Love'. Fame brought him many problems and in 1958 he was fined both for drunkenness and vandalism. This one-time screen extra starred in the 1958 unsuccessful British pop film *The Golden Disc*. Often referred to as 'Britain's Elvis', this singer - with an admitted history of mental disturbance - was inducted into the army with the full press treatment in 1959. A large battalion of media representatives was also present

when he was released as 'medically unfit' just two months later. The end of his short marriage to singer Edna Savage continued to give him the kind of publicity that destroyed what was left of his career. He next joined Larry Parnes stable of stars, but the legendary impresario could not salvage Dene's career. After abandoning pop music, he became a street-singing evangelist, recording three gospel albums. He spent five years living in Sweden and in 1978 a book and album, both called *I Thought Terry Dene Was Dead*, came out. In the 80s he returned to singing and rock 'n' roll with members of his original group, the Dene-Aces, which included Brian Gregg, writer of the classic 'Shakin' All Over'. Despite the fact that Dene was not a great rock 'n' roll original, he was welcomed back like a true legend by many UK fans.

Album: *I Thought Terry Dene Was Dead* (1978).

Further reading: *I Thought Terry Dene Was Dead*, Dan Wooding.

Dennis, Jackie

b. 1942, Edinburgh, Scotland. Dennis was discovered by UK comedians Mike and Bernie Winters, when he was performing at an American Air Force base in Prestwick. They brought him to the attention of top agent Eve Taylor and she instantly booked him on the *6.5 Special* television show. Dennis' impact was immediate and he was quickly added to the cast of the *6.5 Special* film and it was even announced that he was to start filming *The Jackie Dennis Story*. The future looked very bright indeed in 1958 for the kilt-wearing, lively 15-year-old pop singer whose first record 'La Dee Dah', a cover of Billy And Lillie's US hit, had leapt into the UK Top 20 just two weeks after its release. Television and live bookings flooded in and he was even invited to the USA to appear in Perry Como's top-rated television show where he was introduced as 'Britain's Ricky Nelson'. Despite all this, record buyers did not purchase his future releases in any quantity and he faded from the public eye just as quickly as he had arrived.

Dennis, Matt

b. 11 February 1914, Seattle, Washington, USA. A composer, singer and pianist, Dennis was born into a musical family. His father was a well-known singer and his mother played the violin; at one stage they were both part of a vaudeville act called The Five Musical Lovelands. Early in Dennis's life the family moved to Los Angeles, California, where he attended San Rafael High School, eventually directing the school's dance orchestra.

In 1933 he joined Horace Heidt's band as a pianist, and sang with Alice King, one of the King Sisters. Some years later he formed a band with Dick Haymes, and subsequently, served as an arranger and accompanist for Martha Tilton, Margaret Whiting and the Stafford Sisters. In 1940, when Jo Stafford became a member of the Pied Pipers with name band, Tommy Dorsey, she recommended Dennis as a staff arranger and composer. His compositions for the band, with lyrics by Tom Adair, included 'Everything Happens To Me', 'Violets For Your Furs' and 'Free For All', all recorded by Dorsey's boy vocalist, Frank Sinatra; 'Will You Still Be Mine?', sung by Connie Haines; and 'Let's Get Away From It All', which spanned both sides of a 78 rpm disc, and was swung by Sinatra, Jo Stafford, Connie Haines and the Pied Pipers. Stafford and the Dorsey band also performed Dennis's 'Little Man With A Candy Cigar', (lyric by Frank Kilduff). After three and a half years with the Radio Production Unit of the US Army Air Force during World War II, Dennis was much in demand, writing and performing on radio shows such as the *The Alan Young Show, The Chesterfield Supper Club* and the *Seven-Up Show*. He was also a regular performer at the smart Hollywood nightclubs, including the Tally-Ho, Encore and Captain's Table, and had his own NBC television show for a time. When Sinatra began his series of classic Capitol albums in the 50s, he gave the definitive reading to the Dennis/Adair ballad, 'Violets For Your Furs', on *Songs For Young Lovers*, and continued to include several more of the composer's works in his repertoire, such as 'The Night We Called It A Day' (Adair), and 'Angel Eyes' (Earl Brent). Dennis himself sang the latter song in the Iada Lunpino/Howard Duff film, *Jennifer* (1953). His first album, *Matt Dennis Plays And Sings*, was an early on-site recording at the Tally-Ho club, and featured his own songs, including 'Compared To You' (lyric by Paul Herrick), 'Tired Routine Called Love' (Ted Steele), 'It Wasn't In The Stars' (Dave Gillam), 'Junior And Julie' (Adair) and some of the other numbers he wrote for the Dorsey band, such as 'Will You Still Be Mine?', a 'list' song, which was amusingly updated in 1955 on *Buddy Greco At Mr. Kelly's*. Dennis's other compositions include 'Relax', 'Music', 'Show Me The Way To Get Out Of This World', 'Love Turns Winter To Spring', 'Blues For Breakfast', 'Who's Yehoodi?' (a 1940 novelty hit for both Kay Kyser and Jerry Colonna), and 'We Belong Together'. Among his many collaborators have been Jerry Gladstone, Sammy

Cahn, Bob Russell, and his wife, Ginny Maxey Dennis, who also produced *Matt Dennis Is Back!* in 1981. For some years before that he had concentrated on his music publishing interests and piano tutorials such as the 'Matt Dennis Popular Piano Method'. On the 1981 album he retained the inimitable touch and style which has, throughout his life, endeared him to the musical cognisant, but has not made him even nearly-famous. His melodies continue to surface, and one of the best of them, 'Violets For Your Furs', was performed by pianist Kenny Clayton at the 1993 memorial service for the celebrated entertainer, Bernard Braden.
Selected albums: *Matt Dennis Plays And Sings* (1954), *Dennis, Anyone?* (1956) *Welcome, Matt Dennis!* (1958), *Melancholy Baby* (1959), *Some Of My Favourites* (1960), *Matt Dennis Is Back!* (1981).

Diamonds

Dave Somerville (lead), Ted Kowalski (tenor), Bill Reed (bass) and Phil Leavitt (baritone), all born in Toronto, Canada. A white vocal group that specialised in cover versions of black R&B hits, the Diamonds were formed in 1953, and, during the next two years, attracted a good deal of attention on the club circuit in America's mid-west states. In 1955 they cut several sides for Decca's Coral label, including a cover of the Cheers' Top 10 single, 'Black Denim Trousers And Motor Cycle Boots'. Early in the following year they moved to Mercury, a label already highly skilled in re-creating existing hits, such as the Crew-Cuts' version of 'Sh-Boom' (1954), which was first released by the Chords. The Diamonds made their initial impact for Mercury with 'Why Do Fools Fall In Love', a number written by Frankie Lymon and George Goldner, and a Top 10 hit for Lymon and his Teenagers in 1956. The Diamonds' version made the US Top 20, and was followed, in the same year, by further successful substitutes for the originals, such as 'Church Bells May Ring' (Willows), 'Little Girl Of Mine' (Cleftones), 'Love, Love, Love' (Clovers), 'Ka Ding Dong' (G-Clefs), 'Soft Summer Breeze' (Eddie Heywood), and 'A Thousand Miles Away' (Heartbeats). 'Little Darlin'' (1957), written by Maurice Williams when he was lead singer with the Gladiolas, before he went on to the Zodiacs, gave the Diamonds their highest US chart entry (number 2), and subsequently became something of a rock 'n' roll classic. The group's remaining Top 40 hits in the 50s were 'Words Of Love', 'Zip Zip', 'Silhouettes' (also a million-seller for the Rays), 'The Stroll', 'High

Sign', 'Kathy-O' (a ballad, in a more easy listening style), 'Walking Along', and 'She Say Oom Dooby Doom'. In 1958 Phil Leavitt retired and was replaced by Michael Douglas, and, in the following year, two Californians, Evan Fisher and John Felton, took over from Bill Reed and Ted Kowalski. The 'new' Diamonds continued to record through the early 60s and had one Top 30 entry with 'One Summer Night' in 1961. After the group split up, Dave Somerville formed a double act with ex-Four Prep, Bruce Belland, until the Diamonds re-formed in the early 70s. Despite Felton's death in an air crash in 1982, the group continued to tour, and was especially popular on the county fair circuit into the 90s.
Selected albums: *The Diamonds* (1956), *The Diamonds Meet Pete Rugolo* (1958), *Pop Hits* (1960), *The Diamonds Sing The Songs Of The Old West* (1960). Compilation: *The Best Of The Diamonds* (1990).

Dion And The Belmonts

b. Dion DiMucci, 18 July 1939, Bronx, New York, USA. During his peak, from 1958-63, Dion was the quintessential Italian-American New York City rocker and was, perhaps, the first major white rock singer who was not from a southern city. The career of one of America's legendary artists has spanned five decades, during which time he has made numerous musical style changes. Between 1958 and 1960 Dion And The Belmonts were one of the leading doo-wop groups. The Belmonts comprised Angelo D'Aleo (b. 3 February 1940, Bronx, New York, USA), Carlo Mastrangelo (b. 5 October 1938, Bronx, New York, USA), and Freddie Milano (b. 22 August 1939, Bronx, New York, USA). The slick, besuited Italian-look rivalled the black harmony groups that dominated the era. They had nine hits in two years, including two of the all-time great examples of white doo-wop, 'I Wonder Why' and 'No One Knows'. Their classic reading of the Doc Pomus and Mort Shuman song 'Teenager in Love' with the memorable line of teenage despair; 'each night I ask, the stars up above, (bom, bom, bom, bom), why must I be a teenager in love?' It poignantly articulated growing pains in an era when conservative values were being challenged by a new moral climate.
In 1960 they attempted a version of 'When You Wish Upon A Star' from Walt Disney's *Pinocchio* and followed with a worthy cover of Cole Porter's 'In The Still Of The Night'. Dion left for a solo career in 1960 and immediately scored in the USA

with 'Lonely Teenager'. The following year he had two consecutive hits that made him one of America's biggest artists. Both 'Runaround Sue' and 'The Wanderer' are rock classics; the former, warning everybody to keep away from Sue, while the latter warns Flo, Jane and Mary to steer clear of the wanderer. The similarity of the theme can be forgiven as they are both wonderfully uplifting songs, great dance records and two of the finest of the era. Dion sustained an incredible output of hits; in 1963 with seven major singles he was in the US charts for the entire year. In 1964 Dion disappeared from the scene to fight a serious addiction to heroin, a drug to which he had fallen victim in 1960. Although he and the Belmonts reunited briefly in 1967, little was heard of him until December 1968. He returned during a turbulent year in American history, the escalation of the Vietnam War had received strong opposition, particularly from the music world; and the assassination of Robert Kennedy was fresh in peoples' minds. The emotional Dick Holler song, 'Abraham, Martin And John' was a perfectly timed stroke of genius. This lilting folksy ballad barley left a dry eye as it climbed to number 4 in the US charts.
The following year a heroin-free Dion delighted festival and concert audiences with a striking solo act, accompanied on acoustic guitar. That same year the excellent *Dion* was released, including sensitive covers of songs by Bob Dylan, Joni Mitchell, Leonard Cohen, and a brave attempt at Jimi Hendrix's 'Purple Haze'. Dion's critical ranking was high but his commercial standing dwindled, and two acoustic-based albums were commercial disasters. Wily entrepreneurs encouraged another reunion with the Belmonts in 1973, and in 1975 Phil Spector produced 'Born To Be With You'. An album *Born To Be With You* (on Spector's own label), failed, and one underrated album, *The Return Of The Wanderer*, came in 1978 on Lifesong Records. For the next few years Dion became a devout, born-again, Christian and recorded sporadically, releasing Christian albums including *Inside Job* and *Kingdom Of The Street*. He returned to rock 'n' roll in 1988 playing with Bruce Springsteen and released the Dave Edmunds produced *To Frankie*; he toured the UK as recently as 1990. Dion is one of the few survivors from a school of American vocalists who had genuine talent, and should be forever applauded for a series of great uplifting songs that still sound remarkably fresh. He was elected to the Rock and Roll Hall of Fame in 1989.

Albums: Dion And The Belmonts: *Presenting Dion And The Belmonts* (1959), *Wish Upon A Star* (1960), *Together Again* (1967), *By Special Request* (1963), Compilations: *20 Golden Greats* (1980), *Reunion* (1973). Dion: *Alone With Dion* (1961), *Runaround Sue* (1961), *Lovers Who Wander* (1962), *Dion Sings His Greatest Hits* (1962), *Love Came To Me* (1963), *Ruby Baby* (1963), *Donna The Prima Donna* (1963), *Dion Sings To Sandy* (1963), *Dion* (1968), *Sit Down Old Friend* (1969), *Wonder Where I'm Bound* (1969), *You're Not Alone* (1971), *Sanctuary* (1971), *Suite For Late Summer* (1972), *Born To Be With You* (1975), *Sweetheart* (1976), *The Return Of The Wanderer* (1978), *Inside Job* (1980), *Kingdom Of The Street* (1985), *Velvet And Steel* (1986), *Yo Frankie!* (1989), *Bronx Blues: The Columbia Recordings (1962-1965)* (1991).

Further reading: *The Wanderer*, Dion DiMucci with Davin Seay.

Domino, Fats

b. Antoine Domino, February 26 1928, New Orleans, Louisiana, USA. From a large family, he learned piano from local musician Harrison Verrett who was also his brother-in-law. A factory worker after leaving school, Domino played in local clubs such as the Hideaway. It was there in 1949 that bandleader Dave Bartholomew and Lew Chudd of Imperial Records heard him. His first recording, 'The Fat Man', became a Top 10 R&B hit the next year and launched his unique partnership with Bartholomew who co-wrote and arranged dozens of Domino tracks over the next two decades. Like that of Professor Longhair, Domino's playing was derived from the rich mixture of musical styles to be found in New Orleans. These included traditional jazz, Latin rhythms, boogie-woogie, Cajun and blues. Domino's personal synthesis of these influences involved lazy, rich vocals supported by rolling piano rhythms. On occasion his relaxed approach was at odds with the urgency of other R&B and rock artists and the Imperial engineers would frequently speed up the tapes before Domino's singles were released. During the early 50s, Domino gradually became one of the most successful R&B artists in America. Songs like 'Goin' Home' and 'Going To The River', 'Please Don't Leave Me' and 'Don't You Know' were best-sellers and he also toured throughout the country. The touring group included the nucleus of the band assembled by Dave Bartholomew for recordings at Cosimo Matassa's studio. Among the musicians were Lee Allen (saxophone), Frank Field (bass) and Waltet 'Papoose' Nelson (guitar).

By 1955, rock 'n' roll had arrived and young white audiences were ready for Domino's music. His first pop success came with 'Ain't That A Shame' in 1955, though Pat Boone's cover version sold more copies. 'Bo Weevil' was also covered, by Teresa Brewer but the catchy 'I'm In Love Again' with its incisive saxophone phrases from Allen took Domino into the pop Top 10. The b-side was the 20s standard 'My Blue Heaven', which Verrett had sung with Papa Celestin's New Orleans jazz band, given an up-tempo treatment. Domino's next big success also came with a pre-rock 'n' roll song, 'Blueberry Hill'. Inspired by Louis Armstrong's 1949 version, Domino used his creole drawl to perfection. Altogether, Fats Domino had nearly 20 US Top 20 singles in the six years between 1955 and 1960. Among the last of them was the majestic 'Walking To New Orleans', a Bobby Charles composition which became a string-laden tribute to the sources of his musical inspiration. His track record in the *Billboard* R&B lists however is impressive, with 63 records making the charts. He continued to record prolifically for Imperial until 1963, maintaining a consistently high level of performance. There were original compositions like the jumping 'My Girl Josephine' and 'Let the Four Winds Blow' and covers of country songs (Hank Williams' 'Jambalaya') as well as standard ballads like 'Red Sails In The Sunset', his final hit single in 1963. The complex off-beat of 'Be My Guest' was a clear precursor of the ska rhythms of Jamaica, where Domino was popular and toured in 1961. The only unimpressive moments came when he was persuaded to jump on the twist bandwagon, recording a number titled 'Dance With Mr Domino'.

By now, Lew Chudd had sold the Imperial company and Domino had switched labels to ABC Paramount. There he recorded several albums with producers Felton Jarvis and Bill Justis, but his continuing importance was in his tours of North America and Europe which re-created the sound of the 50s for new generations of listeners. The quality of Domino's touring band was well captured on a 1965 live album for Mercury from Las Vegas with Roy Montrell, (guitar), Cornelius Coleman (drums) and the saxophones of Herb Hardesty and Lee Allen. Domino continued this pattern of work into the 70s, breaking the pattern slightly when he gave the Beatles' 'Lady Madonna' a New Orleans treatment. He made further albums for Reprise (1968) and Sonet (1979), the Reprise sides being the results of a reunion session with Dave Bartholomew. In 1991, EMI which now owns the Imperial catalogue, released a scholarly box-set of Domino's remarkable recordings. He remains a giant figure of R&B musically and physically.

Selected albums: *Carry On Rockin'* (1955), *Fats Domino - Rock and Rollin'* (1956), *This Is Fats Domino!* (1957), *Here Stands Fats Domino* (1958), *Fabulous Mr D* (1958), *Let's Play Fats Domino* (1959), *Fats Domino Sings* (1960), *I Miss You So* (1961), *Twistin' The Stomp* (1962), *Just Domino* (1963), *Here Comes Fats Domino* (1963), *Fats On Fire* (1964), *Fats Domino '65* (1965), *Getaway With Fats Domino* (1966), *Fats Is Back* (1968), *Sleeping On The Job* (1979). Numerous compilations are always available.

Dominoes (see Ward, Billy, And The Dominoes)

Donegan, Lonnie

b. Anthony Donegan, 29 April 1931, Glasgow, Scotland. Donegan as 'The King Of Skiffle' became a more homogeneous UK equivalent to Elvis Presley than Tommy Steele. Steeped in traditional jazz and its by-products, he was a guitarist in a skiffle band before a spell in the army found him drumming in the Wolverines Jazz Band. After his discharge, he played banjo with Ken Colyer and then Chris Barber. With his very stage forename a tribute to a black bluesman, both units allowed him to sing a couple of blues-tinged American folk tunes as a 'skiffle' break. His version of Leadbelly's 'Rock Island Line', issued from Barber's *New Orleans Joys* in 1954 as a single after months in the domestic hit parade, was also a US hit. Donegan's music inspired thousands of teenagers to form amateur skiffle combos, with friends playing broomstick tea chest bass, washboards and other instruments fashioned from household implements. The Beatles, playing initially as the Quarrymen, were a foremost example of an act traceable to such roots.

With his own group, Donegan was a prominent figure in skiffle throughout its 1957 prime; he possessed an energetic whine far removed from the gentle plumminess of other native pop vocalists. Donegan could dazzle with his virtuosity on 12-string acoustic guitar and his string of familiar songs have rarely been surpassed: 'Don't You Rock Me

Lonnie Donegan (second right)

Daddy-O', 'Putting On The Style' ('putting on the agony, putting on the style'), 'Bring A Little Water Sylvie', 'Grand Coulee Dam', 'Does Your Chewing Gum Lose Its Flavour On The Bedpost Over Night' and 'Jimmy Brown The Newsboy', were but a few of Donegan's gems. He arguably made the traditional song 'Cumberland Gap' his own (his first UK number 1) and 1959's 'Battle Of New Orleans' was the finest-ever reading. He delved deeper into Americana to embrace bluegrass, spirituals, Cajun and even Appalachian music, the formal opposite of jazz. However, when the skiffle boom diminished, he broadened his appeal - to much purist criticism - with olde tyme music hall/pub singalong favourites, and a more pronounced comedy element. His final chart-topper was with the uproarious 'My Old Man's A Dustman', which sensationally entered the UK charts at number 1 in 1960. The hit was an adaptation of the ribald Liverpool folk ditty, 'My Old Man's A Fireman On The Elder-Dempster Line'. He followed it with further comedy numbers including 'Lively' in 1960. Two years later, Donegan's Top 20 run ended as it had started, with a Leadbelly number ('Pick A Bale Of Cotton'). However, between 1956 and 1962 he had numbered 34 hits.

He finished the 60s with huge sales of two mid-price *Golden Age Of Donegan* volumes, supplementing his earnings in cabaret and occasional spots on BBC television's *The Good Old Days*. The most interesting diversion of the next decade was Adam Faith's production of *Putting On The Style*. Here, at Paul McCartney's suggestion, Donegan re-made old smashes backed by an extraordinary glut of artists who were lifelong fans, including; Rory Gallagher, Ringo Starr, Leo Sayer, Zoot Money, Albert Lee, Gary Brooker, Brian May, Nicky Hopkins, Elton John and Ron Wood. While this album brushed 1978's UK album list, a 1982 single, 'Spread A Little Happiness', was also a minor success - and, as exemplified by the Traveling Wilburys 'skiffle for the 90s', the impact of Donegan's earliest chart entries continues to exert its influence on pop music. Although no longer enjoying the best of health, Donegan continues to entertain. He has long been an influential legend and clearly the man who was British skiffle music.

Selected albums: *Showcase* (1956), *Lonnie* (1958), *Tops With Lonnie* (1959), *Lonnie Rides Again* (1959), *More Tops With Lonnie* (1960), *Sings Hallelujah* (1962), *The Lonnie Donegan Folk Album* (1965), *Golden Hour Of Donegan Vol 1 & 2* (c.60s), *Lonniepops-Lonnie Donegan Today* (1970), *Lonnie Donegan Meets Leineman* (1974), *Lonnie Donegan* (1975), *Lonnie Donegan Meets Leineman-Country Roads* (1976), *Putting On The Style* (1977), *Sundown* (1978), *Jubilee Concert* (1981), *Greatest Hits: Lonnie Donegan* (1983), *Rare And Unissued Gems* (1985), *Rock Island Line* (1985), *The Hit Singles Collection* (1987), *The Best Of Lonnie Donegan* (1989), *The Collection: Lonnie Donegan* (1989), *Putting On The Styles* (1992, 3 CD set).

Dot Records

Formed in 1951 in Gallatin, Tennessee, USA by Randy Wood, proprietor of one of the region's largest mail-order record stores. Although initially an R&B outlet, Dot enjoyed a pop hit the following year with the Hilltoppers' 'Trying'. Group member Billy Vaughn became the company's musical director, as crooner Pat Boone and actor Tab Hunter established themselves as Dot's major signings. The former built his reputation by sanitizing material plundered from Little Richard and Fats Domino, before establishing an MOR/pop career with 'I'll Be Home', 'I Almost Lost My Mind' (1956), 'Love Letters In The Sand' and 'April Love' (1957). Thirteen of the artist's singles sold in excess of 1 million copies, and his rather languorous singing style set the tone for much of Dot's later, often conservative, output. The company did record Nervous Norvus, a novelty-cum-rockabilly act best recalled for the gruesome 'Transfusion', and Gale Storm, but was unable, or unwilling, to shake of an increasingly staid image. By the end of the 50s Wood had moved his operation to Los Angeles and he later sold the entire company to the Gulf Western/Paramount conglomerate. The Dot catalogue was later acquired by the ABC group. Compilation: *Golden Instrumentals* (1967).

Douglas, Craig

b. Terence Perkins, 12 August 1941, Newport, Isle Of Wight, England. After moving to London in the mid-50s, Douglas came under the wing of agent Bunny Lewis, appeared on the television show *6.5 Special*, and won a record contract with Decca before moving to Dick Rowe's label, Top Rank. Covering American hits was the classic route to chart success, and in 1959 Douglas scored with Dion's 'A Teenager In Love' and reached number 1 with Sam Cooke's 'Only Sixteen'. He co-starred with Helen Shapiro in the film *It's Trad Dad* (1961). Several more hits followed but after four consecutive number 9s with 'A Hundred

Pounds Of Clay', 'Time', 'When My Little Girl Is Smiling' and 'Our Favourite Melodies', Craig felt the sting of the approaching beat boom. He then travelled the world, returning for a career in cabaret in the UK, where he still resides. In 1992 he joined another 60s survivor, Helen Shapiro, on the Walkin' Back To Happiness Tour.
Albums: *Craig Douglas* (1960), *Bandwagon Ball* (1961), *Our Favourite Melodies* (1962). Compilation: *The Best Of The EMI Years* (1993).

Drake, Charlie

b. Charles Sprigall, 19 June 1925, London, England. Actor/comedian Charlie Drake was instantly recognizable with his shock of red hair, diminutive 5 feet 1 inch frame and distinctive cockney voice. In 1958, he hit the UK charts, outselling Bobby Darin with a cover version of 'Splish Splash'. Further hits followed over the next three years, including 'Volare', 'Mr. Custer' and 'My Boomerang Won't Come Back'. The latter was co-written by Drake, in collaboration with Max Diamond. The duo also provided Drake's theme song and catchphrase 'Hullo, My Darlings!'. With strong managerial backing from Colonel Bill Alexander and the producing talents of George Martin, Drake was in good hands and his comedy workouts translated well on to disc. Although he continued recording, acting commitments increasingly took precedence, although he did make a brief chart reappearance in 1972 with 'Puckwudgie'.

Draper, Rusty

b. Farrell Draper, Kirksville, Missouri, USA. Draper entered show business at the age of 12, singing and playing his guitar on radio in Tulsa, Oklahoma. For the next five years, he worked on various stations including Des Moines, Iowa and Quincy, Illinois. He then became the Master of Ceremonies and vocalist at the Mel Hertz Club in San Francisco. He eventually moved to Hermie King's Rumpus Room in the same city, where he stayed for the next seven years. In 1953, his recording of 'Gambler's Guitar' reached number 6 on both the US country and pop charts and gave him his first million-seller. A second gold record followed in 1955 for his version of 'Shifting Whispering Sands', which reached number 3 in the pop charts but surprisingly did not even make the country chart at all. (A cover version by Eamonn Andrews made the UK Top 20). During the 50s, he had further US Top 40 pop hits with 'Seventeen' (1955), 'Are You Satisfied' (1955), 'In

The Middle Of The House' (1956) and a US cover version of the UK skiffle hit 'Freight Train' (1957). He did, however, have modest UK pop chart success in 1960 with his version of 'Muleskinner Blues', which peaked at number 39. In 1962, he joined Monument Records and made the US pop charts with 'Night Life' in 1963. He did not achieve further US country chart successes until the late 60s, when he had very minor hits with 'My Elusive Dreams', 'California Sunshine' and 'Buffalo Nickel'. 'Two Little Boys' gave him another minor US hit in 1970, the last for 10 years, when 'Harbour Lights', an unlikely country song, became his last chart entry. During his career, he has also played several acting roles, including appearances in some television western series such as *Rawhide* and *Laramie*, and stage musicals including *Oklahoma!* and *Annie Get Your Gun*.
Albums: *Hits That Sold A Million* (c.60s), *Sing Along* (c.60s), *Country Classics* (c.60s), *Rusty Draper Plays Guitar* (c.60s), *Night Life* (c.60s), *Something Old Something New* (1969).

Dream Weavers

A vocal group consisting of three college students, two men and a girl, based in Miami, Florida, USA. The Dream Weavers were born out of necessity when Wade Buff and Eugene Atkinson were unable to find an artist to record their composition, 'It's Always Tomorrow'. After exposure on the college radio station, their own self-financed recording was picked up by Decca Records and entered the US Top 10 in 1955. It did even better in the UK, climbing to the very top of the charts in the following year. Subsequently, the Dream Weavers had a minor hit with Sammy Fain and Paul Francis Webster's 'A Little Love Can Go A Long, Long Way', from the film, *Ain't Misbehavin'*, but then disappeared without a trace. 'It's Always Tomorrow' also charted in the US for Jo Stafford, Snooky Lanson and David Carroll in the 50s, and was a UK hit for Mark Wynter in 1963.

Drifters

Formed in 1953 in New York, USA, at the behest of Atlantic Records, this influential R&B vocal group was initially envisaged as a vehicle for ex-Dominoes' singer, Clyde McPhatter, Gerhart Thrasher, Andrew Thrasher and Bill Pinkney completed the new quartet which, as Clyde McPhatter And The Drifters, scored a number 1 R&B hit with their debut single, 'Money Honey'. Follow-up releases, including 'Such A Night', 'Lucille' and 'Honey Love' (a second chart-topper), also proved highly successful, while the juxtaposition of McPhatter's soaring tenor against the frenzied support of the other members provided a link between gospel and rock 'n' roll styles. The leader's interplay with bassist Pinkey breathed new life into 'White Christmas', the group's sixth R&B hit, but McPhatter's induction into the armed forces in 1954 was a blow the Drifters struggled to withstand. The vocalist opted for a solo career upon leaving the services, and although his former group did enjoy success with 'Adorable' (number 1 R&B 1955), 'Steamboat' (1955), 'Ruby Baby' (1956) and 'Fools Fall In Love' (1957), such recordings featured a variety of lead singers, including David Baughn and Johnny Moore. A greater emphasis on pop material ensued, but tension between the group and manager, George Treadwell, resulted in an irrevocable split. Having fired the extant line-up in 1958, Treadwell, who owned the copyright to the Drifters' name, invited another act, the Five Crowns, to adopt the appellation. Ben E. King (tenor), Charlie Thomas (tenor), Doc Green Jnr. (baritone) and Elsbury Hobbs (bass), plus guitarist Reggie Kimber, duly became 'the Drifters', and declared their newfound role with 'There Goes My Baby'. Written and produced by Leiber And Stoller, this pioneering release contained a Latin rhythm and string section, the first time such embellishments had appeared on an R&B recording. The single not only topped the R&B chart, it also reached number 2 on the US pop listings, and anticipated the 'symphonic' style later developed by Phil Spector.

Further excellent releases followed, notably 'Dance With Me' (1959), 'This Magic Moment' (1960) and 'Save The Last Dance For Me', the last-named of which topped the US pop chart and reached number 2 in the UK. However, King left for a solo career following 'I Count The Tears' (1960), and was replaced by Rudy Lewis, who fronted the group until his premature death in 1964. The Drifters continued to enjoy hits during this period and songs such as 'Sweets For My Sweet', 'When My Little Girl Is Smiling', 'Up On The Roof' and 'On Broadway' were not only entertaining in their own right, but also provided inspiration, and material, for many emergent British acts, notably the Searchers, who took the first-named song to the top of the UK chart. Johnny Moore, who had returned to the line-up in 1963, took over the lead vocal slot from Lewis. 'Under The Boardwalk', recorded the day after the latter's passing, was the Drifters' last US Top 10 pop hit, although the

group remained a popular attraction. Bert Berns had taken over production from Leiber and Stoller, and in doing so brought a soul-based urgency to their work, as evinced by 'One Way Love' and 'Saturday Night At The Movies' (1964). When he left Atlantic to found the Bang label, the Drifters found themselves increasingly overshadowed by newer, more contemporary artists and, bedevilled by lesser material and frequent changes in personnel, the group began to slip from prominence. However their career was revitalized in 1972 when two re-released singles, 'At The Club' and 'Come On Over To My Place', reached the UK Top 10. A new recording deal with Bell was then secured and British songwriters/producers Tony Macauley, Roger Cook and Roger Greenaway fashioned a series of singles redolent of the Drifters' 'classic' era. Purists poured scorn on their efforts, but, between 1973 and 1975, the group, still led by Moore, enjoyed six UK Top 10 hits, including 'Come On Over To My Place', 'Kissin' In The Back Row Of The Movies', 'Down On The Beach Tonight' and 'There Goes My First Love'. This success ultimately waned as the decade progressed, and in 1982 Moore left the line-up. He was replaced, paradoxically, by Ben E. King who in turn brought the Drifters back to Atlantic. However, despite completing some new recordings, the group found it impossible to escape its heritage, as evinced by the numerous 'hits' repackages and corresponding live appearances on the cabaret and nostalgia circuits.

Selected albums: *Save The Last Dance For Me* (1961), *The Good Life With The Drifters* (1964), *I'll Take You Where The Music's Playing* (1965), *Souvenirs, Love Games* (1975), *There Goes My First Love* (1975), *Every Night's A Saturday Night* (1976), *Greatest Hits Live* (1984). Selected compilations: *The Drifters Greatest Hits, Our Biggest Hits* (1964), *The Drifters' Golden Hits, Rockin' And Driftin', Good Gravy* (1964), *The Drifters' Story, 24 Original Hits, Diamond Series: The Drifters* (1988), *Kissin' In The Back Row: The 70s Classics* (1993).

Duncan, Johnny, And The Blue Grass Boys

b. John Franklin Duncan, 7 September 1931, Oliver Springs, near Knoxville, Tennessee, USA. Duncan sang from an early age in a church choir and then, when aged 13, he joined a gospel quartet. At 16, he left Tennessee for Texas and whilst there, he formed a country group. Duncan was conscripted into the US army in 1952 and posted to England. He married an English woman,

Betty, in 1953. After his demobilization, they went to the USA. Betty returned home for Christmas 1955 and, as she fell ill and needed an operation, Duncan worked in the UK for his father-in-law. He met jazz bandleader Chris Barber, who was looking to replace Lonnie Donegan. Donegan had formed his own skiffle group, a fashion he had started with Barber's band. Barber was impressed by Duncan's nasal vocal delivery and physical resemblance to Donegan and immediately recruited him, and he joined them the following night at London's Royal Festival Hall. In 1957 Duncan left the band and called his own group, the Blue Grass Boys, in homage to Bill Monroe, but they were all British - Denny Wright (guitar), Jack Fallon (bass), Danny Levan (violin), Lennie Hastings (drums). Although promoted as a skiffle artist, Duncan was a straight country performer, both in terms of arrangements and repertoire. 'Last Train To San Fernando', a Trinidad calypso he re-arranged, steamed up the UK charts but the communication cord was pulled just before it reached the top. The b-side, 'Rock-A-Billy Baby', was equally strong. Duncan was featured on BBC television's *6.5 Special* and hosted radio programmes for the BBC and Radio Luxembourg, but he only had two more Top 30 entries, 'Blue Blue Heartache' and 'Footprints In The Snow', both reaching number 27. Duncan worked as a country singer in UK clubs and encouraged local talent. In 1974 he emigrated to Melbourne, Australia where he has worked as a country singer.
Albums: *Johnny Duncan's Tennessee Songbag* (1957), *Johnny Duncan Salutes Hank Williams* (1958), *Beyond The Sunset* (1961), *Back In Town* (1970), *The World Of Country Music* (1973).

E

Eager, Vince
One of the many UK rock/pop artists of the late 50s Eager was one of the more promising singers in the Larry Parnes stable of stars. Launched in the spring of 1958 and christened Eager because of his enthusiastic personality, the vocalist was featured on several prestigious television shows, most notably Jack Good's pioneering *Oh Boy*. He seemed a strong bet to follow Parnes' other acts, Tommy Steele and Marty Wilde, into the UK charts but, despite a series of singles written by such name writers as Floyd Robinson, Marty Robbins, Conway Twitty and Gene Pitney, chart success proved elusive. Eager also received regular star billing on the BBC Television series *Drumbeat*, but his career prospects receded when he split with Parnes. In later years, he featured in the stage production of the musical *Elvis*.

Earl, Robert
b. 17 November 1926, England. This popular ballad singer enjoyed several UK hits in the late 50s. After becoming a semi-professional with the dance bands of Sidney Lipton and Nat Temple, he turned full-time professional in 1950, and appeared frequently on radio and television programmes such as the *Jack Jackson Show* and *Off The Record*. In 1958, he just beat Perry Como to the UK chart with his version of 'I May Never Pass This Way Again'. Later that year, however, his 'More Than Ever (Come Prima)' was kept out of the Top 10 by Malcolm Vaughan. Earl's last hit was 'Wonderful Secret Of Love', in 1959. During the 60s, he retained a small but faithful audience. Subsequently, Earl's occasional releases, such as *Robert Earl Showcase* and *Shalom*, often featured Jewish favourites, including 'Yaas', 'My Son, My Son' and 'Mom-e-le'. Favourably reviewed in a London cabaret appearance in 1991 the 'veteran song stylist' maintained the Hebrew connection by including 'If I Was A Rich Man' from *Fiddler On The Roof*, among a selection of other nostalgic items.
Earl's son, also named Robert, is listed amongst the UK's Top 100 richest people. In his early 40s, he heads the Hard Rock Cafe chain, and co-owns Planet Hollywood, 'New York's newest eating experience', along with Bruce Willis, Sylvester Stallone and Arnold Schwarzenegger.
Selected album: *Robert Earl Showcase* (1961).

Eckstine, Billy
b. William Clarence Eckstein, 8 July 1914, Pittsburgh, Pennsylvania, USA, d. 8 March 1993, Pittsburgh, Pennsylvania, USA. Eckstine possessed one of the most distinctive voices in popular music, a deep tone with a unique vibrato. He began singing at the age of 11 but until his late teens was undecided between a career as a singer or football player. He won a sporting scholarship but soon

Vince Eager

afterwards broke his collar bone and decided that singing was less dangerous. He worked mostly in the north-eastern states in the early 30s and towards the end of the decade joined the Earl Hines band in Chicago. Although far from being a jazz singer, opting instead for a highly sophisticated form of balladry, Eckstine clearly loved working with jazz musicians and in particular the young experimenters who drifted into the Hines band in the early 40s, among them Wardell Gray, Dizzy Gillespie and Charlie Parker. While with Hines he developed into a competent trumpeter and, later, valve trombonist having first mimed as a trumpet player in order to circumvent union rules. In 1943, acting on the advice and encouragement of Budd Johnson, Eckstine formed his own band. Although his original intention was to have a band merely to back his vocals, Eckstine gathered together an exciting group of young bebop musicians and thus found himself leader of what was really the first true bebop big band. During the band's four-year existence its ranks were graced by Gray, Parker, Gillespie, Gene Ammons, Dexter Gordon, Miles Davis, Kenny Dorham, Fats Navarro and Art Blakey, playing arrangements by Gillespie, Johnson, Tadd Dameron, Gil Fuller and Jerry Valentine. Eckstine also hired the Hines band's other singer, Sarah Vaughan. In 1947 the band folded but had already served as an inspiration to Gillespie who formed his own bebop big band that year. Eckstine's commercial recordings during the life of the big band were mostly ballads which he wrapped in his deep, liquid baritone voice and with his bandleading days behind him he continued his career as a successful solo singer. He gained a huge international reputation as a stylish balladeer. During his long career Eckstine had many hit records including 'Jelly, Jelly', recorded in 1940 with Hines, 'Skylark', 'Everything I Have Is Yours', 'I Apologize' (stylistically covered by P.J. Proby to great success), 'Prisoner Of Love', 'Cottage For Sale', 'No One But You' (number three in the UK charts in 1954), 'Gigi' (number eight in 1959), and several duets with Vaughan of which the best-known was 'Passing Strangers' which, although recorded a dozen years earlier, reached number 17 in the 1969 charts. In recent times Eckstine recorded a new single with Ian Levine as part of his Motown revival project on the Motor City label.

Albums: *Live At Club Plantation, Los Angeles* (1945), *Sarah Vaughan And Billy Eckstine: The Irving Berlin Songbook* (1957), *Imagination* (1958), *Basie, Eckstine Inc.* (1959), *Billy's Best* (1959), *Once More With Feeling* (1959), *No Cover, No Minimum* (1959), *Billy Eckstine And Quincy Jones At Basin Street East* (1961), *I Apologize* (c.1960), *Feel The Warm* (c.1971), *The Prime Of My Life* (c.70s), *I'm A Singer* (c.1984), *Billy Eckstine Sings With Benny Carter* (1986). Compilations: *Mr B And The Band* (1945-47), *Together* (1945-47), *Everything I Have Is Yours* (1949-57).

Eddy, Duane

b. 26 April 1938, Corning, New York, USA. The legendary simple 'twangy' guitar sound of Duane Eddy has made him one of rock 'n' roll's most famous instrumental artists. The sound was created after hearing Bill Justis's famous 'Raunchy' (the song that George Harrison first learned to play). Together with producer Lee Hazelwood, Eddy co-wrote a deluge of hits mixed with versions of standards, using the bass strings of his Grestch guitar recorded through an echo chamber. The debut 'Movin' 'N' Groovin'' made the lower end of the US chart, and for the next six years Eddy repeated this formula with greater success. His backing group, the Rebel Rousers was a tight, experienced unit with a prominent saxophone sound played by Jim Horn and Steve Douglas, completed by pianist Larry Knechtel. Among their greatest hits were 'Rebel-Rouser', 'Shazam', 'Peter Gunn', 'Ballad Of Paladin' and 'Theme From Dixie'. The latter was a variation on the Civil War standard written in 1860. One of Eddy's most memorable hits was the superlative theme music for the film *Because They're Young*, brilliantly combining his bass notes with evocative strings. The song has been used by UK disc jockey Johnny Walker as his theme music for over 25 years and this classic still sounds fresh. Eddy's '(Dance With The) Guitar Man' was another major hit, which was unusual for the fact that the song had lyrics, sung by a female group. Eddy's albums played heavily on the use of 'twang' in the title, but that was exactly what the fans wanted.

The hits dried up in 1964 at the dawn of the Beatles' invasion, and for many years his sound was out of fashion. An attempt in the contemporary market was lambasted with *Duane Goes Dylan*. Apart from producing Phil Everly's excellent *Star Spangled Springer* in 1973, Eddy travelled the revival circuit, always finding a small but loyal audience in the UK. Tony Macauley wrote 'Play Me Like You Play Your Guitar' for him in 1975, and after more than a decade he was back in the UK Top 10. He slipped back into relative obscurity but returned to the charts in 1986 when he was flattered to be

Billy Eckstine

asked to play with the electro-synthesizer unit Art Of Noise, all the more complimentary was that it was his song, 'Peter Gunn'. The following year Jeff Lynne produced his first album for many years, being joined by Paul McCartney, George Harrison and Ry Cooder, all paying tribute to the man who should have legal copyright on the word 'twang'.
Selected albums: *Have Twangy Guitar Will Travel* (1958), *Especially For You* (1958), *The 'Twang's The 'Thang'* (1959), *Songs Of Our Heritage* (1960), *$1,000,000 Worth Of Twang* (1960), *Girls! Girls! Girls!* (1961), *$1,000,000 Worth Of Twang Volume 2* (1962), *Twistin' And Twangin'* (1962), *Twisting With Duane Eddy* (1962), *Twangy Guitar-Silky Strings* (1962), *Dance With The Guitar Man* (1963), *In Person* (1963), *Surfin' With Duane Eddy* (1963), *Twang A Country Song* (1963), *Twanging Up A Storm!* (1963), *Lonely Guitar* (1964), *Water Skiing* (1964), *Best Of* (1965), *Twangsville* (1965), *Duane Goes Bob Dylan* (1965), *Duane A Go Go* (1965), *Biggest Twang Of Them All* (1966), *Roaring Twangies* (1967), *Twangy Guitar* (1970), *Legends Of Rock* (1975), *Twenty Terrific Twangies* (1981), *Duane Eddy* (1987), *Greatest Hits* (1991).

Edelhagen, Kurt

b. 5 June 1920, Herne, Germany, d. 8 February 1982. Edelhagen first came to prominence in the years immediately following World War II. Although the prompt formation of a symphony orchestra is often cited as a notable attempt to re-establish an element of culture in post-war German society, the formation of a radio big band is rather more striking. The Berlin Philharmonic Orchestra had never really stopped playing, but dance music, especially that with a jazz-orientation, had been frowned upon by the defeated regime. In these circumstances the speed with which Edelhagen, who had been playing piano in clubs for the Allied armies, formed a big band of such a high quality was quite remarkable. His first band was in operation before the end of 1946 and thereafter he developed a series of radio big bands that continued into the early 70s. He was one of the first post-war European bandleaders to bring in foreign jazz musicians and among those who were featured in his bands were Jimmy Deuchar, Derek Humble, Dusko Goykovich and Jiggs Whigham. The various orchestras Edelhagen led featured a wide range of big-band music, with a bias towards a powerful brassy ensemble playing that reflected his love for Stan Kenton's style.
Albums: *Big Band Jazz From Germany* (1955), *Big Band Jazz* (1957), *Kurt Edelhagen And His Orchestra* i (1959), *Kurt Edelhagen And His Orchestra* ii (1959), *Kurt Edelhagen And His Orchestra* iii (1964), *Live At Lucerna Hall, Prague* (1965), *Swing Goodies* (1965), *Kurt Edelhagen And His Orchestra* iv (1972), *Heidelberger Jazztage 1972* (1972).

Edsels

This R&B five-piece from Youngstown, Ohio, USA led by George Jones Jnr. (lead vocal), also included Marshall Sewell (bass/vocals). They were named after the popular make of car. In 1959 they auditioned for a local music publisher who helped them get a deal. Their debut single was the fast doo-wop outing 'Rama Lama Ding Dong' (written by Jones), originally released under the incorrect title of 'Lama Rama Ding Dong'. It was a local hit but flopped nationally. Two years later when Marcels had a big hit with the similar sounding doo-wop version of 'Blue Moon', a disc jockey was reminded of 'Rama Lama Ding Dong' and started playing it. Demand grew and it was re-released under its correct title and became a hit in the US. By this time the Edsels had moved on and could not capitalize on their success. Although the original failed in the UK the song was a hit in 1978 when it was covered by Rocky Sharpe And The Replays.

Edwards, Tommy

b. 17 February 1922, Richmond, Virginia, USA. d. 22 October 1969, Virginia, USA. This jazz/pop/R&B singer-songwriter, began his professional career in 1931. He wrote the hit 'That Chick's Too Young To Fry' for Louis Jordan in 1946. A demo recording of his own 'All Over Again' later won Edwards an MGM contract. Early releases included 'It's All In The Game' (US number 18 in 1951), a tune based on a 1912 melody by future US Vice-President Charles Gates Dawes. Edwards re-recorded the song in 1958 in a 'beat-ballad' arrangement, hitting number 1 on both sides of the Atlantic and eventually selling 3.5 million. The song was an indisputable classic of its era, highlighted by Edwards's strong, masterful vocal. The song was covered many times and provided hits for Cliff Richard (1963-64) and the Four Tops (1970) and was a notable album track by Van Morrison (1979). Edwards himself scored five more hits during the next two years, including 'Love Is All We Need' and remakes of earlier successes 'Please Mr. Sun' and 'The Morning Side Of The Mountain'.
Selected albums: *For Young Lovers* (1958), *You Started Me Dreaming* (1959), *Sings* (1960), *It's All In*

Duane Eddy

The Game (1960), *Step Out Singing* (1960), *Golden Country Hits* (1961), *Stardust (*1962), *Tommy Edwards* (1965). Compilations: *Greatest Hits* (1961), *The Very Best Of* (1963).

Elegants

Formed in the mid-50s in Staten Island, New York City, New York, USA, the Elegants were a white doo-wop group. They gained a US number 1 single, 'Little Star', only to disappear from the charts permanently thereafter. The group consisted of lead vocalist Vito Picone (b. 17 March 1940), Carman Romano (b. 17 August 1939), James Moschella (b. 10 May 1938), Frank Tardogono (b. 18 September 1941) and Arthur Venosa (b. 3 September 1939). Picone and Romano had recorded unsuccessfully with another group, the Crescents, before forming with new singers as the Elegants. Their 'Little Star', built around the Mozart melody 'Twinkle, Twinkle Little Star', was a favourite of audiences and the group recorded it in mid-1958. The Elegants did not follow up their success for over a year, and further releases did not chart. Although the members went their separate ways, Picone was still leading an version of the group in the early 90s. They did not record any albums.

Elektra Records

Founded in New York, USA in 1950 by student and traditional music enthusiast Jac Holtzman, this much respected label initially showcased recordings drawn from America's rich heritage. Early releases included Jean Ritchie's *Songs Of Her Kentucky Mountain Family* and Ed McCurdy's *Songs Of The Old West*, but the catalogue also boasted collections encompassing material from international sources. Elektra also made several notable jazz and blues recordings but, as the 50s progressed, became renowned for its interest in contemporary folk. It thus attracted many of the performers from the Greenwich Village and New England enclaves, notably Judy Collins, Tom Paxton, Koerner, Ray And Glover, Fred Neil and Phil Ochs, before embracing electric styles in 1966 with the Paul Butterfield Blues Band and Love. Elektra then became established on America's west coast and its transformation from folk to rock was confirmed the following year with the Doors. Subsequent signings included the MC5, Rhinoceros, the Stooges and Earth Opera, while the label achieved concurrent commercial success with Bread. Elektra also became an important outlet for many singer-songwriter's, and its catalogue included superior releases by David Ackles, Tom Rush, Tim Buckley, Harry Chapin, Incredible String Band and Carly Simon. In 1971 Elektra was absorbed into the WEA conglomerate and incongruous releases by the New Seekers and Queen robbed the company of its individuality. Two years later, and with the departure of Holtzman, the label was amalgamated with Asylum and for much of the decade remained the junior partner. Television's *Marquee Moon* rekindled memories of the outlet's classic era, while during the 80s Elektra was responsible for releases by 10,000 Maniacs, the Screaming Blue Messiahs and the Pixies (the latter US only). The label was unwilling, or unable, to shake off its early heritage which was commemorated in a series of boxed sets under the umbrella title *The Jac Holtzman Years*. Elektra's 40th anniversary was celebrated with *Rubiayat*, in which representatives from the current roster performed songs drawn from the 'classic' era.
Recommended listening: *What's Shakin'* (1966), *Select Elektra* (1967), *Begin Here* (1969), *O Love Is Teasing: Anglo-American Mountain Balladry* (1983), *Bleecker & MacDougal: The Folk Scene Of The 60s* (1983), *Crossroads: White Blues In The 60s* (1985), *Elektrock: The Sixties* (c.1985).

Ellington, Ray

b. 1915, London, England, d. 28 February 1985. Ellington began playing drums as a teenager and by 1937 was sufficiently proficient to replace Joe Daniels in Harry Roy's popular band. He remained with Roy for almost five years, although his personal musical taste tended more towards the new jazz styles, and soon after the end of World War II he was playing bop in London clubs. He led his own quartet at this time and made a number of records, and sometimes accompanied visiting American jazzmen. He began to incorporate comedy and novelty material into his repertoire but the group's musical base was always strongly bop-influenced. Throughout the 50s the quartet was regularly featured on *The Goon Show* on BBC radio, usually with Ellington singing, and he also took small acting roles in the programme. By the 60s and with the passing of *The Goon Show*, Ellington was much less in demand, but he continued playing until shortly before his death in February 1985. His son, Lance Ellington, played trombone with the National Youth Jazz Orchestra and also sang as a member of the pop duo Coffee And Cream.
Album: *Goon Show Hits* (1958), *You're the Talk Of The Town* (1975).

Everly Brothers

Don (b. 1 February 1937, Brownie, Kentucky, USA) and Phil (b. 19 January 1939, Chicago, Illinois, USA), the world's most famous rock 'n' roll duo had already experienced a full career before their first record 'Bye Bye Love' was released. As sons of popular country artists Ike and Margaret, they were pushed into the limelight from an early age. They would regularly appear on their parents' radio shows throughout the 40s and accompanied them on many tours. In the mid-50s as rockabilly was evolving into rock 'n' roll the boys moved to Nashville, the mecca for such music. Don had a minor hit when Kitty Wells recorded his composition 'Thou Shalt Not Steal' in 1954.

In 1957 they were given a Felice and Boudleaux Bryant song that was finding difficulty in being placed. They took 'Bye Bye Love' and made it their own; it narrowly missed the US number 1 position and scored in the UK at number 6. The brothers then embarked on a career that made them second only to Elvis Presley in the rock 'n' roll popularity stakes. Their blend of country and folk did much to sanitize and make respectable a phenomenon to which many parents showed hostility. America, then still a racially segregated country, was not ready for its white teenagers to listen to black-based rock music. The brothers' clean looks and even cleaner harmonies did much to change people's attitudes. They quickly followed this initial success with more irresistible Bryant songs, 'Wake Up Little Susie', 'All I Have To Do Is Dream', 'Bird Dog', 'Problems', 'So Sad' and the beautiful 'Devoted To You'. The brothers were supremely confident live performers both with their trademark Gibson Dove and later black J50 guitars. By the end of the 50s they were the world's number 1 vocal group.

Amazingly, their career gained further momentum when, after signing with the newly-formed Warner Brothers Records for $1 million, they delivered a song that was catalogued WB1. This historical debut was the superlative 'Cathy's Clown', written by Don. No Everly record had sounded like this before; the echo-laden production and the treble-loaded harmonies stayed at number 1 in the US for 5 weeks. In the UK it stayed on top for over two months, selling several million and making it one of the most successful records of all time. The brothers continued to release immaculate records, many of them reached the US Top 10, although in England their success was even greater, with two

further number 1's during 1961. Again the echo and treble dominated in two more classics, 'Walk Right Back' and a fast-paced reworking of the former Bing Crosby hit 'Temptation'. At the end of 1961 they were drafted into the US Marines, albeit for only six months, and resumed by making a European tour. Don became dependent on drugs, the pressures from constant touring and recording began to show; during one historic night at London's East Ham Granada, in England, a nervous Phil performed solo. The standard 'food poisoning/exhaustion' excuse was used. What was not known by the doting fans, was that Don had attempted a suicidal drug overdose twice in 48 hours. Phil completed the tour solo. Don's addiction continued for another three years, although they were able to work during part of this time.

The advent of the beat boom pushed the brothers out of the spotlight and while they continued to make hit records, none came near their previous achievements. The decline was briefly halted in 1965 with two excellent major UK hits, 'The Price Of Love' and 'Love Is Strange'. The former, a striking chart-topper, sounded like their early Warner sound, while the latter harked back even earlier, with a naive but infectious call and answer, talking segment. In 1966 they released *Two Yanks In England*, a superb album which contained eight songs by Nash/Clarke/Hicks of the Hollies; surprisingly the album failed to chart. The duo were recognized only for their superb singles, and many of their albums were less well-received. The stunning *Stories We Could Tell*, with an array of guest players, threatened to extend their market into the rock mainstream, but it was not to be. After a few years of declining fortunes and arrival at the supper-club circuit, the brothers acrimoniously parted. Following a show at Knotts Berry Farm, California in 1973 during which a drunken Don had insulted Phil, the latter walked off, smashed one of his beloved Gibsons and vowed, 'I will never get on a stage with that man again'. The only time they met over the next 10 years was at their father's funeral. Both embarked on solo careers with varying degrees of accomplishment. Their country-flavoured albums found more favour with the Nashville audience of their roots. Don and his band, the Dead Cowboys, regularly played in Nashville, while Phil released the critically acclaimed *Star Spangled Springer*. Inexplicably the album was a relatively poor-seller, as was his follow-up *Mystic Line*. Phil made a cameo appearance in the film *Every Which Way But*

Everly Brothers

Loose, performing with actress Sondra Locke. While Don maintained a steady career, playing with ex-Heads, Hands And Feet maestro Albert Lee, Phil concentrated on writing songs. 'She Means Nothing To Me' was a striking duet with Cliff Richard which put the Everly name back in the UK Top 10. Rumours began to circulate of a reunion, which was further fueled by a UK television advertisement for an Everlys' compilation. In June 1983 they hugged and made up and their emotional reunion was made to an ecstatic wet-eyed audience at London's Royal Albert Hall. The following year *EB84* was released and gave them another major hit with Paul McCartney's 'Wings Of A Nightingale'. In 1986 they were inducted into the Rock 'n' Roll Hall Of Fame and the following year Phil gave Don a pound of gold and a handmade guitar for his 50th birthday. The Everly Brothers' influence over a generation of pop and rock artists is inestimable; they set the standard for close harmony singing which has rarely been bettered. They now perform regularly together, and to date the ceasefire has held.

Albums: *The Everly Brothers* (1958), *Songs Our Daddy Taught Us* (1958), *It's Everly Time* (1960), *The Fabulous Style Of The Everly Brothers* (1960), *A Date With The Everly Brothers* (1961), *Both Sides Of An Evening* (1961), *Instant Party* (1962), *Christmas With The Everly Brothers And The Boys Town Choir* (1962), *The Everly Brothers Sing Great Country Hits* (1963), *Gone Gone Gone* (1965), *Rock 'N' Soul* (1965), *Beat 'N' Soul* (1965), *In Our Image* (1966), *Two Yanks In England* (1966), *The Hit Sound Of The Everly Brothers* (1967), *The Everly Brothers Sing* (1967), *Roots* (1969), *The Everly Brothers Show* (1970), *End Of An Era* (1971), *Stories We Could Tell* (1972), *Pass The Chicken And Listen* (1973), *The Most Beautiful Songs Of The Everly Brothers* (1973), *Don's And Phil's Fabulous Fifties Treasury* (1974), *The Exciting Everly Brothers* (1975), *Living Legends* (1977), *The New Album* (1977), *The Sensational Everly Brothers* (1979), *The Everly Brothers Reunion Concert* (1984), *Nice Guys* (1984), *EB84* (1984), *Born Yesterday* (1986), *Some Hearts* (1989). Selected compilations: *The Very Best Of The Everly Brothers* (1965), *The Golden Hits Of The Everly Brothers* (1962), *The Everly Brothers Original Greatest Hits* (1970), *The Very Best Of The Everly Brothers* (1964), *Walk Right Back With The Everlys* (1976), *Hidden Gems* (1990), *Perfect Harmony* (1990). Solo albums: Don Everly *Don Everly* (1970), *Sunset Towers* (1974), *Brother Juke Box* (1977). Phil Everly *Star Spangled Springer* (1973), *Phil's Diner (There's*

Nothing Too Good For My Baby) (1974), *Mystic Line* (1975), *Living Alone* (1979), *Phil Everly* (1983). Further reading: *Walk Right Back*, Roger White.

F

Fabian

b. 6 February 1943, Philadelphia, USA. Fabiano Forte Bonaparte, almost despite himself, was among the more endurable products of the late 50s when the North American charts were infested with a turnover of vapid boys-next-door - all hair spray, doe eyes and coy half-smiles - groomed for fleeting stardom. Fabian was 'discovered' by two local talent scouts, Peter De Angelis and Bob Marucci, in Frankie Avalon's Teen And Twenty youth club in 1957. Enthralled by the youth's good looks, the pair shortened his name and contracted him to their Chancellor Records where a huge budget was allocated to project him as a tamed Elvis Presley. Accompanied by the Four Dates, Fabian's first two singles - 'I'm In love' and 'Lilly Lou' - were only regional hits but a string of television performances on Dick Clark's nationally-broadcast *American Bandstand* plus a coast-to-coast tour had the desired effect on female teenagers, and Fabian found himself suddenly in *Billboard*'s Top 40 with 'I'm A Man,' composed by the top New York songwriting team, Doc Pomus/Mort Shuman who also delivered more lucrative hits in 'Turn Me Loose' and 'Hound Dog Man', the main theme from Fabian's silver screen debut of the same name.

More substantial movie roles came Fabian's way after his recording career peaked with 1959's million-selling 'Tiger' and *Hold That Tiger*. As well as the predictable teenpics with their vacuous story-lines and mimed musical sequences, he coped surprisingly well as John Wayne's sidekick in 1960's *North To Alaska* and with Bing Crosby and Tuesday Weld in *High Time*. Fabian's decline was as rapid as his launch after Congress pinpointed him as an instance of one of the exploited puppets in the payola scandal. Questioned at the time, Fabian made matters worse by outlining the

considerable electronic doctoring necessary to improve his voice on record. 1960 brought his first serious miss in 'About This Thing Called Love' and an irredeemable downward spiral mitigated by 1962's 'Kissin' And Twistin'' and other small hits. Nevertheless, he could be spotted in in films like the 1962 war epic *The Longest Day* but more commensurate with his talent were such as *Fireball 500* (a 1966 hot-rod epic with his old friend Frankie Avalon) and 1965's *Ride The Wild Surf*.
Selected albums: *Hold That Tiger* (1959), *Fabulous* (1960), *Facade* (1961), *Good Old Summertime* (1961), *Rockin' Hot* (1961). Compilation: *16 Fabulous Hits* (1962).

Faith, Adam

b. Terence Nelhams, 23 June 1940, Acton, London, England. During the British 'coffee bar' pop music phenomenon of the late 50s two artists reigned supreme; Cliff Richard and Adam Faith. While the former has shown astonishing staying power the young Faith had a remarkable run of hit records during the comparatively short time before he retired from singing. In seven years he made the UK chart 24 times, opening his career with two chart toppers. Both, 'What Do You Want' and 'Poor Me' lasted only two minutes; both featured the infectious pizzicato strings of John Barry's orchestra, both were written by Les Vandyke (alias Johnny Worth) and both featured the hiccuping delivery with the word, 'baby' pronounced 'bybeee'. This became Adam's early 'gimmick'. Faith's continued success rivalled that of Cliff's, when in a short period of time he appeared in three films *Beat Girl*, *Never Let Go* and *What A Whopper*, and made a surprisingly confident appearance, being interviewed by John Freeman in a serious BBC television programme, *Face To Face*. Adults were shocked to find that during this conversation, this lucid teenager admitted to pre-marital sex and owned up to listening to Sibelius. The following year, still enjoying chart hits, he appeared in the film *Mix Me A Person*. His career continued until the dawn of the Beatles, then Faith was assigned the Roulettes (featuring a young Russ Ballard). Songwriter Chris Andrews proceeded to feed Adam with a brief second wave of infectious beat-group hits most notably 'The First Time'. In the mid-60s he gave up singing and went into repertory theatre and in 1971 became an acting star in the UK television series *Budgie*. Additionally Faith has produced records for Roger Daltrey and Lonnie Donegan and managed Leo Sayer. His two supporting actor roles in *Stardust* and *McVicar*

bought him critical success in addition to appearing in *Yesterday's Hero*. For a number of years he has been a wealthy financial consultant, although in the 90s he returned to the stage with *Budgie* and *Alfie*, and to television, as lead actor in *Love Hurts*. Faith still works on the perimeter of the musical world. While he will readily admit that his vocal range was limited, his contribution to popular music was significant insofar that he was the first British teenager to confront a hostile world of respectable parents and adults and demonstrate that pop singers were not all mindless layabouts and boneheads.
Selected albums: *Adam* (1960), *Beat Girl* (1961, film soundtrack), *Adam Faith* (1962), *Faith Alive* (1965), *I Survive* (1974). Compilations: *20 Golden Greats* (1981), *Not Just A Memory* (1983), *The Adam Faith Singles Collection: His Greatest Hits* (1990). Further reading: *Poor Me*, Adam Faith.

Faith, Percy

b. 7 April 1908, Toronto, Ontario Canada, d. 9 February 1976, Ericino, California, USA. During the 30s Faith worked extensively on radio in Canada. He moved to the USA in 1940 to take up a post with NBC. During the 50s he was musical director for Columbia Records, for whom he made a number of popular albums, mostly of mood music. He worked with Tony Bennett, with whom he had three million-selling singles, and, from 1950, also had several hits in his own right, including 'Cross My Fingers', 'All My Love', 'On Top Of Old Smoky' (vocal by Burl Ives), 'Delicado', 'Song From The Moulin Rouge (Where Is Your Heart)' (US number 1 in 1953), 'Return To Paradise' (1953), and 'Theme From A Summer Place', which reached number 1 in the US and number 2 in the UK charts in 1960. In Hollywood in the 50s, Faith had written several background film scores, including *Love Me Or Leave Me* (1955), a bio pic about Ruth Etting which starred Doris Day. His film credits in the 60s included *Tammy Tell Me True* (1961), *I'd Rather Be Rich* (1964), *The Third Day* (1965), and *The Oscar* (1966). For *The Love Goddesses*, Faith wrote the title song, with Mack David. His other compositions included 'My Heart Cries For You' (with Carl Sigman), which was a big hit for Guy Mitchell, Dinah Shore, Vic Damone and others in 1951.
Selected albums: *Continental Music* (1956), *Passport To Romance* (1958), *Touchdown!* (1958), *North & South Of The Border* (1958), *Music From My Fair Lady* (1959), *Viva!* (1959), *Hallelujah* (1959), *Music Of George Gershwin* (1959), *Malaguena* (1959), *Music*

Eddie Fisher and Elizabeth Taylor

From South Pacific (1960), *Music Of Victor Herbert* (1958), *A Night With Sigmund Romberg* (1959), *Bouquet* (1959), *Porgy And Bess* (1960), *Bon Voyage!* (1960), *Continental Souvenirs* (1960), *Jealousy* (1960), *A Night With Jerome Kern* (1960), *Camelot* (1961), *Carefree* (1961), *Mucho Gusto!* (1961), *Tara's Theme* (1961), *Bouquet Of Love* (1962), *Subways Are For Sleeping* (1962), *Music Of Brazil* (1962), *Hollywood's Themes* (1963), *American Serenade* (1963), *Exotic Strings* (1963), *Shangra-La!* (1963), *More* (1964), *Great Folk Themes* (1964), *Latin Themes* (1965), *Broadway Bouquet* (1965), *Themes For The 'In' Crowd* (1966), *Today's Themes* (1967), *Forever Young* (1970).

Fisher, Eddie

b. Edwin Jack Fisher, 10 August 1928, Philadelphia, Pennsylvania, USA. One of the most popular US singers of the 50s, with a strong, melodic voice; a 'bobby sox idol'. Fisher sang with the bands of Buddy Morrow and Charlie Ventura at the age of 18. His nickname was 'Sonny Boy' because of his affection for Al Jolson songs. In 1949 he got nationwide exposure on Eddie Cantor's radio show. Signed to RCA-Victor Records, and accompanied by Hugo Winterhalter, Fisher had a string of US Top 10 hits through to 1956, including 'Thinking Of You', 'Turn Back The Hands Of Time', 'Tell Me Why', 'I'm Yours', 'Maybe'/'Watermelon Weather' (duets with Perry Como), 'Wish You Were Here' (number 1), 'Lady Of Spain', 'I'm Walking Behind You' (number 1), 'Oh My Pa-Pa' (number 1), 'I Need You Now' (number 1), 'Count Your Blessings', 'Heart', 'Dungaree Doll' and 'Cindy, Oh Cindy'. Five of those won gold discs. He also made the US Top 40 album charts in 1955 with *I Love You*. His career was interrupted from 1952-53 when he served in the US Armed Forces Special services, and spent some time in Korea. After his discharge he became immensely popular singing in top nightclubs, and on his own television series, *Coke Time* and *The Chesterfield Supper Club*, with George Gobel. In 1956 he co-starred with his first wife, Debbie Reynolds, in the film musical *Bundle Of Joy*; and had a straight role in *Butterfield 8* (1960), in which his second wife, Elizabeth Taylor won an Academy Award for Best Actress. During the 60s, beset by drug and financial problems, he switched record labels and was recorded *Live At The Winter Garden* for his own Ramrod Records, and *Eddie Fisher Today* for Dot Records. He returned to RCA and had a minor singles hit in 1966 with 'Games That Lovers Play', and it became the title of a best-selling album. His last album for RCA was a Jolson tribute, *You Ain't Heard Nothing Yet*. During the late 60s he married, and divorced, actress Connie Stevens, and in the 70s attempted several unsuccessful comebacks. In 1990, following extended periods of treatment at the Betty Ford Centre, Fisher announced that he was finally cured of his drug problems and intended to resume work. His daughter, by Debbie Reynolds, actress Carrie Fisher, appeared in the hit movies, *Star Wars*, *The Empire Strikes Back*, and *When Harry Met Sally*. The film, *Postcards From The Edge*, reputedly based on her drug problems, and her life with Debbie Reynolds, was released in 1990.
Albums: *I Love You* (1955), *I'm In The Mood For Love* (1955), *May I Sing To You?* (1955), *Bundle Of Joy* (1956, film soundtrack), *Thinking Of You* (1957), *As Long As There's Music* (1958), *Scent Of Mystery* (1960, film soundtrack), *Eddie Fisher At The Winter Garden* (1963), *Eddie Fisher Today!* (1965), *When I Was Young* (1965), *Games That Lovers Play* (1966), *People Like You* (1967), *You Ain't Heard Nothing Yet* (late 60s). Compilations: *Eddie Fisher's Greatest Hits* (1962), *His Greatest Hits* (1965), *The Very Best Of Eddie Fisher* (1988, CD only release).
Further reading: *Eddie, My Life And Loves*, Eddie Fisher.

Fitzgerald, Ella

b. 25 April 1918, Newport News, Virginia, USA. Following the death of her father, Fitzgerald was taken to New York City by her mother. At school she sang with a glee club and showed early promise, but preferred dancing to singing. Even so, chronic shyness militated against her chances of succeeding as an entertainer. Nevertheless, she entered a talent contest as a dancer, but last minute nerves forced her to either just stand there or sing. She sang. Her unexpected success prompted her to try other talent contests and she began to win often enough to keep trying. Eventually, she reached the top end of the talent show circuit, singing at the Harlem Opera House where she was heard by several important people. In later years many claimed to have 'discovered' her, but among those most likely to have had a hand in trying to establish her as a professional singer with the Fletcher Henderson band were Benny Carter and John Hammond. These early efforts were unsuccessful, however, and she continued her round of the talent shows. An appearance at Harlem's Apollo Theater, where she won, was the most important stepping stone in her life. She was heard by Bardu

Ella Fitzgerald

Love Easy (1974), *Ella In London* (1974), *Fine And Mellow* (1974), *Ella - At The Montreux Jazz Festival 1975* (1975), with Oscar Peterson *Ella And Oscar* (1975), with Joe Pass *Again* (1976), *Montreux '77* (1977), *Lady Time* (1978), with Count Basie *A Classy Pair* (1979), *A Perfect Match - Basie And Ella* (1979), *Ella Fitzgerald Sings The Antonio Carlos Jobim Songbook* (1981), *The Best Is Yet To Come* (1982), *Easy Living* (1983), *Speak Love* (1983), *Nice Work If You Can Get It* (1983), *A 75th Birthday Tribute* (1993).

Further reading: *Ella Fitzgerald - A Life Through Jazz*, Jim Haskins. *Ella Fitzgerald*, Stuart Nicholson.

Five Keys

This US R&B vocal group helped shape the rhythm and blues revolution of the early 50s. The ensemble was formed as the Sentimental Four in Newport News, Virginia, USA, in the late 40s, and originally consisted of two sets of brothers - Rudy West (b. 25 July 1932, Newport News, Virginia, USA) and Bernie West (b. 4 February 1930, Newport News, Virginia, USA), and Ripley Ingram (b. 1933) and Raphael Ingram. After Ralph Ingram left and Maryland Pierce (b. 1933) and Dickie Smith became members in 1949, the name of the group was changed to Five Keys. With Pierce doing the lead work, the Five Keys joined Los Angeles-based Aladdin Records in 1951 and the same year hit with a remake of the old standard, 'Glory Of Love', which became a US R&B number 1. Despite recording an appealing combination of old standards and R&B originals, further chart success on Aladdin, eluded the Five Keys.

In 1952 Rudy West went into the army, and was replaced by Ulysses K. Hicks, and in 1954 Dickie Smith left and was replaced with Ramon Loper. This new line-up of Five Keys was signed to Capitol Records, which brought the group to stardom, albeit with some modification in their style from a deep rhythm and blues sound to a more pop vein with greater instrumentation in support. The group's first hit for Capitol was the novelty pop jump, 'Ling Ting Tong', (US R&B number 5 and US pop Top 30 in 1955). Following the first Capitol recording session, Rudy West rejoined the Five Keys in October, 1954, replacing the ailing Hicks, who died a few months later. Further hits on Capitol included some spectacular R&B ballads: the Chuck Willis-composed 'Close Your Eyes' (R&B number 5, 1955), 'The Verdict' (R&B number 13, 1955), and 'Out Of Sight, Out Of Mind' (R&B number 12 and pop Top 30 in

1956). The Capitol material also featured old standards, such as a marvellous remake of the Ink Spots' 'The Gypsy' (1957). Rudy West retired in 1958, and an unsuccessful stay at King Records, from 1958 to 1961 produced more personnel changes and no hits and few songs that could compete with the new rock 'n' roll sounds. Periodic sessions were recorded by various reunion groups in subsequent years, but the basic legacy of the Five Keys rests in their Aladdin, Capitol, and King sessions.

Albums: *The Best Of The Five Keys* (1956), *The Five Keys On The Town* (1957), *The Five Keys On Stage* (1957), *The Five Keys* (1960), *Rhythm And Blues Hits Past And Present* (1960), *The Fantastic Five Keys* (1962). Compilations: *The Five Keys* (1978), *Collector's Series* (1989), *Five Keys And The Nitecaps* (1990), *Dream On* (1991), *The Aladdin Years* (1991).

Five Satins

This R&B vocal group was formed in New Haven, Connecticut, USA in 1955. The Five Satins' first hit, 'In The Still Of The Night', (US R&B number 3 and pop Top 30 pop in 1956) was one of the definitive songs of the early rock 'n' roll era with its strong chanting of doo-wop riffs in the background and impassioned lead work. The group on this record were lead Parris, Al Denby, Ed Martin, bass Jim Freeman, and pianist Jessie Murphy. Parris, who wrote the tune, brought a lot of experience to the Five Satins, having formed the Scarlets (Parris, Al Denby, Bill Powers, Sylvester Hopkins and Nate Mosely) in 1953, a group that hit regionally with 'Dear One' in 1954. The long cherished national success for Parris was initially denied him, because he was in the army stationed in Japan when 'In The Still Of The Night' hit, and the wonderful follow-up, 'To The Aisle', (US R&B number 5 and pop Top 30 in 1957) featured a reorganized group with Bill Baker as lead. Parris returned from Japan in 1958 and again re-organized the Five Satins, recruiting tenor Richie Freeman (b. December 1940), second tenor West Forbes (b. 1937), Sylvester Hopkins (b. 1938) and Lou Peeples. This group was not able to get another big hit, although 'Shadows' (US R&B number 27, 1959) kept their name visible. Their visibility was significantly enhanced with the release of Art Laboe's first *Oldies But Goodies* which included 'In The Still Of The Night'. As result the song helped to create the doo-w revival in the early 60s and re-entered the nat' pop chart in 1961. The Five Satins broke up early 60s, but re-formed and became a perer

Ali, who fronted the Chick Webb band at the Savoy Ballroom. Later, when the Webb band was appearing at the Apollo, Ali persuaded Webb to listen to the singer. Webb took her on, at first paying her out of his own pocket, and for the fringe audience she quickly became the band's main attraction. She recorded extensively with Webb, with a small group led by Teddy Wilson, with the Ink Spots and others, and even recorded with Benny Goodman. Her hits with Webb included 'Sing Me A Swing Song', 'Oh, Yes, Take Another Guess', 'The Dipsy Doodle', 'If Dreams Come True', 'A-Tisket, A-Tasket', (a song on which she collaborated on the lyric), 'F.D.R. Jones' and 'Undecided'. After Webb's death in 1939 she became the nominal leader of the band, a position she retained until 1942. Fitzgerald then began her solo career, recording numerous popular songs, sometimes teaming up with other artists, and in the late 40s signing with Norman Granz. It was Granz's masterly and astute control of her career that helped to establish her as one of America's leading jazz singers. She was certainly the most popular jazz singer with non-jazz audiences, and through judicious choice of repertoire, became the foremost female interpreter of the Great American Popular Song Book. With Granz she worked on the 'songbook' series, placing on record definitive performances of the work of America's leading songwriters, and she also toured extensively as part of his Jazz At The Philharmonic package.

Ella has a wide vocal range, but her voice retained a youthful, light vibrancy throughout the greater part of her career, bringing a fresh and appealing quality to most of her material especially 'scat' singing. Although it proved less suited to the blues, a genre which, for the most part, she wisely avoided. Indeed, in her early work the most apparent musical influence is Connee Boswell. As a jazz singer, Fitzgerald performed with elegantly swinging virtuosity and her work with accompanists such as Ray Brown, to whom she was married for a while (they have an adopted son, Ray Brown Jnr., a drummer), Joe Pass and Tommy Flanagan was always immaculately conceived. However, her recordings with Louis Armstrong reveal the marked difference between her conception and that of a singer for whom the material was always of secondary importance to the improvisation he could weave upon it. For all the enviably high quality of her jazz work, it is as a singer of superior popular songs that Fitzgerald's importance and influence is most profound. Her respect for her material, beautifully displayed in the 'songbook' series, helped her to estab[lish] her place as the finest vocalist of her [era in popular] music. Due largely to deteriorating h[ealth by the] mid-80s Fitzgerald's career was a[t a] standstill, although a 1990 appearance [in the UK] was well-received by an ecstatic audi[ence. Her] most obvious counterpart among male [singers is] Frank Sinatra and, as the careers of b[oth] artists draw to a close, questions inevita[bly arise] about the fate of the great popular songs o[f the 30s] and 40s. While there are numerous ex[cellent] interpreters still around in the early 90s, and [many] whose work has been strongly influenc[ed by] Fitzgerald, it is hard to see any single singer [who] can take her place emerging in the foresee[able] future. This is not a view conceived ou[t of] blinkered nostalgia but rather an acute awaren[ess] that the conditions which helped to crea[te] America's First Lady of Song no longer exist. [It] seems highly unlikely, therefore, that we shall eve[r] see or hear her like again.

Selected albums: *The Chronological Ella Fitzgerald Vols 1-3* (1935-39 recordings), *Webb On The Air* (1940 recordings), *Live From The Roseland Ballroom* (1940 recordings), *Ella And Ray* (1948), *The Ella Fitzgerald Set* (1949), *Ella Sings Gershwin* (1950), *Ella Fitzgerald Sings The Cole Porter Songbook* (1956), *Ella Fitzgerald Sings The Rodgers And Hart Songbook* (1956), with Louis Armstrong *Ella And Louis* (1956), with Armstrong *Porgy And Bess* (1956), *Ella Fitzgerald Sings The Duke Ellington Songbook* (1957), *Ella Fitzgerald At Newport* (1957), *Ella And Louis Again Vols 1 & 2* (1957), *Ella Fitzgerald At The Opera House* (1957), *Ella Fitzgerald Sings The Irving Berlin Songbook* (1958), *Ella Sings Sweet Songs For Swingers* (1958), *Ella Swings Lightly* (1958), *Ella Fitzgerald Sings The George And Ira Gershwin Songbook* (1959), *Mack The Knife - Ella In Berlin* (1960), *Ella Wishes You A Swinging Christmas* (1960), *The Intimate Ella* (1960), *Ella Fitzgerald Sings The Harold Arlen Songbook* (1961), *Ella Swings Gently With Nelson* (1962), *Ella Fitzgerald Sings The Jerome Kern Songbook* (1963), *These Are The Blues* (1963), *Ella At Juan-Les-Pins* (1964), *Hello, Dolly!* (1964), *Ella Fitzgerald Sings The Johnny Mercer Songbook* (1964), *Ella At Duke's Place* (1965), *Ella In Hamburg* (1965), with Ellington *The Stockholm Concert* (1966), *Ella And Duke On The Cote D'Azure* (1966), *Whisper Not* (1966), *Brighten The Corner* (1967), *Misty Blue* (1967), *30 By Ella* (1968), *Sunshine Of Your Love/Watch What Happens* (1969), *Things Ain't What They Used To Be* (1970), *Ella A Nice* (1971), *Ella Fitzgerald And Cole Porter* (1972), *Ella Fitzgerald At Carnegie Hall* (1973), *Take*

Five Keys

the oldies circuit in the 70s. The new group consisted of Fred Parris, Richie Freeman, Jimmy Curtis, and Nate Marshall. Briefly under the name Black Satin, they got a number 49 R&B hit in 1975 with 'Everybody Stand And Clap Your Hands (For The Entertainer)'.

Albums: *The Five Satins Sing* (1957), *Encore, Volume 2* (1960). Compilations: *The Best Of The Five Satins* (1971), *In The Still Of The Night* (1990).

Five Sharps

Formed in the early 50s in Jamaica, New York, USA, the Five Sharps were a vocal harmony group whose sole claim to fame is the fact that their only record, Harold Arlen's 'Stormy Weather', is acknowledged by collectors to be the rarest in the world. The group consisted of Ronald Cuffey (lead vocals), Clarence Bassett and Robert Ward (both tenors), Mickey Owens (bass vocals) and Tom Duckett (piano). In late 1952 the group recorded the standard 'Stormy Weather' for Jubilee Records. The record failed to gain any significant airplay or sales and the Five Sharps broke up. Virtually no one remembered their recording until a collector found a 78 rpm copy at a Brooklyn record store in 1961. When no others turned up, the value of the surviving original rose steadily; a second copy was finally located in 1977 and sold for nearly $4,000. No 45s were ever discovered and should another 78 turn up in the 90s its value is now estimated at over $10,000 by record value experts.

Flamingos

This R&B vocal group, formed in Chicago, Illinois, USA in 1951, was renowned for producing the tightest and most gorgeous harmonies of the rock 'n' roll era. For much of their history they consisted of Zeke Carey (b. 24 January 1933, Bluefield, Virginia, USA), Jake Carey (b. 9 September 1926, Pulaski, Virginia, USA), Paul Wilson (b. 6 January 1935, Chicago, Illinois, USA, d. May 1988) and Johnny Carter (b. 2 June 1934, Chicago, Illinois, USA). The group's first lead was Sollie McElroy (b. 16 July 1933, Gulfport, Mississippi, USA) who brought the group regional fame on 'Golden Teardrops' for the Chance label in 1954. He was replaced by Nate Nelson (b. 10 April 1932, Chicago, Illinois, USA, d. 10 April 1984) who brought the group into the rock 'n' roll era with the magnificent ballad, 'I'll Be Home', a number 5 R&B hit in 1956 on the Chess label. There then followed a period of disarray, in which Carter and Zeke Carey were lost to the draft. The Flamingos brought into the group Tommy Hunt

(b. 18 June 1933, Pittsburgh, Pennsylvania, USA) and Terry Johnson (b. 12 November 1935, Baltimore, Maryland, USA) and moved to New York where they signed with End Records in 1958.

At End the Flamingos got their biggest US hits 'Lovers Never Say Goodbye' (R&B number 25 in 1958), 'I Only Have Eyes For You' (R&B number 3 and pop number 11 in 1959), 'Nobody Loves Me Like You' (R&B number 23 and pop Top 30 in 1960), the latter song written by Sam Cooke. One of the group's last outstanding records was 'I Know Better' (1962), a Drifters' sound-alike that captured top spots in many markets. During the early 60s the Flamingos lost the remaining of their original members, except for Jake and Zeke Carey. The cousins managed to get some minor hits during the soul era, notably 'Boogaloo Party' which was the group's only UK chart hit when it reached number 26 in 1969 (three years earlier it was a US R&B number 22 hit). The Flamingos' last US chart record was 'Buffalo Soldier' 1970 (R&B Top 30). Nate Nelson died in 1984 and Paul Wilson in 1988. Sollie McElroy, after leaving the Flamingos in 1955, joined the Moroccos, with whom he recorded for three years, and Johnny Carter joined the Dells in 1960.

Albums: *The Flamingos* (1959), *Flamingos Serenade* (1959), *Flamingos Favorites* (1960), *Requestfully Yours* (1960), *The Sound Of The Flamingos* (1962), *The Spiritual And Folk Moods Of The Flamingos* (1963), *Their Hits - Then And Now* (1966), *Flamingos Today* (1971). Compilations: *The Flamingos* (1964), *Golden Teardrops* (1982), *The Chess Sessions* (1987), *The Best Of The Flamingos* (1990), *The Flamingos: I Only Have Eyes For You* (1991).

Flanders And Swann

The son of an actor father, and a mother who had been a concert-violinist before she married, Michael Flanders (b. 1 March 1922, London, England, d. 14 April 1975), was brought up in a musical household. He learned to play the clarinet and made his stage debut at the age of seven in a singing contest with *Uncle Mac's Minstrel Show*. At Westminster School in London, where Peter Ustinov was one of his classmates, he started to write and stage revues. His search for a pianist led him to Donald Swann, and their first revue together was *Go To It*. At Oxford University in 1940 Flanders played in and directed several productions for the Dramatic Society and made his professional debut as Valentine in Shaw's *You Never Can Tell*, at the Oxford Playhouse. In 1943, while

serving in the Royal Navy Volunteer Reserve, having survived the infamous convoys to Russia, he was struck down by poliomyelitis. Three years later he was discharged from hospital, in a wheelchair, and with a full beard which he retained for the rest of his life. Unable to resume a normal acting career, Flanders turned to writing and broadcasting. He contributed lyrics to several West End revues, in collaboration with Swann, including *Penny Plain* (1951), *Airs On A Shoestring* (1953) and *Fresh Airs* (1956). Flanders also appeared extensively on radio, and later, television, in programmes ranging from sports commentary to poetry readings, and including a spell of two years as chairman of *The Brains Trust*. His translation of Stravinsky's *Soldier's Tale* (with Kitty Black), became the standard English version, and his concert performance of it with Peter Ustinov and Sir Ralph Richardson was a surprise sell-out at the Royal Festival Hall in 1956. After successfully entertaining their friends at parties with their own songs, Flanders and Swann decided to perform professionally, so on New Years Eve 1956 they opened their own two-man show, *At The Drop Of A Hat*, at the intimate New Lindsey Theatre, Notting Hill, west London, moving three weeks later into the West End's Fortune Theatre. The show was a smash hit and ran for over three years. It is said that Princess Margaret attended a performance, and came back the following week with the Queen and the Duke of Edinburgh. With Flanders' urbane image contrasting with Swann's almost schoolboy enthusiasm, they introduced songs such as 'The Hippopotamus ('Mud, Mud, Glorious Mud')', 'Misalliance', 'A Gnu', and 'Madeira M'Dear?'. Two albums from the show were released; the earlier mono recording being preferable to the later stereo issue. In 1959 the show opened on Broadway, billed as 'An After-Dinner Farrago', and later toured the USA, Canada and the UK. In 1963 at the Haymarket Theatre, London, they presented a fully revised version entitled *At The Drop Of Another Hat*, which included songs such as 'The Gas-Man Cometh', 'First And Second Law' and 'Bedstead Men'. During 1964 and 1965 they toured Australia, New Zealand and Hong Kong, before returning to the West End in 1965, and yet again, to New York in the following year. Meanwhile, Flanders was still continuing with his other work, writing, broadcasting and theatrical speech recitals. He published *Creatures Great And Small*, a children's book of verses about animals and, together with Swann, released an album of animal songs entitled *The Bestiary Of Flanders And Swann*. Flanders was awarded the OBE in 1964, and died in April 1975.
Albums: *At The Drop Of A Hat* (1957), *Bestiary Of Flanders And Swan* (1961), *At The Drop Of Another Hat* (1964), *A Review Of Revues* (1975), *Tried By Centre Court* (1977), *The Complete Flanders & Swann* (1991, 3 CD set).

Fleetwoods

One of America's most popular doo-wop groups in the late 50s comprised Gary Troxell (b. 28 November 1939, Centralia, Washington, DC, USA), Gretchen Christopher (b. 29 February 1940, Olympia, Washingtion, DC, USA) and Barbara Ellis (b. 20 February 1940, Olympia, Washington, USA). They met when seniors at high school in the girls' home town. Originally a female duo, they recruited Troxell initially to play trumpet. The girls had composed a song, while independently Troxell had written a hook that went something like; 'Mmm Dooby Doo, Dum Dim Dum Doo Dum'; they put them together and 'Come Softly To Me' was born. Their first monicker, Two Girls and a Guy, was changed by a Seattle record distributor, Bob Reisdorff, who became their manager and founded Dolphin Records (later called Dolton) which released the single. Chart fame was instant for the distinctive trio and the haunting and catchy song, (on which the vocal was recorded a cappella), shot to the top in the US charts and made the UK Top 10 despite a hit cover by Frankie Vaughan and the Kaye Sisters.
Their third release, 'Mr. Blue', a Dewayne Blackwell song originally written for the Platters, was also a US number 1 (in the UK two covers took the honours) and made Troxell one of the leaders in the teen idol stakes. In the midst of their success he was drafted into the navy, his place being taken when necessary by later solo star Vic Dana. Despite Troxell's absence, the US hits continued and they totalled nine Top 40 hits between 1959 and 1963 which included the number 10 hit 'Tragedy', a revival of the Thomas Wayne song. The unmistakable close-harmony trio surfaced again in 1973 when they signed with the noted producer Jerry Dennon but no hits came from this collaboration.
Compilation: *The Fleetwoods Greatest Hits* (1962).

Fontane Sisters

The line-up of this close-harmony 50s US vocal group comprised Marge Rosse (b. New Milford, New Jersey, USA; lead), Bea Rosse (b. New Milford, New Jersey, USA; low harmony) and

Fontane Sisters

Geri Rosse (b. New Milford, New Jersey, USA; harmony). Their initial success was achieved by making cover versions of black R&B records. Their mother was a choral director and organist. After leaving high school they joined an all-girl troupe and went on an eight-month tour. Later, they were joined by their brother Frank, on guitar, and appeared on radio and in theatres and clubs. After Frank was killed in World War II, the girls re-formed in 1944 as a trio and worked for several years on Perry Como's radio and television shows, and backed him on several records, including the US number 1 hits, 'You're Adorable', and 'Hoop-Dee-Doo'. Signed for RCA-Victor in 1949, they had several minor hits in the early 50s, including 'Tennessee Waltz', 'Let Me In' (with Texas Jim Robertson) and 'Cold, Cold Heart'. In 1954 they switched to Dot Records, a label which specialized in making cover versions of established hits, and came under the influence of Dot's musical director, Billy Vaughn, who, with his orchestra, provided the backing for most of their successful records. Early that year, they made the US charts with 'Happy Days And Lonely Nights', a 1929 song by Fred Fisher and Billy Rose, and in December 1954 they went to number 1 with 'Hearts Of Stone'. The original version was the debut disc of the R&B Cincinnati group, Otis Williams And The Charms. Other successful covers of black artists' records included 'Rock Love', 'Rollin' Stone' (original by the Marigolds) and 'Eddie, My Love' (originally by the sisters Betty and Rosie Collins' group, the Teen Queens). Other 'white' covers included Boyd Bennett And His Rockets' 'Seventeen', which the Fontanes took to number 3 in the US chart, and 'Daddy-O', a song said to have been inspired by a character in the 1955 movie, *Blackboard Jungle*, and which was originally a US Top 20 hit for Bonnie Lou. The Fontane's 1957 version of 'Banana Boat Song' also made the Top 20, but was prevented from rising higher by a version by the Tarriers; another version, by Steve Lawrence, was his first chart entry. By the late 50s, with more and more black artists making the charts themselves, the Fontanes faded from their position as one of the top girl groups of the 50s. Their last two hits, 'Chanson D'Amour' and 'Jealous Heart' came in 1958.
Albums: *The Fontane Sisters* (1956), *The Fontanes Sing* (1957), *Tips Of My Fingers* (1963). Compilations: *Rock Love* (1984), *Rock Again Love* (1986).

Ford, Frankie

A rocker from a suburb of New Orleans, Frankie Ford (b. Francis Guzzo, 4 August 1939, Gretna, Louisiana, USA) was a second cousin to that other New Orleans legend Dr. John. His first major appearance was on *Ted Mack's Amateur Hour Talent Show*, where he sang with Carmen Miranda and Sophie Tucker. After winning a scholarship to South Eastern College, Hammond, he started his first band with school friends. By 1958 he was singing with the Syncopators when he was asked to audition for Ace Records. Subsequently he released his first single 'Cheatin' Woman' as Frankie Ford. Fellow musician Huey 'Piano' Smith (b. 26 January 1934, New Orleans, Louisiana, USA) was a pianist. With his group the Clowns he had recorded a self-penned song called 'Sea Cruise' but Ace persuaded him to let Ford record a new vocal over Bobby Marcham's original. They also added a few extra effects such as paddle steamer whistle blows, which altered the song enough for Ford to claim a co-writing credit. Released under the title Frankie Ford with Huey 'Piano' Smith and his Clowns, it sold over a million copies and docked in the national Top 20. It was perceived in retrospect as a rock 'n' roll classic to be revived by Jerry Lee Lewis, Herman's Hermits, Sha Na Na, John Fogerty and Shakin' Stevens. Both 'Sea Cruise' and its follow-up 'Alimony' were taped originally by composer Huey Smith with the Clowns. The lead vocals were then erased and Ford's singing superimposed. As Morgus And The Ghouls' Ford and the Clowns also recorded 'Morgus The Magnificent', a novelty tribute to a local television personality. There was also an unissued homage to Fats Domino written and recorded by Ford and Dave Bartholomew. Ford left Ace in 1960 to form his own Spinet Records and signed to Liberty in 1960 but never repeated the success of 'Sea Cruise'. He also formed a 'supergroup' with Huey Smith, Robert Parker (hitmaker of 'Barefootin'') and Dr. John (under various pseudonyms due to contractual problems). They recorded various old New Orleans favourites. He continued to record for obscure labels throughout the 70s. In 1971, he opened a club in New Orleans' French Quarter where he became a cabaret fixture and a tourist attraction. Moreover, he still looked youthful enough to play his younger self in the 1978 movie *American Hot Wax*, set in the late 50s. As part of a package he toured the UK in 1985 along with Rick Nelson, Bobby Vee and Bo Diddley. Ford resents the term one-hit-wonder, and rightly pointed out that his four recordings of 'Sea Cruise' have now sold over 30 million copies worldwide.

Tennessee Ernie Ford

Albums: *On A Sea Cruise With Frankie Ford* (1959), *Frankie Ford* (1976), *New Orleans Dynamo* (1989).

Ford, Tennessee Ernie

b. Ernest Jennings Ford, 13 February 1919, Bristol, Tennessee, USA, d. 17 October 1991, Reston, Virginia, USA. It is difficult to categorize a performer with so many varied achievements, but Ford can be summarized as a master interpreter of melodic songs and hymns. The fact that he has been able to combine singing with his strong faith gives America's best-loved gospel singer great satisfaction. When only four years old, he was singing 'The Old Rugged Cross' at family gatherings, and from an early age, he wanted to be an entertainer. He pestered the local radio station until they made him a staff announcer in 1937 and he also took singing lessons. He subsequently worked for radio stations, WATL in Atlanta and WROL in Knoxville, where he announced the attack on Pearl Harbour. He joined the US Army Air Corps in 1942 and married a secretary, Betty Heminger, whom he met at the bombardier's school. After the war, they moved to California and he worked as an announcer and a disc jockey of hillbilly music for KXFM in San Bernardino. He rang cowbells and added bass harmonies to the records he was playing and so developed a country yokel character, Tennessee Ernie. He continued with this on KXLA Pasadena and he became a regular on their *Hometown Jamboree*, which was hosted by bandleader Cliffie Stone. He was also known as the Tennessee Pea-Picker using the catchphrase 'Bless your pea-pickin' hearts' and appearing on stage in bib overalls and with a blacked-out tooth. Lee Gillette, an A&R for Capitol Records, heard Ford singing along with a record on air and asked Stone about him. His first record, in 1949, was 'Milk 'Em In The Morning Blues'. Ford began his chart success with 'Tennessee Border', 'Country Junction' and 'Smokey Mountain Boogie', a song he wrote with Stone. 'Mule Train' despite opposition from Frankie Laine, Gene Autry and Vaughn Monroe, was a national hit and a US country number 1. An attempt to write with Hank Williams did not lead to any completed songs, but Ford wrote 'Anticipation Blues' about his wife's pregnancy and it made the US charts in 1949. Capitol teamed him with many of their female artists including Ella Mae Morse, Molly Bee and the Dinning Sisters, and his most successful duets were 'Ain't Nobody's Business But My Own' and 'I'll Never Be Free', a double-sided single with Kay Starr. The duet just

missed a gold record but he secured one, also in 1950, with his own song, 'Shotgun Boogie', which capitalized on the boogie craze and can be taken as a forerunner of rock 'n' roll. Its UK popularity enabled him to top a variety bill at the London Palladium in 1953. Ford recalls, 'When somebody told me that 'Give Me Your Word' was number 1 in your charts, I said, "When did I record that?" because it wasn't big in America and I had forgotten about it!' Ford also had success with 'The Cry Of The Wild Goose' and the theme for the Marilyn Monroe film, *The River Of No Return*, while the superb musicians on his records included Joe 'Fingers' Carr, who was given equal billing on 'Tailor Made Woman' in 1951, Speedy West and Jimmy Bryant. Ford hosted a USA daytime television show for five days a week and, in 1955, Capitol informed him that he would be in breach of contract if he did not record again soon. He chose a song he had been performing on the show, Merle Travis' 'Sixteen Tons'. Ford says, 'The producer, Lee Gillette, asked me what tempo I would like it in. I snapped my fingers and he said, "Leave that in." That snapping on the record is me.' 'Sixteen Tons' topped both the US and the UK charts, and Ford was also one of many who recorded 'The Ballad Of Davy Crockett', the theme of a Walt Disney western starring Fess Parker, which made number 3 in the UK. His half-hour US television show, *The Ford Show* (guess the sponsor) ran from 1956-61. He closed every television show with a hymn, which led to him recording over 400 gospel songs. One album *Hymns*, made number 2 in the US album charts and was listed for over five years. He has shared his billing with the Jordanaires on several albums including *Great Gospel Songs* which won a Grammy in 1964. Ford says, 'Long before I turned pro, it was a part of my life. There are many different types of gospel music, ranging from black music to the plain old Protestant hymns. I've shown that you don't have to sing them with a black robe on.' Ford had further USA hits with 'That's All', 'In The Middle Of An Island' and 'Hicktown' but, for many years, he concentrated on gospel. In 1961 he decided to spend more time with his family and moved to a ranch in the hills of San Francisco. He recorded albums of well-known songs, be they pop or country, and he rates *Country Hits - Feelin' Blue* and *Ernie Sings And Glen Picks*, an album which showcases his deep, mellow voice with Glen Campbell's guitar, amongst his best work. Many collectors seek original copies of his albums of Civil War songs. Ford, who was elected to the Country

Music Hall of Fame in 1990, remarked; 'People say to me, "Why don't you record another 'Sixteen Tons'" and I say, "There is no other 'Sixteen Tons'."

Albums: *This Lusty Land* (1956), *Hymns* (1956), *Spirituals* (1957), *C-H-R-I-S-T-M-A-S* (1957), *Tennessee Ernie Ford Favourites* (1957), *Ol' Rockin' 'Ern* (1957), *The Folk Album* (1958), *Nearer The Cross* (1958), *The Star Carol* (1958), with the Jordanaires *Gather 'Round* (1959), with the Jordanaires *A Friend We Have* (1960), *Sing A Hymn With Me* (1960), *Sixteen Tons* (1960), *Sing A Spiritual With Me* (1960), *Come To The Fair* (1960), *Sings Civil War Songs Of The North* (1961), *Sings Civil War Songs Of The South* (1961), *Ernie Ford Looks At Love* (1961), *Hymns At Home* (1961), *Here Comes The Tennessee Ernie Ford Mississippi Showboat* (1962), *I Love To Tell The Story* (1962), *Book Of Favourite Hymns* (1962), *Long, Long Ago* (1963), with the San Quentin Prison Choir *We Gather Together* (1963), with the Roger Wagnor Chorale *The Story Of Christmas* (1963), with the Jordanaires *Great Gospel Songs* (1964), *Country Hits - Feeling Blue* (1964), *Let Me Walk With Thee* (1965), *Sing We Now Of Christmas* (1965), *My Favourite Things* (1966), *Wonderful Peace* (1966), *God Lives* (1966), *Aloha From Tennessee Ernie Ford* (1967), *Faith Of Our Fathers* (1967), with Marilyn Horne *Our Garden Of Hymns* (1967), *The World Of Pop And Country Hits* (1968), *O Come All Ye Faithful* (1968), *Songs I Like To Sing* (1969), *New Wave* (1969), *Holy Holy Holy* (1969), *America The Beautiful* (1970), *Sweet Hour Of Prayer* (1970), *Tennessee Ernie Ford Christmas Special* (1970), *Everything Is Beautiful* (1970), *Abide With Me* (1971), *Mr. Words And Music* (1972), *It's Tennessee Ernie Ford* (1972), *Country Morning* (1973), *Ernie Ford Sings About Jesus* (1973), *Precious Memories* (1975), with Glen Campbell *Ernie Sings And Glen Picks* (1975), *Tennessee Ernie Ford Sings His Great Love* (1976), *For The 83rd Time* (1976), *He Touched Me* (1977), with the Jordanaires *Swing Wide Your Golden Gate* (1978), *Tell The Old, Old Story* (1981), *Sunday's Still A Special Day* (1984).

Four Aces

A close-harmony vocal group of the pre rock 'n' roll era, the quartet was founded in Pennsylvania, USA, in 1949 by baritone lead singer Al Alberts (b. Chester, Pennsylvania, USA). With Dave Mahoney, Lou Silvestri and Sol Vocare (both born in Chester) he recorded a self-financed single on the local Victoria label in 1951. 'Sin (Not a Sin)' went on to sell a million copies and the Four Aces

were subsequently signed to Decca. Alberts and Martin Gold co-wrote 'Tell Me Why' which began a string of hit singles during the mid-50s. Among them were the 1952 revival of Hoagy Carmichael and Frank Loesser's 1938 song, 'Heart And Soul', 'Stranger In Paradise' (from the stage musical *Kismet*), 'Mister Sandman' (1954), 'Heart' and 'Melody Of Love' (1955).

The group's only number 1 record was the Oscar-winning 'Love Is A Many Splendoured Thing', the title song from the 1955 film starring Jennifer Jones and William Holden. The Four Aces also recorded versions of the theme from *Three Coins In A The Fountain* and 'The World Outside' from the film *Suicide Squadron*. In 1956, the group suffered a double blow as Alberts left to follow a solo career and rock 'n' roll arrived. The Four Aces tried various strategies to survive including covering a Pat Boone song ('Friendly Persuasion') and jumping on the calypso and rock bandwagons with 'Bahama Mama' and 'Rock And Roll Rhapsody'. However, few of these records were even minor hits and by the end of the 50s the Four Aces had disappeared from view. Alberts did little better, although 'Willingly' (1958) was only a minor success.

Albums: *The Four Aces* (1956), *The Mood For Love* (1956), *Sentimental Souvenirs* (1956), *Heart And Soul* (1957), *Hollywood Hits* (1957), *Shuffling Along* (1958), *The Swingin' Aces* (1958), *Hits From Broadway* (1959), *Beyond The Blue Horizon* (1959).

Four Coins

Formed in Canonsburg, Pennsylvania, USA in 1952, the vocal harmony group the Four Coins consisted of George Mantalis, James Gregorakis and brothers George and Michael Mahramas. Originally the quartet were horn players in an orchestra with Bobby Vinton, who was an unknown at the time. At the end of 1952 the foursome began harmonizing together, and in January 1953 appeared on an 'amateur hour' radio programme, which they won. They left Vinton in 1953 and began a residency at a Pittsburgh club called the Blue Ridge Inn, calling themselves the Four Keys. They recorded their first singles in November 1953 for Corona Records, which led to a contract with Epic Records, a branch of the larger Columbia Records. Taking their cue from another quartet, the Four Aces, the group changed its name to the Four Coins. The group's first Epic single, 'We'll Be Married (In The Church In The Wildwood)', sold well but it was not until 1957 that they recorded their biggest hit, 'Shangri-La',

which reached number 11 in the US charts and earned a gold record. The group had charted seven times by 1959. In 1960 they changed labels to MGM Records and continued to record for Jubilee Records, VeeJay Records, and Roulette Records, undergoing personnel changes along the way. They disbanded in 1970.

Albums: *The 4 Coins* (1955), *The Four Coins In Shangri-La* (1958), *Greek Songs By The Four Coins* (1961), *Greek Songs Mama Never Taught Me* (1964).

Four Freshmen

Formed at Arthur Jordan Conservatory of Music in Indianapolis, Indiana, USA, in 1948, the Four Freshmen were a ground-breaking vocal group which influenced the Hi-Lo's, the Beach Boys,

Manhattan Transfer and countless other close-harmony outfits. The group originally consisted of lead vocalist Bob Flanigan (b. 22 August 1926, Greencastle, Indiana, USA), his cousins Ross Barbour (b. 31 December 1928, Columbus, Indiana, USA) and Don Barbour (b. 19 April 1929, Columbus, Indiana, USA, d. 5 October 1961), and Hal Kratzsch (b. Warsaw, Indiana, USA, d. 18 November 1970). Prior to the formation of the Four Freshmen, the Barbour brothers and Kratzsch, along with lead singer Marvin Pruitt, had been in a barbershop quartet called Hal's Harmonizers, each member playing an instrument. The same line-up formed a more jazz-oriented second group, called the Toppers in 1948. Pruitt left that same year at which point Flanigan

returned from Florida, where he had gone for the summer. Inspired by Mel Torme's Mel-Tones, the new group, renamed the Four Freshmen, was discovered in September 1949 by Woody Herman. In 1950 Stan Kenton saw the quartet in concert in Dayton, Ohio and arranged for them to audition for Capitol Records, which signed them. Their first hit single came in 1952, 'It's A Blue World', which reached number 30 in the USA. Spring 1953 saw a personnel change when Kratzsch left, replaced by Ken Errair (b. 23 January 1930, d. 14 June 1968). Errair also departed in 1955, replaced by Ken Albers. By that time the group had logged two more Top 40 hits, 'It Happened Once Before' and 'Mood Indigo'. Three final chart singles were issued in 1955-56, including the number 17 'Graduation Day', later covered by the Beach Boys. The group had seven album hits, including the Top 10 *Four Freshmen And 5 Trombones* in 1956 and *4 Freshmen And 5 Trumpets* the following year. Further personnel changes marked the group's career. Don Barbour left in 1960, replaced by Bill Comstock (who left in 1972). Ross Barbour stayed on until 1977 and Ken Albers in 1982. Flanigan remained with the group into the early 90s. Don Barbour was killed in a car crash in 1961, Kratzsch died of cancer in 1970 and Errair died in a plane crash in 1968. The latest Four Freshman line-up toured the UK in 1992, backed by Ray McVay's UK All-Star Big Band.
Selected albums: *Four Freshmen And 5 Trombones* (1956), *Freshmen Favorites* (1956), *4 Freshmen And 5 Trumpets* (1957), *Four Freshmen And Five Saxes* (1957), *The Four Freshmen In Person* (1958), *Voices In Love* (1958), *The Four Freshmen And Five Guitars* (1960), *Got That Feelin'* (1963), *More With 5 Trombones* (1964), *Time Slips Away* (1964).

Four Knights

The singing of Gene Alford was framed by the backing harmonies of Oscar Broadway, Clarence Dixon and John Wallace (who also strummed guitar). From regular performances in the late 40s on radio stations local to their native Charlotte, North Carolina, USA, the Knights graduated to television, providing musical interludes on nationally broadcast situation comedies starring Arthur Godfrey and Red Skelton. This exposure aided the combo's procurement of a Capitol contract and much airplay for their debut single, 1951's 'It's No Sin' on which Broadway's bassman grumblings were conspicuous. In 1953, they entered the national hit parade with 'Oh Happy Day' - lush with orchestral accompaniment - and

the following year, came up with the million-selling 'I Get So Lonely', a clever uptempo reworking of a hillbilly ballad. After 'O Falling Star' slipped from the charts, the quartet teamed up with Nat 'King' Cole for a 1956 smash with 'That's All There Is To That' - and so it was for the Four Knights who never had another hit.
Selected album: *Million $ Baby* (1960).

Four Lads

The line-up comprised Frank Busseri (b. Toronto, Canada; baritone), Bernard Toorish (b. Toronto, Canada; second tenor), James Arnold (b. Toronto, Canada; first tenor) and Connie Codarini (b. Toronto, Canada; bass). They were a versatile, vocal quartet, popular in the USA in clubs, theatres, television and on records, especially during the 50s. The Lads formed their group while attending St. Michael's Choir School in Toronto. Aided by 'Dad' Wilson, a member of the Golden Gate Quartet, the Lads played a try-out engagement at Le Ruban Bleu in New York, stayed for some 30 weeks, and then toured extensively. They were signed by Columbia Records as a background group, and in 1951 accompanied Johnnie Ray on his first big hit, 'Cry', which sold over two million copies. Their first solo success was in 1952 with 'Mocking Bird', followed by 'He Who Has Love', 'Down By The Riverside', 'Istanbul (Not Constantinople)', 'Gilly, Gilly, Ossenfeffer, Katzenellen Bogen By The Sea' and 'Skokiian', a South African song. In 1955 they had one of their biggest hits with 'Moments To Remember', written by Robert Allen and Al Stillman. The songwriters also provided the Lads with several other successful singles such as 'No, Not Much', 'Who Needs You', 'Enchanted Island' and 'There's Only One Of You'. Allen and Stillman also contributed to Johnny Mathis's early success with numbers such as 'Chances Are' and 'It's Not For Me To Say'. Other Four Lads' US Top 20 entries, through until 1958 included 'The Bus Stop Song (A Paper Of Pins)', 'A House With Love In It', 'Put A Light At The Window' and 'Standing On The Corner', from Frank Loesser's Broadway show, *The Most Happy Fella*. In 1957, the group recorded the album *The Four Lads Sing Frank Loesser*, which contained medleys from three of his successful scores: *Where's Charley?*, *Hans Christian Andersen* and *Guys and Dolls*. Other successful albums were their US Top 20 entry, *On The Sunny Side*, with the Claude Thornhill Orchestra; *Breezin' Along*, conducted by Ray Ellis and *Four On The Aisle*, a collection of extended

Four Preps

medleys from the musical shows, *Annie Get Your Gun*, *Babes In Arms* and *Kiss Me Kate*. A modified version of the group was still working in the 80s, Jimmy and Frank performing with two new members. Bernie was to be found singing with the Vince Mastro Quartet.

Albums: *On The Sunny Side* (1956), *The Stingiest Man In Town* (1956, film soundtrack), *The Four Lads Sing Frank Loesser* (1957), *Breezin' Along* (1959), *Four On The Aisle* (1959), *The Four Lads Swing Along* (1959), *High Spirits!* (1959), *Love Affair* (1960), *Everything Goes* (1960), *Dixieland Doin's* (1961), *Hits Of The 60's* (1962), *Oh, Happy Day* (1963), *This Year's Top Movie Hits* (1964), *Songs Of World War I* (1964). Compilations: *The Four Lads' Greatest Hits* i (1958), *Twelve Hits* (1961), *The Four Lads' Greatest Hits* ii (1983).

Four Preps

Formed in the early 50s in Hollywood, California, USA, the Four Preps were a vocal group consisting of Bruce Belland, Glen Larson, Marvin Inabnett and Ed Cobb. Recording for Capitol Records they placed 13 singles in the US charts between 1956-64, two of which made the Top 5 in 1958. The quartet began singing together during their high school years, influenced by the Mills Brothers, Four Aces, and Four Freshmen acts. Impressed by a demo tape the group recorded Mel Shauer, manager of Les Paul And Mary Ford, took the group under his wing and arranged a recording contract with Capitol. Their first session, in late 1956, yielded 'Dreamy Eyes', which was a minor hit, but the follow-up, '26 Miles (Santa Catalina)', written by Belland and Larson years earlier, reached number 2 and their next single, 'Big Man', made number 3. Subsequent singles failed to make the US Top 10 although the group did score a Top 10 album, *The Four Preps On Campus*, in 1961 during the height of the folk music revival in the USA. The group's final charting single, 1964's 'A Letter To The Beatles', parodied Beatlemania but was allegedly withdrawn from distribution by Capitol upon request by the Beatles' management. The group continued until 1967. Cobb went on to join the group Piltdown Men, and later to produce such records as the Standells' 'Dirty Water' and wrote 'Tainted Love', a hit for Soft Cell in 1982. In 1988, the Four Preps were back on the road, with two of the original members, Belland and Cobb, being joined by David Somerville, former lead singer of the Diamonds and Jim Pike, founder of the Lettermen.

Albums: *Four Preps* (1958), *The Things We Did Last Summer* (1958), *Dancing And Dreaming* (1959), *Early In The Morning* (1960), *Those Good Old Memories* (1960), *Four Preps On Campus* (1961), *Campus Encore* (1962), *Campus Confidential* (1963), *Songs For A Campus Party* (1963), *How To Succeed In Love!* (1964). Compilations: *Best Of The Four Preps* (1967), *Capitol Collectors Series* (1989), *Three Golden Groups In One* (1993).

Francis, Connie

b. Concetta Rosa Maria Franconero, 12 December 1938, Newark, New Jersey, USA. A popular singer of tearful ballads and jaunty up-tempo numbers, Francis was one of the most successful female artists of the 50s and 60s. She began playing the accordion at the age of four, and was singing and playing professionally when she was 11. After winning an *Arthur Godfrey Talent Show*, she changed her name, at Godfrey's suggestion. Signed for MGM Records in 1955, her first record was a German import, 'Freddy', which was also recorded by Eartha Kitt and Stan Kenton. 'Majesty Of Love', her 10th release, a duet with Marvin Rainwater, was her first US chart entry. In 1957 she was persuaded by her father, against her will, to record one of his favourites, the 1923 song 'Who's Sorry Now', by Harry Ruby, Bert Kalmar and Ted Snyder. It went to number 4 in the US charts and number 1 in the UK, and was the first of a string of hits through to 1962. These included re-workings of more oldies, such as 'My Happiness', 'Among My Souvenirs' and 'Together'. Among her more jaunty, upbeat songs were 'Stupid Cupid' (another UK number 1 coupled with 'Carolina Moon') and 'Where The Boys Are' by the new songwriting team of Neil Sedaka and Howard Greenfield. Her other US Top 10 entries included 'Lipstick On Your Collar', 'Frankie', 'Mama', 'Everybody's Somebody's Fool' (her first US number 1), 'My Mind Has A Heart Of Its Own' (another US number 1), 'Many Tears Ago', 'Breakin' In A Brand New Broken Heart', 'When The Boy In Your Arms (Is The Boy In Your Heart)', 'Don't Break The Heart That Loves You' (US number 1), 'Second Hand Love' and 'Vacation'. Francis made her film debut in 1960 with *Where The Boys Are*, and followed it with similar 'frothy' comedy musicals such as *Follow The Boys* (1963), *Looking For Love* (1964) and *When The Boys Meet The Girls* (1965). Outdated by the 60s beat boom, she worked in nightclubs in the late 60s, and did much charity work for UNICEF and similar organizations, besides entertaining US troops in Vietnam. She also extended her repertoire, and kept her options open, by recording albums in several languages, including French, Spanish and Japanese, and one entitled, *Connie Francis Sings Great Jewish Favorites*. Late 70s issues included more country music selections, including *Great Country Hits* with Hank Williams Jnr.

In 1974 she was the victim of a rape in her motel room after performing at the Westbury Theatre, outside New York. She later sued the motel for negligence, and was reputedly awarded damages of over three million dollars. For several years afterwards she did not perform in public, and underwent psychiatric treatment for long periods. She returned to the Westbury in 1981, to an enthusiastic reception, and resumed performing in the USA and abroad, including appearances at the London Palladium in 1989; and in Las Vegas in the same year, where she received a standing ovation after a mature performance ranging from her opening number, 'Let Me Try Again', to the climactic, 'If I Never Sing Another Song'. While at the Palladium, her speech became slurred and she was suspected of being drunk. In 1991 she had trouble speaking on a US television show, and, a year later, collapsed at a show in New Jersey. She was diagnosed as suffering from 'a complex illness', and of 'having been toxic for 18 years'. After drastically reducing her daily lithium intake, in 1993 she signed a new recording contract with Sony, buoyed up by the fact that her 1959 hit, 'Lipstick On Your Collar', was climbing high in the UK charts, triggered by its use as the title of a Dennis Potter television series.

Albums: *Who's Sorry Now?* (1958), *The Exciting Connie Francis* (1959), *My Thanks To You* (1959), *Christmas In My Heart* (1959), *Italian Favorites* (1960), *More Italian Favorites* (1960), *Rock 'N' Roll Million Sellers* (1960), *Country And Western Golden Hits* (1960), *Spanish And Latin American Favorites* (1960), *Connie Francis At The Copa* (1961), *Connie Francis Sings Great Jewish Favorites* (1961), *Songs To A Swingin' Band* (1961), *Never On Sunday And Other Title Songs From Motion Pictures* (1961), *Folk Song Favorites* (1961), *Do The Twist* (1962), *Second Hand Love And Other Hits* (1962), *Country Music Connie Style* (1962), *Modern Italian Hits* (1963), *Follow The Boys* (1963, film soundtrack), *German Favorites* (1963), *Award Winning Motion Picture Hits* (1963), *Great American Waltzes* (1963), *In The Summer Of His Years* (1964), *Looking For Love* (1964, film soundtrack), with Hank Williams Jnr. *Great Country Favorites* (1964), *A New Kind Of Connie* (1964), *Connie Francis Sings For Mama* (1965), *When The Boys Meet The Girls* (1965, film

soundtrack), *Movie Greats Of The Sixties* (1966), *Live At The Sahara In Las Vegas* (1966), *Love Italian Style* (1967), *Happiness* (1967), *My Heart Cries For You* (1967), *Hawaii Connie* (1968), *Connie And Clyde* (1968), *Connie Sings Bacharach And David* (1968), *The Wedding Cake* (1969), *Connie Francis Sings Great Country Hits, Volume Two* (1973), *Sings The Big Band Hits* (1977), *I'm Me Again - Silver Anniversary Album* (1981), *Connie Francis And Peter Kraus, Volumes 1 & 2* (1984), *Country Store* (1988). Compilations: *Connie's Greatest Hits* (1960), *More Greatest Hits* (1961), *Mala Femmena And Connie's Big Hits From Italy* (1963), *The Very Best Of Connie Francis* (1963), *The All Time International Hits* (1965), *20 All Time Greats* (1977), *Connie Francis In Deutschland* (1988, eight-album box set), *The Very Best Of Connie Francis, Volume Two* (1988), *The Singles Collection* (1993).

Further reading: *Who's Sorry Now?*, Connie Francis.

Franz, Johnny

b. John Charles Franz, 23 February 1922, London, England, d. 29 January 1977, London, England. An extremely successful and highly regarded pianist, and A&R producer for Philips Records in the UK. Franz began to study the piano when he was 13, and, two years later, joined the music publishers, Francis, Day and Hunter. In parallel with his day job, Franz worked in the evenings with artists such as Jack Jackson, George Elrick and Nat Allen. He also served as accompanist to harmonica soloist, Ronald Chesney, on his radio series. In 1940 Franz played the piano for the band singer Bernard Hunter's first stage appearance, at Collins Music Hall, and, by the late 40s, had established a reputation as one of the leading accompanists in Britain, working with Adelaide Hall, Benny Lee and visting American star, Vivian Blaine. One of his most enduring associations was with Anne Shelton, and they were part of an entertaintment 'package' that was flown on a round trip of 1,500 miles to play three dates in the American zone of Nuremborg, West Germany, in 1950. Ironically, not long afterwards, Franz was a passenger in a Rapide small aircraft that up-ended on a runway in Jersey, and he was reluctant to fly again. In 1954, after spending 17 years with Francis, Day and Hunter, whilst also discovering and coaching new talent, Franz was appointed the A&R Manager of Philips Records in 1954. His previous background meant that he was ideally suited to the job. He was able to select the right kind of material for his roster of artists, routine them, and explain to the musical arrangers precisely the sound that he wanted to hear on the finished records. Blessed with perfect pitch, he could also spot a clinker in the string section from the other side of the control room. In the late 50s Franz was responsible for the output of some of the most successful artists in the UK, such as Frankie Vaughan, Shirley Bassey, Harry Secombe, the Beverley Sisters, the Kaye Sisters, Robert Earl, Ronnie Carroll, Susan Maughan, Julie Rogers and, of course, Anne Shelton. It was his idea, when recording Shelton's 1956 chart-topper, 'Lay Down Your Arms', to add the sound of martial marching feet by having one of the studio staff shuffling about in a sand tray - recorded 'live', too - no over-dubbing in those days. In complete contrast, he worked with the risque American cabaret star, Ruth Wallis, and also produced the sophisticated *Mel Tormé Meets The British*, which was arranged by Wally Stott, one of Franz's key conductor/arrangers along with Ivor Raymonde and Peter Knight. In the late 50s, Marty Wilde was at the forefront of Philips's assault on the charts, as Franz adapted to the radical musical changes that were happening all around him. Early in the 60s he nurtured the vocal/instrumental group, the Springfields, from which emerged one of the decade's superstars, Dusty Springfield, with a string of hits which included the million-sellers, 'I Only Want To Be With You' (written by her musical director, Ivor Raymonde, with Mike Hawker), and 'You Don't Have To Say You Love Me'. The Four Pennies were another successful Franz act around that time, with their UK number 1, 'Juliet'. So to were the Walker Brothers, who introduced the pop world to another 60s icon, Scott Walker. The sound that Franz created for Walker Brothers hits such as 'Make It Easy On Yourself' 'My Ship Is Coming In' and 'The Sun Ain't Gonna Shine Any More', is sometimes called 'Phil Spectorish'. That may well be true, although the two producers were very different in appearance and style: Franz could easily have been mistaken for a bank manager - albeit one who chain-smoked and devoured copious amounts of tea. As well as producing Scott Walker's chart hits, 'Jackie', 'Joanna' and 'Lights Of Cincinatti', Franz's influence was also apparent on *Sings Songs From His T.V. Series,* which, with show numbers such as 'I Have Dreamed', 'The Song Is You' and 'If She Walked Into My Life', showed Walker to be a romantic balladeer of the old school. In a way, it was the 'old pals' act' that brought much of the best commercial material Franz's way. His contacts in the music publishing

business, such as Cyril Shane, ensured that Philips were offered many potential hit songs, some of them from abroad. Dusty Springfield's 'I Only Want To Be With You' came to London from the 1965 San Remo Song Festival, and, in 1973, Franz placed 'Welcome Home' ('Vivre'), a French number with an English lyric by Bryan Blackburn, with *Opportunity Knocks* winners, Peters And Lee. It gave them a UK number 1, and they hit the top spot again in the same year with *We Can Make It,* the first of their four Top 10 albums in the 70s. Among the most fondly remembered television and recording performers of the decade, the duo were a part of the final flourish in the life of a man who has been called 'the last of the great pro's'. Johnny Franz died in 1977, at the age of 55, in a Chelsea hospital.

Freberg, Stan

b. Stanley Victor Freberg, 7 August 1926, Los Angeles, California, USA. Stan Freberg was a satirist who experienced great popularity during the early 50s in the USA. Freberg pioneered the style of satire and parody later used on such television programmes as *Saturday Night Live*. He performed on radio and television, acted, wrote books as well as his own comedy material, worked in advertising and was even an accomplished puppeteer. Freberg grew up the son of a Baptist minister in Pasadena, California. His first showbusiness experience was at the age of 11 as an assistant to his uncle, a magician. Freberg became enthralled with the radio during his youth. As well as performing, he wrote and produced student shows and became his high school's speech champion, going on to win a statewide competition. He was awarded a drama scholarship but turned it down to work with Mel Blanc, who provided the voices of Warner Brothers cartoon characters such as Bugs Bunny and Porky Pig. Freberg provided voice-overs for other characters.

In the mid-40s he appeared on radio for the first time and soon became a regular on such programmes as the *Jack Benny Show* and on the Armed Forces Radio Network. He spent two years in the army and then joined a small orchestra, Red Fox And His Musical Hounds, as comedian/guitarist. He and actor Daws Butler (later the voice of Yogi Bear and Huckleberry Hound) then wrote and performed for the cartoon show *Time For Beany,* an Emmy-winning programme which served as inspiration to *Muppets* creator Jim Henson. In 1951 Freberg signed to Capitol Records and recorded 'John And Marsha', a spoof of soap operas in which the only lyrics were the two names of the title, repeated dramatically throughout the record. The record became a US hit, and was followed by parodies of Cole Porter's 'I've Got You Under My Skin', Johnnie Ray's 'Cry' and others. In 1953 Freberg scored a number 1 record with 'St. George And The Dragonet', a parody of the *Dragnet* television series.

As the rock 'n' roll era began in 1954 Freberg lampooned such hits as 'Sh-Boom' and 'The Great Pretender', with orchestration by Billy May, who remains Freberg's arranger/conductor in the 90s. In 1956 Freberg took on Elvis Presley's 'Heartbreak Hotel' and British skiffle artist Lonnie Donegan's 'Rock Island Line', while the following year found him satirizing Harry Belafonte's 'Banana Boat Day-O'. Other Freberg targets were Lawrence Welk, Mitch Miller and the television medium itself. In 1957 Freberg was given his own 17-week radio programme, some of which was collected on the Grammy-winning album *The Best Of The Stan Freberg Shows*. Freberg's 1958 single 'Green Chritma' brilliantly attacked the commercialization of Christmas and was banned by many radio stations. His final chart hit, 1960's 'The Old Payola Roll Blues (Side 1)' was another controversial release. Freberg continued to release albums throughout the 60s, his most successful being 1961's *Stan Freberg Presents The United States Of America*. He is active as an advertising writer in the 90s and still lends his voice to advertisement and voice-overs, and the occasional cartoon, such as the CBS television animation anthology *Toon Night* (1991).

Albums: *Comedy Caravan* (1956), *A Child's Garden Of Freberg* (1957), *The Best Of The Stan Freberg Shows* (1958), *With The Original Cast* (1959), *Face The Funnies* (1962), *Presents The United States Of America* (1961), *The Madison Avenue Werewolf* (1962), *Mickey Mouse's Birthday Party* (1963), *Underground Show #1* (1966). Compilations: *The Best Of Stan Freberg* (1964), *The Capitol Years* (1989).

Further reading: *It Only Hurts When I Laugh*, Stan Freberg.

Freed, Alan

b. 15 December 1926, Johnstown, Pennsylvania, USA, d. 20 January 1965. Freed was one of several key individuals who helped to create the audience for rock 'n' roll. As an influential disc jockey, he made enemies among the music business establishment by championing the cause of black artists but his career ended tragically when he was found to be guilty of payola in 1962. The son of European immigrants, he played trombone in a high school band named the Sultans Of Swing. After US Army service, he got his first radio job in 1946, playing classical records. He moved on to Akron, Ohio to play current pop material and in 1951 joined WJW Cleveland. There Freed hosted a show sponsored by local record store owner Leo Mintz, consisting of R&B originals rather than white pop cover versions. Entitled *Moondog's Rock 'N' Roll Party*, the show attracted large audiences of white teenagers who swamped a 1952 concert by the Moonglows, a group Freed had discovered and signed to his own short-lived Champagne label. His local success led him to New York and WINS in 1953. He was stopped from using the Moondog title after litigation with the blind Manhattan street musician Moondog (Louis Hardin). Still a champion of black artists such as Chuck Berry and Fats Domino, Freed hosted major live shows at the Paramount Theatre and in 1956-57 appeared in the films *Rock Around The Clock*, *Rock Rock Rock* and *Don't Knock The Rock*. However, with the rise of Bill Haley, Elvis Presley and Pat Boone (whose cover versions he frequently ignored), Freed's power as a disc jockey was weakened. In particular, he became a target of opponents of rock 'n' roll such as Columbia's A&R chief Mitch Miller, and when Freed refused to play Columbia releases he was fired by WINS. He then joined WABC and hosted a televised *Dance Party* show on WNEW-TV based on Dick Clark's *American Bandstand*.

Freed's arrest on a charge of inciting a riot at a Boston concert left him ill-prepared to deal with the accusations of payola laid by a Congressional investigation in 1959. It emerged that independent labels had provided cash or publishing rights to Freed in return for the airplay they were denied by the prejudices of other radio stations. In 1962 Freed was found guilty of bribery and this was followed by charges of tax evasion. He died of uremic poisoning in January 1965.

Freed, Arthur

b. 9 September 1894, Charleston, South Carolina, USA, d. 12 April 1973. While still at school Freed began to write song lyrics. He was already an accomplished pianist and was determined to make his way as a songwriter. His first job was as a demonstrator in a Chicago music shop where he met Minnie Marx, mother of the Marx Brothers. With her encouragement he quit his job and

Alan Freed

joined her sons' show as a singer. He later teamed up with Gus Edwards as a musical act in vaudeville. During this period he wrote many songs of variable quality and after World War I continued with different collaborators, including Gus Arnheim and Abe Lyman with whom he wrote 'I Cried For You', his first huge hit. By the end of the 20s Freed was in Los Angeles, where he wrote the score for *The Broadway Melody* (1929). He stayed on in Hollywood, writing scores for films before moving into production. He subsequently produced many of MGM's best musicals, including *Babes In Arms*, *The Wizard Of Oz* (both 1939), *Lady Be Good* (1941), *Meet Me In St Louis*, *The Ziegfeld Follies* (both 1944), *The Pirate* (1947), *The Barkleys Of Broadway*, *Easter Parade*, *Take Me Out To The Ball Game*, *Words And Music* (all 1948), *Annie Get Your Gun*, *On The Town* (both 1949), *An American In Paris*, *Show Boat* (both 1951, with the former winning the Oscar for Best Film), *Singin' In The Rain* (1952), *Brigadoon*, *Kismet* (both 1955), *Silk Stockings* (1956) and *Gigi*, which won an Oscar for Best Film of 1958. During his long stay at MGM Freed collaborated extensively with composer Herb Nacio Brown, writing songs such as 'You Were Meant For Me', 'The Wedding Of The Painted Doll', 'The Broadway Melody', 'Singin' In The Rain', 'Pagan Love Song', 'Alone', 'Good Morning' and 'All I Do Is Dream Of You'. Although written for many different films, several of their best songs were reprised in *Singin' In The Rain*, for which they wrote a new song, 'Make 'Em Laugh'. During his days as a producer, Freed was responsible for substantially furthering the careers of dancer Gene Kelly, André Previn, and director Vincente Minnelli. For a number of years in the 60s Freed was president of the American Academy of Motion Picture Arts and Sciences, from whom he received the Irving Thalberg Award in 1961 and a further award in 1968, the year he retired from MGM.

G

Garland, Judy

b. Frances Gumm, 10 June 1922, Grand Rapids, Minnesota, USA, d. 22 June 1969. The Gumms were a theatrical family. Parents, Frank and Ethel, had appeared in vaudeville as Jack and Virginia Lee and, later, with the addition of their first two daughters, Mary Jane and Virginia, appeared locally as 'The Four Gumms'. 'Baby Frances' joined the troupe when she was a little over two years of age and it was quickly apparent that with her arrival, even at that early age, the Gumm family had outgrown their locale. The family moved to Los Angeles, where all three girls were enrolled in a dance school. When Frank Gumm bought a run-down theatre in Lancaster, a desert town north of Los Angeles, the family moved again. Domestic problems beset the Gumm family throughout this period and Frances's life was further disrupted by Ethel Gumm's determined belief in her youngest daughter's show-business potential. The act had become the Gumm Sisters, although Baby Frances was clearly the one audiences wanted to see and hear. In 1933 Ethel Gumm returned to Los Angeles, taking the girls with her. Frances was again enrolled in a theatrical school. A visit to Chicago was an important step for the girls, with the youngest once more attracting the most attention; here too, at the urging of comedian George Jessell, they changed their name to the Garland Sisters. On their return to Los Angeles in 1934 the sisters played a successful engagement at Grauman's Chinese Theater in Hollywood. Soon afterwards Frances was personally auditioned by Louis B. Mayer, head of MGM. Deeply impressed by what he saw and heard, Mayer signed the girl before she had even taken a screen test. With another adjustment to her name, Frances now became Judy Garland. She made her first film appearance in *Every Sunday* (1936), a short musical film which also featured Deanna Durbin. Her first major impact on audiences came with her third film, *Broadway Melody Of 1938*, in which she sang 'Dear Mr Gable' (to a photograph of Clark Gable), seguing into 'You Made Me Love You'. She was then teamed with MGM's established child star, Mickey Rooney, a partnership which brought a succession of popular films in the 'Andy Hardy' series. By now, everyone at MGM knew that they had a star on their hands. This fact was

Judy Garland with Gene Kelly

triumphantly confirmed with her appearance in *The Wizard Of Oz* (1939), in which she sang 'Somewhere Over The Rainbow', the song with which she would subsequently always be associated. Unfortunately, this period of frenzied activity came at a time when she was still developing physically. Like many young teenagers, she tended to put on weight and this was something film-makers could not tolerate. On the one hand they did not want a pudgy celebrity; on the other it was the practical effect of not wanting their star to change appearance during the course of a film. Whatever the reason, she was prescribed some drugs for weight control, others to ensure she was bright and perky for the long hours of shooting, and still more to bring her down at the end of the day so that she could sleep. These were the days before the side effects of amphetamines (which she took to suppress her appetite) were understood, and no one at the time knew that the pills she was taking in such huge quantities were habit-forming. Adding to the growing girl's problems were emotional difficulties which had begun during her parents' stormy relationship, and which were exacerbated by the high pressure of her new life. In 1941, against the wishes and advice of her mother and the studio, she married David Rose and soon afterwards became pregnant but was persuaded, by her mother and Mayer, to have an abortion. With her personal life firmly on the downward slide towards later disasters, Garland's successful film career now took a further upswing. In 1942 she appeared in *For Me And My Gal*, then made *Presenting Lily Mars, Thousands Cheer, Girl Crazy* (all 1943), *Meet Me In St Louis* (1944), *The Harvey Girls, Ziegfeld Follies* and *Till The Clouds Roll By* (all 1946). Garland's popularity extended beyond films into radio and records, but her private life was still in disarray. In 1945 she divorced Rose and married Vincente Minnelli, who had directed her in *Meet Me In St Louis*. In 1946 her daughter, Liza Minnelli, was born. The late 40s brought more film successes with *The Pirate, Easter Parade, Words And Music* (all 1948) and *In The Good Old Summertime* (1949). Although Garland's career appeared to be in splendid shape, in 1950 her private life was fast deteriorating. Pills and alcohol and severe emotional disturbances led to her failing to appear before the cameras on several occasions and resulted in the ending of her contract with MGM. In 1951 her marriage to Minnelli also finished and she attempted suicide. Her subsequent marriage to Sid Luft and his handling of her career brought an upturn both emotionally and professionally. She made a trip to Europe, appearing at the London Palladium to great acclaim. On her return to the USA she played the Palace Theater in New York for a hugely successful 19-week run. Her film career resumed with a dramatic/singing role in *A Star Is Born* (1954), for which she was unsuccessfully nominated for an Oscar. By the late 50s all the problems were back, and in some cases had worsened. She suffered nervous and emotional breakdowns, her marriage was on the rocks, and she made further suicide attempts. A straight dramatic role, in *Judgement At Nuremberg* (1961), for which she was again nominated for an Oscar, enhanced her reputation. However, her marriage was still in trouble, although she and Luft made repeated attempts to hold it together (they had two children, Lorna and Joey). Despite the personal traumas and the professional ups and downs, Garland achieved another huge success with a personal appearance at New York's Carnegie Hall on 23 April 1961, the subsequent album of the concert winning five Grammy Awards. A 1963 television series was disappointing and, despite another good film performance in a dramatic role, in *A Child Is Waiting* and a fair dramatic/singing appearance in *I Could Go On Singing* (both 1963), her career remained plagued with inconsistencies. The marriage with Luft ended in divorce, as did a subsequent marriage. Remarried again in 1968, Garland attempted a comeback with a club appearance in London but suffered the indignity of a major flop. On 22 June 1969 she was found dead, apparently from an overdose of sleeping pills. She was at her best in such films as *Meet Me In St Louis* and *The Wizard Of Oz* and on stage for the superb Carnegie Hall concert, and had she done nothing else, she would have earned a substantial reputation as a major singing star. To her powerful singing voice she added great emotional depths, which came not only through artifice but from the sometimes cruel reality of her life. When the catalogue of personal tragedies was added to Garland's performing talent she became something else, a cult figure, a show business legend. She was a figure that only Hollywood could have created and yet, had she been a character in a melodrama, no one would have believed such a life was possible.

Selected albums: *Judy* (1956) *Judy In Love* (1958), *Garland At The Grove* (1959), with John Ireland *The Letter* (1959), *Judy At Carnegie Hall* (1961, 2-LP set), *Judy! That's Entertainment* (1961), *Star Years* (1961), *Magic* (1961), *Our Love Letter* (1963), *Alone*

(1963), *Miss Show Business* (1963), *Just For Openers* (1964), with Liza Minnelli *Live At The London Palladium* (1965), *Judy Garland* (1965), *The Last Concert 20-7-68* (1968). Compilations: *The Young Judy Garland* (c.1938-42), *The Beginning* (1979).

Further reading: *Judy Garland*, Anne Edwards. *Judy And Liza*, James Spada with Karen Swenson. *The Other Side Of The Rainbow: With Judy Garland On The Dawn Patrol*, Mel Tormé. *Judy Garland*, David Shipman. *World's Greatest Entertainer*, John Fricke.

Gibbs, Georgia

b. Freda Gibbons, 17 August 1920, Worcester, Massachusetts, USA. Gibbs has been unfairly maligned by rock critics for building her career in the 50s by covering R&B hits of LaVern Baker and Etta James. In reality she was a genuinely talented pop vocalist, whose jazz-tinged approach reflected years of experience in the big band era, a period when there was no stigma attached to covers. Her big break in the business came in 1936 when she joined the Hudson-DeLange Orchestra, recording for Brunswick Records. That led to a radio career in 1937, including *Your Hit Parade*. There were also recording stints with the bands of Frankie Trumbauer (1940), Artie Shaw (1942), and Tommy Dorsey (1944). On the *Jimmy Durante Camel Caravan* radio show 1943-47, she received her trademark nickname when host Garry Moore dubbed her 'Her Nibs, Miss Gibbs'. Gibbs first entered the charts in 1950 with a cover of Eileen Barton's 'If I Knew You Were Comin' I'd've Baked A Cake' (number 5 pop), and had her first number 1 hit with 'Kiss Of Fire', a vocal version of the 30s tango instrumental 'El Choclo'. After hitting with 'Seven Lonely Days' (number 5 pop 1953), Gibbs achieved notoriety in 1955 when she hit with two note-for-note covers of R&B tunes – 'Tweedledee' (US pop number 2) by Baker and 'Dance With Me Henry' (US pop number 1) by James. 'Kiss Me Another' (US pop number 30) and 'Tra La La' (US pop number 24) kept her in the public eye in 1956, but not for long. Her last chart record was 'The Hula Hoop Song' (US pop Top 40 1958), which tried to ride the success of the silly toy fad. In the UK, Gibb's chart success was minuscule; two one-week appearances by 'Tweedle Dee' and 'Kiss Me Another' respectively. Albums: *Ballin' The Jack* (1951), *Georgia Gibbs Sings Oldies* (1953), *The Man That Got Away* (1954), *Music And Memories* (1956), *Song Favorites* (1956), *Swingin' With Her Nibs* (1956), *Her Nibs* (1957), *Something's Gotta Give* (1964), *Call Me* (1966). Compilation: *Georgia Gibbs' Greatest Hits* (1963).

Gleason, Jackie

b. Herbert John Gleason, 26 February 1916, Brooklyn, New York, USA, d. 24 June 1987. Gleason was primarily a comedian, starring on stage, screen and television, but he also recorded a number of albums in the 50s and 60s. He established his persona with early films like *Orchestra Wives* (1942) and several appearances on Broadway (*Artists And Models, Follow The Girls* and *Along Fifth Avenue*). However, stardom came with the dawn of the 50s. The formative television series *The Life Of Riley* led to *Cavalcade Of Stars* in 1949, from which Gleason, alongside Art Carney, launched a series of sketches and basic comedy routines. He then fronted a variety/new talent CBS programme *Stageshow* before Tommy and Jimmy Dorsey took over. The programme was notable for introducing Elvis Presley to a television audience. The enormously popular television show *The Honeymooners* followed in 1955, before a series of films leading in to the 60s. Notable amongst these were *The Hustler* (1961), alongside Paul Newman, for which Gleason was nominated for an Oscar as best supporting actor, and *Requiem For A Heavyweight*, the first major play by *The Twilight Zone's* creator Rod Serling. Gleason also appeared as Buford T. Ford, a law officer prone to mishap in the Burt Reynolds vehicle *Smokey And The Bandit* in 1977. By this time his recording career had largely ended. He had previously written the score for *Gigot* (1962), and his own television theme 'Melancholy Serenade'. In addition there were several 'mood music' albums on Capitol, which represented his most successful material, and a projected ballet. A string of Top 10 US albums between 1956 and 1957 featured Bobby Hackett and Pee Wee Erwin in his studio orchestras. Selected albums: *Music For Lovers Only* (1953), *Music To Make You Misty* (1954), *Music To Remember Her* (1955), *Lonesome Echo* (1955), *Romantic Jazz* (1955), *Music To Change Her Mind* (1956), *Night Winds* (1956), *Merry Christmas* (1956), *Music For The Love Hours* (1957), *Velvet Brass* (1957), *Jackie Gleason Presents 'OOO!'* (1957).

Further reading: *The Great One: The Life And Legend Of Jackie Gleason*, William A. Henry III, *Jackie Gleason: An Intimate Portrait Of The Great One*, W.J. Weatherby.

Good, Jack

b. 1931, London, England. This founder of British pop television was president of Oxford University Drama Society and then a stand-up comic before enrolling on a BBC training course. Good's final test film was centred on Freddie Mills. The late boxer was also an interlocutor on 1957's *6.5 Special*, a magazine series for teenagers produced by Good and Josephine Douglas. While he became evangelical about rock 'n' roll, Good's staid superiors obliged him to balance the pop with comedy sketches, string quartets and features on sport and hobbies. He was fired for flaunting Corporation dictates by presenting a stage version of the show. Snapped up by ITV, he broke ground with *Oh Boy!* which introduced Cliff Richard, Marty Wilde and other homegrown rockers to the nation. So swiftly did its atmospheric parade of idols - mostly male - pass before the cameras that the screaming studio audience, urged on by Good, scarcely had pause to draw breath. While overseeing the less exciting *Boy Meets Girls* and *Wham!*, Good branched out into publishing - and record production of such as Billy Fury's *Sound Of Fury*.

1962 found Good in North America where he worked intermittently as an actor - notably on Broadway in C.P. Snow's *The Affair* and, in 1967, as a hotelier in *Clambake*, an Elvis Presley vehicle. His self-financed pilot programme, *Young America Swings The World*, fell on stony ground but, after Brian Epstein commissioned him for *Around The Beatles*, he superintended the nationally-broadcast pop showcase *Shindig* which, as well as 'discoveries' like the Righteous Brothers and Sonny And Cher, represented a media breakthrough for black artists as diverse as Howlin' Wolf to the Chambers Brothers - and held its own in a ratings war against *The Beverley Hillbillies* on a main rival channel. Leaving *Shindig* to fend for itself, his most interesting career tangent of the later 60s was *Catch My Soul*, 1968's rock adaptation in a Los Angeles theatre of Shakespeare's *Othello* with Jerry Lee Lewis as Iago. For a season in London, P.J. Proby assumed the Lewis role with Good himself as the Moor. Back in the USA, he ticked over with one-shot television specials concerning, among others, Andy Williams, the Monkees and 1970's Emmy award-winning classical/pop hybrid of Ray Charles, Jethro Tull, the Nice and the LA Philharmonic. On an extended visit to England from his Santa Fe home, Good put on *Elvis*, a biographical musical starring, initially, Proby and Shakin' Stevens before daring an updated reconstruction of *Oh Boy!* (later transferred to television) at the same London West End theatre. By the 80s, income from the inspired Good's less frequent television and stage ventures underwrote

another vocational episode - as a painter. In the early 90s it was reported that Good was taking up the priesthood with the aim of becoming a monk, but, while he was contemplating it, he travelled to London to oversee the West End launch of his own autobiographical musical, *Good Rockin' Tonite*, which had them dancing in the aisles - just like the old days.

Goons

Mutating from Britain's radio show *Crazy People* in 1951, the high summer of the BBC's Light Programme's *Goon Show* was reflected in UK hit parade entries in 1956 for its spin-off double a-sides, 'I'm Walking Backwards For Christmas'/'Bluebottle Blues' and 'Bloodnok's Rock 'N' Roll'/'Ying Tong Song' - which encapsulated the off-beat humour, topical parodies and musical interludes (under the baton of bandleader Ray Ellington) of the radio series starring Terence 'Spike' Milligan, Peter Sellers, Harry Secombe and, briefly, Michael Bentine. As well as ushering in that strata of comedy that culminated in the late 60s with *Monty Python's Flying Circus*, aspects of the Goons became apparent in the stylistic determination of the Scaffold, the Bonzo Dog Doo-Dah Band and, less directly, the Beatles - particularly in their first two films and in John Lennon's literary output. In reciprocation, a cod-Shakespearian recitation of 'A Hard Day's Night' was among the late Sellers' solo hits. However, Secombe - whose chart career began before that of the Goons - enjoyed greater success with sonorous ballads, almost topping the British list in 1967 with 'This Is My Song'. Nevertheless, Secombe's next - and last - Top 10 penetration took place six years later with a re-issue of his Goons' 'Ying Tong Song', shortly after the troupe's one-off radio and television reunion during the BBC's 50 anniversary celebrations.
Selected albums: *The Best Of The Goons* (1960), *The Last Goon Show Of All* (1972).

Gorme, Eydie

b. Edith Gorme, 16 August 1931, New York, USA. Gorme was the youngest of three children. Her parents were of Turkish and Spanish origin, and since Spanish was the family language, she grew up speaking it fluently. At the age of three she made her radio debut, singing in a children's programme from a department store. While at the William Howard Taft High School in the Bronx, Gorme was voted 'the prettiest, peppiest cheerleader', starred in the school musicals, and

Eydie Gorme and Steve Lawrence

sang with her friend Ken Greengrass's band at the weekends. On leaving school, she worked as a Spanish interpreter with the Theatrical Supply Export Company, before deciding to concentrate on a singing career, with Greengrass as her manager. Her first break came in 1950 when she successfully auditioned for bandleader Tommy Tucker, and toured with him for two months. When that tour ended she spent a year with Tex Beneke before going out on her own, appearing in nightclubs, and on radio and television. After being turned down several times by Arthur Godfrey's talent scouts, 'the fourth time I tried, they locked the office door when they saw me coming up the stairs', Gorme signed for Coral Records in 1952. Her singles included 'Frenesi', 'I've Gotta Crow', 'Tea For Two' and 'Fini', which entered the US Top 20. She also hosted her own radio show, *Cita Con Eydie* (*A Date With Eydie*), which was transmitted to Spanish-speaking countries via the *Voice Of America*. In September 1953, she became a permanent member of Steve Allen's top rated *Tonight* show, on which she sang, and wrote and performed sketches with another regular, Steve Lawrence. They also introduced Allen's composition, 'This Could Be The Start Of Something', which became associated with them as their singing partnership blossomed into romance. Lawrence (b. Stephen Leibowitz, 8 July 1935, Brooklyn, New York, USA), was the son of Eastern European parents and had sung in the choir at his cantor father's synagogue. Lawrence *did* make it onto the *Arthur Godfrey Talent Show*, in 1952, and had made an impression with his version of Tony Martin's hit, 'Domino'. An important and influential figure in both Gorme and Lawrence's recording careers was conductor/arranger/producer, Don Costa. In February 1956, Gorme deputized at short notice for Billy Daniels at New York's Copacabana nightclub, and was so well received that she returned in July to headline with her own show. In January 1957, she made her Broadway debut in the *Jerry Lewis Stage Show* at the Palace Theatre, and in December, Gorme and Lawrence were married in Las Vegas. Eydie's success in the the US singles chart upto this period had included 'Too Close For Comfort', 'Mama, Teach Me To Dance' (both 1956), 'Love Me Forever' (1957) and the number 11 hit 'You Need Hands' (1958). During the summer of 1958, they starred in their own weekly one-hour musical variety television show, as a replacement for Steve Allen. Shortly afterwards, Lawrence was inducted into the US Army for two

years. Eydie embarked on a country-wide nightclub tour until 1960 when she was reunited with Lawrence at the Copacabana and the Coconut Grove, Los Angeles, and the Sands and Sahara Hotels in Las Vegas. In 1960 they won a Grammy Award for *We Got Us*, their first complete duet album, which was followed by several others, including *Two On The Aisle*, a set of Broadway show numbers and *At The Movies*. In the singles chart, the couple's most successful joint efforts included 'I Want To Stay Here' (1963) and 'I Can't Stop Talking About You' (1964). Eydie received a Grammy Award for Best Popular Female Vocalist for her version of 'If He Walked Into My Life', from Jerry Herman's musical, *Mame*. In 1968, the couple appeared on Broadway in *Golden Rainbow*, a musical adaptation of Arnold Schulman's play, *A Hole In the Head*, with words and music by Walter Marks. One of the songs, 'I've Gotta Be Me', entitled a Lawrence album, and also became a regular part of Sammy Davis Jnr.'s repertoire. In 1969, Gorme and Lawrence recorded their first musical, *What It Was, Was Love*, written for them by Gordon Jenkins. During the 70s and 80s, the couple continued to record and appear regularly on television. Several of their 'specials', commemorating the music of composers such as Cole Porter and George and Ira Gershwin, won awards; *Steve And Eydie Celebrate Irving Berlin* gained a record-breaking seven Emmys. In 1987, they were in a television production of *Alice In Wonderland*, written by Steve Allen, playing the parts of Tweedledum and Tweedledee. In 1989, they released *Alone Together*, on their own GL label. It was for their live performances, however, that they received the most applause. During the 80s, they appeared at venues such as Carnegie Hall in 1981 and 1983; the Universal Amphitheatre, in Los Angeles; Harrah's, Tahoe; and the 1,400-seater Bally's at Las Vegas. Their skilful blend of classy songs (or, as they put it, 'no punk, no funk, no rock, no schlock'), coupled with a brand of humour which has been honed for over 30 years, make them one of the few consistently successful acts of their kind in the world. In 1991, they saw quite a lot of that world, when they joined Frank Sinatra on his year-long *Diamond Jubilee Tour*, to commemorate his 75th birthday.

Albums: solo *Eydie Gorme* (1957), *Eydie Swings The Blues* (1957), *Eydie Gorme Vamps The Roaring 20s* (1958), *Eydie In Love...* (1958), *Eydie Gorme On Stage* (1959), *Eydie Sings Showstoppers* (1959), *Eydie In Dixie-Land* (1960), *Come Sing With Me* (1961), *I Feel So Spanish* (1962), *Blame It On The Bossa Nova*

Charlie Gracie

(1963), *Let The Good Times Roll* (1963), *Gorme Country Style* (1964), *Amor* (1964), *More Amor* (1965), *Don't Go To Strangers* (1966), with the Trio Los Panchos *Navidad Means Christmas* (1966), *Softly, As I Love You* (1967), *Tonight I'll Say A Prayer* (1970), *Tomame O Dejame* (1985), *Come In From The Rain* (1985), *Sings/Canta* (1987); with Steve Lawrence *We Got Us* (1960), *Cozy* (1961), *On Broadway* (1967), *What It Was, Was Love* (1969), *Real True Lovin'* (1969), *We Can Make It Together* (1975), *Our Best To You* (1977), *Our Love Is Here To Stay* (1977), *I Still Believe In Love* (1985), *Alone Together* (1989). Compilations: solo *The Very Best Of Eydie Gorme* (1961), *Eydie Gorme's Greatest Hits* (1967); with Steve Lawrence *The Golden Hits* (1960), *The Best Of Steve And Eydie* (1977), *20 Golden Performances* (1977).

Gracie, Charlie

b. Charles Anthony Graci, 14 May 1936, Philadelphia, Pennsylvania, USA. When guitarist and songwriter Charlie Gracie recorded the original version of the rock 'n' roll song 'Butterfly' in 1957, he faced stiff competition from Andy Williams' cover. Charlie's 'Elvis Presley-like vocal' took the song to number 5 in the US charts and Top 20 in the UK, but Williams' charted higher, number 1 in the UK and US. They both sold over a million copies. He started out appearing as a teenager on Paul Whiteman's top-rated American television show. Gracie's subsequent singles were styled to suit his voice, including the ballads, 'Fabulous' and 'Wanderin' Eyes', both Top 10 smashes in the UK in the same year. For many years he has been a legend rather than a performing artist. Often controversial he has changed record labels countless times and still performs in the UK and the USA.
Selected albums: *Early Recordings* (1979), *Rockin' Philadelphia* (1982), *Amazing Gracie* (1982), *Live At The Stockton Globe 1957* (1983). Compilation: *Best Of Charlie Gracie* (1988).

Grant, Gogi

b. Myrtle Audrey Arinsberg, 20 September 1924, Philadelphia, Pennsylvania, USA. Pop vocalist Grant was apparently named after a New York restaurant called Gogi's La Rue, which was frequented by Dave Kapp, head of A&R at RCA Records. She had previously recorded, without success, as Audrey Brown and Audrey Grant, but as Gogi Grant she hit the US Top 10 in 1955 with the ballad 'Suddenly There's A Valley'. Her biggest hit came a year later with the sad ballad about lost love, 'The Wayward Wind', which shot to number 1 in the US and made Top 10 in the UK. She provided all the vocals for actress Ann Blyth's portrayal of 1920s torch singer Helen Morgan, in the 1957 bio-pic *The Helen Morgan Story*.
Selected albums: *The Helen Morgan Story* (1957, film soundtrack), *If You Want To Get To Heaven* (1960).

Greco, Buddy

b. Armando Greco, 14 August 1926, Philadelphia, Pennsylvania, USA. As a singer, Greco's strong suit was always swinging, ultra-hip interpretations of classy songs. The son of a music critic who had his own radio show on station WPEN, Buddy himself appeared on WPEN at the age of five, initially making his mark as a singer and actor. Later on, like his two brothers, he studied to become a pianist, practising and playing at the Philadelphia Settlement House, a 10-block complex of recreational and hobby facilities, where so many of the city's youthful musicians congregated. Greco led his own trio during 1944-49, and recorded a major hit version of Carmen Lombardo's 'Ooh, Look-A There Ain't She Pretty', though the singer received only $32 for recording the single. Heard by Benny Goodman while playing at Philadelphia's Club 13, he was offered a job by the bandleader and subsequently became pianist-vocalist-arranger with the Goodman orchestra, appearing with Goodman's sextet at the London Palladium in 1949, embarking on several tours with the band and gracing such Goodman Capitol sides as 'It Isn't Fair', 'Don't Worry 'Bout Me', 'The Land of Oo-Bla-Dee' and 'Brother Bill' with his vocals. By 1951 Greco had become a solo act once more, gaining a regular spot on the *Broadway Open House* television show and providing Coral with a hit record in 'I Ran All The Way Home'. He also won many lucrative nightclub engagements, one of which provided the best-selling album *Buddy Greco At Mister Kelly's*, a superb document of his appearances at the Chicago club in 1955. Greco's biggest hit was still to come, a non-stop, grab-at-the-lyrics version of Richard Rodgers and Lorenz Hart's 'The Lady Is A Tramp', cut for Epic Records in 1960. This track sold over a million copies worldwide and gave Buddy his first UK chart entry. During the late 60s and 70s Greco became increasingly associated with the British showbusiness scene, playing dates at London's Talk Of The Town, appearing on the Royal Command Performance and cutting an instrumental album with the London Symphony Orchestra. This well-

Gogi Grant

travelled and appreciated performer has claimed to have played every major club in the world on at least two occasions, and was still going round to some of them again in the late 80s.

Albums: *At Mister Kelly's* (1955), *My Buddy* (1960), *Songs For Swinging Losers* (1960), *Buddy's Back In Town* (1961), *I Like It Swinging* (1961), *Let's Love* (1962), *I Love A Piano* (1966), *Let The Sunshine In* (1970), *Live At Pullen's Talk Of North, April 1974* (1974), *For Once In My Life* (1982). Compilations: *Golden Hour Presents Buddy Greco* (1978), *Greatest Hits* (1984).

Grenfell, Joyce

b. Joyce Irene Phipps, 10 February 1910, London, England, d. 30 November 1979, London, England. An actress, singer and author - a brilliant exponent of the monologue and witty song. The daughter of American parents - her mother's sister was Nancy Astor - Joyce Phipps used to describe herself as 'three fourths American'. She became interested in the theatre at an early age, and spent a term at RADA before marrying Reginald Grenfell in 1929. Subsequently, she worked for a time in commercial art, contributed to *Punch* and *Country Life*, and spent over three years as radio critic for the *Observer*. After impressing the humourist Steven Potter with her own charming recollection of a lecture that she had recently attended at a Women's Institute, she was engaged by the theatrical producer, Herbert Farjeon, for *The Little Revue* (1939). In the early 40s she appeared in other Farjeon revues, *Diversion*, *Diversion No. 2* and *Light And Shade*, and then, in 1944, toured extensively with ENSA, in the Near and Far East, and in India, entertaining the troops in British forces' hospitals, with comic monologues and songs. Two years later she was awarded the OBE. In *Sigh No More* (1945), at London's Piccadilly Theatre, Grenfell dressed as a schoolgirl for Noel Coward's witty 'That Is The End Of The News', and, in the same show, introduced 'Du Maurier', a song she had written with composer Richard Addinsell. They collaborated again on material for the revues, *Tuppence Coloured* (1947) and *Penny Plain* (1951), in which Grenfell also appeared. It was the beginning of a significant and enduring professional relationship. By the late 40s and early 50s, Grenfell was working more and more in radio - as a panellist on *We Beg To Differ*, and as the British host of *Transatlantic Quiz*. She made a couple of propaganda films during the war, but her movie career proper began in 1943 with a comedy, *The Demi-Paradise*, which starred Laurence Olivier

and Margaret Rutherford. Grenfell appeared with Rutherford again, in *The Happiest Days Of Your Life* (1949), which also starred the lugubrious Alastair Sim. He and Grenfell managed to emerge unscathed from the *St. Trinians* film series. during the late 50s. Grenfell's other film roles, some of them highly telling cameos, were in such as *Here Comes The Bride*, *The Galloping Major*, *Pickwick Papers*, *The Million Pound Note* and *The Americanization Of Emily*. It was on stage, though, that she really came into her own. In 1954 she wrote the book and lyrics, with Addinsell's music, for *Joyce Grenfell Requests The Pleasure*, which ran for nearly a year in London before transferring to Broadway in the following year. In America, Grenfell developed her one-woman show, toured US cities, and appeared on the *Ed Sullivan Show* several times in the late 50s. One Sullivan date saw her on the same bill with Elvis Presley ('a pasty-faced plump boy', as she recalled). She presented her solo effort in London for the first time in 1957, at the Lyric theatre, under the title of *Joyce Grenfell - A Miscellany*, and later took the show to Australia where it was called *Meet Joyce Grenfell*. Throughout the 60s she continued to tour extensively at home and abroad, and went back to Australia three times. In the early 70s she lost the sight of one eye and retired from the stage. During the next six years she published two volumes of autobiography, *Joyce Grenfell Requests The Pleasure* and *In Pleasant Places*, before cancer affected her other eye, too, and she died in 1979. Always an effective broadcaster, from 1966 she was an essential member of television's *Face The Music*, a general knowledge quiz about music, and had her own series on BBC2 for a time. As a performer she was unique, and impossible to pigeon-hole. The wonder is that, because of her 'terribly English' image, she was so popular around the world, particularly in America. With the gentle 'I'm Going To See You Today', which became her theme, the pomp of 'Stately As A Galleon', and many other favourites such as 'Maude', 'Nursery School', 'A Terrible Worrier', 'Time', 'Three Brothers', 'It's Almost Tomorrow', and two recorded duets with Norman Wisdom, 'Narcissus' and 'I Don't 'Arf Love You', she presented a refined, humorous, perceptive, yet never unkind view of society. One of her best remembered pieces is 'I Like Life', which accords with her own philosophy: 'I am not interested in the pursuit of happiness, but only in the discovery of joy'. Her companion on that journey, Reginald Grenfell, who edited some of her books, died in 1993.

Selected albums: *Requests The Pleasure* (1955), *At*

Home (1957), *The Collection* (1976), *The New Collection* (1978), *Joyce Grenfell Talking* (1981), *Keepsake* (1986), *Re: Joyce* (1988), *The Second Collection* (1988), *Songs And Monologues* (1991), *Requests The Plaeasure* (3-CD set, 1992). Maureen Lipman and Denis King *Re: Joyce!* (stage cast, 1989).

Further reading: *Darling Ma: Letters To Her Mother, 1932-1944*, Edited by James Roose-Evans. *George - Don't Do that...* (sketches and songs). *Stately As A Galleon* (sketches and songs). *Time Of My Life - Entertaining The Troops: Her Wartime Journals*, Joyce Grenfell. *Joyce Grenfell Requests The Pleasure*, Joyce Grenfell. *Joyce: By Herself And Her Friends*, Edited by Reggie Grenfell and Richard Garnett. *In Pleasant Places*, Joyce Grenfell.

Guys And Dolls

Opening on 24 November 1950, the stage musical *Guys And Dolls* was a predicted success. With music and lyrics by Frank Loesser, and a book by Abe Burrows, out-of-town tryouts were hugely successful and by the time of its opening night on Broadway the word was out that the show was a winner. Based upon the risque yarns of Damon Runyon, the dialogue and lyrics effectively captured the speech patterns of Runyon's larger-than-life characters and the music perfectly matched the show's mood. The story presents an account of a love affair between compulsive gambler Nathan Detroit and dancer Miss Adelaide, alongside of which develops another love story, this one between another gambler, Sky Masterson, and Miss Sarah Brown, a member of the 'Save A Soul Mission'. Other Runyonesque characters fill out the cast, notably Nicely-Nicely Johnson, and Harry The Horse. During the course of the show true love eventually finds its way despite many obstacles, not least of which is police lieutenant Brannigan's desperate attempts to locate and close down Nathan's floating crap game, the oldest established in New York. By the end, Masterson is a reformed character and has married Sarah while Nathan and Miss Adelaide are about to marry after a 14-year long courtship. Loesser's songs included 'Fugue For Tinhorns', 'The Oldest Established' 'Take Back Your Mink', 'A Bushel And A Peck', 'Adelaide's Lament', 'Marry The Man Today', 'Sue Me', 'If I Were A Bell', 'More I Cannot Wish You', 'Luck Be A Lady', 'I'll Know', 'I've Never Been In Love Before' and the title number. Complementing the show's strong characterization and dramatic storyline, the producers cast actors rather than singers in the key roles, amongst them Sam Levene as Nathan, Vivian Blaine, who had worked in Hollywood musicals, as Miss Adelaide, Robert Alda as Sky, Isabel Bigley as Sarah, and Stubby Kaye as Nicely-Nicely Johnson, who stopped the show every night with his exuberant singing of 'Sit Down, You're Rockin' The Boat'. Critics and public loved it, and the show ran for 1,200 performances. The London production opened in 1953 with most of the principals recreating their roles, including Stubby Kaye, who repeatedly stopped the show in the West End, just as he had in Manhatten. *Guys And Dolls* was revived in the 70s by the National Theatre and again in the mid-80s. The 1955 film version, directed by Joseph L. Mankiewicz, starred Marlon Brando as Sky (one of Sky's songs, 'My Time Of Day', was dropped because the actor was unable to sing it, although he managed to handle a new one, 'Woman In Love'), with Jean Simmons as Sarah, Frank Sinatra as Nathan, and Vivian Blaine and Stubby Kaye reprising their roles. Sinatra introduced 'Adelaide', another number Loesser wrote for the film, which became popular on record for Sammy Davis Jnr.

Gypsy

Purporting to tell the true story of burlesque queen Gypsy Rose Lee, *Gypsy* opened on Broadway on 21 May 1959. With songs composed by Jule Styne, lyrics by Stephen Sondheim, plus direction and choreography by Jerome Robbins, the show looked strong but the story's construction demanded a powerful lead in the role of Mamma Rose. She was the ambitious mother of the two aspiring entertainers who grew up to be 'Louise' and 'June'; in real life Gypsy Rose Lee and her much more talented younger sister, screen actress June Havoc. In casting Ethel Merman not only did the producers get the best woman for the job, they also got an artist who audiences would flock to see. Songs from the show included 'May We Entertain You'/'Let Me Entertain You', 'Together, Wherever We Go', 'Small World', 'All I Need Is The Girl', and Merman's big song, 'Everything's Coming Up Roses'. Other cast members included Sandra Church and Jack Klugman. The show ran for slightly over 700 performances and was revived in 1974 with Angela Lansbury as Mamma Rose. The 1962 film version mysteriously miscast an over-demure Natalie Wood as Louise and an ultra-refined Rosalind Russell as Mamma Rose, a part that screamed out for a singer who could belt out a song as only Merman knew how.

H

Haley, Bill, And His Comets

b. William John Clifton Haley, 6 July 1925, Highland Park, Michigan, USA, d. 9 February 1981. Haley was one of the great pioneers of rock 'n' roll and was the first artist to take the new musical form to the world stage. His roots were in country music and he began his career as a yodelling cowboy. After playing in such country groups as the Downhomers and the Range Drifters, he formed the Four Aces Of Western Swing in 1948. At that point, his repertoire included compositions by both Red Foley and Hank Williams. His next group was the Saddlemen, who played a stirring mixture of western swing, mixed with polka. In 1951, he recorded the R&B hit 'Rocket 88', which indicated how far he had already travelled in assimilating the styles of rock 'n' roll. Haley's fusion of country, R&B and a steady beat was to provide the backbone of the musical genre, which he immortalized. The jive talk used on the following year's 'Rock The Joint', coupled with the distinctive slap bass playing on the record, continued the experiment.

In 1953, Haley abandoned the cowboy image and formed a new group, Bill Haley And His Comets. The line-up of the group would change frequently over the years, but Haley would always remain. Their first single, the exuberant 'Crazy Man Crazy' crossed over into the national charts and was the first rock 'n' roll Top 20 US hit. After signing to Decca in May 1954, Haley recorded a series of songs that was historically crucial in bringing rock 'n' roll to the world. 'Rock Around The Clock' was a staggering achievement, a single whose timing, vocal, spine-tingling guitar breaks and inspired drumming was quite unlike any other commercial recording up until that time. Amazingly, it was initially issued as a b-side and, even when the sides were flipped, it initially became only a minor hit. Haley returned to the studio to record a follow-up, 'Shake Rattle And Roll'. This was another seminal work, whose jive-style lyrics and brilliant employment of saxophone and upright bass brought a new sound into the US Top 20. Haley enjoyed further, though less important hits, during the next year with 'Dim Dim The Lights' and 'Mambo Rock'. Then, in the spring of 1955, his career took a dramatic upswing when the previously-issued 'Rock Around The Clock' was included in the controversial film, *The Blackboard Jungle*. Suddenly, the world woke up to the importance of 'Rock Around The Clock' and it became a veritable rock 'n' roll anthem and rallying cry. It soared to the top of the US charts for a lengthy spell and achieved the same feat in the UK. When *The Blackboard Jungle* was shown in Britain, enthusiastic youths jived in the aisles and ripped up seats in their excitement. Haley was crowned the king of rock 'n' roll and dominated the US/UK chart listings throughout 1955-56 with such songs as 'Rock-A-Beatin' Boogie', 'See You Later Alligator', 'The Saints Rock 'N' Roll', 'Razzle Dazzle', 'Burn That Candle', 'Rip It Up' and 'Rudy's Rock'. The latter was an instrumental which focused attention on Haley's saxophone player, the excellent Rudy Pompilli, who often played onstage lying on his back. His brother, Al Pompilli, was another important component in the group, renowned for his acrobatic displays on the stand-up bass. Haley's exciting stage act provoked hysteria among youth, which soon became pandemic. In February 1957, he travelled to England, the first rock 'n' roll star to tour abroad. He was mobbed when his train arrived in London and there were rabid scenes of fan mania when he performed at the Dominion Theatre, London. Inevitably, the moral pundits criticized such performances but Haley proved himself an adept apologist and emphasized the point by recording the protest 'Don't Knock The Rock', the title theme of an Alan Freed film.

Haley's star burned brightly for a couple of years, but his weakness was his age and image. At the age of 32, he was a little too old to be seen as the voice of teendom and his personality was more avuncular than erotic. Once Elvis Presley exploded onto the scene, Haley seemed a less authentic rock 'n' roll rebel and swiftly lost his standing among his young audience. He was still respected as a kind of elder statesman of rock - the man who first brought the music to the masses. Not surprisingly, he maintained his popularity by constantly touring and his recordings veered from Latin dance excursions to novelty and straight country. He was always called upon to carry the rock 'n' roll mantle whenever there was a nostalgic outbreak of 50s revivalism. It is a testament to the power of Haley's influence that 'Rock Around The Clock' returned to the UK Top 20 on two separate occasions: in 1968 and 1974. His music effectively transcended the generation gap by reaching new listeners over

Russ Hamilton

three decades. By the late 70s, Haley was reportedly ill and drinking heavily. He returned to England in November 1979 for a memorable performance at the *Royal Variety Show*. The following year reports filtered through that he was suffering from a brain tumour. On 9 February 1981, he died of a heart attack in Harlingen, Texas, USA. His inestimable influence on rock 'n' roll still continues.

Selected albums: *Live It Up* (1955), *Rock Around The Clock* (1956), *Rock And Roll Stage Show* (1956), *Rock The Joint* (1957), *Rocking The Oldies* (1957), *Rocking The Joint* (1958), *Bill Haley's Chicks* (1959), *Strictly Instrumental* (1960), *Bill Haley's Jukebox* (1960), *Twistin' Knights At The Round Table* (1962), *Bill Haley And The Comets* (1965), *Rip It Up* (1968), *On Stage* (1970), *Golden King Of Rock* (1972), *Just Rock And Roll Music* (1973), *Live In London '74* (1974), *Rock Around The Country* (1974), *The Bill Haley Collection* (1976), *R-O-C-K* (1976), *Armchair Rock 'N' Roll* (1978), *Everyone Can Rock 'N' Roll* (1980), *A Tribute To Bill Haley* (1981), *Rock And Roll Stage Show* (1983), *The Essential Bill Haley* (1984), *Hillbilly Haley* (1984), *Boogie With Bill Haley* (1985), *Golden Greats* (1985), *The Original Hits '54-'57* (1987), *Greatest Hits* (1988), *Rip It Up Rock 'N' Roll* (1988). CDs: *Greatest Hits* (1985), *From The Original Master Tapes* (1985), *Rock The Joint* (1989), *Golden CD Collection* (1989), *The Original Hits '54-'57* (1990), *Bill Haley's Rock 'N' Roll Scrapbook* (1990), *The Decca Years And More* (1991, 5-CD boxed set).

Hamilton, Russ

b. Ronald Hulme, 1933, Liverpool, England. This singer-songwriter was the first Liverpool artist to make the US Top 10 in the 50s. In 1956, this Korean War veteran (he was in the Royal Air Force), entertained children as a Redcoat at Butlins Holiday Camps in Blackpool and Brighton, and when at the latter, formed a skiffle group and recorded his first single for Oriole in. The a-side 'We Will Make Love', written after splitting up with girlfriend Pat Hichin, made number 2 in the UK, staying in the Top 10 for 15 weeks. The b-side 'Rainbow', which he says took only a couple of minutes to write, made him a US one-hit wonder and shot to number 7, becoming the biggest hit to date there by a UK male artist. In the summer of 1957 he was a transatlantic star commuting between the USA and Clacton, Essex where he was entertaining Butlins holidaymakers. His follow-up, 'Wedding Ring', again written about Miss Hitchin, gave him his last UK chart

entry. He joined MGM Records in 1960, but even recording in Nashville did not help him return to the charts. Despite having such a spectacular start to his career, it seemed that either Hamilton's face, distinctive lisp or seemingly unfashionable ballad singing style did not fit any more.
Selected album: *We Will Make Love* (1959).

Harris, Wee Willie

'Discovered' in London's famous coffee bar club the 2 I's - shrine of early UK pop - he was promoted by his manager as the kingdom's very own Jerry Lee Lewis - though he was less a teen idol than a television gimmick in loud attire and hair dyed a funny colour - usually shocking pink, green or orange - for regular appearances on the television pop show *6.5 Special*. Neither was he above banal publicity stunts like a 'feud' with blue-rinsed Larry Page, another 50s hopeful. Though Harris composed 'Rockin' At The 2 I's' as a debut single, he relied mostly on US covers - albeit delivered with more enthusiasm than many other native contemporaries. Nevertheless, home consumers preferred the original versions of 'Riot In Cell Block Number Nine' (the Robins) and 'Wild One' (Bobby Rydell), though they were unlikely to have heard Timmie Rogers' 'Back To School Again' or Gerry Granahan's 'No Chemise Please' before Harris rehashed them. If a less enduring clown than Screaming Lord Sutch, he resurfaced as a nostalgia act in the late 70s when it transpired that he was still remembered by Ian Dury who dropped his name in the lyrics of 1979's 'Reasons To Be Cheerful (Part Three)'.
Album: *Goes Ape* (1986).

Haymes, Dick

b. Richard Benjamin Haymes, 13 September 1916, Buenos Aires, Argentina, d. 28 March 1980, Los Angeles, California, USA. One of the outstanding ballad singers to emerge from the swing era of the late 30s/early 40s, with a deep, warm baritone voice and a straighforward style similar to Bob Manning, another singer who was popular in the 50s. Son of a Scottish father, and an Irish mother who was a concert singer and vocal coach, Haymes was educated in several countries including France, Switzerland and the USA. After working as a radio announcer, film extra and stuntman, and taking small parts in vaudeville, he replaced Frank Sinatra in the Harry James Band in 1941 and worked briefly for Benny Goodman and Tommy Dorsey before going out as a solo act in 1943. Signed for US Decca, he had a string of hits through to 1951,

Wee Willie Harris (left) with Johnny Duncan and Cliff Richard

including 'It Can't Be Wrong' (number 1), 'You'll Never Know' (number 1), 'Wait For Me Mary', 'Put Your Arms Around Me Honey', 'How Blue The Night', 'Laura', 'The More I See You', 'I Wish I Knew', 'Till The End Of Time', 'Love Letters', 'That's For Me', 'It's A Grand Night For Singing', 'It Might As Well Be Spring', 'How Are Thing In Glocca Morra?', 'Mamselle', 'I Wish I Didn't Love You So', 'Little White Lies', 'You Can't Be True Dear', 'It's Magic', 'Room Full Of Roses', 'Maybe It's Because', 'The Old Master Painter' and 'Count Every Star'. During this time he also recorded duets with Judy Garland, such as in 'For You, For Me, Forever More' (1947), as well as joining Bing Crosby and the Andrews Sisters in 'There's No Business Like Show Business' (1947), and Ethel Merman in 'You're Just In Love', (1951). He also had several hits with another ex-Harry James singer, Helen Forrest, which included 'Long Ago And Far Away', 'It Had To Be You', 'Together', 'I'll Buy That Dream', 'Some Sunday Morning', 'I'm Always Chasing Rainbows' and 'Oh! What It Seemed To Be'. Haymes was also successful on radio with his *Here's To Romance*, and the *Autolite* shows. Haymes' first starring role in films was in *Irish Eyes Are Smiling* (1944), a musical bio-pic of composer Ernest R. Ball ('When Irish Eyes Are Smiling', 'Dear Litle

Boy Of Mine', 'A Little Bit Of Heaven' and 'Let The Rest Of The World Go By'). His other film musicals included *Billy Rose's Diamond Horseshoe* (1945), *State Fair* (1945), *Do You Love Me?* (1946), *The Shocking Miss Pilgrim* (1947), *Up In Central Park* and *One Touch Of Venus* (both 1948). In most of the movies he featured opposite some of the most glamorous leading ladies of the day, including June Haver, Betty Grable, Jeanne Crain, Maureen O'Hara, Deanna Durbin and Ava Gardner. His career waned somewhat in the 50s, hampered by tax problems and immigration departments. He also had financial troubles over the years with some of his various wives, who included film stars Rita Hayworth and Joanne Dru, singers Edith Harper and Fran Jeffries, Errol Flynn's ex-wife Nora, and finally, model Wendy Patricia Smith. A switch from Decca to Capitol Records in 1955 produced two albums of standard ballads, *Rain Or Shine* and *Moondreams*, with arrangements by Johnny Mandel and Ian Bernard, which are generally considered to be classics of their kind. Both are now available together on one CD in the UK. During the 60s Haymes lived and worked mostly in Europe and in 1969 made an album in the UK entitled *Now And Then*, a mixture of his old favourites and more contemporary material. In the 70s he returned to the USA and undertook television and cabaret dates. He recorded a live album, *Dick Haymes Comes Home! First Stop: The Coconut Grove*, on which he was backed by an old name from the swing era, the Les Brown Band of Renown.

Albums: *Rain Or Shine* (1955), *Moondreams* (1957), *Now And Then* (1969), *Dick Haymes Comes Home! First Stop: The Coconut Grove* (early 70s). Compilations: *The Special Magic Of Dick Haymes* (1979), *The V-Disc Years* (1979), *The Best Of Dick Haymes* (1982), *The Last Goodbye* (1983), *Great Song Stylists, Volume One* (1983), *Dick Haymes Sings Irving Berlin* (1984), *Golden Greats* (1985).

Heath, Ted

b. 30 March 1900, Wandsworth, London, England, d. 18 November 1969, Surrey, England. After playing tenor horn at the age of six, Heath later switched to trombone and throughout the 20s and 30s played with top orchestras such as Jack Hylton, Al Sarita, Sydney Lipton, and in the early 40s with Geraldo. On 7 May 1945, (VJ Day), he formed his own band, some of the early finance being provided by royalties from the songs, 'That Lovely Weekend' and 'I'm Gonna Love That Guy', written by Heath and his wife, Moira.

Kenny Baker, Jack Parnell, Ronnie Chamberlain and Don Lusher were just some of the top musicians to play for him, plus vocalists Paul Carpenter and Beryl Davis. In 1946 the band provided the musical background for the first major British movie musical, *London Town*. Taking a big chance, Heath hired the London Palladium for a *Sunday Night Swing Session*, which proved to be so successful, that it ran for several years. The addition of singers Lita Roza, Dennis Lotis and Dickie Valentine in the early 50s gave the band more teenage appeal, and they appeared in three more films, *Dance Hall* (1950), *It's A Wonderful World* (1956) and *Jazz Boat* (1960). Their theme, 'Listen To My Music', introduced many specialities including 'Opus One', 'The Champ', 'Dragnet', 'Skin Deep', 'Hot Toddy' and 'Swingin' Shepherd Blues'. The Heath band was the first unit to go to the USA when Musicians' Union restrictions were relaxed and Anglo-American exchanges began in 1955. Subsequently, they toured there many times after that. The Heath band compared favourably with even America's top bands, and is accepted as the best swing band that Britain ever produced. Heath died in 1969. Many of his original personnel

Ted Heath (centre)

still play together, usually under the direction of Jack Parnell or Don Lusher.

Albums: *Big Band Percussion* (1961), *Big Band Bash* (1962), *Satin Saxes And Bouncing Brass* (1963), *Big Band Spirituals* (1964), *Coast To Coast* (1964), *Palladium Revisted* (1964), with Edmundo Ros *Heath Versus Ros* (1964), *The Sound Of Music* (1965), with Ros *Heath Versus Ros, Round Two* (1967), *Ted Heath Recalls The Fabulous Dorseys* (1969), *Fever* (1966), *Beatles, Bach And Bacharach* (1971), *100th London Palladium Sunday Concert 1954* (1971), *Salute To Glenn Miller* (1973), *Big Band Themes Remembered, Volume One* (1974), *Ted Heath At The London Palladium 1953* (1976), *Big Band Themes Remembered, Volume Two* (1974), *Salutes The Duke* (1975), *Salutes Benny Goodman* (1976), *Smooth 'N' Swinging* (1981, recordings from 1959-62). Compilations: *Big Band World Of Ted Heath* (1970), *Swing Meets Latin* (1974), with Denis Lotis, Lita Roza *The Ted Heath Years* (1977), *Focus On Ted Heath* (1978), *All Time Top Twelve* (1979), *Ted Heath At The BBC* (1983), *Big Band Favourites* (1984), *Big Band Bash, Volumes 1-4* (all 1988).

Helms, Bobby

b. Robert Lee Helms, 15 August 1933, Bloomington, Indiana, USA. Helms was something of a child prodigy, who was playing guitar and singing a mixture of pop and country on local radio at the age of 12 and from 1946-54, he regularly appeared on WWTV Bloomington. He made his debut on the *Grand Ole Opry* in 1950, having impressed WSM officials so much that they had him flown to Nashville to appear. He signed with Decca and in 1957, his recording of Lawton Williams' 'Fraulein', his first US country chart entry, was a number 1 (even reaching number 36 in the US pop charts). The song stayed in the country charts for 52 weeks, which, according to Joel Whitburn's *Record Research*, is the second longest chart tenure of all time. The same year also saw him with two further hits, 'My Special Angel' and the original version of 'Jingle Bell Rock', both of which became million sellers and made the Top 10 in the US pop charts. The former, another US country number 1, managed a Top 30 appearance in the UK charts but lost out to the Top 10 cover version by Malcolm Vaughan. (Max Bygraves made the UK Top 10 with his version of 'Jingle Bell Rock' in 1959.) Helms had further country/pop success the following year with 'Jacqueline', from the film *The Case Against Brooklyn* (which also charted in the UK) and a US country number 10 with 'Just A Little Lonesome'.

In the late 60s, he left Decca and recorded for Little Darlin' but achieved no further major chart hits. Throughout the 70s and 80s, he continued to tour, often with his wife Dori and he released an album in 1989. He is still remembered because of seasonal appearances of 'Jingle Bell Rock' but his last chart hit, 'Mary Goes Round', was on the Certron label in 1970. Interestingly, it was a cover version of Helms' recording of 'Schoolboy Crush' which became the b-side of Cliff Richard's first recording.

Selected albums: *To My Special Angel* (1957), *Country Christmas* (1958), *Best Of Bobby Helms* (1963), *Bobby Helms* (1965), *I'm The Man* (1966), *Sorry My Name Isn't Fred* (1966), *All New Just For You* (1968), *Greatest Performance* (1970), *Jingle Bell Rock* (1974), *Greatest Hits* (1975), *Pop A-Billy* (1983), *Bobby Helms Country* (1989).

Henderson, Joe 'Mr Piano'

b. 2 May 1920, Glasgow, Scotland, d. 4 May 1980, London, England. A pianist and composer, Henderson formed his own band to play at school dances, and played professionally from the age of 13. In the early 50s, Henderson served as accompanist for former child actress and singer Petula Clark, who featured frequently in the UK charts, and, later, recorded several of her ex-pianist's compositions. Henderson himself became extremely popular on the UK variety circuit, alongside other solo piano acts, such as Winifred Atwell, Russ Conway, and later, Bobby Crush. Henderson survived the radical changes in popular music which began to take place in the late 50s, and still retained an audience. He also featured in *Bumper Bundle* on Radio Luxembourg, and had his own television series, *Sing Along With Joe* and *Mr. Piano Plays*. Henderson's first hits came in 1955, with 'Sing It With Joe' and 'Sing It Again With Joe'. These consisted of short piano medleys of jolly standards, such as 'Margie' and 'Somebody Stole My Gal'. In 1958 he had another UK Top 20 hit with 'Trudie', accompanied by the Beryl Stott Chorus. It was the best known of his mostly bright, catchy compositions, and won an Ivor Novello Award for 'The Year's Best Selling And Most Performed Item'. He earned another 'Ivor' the following year for the movie title song, 'Jazzboat', 'The Year's Most Outstanding Composition In The 'Jazz' Or 'Beat' Idiom'. *Jazzboat* was one of three films that Henderson scored and starred Anthony Newley. The others were *Idle On Parade*, the film that launched Newley's singing career (he co-wrote some of the songs) and *Let's Get Married*.

Joe 'Mr Piano' Henderson with Petula Clark

Henderson's other compositions, published by his own company, included 'Why Don't They Understand?' (a US and UK chart hit for country singer George Hamilton IV), 'Chick', 'Treble Chance' (his last Top 30 entry, in 1959), 'Dear Daddy' (with lyrics by Jack Fishman, featured on *Ruby Murray Successes*), 'Matchbox Samba', 'Coffee Bar Jive', 'What A Day We'll Have', 'I'd Have A Long Way To Go', 'When You're Away', 'Dream Of Paradise', 'First Theme', 'I Need You', 'Somebody' and 'Crinoline Waltz'. His other recordings included Charles Chaplin's 'Smile', Leroy Anderson's 'Forgotten Dreams', 'The Theme From the Threepenny Opera (Moritat)' and a lively version of the novelty, 'Don't Ring-A Da Bell'. On the latter he played harpsichord, with a vocal by actress Shani Wallis, who later played Nancy in the movie of Lionel Bart's *Oliver!*. Henderson's albums, such as *Dancing Cheek To Cheek* and *Bumper Bundle* contained the usual mixture of old, familiar favourites. On *The Hits Of 1968*, he included such evergreen songs as 'Anniversary Waltz' (1942), 'Old Devil Moon' (1947) and 'Careless Hands' (1949). A very likeable and genial personality, Henderson continued to entertain, particularly in that very British institution, the seaside summer season, at top venues such as Blackpool and Bournemouth. He died in May 1980, at his home in London, England.
Albums: *Joe 'Mr. Piano' Henderson* (1961), *Dancing Cheek To Cheek* (60s) *Bumper Bundle* (60s), *The Hits Of 1968* (1968), *Secret Love Hits Of The 50s* (1972), *Sing-A-Long With Joe* (1973), *Swing-A-Long With Joe 'Mr. Piano' Henderson* (1974), *Joe Henderson Recalls The Unforgettable 50s* (1975), *40 All Time Singalong Party Hits* (1975).

Henry, Clarence 'Frogman'

b. 19 March 1937, Algiers, Louisiana, USA. Henry began performing during the 50s with a New Orleans-based R&B group led by Bobby Mitchell. The singer later began work with bandleader Paul Gayten who accompanied him on his 1957 smash 'Ain't Got No Home'. However it was not until 1961 that 'But I Do' provided a follow-up to this novelty song, earning Henry a US number 4 and UK number 3 hit. Co-written by Bobby Charles, the song featured several seasoned New Orleans musicians, including the young Allen Toussaint, and relaunched Henry's career. The same year a further international success, 'You Always Hurt The One You Love' - previously a hit for the Mills Brothers in 1944 - echoed the same effortless style. The following single fared better in the UK, with 'Lonely Street'/'Why Can't You' just missing the Top 40, but it was the artist's last substantial hit. He continued to record for a variety of companies, and the 1969 collection, *Is Alive And Well*, was acclaimed as a fine example of the 'Crescent City' style. Since then Henry has remained a popular live attraction in his adopted city.

Albums: *You Always Hurt The One You Love* (1961), *Is Alive And Well And Living In New Orleans* (1969), *New Recordings* (1979), *Little Green Frog* (1987). Compilation: *Legendary Clarence 'Frogman' Henry* (1983).

Hibbler, Al

b. 16 August 1915, Little Rock, Arkansas, USA. After singing for several years in relative obscurity, Hibbler joined Jay McShann in 1942 and the following year was hired by Duke Ellington, proving to be one of the best singers he had ever employed. Hibbler subsequently recorded with several well-known jazz musicians in his backing groups, among them Harry Carney, Billy Kyle, Count Basie and Gerald Wilson. In the 50s his recordings of songs such as 'It Shouldn't Happen To A Dream', which he had recorded with Ellington, 'The Very Thought Of You' and 'Stardust' proved popular, while his version of 'Unchained Melody' was outstanding. A powerful, rich-toned baritone, Hibbler cannot be regarded as a jazz singer but as an exceptionally good singer of 20th-century popular song who happened to work with some of the best jazz musicians of the time.
Albums: *Al Hibbler Sings Love Songs* (1952), *Melodies By Al Hibbler* (1954), *After The Lights Go Down Low* (1956), *Monday Every Day* (1961), *Early One Morning* (1964), with Rahsaan Roland Kirk *A Meeting Of The Times* (1972), *For Sentimental Reasons* (1982).

Hilliard, Bob

b. 21 January 1918, New York, USA, d. 1 February 1971, Hollywood, California, USA. Hilliard was a lyricist for many popular songs from the mid-40s into the 60s. His first hit, with Dick Miles, came in 1946, when Frank Sinatra recorded their 'Coffee Song'. The singer remembered it again on *Ring-A-Ding-Ding* (1961), the first album for his own Reprise label. In the following year Hilliard contributed 'The Big Brass Band From Brazil' and 'Civilization', with Carl Sigman, to the Broadway show *Angel With Wings*. The latter song, sung by Elaine Stritch in the show, became a massive hit for Danny Kaye and the Andrews Sisters, Ray McKinley and Louis Prima. Hilliard's other 40s hits included 'A Strawberry Moon' (Blue Barron), 'Careless Hands' (with Sigman - revived by Des O'Connor in 1967) and 'Dear Hearts And Gentle People' (a hit for Bing Crosby, Dennis Day, Gordon MacRae and others). In the 50s Hilliard wrote with Jule Styne for *Michael Todd's Peep Show* ('Stay With The Happy People') and *Hazel Flagg*

('Every Street's A Boulevard In Old New York' and 'How Do You Speak To An Angel?'), which was made into one of Dean Martin and Jerry Lewis's best movies, *Living It Up* (1954). Hilliard's other film work around that time included several songs, with Sammy Fain, for Disney's 1952 *Alice In Wonderland* ('It's Late', 'Very Good Advice'). Hilliard's other 50s songs included 'Dearie' (with Dave Mann), 'Be My Life's Companion', 'Jealous Eyes', 'Bouquet Of Roses', 'Downhearted' (a hit for Eddie Fisher), 'Sweet Forgiveness', 'Somebody Bad Stole De Wedding Bells (with Mann) and 'Moonlight Gambler' (with Phil Springer). In 1959 Hilliard had a hit with another novelty song, 'Seven Little Girls Sitting In The Back Seat', by Paul Evans in the US, and the Avons in the UK. In the early 60s, with the advent of the beat boom, his output declined, although he had some success with 'Tower Of Strength' with Burt Bacharach), 'You're Following Me', 'My Summer Love', 'My Little Corner Of The World' (with Le Pockriss) and 'Our Day Will Come' (with Mort Garson), which was a US number 1 for Ruby And The Romantics. Hilliard's other songs included 'Don't You Believe It', 'Any Day Now', 'Red Silk Stockings And Green Perfume', 'The Thousand Islands Song', 'Chocolate Whiskey And Vanilla Gin', 'Castanets And Lace' and 'Baby Come Home'. His other collaborators included Dick Sanford and Sammy Mysels.

Hilltoppers

This vocal quartet formed at the Western Kentucky College in Bowling Green, Kentucky, USA, comprised lead Jimmy Sacca (b. Hazard, Kentucky, USA), baritone Billy Vaughn (b. 12 April 1931, Glasgow, Kentucky, USA), tenor Seymour Speigelman and bass Don McGuire. Sacca and Vaughn formed the group to record 'Trying' in 1952 and named it after their college nickname. Dot Records signed the band, re-recorded 'Trying' in the college auditorium, and it reached the US Top 10 (making the UK charts in 1956). Over the next five years the group, who wore college sweaters and beanies on stage, scored a further nine US Top 20 singles, the biggest being 'P.S. I Love You' in 1953, 'Only You' in 1955 and 'Marianne' in 1957. Vaughn left in 1955 and had a very successful career as musical director for Dot and as an orchestra leader. In the UK, where the Platters' original version of 'Only You' was not released until 1956, they reached number 3 with their recording and were in the Top 20 for six months. They were one of the most successful early 50s vocal groups, but like many other acts they could not survive in a rock 'n' roll world and disbanded in 1963. Since then Sacca has occasionally played dates with new sets of Hilltoppers.

Selected albums: *Tops In Pops* (1957), *The Towering Hilltoppers* (1958), *Love In Bloom* (1958).

Hi-Lo's

The name of this North American vocal unit was born of the contrast in height between its tallest members - leader/arranger Eugene Thomas Puerling (b. 31 March 1929, Milwaukee, Wisconsin) and Robert Morse (b. 27 July 1927, Pasadena, Texas) - and diminutive Clark Burroughs (b. 3 March 1930, Los Angeles, California) and Robert Strasen (b. 1 April 1928, Strasbourg, France). While developing their sophisticated close harmony style, they dwelt in the same Chicago house, making ends meet with menial jobs and engagements at weekends and evenings. Through the offices of bandleader Jerry Fielding, they recorded for several labels while building a reputation as a versatile, technically accomplished act via a Las Vegas hotel season, a tour supporting Judy Garland and replacing the Four Esquires as resident musical turn on comedian Red Skelton's networked television series. Before Strasen was replaced by Dan Shelton in 1958, the four teamed up on disc with the Marty Paich Dektette - and Rosemary Clooney with whom they notched up a US hit with 1957's 'Ring Around Rosie' (with Morse's counter tenor prominent). This breakthrough assisted the passage of *Now Hear This* into the album Top 20. Further collections - some devoted to specific stylistic genres - sold steadily if less remarkably.

After the Hi-Lo's disbanded in 1964, Puerling and Shelton found employment producing advertising jingles with vocalists Len Dressler and Bonnie Herman with whom they formed Singers Unlimited in 1966. An impressed Oscar Peterson recommended them to Germany's BASF/MPS company which released several Singers albums including *Sentimental Journey* and, accompanied by Robert Farnon's orchestra, 1978's *Eventide*. That same year, the Shelton line-up of the Hi-Lo's re-formed as a recording entity and were affectionately applauded at performances in nostalgia revues. The Hi-Lo's had a profound influence on the harmony sound of the Four Freshmen and the Beach Boys.

Albums: *Suddenly It's The Hi-Lo's* (1957), *Love Nest* (1957), *Now Hear This* (1957), with Rosemary Clooney *Ring Around Rosie* (1957), *The Hi-Lo's And All That Jazz*, (1959), *All Over The Place* (1960), *Broadway Playbill* (1960), *The Hi-Lo's, I Presume* (1960), *The Hi-Lo's On Hand* (1960), *The Hi-Lo's Under Glass* (1960), *The Hi-Lo's Happen To Folk* (1962), *This Time It's Love* (1962), *The Hi-Lo's Happen To Bossa Nova* (1963), *Back Again* (1978).

Hilton, Ronnie

b. Adrian Hill, 26 January 1926, Hull, England. Hilton left school at the age of 14 and worked in an aircraft factory during the war before joining the Highland Light Infantry. He was demobilized in 1947 and returned to factory work in Leeds. He sang with the Johnny Addlestone band at the Starlight Roof in Leeds from 1950 and was heard by A&R manager Wally Ridley and signed to HMV. At this point he underwent surgery for a hair lip, changed his name, and in July 1954 made his debut as Ronnie Hilton. His first appearance on stage was at the Dudley Hippodrome in 1955, and soon afterwards he had his own radio series. For the next 10 years he was one of the most popular vocalists in the UK and specialized in romantic ballads. His hits included 'I Still Believe', 'Veni Vidi Vici', 'A Blossom Fell', 'Stars Shine In Your Eyes', 'Yellow Rose Of Texas', 'Young And Foolish', 'No Other Love' (a UK number 1 in 1956), 'Who Are We', 'Two Different Worlds', 'Around The World', 'The World Outside', and the novelty, 'A Windmill In Old Amsterdam'. Since his last hit in 1965 he has remained in demand especially in the north of England. He still performs summer seasons and tours with nostalgia packages which include contemporaries such as Russ Conway, Dennis Lotis and Rosemary Squires, and regularly presents *Sounds Of The 50s* for BBC Radio Two.

Albums: *I'm Beginning To See The Light* (1959). Compilations: *The Very Best Of Ronnie Hilton - 16 Favourites Of The 50s* (1984), *The EMI Years: The Best Of Ronnie Hilton* (1989).

Hockridge, Edmund

b. 9 August 1923, Vancouver, British Columbia, Canada. Hockridge was one of the UK's premier musical comedy leading men, with rugged looks, a sure manner and a big, strong baritone voice. He first visited the UK in 1941 with the Royal Canadian Air Force, and helped set up the Allied Expeditionary Forces Network, which supplied entertainment and news for troops in Europe. He also sang on many of the broadcasts, several of them with fellow Canadian Robert Farnon who was leader of the Canadian Allied Expeditionary Force Band. After the war, he featured in his own coast-to-coast show for the CBC, playing leading roles in operas such as *La Bohème*, *Don Giovanni* and Gilbert And Sullivan operettas. After seeing some Broadway musical shows such as *Brigadoon* and *Carousel*, on a visit to New York, he decided that there was more future for him in that direction. That was certainly the case, for on his return to the UK in 1951, he replaced Stephen Douglass as Billy Bigelow in *Carousel* at the Drury Lane Theatre, London. When the run ended he replaced Jerry Wayne as Sky Masterson in *Guys And Dolls* at the Coliseum, and stayed at that theatre for two more shows, *Can-Can*, and *The Pajama Game*, in which he created for the London stage, the roles of Judge Aristide Forestier and Sid Sorokin. From the latter show he had one of his biggest record hits, 'Hey There'. His other 50s singles included 'Young And Foolish', 'No Other Love', 'The Fountains Of Rome', 'Sixteen Tons', 'The Man From Laramie', 'A Woman In Love', 'More Than Ever' and 'Tonight'. Extremely popular in theatres and on television, he played a six-month season at the London Palladium, appeared in six Royal Command Performances, and was Canada's representative in the Westminster Abbey Choir at the Queen's Coronation in 1953. He headlined the cabaret on the liner QE2's maiden voyage, and toured Europe extensively, both in revivals of musicals, and his own one-man show, which contained over 30 songs.

In the early 80s he toured the UK with successful revivals of *The Sound Of Music* and *South Pacific*, before returning to Canada in 1984 for a concert tour with Robert Farnon and the Vancouver Symphony Orchestra. In 1986, 35 years after he strode onto the Drury Lane stage as young, arrogant Billy Bigelow, he played the part of senior citizen, Buffalo Bill, in a major London revival of *Annie Get Your Gun*, with pop star, Suzi Quatro, as Annie. In the early 90s, Hockridge toured with his show, *The Edmund Hockridge Family*, being joined onstage by his wife, Jackie, and their two sons, Murray and Stephen.

Albums: *Edmund Hockridge Sings* (1957), *In Romantic Mood* (1957), *Hooray For Love* (1958), *Hockridge Meets Hammond* (1975), *Make It Easy On Yourself* (1984), *Sings Hits From Various Musicals* (1985).

Holliday, Michael

b. Michael Milne, 26 November 1928, Liverpool, England, d. 29 October 1963. A popular singer in the UK during the 50s, influenced by, and very similar in style and tone to Bing Crosby. After entertaining his shipmates in the Merchant Navy, Holliday made his first public appearance as a singer when his ship docked in New York. He won a talent contest on the stage of Radio City Music Hall, one of the world's largest theatres. In the absence of offers to star in a big Broadway musical, he returned to the UK, was released from the navy, and obtained work as a singer-guitarist with the Eric Winstone Band, touring UK holiday camps. He was signed for Columbia by Norrie Paramor in 1955, and during the next couple of years, covered several US artists' hits such as 'The Yellow Rose Of Texas' (Mitch Miller), 'Sixteen Tons' (Tennessee Ernie Ford), and 'Hot Diggity' (Perry Como); whilst also reaching the UK Top 30 with 'Nothin' To Do', 'Ten Thousand Miles' and 'The Gal With The Yaller Shoes', from the 1956 movie, *Meet Me In Las Vegas*. In 1958 he had some success with 'In Love', 'Stairway Of Love' and the 1929 number, 'I'll Always Be In Love With You'. He topped the UK chart with 'The Story Of My Life', an early composition by Burt Bacharach and Hal David. On the b-side of that record was one of Holliday's own compositions, 'Keep Your Heart'. Early in 1960 he had another number 1 with 'Starry Eyed', but after 'Skylark' and 'Little Boy Lost' later in the year, the singles hits dried up. On his albums such as *Mike* and *Holliday Mixture* he ignored the contemporary music scene, and sang old standards - as he did on television. With his casual, easy-going style, he was a natural for the small screen, and had his own *Relax With Mike* series, on which he duetted with himself on a tape recorder, in the days when those machines were a domestic novelty in the UK.

His only appearance on the larger screen was in the movie *Life Is A Circus* (1962), with one of Britain's best loved comedy teams, the Crazy Gang. Unfortunately, his relaxed image seems to have been a façade, concealing professional and private problems. When Michael Holliday died in October 1963, at Croydon General Hospital, Surrey, England, the cause of death was believed to be have been an overdose of drugs.

Albums: *Mike* (1960), *Holliday Mixture* (1961), *Happy Holiday* (1962). Compilations: *Story Of My Life* (1973), *To Bing - From Mike* (1978), *A Sentimental Journey* (1988), *The EMI Years: The Best Of Michael Holliday* (1989).

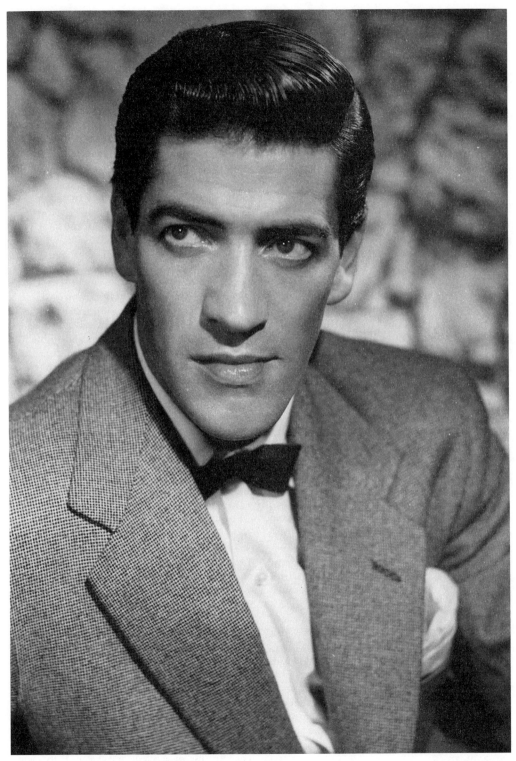

Michael Holliday

Holly, Buddy

b. Charles Hardin Holley, 7 September 1936, Lubbock, Texas, USA. Holly was one of the first major rock 'n' roll groundbreakers, and one of its most influential artists. He wrote his own songs, recorded with a self-contained guitar-bass-drums combo, experimented in the studio and even changed the image of what a rock singer could look like: until he came along, the idea of a bespectacled rock idol was unthinkable. Holly's hiccupping vocal style and mature, melodic compositions inspired many of the rockers who would emerge in the 60s and 70s, from the Beatles and Bob Dylan to the Hollies. Later, British singer-songwriter Elvis Costello would emerge with an unabashed Holly-inspired physical appearance. Like many other early rock 'n' rollers, Holly's musical influences included both C&W music and 'race' music, or R&B. He made his first stage appearance at the age of five, joining with his brothers Larry and Travis in a talent contest; he won $5. During his childhood, Holly learned to play guitar, violin and piano, taking formal lessons but teaching himself boogie-woogie rhythms on the piano. At 12 years old he was entertaining friends with Hank Williams songs and in 1949 formed a bluegrass duo, Buddy and Bob, with friend Bob Montgomery. He learned to play banjo and mandolin during this period. Holly made his first recording on a home tape recorder in 1949, a song called 'My Two Timin' Woman'.

By 1952 Buddy and Bob had become popular around Lubbock; recording two songs together at Holly's home that year and another in 1953. In September of that year Buddy and Bob appeared on KDAV radio, performing two numbers. Adding bass player Larry Welborn, they were given their own programme, *The Buddy And Bob Show.* They performed country material primarily but occasionally stuck in an R&B song. KDAV disc jockey Hipockets Duncan became the trio's manager and secured work for them in the West Texas area. Further recording took place at KDAV but none of it was released. In 1954 the trio added fiddler Sonny Curtis and steel guitarist Don Guess to the group, and together made more recordings in Lubbock and at Nesman Recording Studio in Wichita Falls, Texas. That year the group, now including drummer Jerry Allison, opened concerts for Bill Haley And His Comets and Elvis Presley in Texas. Holly was impressed by Presley and began thinking about performing in the new rock 'n' roll style. However, in the meantime he continued to play country.

In December 1955 Nashville agent Eddie Crandall requested of KDAV disc jockey Dave Stone that Holly and his group record four demo songs, believing he could secure them a contract with Decca Records. The group, now minus Montgomery, sent five songs, and Decca brought them to Nashville where they recorded four songs at Bradley's Barn Studio on 26 January 1956. Decca issued 'Blue Days, Black Nights', backed with 'Love Me', under the name Buddy Holly And The Three Tunes, in April. Several other records were recorded in two sessions for Decca during the autumn of 1956, but Holly, now dissatisfied with Decca's insistence that he continue to play country music, left the label in September. Later that year Holly, Allison and Welborn went to Clovis, New Mexico, where they recorded two songs. Upon returning to Lubbock, Holly formed the Crickets with Allison and Niki Sullivan on rhythm guitar. On 25 February 1957 they went back to Clovis and recorded a rock 'n' roll version of Holly's 'That'll Be The Day', a song from their period in Nashville. The song was a revelation and contained one of the most gripping vocals and distinctive galloping riffs of any record released during the 50s. Joe B. Mauldin joined as the Crickets' bassist following those sessions. A number of record companies turned down the song until it was issued by Brunswick Records, ironically a division of Decca, in May. With Petty as manager, the single underwent heavy promotion until it reached number 1 in September 1957. It also reached number 1 in the UK. Just as the record was being released, the Crickets performed at such venues as the Apollo Theater in New York and the Howard Theater in Washington, D.C., winning over mostly-black audiences and helping to further break down racial barriers in rock. They spent the next three months touring the USA.

The group recorded prolifically in 1957, including such indisputable classics as 'Words Of Love', 'Maybe Baby', 'Not Fade Away', 'Everyday', 'Peggy Sue' (named after Allison's girlfriend) and 'Oh Boy'. Holly was innovative in the studio, making much use of production techniques newly available as overdubbing vocals and double-tracking guitar parts. The vocals on 'Peggy Sue' were a typical example of Holly's technique. Although simple in structure and execution, Holly somehow manages to recite the words 'Peggy Sue' differently in every line, as if fascinated by the very syllables of her name. A seemingly straightforward song like 'Everyday' is similarly transformed by the ingenious use of a celeste (played by Petty's wife

Buddy Holly (right)

Vi) and the decision to include Jerry Allison slapping his knee, in place of drums. Brunswick continued to issue recordings under the Crickets name while Holly signed on as a solo artist to Coral Records. Despite this, most releases featured the entire group, often with other musicians (Vi Petty on piano) and a vocal group (the Picks). Of these releases, 'Peggy Sue' reached number 3 in the US and 'Oh Boy' number 10 US during 1957. Contrary to the legend, Holly and the Crickets only charted 11 times in the USA during their brief career. No albums charted during Holly's lifetime. The Crickets closed out 1957 with an appearance on the influential *Ed Sullivan Show* and again in January 1958, by which time Holly had left the group.

In late January the Crickets recorded 'Rave On' in New York and then toured Australia for six days. Further Clovis recording sessions, including 'Well...All Right' occupied February. This was followed by a UK tour beginning on 2 March at the Trocadero in London which also included appearances on the UK television programmes *Sunday Night At The London Palladium* and *Off The Record*. The UK tour finished on 25 March at the Hammersmith Gaumont. Holly and the group enjoyed immense popularity in Britain, with nine top 10 singles. 'Maybe Baby' became the fourth Holly/Crickets single to chart in the USA in March, eventually peaking at number 17 in the USA (and number 4 in the UK). The group returned to the USA in late March and immediately headed out on a US tour assembled by disc jockey Alan Freed, also featuring such popular artists as Jerry Lee Lewis and Chuck Berry. Coral released the frantic 'Rave On' in May and although it reached only number 37 in the USA, it made number 5 in the UK. Following the tour, on 19 June, Holly recorded two songs written by Bobby Darin in New York without the Crickets; they remained unreleased but would signal an impending split between Holly and the group. While in New York Holly met Maria Elena Santiago, whom he married two months later. During that summer Holly returned to Petty's studio in Clovis and recorded 'Heartbeat', 'Love's Made A Fool Of You' and 'Wishing'. Guitarist Tommy Allsup played on the latter two and was subsequently asked to join the Crickets. During September sessions in Clovis extra musicians including saxophonist King Curtis and guitarist Phil Everly joined Holly. Waylon Jennings, then unknown, provided backing vocals on one track; during the same period, Holly produced Jennings'

debut single. By September three more Holly/Crickets singles had charted in the USA, but none fared very well.

Holly and the Crickets toured the northeast and Canada during October, by which time there was apparently friction between the Hollys and the Pettys. Buddy and Maria Holly travelled apart from the group between dates. During the trip, Holly decided to try recording with strings, but prior to returning to New York for that session in October 1958, he announced to manager/producer Petty that he was leaving him. To Holly's surprise the other Crickets chose to leave Holly and stay with Petty; Holly allowed them use of the group's name and they continued to record without him (Sonny Curtis joined the group after Holly's death). Meanwhile, on 21 October, Holly, producer Dick Jacobs and studio musicians (including a string section) recorded 'True Love Ways', 'It Doesn't Matter Anymore' (written by Paul Anka), 'Raining In My Heart' and 'Moondreams'. They were held for later release while 'It's So Easy' was released; it failed to chart in the US. 'Heartbeat' was issued in December and became the last Holly single to chart in the US during his lifetime. The superb 'It Doesn't Matter Anymore' was released posthumously and its lyrics betrayed an unintended elegiac mood in light of the singer's fate. The song provided Holly with his only UK number 1 hit and served as a perfect memorial. The flip-side, 'Raining In My Heart' was equally inventive, with a touching melody reinforced by the orchestral arrangement in which strings were used to startling effect to suggest tearful raindrops.

In December 1958 Holly, now living in New York with his wife, recorded six songs at home on his tape recorder, presumably to be re-recorded in the studio at a later date. During Christmas Holly returned to Lubbock and appeared on radio station KLLL with Jennings. Back in New York during January 1959 he made other demos at home by himself. That month he began assembling a band to take on the 'Winter Dance Party' tour of the US midwest. Allsup was hired on guitar, Jennings on bass and Carl Bunch on drums. They were billed as the Crickets despite the agreement to give Holly's former band mates that name. Also starring Ritchie Valens, the Big Bopper, Dion And The Belmonts and unknown Frankie Sardo, the tour began 23 January 1959 in Milwaukee, Wisconsin. On the afternoon of 1 February the tour played in Green Bay, Wisconsin but an evening show was cancelled owing to bad weather. The 2 February date at the Surf Ballroom in Clear Lake, Iowa went ahead. It was following this show that Holly, Valens and the Big Bopper chartered a small plane to take them to the next date in Moorhead, Minnesota, rather than travel on the tour bus, which had a defective heater and had previously broken down several times. Owing to the snowy weather the plane crashed minutes after takeoff, killing all three stars and the pilot. (The tour actually continued after their deaths, with Bobby Vee, Jimmy Clanton and Frankie Avalon filling in.)

Holly's popularity increased after his death, and his influence continues to this day. Even as late as the 80s unreleased material was still being released. Several of the posthumous releases fared particularly well in the UK. In 1962 Norman Petty took the demos Holly had recorded at home in 1958 and had the instrumental group the Fireballs along play to them, creating new Buddy Holly records from the unfinished tapes. In 1965, *Holly In The Hills*, comprised of the early Buddy and Bob radio station recordings, was released and charted in the UK. Compilation albums also charted in both the USA and the UK, as late as the 70s. During the 70s the publishing rights to Holly's song catalogue were purchased by Paul McCartney, who began sponsoring annual Buddy Holly Week celebrations. A Buddy Holly Memorial Society was also formed in the USA to commemorate the singer. In 1978, a film called *The Buddy Holly Story* and starring actor Gary Busey as Holly, premiered; members of the Crickets, in particular, denounced it as containing many inaccurate scenes. The following year, a six-record boxed set called *The Complete Buddy Holly* was released in the UK (it was issued in the USA two years later). A 1983 release, *For The First Time Anywhere*, contained original Holly recordings prior to overdubbing. As of the early 90s a group called the Crickets and including at least one original member (and usually more) was still touring. In 1990, *Buddy*, a musical play which had previously been staged in London, opened on Broadway in New York. Buddy Holly's legacy lives on not only with tributes such as these, but in the dozens of cover versions of his songs that have been recorded over the years. Holly was an initial inductee into the Rock and Roll Hall of Fame in 1986.

Selected albums: *The 'Chirping' Crickets* (1957), *That'll Be The Day* (1958), *Buddy Holly* (1958), *The Buddy Holly Story* (1959), *The Buddy Holly Story, Vol. 2* (1959), *Buddy Holly And The Crickets* (1962), *Reminiscing* (1963), *Showcase* (1964), *Holly In The Hills* (1965), *The Best Of Buddy Holly* (1966), *Buddy Holly's Greatest Hits* (1967), *The Great Buddy Holly* (1968), *Giant* (1969), *Good Rockin'* (1971), *A Rock And Roll Collection* (1972), *The Nashville Sessions* (1975), *20 Golden Greats* (1978), *The Complete Buddy Holly* (1979), *For The First Time Anywhere* (1983), *From The Original Master Tapes* (1985), *Legend* (1986), *Special Limited Edition* (1992), *Words Of Love* (1993).

Hollywood Flames

Formed as the Flames in 1949, this R&B group went through a variety of name changes - Four Flames, Hollywood Four Flames, Jets, Ebbtides and Satellites - during its career. But it was as the Hollywood Flames that it had its biggest success, the 1957 hit 'Buzz, Buzz, Buzz'. The song was written by founding member Bobby Byrd, who also had a solo career as Bobby Day. The vocal on the song was not by Day, however, but by group member Earl Nelson, who also recorded as Jackie Lee and as half of Bob And Earl. The other members of the group at the time of the hit, which reached number 11 in the US pop charts and number 5 in the R&B charts, were founding member David Ford and baritone Curtis Williams, co-writer of the hit 'Earth Angel' and a former member of the group that recorded it, the Penguins. 'Buzz, Buzz, Buzz' was released on Ebb Records, run by Lee Rupe, wife of Specialty Records owner Art Rupe. Released in November 1957, the single spent 17 weeks in the charts. Follow-up singles were issued under Day's name, but by 1959 Ebb had folded. The group continued to record with various personnel for several years.

Horne, Lena

b. 30 June 1917, Brooklyn, New York, USA. A dynamic performer, of striking appearance and elegant style. The daughter of an actress and a hotel operator, she was brought up mainly by her paternal grandmother, Cora Calhoun Horne. She made her professional debut at the age of 16 as a singer in the chorus at Harlem's Cotton Club, learning from Duke Ellington, Cab Calloway, Billie Holiday and Harold Arlen, the composer of a future big hit, 'Stormy Weather'. From 1935-36 she was featured vocalist with the all-black Noble Sissle's Society Orchestra, (the same Noble Sissle who, with Eubie Blake wrote several hit songs including 'Shuffle Along' and 'I'm Just Wild About Harry') and later toured with the top swing band of Charlie Barnet, singing numbers such as 'Good For Nothin' Joe' and 'You're My Thrill'. Sometimes, when Barnet's Band played the southern towns, Horne had to stay in the band bus.

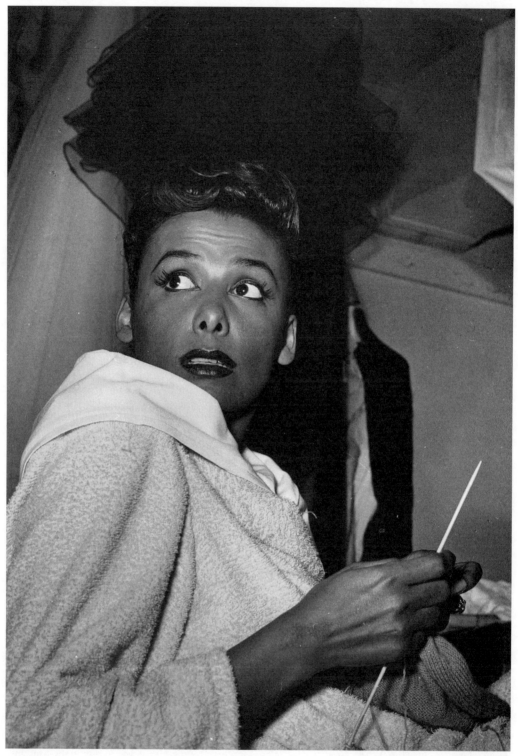

Lena Horne

She made her Broadway debut in 1934 as 'A Quadroon Girl' in *Dance With Your Gods*, and also appeared in Lew Leslie's *Blackbirds Of 1939*, in which she sang Mitchell Parish and Sammy Fain's, 'You're So Indifferent' - but only for the show's run of nine performances.

After a spell at the Café Society Downtown in New York, she moved to Hollywood's Little Troc Club and was spotted by Roger Edens, musical supervisor for MGM Pictures, and former accompanist for Ethel Merman, who introduced her to producer, Arthur Freed. In her first film for MGM, *Panama Hatti* (1942), which starred Merman, Horne sang Cole Porter's 'Just One Of Those Things', and a rhumba number called 'The Sping'. To make her skin appear lighter on film, the studio used a special make-up called 'Light Egyptian'. Horne referred to herself as 'a sepia Hedy Lamarr'. Her next two films, *Cabin In The Sky* and *Stormy Weather* both 1943, are generally regarded as her best. In the remainder of her 40s and 50s movie musicals (which included *Thousands Cheer*, *Swing Fever*, *Broadway Rhythm*, *Two Girls And A Sailor*, *Ziegfeld Follies*, *Till The Clouds Roll By*, *Words And Music*, *Duchess Of Idaho* and *Meet Me In Las Vegas*); she merely performed guest shots which were easily removable, without spoiling the plot, for the benefit of southern-state distributors.

Her 40s record hits included her theme song, 'Stormy Weather' and two other Arlen songs, ''Deed I Do' and 'As Long As I Live'. She also recorded with several big swing era names such as Artie Shaw, Cab Calloway and Teddy Wilson. During World War II, she became the pin-up girl for many thousands of black GIs and refused to appear on US tours unless black soldiers were admitted to the audience. In 1947 she married pianist/arranger/conductor Lennie Hayton, who also became her manager and mentor until his death in 1971. For a time during the 50s Lena Horne was blacklisted, probably for her constant involvement with the Civil Rights movement, but particularly for her friendship with Communist sympathizer Paul Robeson. Ironically she was at the peak of her powers at that time, and although she was unable to appear much on television and in films, she continued to make records and appear in nightclubs which were regarded as her special forte. Evidence of that was displayed on *Lena Horne At The Waldorf Astoria*. The material ranged from the sultry 'Mood Indigo', right through to the novelty 'New Fangled Tango' and *Lena At The Sands*, with its medleys of songs by Richard Rodgers/Oscar Hammerstein II, Jule Styne and

'Yip' Harburg. Other US Top 30 chart albums included *Give The Lady What She Wants* and *Porgy And Bess*, with Harry Belafonte. Horne also made the US Top 20 singles charts in 1955 with 'Love Me Or Leave Me', written by Gus Kahn and Walter Donaldson for Ruth Etting to sing in the 1928 Broadway Show, *Whoopee*.

In 1957 Horne had her first starring role on Broadway when she played Savannah, opposite Ricardo Montalban, in the Arlen/Harburg musical, *Jamaica*. In the 60s, besides the usual round of television shows and records, she appeared in a dramatic role, with Richard Widmark, in *Death Of A Gunfighter* (1969). After Hayton's death in 1971 she worked less, but did feature in *The Wiz*, an all-black film version of *The Wizard Of Oz*, starring Diana Ross and Michael Jackson, and in 1979 she received an honorary doctorate degree from Harvard University. In May 1981, she opened on Broadway in her own autobiographical show, *Lena Horne: The Lady And Her Music*. It ran at the Nederland Theatre to full houses for 14 months, a Broadway record for a one-woman show. Horne received several awards including a special Tony Award for 'Distinguished Achievement In The Theatre', a Drama Desk Award, New York Drama Critics' Special Award, New York City's Handel Medallion, Dance Theatre of Harlem's Emergence Award, two Grammy Awards and the NAACP Springarn Award. She took the show to London in 1984, where it was also acclaimed. In 1993, after not singing in public for several years, Lena Horne agreed to perform the songs of Billy Strayhorn at the US JVC Jazz Festival.

Selected albums: *Lena Horne At The Waldorf Astoria* (1957), *Give The Lady What She Wants* (1958), with Harry Belafonte *Porgy And Bess* (1959), *Lena At The Sands* (1961), *Lena On The Blue Side* (1962), *Lena...Lovely And Alive* (1963), *Lena Goes Latin* (1963), with Gabor Szabo *Lena And Gabor* (1970), *Lena* (1974), *Lena, A New Album* (1976), *The Twenty Golden Pieces Of Lena Horne* (1979), *Lena Horne And Pearl Bailey* (1979), *Lena Horne: The Lady And Her Music* (1981, stageshow soundtrack), *Lena Horne And Frank Sinatra* (1984), *A Song For You* (1992)

Further reading: *In Person*, Lena Horne. *Lena*, Lena Horne with Richard Schikel.

Howard, Eddy

b. 12 September 1914, Woodland, California, USA, d. 23 May 1963, Palm Desert, California, USA. Howard attended San Jose State College and Stanford University Medical School. After various singing stints on radio he worked with bands led by George Olsen, Tom Gerun and Ben Bernie, becoming the resident crooner with the Dick Jurgens Orchestra in 1934. Howard spent nearly six years with Jurgens, and had hits with 'My Last Goodbye' and 'Careless', both his own compositions. In 1941, after a short spell as a solo act, he formed his own band, basing its style on the popular Isham Jones Orchestra. This brought him success with 'To Each His Own', 'My Adobe Haçienda', 'I Wonder, I Wonder', 'An Apple Blossom Wedding' and 'Now Is The Hour', all Top 20 recordings. In 1949 Howard signed to Mercury Records, and during the early 50s supplied the label with such major hits as 'Maybe It's Because', 'Be Anything, But Be Mine', 'Auf Wiederseh'n Sweetheart' and 'Sin'. Beset by ill health, Howard decided to go solo again, though he did re-form his band later and made a slight impression on a rapidly changing music scene with his final success, 'The Teenagers Waltz'.

Selected albums: *Paradise Isle* (1957), *Saturday Nite Dance Date* (1958), *Words Of Love* (1958), *Great For Dancing* (1959), *Sleepy Serenade* (1960), *Great Old Waltzes* (1962), *Great Band Hits* (1963), *The Velvet Voice Of Eddy Howard* (1963), *Intimately Yours* (1964), *Sings The Great Ones* (1965), *Softly And Sincerely* (1965). Compilations: *Golden Hits* (1961), *Eddie Howard And His Orchestra 1949-53* (1986), *His Top Hits* (1987), *Eddy Howard 1946-51* (1988), *To Each His Own 1946-56* (1988).

Hughes, David

b. 11 October 1929, Birmingham, England, d. 19 October 1972. Hughes was a ballad singer with a fine tenor voice, who had success in the popular field in the UK during the 50s and early 60s, before he went on to become a star in opera. After studying at the Royal Academy, Hughes made his West End debut in the romantic musical, *Belinda Fair* (1949). During the 50s, he was a regular on radio and television, in programmes such as *The Passing Show, Come To Charlie, Henry Hall's Guest Night, Presenting David Hughes, TV Starlight, Sunday Night At The London Palladium, Spring Song, Boy Meets Girls* (from Paris), and his own series, *Make Mine Music*. He also appeared, with Ginger Rogers, Lizabeth Webb and Brian Reece, in a television version of the 1948 West End musical, *Carissima*, and was back on the London stage himself in 1956, in *Summer Song*. Hughes was also popular on the UK variety circuit, and had several successful records, including 'By The Fountains Of Rome', which won an Ivor Novello Award as 'the most

outstanding song of the year' in 1956, for its writers, Matyas Seiber and Norman Newell. Around this time, with his good looks and romantic delivery, he was dubbed 'Mr. Hearthrob'. In 1962 he appeared in Scapa, a musical version of the 1950 hit comedy, *Seagulls Over Sorrento* and, shortly afterwards, decided to forsake the world of pop for light music and opera. In 1964 he made an album of 16th-century songs. Appearances at Glyndebourne the following year eventually led to work with the Sadler's Wells Company. From then on, encouraged by the legendary Sir John Barbarolli, he sang many leading roles in opera, in the UK and abroad, including Lieutenant Pinkerton in *Madame Butterfly*.

Albums: *Favourite Opera And Operetta Arias* (1970), *World Of Classic Love Songs* (1973).

Hunter, Tab

b. Arthur Andrew Kelm, 11 July 1931, New York City, New York, USA. This blond-haired, blue-eyed pop vocalist/actor used his mother's maiden name, Gelien, until he was spotted in 1948, working at a stable, by talent scout Dick Clayton. He introduced him to Rock Hudson's Hollywood agent Harry Wilson, who said 'We've got to tab you something' then named him Tab Hunter. He made his screen debut in the 1950 film *The Lawless* and two years later co-starred with Linda Darnell, in the British film *Island Of Desire*. In late 1956 he received a phone call from Randy Wood, president of Dot Records, asking him to record a song, recently cut by US country star Sonny James, the lilting ballad, 'Young Love'. Both versions made the US charts, Hunter reached number 1 and James peaked at 2. He also topped the UK chart but James lagged behind at number 11. He continued recording for Dot and hit with the slightly uptempo '99 Ways', which narrowly missed the US Top 10 but made the UK Top 5 (1957). In the following year he appeared in the film version of the Broadway show, *Damn Yankees*, with Gwen Verdon and Ray Walston. As Warner Brothers had him under contract to make films, they resented him recording for Dot and established their own record label in 1958. He signed, with moderate success, and in 1960 starred in his own NBC US television series. He kept up his acting and appeared opposite Fabian in the 1964 'beach party' film, *Ride The Wild Surf*. He was still acting in the 80s, notably in *Polyester* and *Lust In The Dust* and also in the *Grease* sequel, *Grease 2*.

Selected albums: *Young Love* (1961), *R.F.D.* (1962).

Husky, Ferlin

b. 3 December 1925, on a farm near Flat River, Missouri, USA. He learned to play guitar as a child and during World War II served in the US Merchant Navy. His mother wanted him to be a preacher and his father a farmer but, after discharge, he found radio work as an announcer and disc jockey but gradually turned to performing while at KXLW St. Louis. In the late 40s he moved to California, where he appeared on the Los Angeles *Hometown Jamboree* and played clubs in the Bakersfield area. Believing that Ferlin Husky, though his real name, was unsuitable he first called himself Tex Preston, then changed again to Terry Preston. He also developed an alter ego country philosopher character, Simon Crum, who he introduced into his act. (A few years later, Sheb Wooley also adopted a similar practice with his character Ben Colder, who sought to entertain with his supposed humorous parodies on popular and country songs.)

In the early 50s, he recorded for Capitol and worked with Tennessee Ernie Ford. In 1953, as Ferlin Huskey, he recorded 'A Dear John Letter' with Jean Shepard, which became a smash US country number 1, as well as reaching number 4 on the US pop charts. An answer version called 'Forgive Me John', also had success in both charts. Following success with his self-penned 'Hank's Song' (a tribute to Hank Williams), Huskey finally dropped the name of Terry Preston. In 1957, now minus the 'e' again, Husky joined the *Grand Ole Opry* and achieved another smash hit number 1 with his million selling recording of 'Gone', which, ironically, he had first recorded unsuccessfully as Preston five years earlier. In 1960, he charted a further country number 1 with the gospel/country 'Wings Of A Dove', which also became a Top 20 pop hit. He recorded 'The Drunken Driver', a tear-jerking narration about a father who runs over his son, which has been rated a classic by some and one of the worst recordings ever made by others. He became a popular entertainer on many network television shows including hosting the *Arthur Godfrey Show* and appearing as a dramatic actor on *Kraft TV Theatre*.

Whilst not always singing traditional country material, he maintained his country popularity through the character of Simon Crum. In this guise, he demonstrated a great talent for impersonating other country stars, presenting rustic comedy and even managed a number 2 country hit with 'Country Music's Here To Stay'. He recorded an album of pop songs called *Boulevard Of Broken Dreams* in 1957 and also recorded one or two rock 'n' roll singles such as 'Wang Dang Do'. Husky has appeared in several films including *Mr. Rock & Roll* and *Country Music Holiday*. From the 60s to the mid-70s, he toured extensively with his band, the Hush Puppies, and had regular country chart entries including 'Once', 'Just For You', 'True True Lovin'' and 'Freckles And Polliwog Days'. He moved to ABC Records in 1973 and on that label, achieved country chart entry number 51 (and last) in 1975 with 'An Old Memory Got In My Eye'. Husky has been married six times and has nine children, one not surprisingly being called Terry Preston. His career was slowed in 1977 by a heart operation but he recovered and continued to perform and later again recorded.

Albums: *Songs Of The Home And Heart* (1956), *Boulevard Of Broken Dreams* (1957), *Born To Lose* (1959), *Country Tunes From The Heart* (1959), *Sittin' On A Rainbow* (1959), *Favorites of Ferlin Huskey* (1959), *Gone* (1960), *Easy Livin'* (1960), *Ferlin's Favorites* (1960), *Some Of My Favorites* (1960), *Walkin' & Hummin'* (1961), *Memories Of Home* (1961), *The Heart & Soul Of Ferlin Husky* (1963), *The Unpredictable Simon Crum* (1963), *By Request* (1964), *True True Lovin'* (1965), *I Could Sing All Night* (1966), *Songs Of Music City, USA* (1966), *Christmas All Year Long* (1967), *What Am I Gonna Do Now* (1967), *Where No One Stands Alone* (1968), *White Fences And Evergreen Trees* (1968), *Just For You* (1968), *That's Why I Love You So Much* (1969), *Your Love Is Heavenly Sunshine* (1970), *Your Sweet Love Lifted Me* (1970), *One More Time* (1971), *Just Plain Lonely* (1972), *Sweet Honky Tonk* (1973), *True True Lovin'* (1973), *Champagne Ladies & Blue Ribbon Babies* (1974), *Freckles & Polliwog Days* (1974), *Mountain Of Everlasting Love* (1974), *The Foster & Rice Songbook* (1975), *Ferlin Husky* (1982), *Live* (1983).

I

Impalas

With sweet-voiced lead singer Joe 'Speedo' Frazier, b 5 September 1943, New York City, New York, USA, this New York doo-wop group had an overnight success with their first record '(Sorry) I Ran All The Way Home'. From the Carnesie section of Brooklyn, the rest of the Impalas were Richard Wagner, Lenny Renda and Tony Calouchi. They were discovered by disk jockey Alan Freed and Artie Zwirn who co-wrote the bright, brash novelty tune with Gino Giosasi, (of the Gino And Gina vocal duo). With an arrangement by Ray Ellis, '(Sorry) I Ran All The Way Home' was released in 1959 on the MGM subsidiary label Cub, reaching number 2 in America and entering the UK Top 30. The follow-up, 'Oh What A Fool' was a smaller hit. The Impalas made later records for Hamilton and 20th Century Fox before splitting up. Frazier went on to sing with Love's Own in 1973.
Album: *Sorry I Ran All The Way Home* (1959).

Imperial Records

Formed in Los Angeles, California, USA by Lew Chudd in 1947. Imperial emerged as one of the most influential independent R&B labels of the 50s. Despite the company's devotion to the R&B market, for many years their only major hit was by the C&W artist Slim Whitman, with 'Indian Love Call' in 1952. Having secured the New Orleans R&B bandleader Dave Bartholomew as house producer, a former Bartholomew band member, Fats Domino was signed to record for the label and his first release, 'The Fat Man' became a US R&B chart hit. The subsequent and consistent success of Domino's career in the national US chart between 1955 and 1962 was, for some time, crucial to Imperial's ability to promote other R&B artists, such as Roy Brown ('Let The Four Winds Blow'), Smiley Lewis ('I Hear You Knockin''), Chris Kenner ('Sick And Tired') and Ernie Freeman ('Raunchy'). In 1957 Chudd found his new pop star in Rick Nelson, who provided the label with a string of 16 hits up until 1962. An effort to cash-in on Phil Spector's Teddy Bears success with 'To Know Him Is To Love Him' (having been recorded on the Dore label) came to nought, with the exception that the group did release their only

(and very rare) album on the Imperial label. Other US hits during this period were supplied by Garry Mills (a 1960 Top 30 hit with 'Look For A Star - Part 1') and the rock 'n' roll drummer Sandy Nelson with his instrumental hits 'Let There Be Drums' (1961) and 'Drums Are My Beat' (1962). Throughout this time the label was well served by the steady success of Slim Whitman, particularly in the UK, where the Imperial label was licensed to London Records.
In the early 60s Chudd acquired the New Orleans label, Minit. He sold the company to Liberty Records in 1963, after which Imperial concentrated more on the mainstream pop market, releasing many British acts in the USA, including Billy J. Kramer (a Top 10 hit with 'Little Children'/'Bad To Me' in 1964), Georgie Fame (a Top 30 hit in 1965 with 'Yeh Yeh') and the Hollies, (notably two Top 10 hits in 1966 with 'Bus Stop' and 'Stop Stop Stop'). Cher had begun her solo career with Imperial scoring 5 US Top 40 hits between 1965 and 1967, including 'Bang Bang (My Baby Shot Me Down)' (number 2), 'You Better Sit Down Kids' (number 9), and former rock 'n' roll singer-turned MOR act, Johnny Rivers, had an impressive string of 13 hit singles from 1964-67, including the number 1 'Poor Side Of Town' in 1966. A link with the R&B past was maintained with Irma Thomas's Top 20 hit 'Wish Someone Would Care' (1964) and with Mel Carter's three Top 40 hits during 1965-66, which included the Top 10 'Hold Me, Thrill Me, Kiss Me' (1965). Songwriter Jackie DeShannon's occasional excursion into the recording studio rewarded Imperial with two Top 10 hits with the classic Burt Bacharach song 'What The World Needs Now Is Love' (1965) and 'Put A Little Love In Your Heart' (1969). Classic IV rounded off the label's list of Top 10 hits during 1968-69 with 'Spooky' (number 3), 'Stormy' (number 5) and 'Traces' (number 2). By the end of the 60s, the machinations of the corporate music industry had forced Liberty and Imperial to merge with the United Artists label who, in turn, were swallowed up by the giant EMI conglomerate by 1979.
Compilations: *Imperial Rockabillies* (1977), *Imperial Rockabillies Volume 2* (1979), *Imperial Rockabillies Volume 3* (1980), *Imperial Musicians 1951-1962: The Rhythm In Rhythm & Blues* (1987).

Irwin, Big Dee

b. Defosca Erwin, 4 August 1939, New York City, New York, USA. The corpulent R&B singer first made his mark as lead for the doo-wop group, the

Pastels, who hit with two sumptuous ballads, 'Been So Long' (1957) and 'So Far Away' (1958). As a solo artist, he is recalled for a series of tongue-in-cheek singles, the most successful of which was a version of the Bing Crosby hit 'Swingin' On A Star' in 1963, an irreverent performance on which he was joined by a perky, Little Eva. Irwin's other releases included 'Everybody's Got A Dance But Me', on which he begrudged the dance-based releases of other artists, and 'Happy Being Fat', where Eva, once again, provided the spiky interjections. Irwin later enjoyed intermittent success as a songwriter, including 'What Kind Of Boy', recorded on the Hollies' debut album.

J

Jacobs, Dick

b. 29 March 1918, New York, USA. A graduate from the city university, Jacobs was to be one of the few producers for a major US record company in the 50s who catered for rock 'n' roll consumers without finding the form personally objectionable. With his orchestra, he had a US Top 30 entry with Elmer Bernstein's jazzy main theme to 1956's *The Man With The Golden Arm* (starring Frank Sinatra) but after serving as musical director for the nationally televised Hit Parade, he became recording manager for Coral, a Decca subsidiary. Among his clients were Jackie Wilson, Bobby Darin and Buddy Holly, for whom Jacobs cut corners by duplicating the Darin arrangement of 'Early In The Morning'. By contrast, 'the most unplanned thing I have ever written' was the pizzicato string section that embroidered Holly's posthumous smash, 'It Doesn't Matter Any More', taped in the New York's Pythian Temple studio. During the 60s, Jacobs functioned in a more administrative capacity in the music industry, working for New York's Springboard Records prior to his retirement in the late 70s.

James, Dick

b. Isaac Vapnick, 1919, London, England, d. 1 February 1986, London, England. Originally a dance band singer under the name Lee Sheridan, he sang with several of the major bandleaders of the 40s and 50s, including Geraldo and Cyril Stapleton. After changing his name to Dick James he was signed to EMI's Parlophone label and achieved a memorable UK Top 20 with 'Robin Hood'. The song was commissioned for a long-running television series, *The Adventures Of Robin Hood*, and a generation of children were entranced by James lusty, barrel-voiced, perfectly enunciated vocal. The singer enjoyed a further hit with the much-covered 'Garden Of Eden' before retiring from recording, and launched himself as a music publisher. In November 1962, James, to his lasting fortune, was visited by entrepreneur Brian Epstein, and acquired the most lucrative songwriting catalogue of modern times. With the Beatles, James changed irrevocably Tin Pan Alley music publishing in the UK. Instead of offering the group the traditional 10 per cent retail price of sheet music, he suggested that they form Northern Songs, a separate company that would deal exclusively with the songs of John Lennon and Paul McCartney. The offer was a 50/50, half to James and his partner, 20 per cent each to Lennon/McCartney and 10 per cent to Epstein. The success of the Beatles' songwriting team eroded the power of the old Tin Pan Alley songsmiths, but James remained a prominent figure. He had the cream of the Merseybeat groups as part of his company, and also published Manchester's major pop act, the Hollies, and Birmingham's Spencer Davis Group. During the late 60s, he oversaw the publishing side of Larry Page's record company, Page One. After many successful years with the Beatles, James eventually sold his major shareholding in Northern Songs to Lew Grade's ATV company in 1969. His major concern during the early 70s was the extension of Dick James Music into DJM Records. As a publisher and record company mogul, he hit new peaks after signing the songwriting team of Elton John and Bernie Taupin. Their catalogue proved one of the most valuable of the era. James finally retired from the business but was forced to return to the fray when Elton John belatedly began legal proceedings in a vain attempt to win back his songs. Three months after the lengthy court proceedings ended, James died at his St. John's Wood home in February 1986.
Selected album: *Fun And James* (1958).

James, Joni

b. Joan Carmello Babbo, 22 September 1930,

Chicago, Illinois, USA. Growing up during the Depression years, James attended drama and dance lessons and organized a ballet club in high school. Following graduation, she worked as a dancer and began singing. In 1952 she recorded her first tracks for MGM Records, with the second single, 'Why Don't You Believe Me', becoming a million-seller and a number 1 hit on the US pop charts. The hit was later covered by both Patti Page and Margaret Whiting. James next two singles, the double-sided hit 'Have You Heard'/'Wishing Ring' and a cover of Hank Williams' 'Your Cheatin' Heart', were also major hits. James hit the Top 10 four more times up to 1955 with 'Almost Always', 'My Love, My Love', 'How Important Can It Be?' and 'You Are My Love'. Joni continued to record for MGM until 1964; when the hits stopped coming she retired from show business.

Selected albums: *Let There Be Love* (1953), *The Joni James Award Winning Album* (1954), *Little Girl Blue* (1955), *When I Fall In Love* (1955), *In The Still Of The Night* (1956), *Among My Souvenirs* (1958), *Songs Of Hank Williams* (1959), *Joni Sings Sweet* (1959), *At Carnegie Hall* (1960), *I'm In The Mood for Love* (1960), *Sings Hollywood* (1960), *100 Strings And Joni* (1960), *100 Voices, 100 Strings* (1961), *Mood Is Blue* (1961), *Mood Is Romance* (1961), *Mood Is Swinging* (1961), *Sings Folk Songs* (1961), *After Hours* (1962), *I'm Your Girl* (1962), *Something For The Boys* (1963), *Beyond The Reef* (1964), *Sings The Gershwins* (1964), *My Favourite Things* (1964), *Put On A Happy Face* (1964), *Italianissime* (1964), *Bossa Nova Time* (1965).

Johnson, Teddy (see Carr, Pearl, And Teddy Johnson)

Jordanaires

This renowned harmony-vocal quartet is best-known for a lengthy working relationship with Elvis Presley. The group first accompanied the youthful rock 'n' roll star in 1956 during a performance on the pivotal *Louisiana Hayride*. Lead vocalist Gordon Stocker was subsequently featured on Presley's first recordings for RCA Victor, notably 'Heartbreak Hotel', while the remaining trio - Neal Matthews (tenor), Hoyt Hawkins (baritone) and Hugh Jarrett (bass) - joined him on the session producing 'Hound Dog' and 'Don't Be Cruel'. The Jordanaires also supported Presley on the *Steve Allen* and *Milton Berle* television shows where their clean-cut, conservative appearance contrasted the impact of the singer's explosive personae. The quartet continued to accompany

him throughout the 50s and 60s, although they were noticeably absent from the 'comeback' NBC-TV spectacular, *Elvis* (1968), where their role was taken by girl-group, the Blossoms. The Jordanaires did not feature on the fruitful sessions spawning 'Suspicious Minds' and 'In The Ghetto', nor the subsequent live appearances, but returned to the fold for recordings undertaken in Nashville during June and September 1970. These marked the end of the Jordanaires' relationship with Presley, but the group remained an integral part of the city's music industry. In 1972 they contributed to *Guitar That Shook The World*, the solo debut by longtime Elvis' guitarist Scotty Moore, and were heavily featured on sessions with Johnny Cash, Kris Kristofferson, Don McLean, Tracy Nelson and Billy Swan. The Jordanaires - by this point comprising of Stocker, Hawkins, Matthews, and new bass player Lovis Nunley - also released several albums in their own right, many of which featured gospel material, but their career remains inextricably linked to that of Elvis Presley.

Selected albums: *We'd Like To Teach The World To Sing* (1972), *The Jordanaires Sing Elvis' Favorite Spirituals* (1985), *The Jordanaires Sing Elvis' Gospel Favorites* (1986).

K

Kaye Sisters

This UK pop trio comprised Sheila Jones (b. 21 October 1936, Lewisham, London, England), Shirley 'Shan' Palmer (b. 15 August 1938, Hull, England) and Carole Young (b. 12 April 1930, Oldham, Lancashire, England). Formed in 1954 by Carmen Kaye and originally known as the Three Kayes, their big break came when they appeared on television's *In Town Tonight* in 1956. They followed this with two weeks at the London Palladium and then their debut single, a cover of the Charms' 'Ivory Tower' on HMV, made the UK Top 20. They joined the Philips label in 1957 and their first two Top 10 hits, which came in the company of Frankie Vaughan, were covers of Bob Jaxon's 'Gotta Have Something In The Bank

Kaye Sisters

Frank' (their royalties going to the Boys Clubs, an organization with which Vaughan has been involved for many years) and the Fleetwoods 'Come Softly To Me'. Of the many singles they released, their only solo Top 10 was their version of Anita Bryant's US hit 'Paper Roses' in 1960. Jones retired in the late 60s and was replaced by Gilly. They continued to work, often supporting Max Bygraves. Young left in the late 70s to pursue an acting career, and appeared in the ITV series *Albion Market* and top soap, *Coronation Street*. 'Shan and Gilly Kaye', appeared in the 1978 Royal Command Performance of 1978, and sang together in theatres and cabaret during the 80s. The original three members were reunited in 1992 and 1993, singing numbers made famous by the Andrews Sisters, in UK tours of *In The Mood*, a tribute to Glenn Miller.
Album: *Shan, Gill And Carole* (1973).

Kaye, Danny

b. David Daniel Kominsky, 18 January 1913, Brooklyn, New York, USA, d. 3 March 1987, Los Angeles, California, USA. Kaye was an extraordinary entertainer and an apparently inexhaustible comedian, mimic and dancer who seemed to be able to twist his face and body into any shape he wanted. As a singer, he specialized in very fast double talk and tongue-twisters, but could present a gentle ballad equally well. He was also an indefatigable ambassador for numerous charities, especially the United Nations International Children's Emergency Fund (now UNICEF), for which he travelled and worked for many years. A son of Jewish immigrant parents from Russia, Kominsky originally wanted to join the medical profession, but dropped out of high school when he was 14 years old, and hitch-hiked to Florida with his friend, Louis Eilson, where they sang for money. On their return to New York, they formed an act called Red And Blackie, and performed at private functions. During the day, Kominski worked as a soda-jerk, and then as an automobile appraiser with an insurance company. The latter job was terminated after he made a mistake which is said to have cost the company some $40,000. Kominski and Eilson then obtained summer work as 'toomlers', creators of tumult or all-round entertainers, in the Borscht Circuit summer hotels and camps in the Catskill Mountains. After five years, Kominski was earning $1,000 per season.

In 1933, he joined David Harvey and Kathleen Young on the vaudeville circuit in their dancing act, the Three Terpsichoreans, and was billed for the first time as Danny Kaye. An early on-stage accident in which he split his trousers, elicited much laughter from the audience and was incorporated into the act. Signed by producer A.B. Marcus, the group toured the USA for five months in the revue, *La Vie Paree*, before sailing for the Orient in February 1934. It is often said that during this period of playing to non-English speaking audiences in Japan, China and Malaya, was when Kaye developed his face-making and pantomiming techniques, and his 'gibberish' singing with the occasional recognized word. Back in the USA in 1936, Kaye worked with comedian Nick Long Jnr. and toured with Abe Lyman's Band, before being booked by impresario Henry Sherek, to appear in cabaret at London's Dorchester Hotel. The engagement, in 1938, was not a success. Kaye commented: 'I was too loud for the joint'. (Ten years later in London, it would be an entirely different story.) While appearing in Max Liebman's *Sunday Night Varieties* in New York, Kaye met pianist-songwriter Sylvia Fine, who had been raised in the same Brooklyn neighbourhood, and majored in music at Brooklyn College. She became a powerful influence throughout his career, as his director, coach and critic. Working with Liebman's Saturday night revues at Camp Taimiment in the Pennsylvania Hills, during the summer of 1939, they started their collaboration, with Fine accompanying Kaye on the piano, and writing special material which included three of his most famous numbers, 'Stanislavsky', 'Pavlova' and the story of the unstable château designer, 'Anatole Of Paris'. The best of the material was assembled in *The Straw Hat Revue* in which Kaye appeared with Imogene Coca, and opened on Broadway in September 1939. The show also featured a young dancer named Jerome Robbins. After Fine and Kaye were married in January 1940, Kaye appeared in a smash hit engagement at La Martinique nightclub in New York, which led to a part in *Lady In The Dark*, starring Gertrude Lawrence. On the first night, Kaye stopped the show with the Kurt Weill and Ira Gershwin tongue-twister 'Tchaikovsky', in which he reeled off the names of 50 real, or imagined, Russian composers in 38 seconds. After playing a return engagement at La Martinique, and a five-week stint at the Paramount Theatre, Kaye appeared again on Broadway, starring in the Cole Porter musical, *Let's Face It*, which opened in October 1941. Porter allowed Sylvia Fine and Max Liebman to interpolate some special material for Kaye, which included a 'jabberwocky of song, dance, illustration and double-talk' called 'Melody In 4F'. Kaye had to leave the show early in 1942, suffering from nervous exhaustion, but having recovered, he toured on behalf of the war effort and is said to have sold a million dollars worth of government

bonds in six months. Rejected by the US Army because of a back ailment, he entertained troops with his two-hour shows in many theatres of operations including the South Pacific.
In 1944, Kaye made his feature film debut in *Up In Arms*, the first of a series of five pictures for Sam Goldwyn at MGM. His performance as a hypochondriac elevator boy, involving yet another memorable Fine-Liebman piece, 'Manic Depressive Pictures Presents: Lobby Number', moved one critic to hail his introduction as 'the most exciting since Garbo's'. Goldwyn was criticized, however for having Kaye's red hair dyed blonde. His remaining films for the studio included *Wonder Man*, in which he gave his impression of a sneezing Russian baritone with 'Orchi Tchornya'. This was the first of several films in which he played more than one character; *The Kid From Brooklyn* (1946), which featured 'Pavlova', *The Secret Life Of Walter Mitty* (1947), one of his best-remembered roles (six of them), and *A Song Is Born* (1948), one of his least remembered. In 1945, Kaye appeared for a year on his own CBS radio show with Harry James and Eve Arden, and during the following year the Kayes' daughter, Dena was born. When Kaye recorded the old standard, 'Dinah', he changed some of the 'i' sounds to 'e', so that the song ran: 'Denah, is there anyone fener? In the State of Carolena . . .' etc. His other hit songs included 'Tubby The Tuba', 'Minnie The Moocher', 'Ballin' The Jack', 'Bloop Bleep', 'Civilization' and 'The Woody Woodpecker Song', both with the Andrews Sisters; 'C'est Si Bon'; and 'Blackstrap Molasses', recorded with Jimmy Durante, Jane Wyman and Groucho Marx. In 1948, Kaye returned to England, to appear at the London Palladium. His enormously successful record-breaking performances began an affectionate and enduring relationship with the British public. He is said to have received over 100,000 letters in a week. His shows were attended by the Royal Family; he met both Winston Churchill and George Bernard Shaw, and was cast in wax for London's Madame Tussauds Museum. He returned in 1949 for the first of several Royal Command Performances, and also toured provincial music halls throughout 1952. He endeared himself to the British by singing some of their parochial songs such as the novelty 'I've Got A Lovely Bunch Of Coconuts' and 'Maybe It's Because I'm A Londoner'. During one performance at the Palladium, when a member of the audience enquired after the state of Kaye's ribs, following a car accident, he ordered the lights to be

lowered while he displayed the actual X-ray plates! Kaye went to Canada in 1950 and became the first solo performer to star at the Canadian National Exhibition, where he sold out the 24,000-seater stadium for each of his 14 performances.

He returned to his multiple roles in films such as *The Inspector General* (1949) and *On The Riviera* (1951), before embarking on the somewhat controversial, *Hans Christian Andersen* (1952). After 16 different screenplays over a period of 15 years, and protests in the Danish press about the choice of Kaye to play their national hero, the film, with a final screenplay by Moss Hart, was the third biggest money-spinner in MGM's history. Frank Loesser's score produced several appealing songs, including 'No Two People', 'Anywhere I Wander', 'Inchworm', 'Thumbelina', 'The Ugly Duckling' and 'Wonderful Copenhagen', the latter reaching the UK Top 5. Kaye's other films during the 50s and early 60s included *Knock On Wood* (1954), said to be his favourite, in which he sang two more Fine numbers, the title song, and 'All About Me', *White Christmas* (1954), co-starring with Bing Crosby, Rosemary Clooney and Vera Ellen, *The Court Jester* (1956), *Me And The Colonel* (1958), *Merry Andrew* (1958), *The Five Pennies* (1959), a bio-pic of 20s cornet player Red Nichols (including a rousing version of 'When The Saints Go Marching In', with Louis Armstrong), *On The Double* (1961) and *The Man From The Diners' Club* (1963). After a break, he came back for *The Madwoman Of Chailliot* (1969), and the following year, returned to Broadway in the role of Noah, in the Richard Rodgers and Martin Charnin musical, *Two By Two*. Shortly after the show opened, Kaye tore a ligament in his leg during a performance, and subsequently appeared on crutches or in a wheel chair, in which he tried to run down the other actors, adapting the show to his injury, much to the distaste of producer and composer, Richard Rodgers.

During the 70s and 80s, Kaye conducted classical orchestras and appeared on several television shows including *Peter Pan*, *Pinocchio* and *Danny Kaye's Look At The Metropolitan Opera*. He also played dramatic roles on television in *Skokie* and *The Twilight Zone*, but concentrated mainly on his charity work. He had started his association with UNICEF in the early 50s, and in 1955 made a 20-minute documentary, *Assignment Children*. He eventually became the organization's ambassador-at-large for 34 years, travelling worldwide on their behalf, and entering the *Guinness Book Of Records* by visiting 65 US and Canadian cities in five days,

piloting himself in his own jet plane. During his career he received many awards including the French Legion d'Honneur, the Jean Hersholt Humanitarian Award, the Knight's Cross of the First Class of the Order of Danneborg, given by the Danish Government. Other awards included a special Academy Award in 1954, along with Tonys for his stage performances, plus Emmys for his successful 60s television series. He died in March 1987, following a heart attack.

Albums: *Hans Christian Andersen* (1953, film soundtrack), *Mommy, Gimme A Drink Of Water* (1958), with Louis Armstrong *The Five Pennies* (1959, film soundtrack), *For Children* (1974), with Ivor Moreton *Happy Fingers* (1977). Compilations: *The Best Of Danny Kaye* (1982), *The Very Best Of Danny Kaye - 20 Golden Greats* (1987).

Further reading: *The Danny Kaye Saga*, Kurt Singer.

Keel, Howard

b. Harold C. Leek, 13 April 1917, Gillespie, Illinois, USA. After starting his career as a singing waiter in Los Angeles, Keel became an 'in-house entertainer' for the huge Douglas aircraft manufacturing company. In 1945, he appeared in *Carousel* on the west coast and then travelled to the UK to appear in the London production of *Oklahoma!*. At this time he was known as Harold Keel, having reversed the spelling of his last name. Now, he changed his first name and after making a non-singing appearance in the film, *The Small Voice* (1948), he returned to the USA where he landed the role of Frank Butler in the film *Annie Get Your Gun* (1950). He continued to make films, mostly musicals, including *Show Boat* (1951), *Kiss Me Kate* and *Calamity Jane* (both 1953), *Rose Marie* and *Seven Brides For Seven Brothers* (both 1954) and *Kismet* (1955). By the 60s he was touring the US in revivals of popular shows, and appearing in mostly to be seen in non-musical low-budget western movies. In 1981 his acting career received a boost when he started to appear in the long-running television soap, *Dallas*. This revived interest in his singing, particularly in the UK, and in 1984 he recorded his first solo album. Although untrained, Keel's rich and powerful baritone voice and commanding stage and screen presence made him a good leading actor for musical comedies. In 1993, with his tongue firmly in his cheek, he announced his Farewell Tour of the UK.

Selected albums: *And I Love You So* (1984), *Reminiscing* (1985), *The Collection* (1989), *The Great MGM Stars* (1991), *Close To My Heart* (1991), and

Howard Keel

the soundtrack albums from the above film musicals.

Keller, Jerry

b. 20 June 1938, Fort Smith, Arkansas, USA. After moving to Tulsa in 1944 Keller formed the Lads Of Note Quartet in the 50s before joining the Tulsa Boy Singers. He won a talent contest organized by bandleader Horace Heidt which earned him the vocalist job with Jack Dalton's Orchestra. He then spent nine months as a disc jockey in Tulsa before moving to New York in 1956. He recorded a series of demos for record companies before fellow performer Pat Boone introduced him to Marty Mills who became his manager. He recorded the self-penned 'Here Comes Summer' for the Kapp record label, and it became a US summer hit in 1959. Ironically it only entered the UK charts in late August as the warmer months lapsed into autumn, but it still went to number 1. Follow-ups such as 'If I Had A Girl', and 'Now Now Now' failed to repeat the success. In 1960, he toured the UK replacing Eddie Cochran in a package tour engagement after Cochran had died in a car crash. Despite the lack of subsequent hits as a singer, his songs charted handsomely for artists such as Andy Williams and the Cyrkle. In 1977, he appeared in the film *You Light Up My Life* and the following year in *If I Ever See You Again*.
Album: *Here Comes Jerry Keller* (1960).

Kelly, Gene

b. Eugene Curran Kelly, 23 August 1912, Pittsburgh, Pennsylvania, USA. An actor, dancer, singer, choreographer, director, producer, and one of the most innovative and respected figures in the history of the screen musical. Kelly was taking dance lessons at the age of eight - albeit against his will - and excelled at sports when he was at high school. During the Depression he worked at a variety of jobs, including gymnastics instructor, and, with his brother, Fred, performed a song-and-dance act in local nightclubs. In the early 30s he spent a few months at law school before opening the Gene Kelly Studios of the Dance and discovered he had a real aptitude for teaching, which would manifest itself throughout his career in some of the most creative choreography ever seen on the big screen. In 1937 he moved to New York and gained a small part as dancer in the musical comedy *Leave It To Me*, in which Mary Martin made her Broadway debut; and a larger one in the revue, *One For The Money*. He also played

Harry, the 'good natured hoofer' in the Pulitzer prize-winning comedy, *The Time Of Your Life*. In 1940, after working in summer stock, and serving as dance director at Billy Rose's Diamond Horseshoe club, he won the title role in the new Richard Rodgers and Lorenz Hart musical, *Pal Joey*. His portrayal of the devious, unscrupulous nightcub entertainer made him a star overnight. After choreographing *Best Foot Forward*, he moved to Hollywood in 1942, and made his screen debut, with Judy Garland, in *For Me And My Gal*. Two more MGM musicals, *DuBarry Was A Lady* and *Thousands Cheer*, followed, before the company loaned him to Columbia for *Cover Girl* (1944). Co-starred with Rita Hayworth and Phil Silvers, the film was a major landmark in Kelly's career, and an indication of the heights he would achieve during the next 10 years. It was memorable in many respects: for Kelly's sensitive rendering of Jerome Kern and Ira Gershwin's 'Long Ago And Far Away'; and his 'Alter Ego' dance, during which Kelly danced with his reflection in shop window. Back at MGM, he was called on to play several straight dramatic roles as well as appearing in *Anchors Aweigh*, (1944), for which he received an Oscar nomination for best actor. As a couple of sailors on leave, Kelly and Frank Sinatra were joined by Kathryn Grayson, a Sammy Cahn and Julé Styne score - and Jerry, an animated mouse, who accompanied Kelly in a live-action/cartoon sequence that is still regarded as a minor classic. After spending two years in the *real* US Navy, supervising training films, Kelly resumed at MGM with *Ziegfeld Follies* (1946), in which he danced with Fred Astaire for the first time on screen, in 'The Babbitt And The Bromide'. He also starred in *The Pirate* (1948), an underrated film at the time, for which he was again teamed with Judy Garland. After choreographing the 'Slaughter On Tenth Avenue' sequence in the Rodgers and Hart biopic, *Words And Music*, for which he was partnered by Vera-Ellen, Kelly joined Sinatra and Jules Munshin, first for the lively *Take Me Out To The Ball Game* (1949), and again, in the following year, for *On The Town*, 'the most inventive and effervescent movie musical Hollywood had thus far produced'. Although criticized for its truncation of the original Broadway score, *On The Town*, with its integrated music and plot, and location filming of the athletic dance sequences on the streets of New York, was acclaimed from all sides. After his triumph in *On the Town*, Kelly went on to *Summer Stock* with Judy Garland, before turning to what many consider to be the jewel in MGM's musical

Gene Kelly

crown - *An American In Paris* (1951). Directed by Vincente Minnelli, and set in an idealised version of Paris, Kelly and his partner, Leslie Caron, danced exquisitely to a Gershwin score which included 'I've Got Rhythm', 'Our Love Is Here To Stay', ''S'Wonderful' and 'I'll Build A Stairway To Paradise'. The film ended with a 17 minute ballet sequence, 'a summation of Gene Kelly's work as a film dancer and choreographer, allowing him his full range of style - classical ballet, modern ballet, Cohanesque hoofing, tapping, jitterbugging and sheer athletic expressionism' It won eight Academy Awards, including one for best picture. Kelly received a special Oscar 'in appreciation of his versatility as an actor, singer, director and dancer, and specifically for his briliant achievements in the art of choreography on film'. If *An American In Paris* was MGM's jewel, then *Singin' In The Rain* (1952) was probably its financial plum - arguably the most popular Hollywood musical of them all. Produced by Arthur Freed, who also wrote the songs with Nacio Herb Brown, Comden and Green's witty screenplay dealt with the Hollywood silent movie industry, trying to come to terms with talking pictures. Debbie Reynolds and Donald O'Connor joined Kelly in the joyous spoof, and sang and danced to a score which included 'You Were Meant For Me', 'Make 'Em Laugh', 'Good Mornin'', 'Moses Supposes'. The sequence, in which Kelly sings the title song while getting completely drenched, is probably the most requested film clip in the history of the musical cinema. For *Deep In My Heart* (1955), the Sigmund Romberg bio-pic, Kelly went back to his roots and danced with his younger brother, in one of film's highspots, 'I Love To Go Swimmin' With Wimmen'. Kelly's final major musical projects for MGM were *Brigadoon* (1954) and *It's Always Fair Weather* (1955). In the former, 'the magical story of a Scottish village long lost to history and coming to life once every hundred years for a single day', Kelly co-starred with Cyd Charisse and Van Johnson in a production that was critisized for being shot in CinemaScope, and in the studio, rather than on location. For the latter, Kelly joined Dan Dailey and Phil Silvers for what was, essentially, a satirical swipe at the cynical commercialism of the US television industry - with music. *Invitation To The Dance* (1956), with script, choreography and direction by Kelly, was a film consisting of three unrelated episodes, all entirely danced, with Kelly accompanied by a classically trained troupe. A commercial failure in the US, it was acclaimed in parts of Europe, and awarded the grand prize at the West Berlin film festival in 1958. Following its success there, Kelly choreographed a new ballet for the Paris Opera's resident company, and was made a Chevalier of the Legion of Honor by the French government. *Les Girls* (1956) was Kelly's final MGM musical, and Cole Porter's last Hollywood score - the golden era of screen musicals was over. Subsequently, he played several straight roles in films such as *Marjorie Morningstar* and *Inherit The Wind*, but spent much of his time as a director, on projects such as Rodgers and Hammerstein's Broadway musical, *Flower Drum Song*, and 20th Century Fox's $20,000,000 extravaganza, *Hello Dolly* (1969), which starred Barbra Streisand, Walter Matthau and a young Michael Crawford. In 1974, *That's Entertainment*, 'a nostalgia bash, featuring scenes from nearly 100 MGM musicals', became a surprise hit, and two years later, in *That's Entertainment Part Two*, Kelly and Astaire hosted the inevitable sequel. After all that, it would be interesting to know what Kelly really thought about a more modern musical film, *Xanadu* (1980), in which he appeared with Olivia Newton-John. Long before then, together with director Stanley Donen and the whole Arthur Freed Unit, which produced most of his musicals at MGM, Kelly, with his athletic performance, choreography and direction, had completed a body of work equivalant to that of the other master of dance on film, Fred Astaire. - but different. Whereas Astaire had the smooth, top hat, white tie and tails image, Kelly's 'concept of a cinema dancer was an "ordinary Joe" in sports shirt, slacks and white socks (to draw attention to the feet)'. As he said himself: 'Astaire represents the aristocracy when he dances - I represent the proletariat'.

Selected albums: *Song And Dance Man* (c.50s), *Singin' In The Rain Again* (1978), and film soundtracks.

Further reading: *Gene Kelly: A Biography*, Clive Hirschhorn. *The Films Of Gene Kelly*, Tony Thomas. *Gene Kelly*, J. Basinger.

Kenton, Stan

b. 15 December 1911, Wichita, Kansas, USA, d. 25 August 1979. After playing piano in various dance bands, including those of Everett Hoagland and Vido Musso, mostly on the west coast, Kenton decided to form his own band in 1941. Although geared partially to the commercial needs of the dancehall circuit of the time, Kenton's band, which he termed the 'Artistry In Rhythm' orchestra, also featured powerful brass section work and

Stan Kenton

imaginative saxophone voicings, unlike those of his more orthodox competitors. The band developed a substantial following among the younger elements of the audience who liked their music brash and loud. During the remainder of the 40s Kenton's popularity increased dramatically, seemingly immune to the declining fortunes that affected other bands. A succession of exciting young jazz musicians came into the band, among them Buddy Childers, Art Pepper, Kai Winding, Shelly Manne, Bob Cooper and Laurindo Almeida, playing arrangements by Kenton, Gene Roland and Pete Rugolo. His singers included Anita O'Day, June Christy and Chris Connor. In the 50s, his enthusiasm undimmed, Kenton introduced a 43-piece band, his 'Innovations In Modern Music' orchestra, again featuring Pepper and Manne as well as newcomers such as Maynard Ferguson and Bud Shank. Complex, quasi-classical arrangements by Bob Graettinger and others proved less appealing, but a 1953 tour of Europe ensured Kenton's international reputation. Reduced to a more manageable 19-piece, his New Concepts In Artistry In Rhythm band continued playing concerts and recording, using arrangements by Roland, Gerry Mulligan and Johnny Richards. Always eager to try new ideas, and to clearly label them, in the 60s Kenton introduced his 'New Era In Modern Music' orchestra, a 23-piece band using mellophoniums, and the 'Neophonic' orchestra, five pieces larger and tempting fate with neo-classical music. In the 70s, he embraced rock rhythms and looked as if he might go on forever. By 1977, however, his health had begun to deteriorate and although he returned from hospitalization to lead his band until August 1978, his bandleading days were almost over. He died in August 1979.

More than most bandleaders, Kenton polarized jazz fans, inspiring either love or hatred and only rarely meeting with indifference. Almost half a century after the event it is hard to understand what all the fuss was about. Certainly the band did not swing with the grace of, say, the Jimmie Lunceford band but it was just as wrong to declare, as did many critics, that Kenton never swung at all. Certainly if some of the arrangements were too monolithic for effective jazz performances, the abilities of some of his key soloists were seldom buried for long. Kenton's band was important for bringing together many excellent musicians and for allowing arrangers free rein to experiment in big band concepts that few other leaders of the period would tolerate. As a leader, Kenton brought to jazz an unbridled enthusiasm that persisted long after he could have retired in comfort to study psychology, the other consuming passion in his life.

Albums: *Stan Kenton At The Hollywood Palladium* (1945), *Progressive Jazz* (1946-47), *One Night Stand With Nat 'King' Cole And Stan Kenton* (1947), *One Night Stand At The Commodore* (1947), *Stan Kenton And His Orchestra With June Christy* (c.1949), *Innovations In Modern Music* (1950), *One Night Stand With Stan Kenton* i (1950), *Nineteen Fifty-One* (1951), *One Night Stand With Stan Kenton* ii (1951), *Carnegie* (1951), with Charlie Parker *Kenton And Bird* (1951-54), *Artistry In Tango* (1951-52), *Concert In Miniature* (1952), *Concert In Miniature No 9 And 10* (1952), *Concert In Miniature No 11 And 12* (1952), *Concert In Miniature No 13 And 14* (1952), *New Concepts Of Artistry In Rhythm* (1952), *Concert Encores* (1953), *The Definitive Stan Kenton With Charlie Parker And Dizzy Gillespie* (1953-54), *Stan Kenton In Berlin* (1953), *Europe Fifty Three Part One And Two* (1953), *Paris, 1953* (1953), *Sketches On Standards* (1953-54), *Artistry In Kenton* (1954), *Stan Kenton Festival* (1954), with June Christy *Duet* (1955), *Contemporary Concepts* (1955), *Stan Kenton In Hi-Fi* (1956), *Kenton In Concert* (1956), *Kenton In Stereo* (1956), *In Stockholm* (1956), *Cuban Fire* (1956), *Kenton '56* (1956), *Rendez-vous With Kenton/At The Rendezvous Vol. 1* (1957), *Back To Balboa* (1958), *The Ballad Style Of Stan Kenton* (1958) *Lush Interlude* (1958), *The Stage Door Swings* (1958), *On The Road* (1958), *The Kenton Touch* (1958), *Stan Kenton At The Tropicana* (1959), *In New Jersey* (1959), *At Ukiah* (1959), *Viva Kenton* (1959), *The Road Show Vols 1 & 2* (1959), with Ann Richards *Two Much* (1960), with Christy *Together Again* (1960), *Stan Kenton's Christmas* (1961), *The Romantic Approach* (1961), *Stan Kenton's West Side Story* (1961), *Mellophonium Magic* (1961), *Sophisticated Approach* (1961), *Adventures In Standards* (1961), *Adventures In Blues* (1961), *Adventures In Jazz* (1961), *The Sound Of Sixty-Two* (1962), *Adventures In Time* (1962), *Stan Kenton's Mellophonium Band* (1962), *Artistry In Bossa Nova* (1963), *Artistry In Voices And Brass* (1963), *The Best Of Brant Inn* (1963), *Kenton In England* (1963), *Wagner* (1964), *Stan Kenton Conducts The Los Angeles Neophonic Orchestra* (1965), *Rhapsody In Blue* (1965), *Stan Kenton Conducts The Jazz Compositions Of Dee Barton* (1967), *Live At Redlands University* (1970), *Live At Brigham Young University* (1971), *Live At Fairfield Hall, Croydon* (1972), *Live At Butler University* (1972), *National Anthems Of The World* (1972), *Stan Kenton Today* (1972), *Birthday In Britain* (1973), *7.5 On The Richter Scale* (1973),

Solo: *Stan Kenton Without His Orchestra* (1973), *Stan Kenton Plays Chicago* (1974), *Fire, Fury And Fun* (1974), *Kenton 1976* (1976), *Journey Into Capricorn* (1976), *Stan(dard) Kenton: Stan Kenton In Warsaw* (1976), *Stan Kenton In Europe* (1976). Compilations: *The Kenton Era (1940-53)* (1955, reissued 1985), *Stan Kenton's Greatest Hits (1943-51)* (1983), *The Christy Years (1945-47)* (1985), *The Fabulous Alumni Of Stan Kenton (1945-56)* (1985), *Collection: 20 Golden Greats* (1986), *Retrospective 1943 - 1968* (1992, 4-CD), *7.5 On The Richter Scale* (1993).

Further reading: *Straight Ahead: The Story Of Stan Kenton*, Carol Easton. *Stan Kenton: Artistry In Rhythm*, William F. Lee. *Stan Kenton: The Man And His Music*, Lillian Arganian.

King And I, The

With music by Richard Rodgers and book and lyrics by Oscar Hammerstein II, *The King And I* opened on Broadway on 29 March 1951. It starred Yul Brynner as the King of Siam and Gertrude Lawrence as Anna Leonowens, a schoolteacher hired to educate the royal children. Set in the 1860s, the story of *The King And I* was based upon Anna Leonowens's book, *The English Governess At The Siamese Court* (Margaret Landon's novel, *Anna And The King Of Siam*, was also based upon the same source material). The project was Lawrence's brainchild and once she had set the wheels in motion and Rodgers and Hammerstein were hired to write it, the show was scheduled to become one of the great money spinners of Broadway. There is a strong storyline which contrasts an Oriental nation's attempts to advance towards the progressive ideologies of the west while still shackled to the concepts of a slave-owning, male-dominated society. With settings of Oriental opulence, a masterly score and superb central performances, *The King And I* was a great hit. Among the songs were 'I Whistle A Happy Tune', 'Hello, Young Lovers', 'Getting To Know You', 'Shall We Dance', 'I Have Dreamed', 'We Kiss In The Shadow' and 'Something Wonderful', which was sung by Dorothy Sarnoff as Lady Thiang. Additionally, there was the engaging 'March Of The Siamese Children' in which Rodgers effectively captured an Oriental flavour while using orthodox western musical forms. Fittingly, given her involvement in its creation, *The King And I* was a triumph for Lawrence. It was also her swan song; she died 18 months after the show's opening. For the 1956 screen version, Brynner reprised his bravura performance as the king, winning the

Oscar as Best Actor, and Deborah Kerr appeared as Anna, her singing being dubbed by Marni Nixon. *The King And I* opened in London in 1953, starring Herbert Lom and Valerie Hobson and enjoyed revivals in the late 70s and mid-80s, the latter starring Brynner. In 1992, Julie Andrews, who many consider would have been the perfect Anna, sang the role for a studio cast CD, with British actor Ben Kingsley as the King.

King Brothers

Brothers Michael (b. 1936; guitar), Tony (b. 1937; bass) and Denis King (b. 1939; piano) from Hornchurch, Essex, England, were one of Britain's top groups in the 50s. The trio, fronted by Denis, made their television debut in 1953 on *Shop Window* and were often seen on mid-50s children's programmes. In 1954, they appeared at London's famous Astor and Embassy clubs, played a season at the Windmill Theatre and performed at the Palladium in 1955 - all before any of them was 21 years old. After recording unsuccessfully for World Record Club and Conquest, the old-fashioned styled young trio, who were mistakenly tagged 'Britain's Rock 'n' Roll Kids', joined Parlophone. In 1957, they charted with covers of 'A White Sport Coat', 'In The Middle Of An Island' and even the Everly Brothers' 'Wake Up Little Susie' and were voted Britain's Top Vocal Group by *New Musical Express* readers. They obtained four more Top 40 hits in 1960-61, again with Norman Newell-produced covers of songs popular in the USA. The biggest of these being 'Standing On The Corner' from the musical *The Most Happy Fella*, which reached number 4 in 1960. Their final chart hit came a year later with '76 Trombones'. In those days, when UK vocal groups were rare, these successes helped them regain the *New Musical Express* Vocal Group award in 1960 and to pick up *Melody Maker*'s similar award a year later. When they decided to record their own compositions the hits stopped for the trio who disliked being associated with rock 'n' roll. They were the last of the old-school vocal groups to be successful in the UK and were perhaps fortunate to be around when Britain badly needed a vocal group to call its own. They recorded for Pye in 1963, Oriole in 1964 and CBS and Page One in 1966. Denis King has since become one of the best known television music writers in the UK composing the themes for such successful television series as *Bouquet Of Barbed Wire*, *Within These Walls* and *Black Beauty*.

Selected albums: *Three Kings And An Ace* (1959), *Kings Of Song* (1962).

King Brothers

King, Dave

b. Twickenham, Middlesex, England. King was a very popular comedian/singer in the UK in the 50s. At the age of 15, he had been a stooge and washboard player in the bill-topping variety act, Morton Fraser's Harmonica Gang. He joined the Royal Air Force in 1950 and returned to the Gang afterwards. His big solo break came with appearances on UK television's *Showcase* and *Television Music Hall*. These led to him headlining a London West End show and to host his own television variety series. King first recorded in 1955 with producer George Martin for Parlophone and his debut hit came in 1956, with a cover of 'Memories Are Made Of This' on Decca, which gave the Dean Martin original strong competition in the UK charts. King also reached the UK Top 20 with 'You Can't Be True To Two' in 1956 and 'Story Of My Life', which was one of three versions of the Burt Bacharach song to make the UK Top 20 in 1958. King was one of the rare UK comedians to make any impact in the USA having his own summer television series there in the late 50s. He joined Pye in 1959 but no more hits came the way of this easy-going, relaxed ballad singer whose television appearances also dried up in the 60s. Subsequently, King became a respected character actor in UK films and television.
Selected album: *Memories Are Made Of This* (1962).

Kingston Trio

An influential part of America's folk revival, the Kingston Trio was formed in San Francisco in 1957 and were popular in the late 50s. The group consisted of Bob Shane (b. 1 February 1934, Hilo, Hawaii), Nick Reynolds (b. 27 July 1933, Coronado, California, USA) and Dave Guard (b. 19 October 1934, San Francisco, California, USA, d. 22 March 1991). The Kingston Trio had limited singles successes and are most often remembered for 'Tom Dooley' which reached number 5 in the UK charts, and number 1 in the US chart in 1958. The song, written by Guard, was based on an old folk tune, from the 1800s called 'Tom Dula'. *The Kingston Trio*, from which 'Tom Dooley' came, also reached number 1 in the US. The group had a line of successful albums in 1959, with *From The Hungry i*, a live recording, reaching number 2, and *The Kingston Trio At Large*, and *Here We Go Again* both achieving top placings. Further chart-toppers followed with *Sold Out*, and *String Along*. Their fresh harmonies and boyish enthusiasm endeared the trio to an America suspicious of the genre's New Left sympathies, but in the process paved the way for a generation of more committed performers. Guard was replaced by John Stewart (b. 5 September 1939, San Diego, California, USA) in May 1961, having left to pursue a solo career and form the Whiskeyhill Singers. *Close-Up* was the first release featuring Stewart, who had previously been with the Cumberland Three, and it reached number 3 in the US charts. 'San Miguel', the follow-up to 'Tom Dooley', only just managed to reach the Top 30 in the UK the following year. 'The Reverend Mr Black' achieved a Top 10 placing in the US chart in 1963. The line-up with Stewart continued until 1967.

Shane later re-formed the group, as the New Kingston Trio, with Roger Gamble and George Grove. The group continued to enjoy widespread popularity and their output, if stylistically moribund, was certainly prolific. However, the success of more exciting folk and folk-rock acts rendered them increasingly old-fashioned, and the Trio was disbanded in 1968. A group reunion was hosted on television, by Tom Smothers in 1981, when all six members were brought together for the first time. Stewart went on to achieve a cult following as a soloist, and continues to record and perform. In 1987 the Trio was on the road again, with Shane, Grove, and new member, Bob Haworth.

Albums: *The Kingston Trio* (1958), *From The Hungry i* (1959), *The Kingston Trio At Large* (1959), *Stereo Concert* (1959), *Here We Go Again* (1959), *Sold Out* (1960), *String Along* (1960), *The Last Month Of The Year* (1960), *Make Way!* (1961), *Goin' Places* (1961), *Close-Up* (1961), *College Concert* (1962), *Something Special* (1962), *New Frontier* (1963), *The Kingston Trio No. 16* (1963), *Sunny Side* (1963), *Sing A Song With The Kingston Trio* (1963), *Time To Think* (1963), *Back In Town* (1964), *The Folk Era* (1964), *Nick-Bob-John* (1965), *Stay Awhile* (1965), *Somethin' Else* (1965), *Children Of The Morning* (1966), *Once Upon A Time* (1969), *American Gold* (1973), *The World Needs A Melody* (1973), *Aspen Gold* (1979). Compilations: *Encores* (1961), *The Best Of The Kingston Trio* (1962), *Folk Era* (1964), *The Best Of The Kingston Trio Vol. 2* (1965), *The Best Of The Kingston Trio Vol. 3* (1966), *Once Upon A Time* (1969), *The Kingston Trio* (1972), *Where Have All The Flowers Gone* (1972), *The Historic Recordings Of The Kingston Trio* (1975), *The Very Best Of The Kingston Trio* (1987).
Further reading: *The Kingston Trio On Record*, Kingston Korner.

Kinsey, Tony

b. 11 October 1927, Sutton Coldfield, West Midlands, England. Kinsey was a key drummer in the London jazz scene of the 50s, having studied formally in the UK and USA before joining the Johnny Dankworth Seven in 1950. He later formed his own groups, working with many leading jazz musicians, including Joe Harriott, Peter King and a succession of visiting American stars. Kinsey's early musical studies had extended into composition, and he has written many longer works for jazz orchestra and for classical groups. He has also written for films and television, but in the late 80s was still leading his small jazz groups around London clubs. As a skilful technician, Kinsey is comfortable playing in bebop or mainstream settings and is an outstanding jazz drummer.

Albums: *Starboard Bow* (1955), *Jazz At The Flamingo* (1956), *The Tony Kinsey Quartet* (1957), *The Tony Kinsey Quintet* i (1957) *The Tony Kinsey Quintet* ii (1958), *The Tony Kinsey Quintet* iii (1959), *Foursome* (1959), *The Tony Kinsey Quintet* iv (1961), *How To Succeed In Business* (1963), *The Thames Suite* (1976).

Kismet

Unusually for a Broadway musical comedy, the music for *Kismet* was adapted by George Forrest and Robert Wright from the classical compositions of Alexander Borodin. With book by Charles Lederer and Luther Davis and lyrics by Forrest and Wright, the show opened on 3 December 1953. Forrest and Wright had previously adapted the classics for Broadway with their use in 1944 of Edvard Grieg's music for *Song Of Norway*. *Kismet* met with a measure of indifference from the critics. However, by a fortuitous quirk of fate, there was a newspaper strike at the time and before reviews were printed, the show was already a success. Audiences liked it and *Kismet* ran for almost 600 performances. Drawing its storyline from the *Arabian Nights* fantasies, *Kismet* was very well staged. Of the songs from the show the biggest hit was 'Stranger In Paradise' with success for 'Baubles, Bangles And Beads', 'And This Is My Beloved', 'Not Since Nineveh', 'Gesticulate', 'The Olive Tree' and 'Night Of My Nights'. Original cast members included Alfred Drake, Richard Kiley and Doretta Morrow. The 1955 film version starred Howard Keel, Ann Blyth, Dolores Gray and Vic Damone. A 1978 version of the show, retitled *Timbuktu*, featured an all-black cast.

Eartha Kitt

Kitt, Eartha

b. 26 January 1928, Columbia, South Carolina, USA. Raised in New York's Harlem, Kitt attended the High School for Performing Arts before joining Katharine Dunham's famed dancing troupe. At the end of a European tour Kitt decided to stay behind, taking up residence in Paris. Having added singing to her repertoire she was a success and on her return to New York appeared at several leading nightclubs. She appeared on Broadway in *New Faces Of 1952* and was later seen more widely in the film version of the show. She continued to work in cabaret, theatre and television, singing in her uniquely accented manner and slinkily draping herself across any available object, animate or otherwise. She made a few more films over the years, including playing leading roles in *St Louis Blues* (1958), with Nat 'King' Cole, and an all-black version of *Anna Lucasta* (1959), opposite Sammy Davis Jnr. Although her highly-mannered presentation of songs is best seen rather than merely heard, Kitt has made some songs virtually her own property, amongst them 'I'm Just An Old-Fashioned Girl', a claim which is patently untrue. In the late 70s Kitt appeared on Broadway in an all-black version of *Kismet* entitled *Timbuktu*. Her career has continued along similar lines on both sides of the Atlantic throughout the 80s and into the 90s although she was courted by a much younger audience (witness her collaboration with Bronski Beat in 1989) who were suitably impressed by her irreverent coolness. In 1992 Kitt toured the UK with the Inkspots, in a revue, *A Night At The Cotton Club*.

Selected albums: *Revisited* (1961), *At The Plaza* (1965), *Bad But Beautiful* (1976), *At Her Very Best* (1982), *C'est Si Bon* (1983), *I Love Men* (1984), *Love For Sale* (1984), *The Romantic Eartha Kitt* (1984), *St. Louis Blues* (1985), *That Bad Eartha* (1985), *Eartha Kitt In Person At The Plaza* (1988), *I'm A Funny Dame* (1988), *My Way* (1988), *Primitive Man* (1989), *I'm Still Here* (1989), *Live In London* (1990), *Thinking Jazz* (1992). Compilations: *Diamond Series: Eartha Kitt* (1988), *Best Of Eartha Kitt* (1990).

Further reading: *I'm Still Here*, Earth Kitt.

Knox, Buddy

b. Wayne Knox, 14 April 1933, Happy, Texas, USA. Knox was one of the first 'pop-abilly' hitmakers in the 50s. With bassist Jimmy Bowen, he formed the country band the Rhythm Orchids in 1956, adding Don Lanier (guitar) and Dave Alldred (drums). The following year Knox sang lead vocals on 'Party Doll', recorded at Norman Petty's Oklahoma studio. First issued locally on the Triple-D label, it became the first release on Roulette, formed by New York nightclub owner Maurice Levy. 'Party Doll' went to number 1 in the USA. At the same session Bowen recorded another hit, 'I'm Stickin' With You'. With his light voice skimming over the insistent rhythms, Knox was the first in a line of Texan rockers which included Buddy Holly and Roy Orbison. Both 'Rock Your Little Baby To Sleep' and the gimmicky 'Hula Love' were Top 20 hits later in 1957, when he also appeared in the film *Disc Jockey Jamboree*. Although he toured frequently with Alan Freed's package shows, 'Somebody Touched Me' (1958) was his only later hit and in 1960, Knox and Bowen moved to Los Angeles. There, Knox turned to 'teenbeat' material like 'Lovey Dovey', 'Ling Ting Tong' and 'She's Gone' (a minor UK hit in 1962) with producer Snuff Garrett. During the mid-60s he returned to country music, recording in Nashville for Reprise and had a hit with 'Gypsy Man', composed by ex-Crickets' Sonny Curtis. This led to film appearances in *Travellin' Light* (with Waylon Jennings) and *Sweet Country Music* (with Boots Randolph and Johnny Paycheck). Knox was now based in Canada, where he set up his own Sunnyhill label. He also visited Europe with rockabilly revival shows during the 70s and early 80s. Jimmy Bowen became one of Nashville's most powerful A&R men, working for Dot, MCA and latterly Capitol.

Albums: *Buddy Knox* (1957), *Buddy Knox And Jimmy Bowen* (1958), *Buddy Knox In Nashville* (1967), *Gypsy Man* (1969), *Four Rock Legends* (1978), *Sweet Country Music* (1981), *Texas Rockabilly Man* (1987), *Travellin' Light* (1988). Compilations: *Buddy Knox's Golden Hits* (1963), *Greatest Hits* (1985), *Liberty Takes* (1986), *Party Doll And Other Hits* (1988).

L

Laine, Frankie

b. Frank LoVecchio, 13 March 1913, Chicago, Illinois, USA. Laine had been a chorister at the Immaculate Conception Church in his city's Sicilian quarter before entering showbusiness proper on leaving school. For nearly a decade he travelled as a singing waiter, dancing instructor (with victory in a 1932 dance marathon his principal qualification) and other lowly jobs, but it was as one of a New Jersey nightclub quartet that he got his first big break - replacing Perry Como in Freddie Carlone's touring band in 1937. This was a springboard to a post as house vocalist with a New York radio station until migration to Los Angeles where he was 'discovered' entertaining in a Hollywood spa by Hoagy Carmichael. The songwriter persuaded him to adopt an Anglicised *nom de theatre*, and funded the 1947 session that resulted in 'That's My Desire', Laine's first smash. This was followed by 'Shine' (written in 1924) and a revival again in Louis Armstrong's 'When You're Smiling'. This was the title song to a 1950 movie starring Laine, the Mills Brothers, Kay Starr and other contributors of musical interludes to its 'backstage' plot. His later career on celluloid focused largely on his disembodied voice carrying main themes of cowboy movies such as *Man With A Star*, the celebrated *High Noon*, *Gunfight At The OK Corral* and the *Rawhide* television series. Each enhanced the dramatic, heavily masculine style favoured by Laine's producer, Mitch Miller, who also spiced the artist's output with generous pinches of C&W. This was best exemplified in the extraordinary 1949 hit, 'Mule Train', one of the most dramatic and impassioned recordings of its era. Other early successes included 'Jezebel', 'Jalousie' and 'Rose Rose, I Love You', an adaptation by Wilfred Thomas of Hue Lin's Chinese melody 'Mei Kuei'.

Laine proved a formidable international star, particularly in the UK, where his long chart run began in 1952 with 'High Noon'. The following year he made chart history when his version of 'I Believe' topped the charts for a staggering 18 weeks, a record which has never been eclipsed, despite a valiant run of 16 weeks by Bryan Adams 28 years later. Laine enjoyed two further UK chart-toppers in 1953 with 'Hey Joe' and 'Answer Me'. Incredibly, he was number 1 for 27 weeks that year, another fact of chart domination that is difficult to envisage ever being equalled. No less than 22 UK Top 20 hits during the 50s emphasized the popularity of Laine, including such memorable songs as 'Blowing Wild', 'Granada', 'The Kid's Last Fight', 'My Friend', 'Rain Rain Rain', 'Cool Water', 'Hawkeye', 'Sixteen Tons', 'A Woman In Love' and 'Rawhide'. Laine was also a consummate duettist and enjoyed additional hits with Johnnie Ray, Doris Day and Jimmy Boyd. After a hit parade farewell with 1961's 'Gunslinger', he found a full life commuting around the world as a highly-waged cabaret performer with a repertoire built round selections from hit compilations, one of which (*The Very Best Of Frankie Laine*) climbed into international charts as late as 1977. New material tended to be of a sacred nature - though in the more familiar 'clippetty-clop' character was his 'Blazing Saddles' in Mel Brooks' (the lyricist) 1974 spoof-western of the same name. By the mid-80s, he was in virtual semi-retirement in an opulent ocean-front dwelling in San Diego, California with his wife, former actress Nanette Gray. With sales in excess of 100 million, Laine was a giant of his time and one of the most important solo singers of the immediate pre-rock 'n' roll period.

Selected albums: *Songs By Frankie Laine* (1955), *That's My Desire* (1955), *Frankie Laine Sings For Us* (1955), *Concert Date* (1955), *With All My Heart* (1955), *Command Performance* (1956), *Jazz Spectacular* (1956), *Rockin'* (1957), *Foreign Affair* (1958), *Torchin'* (1960), *Reunion In Rhythm* (1961), *You Are My Love* (1961), *Frankie Laine, Balladeer* (1961), *Hell Bent For Leather!* (1961), *Deuces Wild* (1962), *Call Of The Wild* (1962), *Wanderlust* (1963), *I'll Take Care Of Your Cares* (1967), *I Wanted Someone To Love* (1967), *To Each His Own* (1968), *You Gave Me A Mountain* (1969), with Erich Kunzel And The Cincinnati Pops Orchestra *Round Up* (1987). Compilations: *The Very Best Of Frankie Laine* (1977), *Songbook* (1981), *All Of Me* (1982), *The Uncollected* (1986), *Rawhide* (1986), *Evergreens* (1988), *Country Store* (1988), *Portrait Of A Song Stylist* (1989), *On The Trail Again* (1993).

Further reading: *That Lucky Old Son*, Frankie Laine and Joseph F. Laredo.

Lambert, Hendricks And Ross

In the late 50s a group of singers began informal 'vocalese' jam sessions at the New York apartment of Dave Lambert (b. 19 June 1917, Boston, Massachusetts, USA). At these sessions singers

Frankie Laine

would improvise vocal lines in much the same manner as jazz instrumentalists. Ten years previously, Lambert had worked as arranger and singer in Gene Krupa's band, recording 'What's This?', an early example of a bop vocal. In 1955, Lambert teamed up with Jon Hendricks (b. 16 September 1921, Newark, Ohio, USA) to record a vocalized version of 'Four Brothers'. In 1958, Lambert and Hendricks added to their duo the highly distinctive singer Annie Ross (b. Annabelle Short Lynch, 25 July 1930, Mitcham, Surrey, England) to record the album, *Sing A Song Of Basie*. The concept of the Lambert, Hendricks And Ross recordings was simple although highly complex in execution. The singers performed wordless vocal lines, matching the brass and reed section parts of the Count Basie band's popular recordings. With this formula they enjoyed great success in the late 50s and early 60s. In 1962, Ross left the trio and was replaced by Yolande Bavan (b. 1 June 1940, Colombo, Ceylon). Two years later Lambert also left and soon thereafter the trio concept was abandoned. Subsequently, Lambert worked briefly as a studio arranger before his death on 3 October 1966.
Albums: *Sing A Song Of Basie* (1957), *The Swingers* (1959), *The Hottest Group In Jazz/Everybody's Boppin'/The Best Of Lambert, Hendricks And Ross* (1959), *Lambert, Hendricks And Ross Sing Ellington* (1960), *High Flying* (1960), *Lambert, Hendricks And Bavan: Having A Ball At The Village Gate* (1963).

Lang, Don

b. Gordon Langhorn, 19 January 1925, Halifax, Yorkshire, England, d. 3 August 1992, London, England. Lang started as a dance band trombonist working with the bands of Peter Rose, Teddy Foster and Vic Lewis. It was with Lewis that he made his first recordings. He began singing with Ken Mackintosh's Band and is credited under his real name on some of their records and also one recording with the Cyril Stapleton Orchestra. Lang went solo in the mid-50s and after a couple of singles on Decca he made the UK Top 20 with a 'vocalese' (scat jazz) version of 'Cloudburst' in 1956/56 on HMV Records. Together with his Frantic Five (which included the late saxophonist Red Price) he was one of the first UK acts to get involved with rock 'n' roll and skiffle, although his jazz roots were always audible. The group appeared regularly on UK television's seminal *6.5 Special* and sang the theme song over the credits. After many unsuccessful singles he charted with a cover of Chuck Berry's 'School Day' and reached the Top

10 with a version of David Seville's 'Witch Doctor' (with the curious lyric, 'ooh ee ooh aha bing bang walla walla bing bang'). When the hits dried up for this elder statesman of UK pop, he formed a new band and played the dancehall and club circuit for many years. At times he sang alongside such notable acts as the Mike Sammes and Cliff Adams Singers and played on records like the Beatles', 'white album' (*The Beatles*). Alongside 50s acts like Wee Willie Harris and Tommy Bruce, he could still be seen on the UK rock 'n' roll circuit. For a time he returned to his first love - jazz, but for the last few years of his life he was in virtual retirement, emerging for the occasional rock 'n' roll revival show or recording session. He died of cancer in the Royal Marsden Hospital in August 1992. His son Brad has played bass for ABC and Toyah.
Albums: *Skiffle Special* (1957), *Introducing The Hand Jive* (1958), *Twenty Top 20 Twists* (1962). Compilation: *Rock Rock Rock* (1983), with the Twisters *20 Rock 'n' Roll Twists* (1988).

Lanza, Mario

b. Alfredo Cocozza, 31 January 1921, Philadelphia, Pennsylvania, USA, d. 7 October 1959. Lanza was an enormously popular star of film musicals and on records during the 50s, with a magnificent operatic tenor voice. The son of Italian immigrants, he took his stage name from his mother's maiden name, Maria Lanza. From the age of 15, Lanza studied singing with several teachers, and was introduced into society circles with the object of gaining a patron. He was signed to Columbia Artistes Management as a concert singer, but their plans to send him on an introductory tour were quashed when Lanza was drafted into the US Army in 1943. He appeared in shows, billed as 'the Service Caruso', and sang in the chorus of the celebratory Forces show *Winged Victory*. After release, he lived in New York, gave concerts and worked on radio shows. One of the audition recordings that he made for RCA found its way to the MGM Film Studios, and when he deputized for another tenor at the Hollywood Bowl, MGM chief Louis B. Mayer was in the audience. Soon afterwards Lanza was signed to a seven-year MGM contract by Hungarian producer, Joe Pasternak, who was quoted as saying: 'it was the most beautiful voice I had ever heard - but his bushy hair made him look like a caveman!'
Lanza's contract allowed him to continue with his concert career, and in April 1948 he made his first, and last, appearance on the professional operatic

stage, in two performances of *Madame Butterfly*, with the New Orleans Opera. Lanza's first film in 1949 for MGM, *That Midnight Kiss*, co-starred Kathryn Grayson and pianist Jose Iturbi, and contained a mixture of popular standards as diverse as 'They Didn't Believe Me' and 'Down Among The Sheltering Palms', and classical pieces, including 'Celeste Aida', (from Verdi's *Aida*), which gave Lanza one his first record hits. The film was a big box-office success, and was followed by *The Toast Of New Orleans*, also with Grayson, which, along with the operatic excerpts, contained some songs by Sammy Cahn and Nicholas Brodszky, including one of Lanza's all-time smash hits, the million-seller, 'Be My Love'. Lanza starred in the bio-pic *The Great Caruso* (1951), performing several arias associated with his idol. He also introduced 'The Loveliest Night Of The Year', a song adapted by Irving Aaronson from 'Over the Waves', by Juventino Rosas, with a new lyric by Paul Francis Webster; it gave Lanza his second million-selling record.

By now, he was one of Hollywood's hottest properties, and as his career blossomed, so did his waistline. There were rumours of breakfasts consisting of four steaks and six eggs, washed down with a gallon of milk, which caused his weight to soar to 20 stone. He claimed that 'nervousness' made him eat. In 1951, Lanza embarked on a country-wide tour of 22 cities, and also appeared on his own CBS radio series. Back in Hollywood, he initially turned down MGM's next project, *Because You're Mine*, because of its 'singer-becomes-a-GI' storyline. After some difficulties, the film was eventually completed, and was chosen for the 1952 Royal Film Premiere in the UK. The title song, by Cahn and Brodszky, was nominated for an Academy award in 1952, and became Lanza's third, and last, million-selling single.

He had already recorded the songs for his next MGM project, *The Student Prince*, when he walked out on the studio following a disagreement with the director. He avoided damaging breach of contract lawsuits by allowing MGM to retain the rights to his recordings for the film. British actor, Edmund Purdom took his place, miming to Lanza's singing voice. Ironically, Lanza's vocal performances for the film were considered to be among his best, and *Songs From The Student Prince And Other Great Musical Comedies* (containing 'The Drinking Song'), was number 1 in the USA for several weeks. Beset by problems with alcohol, food, tranquillizers and the US tax authorities, Lanza became a virtual recluse, not performing for

over a year, before appearing on CBS Television with Betty Grable and Harry James. He was criticized in the press for miming to his old recordings on the show, but proved the voice was still intact by resuming his recording career soon afterwards. In 1956, Lanza returned to filming, this time for Warner Brothers. *Serenade*, adapted from the novel by James M. Cain, in which Lanza co-starred with Joan Fontaine, was considered by the critics to be one of his best movies. Once again, the operatic excerpts were interspersed with some romantic songs by Cahn and Brodszky, including 'Serenade' and 'My Destiny'. In 1957, tired of all the crash diets, and disillusioned by life in the USA, Lanza moved to Italy, and settled in Rome. He made one film there, *The Seven Hills Of Rome* (1958). Apart from the sight of Lanza playing an American entertainer doing impersonations of Dean Martin, Frankie Laine and Louis Armstrong, the film is probably best remembered for the inclusion of the 1955 hit song, 'Arrivederci, Roma', written by Renato Rascel (Ranucci) and Carl Sigman, impressively sung in the film by Lanza, and which became the accompaniment to many a backward glance by tourists ever since. In 1958, Lanza visited the UK, making his first stage appearances for six years, in concert at London's Royal Albert Hall and on the Royal Variety Show. From there, he embarked on a European tour. While on the Continent, he made *For The First Time* (1959), which was the last time he was seen on film. He appeared relatively slim, and was still in excellent voice. In the autumn of 1959 he went into a Rome clinic; a week later, he died of a heart attack. Much later it was alleged that he was murdered by the Mafia because he refused to appear at a concert organized by mobster, Lucky Luciano. The city of Philadelphia officially proclaimed 7 October as 'Mario Lanza Day'. His wife, Betty, died five months later. Opinions of his voice, and its potential, vary. José Carreras is quoted as saying that he was 'turned on' to opera at the age of 16 by seeing Lanza in *The Great Caruso*. Arturo Toscannini is supposed to have called it the greatest voice of the 20th century. On the other hand, one critic, perhaps representing the majority, said: 'He just concentrated on the big 'lollipops' of the opera repertoire, he had a poor musical memory, and would never have been an opera star.'

Selected albums: *Songs From The Student Prince And Other Great Musical Comedies*, *Serenade* (1956, film soundtrack), *Seven Hills Of Rome* (1958, film soundtrack), *Songs From The Student Prince/The*

Great Caruso (1958), *For The First Time* (1959, film soundtrack), *Lanza Sings Christmas Carols* (1959), *Mario Lanza Sings Caruso Favourites/The Great Caruso* (1960), *You Do Something To Me* (1969). Compilations: *I'll Walk With God* (1962), *His Greatest Hits, Volume 1* (1971), *His Greatest Hits From Operettas And Musicals, Volumes One, Two & Three* (all 1981), *20 Golden Favourites* (1981), *The Legendary Mario Lanza* (1981), *A Portrait Of Mario Lanza* (1987), *Diamond Series: Mario Lanza* (1988). Further reading: *Mario Lanza*, Matt Bernard. *Mario Lanza*, Michael Burrows. *Lanza - His Tragic Life*, Raymond Strait.

Lawrence, Lee

b. Leon Siroto, c.1921, Salford, Lancashire, England, d. February 1961. This former ENSA entertainer's quasi-operatic tenor was similar to that of Ronnie Hilton whom he rivalled as the BBC Light Programme's most omnipresent vocalist in the early 50s. Both of his parents were members of the Carl Rosa Opera Company, and, at the age of 16, Lawrence went to Italy to study opera. After service in World War II he sang with various bands, and made his broadcasting debut on *Beginners Please*. After his 1953 cover of Rex Allen's 'Crying In The Chapel' peaked at number 7 in the UK Top 10, Lee's chart career slumped until a transfer from Decca to EMI in 1955 brought a second - and final - entry with a version of 'Suddenly There's A Valley' (1955). This, like many other of his recordings, was produced by Ray Martin, and followed a false dawn with an arrangement of Tennessee Ernie Ford's 'Give Me Your Word'. He is fondly remembered for his powerful versions of songs such as 'Fascination', 'The Story Of Tina'. 'Lonely Ballerina', 'Falling In Love With Love' and his theme, 'The World Is Mine Tonight'. In the late 50s he moved to the USA and played in cabaret and appeared on television. Before his death in February 1961, among the more interesting of Lawrence's later releases were Anisteen Allen's 'Don't Nobody Move' and 1956's opportunist 'Rock 'N' Roll Opera' a spoof that mentioned Elvis Presley, Gene Vincent, Tommy Steele and other newcomers who were lessening the chances of Lee ever returning to the charts.
Selected albums: *Presenting Lee Lawrence* (1953), *Fascination* (1985).

Lee, Brenda

b. Brenda Lee Tarpley, 11 December 1944, Lithonia, Georgia, USA. Even in early adolescence, she had an adult husk of a voice that could slip from anguished intimacy through sleepy insinuation to raucous lust even during 'Let's Jump The Broomstick', 'Speak To Me Pretty' and other jaunty classics that kept her in the hit parade from the mid-50s to 1965. Through local radio and, by 1956, wider exposure on Red Foley's Ozark Jubilee broadcasts, 'Little Brenda Lee' was ensured enough airplay for her first single, a revival of Hank Williams' 'Jambalaya', to crack the US country chart before her *Billboard* Hot 100 debut with 1957's 'One Step At A Time'. The novelty of her extreme youth facilitated bigger triumphs for 'Little Miss Dynamite' with the million-selling 'Rockin' Around The Christmas Tree' and later bouncy rockers before the next decade brought a greater proportion of heartbreak ballads such as 'I'm Sorry', 'Thanks A Lot' and 'Too Many Rivers' - plus an acting role in the children's fantasy movie, *The Two Little Bears*. 1963 was another successful year - especially in the UK with the title song of *All Alone Am I*, 'Losing You' (a French translation), 'I Wonder' and 'As Usual' each entering the Top 20. While 1964 finished well with 'Is It True' and 'Christmas Will Be Just Another Lonely Day', only minor hits followed. Though she may have weathered prevailing fads, family commitments caused Brenda to cut back on touring and record only intermittently after 1966's appositely-titled *Bye Bye Blues*.
Lee resurfaced in 1971 with a huge country hit in Kris Kristofferson's 'Nobody Wins' and later recordings that established her as a star of what was then one of the squarest seams of pop. When country gained a younger audience in the mid-80s, respect for its older practitioners found her guesting with Loretta Lynn and Kitty Wells on k.d. lang's *Shadowland*. - produced in 1988 by Owen Bradley (who had also supervised many early Lee records). In Europe, Brenda Lee remained mostly a memory - albeit a pleasing one as shown by Coast To Coast's hit revival of 'Let's Jump The Broomstick', a high UK placing for 1980's *Little Miss Dynamite* greatest hits collection and Mel Smith And Kim Wilde's 'Rockin' Around The Christmas Tree'. Lee is fortunate in having a large rock 'n' roll catalogue destined for immortality in addition to her now-high standing in the country music world. In 1993, billed as 'the biggest-selling female star in pop history', Brenda Lee toured the UK and played the London Palladium, headlining a nostalgia package that included Chris Montez, Len Barry and Johnny Tillotson. From her opening 'I'm So Excited', through to the closing 'Rockin'

All Over The World', she fulfilled all expectations, and won standing ovations from packed houses.

Albums: *Grandma, What Great Songs You Sang* (1959), *Brenda Lee* (1960), *This Is ... Brenda* (1960), *Emotions* (1961), *All The Way* (1961), *Sincerely* (1962), *Brenda, That's All* (1962), *The Show For Christmas Seals* (1962), *All Alone Am I* (1963), *Let Me Sing* (1963), *By Request* (1964), *Merry Christmas From Brenda Lee* (1964), *Top Teen Hits* (1965), *The Versatile Brenda Lee* (1965), *Too Many Rivers* (1965), *Bye Bye Blues* (1966), *Coming On Strong* (1966), with Pete Fountain *For The First Time* (1968), *Johnny One Time* (1969), *LA Sessions* (1977), *Even Better* (1980), *Brenda Lee* (1991). Compilations: *10 Golden Years* (1966), *The Brenda Lee Story* (1974), *Little Miss Dynamite* (1980), *25th Anniversary* (1984), *The Golden Decade* (1985), *The Best Of Brenda Lee* (1986), *Love Songs* (1986), *Brenda's Best* (1989), *Very Best Of Brenda Lee Vol 1* (1990), *Very Best Of Brenda Lee Vol 2* (1990).

Lee, Peggy

b. Norma Deloris Egstrom, 26 May 1920, Jamestown, North Dakota, USA. Lee is of Scandinavian descent, her grandparents were Swedish and Norwegian immigrants. She endured a difficult childhood and her mother died when she was four; when her father remarried she experienced a decidedly unpleasant relationship with her stepmother. Her father took to drink, and at the age of she 14 found herself carrying out his duties at the local railroad depot. Despite these and other hardships, she sang frequently and appeared on a local radio station. She took a job as a waitress in Fargo where the manager of the radio station changed her name to Peggy Lee. In 1937, she took a trip to California to try her luck there but soon returned to Fargo. Another California visit was equally unsuccessful and she then tried Chicago where, in 1941, as a member of a vocal group, The Four Of Us, she was hired to sing at the Ambassador West Hotel. During this engagement she was heard by Mel Powell, who brought Benny Goodman in to hear her. Goodman's regular singer, Helen Forrest, was about to leave and Lee was hired as her replacement. She joined the band for an engagement at the College Inn and within a few days sang on a record date. A song from this date, 'Elmer's Tune', was a huge success. Amongst other popular recordings she made with Goodman were 'How Deep Is The Ocean?', 'How Long Has This Been Going On?', 'My Old Flame' and 'Why Don't You Do Right?'. Later, Lee married Goodman's guitarist, Dave Barbour. After she quit

Goodman in 1943, she had more successful records including 'That Old Feeling' and three songs of which she was co-composer with Barbour, 'It's A Good Day', 'Don't Know Enough About You' and 'Mañana'. She also performed on radio with Bing Crosby. In the 50s she made several popular recordings for Capitol, the orchestral backings for many of which were arranged and conducted by Barbour with whom she maintained a good relationship despite their divorce in 1952. Her 1958 hit single 'Fever' was also a collaboration with Barbour. Her *Black Coffee* album of 1953 was particularly successful as was *Beauty And The Beat* a few years later. On these and other albums of the period, Lee was often accompanied by jazz musicians, including Jimmy Rowles, Marty Paich and George Shearing. During the 50s Lee was also active in films. In some, such as *Johnny Guitar* (1954), she performed the title song, for others, like *Tom Thumb* (1958), she wrote songs. She also made a number of on-screen appearances in acting roles, including *The Jazz Singer* (1953) and for one, *Pete Kelly's Blues* (1955), she was nominated for an Acadamy Award as Best Supporting Actress. However, her most lasting fame in films lies in her off-screen work on Walt Disney's *Lady And The Tramp* (1955) for which Lee wrote the song 'He's A Tramp' and provided the voice for the characters of 'Peg', the Siamese cats, and one other screen feline. Her recording successes continued throughout this period even if, on some occasions, she had to fight to persuade Capitol to record them. One such argument surrounded 'Lover', which executives felt would compete directly with the label's currently popular version by Les Paul. Lee won out and her performance of her own arrangement, played by a studio orchestra under the direction of Gordon Jenkins, was a sensation. Towards the end of the 50s the intense level of work began to have its effect upon her and she suffered a period of ill health. Throughout the 60s and succeeding decades Lee performed extensively, singing at concerts and on television and, of course, making records, despite being frequently plagued with poor health. Her voice is light with a delicate huskiness which provides intriguing contrasts with the large orchestral accompaniment that is usually a part of a Lee performance. Over the years her repeated use of previously successful settings for songs has tended to make her shows predictable but she remains a dedicated perfectionist in everything that she does. In the early 80s she attempted a stage show, *Peg*, but it proved unpopular and closed quickly. In late 80s she again suffered poor health and on some of her live performances her voice was starting to display the ravages of time. For her many fans, it did not seem to matter. Paraphrasing the title of one of her songs, they just loved being there with Peg. In 1992, wheelchair bound for the past two years, Lee was persisting in a law suit, begun in 1987, against the Walt Disney Corporation for her share of the video profits from *Lady And The Tramp*. A year later, dissatisfied with the 'paltry' £2 million settlement for her six songs (written with Sonny Burke) and character voices, she was preparing to write a book about the whole affair. Meanwhile, she continued to make occasional cabaret appearances at New York venues such as Club 53. In 1993 she recorded a duet with Gilbert O'Sullivan for his album *Sounds Of The Loop*. Lee is one of the greatest 'classy' vocalists of the century, alongside Ella Fitzgerald, Billie Holiday, Sarah Vaughan and Betty Carter.

Albums: *Rendezvous* (1952), *My Best To You* (1952), *Song In Intimate Style* (1953), *Black Coffee* (1953), *The Lady And The Tramp* (1955, film soundtrack), with Ella Fitzgerald *Pete Kelly's Blues* (1955, film soundtrack), *Dream Street* (1956), *The Man I Love* (1957), *Jump For Joy* (1958), *Sea Shells* (1958), *Things Are Swingin'* (1958), *Beauty And The Beat* (1959), *I Like Men* (1959), *Miss Wonderful* (1959), *Pretty Eyes* (1960), *Latin A La Lee!* (1960), *All Aglow Again* (1960), *Olé A La Lee* (1960), *Christmas Carousel* (1960), *At Basin Street East* (1960), *Blues Cross Country* (1961), *Sugar 'N' Spice* (1962), *If You Go* (1961), *I'm A Woman* (1963), *Mink Jazz* (1963), *In Love Again* (1963), *Lover* (1964), *In The Name Of Love* (1964), *Pass Me By* (1965), *That Was Then, This Is Now* (1965), *Big Spender* (1966), *Extra Special* (1967), *Is That All There Is?* (1969), *Bridge Over Troubled Water* (1970), *Make It With You* (1970), *Let's Love* (1976), *Mirrors* (1976), *Close Enough For Love* (1979), *Peggy Sings The Blues* (1988), with Quincy Jones *P'S & Q'S* (1992), *Love Held Lightly* (1993), *Moments Like These* (1993). Compilations: *Bewitching-Lee!* (1962), *Peggy Lee Sings With Benny Goodman (1941-43)* (1984), *The Peggy Lee Collection - 20 Golden Greats* (1985), *The Capitol Years* (1988), *Peggy Lee - Fever* (1992), *The Best Of* (1993).

Further reading: *Miss Peggy Lee*, Peggy Lee.

Lehrer, Tom

b. Thomas Andrew Lehrer, 9 April 1928, New York City, New York, USA. Lehrer was a song satirist who also recorded a number of albums during the 50s and 60s. Having graduated from Harvard University, Lehrer then taught mathematics there. Having trained on piano, he began to perform song satires of his own for colleagues at the college. They enjoyed his songs, so Lehrer recorded a dozen of them in 1953 and had 400 copies pressed on a 10-inch album, on his own Lehrer label. An instant success on campus, Lehrer was forced to press more copies to meet the demand. He then began entertaining in clubs and writing songs for television programmes. Before the end of the 50s he had recorded three more albums on his own label and had begun to tour extensively, even gaining a following in Europe. His sense of black humour is encapsulated in the titles 'Poisoning Pigeons In The Park', 'The Old Dope Peddler' and 'The Masochism Tango' - which could be described as something between *Mad* magazine and Lenny Bruce. He stopped making live appearances in 1960 but continued to record, signing with Reprise Records in 1965. He also wrote for the US editions of the television programme, *That Was The Week That Was* in 1964-65, lampooning current news events. His album *That Was The Year That Was* collected songs which had been heard on that programme. He largely stopped writing in the late 60s although he did contribute songs to the television show *The Electric Company* in 1972. A British musical revue, *Tomfoolery*, in 1980, was based on his songs. He returned to teaching in the late 70s.

Albums: *Songs By Tom Lehrer* (1953), *More Of Tom Lehrer* (1959), *An Evening Wasted With Tom Lehrer* (1959), *Tom Lehrer Revisited* (1960), *That Was The Year That Was* (1965), *Songs By Tom Lehrer* (1966, re-recorded versions of first album's songs). Compilation: *Too Many Songs By Tom Lehrer* (1981).

Leiber And Stoller

Jerry Leiber (b. 25 April 1933, Baltimore, Maryland, USA) and Mike Stoller (b. 13 March 1933, New York City, New York, USA) began their extraordinary songwriting and production partnership at the age of 17. Leiber was a blues enthusiast and record store assistant, while Stoller played jazz piano. Based in Los Angeles, they provided numerous songs for the city's R&B artists during the early 50s. 'Hard Times' by Charles Brown was the first Leiber and Stoller hit, but their biggest songs of the era were 'Hound Dog' and 'K.C. Lovin'' (later renamed 'Kansas City'). Originally recorded by Big Mama Thornton, 'Hound Dog' was one of the songs which defined rock 'n' roll when Elvis Presley performed it.

'Kansas City' had its greatest success in a version by Wilbert Harrison, and went on to become part of every UK beat group's repertoire. In 1954, the duo set up their own Spark label to release material by the Robins, a vocal group they had discovered. Renamed the Coasters a year later, when Leiber and Stoller moved to New York, the group was given some of the songwriters' most clever and witty compositions. Songs like 'Smokey Joe's Cafe', 'Searchin'', 'Yakety Yak' and 'Charlie Brown' bridged the gap between R&B and rock 'n' roll, selling millions in the mid to late 50s, while Leiber And Stoller's innovative production techniques widened the scope of the R&B record, prompting hosts of imitators. In New York, Leiber and Stoller had a production deal with Atlantic Records, where they created hits for numerous artists. They wrote 'Lucky Lips' for Ruth Brown and 'Saved' for Lavern Baker, but their most notable productions were for the Drifters and the group's lead singer Ben E. King. Among these were 'On Broadway', 'Spanish Harlem', 'There Goes My Baby', 'I (Who Have Nothing)' and 'Stand By Me', which was an international hit when reissued in 1986. Away from Atlantic, Leiber and Stoller supplied Elvis Presley with songs like 'Jailhouse Rock', 'Baby I Don't Care', 'Loving You', 'Treat Me Nice' and 'His Latest Flame'. They also wrote hits for Perry Como, Peggy Lee ('I'm A Woman') and Dion. In 1964, the duo set up the Red Bird and Blue Cat record labels with George Goldner. Despite the quality of many of the releases (Alvin Robinson's 'Down Home Girl' was later covered by the Rolling Stones), the only big hits came from the Shangri-Las, who were produced by George 'Shadow' Morton rather than Leiber and Stoller. Subsequently, the duo took several years away from production, purchasing the King Records group and creating the *Cabaret*-like songs for Peggy Lee's album *Mirrors* (1976). They returned to the pop world briefly in 1972, producing albums for UK acts like Stealer's Wheel and Elkie Brooks, for whom they part-wrote 'Pearl's A Singer'. During the 70s, they were in semi-retirement, developing *Only In America*, a stage show involving 30 of their compositions. Another musical based on their work - *Yakety Yak* - was presented in London with oldies band Darts. During the 80s Leiber and Stoller's songs were featured in the cartoon film *Hound Dog* and they were reported to be working on a musical. However, their public appearances seemed to be confined to awards ceremonies where they were made members of several Halls of Fame, including

that of Rock 'n' Roll in 1987. In 1979, Robert Palmer wrote a highly-praised biography of the duo.

Further reading: *Baby, That Was Rock & Roll: The Legendary Leiber And Stoller*, Robert Palmer.

Lewis, Jerry Lee

b. 29 September 1935, Ferriday, Louisiana, USA. The 'Killer' is the personification of 50s rock 'n' roll at its best. He is rowdy, raw, rebellious and uncompromising. The outrageous piano-pounder has a voice that exudes excitement and an aura of arrogance that becomes understandable after witnessing the seething hysteria and mass excitement at his concerts. As a southern boy, Lewis was brought up listening to many musical styles in a home where religion was as important as breathing. In 1950, he attended a fundamentalist bible school in Waxahachie, Texas, but was expelled. The clash between the secular and the religious would govern Lewis's life and art for the remainder of his career. He first recorded on the *Louisiana Hayride* in 1954 and decided that Elvis Presley's label, Sun Records was where he wanted to be. His distinctive version of country star Ray Price's 'Crazy Arms' was his Sun debut, but it was his second single, a revival of Roy Hall's 'Whole Lotta Shakin' Goin' On' in 1957 that shot him to international fame. The record, which was initially banned as obscene, narrowly missed the top of the US chart, went on to hit number 1 on the R&B and country charts and introduced the fair-haired, one-man piano wrecker to a world ready for a good shaking up. He stole the show from many other stars in the film *Jamboree* in which he sang the classic 'Great Balls Of Fire', which became his biggest hit and topped the UK chart and made number 2 in the USA. He kept up the barrage of rowdy and unadulterated rock with the US/UK Top 10 single, 'Breathless' which, like its predecessor, had been written by Otis Blackwell. Problems started for the flamboyant 'god of the glissando' when he arrived in Britain for a tour in 1958, accompanied by his third wife Myra, who was also his 13-year-old second cousin. The UK media stirred up a hornet's nest and the tour had to be cancelled after only three concerts, even though the majority of the audience loved him. The furore followed Lewis home and support for him in his homeland also waned and he never returned to the Top 20 pop chart in the UK. His last big hit of the 50s was the title song from his film *High School Confidential* which made the UK Top 20 in 1959 and number 21 in the USA. Despite a continued high standard of output, his records either only made the lower chart rungs or missed altogether. When his version of Ray Charles' 'What'd I Say' hit the UK Top 10 in 1960 (US number 30) it looked like a record revival was on the way, but it was not to be. The fickle general public may have disowned the hard-living, hell-raiser, but his hardcore fans remained loyal and his tours were sell outs during the 60s. He joined Smash Records in 1963 and although the material he recorded with the company was generally unimaginative, there were some excellent live recordings, most notably, *The Greatest Live Show On Earth* (1964).

In 1966, Lewis made an unexpected entry into rock music theatre when he was signed to play Iago in Jack Good's *Catch My Soul*, inspired by *Othello*. After a decade playing rock 'n' roll, Lewis decided to concentrate on country material in 1968. He had often featured country songs in his repertoire so his new policy was not an about-face. This changeover was an instant success - country fans welcomed back their prodigal son with open arms. Over the next 13 years Lewis was one of country's top-selling artists and was a main attraction wherever he put on his 'Greatest Show On Earth'. He first appeared at the *Grand Ole Opry* in 1973 playing an unprecedented 50-minute set. He topped the country chart with records like 'There Must Be More To Love Than This' in 1970, 'Would You Take Another Chance On Me?' in 1971 and a revival of 'Chantilly Lace' a year later. The latter also returned him briefly to the transatlantic Top 40. However, he also kept the rock 'n' roll flag flying by playing revival shows around the world and by always including his old 50s hits in his stage shows. In fact, old fans have always been well catered for as numerous compilations of top class out-takes and never previously issued tracks from the 50s have regularly been released over the last 20 years. On the personal front, his life has never been short of tragedies often compounded by his alcohol and drug problems. His family has been equally prone to tragedy. In November 1973, his 19-year-old son, Jerry Lee Jnr. was killed in a road accident following a period of drug abuse and treatment for mental illness. Lewis's own behaviour during the mid-70s was increasingly erratic. He accidentally shot his bass player in the chest - the musician survived and sued. Late in 1976, Lewis was arrested for waving a gun outside Elvis Presley's Gracelands home. Two years later, Lewis signed to Elektra Records for the appropriately titled, *Rockin' My Life Away*. Unfortunately, his association with the company ended with much-publicized lawsuits. In 1981, Lewis was hospitalized and allegedly close to death from a haemorrhaged ulcer. He survived that ordeal and was soon back on the road. In 1982, his fourth wife drowned in a swimming pool. The following year, his fifth wife was found dead at his home following a methodone overdose. The deaths brought fresh scandal to Lewis's troubled life. Meanwhile, the IRS were challenging his earnings from the late 70s in another elongated dispute. A sixth marriage followed along with more bleeding ulcers and a period in the Betty Ford Clinic for the treatment of a pain-killer addiction. Remarkably, Lewis's body and spirit have remained intact, despite these harrowing experiences. During his career he has released dozens of albums, the most successful being *The Session* in 1973, his sole US Top 40 album on which many pop names of the period backed him, including Peter Frampton and Rory Gallagher. Lewis was one of the first people inducted into the 'Rock 'n' Roll Hall Of Fame' in 1986. In 1989, a bio-pic of his early career *Great Balls Of Fire*, starring Dennis Quaid, brought him briefly back into the public eye. In 1990, a much awaited UK tour had to be cancelled when Jerry and his sixth wife (who was not even born at the time of his fateful first tour) failed to show.

His cousin Mickey Gilley is an accomplished country artist, while another cousin, Jimmy Lee Swaggart has emerged as one of America's premier television evangelists. Any understanding of the career of Jerry Lee Lewis is inextricably linked with the parallel rise and fall of Jimmy Lee. They were both excellent piano players but whereas Jerry Lee devoted his energies to the 'devil's music', Jimmy Lee damned rock 'n' roll from the pulpit and played gospel music. Jerry Lee has often described his career as a flight from God, with Jimmy Lee cast in the role of his conscience and indefatigable redeemer. The relationship, however, was more complex than that, and the spirits of these two American institutions were latterly revealed as more complementary than antithetical. When Jimmy Lee was discovered with a prostitute in a motel, the evangelist created a scandal that surpassed even his cousin's series of dramas. Tragedy, scandal and, above all, rock 'n' roll have seldom been so intrinsically a part of one musician's life.

Albums: *Jerry Lee Lewis* (1957), *Jerry Lee's Greatest* (1961), with the Nashville Teens, *Live At The Star Club, Hamburg* (1965), *The Greatest Live Show On Earth* (1965), *The Return Of Rock* (1965), *Whole*

Lotta Shakin' Goin' On (1965), *Country Songs For City Folks* (1965), *By Request - More Greatest Live Show On Earth* (1967), *Breathless* (1967), *Soul My Way* (1967), *Got You On My Mind* (1968), *Another Time, Another Place* (1969), *She Still Comes Around* (1969), *I'm On Fire* (1969), with Linda Gail Lewis *Together* (1970), *She Even Woke Me Up To Say Goodbye* (1970), *A Taste Of Country* (1971), *There Must Be More To Love Than This* (1971), *Rockin' Rhythm And Blues* (1971), *Johnny Cash And Jerry Lee Lewis Sing Hank Williams* (1971), *Monsters* (1971), *Would You Take Another Chance On Me* (1972), *The Killer Rocks On* (1972), *Old Tyme Country Music* (1972), with Johnny Cash *Sunday Down South* (1972), *The Session* (1973), *Live At The International, Las Vegas* (1973), *Great Balls of Fire* (1973), *Southern Roots* (1974), *Rockin' Up A Storm* (1974), *Rockin' And Free* (1974), *I'm A Rocker* (1975), *Live At The Star Club, Hamburg* (1980), *When Two Worlds Collide* (1980), *My Fingers Do The Talking* (1983), *I Am What I Am* (1984), *Keep Your Hands Off It* (1987), *Don't Drop It* (1988), *Great Balls Of Fire!* (1989, film soundtrack), *Rocket* (1990). Compilations: *Golden Hits* (1974), *Country Music Hall Of Fame Hits Vol. 1* (1969), *Country Music Hall Of Fame Hits. Vol. 2* (1969), *The Best Of Jerry Lee Lewis* (1970), *Original Golden Hits Vol. 1* (1970), *Original Golden Hits Vol. 2* (1971), *Rockin' With Jerry Lee Lewis* (1972), *Original Golden Hits Vol. 3* (1973), *Fan Club Choice* (1974), *Whole Lotta Shakin' Goin' On* (1974), *Good Rockin' Tonight* (1975), *Jerry Lee Lewis And His Pumping Piano* (1975), *Rare Jerry Lee Lewis Vol. 1* (1975), *Rare Jerry Lee Lewis Vol. 2* (1975), *I'm A Rocker* (1975), *The Jerry Lee Lewis Collection* (1976), *Golden Hits* (1976), *The Original Jerry Lee Lewis* (1976), *Nuggets* (1977), *Nuggets Vol. 2* (1977), *The Essential Jerry Lee Lewis* (1976), *Shakin' Jerry Lee* (1978), *Back To Back* (1978), *Duets* (1979), *Jerry Lee Lewis* (1979), *Good Golly Miss Molly* (1980), *Trio Plus* (1980), *Jerry Lee's Greatest* (1981), *Killer Country* (1981), *Jerry Lee Lewis* (1982), *The Collection* (1986), *The Pumpin' Piano Cat* (1986), *The Great Ball Of Fire* (1986), *The Wild One* (1986), *At The Country Store* (1987), *The Very Best Of Jerry Lee Lewis* (1987), *The Classic Jerry Lee Lewis* (1989), *Killer's Birthday Cake* (1989), *Killer's Rhythm And Blues* (1989), *The EP Collection* (1990), *Pretty Much Country* (1992), *The Sun Years* (1993).

Liberace

b. Wladziu Valentino Liberace, 16 May 1919, West Allis, Wisconsin, USA, d. 4 February 1987. This larger-than-life pianist had no major chartbusters - but had an indefinable charm and talent that gave delight to multitudes of fans across the globe. Of Polish-Italian extraction, he was raised in a household where there was always music - particularly from father Salvatore who blew French horn in both John Philip Sousa's Concert Band and the Milwaukee Symphony Orchestra. George and the younger Wladziu seemed keenest on likewise becoming professional players. Wladziu's piano skills were praised by no less than Paderewski, and he won a place at Wisconsin College of Music at the age of seven. During a 17-year scholarship - the longest ever awarded by the academy - he made a concert debut as a soloist at 11 and was fronting renowned symphony orchestras before leaving adolescence. A fulfilling career of classical recitals and university master classes might have beckoned but for the artist's underlying sense of humour and flair for self-promotion. In 1934, he had elocution lessons to dilute his Polish accent to better facilitate the surfacing of a natural showmanship. After service in an overseas entertainments unit during World War II, he played and sang in club dance bands and it was during a residency at the Wunderbar in Warsaw, Wisconsin, that he was first introduced as plain 'Liberace'. At New York's Persian Rooms, an experiment whereby he played counterpoints to records - including his own one-shot single for the Signature label - played on the venue's sound system was curtailed by a Musicians Union ban. A happier season in a Californian hotel resulted in a Decca contract for which he was visualized as a second Frankie Carle. However, wishing to develop a more personal style, he moved to Columbia Records where, supervised by Mitch Miller, he cut a flamboyant version of 'September Song' which, supplemented by an in-concert album, brought Liberace to a national audience. By the early 50s, his repertoire embraced George Gershwin favourites, cocktail jazz, film themes ('Unchained Melody'), boogie-woogie and self-composed pieces ('Rhapsody By Candlelight') as well as adaptations of light-classics such as 'Story Of Three Loves' - borrowed from a Rachmaninov variation on a tune by Paganini. Nevertheless, Liberace struck the most popular chord with encores in which doggerel like 'Maizy Doats' or 'Three Little Fishes' were dressed in arrangements littered with twee arpeggios and trills. He also started garbing himself from a wardrobe that would stretch to rhinestone, white mink, sequins, gold lame and similar razzle-dazzle. Crowned with a carefully-waved coiffeur, he oozed charm and

Liberace (left) with Marion Ryan and Nat 'King' Cole

extravagant gesture with a candelabra-lit piano as the focal point of the epic vulgarity that was *The Liberace Show*, televised coast-to-coast from Los Angeles, which established a public image that he later tried in vain to modify. His fame was such that he was name-checked in 'Mr. Sandman' a 1954 million-seller by the Chordettes, and, a year later, starred (as a deaf concert pianist) in a film, *Sincerely Yours*, with brother George (future administrator of the Liberace Museum in Las Vegas) as musical director. Another spin-off would be the publication of a Liberace cookbook. Following a celebration of a quarter century in showbusiness with a Hollywood Bowl spectacular in 1956, Liberace crossed to England - where a vocal outing, 'I Don't Care', was lodged in the Top 30 - for the first of three Royal Command Performances. While in the UK, he instigated a High Court action, successfully suing the *Daily Mirror*, whose waspish columnist, Cassandra had written an article on the star, laced with sexual innuendo. During the next decade, a cameo in the film satire, *The Loved One* was favourably reviewed - as would be one of his early albums for RCA in which he aimed more directly at the contemporary market. This, however, was a rare excursion for his work maintained a certain steady consistency - 'squareness' his detractors would say - that deviated little from the commercial blueprint wrought in the 50s. Nonetheless, Liberace's mode of presentation left its mark on stars such as Gary Glitter, Elton John, Queen - and, in an inverted sense, Nigel Kennedy who also thrived on bringing the classics to the masses. Although attendant publicity boosted box office takings on a world tour, embarrassing *Mirror*-type allegations by a former employee placed his career in a darker perspective. When the singer died on 4 February 1987 at his Palm Springs mansion, the words 'kidney complaint' were a euphemism for an AIDS-related illness.

Selected albums: *Liberace At The Palladium* (1961), *My Parade Of Golden Favourites* (1961), *As Time Goes By* (1962), *Mr. Showmanship* (1963), *Christmas* (1963), *My Most Requested* (1964), *Liberace At The American* (1964), *Golden Themes From Hollywood* (1964), *Liberace Now* (1967), *Brand New Me* (1970), *Candlelight Classics* (1973), *Piano Gems* (1976), *Mr. Showmanship - Live* (1978), *New Sounds* (1979). Compilations: *Best Of Liberace* (1983), *Collection* (1988).

Further reading: *Liberace*, Liberace. *Liberace: The True Story*, B. Thomas.

Liberty Records

Founded in Los Angeles in 1955 by Al Bennett, Sy Waronker and Theodore Keep, Liberty became one of the most successful post-rock 'n' roll independent labels. Their most notable early signing was Eddie Cochran, whose short, but influential, career included such seminal recordings as 'Summertime Blues' (1958) and 'C'mon Everybody' (1959). The finely-honed commercial productions of Snuff Garrett proved successful for early 60s signings Johnny Burnette and Bobby Vee, while the acquisition of the Imperial label in 1963 brought Fats Domino, Ricky Nelson, Sandy Nelson and discotheque star Johnny Rivers to the label. Aware of the success of New York's Aldon publishing house, Waronker supervised Liberty's Metric Music subsidiary, which introduced the talents of contract songwriters Jackie DeShannon, Randy Newman, David Gates and Russ Titleman to the company. Liberty enjoyed considerable commercial success with Jan And Dean and Gary Lewis And The Playboys, while an association with the Ventures, through their distribution of the Dolton label, also proved fruitful. Despite the acquisition of leading blues group Canned Heat, Liberty was generally unable to sustain its eminent position in the face of underground rock, although its UK office, under the aegis of A&R director Andrew Lauder, made several astute signings, including the Groundhogs, Brinsley Schwarz and Hawkwind. By 1972, the label's roster and back catalogue had been absorbed by the United Artists conglomerate and Liberty's brief tenure was ended.

Little Richard

b. Richard Wayne Penniman, 5 December 1935, Macon, Georgia, USA. The wildest and arguably the greatest and most influential of the 50s rock 'n' roll singers and songwriters. He first recorded in late 1951 in Atlanta for RCA, cutting eight urban blues tracks with his mentor Billy Wright's Orchestra; 'Taxi Blues' being the first of four unsuccessful single releases on the label. He moved to Houston, Texas in 1953 and with the Tempo Toppers (vocals) and the Duces of Rhythm (backing) recorded four R&B tracks including 'Ain't That Good News'. Eight months later he recorded another four with Johnny Otis' Orchestra but none of these were released at the time. In February 1955, at the suggestion of Lloyd Price, he sent a demo to Specialty Records who realized his potential and in September, under the guidance of producer Robert 'Bumps' Blackwell, recorded a dozen tracks in New Orleans. The classic 'Tutti

Little Richard

Frutti', which was amongst them gave him his first R&B and pop hit in the USA. The follow-up 'Long Tall Sally' topped the R&B chart and was the first of his three US Top 10 hits, despite being covered by Pat Boone whose previous record, a cover of 'Tutti Frutti', was still charting. Richard's string of Top 20 hits continued with the double-sider 'Rip It Up'/'Ready Teddy', the former being his first UK release and chart entry in late 1956. Richard's frantic, no-holds barred performance of his first two hits 'Long Tall Sally' and 'Tutti Frutti' in the film *Don't Knock The Rock* undoubtedly helped push his next UK single, which coupled the tracks, into the Top 3.

His next film and single was *The Girl Can't Help It* which missed the US Top 40 but together with its b-side 'She's Got It' (a re-working of his earlier track 'I Got It') gave him two more UK Top 20

hits. The remainder of 1957 saw him notch up three more huge transatlantic hits with the rock 'n' roll classics 'Lucille', 'Keep A Knockin'' (he featured both in the movie *Mr. Rock & Roll*) and 'Jenny Jenny' and a Top 20 album with *Here's Little Richard*. At the very height of his career, the man with the highest pompadour in the business, shocked the rock world by announcing, during an Australian tour, that he was quitting music to go into a theological college. In 1958, previously recorded material like the transatlantic Top 10 hit 'Good Golly Miss Molly' kept his name on the chart and a year later he had his biggest UK hit with a 1956 recording of the oldie 'Baby Face' which reached number 2. Between 1958 and 1962 Richard recorded only gospel music for Gone, Mercury (with producer Quincy Jones) and Atlantic. In late 1962, Richard toured the UK for the first time and the now short-haired wild-man who pounded pianos and pierced eardrums with his manic falsetto was a huge success. In 1963, he worked in Europe with the Beatles and the Rolling Stones, who were both great admirers of his music. His first rock recordings in the 60s were made back at Speciality and resulted in the UK Top 20 hit 'Bama Lama Bama Loo'. In 1964, he signed with VeeJay where he re-recorded all his hits, revived a few oldies and cut some new rockers - but the sales were unimpressive. In the mid-60s, soul music was taking hold worldwide and Richard's soulful VeeJay tracks, 'I Don't Know What You've Got But It's Got Me' (which included Jimi Hendrix on guitar) and 'Without Love', although not pop hits, were among the best recordings of the genre. For the rest of the 60s he continued to pack in the crowds singing his old hits and in the studios mixed 50s rock and 60s soul for Modern in 1965, OKeh a year later and Brunswick in 1967. The best of these were his OKeh tracks which included 'Poor Dog', 'Hurry Sundown' and the UK recorded 'Get Down With It' (which gave Slade their first hit in the 70s).

Reprise Records, whom he joined in 1970, tried very hard to get him back at the top and under the expertise of producer Richard Perry he managed minor US hits 'Freedom Blues' and 'Greenwood, Mississippi' but his three albums sold poorly. The rest of the 70s was spent jumping from label to label, recording in supergroup-type projects and playing oldies shows. When he desired, he could still 'out rock' anyone, but often there was too much Las Vegas glitter, excessive posturing and an element of self-parody. In 1976, he re-joined the church and for the next decade preached throughout America. In 1986, Richard was among the first artists inducted into the Rock 'n' Roll Hall of Fame and he successfully acted in the film *Down And Out In Beverly Hills* which included the rocking 'Great Gosh A'Mighty', which just missed the US Top 40. Renewed interest, spurred WEA to sign him and release, *Lifetime Friend*, which included the chart record 'Operator'. Since the mid-80s he has become a frequent visitor on chat shows, an in-demand guest on other artist's records and an often seen face on videos (of acts ranging from Hank Williams Jnr. to Living Colour to Cinderella), He even has his own star on the Hollywood Walk of Fame and a boulevard named after him in his hometown. Nowadays a regular presenter of music awards, he has also been the star of Jive Bunny hits. The leader of rebellious 50s rock 'n' roll, the man who shook up the music

business and the parents of the period, is now a much-loved personality accepted by all age groups.
Selected albums: *Here's Little Richard* (1957), *Little Richard Volume 2* (1958), *The Fabulous Little Richard* (1959), *Little Richard Is Back* (1965), *The Explosive Little Richard* (1967), *The Little Richard Story* (1970), *Good Golly Miss Molly* (1969), *Rock Hard Rock Heavy* (1970), *Mr Big* (1971), *The Original Little Richard* (1972), *Rip It Up* (1973), *Slippin' And Slidin'* (1973), *Keep A Knockin'* (1975), *Dollars Dollars* (1975), *The Great Ones* (1976), *Little Richard And Jimi Hendrix Together* (1977), *Whole Lotta Shakin' Goin' On* (1977), *Greatest Hits Recorded Live* (1977), *The Georgia Peach* (1980), *Little Richard And His Band* (1980), *Get Down With It* (1982), *Ooh! My Soul* (1982), *The Real Thing* (1983), *He's Got It* (1984). Compilations: *20 Classic Cuts* (1986), *The Collection* (1989), *The Specialty Sessions* (1989, CD box set), *The Formative Years, 1951-53* (1989), *The EP Collection* (1993).

Locke, Josef

b. Joseph McLaughlin, 23 March 1917, Londonderry, Northern Ireland. Locke was an extremely popular ballad singer in the UK from the 40s through to the 60s, with an impressive tenor voice and substantial stage presence. He sang in local churches as a child, and, when he was 16, added two years to his age in order to enlist in the Irish Guards. Later, he served abroad with the Palestine Police before returning to Ireland in the late 30s to join the Royal Ulster Constabulary. Nicknamed the 'Singing Bobby', he became a local celebrity in the early 40s, and then toured the UK variety circuit. In the following year, he played the first of 19 seasons at the popular northern seaside resort of Blackpool. He made his first radio broadcast in 1949 on the popular *Happydrome*, which starred the trio of 'Ramsbottom, Enoch and Me', and subsequently appeared on television programmes such as *Rooftop Rendezvous*, *Top Of The Town*, *All-Star Bill* and the *Frankie Howerd Show*. In 1947, Locke released 'Hear My Song, Violetta', which became forever associated with him. His other records were mostly a mixture of Irish ballads such as 'I'll Take You Home Again Kathleen', 'Dear Old Donegal' and 'Galway Bay'; excerpts from operettas, including 'The Drinking Song', 'My Heart And I' and 'Goodbye'; along with familiar Italian favourites such as 'Come Back To Sorrento' and 'Cara Mia'. He also made several films, including the comedy *Holidays With Pay*. In 1958, after appearing in five Royal Command Performances, and while still at the peak of his career, the Inland Revenue began to make substantial demands that Locke declined to meet. Eventually he 'fled from public view to avoid tax-evasion charges'. Meanwhile, on the television talent show, *Opportunity Knocks*, Hughie Green introduced 'Mr. X', a Locke look-alike, as a 'is-he-or-isn't-he' gimmick. He was in reality, Eric Lieson, who carved a long and lucrative career out of the impersonation. When Locke's differences with the tax authorities were settled, he retired to Co. Kildare, emerging for the occasional charity concert. In 1984, he was the subject of a two-hour birthday tribute on Gay Bryne's talk show, *The Late, Late Show*, on Irish television. In 1992, the Peter Chelsom film, *Hear My Song*, was released in the UK. It was an 'unabashed romantic fantasy based on the exuberant notion of Locke returning to Britain to complete an old love affair and save an Liverpool-based Irish night-club from collapse'. Locke was flown to London for the royal premiere, attended by Princess Diana, and became the 'victim' of television's *This Is Your Life*. In the movie, the songs were dubbed by the operatic tenor, Vernon Midgely. During the spring of 1992, Locke found himself in the UK Top 10 album chart with *Hear My Song*.

Selected albums: *My Many Requests* (1964), *I'll Sing It My Way* (1974), *Josef Locke Sings Favourite Irish Songs* (1978), *Let There Be Peace* (1980), *In Concert* (1989). Compilations: *The World Of Josef Locke Today* (1969), *Hear My Song* (1983), *34 Great Singalong Songs* (1988), *Hear My Song: The Best Of* (1992), *Take A Pair Of Sparkling Eyes* (1992), *A Tear, A Kiss, A Smile* (1993).

London Records

Founded in 1947, this renowned label was established in the USA by British Decca to provide an outlet for its domestic releases. The UK counterpart was introduced in 1949 when the parent company began recording American acts, including Teresa Brewer and Josh White. London began licensing material from other US outlets in October 1951 and within two years had acquired the rights to Essex and Imperial, with which it laid the foundations of its impressive rock 'n' roll catalogue. Bill Haley And His Comets and Fats Domino were an important part of its early roster, but the label enjoyed commercial success with releases by Slim Whitman and the bright pop of Pat Boone. The addition of Atlantic Records (1955), Chess, Specialty (both 1956) and Sun (1957) ensured a virtually peerless position. Little Richard, Chuck Berry, Bo Diddley, Jerry Lee

Lewis, the Everly Brothers, Rick Nelson and the Coasters were among the many artists introduced to British audiences by this cogent outlet whose reputation flourished as the 50s progressed.

London's eminent position continued into the 60s. Success with Duane Eddy, Del Shannon and Roy Orbison was derived by distributing the Jamie, Big Top and Monument labels and the girl-group genre was satisfied through releases drawn from Phil Spector's Philles label. However, several other licencees felt the wide roster jeopardized their individuality. Berry Gordy removed his fledgling Tamla/Motown empire after a mere handful of releases, EMI acquired the rights to Liberty, United Artists, Imperial and Minit, while the defection of Chess to Pye International was particularly ill-timed, given that the emergent British R&B movement brought renewed interest to a catalogue London had failed to exploit fully. Another crucial loss was that of Atlantic and although London had secured a measure of success with Otis Redding, the US company took its catalogue to Polydor in 1966, just as the soul style it contained began a commercial ascendancy. Elektra made a similar move, thus depriving London of a prime outlet for folk-rock and the emergent US underground scene, and by 1967 releases on this once-prolific outlet had lessened dramatically. Minor labels - White Whale, Bang and Laurie - provided occasional hits, but London's sole remaining jewel was the Memphis-based Hi Records, home of Al Green, Ann Peebles and Willie Mitchell. Releases by these artists provided commercial and artistic success, but the company's decline during the 70s mirrored that of Decca itself. This once-mighty concern had failed to adapt to the changing face of pop and was sold to Phonogram in 1980 upon the death of its patriarch, Sir Edward Lewis. Although initially reserved - two singles were released bearing the London imprint between 1980 and 1981 - the new owners resurrected the name fully in 1982 for a new generation of British-based acts. Hits for the Bluebells, New Edition, Blancmange, Bronksi Beat, Communards and Glenn Medeiros ensued, but Bananarama enjoyed the most comprehensive success with a run of 17 Top 40 hits for the label between 1982 and 1988.

Albums: *London American Legend, Part One* (1975), *London American Legend, Part Two* (1976).

London, Julie

b. June Webb, 26 September 1926, Santa Rosa, California, USA. Actress-singer London is inextricably linked to the sultry Andy Hamilton song, 'Cry Me A River' which gave the artist her sole million-seller in 1955. Her memorable performance of the song in the film *The Girl Can't Help It*, defined a lachrymose delivery best exemplified on *Julie Is Her Name*, which also featured the talent of jazz guitarist Barney Kessel. London continued to record prodigiously throughout the late 50s to the mid-60s, but this aspect of her career vied with roles in films, notably: *The Great Man* and *A Question Of Adultery*. She later appeared in several television series, often alongside longtime producer and songwriter Bobby Troup. Her popularity underwent a revival in the UK in the early 80s after Mari Wilson scored a hit with London's classic lament.

Albums: *Julie Is Her Name* (1955), *Lonely Girl* (1956), *Calendar Girl* (1956), *About The Blues* (1957), *Make Love To Me* (1957), *Julie* (1957), *Julie Is Her Name, Volume 2* (1958), *London By Night* (1958), *Sing Me An Old Song* (1959), *Your Number Please* (1959), *Julie London At Home* (1959), *Around Midnight* (1960), *Send For Me* (1960), *Whatever Julie Wants* (1961), *Sophisticated Lady* (1962), *Love Letters* (1962), *Latin In A Satin Mood* (1963), *The End Of The World* (1963), *The Wonderful World Of Julie London* (1963), *Julie London* (1964), *In Person At The Americana* (1964), *Our Fair Lady* (1965), *All Through The Night* (1965), *For The Night People* (1966). Compilations: *Julie's Golden Greats* (1963), *Great Performances* (1968), *The Best Of Julie London* (1984).

Lord Rockingham's XI

Scottish bandleader Harry Robinson and his band took the pseudonym of Lord Rockingham's XI (after a genuine historical character) to appear on the Jack Good UK television pop programme, *Oh Boy*, playing 'novelty' rock instrumentals. Other key members were Chery Wainer (organ), and Red Price (saxophone) as well as renowned British rock 'n' roll drummer Rory Blackwell, the former two of which would feature in their own spots on *Oh Boy*. The first release was 'Fried Onions' in May 1958 but in September Decca released the Robinson penned 'Hoots Mon' complete with Scottish accented cries of 'Hoots mon, there's a moose in the hoose!'. It was a UK number 1 hit but the follow-up, 'Wee Tom', only made number 16. They featured on an *Oh Boy* EP but after a further attempt to have a hit with 'Ra Ra Rockingham' failed, Robinson reverted to more straight forward orchestra names like Harry Robinson's XV and the Robinson Crew. He later

revived the Lord Rockingham monicker in an attempt to cash in on the 1962 Twist phenomenon with 'Newcastle Twist'/'Rockingham Twist'. Benny Green played tenor sax with Rockingham before he realized he could make more money writing and talking about jazz than performing. He is now a respected author and broadcaster, but still plays saxophone semi-professionally. Robinson was later involved with another UK number 1 when he provided the musical accompaniment to Millie's 'My Boy Lollipop'.

Lotis, Dennis

b. 8 March 1925, Johannesburg, South Africa. Lotis was an extremely popular singer in the UK in the 50s, with a sophisticated style which was particularly attractive to the young female population. Lotis trained for four years as a boy soprano, and won several cups and medals. He made his first stage appearance at the age of seven, and his first broadcast at the age of nine. After leaving school, he worked as a bus conductor and electrician, and sang in cinemas and nightclubs in Johannesburg, before moving to the UK in the early 50s, carrying a letter of introduction to Ted Heath from the former London saxophonist and bandleader, Don Barrigo. Following a couple of broadcasts with Henry Hall, Lotis joined the Heath band and, together with other resident vocalists Lita Roza and Dickie Valentine, became one of the most popular singers on the circuit. Lotis's vocal talents were evident on such records as 'Sam's Song', 'Goodnight Irene', 'Nevertheless', and 'She's A Lady' (with Roza and Valentine). After scoring a hit with 'Cuddle Me', he went solo, and during the late 50s toured the UK variety circuit, appeared in his first Royal Command Performances, and rejoined the Heath band for a tour of the USA, including an appearance at Carnegie Hall. In 1956, he appeared in a touring production of the stage musical, *Harmony Close* and, two years later, starred in John Osborne's *The World Of Paul Slickey*, a musical comedy that was poorly-received in Britain. Lotis also made several films, a mixture of drama, comedy, musicals and horror, including *The Extra Day*, *It's A Wonderful World*, *City Of The Dead* and *She'll Have To Go*. His other stage appearances included the role of Lucio in John Neville's Playhouse Production of Shakespeare's *Measure For Measure*. Adversely affected by the changing face of popular music, he played the working men's clubs, and ran his own antiques business for a time, from a shop in Kent. Eventually, in the 80s and 90s, he returned to

Dennis Lotis

Lymon, Frankie

theatre, singing in nostalgic shows with contemporaries such as Joan Regan and Russ Conway, and joined Lita Roza, and many other mature musicians, in concerts commemorating the great Ted Heath band.
Selected albums: *How About You?* (1958), *Bidin' My Time* (1959), *Night And Day* (1983).

Lutcher, Nellie
b. 15 October 1915, Lake Charles, Louisiana, USA. A singer/pianist notable for her percussive piano playing and distinctive scat-vocal approach. Initially, Lutcher played in a big band with her bass-playing father before moving on to join the Southern Rhythm Boys band. She played clubs on the west coast during the late 30s/early 40s and signed to Capitol Records in 1947 following an appearance on a *March Of Dimes* charity show. Her first release, the R&B styled 'Hurry On Down', became a US Top 20 hit that same year and was followed by 'He's A Real Gone Guy', 'The Song Is Ended' and 'Fine Brown Frame'. The latter was a cover of an earlier hit by bandleader Buddy Johnson. She later moved on to Liberty Records recording a highly-rated album, *Our New Nellie*. But her popularity had faded and during the late 60s and early 70s she took a staff job with the Hollywood Local Branch of the Musician's Union, still occasionally playing clubs such as the New York Cookery.
Albums: *Real Gone* (mid-50s), *Our New Nellie* (mid-50s). Compilations: *Real Gone Gal* (1985), *My Papa's Got To Have Everything* (1985), *Ditto From Me To You* (1987).

Lymon, Frankie, And The Teenagers
b. 30 September 1942, Washington Heights, New York, USA, d. 28 February 1968, New York City, New York, USA. Often billed as the 'boy wonder', Lymon first entered the music business after teaming-up with a local all-vocal quartet the Premiers. The latter comprised Jimmy Merchant (b. 10 February 1940, New York, USA), Sherman Garnes (b. 8 June 1940, New York, USA, d. 1978), Herman Santiago (b. 18 February 1941, New York, USA) and Joe Negroni (b. 9 September 1940, New York, USA, d. 1977). Lymon joined them in 1954 and soon after they were signed to the Gee label as the Teenagers. Their debut, the startling 'Why Do Fools Fall In Love?' was issued on 1 January 1956 and soon climbed into the US Top 10, alongside the early recordings of Elvis Presley and Carl Perkins. The song went on to reach number 1 in the UK and

sold two million copies. Lymon soon left school and the group toured extensively. For their second single, 'I Want You To Be My Girl', the 13-year-old boy wonder was given superior billing to the group. With their use of high tenor, deep bass and soprano and teenage-orientated lyrics, the Teenagers boasted one of the most distinctive sounds in 50s pop. After registering chart entries in the USA with 'I Promise To Remember' and 'The ABCs Of Love', they found greater acclaim in England. The soaring 'I'm Not A Juvenile Delinquent' (from the film *Rock Rock Rock*) hit the UK Top 12 and Lymon was afforded the honour of appearing at the London Palladium. So strong was his appeal at this point that the single's b-side 'Baby Baby' received separate promotion and outshone the a-side by climbing to number 4. During his celebrated UK tour, Lymon recorded as a soloist with producer Norrie Paramor and the resulting 'Goody Goody' reached the Top 30 on both sides of the Atlantic. By the summer of 1957, he had split from the Teenagers, and thereafter his career prospects plummeted. He enjoyed the excesses of stardom, smoking cigars, drinking heavily and enjoying under-age sex with women old enough to be his mother. Despite recording a strong album, his novelty appeal waned when his voice broke. By 1961, the teenager was a heroin addict and entered Manhattan General Hospital on a drug rehabilitation programme. Although he tried to reconstruct his career with the help of Dizzy Gillespie and even took dancing lessons and studied as a jazz drummer, his drug habit remained. In 1964, he was convicted of possessing narcotics and his finances were in a mess. His private life was equally chaotic and punctuated by three marriages. In February 1968, he was discovered dead on the bathroom floor of his grandmother's New York apartment with a syringe by his side. The Teenager who never grew up was dead at the tragically early age of 25. His former group continued to record sporadically and in the 80s, surviving members Santiago and Merchant formed a new Teenagers and Pearl McKinnon took Lymon's part.
Album: *The Teenagers Featuring Frankie Lymon* (1956), *The Teenagers At The London Palladium* (1958), *Rock 'N' Roll With Frankie Lymon* (1960). Compilations: *Frankie Lymon And The Teenagers* (1987, 61 track set), *The Best Of* (1990).

Lynn, Vera
b. Vera Welch, 20 March 1917, London, England. For many years Lynn has been a leading UK singer with a clear, strong, plaintive voice, held in great

Vera Lynn

esteem by home audiences because of her work in entertaining service personnel during World War II. At the age of seven she was singing regularly in working men's clubs, and later joined a dancing troupe until she was 15. She made her first broadcast in 1935, singing with the Joe Loss Orchestra, and later worked with Charlie Kunz and Ambrose. While she was with Ambrose she met saxophonist Harry Lewis, who later became her husband and manager. She went solo in 1940, and with the help of producer Howard Thomas, launched her own BBC radio series, *Sincerely Yours*. With its signature tune of, 'Wishing', in which she attempted to become the musical link between the girls 'back home' and their men overseas, by reading out personal messages and singing sentimental favourites such as 'Yours', 'We'll Meet Again' and 'White Cliffs Of Dover'. In 1941, she appeared in the revue, *Applesauce* at the London Palladium, with Florence Desmond and 'the cheekie chappy', comedian Max Miller. By now, she was the most popular female vocalist in Britain, and with UK Forces overseas, to whom she was known as 'The Forces Sweetheart'. One comedian was heard to say: 'The war was started by Vera Lynn's agent!'.

She also made three films, *We'll Meet Again* (1942), which also featured Geraldo's Orchestra, *Rhythm Serenade* (1943), with comedy duo Jewell and Warriss, and *One Exciting Night* (1944), with top wartime comic, Richard Murdoch. Lynn toured Burma with ENSA, entertaining the troops, early in 1944, (arriving home on D-Day), and the following year she retired, temporarily. She returned to the UK variety circuit in 1947, and soon had her own BBC radio series again, this time with Canadian Robert Farnon as musical director. Partly because a musicians strike was causing disruption in the USA, UK Decca Records decided to issue some of her material on their US London label. From 1948-54, she had several US Top 30 hits there, including 'You Can't Be True, Dear', 'Again', 'Auf Wiederseh'n Sweetheart' (the first record by a UK artist to top the US charts), 'Yours', 'We'll Meet Again', 'If You Love Me, Really Love Me' and 'My Son, My Son'. She promoted the records by making regular guest appearances on Tallulah Bankhead's US radio programme, *The Big Show*.

In the UK during the 50s, besides 'Auf Wiederseh'n' and 'My Son, My Son' (which was a UK number 1), Lynn had Top 30 entries including 'Homing Waltz', 'Forget Me Not', 'Windsor Waltz', 'Who Are We', 'A House With Love In It', 'The Faithful Hussar (Don't Cry My Love)' and 'Travellin' Home'. From 1952-54, Lynn appeared at London's Adelphi Theatre in the revue, *London Laughs*, which also featured young English comedians Jimmy Edwards and Tony Hancock. In the late 50s, with the decline of the UK variety theatres, Lynn appeared mainly on radio and television. In 1960, after 20 years, she left Decca, the recording company she had been with for 20 years, and joined EMI. This move prompted the album, *Hits Of The Sixties*, containing contemporary ballads such as 'By the Time I Get To Phoenix', 'Everybody's Talking' and 'Fool On The Hill'. In 1962, it was her recorded voice that was used to evoke memories of the war years in Lionel Bart's West End musical, *Blitz*. In 1969, she launched her first television series for seven years, for the BBC, and in the following year was unable to sing for four months after developing the lung condition emphysema. In the same year she was awarded the OBE. Since then she has worked less and less, preferring to save her performances for bodies such as the Burma Star Association at London's Royal Albert Hall, and nostalgic occasions such as June 1984, the 40th anniversary of the D-Day landings, and in 1989, the 50th anniversary of the start of World War II. She has continued to record suitable contemporary material. She was created a Dame of the British Empire in 1975, and is still regarded as a legend by a large proportion of the British public. The Pink Floyd wrote 'Vera' for *The Wall*, which accurately satirised her importance during World War II.

Selected albums: *Hits Of The Blitz* (1962), *The Wonderful Vera* (1963), *Favourite Sacred Songs* (1972), *Unforgettable Songs* (1972), *Remembers The World At War* (1974), *Sing With Vera* (1974), with Kenneth McKellar *World Nursery Rhymes* (1976), *I'll Be Seeing You* (1976), *Christmas With Vera Lynn* (1976), *Vera Lynn In Nashville* (1977), *Thank You For The Music* (1979), *Singing To The World* (1981), *In Concert: Guard's Depot, Caterham* (1984). Compilations: *The World Of Vera Lynn* (1969), *The World Of Vera Lynn, Volume Two* (1970), *The World Of Vera Lynn, Volume Three* (1971), *The World Of Vera Lynn, Volume Four* (1972), *The World Of Vera Lynn, Volume Five* (1974), *The Great Years* (1975), *Focus On Vera Lynn* (1977), *We'll Meet Again* (1980), *This Is Vera Lynn* (1980), *20 Family Favourites* (1981), *The Vera Lynn Songbook* (1981, five-album box set), *We'll Meet Again* (1989).

Further reading: *Vocal Refrain*, Vera Lynn.

Humphrey Lyttelton (right) with Terry Dene

Lyttelton, Humphrey

b. 23 May 1921, Eton, Buckinghamshire, England. Raised in an academic atmosphere, his father was a Housemaster at Eton College, he taught himself to play a variety of instruments including the banjolele. His prodigious talent was spotted early and he was given formal lessons on piano and, a little later, in military band drumming. Eventually, his education took him back to Eton College this time as a pupil. He joined the school orchestra as a typanist but after a while drifted away from the orchestra and the instrument. At the age of 15 he discovered jazz, thanks to records by trumpeters Nat Gonella and, decisively, Louis Armstrong. By this time Lyttelton had switched to playing the mouth-organ but realizing the instrument's limitations, he acquired a trumpet which he taught himself to play. Forming his own small jazz band at the college, he developed his playing ability and his consuming interest in jazz. With the outbreak of World War II he joined the Grenadier Guards, continuing to play whenever possible. After the war he resumed playing, this time professionally and in 1947 became a member of George Webb's Dixielanders. The following year he formed his own band and quickly became an important figure in the British revivalist movement. In the late 40s and through to the mid-50s Lyttelton's stature in British jazz increased. Significantly, his deep interest in most aspects of jazz meant that he was constantly listening to other musicians, many of whom played different forms of the music. Although he was never to lose his admiration for Armstrong he refused to remain rooted in the revivalist tradition. His acceptance and absorption of music from the jazz mainstream ensured that when the trad boom fizzled out, Lyttelton continued to find an audience. In the mid-50s he added alto saxophonist Bruce Turner to his band, outraging some reactionary elements in British jazz circles, and a few years later added Tony Coe, Joe Temperley and other outstanding and forward-thinking musicians.

In the early 60s Lyttelton's reputation spread far beyond the UK and he also developed another important and long-term admiration for a trumpet player, this time Buck Clayton. By this time, however, Lyttelton's personal style had matured and he was very much his own man. He was also heavily involved in many areas outside the performance of music. In 1954, he had published his first autobiographical volume and in the 60s he began to spread his writing wings as essayist, journalist and critic. He also broadcast on radio and television, sometimes as a performer but also as a speaker and presenter. These multiple activities continued throughout the next two decades, his BBC Radio 2 series, *The Best Of Jazz*, running for many years. His writings included further autobiographical work and his ready wit found outlets in such seemingly unlikely settings such as the quizmaster on the long-running radio comedy-panel series, *I'm Sorry I Haven't A Clue*. During this time he continued to lead a band, employing first-rate musicians with whom he toured and made numerous records. Amongst the sidemen of the 70s and 80s were Dave Green, Mick Pyne, John Surman, John Barnes, Roy Williams and Adrian Macintosh. He also toured and recorded with singers Helen Shapiro, Carol Kidd and Lillian Boutté.

Back in the late 40s Lyttelton had recorded with Sidney Bechet and in the 70s and 80s he made occasional albums with other American jazz stars including Buddy Tate, on *Kansas City Woman*, and Kenny Davern, *Scatterbrains* and *This Old Gang Of Ours*. In the early 80s Lyttelton formed his own recording company, Calligraph, and by the end of the decade numerous new albums were available. In addition to these came others, mostly on the Dormouse label, which reissued his earlier recordings and were eagerly snapped up by fans of all ages. Although he has chosen to spend most of his career in the UK, Lyttelton's reputation elsewhere is extremely high and thoroughly deserved. As a trumpet player and bandleader he has ranged from echoing early jazz to near-domination of the British mainstream. For more than 40 years he has succeeded in maintaining the highest musical standards, all the while conducting himself with dignity, charm and good humour. In the early 90s touring with Kathy Stobart, he showed no signs of letting up and barely acknowledged the fact that he had passed his 70th birthday.

Albums: *Humph At The Conway* (1954), *I Play As I Please* (1957), *Triple Exposure* (1959), *21 Years On* (1969), *South Bank Swing Session* (1973), *Kansas City Woman* (1974), *Spreadin' Joy* (1978), *It Seems Like Yesterday* (1983), *Movin' And Groovin'* (1983), *Scatterbrains* (1984), *Humph At The Bull's Head* (1985), *...This Old Gang Of Ours...* (1985) *Gonna Call My Children Home: The World Of Buddy Bolden* (1986), *The Beano Band* (c.1986), *Movin' And Groovin'* (1986), *Gigs* (1987), *The Dazzling Lillian Boutté* (1988), with Helen Shapiro *I Can't Get Started* (1990), *Rock Me Gently* (1991). Compilations: *Delving Back And Forth With Humph*

(1948-86 recordings), *Bad Penny Blues: The Best Of Humph* (1949-56 recordings), *Tribute To Humph Vols 1-8* (1949-56 recordings), *The Parlophone Years* (1949-56 recordings), *Jazz At The Royal Festival Hall & Jazz At The Conway Hall* (1951-54 recordings), *Dixie Gold* (1960-63 recordings).
Further reading: *I Play As I Please*, Humphrey Lyttelton. *Second Chorus*, Humphrey Lyttelton. *Take It From The Top*, Humphrey Lyttelton.

M

McDevitt, Chas
b. 1935, Glasgow, Scotland. McDevitt was the banjo player with the Crane River Jazz Band in 1955 before forming a skiffle group which won a talent contest organised by Radio Luxembourg. Another contestant, vocalist Nancy Whiskey (b. 1936, Glasgow, Scotland) joined the McDevitt group which included guitarists Tony Kohn and Bill Branwell (from the Cotton Pickers skiffle group), Marc Sharratt (d. May 1991; washboard) and Lennie Hanson (bass). The group appeared in the film *The Tommy Steele Story* in 1957, performing 'Freight Train', a song introduced to Britain by Peggy Seeger who had learned it from its composer, black American folk singer Elizabeth Cotten. Issued by Oriole, the McDevitt/Whiskey version was a Top 10 hit in the UK and reached the US charts, although McDevitt did receive a lawsuit from America over the ownership of the copyright. After the release of a version of 'Greenback Dollar' and an EP as follow-ups, Whiskey left the group. With a studio group, the Skifflers, she made a series of singles for Oriole from 1957-59, including 'He's Solid Gone' and the folk song 'I Know Where I'm Going' and also released *The Intoxicating Miss Whiskey*. Having opened a Freight Train coffee bar in London, McDevitt continued to perform and record with new vocalist Shirley Douglas (b. 1936, Belfast, Northern Ireland) whom he later married. He briefly followed the rock 'n' roll trend with conspicuous lack of success and later performed duets with Douglas after the manner of Nina And

Frederik. Among his later efforts were 'It Takes A Worried Man' (Oriole 1957), 'Teenage Letter' (1959) and 'One Love' (HMV 1961). Both McDevitt and Douglas recorded for Joy Records in the 70s enlisting session support from Joe Brown and Wizz Jones.
Albums: *The Intoxicating Miss Whiskey* (1957), *The Six-Five Special* (50s), *Sing Something Old, New, Borrowed & Blue* (1972), *Takes Ya Back Don't It* (1976).

McGuire Sisters
b. Middletown, Ohio, USA. This close-harmony vocal group, popular in the 50s and early 60s, consisted of three sisters, Chris (Christine) (b. 30 July 1929), Dorothy (Dotty) (b. 13 February 1930) and Phyllis (b. 14 February 1931). While in their teens the sisters sang with church choirs, and won an amateur talent contest at their local cinema, for three consecutive weeks. After singing on their local radio station, the McGuires had their first big break, entertaining at army camps and hospitals during a nine-month tour in 1950-51. Then they played club and radio dates in Cincinnati before moving to New York in 1952, and successfully auditioning for the *Arthur Godfrey Talent Scouts* contest. They subsequently became regulars on the show, and also appeared for eight weeks on singer Kate Smith's top-rated radio programme. Signed to the Coral label, they had their first minor hit in 1954, with 'Pine Tree, Pine Over Me', in collaboration with Johnny Desmond and Eileen Barton. During the rest of that year they had further successes with their version of the Spaniels' R&B hit, 'Goodnight Sweetheart, Goodnight', followed by 'Muskrat Ramble', 'Lonesome Polecat' and 'Christmas Alphabet'. In 1955, the sisters had their first million-seller with another cover, 'Sincerely', originally recorded by the Moonglows. The McGuires' version stayed at number 1 in the US for 10 weeks, and accelerated their breakthrough into the big time in clubs, theatres and on television. They sang on the *Red Skelton Show* and the *Phil Silvers Show* and appeared at the Waldorf Astoria, the Desert Inn, Las Vegas and the Coconut Grove, Los Angeles. They made their first visit to London in 1961, and played a season at the Talk Of The Town. Their other hits, up until 1961, included 'No More', 'It May Sound Silly', 'Something's Gotta Give', 'He', 'Moonglow And The Theme From *Picnic*', 'Delilah Jones'; 'Weary Blues' (with Lawrence Welk), 'Ev'ry Day Of My Life', 'Goodnight My Love, Pleasant Dreams', 'Sugartime', 'Ding Dong', 'May You

Always' and 'Just For Old Times Sake'. Among their other releases were *Our Golden Favourites, His And Her's* and *Just For Old Times Sake*. When the McGuires' sweet style was overtaken by the harder sounds of the Crystals, Shirelles and Supremes during the 60s, they turned to cabaret, and eventually disbanded. Phyllis continued as a single, appearing regularly in Las Vegas and other cities. In 1985, the McGuire Sisters re-formed and, in the following year, undertook a national tour, stopping off at Bally's Reno, to headline in Donn Arden's lavish revue, *Hello, Hollywood, Hello*. Their well-received act continued into the 90s, leaning heavily on their old catalogue, along with more contemporary material from *Cats* and *Les Miserables*, and an a cappella version of 'Danny Boy'. In January 1986, Murray Kane, their personal manager and arranger since 1952, died in Las Vegas. He was responsible for writing the arrangements that won the sisters a spot on the *Arthur Godfrey Show*, their first break in New York. Prior to that, Kane had worked with Fred Waring, and had been a member of the Crew Chiefs, Glenn Miller's vocal group during World War II.
Selected albums: *By Request* (1955), *Children's Holiday* (c.50s), *Do You Remember When?* (c.50s), *He* (c.50s), *Sincerely* (c.50s), *Teenage Party* (c.50s), *When The Lights Are Low* (1958) *Musical Magic* (c.50s), *Sugartime* (1958), *Greetings From The McGuire Sisters* (late 50s), *Our Golden Favourites* (late 50s), *May You Always* (1959), *In Harmony With Him* (1960) *His And Her's* (early 60s), *Just For Old Times Sake* (1961), *Subways Are For Sleeping* (1962), *Songs Everybody Knows* (1962), *Showcase* (early 60s), *The McGuire Sisters Today* (1966). Compilation: *The Best Of The McGuire Sisters* (1982).

Mackintosh, Ken

b. 4 September 1919, Liversedge, West Yorkshire, England. Mackintosh began playing alto saxophone as a child and worked with various bands in Yorkshire in his teens. In 1939, he joined the army and towards the end of the war was playing in military bands. He formed his own unit in 1948 and enjoyed a measure of local popularity in dancehalls and on regional radio. In 1950, his band was booked to open the Wimbledon Palais in London and met with immediate success. The band broadcast regularly and won a recording contract with HMV. The Wimbledon engagement lasted three years. During the last year, Mackintosh had a record hit with 'The Creep', his own composition, and this led to a bill-topping tour of the UK. Throughout the 50s the band toured,

recorded, broadcast extensively on radio and television, where it headlined its own show, *Flying Standards*, and was featured in a film, *An Alligator Named Daisy* (1955). Mackintosh was able to give an early career boost to Frankie Vaughan and Alma Cogan, making records with both artists. Among the band's record successes of the 50s were 'Harlem Nocturne' and 'Raunchy', which reached number 8 in 1958. In 1963, Mackintosh was hired to open the new Empire Ballroom in London's Leicester Square, at the time billed as the world's greatest and most expensive ballroom. This engagement lasted for seven years, after which the band moved to the Hammersmith Palais for a further seven-year stint. Late in the 70s, Mackintosh took his band on the road where he frequently backed touring singers, including Matt Monro, Pat Boone, Tom Jones and Shirley Bassey. Throughout the 80s and into the early 90s, Mackintosh was on the road with his band, playing dances at which he acknowledged contemporary sounds while nostalgically recreating the best popular dance music of earlier years. His son is Andy Mackintosh.
Albums: *Skyliner* (1980s), *The Very Thought Of You* (1985), *Blue Skies* (1990).

MacRae, Gordon

b. 12 March 1921, East Orange, New Jersey, USA, d. 24 January 1986, Lincoln, Nebraska, USA. MacRae was the son of local radio celebrity, Wee Willie MacRae, and often worked on radio as a child actor before joining the Millpond Playhouse, New York. There he met actress Sheila Stephens who became his first wife in 1941. After winning an amateur singing contest at the 1939-40 New York World's Fair, he sang for two weeks with the Harry James and Les Brown bands. While working as a pageboy at NBC Radio, he was heard by bandleader Horace Heidt who signed him for two years, during which time he appeared with Heidt, James Stewart and Paulette Goddard in a movie about Heidt's radio giveaway show, *Pot O' Gold*. After serving in the US Army Air Force Corps in World War II, MacRae returned to New York to take a singing role in the 1946 Broadway revue, *Three To Make Ready*, starring Ray Bolger. In 1947, he signed to Capitol Records and had a string of hits up until 1954, including 'I Still Get Jealous', 'At The Candlelight Cafe', 'It's Magic', 'Hair Of Gold, Eyes Of Blue', 'So In Love', 'Mule Train'/'Dear Hearts And Gentle People' and 'Rambling Rose'. After a four-year gap, he entered the US charts again in 1958 with 'The Secret'.

MacRae also made a series of successful singles with ex-Tommy Dorsey singer, Jo Stafford. These included 'Say Something Sweet To Your Sweetheart', 'Bluebird Of Happiness', 'My Darling, My Darling' (a US number 1), 'A-You're Adorable', 'Need You', 'Whispering Hope', 'Bibbidi-Bobbidi-Boo' and 'Dearie'. MacRae's film career, mostly for Warner Brothers, started in 1948 with a non-singing role in *The Big Punch*. This was followed by a series of musical films such as *Look For The Silver Lining* (1949) and *The Daughter Of Rosie O'Grady* (1950), both co-starring June Haver. He made four films with Doris Day: *Tea For Two* (1950), *West Point Story* (1950), *On Moonlight Bay* (1951) and *By The Light Of The Silvery Moon* (1953). Other films included *The Desert Song*, (1953) co-starring Kathryn Grayson, and *Three Sailors And A Girl* (1953), with Jane Powell. Macrae also appeared in several dramatic roles. In 1955, he hit the movie big time when he played Curly, opposite Shirley Jones, in the successful film of the Broadway show, *Oklahoma!*, complete with Richard Rodgers and Oscar Hammerstein's Oscar award-winning score. He repeated this enormous success, again with Shirley Jones, when he replaced the first choice, Frank Sinatra, as Billy Bigelow in the movie of another Rodgers and Hammerstein stage hit, *Carousel* (1956). That same year, MacRae appeared in his last musical film role as Buddy DeSylva, in *The Best Things In Life Are Free*, the bio-pic of the 20s/30s songwriting team of DeSylva, Brown And Henderson. He made one final film appearance, in a dramatic role in *The Pilot*, in 1979. In the mid-50s, MacRae was also popular on US television, as the singing host of *The Railroad Hour*, *The Colgate Comedy Hour*, and his own *Gordon MacRae Show*. After MacRae divorced his first wife, he was remarried in 1967 to Elizabeth Lambert Schrafft. In the same year he made his first Broadway musical appearance since 1946, when he replaced Robert Preston in *I Do! I Do!*. In the 70s he struggled with alcoholism and, in the early 80s, claimed that he had won the battle. He died from cancer of the mouth and jaw in January 1986.

Albums: with Lucille Norman *New Moon/Vagabond King* (1950), with Jo Stafford *Sunday Evening Songs* (1953), with various artists *The Desert Song* (1953), with Stafford *Memory Songs* (mid-50s), *Romantic Ballads* (1956), *Oklahoma!* (1956, film soundtrack), *Carousel* (1956, film soundtrack), *Operetta Favourites* (1956), *The Best Things In Life Are Free* (1956), *Motion Picture Soundstage* (1957), *Gordon MacRae In Concert* (1958), *Cowboy's Lament* (1958), *Seasons Of Love* (1959), *This Is Gordon MacRae* (1960), with Stafford *Whispering Hope* (1962), with Stafford *Peace In The Valley* (1963), with Stafford *Old Rugged Cross* (1978).

Further reading: *Hollywood Mother Of The Year: Sheila MacRae's Own Story*, Sheila MacRae.

Manning, Bob

b. USA. Manning was a highly accomplished ballad singer during the 50s - although perhaps, underrated - whose career probably suffered because of an uncanny vocal similarity with the more popular Dick Haymes. Nevertheless, Manning had several US hits on Capitol in the early 50s, including an impressive reading of 'The Nearness Of You', 'All I Desire', and 'Venus De Milo'. His other releases included a set of classy ballads, *Lonely Spell* and *Our Wedding Songs*. Like Haymes, Manning did not survive the onslaught of rock 'n' roll and beat music.

Manning, Dick

b. Samuel Medoff, 12 June 1912, Gomel, Russia, d. 11 April 1991, Marietta, Georgia, USA. This popular songwriter, during the late 40s and 50s, sometimes wrote both music and lyrics, and was probably best-known for his novelty songs. Born into a theatrical family, Manning was taken to the USA when he was six years old, and studied at the Philadelphia Conservatory and Juilliard. A gifted pianist at an early age, he gave concerts and, later, served as an accompanist, arranger and music coach for singers, while working in theatre and television as an arranger and conductor. One of his first compositions, with F.D. Marchetti and Maurice De Feraudy, was 'Fascination' (1932). He hosted *Sam Medoff And His Yiddish Swing Orchestra* on radio station WHN, before changing his name in 1948. In the same year his composition, 'The Treasure Of Sierra Madre', written with Buddy Kaye, was a hit for Buddy Cole and Freddie Martin, and became the title song for John Huston's film starring Humphrey Bogart. Manning's other 40s songs included 'While The Angelus Was Ringing', 'A Carnival In Venice', a hit for the Mills Brothers, 'Donna Bella' and the jaunty 'One More Dream (And She's Mine)'. It was the 50s, though, when Manning made the greatest impact, mostly in collaboration with lyricist Al Hoffman, with a mixture of novelty songs such as 'Takes Two To Tango'. This was a hit for Louis Armstrong and, somewhat surprisingly, was recorded in the UK by Hermione Gingold and the grumpy television personality,

Gilbert Harding. 'Papa Loves Mambo' and 'Hot Diggity' were both successful for Perry Como, and the latter song also a hit in the UK for Michael Holliday and the Stargazers. Other ballads by Manning included 'Allegheny Moon' (which Patti Page took almost to the top of the US chart in 1956), 'Hawaiian Wedding Song' (successful for Andy Williams in 1959) and 'The Morning Side Of The Mountain' (a US hit for Tommy Edwards in 1959, and revived by Donny and Marie Osmond in 1975). In the 60s, Manning, with Fred Wise, contributed '(There's) No Room To Rhumba In A Sports Car' to the Elvis Presley movie, *Fun In Acapulco* (1963). His songs are said to have been published in 27 languages, and included 'Like I Do' (Maureen Evans), 'Festival Of Roses', 'I Still Feel The Same About You', 'I Can't Get You Out Of My Heart', 'Redwood Smoke', 'When You Kiss Me', 'Oh, Oh, I'm Falling In Love Again', 'Torero' (a hit for Renato Carosone and Julius La Rosa), 'Jilted' (Teresa Brewer), 'Underneath The Linden Tree', 'Don't Stay Away Too Long', 'Mama, Teach Me To Dance' and 'Nickelodeon Song'. He also wrote the score for the television production *The Boys From Boise*, and a symphonic piece for piano and orchestra,

'Nightbird'. His other collaborators included Kay Twomey and Al Stillman.

Mantovani

b. Annunzio Paolo Mantovani, 15 November 1905, Venice, Italy, d. 30 March 1980, Tunbridge Wells, Kent, England. A violinist, pianist, musical director, conductor, composer and arranger, Mantovani was one of the most successful orchestra leaders and album sellers in the history of popular music. His father was principal violinist at La Scala, Milan, under Arturo Toscanini, and also served under Mascagni, Richter and Saint-Saens and, subsequently, led the Covent Garden Orchestra. It is said that Mantovani received encouragement to become a professional musician from his mother, rather than his father. He began his musical training on the piano, and later learned to play the violin. After the family moved to England in 1912, he made his professional debut at the age of 16, playing the Bruch Violin Concerto Number 1. Four years later he had installed his own orchestra at London's Hotel Metropole, and began his broadcasting career. In the early 30s he formed the Tipica Orchestra and began a series of lunch-time broadcasts from the famous Monseigneur

Mantovani

Restaurant, in Piccadilly, London, and started recording for Regal Zonophone. He had two US hits in 1935-36, with 'Red Sails In The Sunset' and 'Serenade In The Night'. Samples of his work around this time are on *The Young Mantovani 1935-39*. In the 40s, Mantovani served as musical director for several London West End shows, including *Lady Behave, Twenty To One, Met Me Victoria, And So To Bed, Bob's Your Uncle* and *La-Di-Da-Di-Da*. He was also involved in Noel Coward's *Pacific 1860* and *Ace Of Clubs*; conducting from the theatre pit for artists such a Lupino Lane, Pat Kirkwood, Mary Martin, Sally Gray, Leslie Henson and many others. His records, for UK Decca, included 'The Green Cockatoo', 'Hear My Song, Violetta' and 'Tell Me, Marianne' (vocal by Val Merrall). Experimenting with various arrangements with which to target the lucrative USA market, he came up with what has been called variously, the 'cascading strings', 'cascading violins', or 'tumbling strings' effect, said to be an original idea of arranger Ronnie Binge. It became the Orchestra's trademark and was first used to great effect in 1951, on Mantovani's recording of 'Charmaine', a song originally written to promote the 1926 silent film classic, *What Price Glory?*. The Mantovani recording was the first of several million-selling singles for his orchestra, which included 'Wyoming', (another 20s number, written by UK music publisher Lawrence Wright), 'Greensleeves', 'Song From Moulin Rouge' (a UK number 1), 'Swedish Rhapsody' and 'Lonely Ballerina'. Mantovani's own compositions included 'Serenata d'Amore', 'A Poem To The Moon', 'Royal Blue Waltz', 'Dance Of The Eighth Veil', 'Toy Shop Ballet' (Ivor Novello Award 1956), 'Red Petticoats', 'Brass Buttons', 'Tango In The Night' and 'Cara Mia', written with UK record producer/manager, Bunny Lewis. David Whitfield's 1954 recording of 'Cara Mia', with Mantovani's orchestra accompaniment, sold over a million copies, and stayed at number 1 in the UK charts for a record (at the time) 10 weeks. It also made Whitfield one of the earliest UK artists to break into the US Top 10. Mantovani issued an instrumental version of the number, featuring himself on piano. This was most unusual in that the instrument was rarely a part of his 40-piece orchestral set-up. Singles apart, it was as an album artist that Mantovani excelled around the world, and especially in the USA. He is said to have been the first to sell over a million stereo units, aided in no small measure by the superb quality of sound obtained by Decca. Between 1955 and 1966 he

had 28 albums in the US Top 30. Although he toured many countries of the world, including Russia, his popularity in the USA, where his kind of orchestral offerings are often referred to as 'the beautiful music', was unique. An indication of that audience's devotion can be gained from a story by George Elrick, Mantovani's manager of 21 years. Elrick claims that, at the beginning of one tour of the USA, the maestro was taken ill and a few concerts had to be cancelled. The prospective capacity audience at one of them, the University of Minnesota and Minneapolis, refused to claim refunds, preferring to retain their tickets for the following year. Mantovani continued to perform throughout the ever-changing musical climate of the 60s and 70s He was awarded a special Ivor Novello Award in 1956 for services to popular music.

Albums: *Mantovani Plays Tangos* (1953), *Strauss Waltzes* (1953), *Christmas Carols* (1953), *The Music Of Rudolf Friml* (1955), *Waltz Time* (1955), *Song Hits From Theatreland* (1955), *Ballet Memories* (1956), *Waltzes Of Irving Berlin* (1956), *Film Encores* (1957), *Gems Forever* (1958), *Continental Encores* (1959), *Film Encores, Volume 2* (1959), *The American Scene* (1960), *Songs To Remember* (1960), *Mantovani Plays Music From Exodus And Other Great Themes* (1960), *Concert Spectacular* (1961), *Operetta Memories* (1961), *Italia Mia* (1961), *Themes From Broadway* (1961), *Songs Of Praise* (1961), *American Waltzes* (1962), *Moon River And Other Great Film Themes* (1962), *Stop The World - I Want To Get Off/Oliver!* (1962), *Latin Rendezvous* (1963), *Classical Encores* (1963), *Mantovani/Manhattan* (1963), *Christmas Greetings From Mantovani* (1963), *Kismet* (1964), *Folk Songs Around The World* (1964), *The Incomparable Mantovani* (1964), *The Mantovani Sound - Big Hits From Broadway And Hollywood* (1965), *Mantovani Olé* (1965), *Mantovani Magic* (1966), *Mr. Music...Mantovani* (1966), *Mantovani Hollywood* (1967), *Old And New Fangled Tangos* (1967), *The Mantovani Touch* (1968), *Mantovani/Tango* (1968), *Mantovani Memories* (1968), *The Mantovani Scene* (1969), *The World Of Mantovani* (1969), *Mantovani Today* (1970), *Mantovani Presents His Concert Successes* (1971), *To Lovers Everywhere USA* (1971), *To Lovers Everywhere* (1972), *Annunzio Paolo Mantovani* (1972), *Cascade Of Praise* (1985). Compilations: *Mantovani Stereo Showcase* (1959), *All-American Showcase* (1959), *Mantovani's Greatest Hits* (1967), *The World Of Mantovani* (1969), *The World Of Mantovani, Volume 2* (1969), *From Monty, With Love* (1971), *Focus On Mantovani* (1975), *Twenty Golden Greats* (1979), *Young Mantovani*

1935-1939 (1980), *Mantovani Magic* (1985), *The Unforgettable Sounds Of Mantovani* (1984), *Collection: Mantovani* (1987).

Martin, Dean

b. Dino Paul Crocetti, 7 June 1917, Steubenville, Ohio, USA. Martin was always widely admired as a ballad singer with a relaxed style, and also showed talent as a light comedian and dramatic actor. After leaving school in the 10th grade, he worked as a shoe-shine boy and a gas station attendant before becoming an 'amateur' welterweight boxer, 'Kid Crochet', earning 10 dollars a fight. When he retired from the boxing arena, he became a croupier at a local casino. His first singing job is said to have been with the Sammy Watkins band in 1941, in which he was initially billed as Dino Martini, but the name was soon changed to Dean Martin. His earliest recordings were for the Diamond label, and they included 'Which Way Did My Heart Go'/'All Of Me' and 'I Got the Sun In The Morning'/'Sweetheart Of Sigma Chi'. He also recorded some tracks for the Apollo label, well known for its impressive roster of black talent. The Martin recordings included, 'Walkin' My Baby Back Home', 'Oh Marie', 'Santa Lucia', 'Hold Me', 'Memory Lane' and 'Louise'. In 1946, Martin first worked with comedian Jerry Lewis at the 500 Club in Atlantic City. Together they developed an ad-libbing, song and comedy act which became very popular on US television and radio in the late 40s. In 1949, they appeared in supporting roles in the film *My Friend Irma*, and in the sequel, *My Friend Irma Goes West*, the following year. The team then starred in another 14 popular comedies, with Martin providing the songs and romantic interest, and Lewis contributing the zany fun. These films included *At War With The Army* (1950), *Jumping Jacks* (1952), *Scared Stiff* (1953), *The Caddy* (1953), *Living It Up* (1954), *Pardners* (1956) and *Hollywood Or Bust* (1956). Their parting was somewhat acrimonious, and it was widely felt that Martin would be the one to suffer most from the split. In fact, they both did well. Martin, after a shaky start in the comedy movie, *Ten Thousand Bedrooms* (1957), blossomed as a dramatic actor in *The Young Lions* (1958), *Some Came Running* (1958), *Rio Bravo* (1959), *Ada* (1961), *Toys In The Attic* (1963), *The Sons Of Katie Elder* (1965) and *Airport* (1970). He still retained his comedy touch in *Who Was That Lady?* (1960) and *What A Way To Go* (1964) but made surprisingly few musicals. The most notable were *Bells Are Ringing* (1960), with Judy Holliday, and *Robin And The Seven*

Hoods (1964). Meanwhile, Martin had signed to Capitol Records in 1948, and for the next 10 years had a series of US Top 30 chart entries, including 'That Certain Party' (duet with Jerry Lewis), 'Powder Your Face With Sunshine', 'I'll Always Love You', 'If', 'You Belong To Me', 'Love Me, Love Me', 'That's Amore', 'I'd Cry Like A Baby', 'Sway', 'Money Burns A Hole In My Pocket, 'Memories Are Made Of This' (number 1), 'Innamorata', 'Standing On The Corner', 'Return To Me', 'Angel Baby' and 'Volare' ('Nel Blu Dipinto Di Blu'). Martin's version of 'That's Amore' surfaced again when it was featured in the 1987 hit movie, *Moonstruck*.

Although Martin was still a big attraction on film and in nightclubs, his records found difficulty in making the singles charts during the early part of the 60s. In 1961, Frank Sinatra, who had also been with Capitol Records, started his own Reprise Records. Martin, who was a member of Sinatra's 'Clan', or 'Ratpack', was one of the first recruits to the new label. In 1964, Martin was back in the US singles charts with a bang. His recording of 'Everybody Loves Somebody', produced by Jimmy Bowen, had a commercial country 'feel' about it, and knocked the Beatles' 'A Hard Day's Night' off the top of the chart. Martin's subsequent Top 30 entries were all in the same vein - records such as 'The Door Is Still Open To My Heart', 'You're Nobody Till Somebody Loves You', 'Send Me The Pillow You Dream On', 'Houston', 'In The Chapel In The Moonlight' and 'Little Ole Wine Drinker, Me'. The latter number was a fitting selection for an artist whose stage persona was that of a man more than slightly inebriated. 'Everybody Loves Somebody' became the theme song for *The Dean Martin Show* on NBC TV which started in 1964, ran for nine seasons and was syndicated world-wide. As well being a showcase for Martin's singing talents, the show gave him the opportunity to display his improvisation skills in comedy. He continued to be a big draw in clubs, especially in Las Vegas, and played the London Palladium in the summer of 1987, to favourable reviews. Later that year, he joined ex-Rat Pack colleagues, Sinatra and Sammy Davis Jnr., in the 'Together Again' tour, involving 40 performances in 29 cities, but had to withdraw at an early stage because of a kidney ailment.

Albums: *The Stooge* (1956, film soundtrack), *Swingin' Down Yonder* (mid-50s), *Pretty Baby* (mid-50s), *This Is Martin* (late 50s), *Sleep Warm* (1959), *Winter Romance* (1959), *The Bells Are Ringing* (1960, film soundtrack), *This Time I'm Swingin'* (1961),

'21-3

Dean Martin (left) with Janet Leigh and Jerry Lewis

Dean Martin (1961), *Dino - Italian Love Songs* (1962), *French Style* (1962), *Dino Latino* (1963), *Country Style* (1963), *Dean 'Tex' Martin Rides Again* (1963), *Everybody Loves Somebody* (1964), *Hey Brother, Pour The Wine* (1964), *Dream With Dean* (1964), *The Door Is Still Open To My Heart* (1964), *Dean Martin Hits Again* (1965), *Dean Martin Sings, Sinatra Conducts* (1965), *Southern Style* (1965), *Holiday Cheer* (1965), *Lush Years* (1965), *(Remember Me) I'm The One Who Loves You* (1965), *Houston* (1965), *Somewhere There's A Someone* (1966), *Relaxin'* (1966), *Happy In Love* (1966), *The Silencers* (1966, film soundtrack), *The Hit Sound Of Dean Martin* (1966), *The Dean Martin TV Show* (1966), *The Dean Martin Christmas Album* (1966), *At Ease With Dean* (1967), *Happiness Is Dean Martin* (1967), *Welcome To My World* (1967), *Gentle On My Mind* (1968), *I Take A Lot Of Pride In What I Am* (1969), *My Woman, My Woman, My Wife* (1970), *For The Good Times* (1971), *Dino* (1972). Compilations: *The Best Of Dean Martin* (1966), *Dean Martin's Greatest Hits! Volume 1* (1968), *Dean Martin's Greatest Hits! Volume 2* (1968), *The Best Of Dean Martin, Volume 2* (1969), *20 Original Dean Martin Hits* (1976), *The Collection* (1989).
Further reading: *Everybody Loves Somebody*, Arthur Marx. *Dino: Living High In The Dirty Business Of Dreams*, Nick Tosches.

Martin, Ray

b. Raymond Stuart Martin, 11 October 1918, Vienna, Austria, d. February 1988, South Africa. Martin was a composer, arranger, musical director and author. After studying violin, composition and orchestration at the State Academy for Music and Fine Arts, Vienna, he moved to Britain in 1937. Martin joined the *Carroll Levis Discoveries* show as a solo violin act, and toured the UK Variety circuit. He was then chosen as the 'New Voice' in the popular BBC radio series, *Bandwaggon*, which starred Arthur Askey and Richard Murdoch. After appearing in several editions of *Sidney Torch's Half Hour*, he joined the British Army in 1940, and worked in the Intelligence Corps, aided by his fluency in German, French and English. Later, he became musical director of the Variety Department for the British Forces Network in Hamburg, Germany. He started broadcasting his *Melody From The Sky* programme from there, with a German string orchestra culled from the Hamburg Philharmonic Orchestra, and transferred the show to the BBC in December 1946, where it ran for over 500 broadcasts. Martin was also instrumental in founding the BBC Northern Variety Orchestra,

and, from 1949-51, conducted at least six shows a week. He started recording for Columbia Records in 1949 with his own Concert Orchestra accompanying other artists including Julie Andrews, Steve Conway and Jimmy Young. Eventually he became the company's recording manager. His 50s instrumental hits included Leroy Anderson's 'Blue Tango', 'Swedish Rhapsody' and 'Carousel Waltz'. He also released *Lehar, Strauss And Novello, High Barbaree - 12 Famous Sea Shanties, Olives, Almonds And Raisins, Million Dollar Melodies, I Could Have Danced All Night, Boots And Saddles* and *Melodies d'Amour*. Some of his many compositions and film scores are difficult to locate because, besides his own name, he wrote under several pseudonyms, such as Tony Simmonds, Buddy Cadbury, Lester Powell and Marshall Ross. In 1956, he wrote the background score, and served as musical director, for a British musical film called *It's Great To Be Young*, starring John Mills. In addition to the title track, written under his own name, the film contained Martin's (Marshall Ross's), 1952 composition, 'Marching Strings'; and his (Lester Powell's) romantic ballad, 'You Are My First Love', written with Paddy Roberts. It also featured a very early Sammy Cahn-Saul Kaplan-Jimmie Lunceford song, 'Rhythm Is Our Business'. Martin's other compositions included 'Melody From The Sky', 'Once Upon A Winter Time', 'Muriella', 'Begorra', 'Parlour Game', 'Blue Violins' (a US hit for Hugo Winterhalter's Orchestra), 'Any Old Time', 'Waltzing Bugle Boy', 'Airborne', 'Ballet Of The Bells', 'Tango Of The Bells', 'Big Ben Blues', 'Never Too Young' and 'Sounds Out Of Sight'. He composed the incidental music for over 20 BBC Sound cartoons, and wrote the scores for several films, including *Yield To The Night*, a prison melodrama in which ex-'glamour girl', Diana Dors, gave a highly acclaimed dramatic performance; and the 1956 version of *My Wife's Father*. In 1957, Martin moved to America to work in New York and Hollywood. His US film scores included *The Young Graduates* and *The Hoax*. In 1972, he returned to work in the UK and, in 1980, appeared as himself in *The Baltimore Bullit*. During the 80s he settled in South Africa, and died there in 1988.
Selected albums: *Piccadilly 2am* (1956), *Dynamica* (1961), *Favourite TV Themes* (1973), *Favourite TV Themes, Volume 2* (1975), *Viva Mariachi* (1975), *Welcome Home* (1975).

Martin, Tony

b. Alvin Morris, 25 December 1913, Oakland,

Tony Martin (right) with Cyril Stapleton

California, USA. Martin was an extremely popular singer from the 30s until the late 50s, with a powerful voice and an easy, romantic style. As a teenager, Martin became proficient on the saxophone and formed his own band, the Clarion Four. For some years he worked in the San Francisco area at the Palace Hotel, playing saxophone and singing with bands such as Anson Weeks, Tom Coakley, and Tom Guran, whose outfit included Woody Herman. Morris drove across country with Herman and other members of the band to the 1933 Chicago World Fair, and afterwards played the city's Chez Paree Club. In 1934, he changed his name to Tony Martin, and tried to break into films, without success. Two years later, he landed a 'bit' part in the Fred Astaire-Ginger Rogers hit movie, *Follow The Fleet*, along with two other young hopefuls, Lucille Ball and Betty Grable. Later in 1936, he signed for 20th Century Fox, and sang 'When I'm With You' in *Poor Little Rich Girl*, and 'When Did You Leave Heaven?' in *Sing, Baby, Sing*. The following year he married one of the film's stars, Alice Faye.

During the late 30s, he achieved star status thanks to film musicals such as *Pigskin Parade*, with Judy Garland and Betty Grable; *Banjo On My Knee*, with Barbara Stanwyck and Joel McCrea; *The Holy Terror* and *Sing And Be Happy*, with Leah Ray; *You Can't Have Everything* and *Sally, Irene And Mary* with Alice Faye; *Ali Baba Goes To Town*, starring Eddie Cantor; *Kentucky Moonshine* and *Thanks For Everything*. When Martin left Fox, he appeared with Rita Hayworth in *Music In My Heart*, and sang Robert Wright and Chester Forest's 'It's A Blue World', which was nominated for an Academy Award in 1940. In 1941, Martin appeared with the Marx Brothers in *the Big Store*, and sang what was to become one of his 'identity songs', 'The Tenement Symphony', described in some quarters, somewhat unkindly, as the comedy highlight of the film. Martin's other movie that year was *Ziegfeld Girl*, with some spectacular Busby Berkeley production numbers, and starring, amongst others, Judy Garland, Hedy Lamarr and Lana Turner. After the attack on Pearl Harbor in December 1941, Martin enlisted in the US Armed Forces, serving first in the Navy, and then with the Army in the Far East. He also sang for a time with the Army Air Forces Training Command Orchestra, directed by Glenn Miller. While in the Services, Martin received several awards, including the Bronze Star and several citations. At the end of World War II, he returned to showbusiness and starred in the Jerome Kern bio-pic, *Till The Clouds Roll By* (1946), which was followed by *Casbah* (1948), thought by many to have been his best role. The songs were by Harold Arlen and Leo Robin, and included another Martin all-time favourite, 'For Every Man There's A Woman'. In the same year, Martin, having divorced Alice Faye, married dancer-actress Cyd Charisse, and later starred with her in *Easy To Love* (1953). Martin's other films during the 50s included *Two Tickets To Broadway* (with Janet Leigh), *Here Come The Girls* (with Bob Hope and Rosemary Clooney), the all-star Sigmund Romberg bio-pic, *Deep In My Heart*, the 1955 MGM re-make of *Hit The Deck*, and a guest appearance in *Meet Me In Las Vegas* (which starred Cyd Charisse and Dan Dailey). In 1957, Martin starred with Vera Ellen in *Let's Be Happy*, an unsuccessful British attempt to recreate the Hollywood musical. Besides his films, Martin had a very successful recording career. His first hits, 'Now It Can Be Told' and 'South Of The Border', came in the late 30s, and continued through to the mid-50s, with songs such as 'It's A Blue World', 'Tonight We Love', 'To Each His Own', 'Rumours Are Flying', 'It's Magic', 'There's No Tomorrow', 'Circus', 'Marta (Rambling Rose Of The Wildwood)', 'I Said My Pyjamas (And Put On My Prayers)' and 'Take A Letter, Miss Smith' (both duets with Fran Warren), 'La Vie En Rose', 'Would I Love You (Love You Love You)', 'I Get Ideas' (adapted from the Argentine tango 'Adios Muchachos' and thought to be quite racey at the time), 'Over A Bottle Of Wine', 'Domino', 'Kiss Of Fire', 'Stranger In Paradise', 'Here', 'Do I Love You (Because You're Beautiful)' and 'Walk Hand In Hand'. His albums included *Dream Music, A Night At The Copacabana* (a fair example of his club act, containing favourites such as 'Begin the Beguine', 'September Song' and 'Manhattan'), *Tenement Symphony, At Carnegie Hall, Fly Me To The Moon, Mr Song Man, Our Love Affair, At The Desert Inn, In the Spotlight* and *Tonight*. As well as having a very successful cabaret act, which he played around the world, Martin was also very active on radio in the 30s, 40s, and into the 50s, on shows such as Walter Winchell's *Lucky Strike Hour*, and others, featuring Burns And Allen, Andre Kostelanetz and David Rose. Martin appeared in his own programmes. He turned to television in the 50s and 60s, and in 1964 formed a night club act with his wife, Cyd Charisse, touring the cabaret circuit in the USA and abroad. In 1976, they published an autobiography, *The Two Of Us*. In 1986, at the age of 63, Charisse re-created the role first played by Anna Neagle over 20 years earlier in

Al Martino

the David Heneker-John Taylor stage musical, *Charlie Girl*, at London's Victoria Palace. Martin and Charisse had first been in London in 1948, on their honeymoon, when he was playing the first of several London Palladium seasons. He has come a long way since then. Martin is still regarded as one of the most accomplished and stylish vocalists of his era.

Selected albums: *A Night At Copacabana* (1956), *Our Love Affair* (1957), *In The Spotlight* (1958), *Dream Music* (1959), *Mr. Song Man* (1960), *At The Desert Inn* (1960), *Tonight* (1960), *Fly Me To The Moon* (1962), *At Carnegie Hall* (1967). Selected compilations: *Greatest Hits* (1961), *Golden Hits* (1962), *Best Of* (1984), *Tenement Symphony* (1984), *Something In The Air* (1989).

Martino, Al

b. Alfred Cini, 7 October 1927, Philadelphia, Pennsylvania, USA. The son of Italian immigrants, a fact that was always obvious in his style and manner, Martino worked as bricklayer in his father's construction business before being encouraged to become a singer by his friend, Mario Lanza. After singing in local clubs, and winning Arthur Godfrey's *Talent Scouts*, he recorded 'Here In My Heart' for the small BBS record label, which shot to number 1 in the US chart, and reputedly sold over a million copies. It was also the first ever record to top the *New Musical Express* UK listings, inaugurated in 1952. His success led to a contract with Capitol Records, and more hits in 1953 with 'Take My Heart', 'Rachel' and 'When You're Mine'. For several years after that, the US record buyers apparently tired of Martino's soulful ballads, although he remained popular in Europe for a time - particularly in the UK, where he made the Top 20 with 'Now', 'Wanted', 'The Story Of Tina' and 'The Man From Laramie'. After some telling performances on US television, he made his recording comeback in 1963, with country singer Leon Payne's 'I Love You Because', followed by 'Painted, Tainted Rose', 'Living A Lie', 'I Love You More And More Every Day', 'Tears And Roses', 'Always Together', 'Think I'll Go And Cry Myself To Sleep' and 'Mary In The Morning'. His second million-seller, 'Spanish Eyes' (1965), was originally an instrumental piece, 'Moon Over Naples', written by the popular German orchestra leader, Bert Kaempfert. With lyrics by Charles Singleton and Eddy Snyder, Martino's version became, particularly in Europe, a dreamy dance favourite to rival Charles Aznavour's, 'Dance In

The Old Fashioned Way'. In 1964, Martino sang the title song for the Bette Davis/Olivia De Havilland film, *Hush...Hush Sweet Charlotte*, and this led to his playing singer Johnny Fontane in the smash hit movie, *The Godfather* (1972). In the film, Martino sang the Italian number 'O Marenariello' ('I Have But One Heart'). He also recorded the film's love theme, 'Speak Softly Love', and had chart success with another couple of Italian songs, 'To The Door Of The Sun' ('Alle Porte Del Sole') and the old hit for Dean Martin, Domenico Modugno's 'Volare'. In vogue once more, Martino played top night clubs and theatres and continued to record albums with Capitol which, into the 90s, has reissued many of his early albums on CD.

Albums: *The Exciting Voice Of Al Martino* (1962), *The Italian Voice Of Al Martino* (1963), *I Love You Because* (1963), *Painted, Tainted Rose* (1963), *Living A Lie* (1964), *I Love You More And More Every Day/Tears And Roses* (1964), *We Could* (1965), *Somebody Else Is Taking My Place* (1965), *My Cherie* (1965), *Spanish Eyes* (1966), *Think I'll Go Somewhere And Cry Myself To Sleep* (1966), *This Is Love* (1966), *This Love For You* (1967), *Daddy's Little Girl* (1967), *Mary In The Morning* (1967), *This Is Al Martino* (1968), *Love Is Blue* (1968), *Sausalito* (1969), *Jean* (1969), *Can't Help Falling In Love* (1970), *My Heart Sings* (1970), *Love Theme From 'The Godfather'* (1972), *Country Style* (1974), *To The Door Of The Sun* (1975), *Sing My Love Songs* (1977), *The Next Hundred Years* (1978). Compilations: *The Best Of Al Martino* (1968), *The Very Best Of Al Martino* (1974), *The Hits Of Al Martino* (1985).

Mathis, Johnny

b. John Royce Mathis, 30 September 1935, San Francisco, California, USA. In 1956, the 19-year-old Mathis was signed to Columbia Records where he began his career with a jazz-tinged album. A US Top 20 hit with 'Wonderful! Wonderful!' saw him move adroitly towards the balladeer market, and before long he was a major concert attraction, with regular appearances on highly-rated American television shows. In 1957, together with his first hit, Mathis was barely absent from the US best-sellers, and that year had a further five hits, including the number 1 'Chances Are', 'The Twelfth Of Never' and 'It's Not For Me To Say'. Mathis had become a phenomenon; his popularity at that time ranked with that of Frank Sinatra. By May 1958, he was scraping the UK charts with 'Teacher, Teacher', and soon established himself with major hits such as 'A Certain Smile', 'Winter

Johnny Mathis

Wonderland', 'Someone', 'Misty' and 'My Love For You'. His appeal to the adult market ensured spectacular album success, and *Johnny's Greatest Hits* stayed a record 490 weeks in the US chart. With the beat boom and 60's pop explosion making it more difficult for visiting American balladeers to infiltrate the singles chart, Mathis concentrated increasingly on releasing albums. Indeed, he seemed willing to tackle a variety of concepts presented by his various producers and arrangers. *Away From Home*, produced by Norman Newell, saw the singer concentrating on the songs of European composers; *Olé*, the Latin-American outing, was sung in Portuguese and Spanish; *Wonderful World Of Make Believe* consisted entirely of songs based on fairy tales; and there were tribute albums to such composers as Burt Bacharach and Bert Kaempfert. Meanwhile, Mathis suffered serious drug addiction, but fortunately managed to kick the habit.

By the late 60s, Mathis seemed equally adept at tackling MOR standards and John Lennon/Paul McCartney songs, as well as hoping to update his image. He returned to the UK singles chart in 1974 for the first time in a decade with 'I'm Stone In Love With You' and, two years later, secured the Christmas number 1 with 'When A Child Is Born'. Back in the USA, he was still searching for new ideas and in 1978, collaborated with Deniece Williams on 'Too Much, Too Late'. This, his first duet, brought a surprise number 1, his first US chart-topper since 1957. Since then, Mathis has duetted incessantly with a list that includes Gladys Knight, Paulette McWilliams, Stephanie Lawrence, Jane Oliver, Dionne Warwick, Angela B'ofill, Natalie Cole, Barbara Dickson and Nana Mouskouri. What has been overlooked is Mathis's incredible commercial success: he is the third most successful recording artist of all time, behind Sinatra and Elvis Presley and ahead of the Beatles and the Rolling Stones. His remarkable durability and unfailing professionalism demands admiration.

Selected albums: *Johnny Mathis* (1957), *Wonderful! Wonderful!* (1957), *Warm* (1957), *Heavenly* (1958), *Merry Christmas* (1958), *Swing Softly* (1958), *Good Night, Dear Lord* (1958), *Open Fire, Two Guitars* (1959), *Ride On A Rainbow* (1960), *Faithfully* (1960), *The Rhythms And Ballads Of Broadway* (1960), *Johnny's Mood* (1960), *I'll Buy You A Star* (1961), *Portrait Of Johnny* (1961), *Live It Up* (1962), *Rapture* (1962), *Johnny* (1963), *Romantically* (1963), *I'll Search My Heart* (1964), *Sounds Of Christmas* (1964), *Tender Is The Night* (1964), *The Wonderful World Of Make Believe* (1964), *Olé* (1965), *This Is*

Love (1964), *Away From Home* (1965), *Love Is Everything* (1965), *The Sweetheart Tree* (1965), *The Shadow Of Your Smile* (1966), *So Nice* (1966), *Up, Up And Away* (1967), *Johnny Mathis Sings* (1967), *Love Is Blue* (1968), *Those Were The Days* (1968), *Johnny Mathis Sings The Music Of Bert Kaempfert* (1969), *The Impossible Dream* (1969), *Love Theme From 'Romeo And Juliet'* (1969), *People* (1969), *Raindrops Keep Fallin' On My Head* (1970), *The Long And Winding Road* (1970), *Johnny Mathis Sings The Music Of Bacharach And Kaempfert* (1970), *Close To You* (1970), *Love Story* (1971), *Christmas With Johnny Mathis* (1972), *You've Got A Friend* (1971), *Johnny Mathis In Person* (1972), *The First Time Ever I Saw Your Face* (1972), *Make It Easy On Yourself* (1972), *Me And Mrs Jones* (1973), *Killing Me Softly With Her Song* (1973), *I'm Coming Home* (1973), *Johnny Mathis Sings The Great Songs* (1974), *Song Sung Blue* (1974), *The Heart Of A Woman* (1974), *When Will I See You Again* (1975), *Feelings* (1975), *I Only Have Eyes For You* (1976), *Sweet Surrender* (1977), *Mathis Is…* (1977), *You Light Up My Life* (1978), *When A Child Is Born* (1978), *The Best Days Of My Life* (1979), *Mathis Magic* (1979), *Tears And Laughters* (1980), *All For You* (1980), *Different Kinda Different* (1980), *Friends In Love* (1982), *A Special Part Of Me* (1984), *Johnny Mathis Live* (1985), *Right From The Heart* (1985), with Henry Mancini *The Hollywood Musicals* (1986), *Christmas Eve With Johnny Mathis* (1986), *Once In A While* (1988), *In The Still Of The Night* (1989), *Love Songs* (1990), *In A Sentimental Mood: Mathis Sings Ellington* (1991), *How Do You Keep The Music Playing?* (1993, CD).

May, Billy

b. 10 November 1916, Pittsburgh, Pennsylvania, USA. May's first impact on the big band scene came in 1938, when he joined the trumpet section of the Charlie Barnet Band and, most notably, began contributing arrangements. Amongst his best-known charts was Barnet's hit record of the old Ray Noble song, 'Cherokee'. In 1939, he joined Glenn Miller, bringing a previously absent vitality to the trumpet section and more fine arrangements. In 1942, he also wrote arrangements for Les Brown and Alvino Rey. The early 40s found him in great demand in radio and film studios, but he continued to write for popular bands of the day. When Capitol Records was formed, with a policy which called for the highest standards of musicianship, May was employed to write and direct for many major singing stars, including Frank Sinatra, Peggy Lee and Nat 'King' Cole. During the 50s, May also began making big

band albums, on which he gave full rein to his highly distinctive arranging style. Although adept at all kinds of big band music, he had a particular fondness for voicing the reed section in thirds, creating a so-called 'slurping' saxophone sound. Among his band's successes were arrangements of 'All Of Me', 'Lulu's Back In Town', 'Charmaine', 'When My Sugar Walks Down The Street', 'Lean Baby' and 'Fat Man Boogie' (the last two also his own compositions). His recording of the movie theme, 'The Man With The Golden Arm', made the UK Top 10 in 1956. For his studio band, May called upon such reliable sidemen as Murray McEachern, Ted Nash and Alvin Stoller. He also wrote for television, lending musical quality to series such as *Naked City* and to the occasional commercial. More recently, he was musical director on the recording dates on which swing era music was recreated for a series of albums issued by *Time-Life*.
Albums: *A Band Is Born* (1951-55), *Sorta May* (1954), *Sorta Dixie* (1955), *Billy May And His Orchestra i* (1956), *The Great Jimmie Lunceford* (1957), *Billy May And His Orchestra ii* (1958), *The Girls And Boys On Broadway* (1958), *Billy May And His Orchestra iii* (1963), *Billy May And His Orchestra iv* (1966), *I Believe In You* (c.70s), *You May Swing* (1980), *The Capitol Years* (1993).

Melly, George

b. 17 August 1926, Liverpool, Lancashire, England. Deeply involved in the UK trad scene of the late 40s and 50s, Melly sang with Mick Mulligan's band. In the 60s he switched careers, exploiting his interest in and knowledge of both music and art to become one of the UK's most ubiquitous critics and writers. He also became a popular television personality, and published the first volume in a series of three autobiographical works. In the early 70s Melly returned to music, performing regularly with John Chilton's band. He has continued to sing with Chilton, touring extensively and entertaining audiences with his broadly-based repertoire which encompasses early blues, popular songs of 20s and 30s vaudeville, and a smattering of later material, some of it written especially by Chilton, which suits his highly personal, rotund singing style.
Selected albums: *George Melly With Mick Mulligan's Band* (1957), *George Melly* (1961), *Nuts* (1972), *At It Again* (1976), *Melly Sings Hoagy* (1978), *Ain't Misbehavin'* (1979), *It's George* (c.1980), *Let's Do It* (1981), *Like Sherry Wine* (1981), *Makin' Whoopee* (1982), *The Many Moods Of Melly* (1984), *16*

Golden Classics (1986), *Running Wild/Hometown* (1986), *Anything Goes* (c.1988).

Further reading: *Owning Up*, George Melly. *Rum, Bum And Concertina*, George Melly. *Scouse Mouse*, George Melly.

Merrill, Bob

b. H. Robert Merrill Levan, 17 May 1921, Atlantic City, New Jersey, USA. After working at a number of jobs in various parts of the USA, Merrill began singing in clubs and on the stage. He was also an effective mimic. After military service during World War II, he worked in Hollywood as a dialogue director and also made a handful of appearances as an actor. It was while working on a film that he was asked by comedienne Dorothy Shay to write some songs for her forthcoming album. Merrill did as she suggested, and the financial rewards this brought encouraged him to pursue songwriting as a career. Among the early songs he wrote were 'Lover's Gold' (music by Morty Nevins), 'Fool's Paradise' and 'The Chicken Song' (with Terry Shand). In 1950 Merrill had his first hit with 'If I Knew You Were Coming I'd've Baked A Cake' (Al Hoffman and Clem Watts). In the early 50s Merrill's successes included 'Sparrow In The Treetop', 'Truly, Truly Fair' and 'How Much Is That Doggie In The Window?'. Other 50s songs were 'Let Me In', 'Red Feathers' 'Walkin' To Missouri', 'Mambo Italiano', 'Where Will The Dimple Be?' and 'A Sweet Old-Fashioned Girl'. Despite the success of these songs, Merrill wanted to write more serious music and, in 1956, he composed the score for the musical version of Eugene O'Neill's novel, *Anna Christie*, which opened on Broadway in May 1957 under the title, *New Girl In Town*. Merrill followed this with another O'Neill story, *Ah, Wilderness!*, which came to the stage as *Take Me Along*. Both shows had moderate success, each exceeding 400 performances, but his next show was his best. *Carnival* opened on 13 April 1961, and ran for 719 performances. Starring Anna Maria Alberghetti, the show included songs such as 'Love Makes The World Go Round', 'Yes, My Heart' and 'Her Face'. In the mid-60s he collaborated with Jule Styne on *Funny Girl* but, despite several attempts, his theatrical career declined thereafter. In contrast, however, a new career as a screenwriter blossomed and, in addition, he has taught at the University of California in Los Angeles.

Miller, Bob

The instrumental group, Bob Miller And The Millermen, appeared regularly on UK television and radio programmes in the 50s and early 60s. After being noticed at several London gigs, including one at the Locarno Ballroom, Streatham, in London, on Coronation Day, 2 June 1953, Miller appeared on BBC television's *Dig This*. He subsequently toured with current pop stars, including Cliff Richard, Bobby Darin, the Four Freshmen and Shirley Bassey. Later, on shows such as *Drumbeat* (for eight years), and the radio series, *Parade Of The Pops* ('a review of the week's popular music, and prediction of hits to come'), they backed many of the UK's top vocalists, and had their own featured spots. Their records included 'Muchacha', 'Square Bash', 'Dig This', 'The Poacher', 'Little Dipper', 'In The Mood', 'My Guy's Come Back', 'The Busker's Tune', 'Manhunt', '77 Sunset Strip', 'Joey's Song' and *The Exciting Sounds Of Bob Miller*. Miller's abiding interest was yacht racing, and in June 1972, he participated in the Transatlantic Race, providing a day-by-day radio commentary. In 1978, he and the Millermen released *Bob Miller & M*.

Miller, Gary

b. Neville Williams, 1924, Blackpool, Lancashire, England, d. 15 June 1968, London, England. Miller was a popular singer in the UK during the 50s and early 60s, with a smooth and polished style. As a young man, Miller was a talented soccer player and played for Blackpool Football Club as an amateur. During World War II, he served as a lieutenant in the Royal Navy Volunteer Reserve and, on release, enrolled as a student at London University with the intention of becoming a teacher of languages. After performing in college concerts, and with the experience of singing at a Welsh Eisteddfod festival as a schoolboy, Miller embarked on the learning process of small-time cabaret and concert tours, and made his first radio broadcast on *Beginners, Please*. As well as singing, he also included dancing in his act, and was involved in negotiations for a small part in the Ray Bolger movie, *Where's Charley?*, when it was being made in England, but nothing materialized. His first real break came when he was discovered by record executive and songwriter Norman Newell during a Variety appearance at Northampton, which led to him making a few tracks for Columbia. He also made regular appearances, singing and dancing, on television in *Shop Window*, and appeared on the fortnightly *Kaleidoscope* series. By 1954, he was headlining in variety on the Moss Empires circuit. After a spell with Newell at the newly-formed

Gary Miller

Philips Records in 1953, during which he released mostly romantic ballads, Miller switched to another new label, Pye Nixa, and started recording more uptempo material. His first hit, 'Yellow Rose Of Texas', in 1955, was overtaken by the US Mitch Miller version, but 'Robin Hood' made the Top 10 despite opposition from Dick James, who benefitted by having his version played over the titles during the weekly television show. During that era it was commonplace for several versions of the same song to jostle each other in the singles chart. This was the case with Miller's 'Garden Of Eden', which lost out to Frankie Vaughan. There was also strong competition on 'Wonderful, Wonderful' from Ronnie Hilton, and on 'The Story Of My Life' from Michael Holliday. Miller's record of the latter song is said to have suffered in popularity because he was touring North Africa at the time of its release. Perhaps in an effort to avoid the competition, Miller reached back to 1945 for his final chart entry, 'I've Heard That Song Before' (1961); it proved to be one of his best vocal performances. His first album, *Meet Mister Miller*, contained standards such as 'Manhattan', 'April Showers' and 'Stella By Starlight'. This was followed by *Gary On The Ball*, with the Kenny Ball Jazz Band. In 1964, Miller appeared in the West End production of *She Loves Me*, Jerry Bock and Sheldon Harnick's musical based on the Hungarian play, *Perfumerie*. He returned to the London stage in 1966 to play the role of the crooning Agent VO3 in Bryan Blackburn's comedy musical, *Come Spy With Me*, starring female impersonator Danny La Rue, at London's 'home of farce', the Whitehall Theatre. Two years later he died of a heart attack at his south London home.

Miller, Mitch

b. Mitchell William Miller, 4 July 1911, Rochester, New York, USA. Miller was an oboist, record producer, arranger and one of the most commercially successful recording artists of the 50s and early 60s. He learned to play the piano at the age of six, and began studying the oboe when he was 12, and later attended Rochester's Eastman School of Music. After graduating in 1932, Miller played oboe with symphony orchestras in the area, before joining CBS Radio in 1932. For the next 11 years, he was a soloist with the CBS Symphony, and played with Andre Kostelanetz, Percy Faith, the Saidenburg Little Symphony, and the Budapest String Quartet. In the later 40s, he became director of Mercury Records' 'pop' division, and then, in 1950, was appointed head of A&R at Columbia. While at Mercury, Miller was responsible for producing several big hits, including Frankie Laine's 'That Lucky Old Sun', 'Mule Train' and

Mitch Miller

'The Cry Of The Wild Goose'. Miller also conducted the orchestra on Laine's 'Jezebel' and 'Rose, Rose, I Love You'. Shortly after he left the label, Patti Page released 'The Tennessee Waltz', which became one of the biggest-selling singles ever. The original was by R&B singer, Erskine Hawkins, and the Page disc is sometimes credited as being the first really successful example of 'crossover' from country to pop, although Miller had already fashioned Hank Williams' 'Hey, Good Lookin'' into a minor hit for Frankie Laine and Jo Stafford. Miller developed this policy when he moved to Columbia, and recorded Guy Mitchell ('Singing The Blues' and 'Knee Deep In The Blues'), Tony Bennett ('Cold, Cold Heart'), Rosemary Clooney ('Half As Much'), Jo Stafford ('Jambalaya') and the little known Joan Weber ('Let Me Go Lover'). Miller's roster at Columbia also included Johnnie Ray ('Cry', 'The Little White Cloud That Cried', 'Just Crying In The Rain') and Frank Sinatra.

There was little empathy between Miller and Sinatra, and the singer rejected several songs which eventually became successful for Guy Mitchell. After he left Columbia, Sinatra sent telegrams to judiciary and senate committees, accusing Miller of presenting him with inferior songs, and of accepting money from writers whose songs he

(Miller) had used. Certainly, Sinatra recorded some unsuitable material, under Miller's auspices, during his final years with label; although 'American Beauty Rose' and 'Goodnight, Irene', both with Miller's accompaniment, and 'Bim Bam Baby', paled in comparison with perhaps the most bizarre item of all: 'Mama Will Bark', on which Sinatra made barking and growling noises, and duetted with a new Miller signing, a female named Dagmar.

Miller's own hit recordings, mostly credited to 'Mitch Miller And His Gang', started in 1950, with his adaptation of the Israeli folk song, 'Tzena, Tzena, Tzena', complete with a happy vocal chorus which would typify his later work. After 'Meet Mr. Callaghan', 'Without My Lover', 'Under Paris Skies' and 'Napoleon' in the early 50s, he spent six weeks at number 1 with the million-selling, 'The Yellow Rose Of Texas', one of the great marching songs from the American Civil War. This was followed by three instrumentals: 'Lisbon Antigua', 'Song For A Summer Night (Parts 1 & 2)', 'March From The River Kwai And Colonel Bogey'. There was also the novelty 'The Children's Marching Song' from the 1959 film, *The Inn Of The Sixth Happiness*. The previous year, Miller had started his series of *Sing Along With Mitch* albums, which featured an all-male chorus singing old favourites, many from before the turn of the century. Nineteen variations on the theme made the US Top 40 between 1958 and 1962, of which seven titles achieved million-selling status. The phenomenally successful *Sing Along* formula was developed as a popular television series, which ran from 1961-66, and featured several solo singers such as Victor Griffin, Leslie Uggams and Louise O'Brien. Despite the obvious financial gain to Columbia from his records sales, Miller was constantly criticized for his negative attitude towards rock 'n' roll. He turned down Buddy Holly, among others, and was blamed for his company's relatively small market share in the rapidly changing music scene during his tenure as an influential executive. On the other hand, his promotion of the artists already mentioned, plus Doris Day ('Que Sera, Sera'), Johnny Mathis, Percy Faith, and many more, substantially aided Columbia. Out of place in the 'swinging 60s', he nevertheless emerged occasionally to conduct the orchestra on various light, and classical music recordings.

Selected albums: *Sing Along With Mitch* (1958), *Christmas Sing Along...* (1958), *More Sing Along...* (1958), *Still More! Sing Along...* (1959), *Folk Songs Sing Along...* (1959), *Party Sing Along...* (1959), *Fireside Sing Along...* (1959), *Saturday Night Sing Along...* (1960), *Sentimental Sing Along...* (1960), *March Along...* (1960), *Memories Sing Along...* (1960), *Happy Times! Sing Along...* (1961), *TV Sing Along...* (1961), *Your Request Sing Along...* (1961), *Holiday Sing Along...* (1961), *Rhythm Sing Along...* (1962), *Family Sing Along...* (1962). Compilation: *Mitch's Greatest Hits* (1961).

Mills Brothers

The three permanent members of the group comprised Herbert Mills (b. 2 April 1912), Harry Mills (b. 9 August 1913, d. 28 June 1982) and Donald Mills (b. 29 April 1915). John Mills Jnr. (b. 11 February 1889), added vocal notes in string bass form and played guitar. All the brothers were born in Piqua, Ohio, USA, sons of a barber who had been a successful concert singer. By the mid-20s, they were singing in sweet, close harmony in local vaudeville, providing their own backing by accurately imitating saxophones, trumpets, trombones and bass. With the main trio still teenagers, they had their own show on Cincinnati radio before moving to New York in 1930. The brothers signed to Brunswick Records and had a hit in 1931 with their first disc, 'Tiger Rag', which they also sang in the movie *The Big Broadcast*,

featuring Bing Crosby and many other stars of US radio. They appeared in several other musical montage movies such as *Twenty Million Sweethearts* (1934), *Broadway Gondolier* (1935) and *Reveille With Beverly* (1943), *Rhythm Parade* (1943), *Cowboy Canteen* (1944) and *When You're Smiling* (1950). In the early 30s, Crosby featured on several of the brothers' record hits, including 'Dinah'/'Can't We Talk It Over', 'Shine' and 'Gems From George White's Scandals', which also included the Boswell Sisters. On later tracks, the Mills Brothers were also joined by Louis Armstrong, Ella Fitzgerald and Cab Calloway. Their early records were labelled: 'No musical instruments or mechanical devices used on this recording other than one guitar'. Other 30s hits included 'You Rascal, You', 'I Heard', 'Good-Bye, Blues', 'Rockin' Chair', 'St. Louis Blues', 'Sweet Sue', 'Bugle Call Rag', 'It Don't Mean A Thing (If It Ain't Got That Swing)', 'Swing It Sister', 'Sleepy Head' and 'Sixty Seconds Together'.

In 1935, John Mills died suddenly and the brothers' father, John Snr., took over as bass singer, and ex-bandleader Bernard Addison joined the group on guitar. During the late 30s, the Mills Brothers toured the USA and abroad, appearing in two UK Royal Command Performances. Their popularity peaked in 1943 with the record 'Paper Doll', which sold over six million copies. They had consistent chart success throughout the 40s with titles on the Decca label such as 'You Always Hurt The One You Love', 'Til Then', 'I Wish', 'I Don't Know Enough About You', ' Across The Alley From The Alamo', 'I Love You So Much It Hurts', 'I've Got My Love To Keep Me Warm', 'Someday (You'll Want Me To Want You)' and 'Put Another Chair At The Table'.

By 1950, the instrumental impressions having generally been discarded, the brothers were accompanied by ex-Tommy Dorsey arranger Sy Oliver's orchestra on their hit 'Nevertheless (I'm In Love With You)' and again in 1952 on 'Be My Life's Companion'. That same year, 'The Glow Worm', gave them another blockbuster. This was a 1908 song from the German operetta *Lysistrata*, with a new lyric by Johnny Mercer. Other 50s favourites from the brothers included Sy Oliver's own composition 'Opus Number One', 'Say 'Si-Si'', 'Lazy River' and 'Smack Dab In The Middle'. In 1956, John Snr. retired, and the brothers continued as a trio. Their last hit on Decca was 'Queen Of The Senior Prom' in 1957. The switch to the Dot label gave them two US Top 30 entries, 'Get A Job' and their final chart success, 'Cab

Mills Brothers

Driver', in 1968. Harry Mills died on 28 June 1982, but Herbert and Donald continued to perform their brand of highly polished, humorous entertainment with a substitute singer. In 1989, Donald Mills, now walking with a cane, gained excellent reviews and favourable audience reaction when he played nightclubs with his son John, using mainly the old Mill Brothers catalogue, but with additional new material.

Selected albums: *Souvenir Album* (mid-50s), *Singin' And Swingin'* (mid-50s), *Memory Lane* (mid-50s), *One Dozen Roses* (mid-50s), *The Mills Brothers In Hi-Fi* (mid-50s), *Glow With The Mills Brothers* (mid-50s), *Barbershop Harmony* (mid-50s), *Harmonizing With The Mills Brothers* (mid-50s), *Mmmm, The Mills Brothers* (1958), *Great Barbershop Hits* (1959), *Merry Christmas* (1959), *The Mills Brothers Sing* (1960), *Yellow Bird* (1961), *San Antonio Rose* (1961), *Great Hawaiian Hits* (1961), *The Beer Barrel Polka And Other Hits* (1962), *The End Of The World* (1963), *Gems By The Mills Brothers* (1964), *Hymns We Love* (1964), *Say Si Si, And Other Great Latin Hits* (1964), *The Mills Brothers Sing For You* (1964), *These Are The Mills Brothers* (1966), *That Country Feelin'* (1966), *The Mills Brothers Live* (1967), *Fortuosity* (1968), with Count Basie *The Board Of Directors* (1968), *My Shy Violet* (1968), *Dream* (1969). Compilations: *The Mills Brothers Greatest Hits* (1958), *Ten Years Of Hits 1954-1964* (1965), *Greatest Hits* (1987, MCA label), in addition, there are a great many compilations available.

Mineo, Sal

b. Salvatore Mineo, 10 January 1939, New York City, New York, USA. d. 12 February 1976. After a difficult childhood, Mineo studied dancing and made his Broadway debut in *The Rose Tattoo*. He followed this with an appearance in *The King And I* in 1952. In the mid-50s he went to Hollywood and began making films, usually appearing as a troubled teenager. Among his best-known films were *Rebel Without A Cause* (1955), for which he was unsuccessfully nominated for an Oscar as Best Supporting Actor, *Somebody Up There Likes Me* and *Giant* (both 1956) and *Exodus* (1960), another unsuccessful Oscar nomination. He also played the title role in *The Gene Krupa Story* (1959). In the late 50s, Mineo made a number of records, including 'Love Affair', 'Start Moving (In My Direction)', 'Lasting Love' and 'You Shouldn't Do That'. He continued making films during the 60s and also returned to stage work. He directed and starred in *Fortune And Men's Eyes*, a play which

reflected Mineo's own homosexuality. He was returning home from the theatre when he was stabbed to death in a Hollywood street.
Album: *Sal* (c.1957).

Mitchell, George

b. 27 February 1917, Stirling, Scotland. Although he played the piano and sang as a youth, Mitchell intended to be an accountant, and followed his inclinations in the Royal Army Pay Corps during World War II. In his spare time he organized concerts with a mixed choir consisting of 16 ATS girls and Pay Corps personnel. In 1947, after his release, he formed the George Mitchell Choir for the BBC radio programme, *Cabin In The Cotton*, and then, two years later, changed the name to the George Mitchell Glee Club, a group of 32 singers, that performed on popular radio shows such as *Stand Easy*, as well as having its own series. The Glee Club also toured the UK variety circuit and appeared in the Royal Variety Performance of 1950, the first of many in which Mitchell was involved. By 1957 the Mitchell singers were re-creating traditional minstrel shows for television, singing on fixed rostra, and wearing red facial make-up, which appeared to be black when the cameras were fitted with green filters. In 1958, masterminded by Mitchell and producer George Innes, the first *Black And White Minstrel Show* proper was transmitted, and continued, with occasional short breaks, in the Saturday night peak spot for 20 years. The original static format was transformed into 'the fastest moving show on television' when the male singers performed routines with the Television Toppers dance troupe. The company, and its three principal singers, Dai Francis, Tony Mercer and John Boulter, were joined at various times through the years by comedians such as Leslie Crowther, Stan Stennett and George Chisholm. Always at the heart of the show was a series of nostalgic medleys of (mostly) American popular music from the years 1920-50, cleverly arranged by Mitchell so that each number seamlessly segued into the next one. When the medleys were transferred to albums, beginning in 1960, the first three issued went to number 1 in the UK charts. In 1961 the *Black And White Minstrel Show* won the Golden Rose of Montreux for the best light entertainment programme. By then, a stage version, presented by Robert Luff, had toured the provinces, beginning in Bristol, and including a summer season at Scarborough, before moving into London's Victoria Palace in 1962. It stayed there, with a break of a few months, until 1972, by which time it was estimated that over seven million people had seen the show, which traditionally always closed with a half-tempo rendering of 'When The Saints Go Marching In'. During the 60s two more companies toured the UK, Australia and New Zealand. In 1978 the BBC axed the television show on the grounds that 'it might offend black people', and later refused to show clips in programmes celebrating BBC Television's history. Eventually, Mitchell and Luff (regretfully?) issued a statement disassociating themselves from contemporary versions of the concept that had brought them so much success in the past, although the original format continued to tour Australia. A form of 'Minstrel' stage show remained a popular summer season attraction at UK seaside resorts, and, in 1985, undertook a 20-date Silver Anniversary Tour. In 1992, *That Old Minstrel Magic* played to capacity audiences in the provinces, but, following protests from the Commision for Racial Equality, no members of the cast appeared in black-face - an attempt by one of the lead singers to do so was rapidly quashed. By that time, Mitchell had retired and was spending most of each year in Florida, USA. His son, Rob, continued the family musical tradition, becoming a respected musical director on radio, and for various stage productions.

Selected albums: *The Black And White Minstrel Show* (1960), *Another Black And White Minstrel Show* (1961), *On Stage With The George Mitchell Minstrels* (1962), *On Tour With The George Mitchell Minstrels* (1962), *Spotlight On The George Mitchell Minstrels* (1963), *Magic Of The Minstrels* (1965), *Here Come The Minstrels* (1966), *Showtime* (1967), *Sing The Irving Berlin Songbook* (1968), *The Magic Of Christmas* (1970), *30 Golden Greats* (1977).

Mitchell, Guy

b. Albert Cernick, 27 February 1927, Detroit, Michigan, USA. Mitchell was an enormously popular singer in the USA and the UK during the 50s, with a straightforward style and affable personality. Although his birthplace is often given as Yugoslavia, his parents' homeland, Mitchell confirmed in a 1988 UK interview that he was born in Detroit, and brought up there until the family moved to Colorado, and then to Los Angeles, California, when he was 11 years old. In Los Angeles, he successfully auditioned for Warner Brothers and, for the next few years, was groomed for a possible movie career as a child star, besides singing on the Hollywood radio station KFWB. The possibility of the world having another Mickey Rooney was averted when the family moved again, this time to San Francisco. Mitchell became an apprentice saddle maker, and worked on ranches and in rodeos in the San Joaquin Valley, and sang on cowboy singer Dude Martin's radio show. His affection for country music stayed with him for the remainder of his career. After a spell in the US Navy, Mitchell joined pianist Carmen Cavallero, and made his first records with the band, including 'I Go In When The Moon Comes Out' and 'Ah, But It Happens'. He then spent some months in New York, making demonstration records. He also won first place on the *Arthur Godfrey Talent Show*. In 1949, he recorded a few tracks for King Records, which were subsequently reissued on *Sincerely Yours* when Mitchell became successful.

In 1950, he was signed to Columbia Records by Mitch Miller, who is said to have been responsible for changing Cernick to Mitchell, Miller's full Christian name. Their first success came in 1950, with 'My Heart Cries For You' and 'The Roving Kind', which were followed by a string of hits throughout the decade, mostly jaunty novelty numbers, usually with Miller arrangements which used French horns to considerable effect. Several of the songs were written by Bob Merrill, including 'Sparrow In The Tree Top', 'Pittsburgh, Pennsylvania', 'My Truly, Truly Fair', 'Feet Up (Pat Him On The Po-Po)', 'Belle, Belle, My Liberty Belle' and 'She Wears Red Feathers', which contained the immortal Merrill couplet: 'An elephant brought her in, placed her by my side/While six baboons got out bassoons, and played "Here Comes The Bride"'! Other US Top 30 entries during this period included 'You're Just In Love', a duet with another Miller protegee, Rosemary Clooney, 'Christopher Columbus', 'Unless' (a 30s Tolchard Evans' number), 'Sweetheart Of Yesterday', 'There's Always Room At Our House', 'I Can't Help It', 'Day Of Jubilo', "Cause I Love You, That's A-Why', 'Tell Us Where The Good Times Are' (the latter two duets with Mindy Carson), and 'Ninety-Nine Years (Dead Or Alive)'. 'Singing The Blues' (with Ray Conniff And His Orchestra), became his most successful record, which stayed at number 1 in the US charts for 10 weeks in 1956. In the UK, Tommy Steele had a hit with his cover, but Mitchell also succeeded by reaching number 1. Further infectious hits followed: 'Knee Deep In The Blues', the irritatingly catchy 'Rock-A-Billy' ('rock-a-billy, rock-a-billy, rock-a-billy rock, rock-a-billy rock-a-billy, ooh rock rock'), and his last

US chart entry in 1959, 'Heartaches By The Number', (number 1).

Of these, five sold over a million copies. Most of Mitchell's US hits were also successful in the UK, where he was highly popular, touring regularly, appearing at the London Palladium for the first time in 1952, and in the 1954 Royal Variety Performance. Additional chart entries in the UK included 'Pretty Little Black-Eyed Susie', 'Look At That Girl' (number 1), 'Cloud Lucky Seven', 'Cuff Of My Shirt', 'Dime And A Dollar' and 'Chicka Boom'. The latter was featured in Mitchell's first movie, a 3-D musical, *Those Redheads From Seattle* (1953), with Rhonda Fleming, Gene Barry and Teresa Brewer. Brewer and Mitchell proved a pleasant combination on the Johnny Mercer/Hoagy Carmichael song, 'I Guess It Was You All The Time'. In 1954, Mitchell appeared with Gene Barry again, in the spoof western movie, *Red Garters*, which also starred Rosemary Clooney, and contained another Mitchell 'special', 'A Dime And A Dollar'. In contrast to the somewhat perky style, so effective on his singles, some of Mitchell's albums revealed him to be an excellent ballad singer, particularly *A Guy In Love*, with Glenn Osser and his Orchestra, which contained standards such as 'The Moon Got In My Eyes', 'Allegheny Moon', 'East Of The Sun' and 'East Side Of Heaven'. *Sunshine Guitar*, with its guitar choir, was 'carefree and breezy, full of infectious gaiety', with a country 'feel' on several of the numbers. With the 60s beat boom imminent, Mitchell's contract with Columbia ended in 1962, and he released some singles on the Joy and Reprise labels. In 1967, he signed for the Nashville-based Starday label, but shortly after his *Travelling Shoes* and *Singing Up A Storm* were released, the company went out of business. During some periods of the 60s and 70s, Mitchell ceased performing. He issued only a few tracks on his own GMI label - partly because of poor health and serious alcoholic problems.

In 1979, he toured Australia, and started to play nightclubs in the USA. In the 80s he made several appearances in the UK, and released the old Elvis Presley favourite, 'Always On My Mind', backed with 'Wind Beneath My Wings' from the Bette Midler hit movie, *Beaches*. This was followed by *Garden In The Rain*, a set of British numbers which included 'My Kind Of Girl', 'Yesterday', 'I Hadn't Anyone Till You' and Noel Coward's theme tune, 'I'll See You Again'. In the 90s, the old hits were still being repackaged and sold to a younger audience following Guy's appearance in John Byrne's UK television drama, *Your Cheatin' Heart*, in 1990. Mitchell typified 50s pop more than any other performer, and his catalogue of hits remains formidable. His work is destined to endure.

Selected albums: *A Guy In Love* (1958), *Sunshine Guitar* (1961), *A Garden In The Rain* (1985). Compilations: *The Best Of Guy Mitchell* (1968), *An American Legend - 16 Greatest Hits* (1977), *Hit Singles 1950-1960* (1981), *20 Golden Pieces* (1984), *Singing The Blues* (1986), *Portrait Of A Song Stylist* (1989), *16 Most Requested Songs* (1992).

Modern Jazz Quartet

In 1951, four musicians who had previously played together in the Dizzy Gillespie big band formed a small recording group. Known as the Milt Jackson Quartet, the group consisted of Jackson (vibraphone), John Lewis (piano), Ray Brown (bass), and Kenny Clarke (drums). Brown's place was soon taken by Percy Heath, and by the following year, the group had adopted the name, Modern Jazz Quartet. Although initially only a recording group, they then began playing concert engagements. In 1955, Clarke dropped out to be replaced by Connie Kay. The new line-up of Jackson, Lewis, Heath and Kay continued performing as a full-time ensemble for the next few years, later reducing their collective commitments to several months each year. Seen as both a black response to the intellectualism of the Dave Brubeck quartet and New York's answer to west-coast cool jazz, the MJQ were both very popular and very controversial, their detractors claiming that their music was too delicate and too cerebral. Whatever the case, there was certainly no denying that the group brought the dignity and professionalism of a classical quartet to their jazz performances. In 1974, the MJQ was disbanded, but reformed once more in 1981 for a concert tour of Japan. The success of this comeback convinced the members to reunite on a semi-permanent basis, which they did in the following year. Since 1982 they have continued to play concert and festival dates. Among the most sophisticated of all bop ensembles, the MJQ's directing influence has always been Lewis, whose sober performing and composing style was never more apparent than in this context. Lewis's interest in classical music has also been influential in MJQ performances, thus placing the group occasionally, and possibly misleadingly, on the fringes of third-stream jazz. The playing of Heath and Kay in this, as in most other settings in which they work, is distinguished by its subtle swing. Of the four, Jackson is the most musically volatile, and the restraints placed upon him in the MJQ create intriguing formal tensions which are, in jazz terms, one of the most exciting aspects of the group's immaculately played, quietly serious music.

Albums: *Django* (1953), *Concorde* (1955), *The MJQ At Music Inn* (1956), *Fontessa* (1956), *Live* (1956), *One Never Knows* (1957), *Third Stream Music* (1957), *Plus* (1957-71), *Odds Against Tomorrow* (1959), *European Concert* (1960), *The Comedy* (1962), *The Sheriff* (1963), *A Quartet Is A Quartet Is A Quartet* (1963), *Blues At Carnegie Hall* (1966), *Space* (1969), *The Legendary Profile* (1972), *The Last Concert* (1974), *In Memoriam* (1977), *Together Again!* (1982), *Together Again!: The MJQ 1984* (1984), *The Best Of The MJQ* (1984-85), *Under The Jasmine Tree* (1993).

Monotones

Formed in 1955 in Newark, New Jersey, USA, the Monotones recorded one of the most memorable doo-wop novelty songs of the 50s, 'Book Of Love'. The group was a sextet, Warren Davis, George Malone, Charles Patrick, Frank Smith, and John and Warren Ryanes. They had sung in the same church choir as Dionne Warwick and Cissy Houston before forming their own group. In 1956, they appeared on the *Ted Mack's Amateur Hour* television programme, singing the Cadillacs' 'Zoom'. They won first prize and began to think more seriously about a career in music. Inspired by a television commercial for toothpaste ('You'll wonder where the yellow went when you brush your teeth with Pepsodent'), Patrick, Malone and Davis wrote 'Book Of Love' to a similar melody. They recorded it at Bell Studio in New York and it was released on the small Mascot label, a subsidiary of Hull Records. It was then picked up by Argo Records for national distribution and ultimately reached number 5 in the USA. The group was touring when their record entered the charts, and months went by before they had a chance to record a follow-up. A single called 'Tom Foolery' was released but failed to chart; the third, 'The Legend Of Sleepy Hollow', was a fine record and is still played on doo-wop radio programmes today, but also failed to chart in its own time. After a few more singles, the Monotones gave up, although some of the original members still perform under that name in the 90s. (The two Ryanes brothers have died). The Monotones never recorded an album.

Monroe, Marilyn

b. Norma Jean Mortenson, 1 June 1926, Los Angeles, California, USA, d. 5 August 1962, Brentwood, California, USA. As well as being a talented comedienne and the number 1 sex symbol in movies during the 50s, Monroe proved to be an appealing interpreter of flirtacious ballads in several of her most popular films. As one of the *Ladies Of The Chorus* (1949), she made a promising start with Lester Lee and Allan Roberts's 'Every Baby Needs A Da-Da-Daddy', which, with its reference to 'Tiffany's', was a precursor to one of her most celebrated performances a few years later, when the same New York store cropped up 'Diamonds Are A Girl's Best Friend', from Jule Styne and Leo Robin's score for *Gentlemen Prefer Blondes* (1953). In that film Monroe duetted with another of Hollywood's top glamour girls, Jane Russell, on 'Two Little Girls From Little Rock', 'Bye Bye Baby' and a Hoagy Carmichael/Harold Adamson number, 'When Loves Goes Wrong'. Co-starred with Robert Mitchum in *River Of No Return* (1954), Monroe's role as a saloon singer conveniently gave her the opportunity to put over the title song and 'I'm Gonna File My Claim', amongst others, and, in the same year, she registered strongly with a bundle of Irving Berlin numbers in *There's No Business Like Show Business*. These included 'A Man Chases A Girl' (with Donald O'Connor), 'After You Get What You Want You Don't Want It', 'Heatwave', 'Lazy' and 'You'd Be Surprised'. In 1959 she made what was to become her most commercially successful film - arguably the highlight of her career. The classic *Some Like It Hot*, with Tony Curtis, Jack Lemmon and Joe E. (nobody's perfect) Brown, contained some of Monroe's most effective vocal peformances, such as 'I'm Through With Love', 'I Wanna Be Loved By You' and 'Running Wild'. She sang for the last time on screen in *Let's Make Love* (1960). Apart from contributing the film's highspot, a compelling version of 'My Heart Belongs To Daddy', Monroe duetted with a couple of European heart-throbs, Yves Montand and Frankie Vaughan, on Sammy Cahn and Jimmy Van Heusen's 'Specialization', 'Incurably Romantic' and the title song. Her final performance, a sultry rendering of 'Happy Birthday Mr. President' and 'Thanks For The Memory', was given in May 1962 for President Kennedy's birthday celebrations in Madison Square Garden. Just over two months later she died, in mysterious circumstances, at the age of 36. One of the musical selections chosen for her funeral service was a

Moonglows

recording of 'Over The Rainbow', sung by Judy Garland, another show business legend who met a tragic end. Since her death, it has been estimated that over 100 Monroe biographies have been published. She was also the subject of several songs, the most famous being Elton John's 'Crying In the Wind'. Others included James Cunningham's 'Norma Jean Wants To Be A Movie Star' and 'Elvis And Marilyn' by Leon Russell.
Album: *Marilyn Monroe -The Complete Recordings* (1988, 2-CD set).

Moonglows

This R&B vocal group was formed in Cleveland, Ohio, USA, in 1952. If there were any group that best signalled the birth of rock 'n' roll - by which R&B emerged out of its black subculture into mainstream teen culture - it was the Moonglows. The group's career paralleled that of their mentor, legendary disc jockey Alan Freed, who in his rise in rock 'n' roll made the Moonglows the mainstays of his radio programmes, motion pictures, and stage shows. Their membership comprised lead singer Bobby Lester (b. 13 January 1930, Louisville, Kentucky, USA, d. 15 October 1980), Harvey Fuqua (b. 27 July 1929, Louisville, Kentucky, USA), Alexander 'Pete' Graves (b. 17 April 1930, Cleveland, Ohio, USA), and Prentiss Barnes (b. 1921, Cleveland, Ohio, USA). After recording for Freed's Champagne label in 1953, the group signed with Chicago-based Chance,

where the group managed to get a few regional hits, most notably a cover of Doris Day's 'Secret Love' in 1954. Joining the group at this time was guitarist Billy Johnson (b. 1924 Hartford, Connecticut, USA, d. 1987). Freed used his connections to sign the Moonglows to a stronger Chicago label, the fast-rising Chess Records, and the group enjoyed a major hit with 'Sincerely' (number 1 R&B/number 20 pop 1954).
Using a novel technique they called 'blow harmony', other great hits followed: 'Most Of All' (number 5 R&B 1955), 'We Go Together' (number 9 R&B 1956), 'See Saw' (number 6 R&B/number 25 pop 1956), all which featured Lester on lead; a remake of Percy Mayfield's 'Please Send Me Someone To Love' (number 5 R&B/number 73 pop 1957) and 'Ten Commandments Of Love' (number 9 R&B/number 22 pop 1958), which featured Fuqua on lead. The original Moonglows disbanded in 1958, and Fuqua put together a new group that included Marvin Gaye. In 1960 Fuqua disbanded this group and he and Gaye went to Detroit to work in the industry there. Fuqua worked with Berry Gordy's sister, Gwen Gordy on the Anna label and Gaye joined Berry Gordy's Motown operation. Fuqua carved out a very successful career as a producer and record executive, working with Motown artists in the 60s and a stable of Louisville artists in the 70s on the RCA label.
Albums: *Look! It's The Moonglows* (1959), *The*

Jane Morgan

Return Of The Moonglows (1972). Compilations: *The Best Of Bobby Lester And The Moonglows* (1962), *The Flamingos Meet The Moonglows* (1962), *The Moonglows* (1964), *Moonglows* (1976), *Their Greatest Sides* (1984).

Morgan, Jane

b. Jane Currier, Boston, Massachusetts, USA. A popular singer with a clear, strong voice and an ablility to sing in several languages, Morgan was accepted in many parts of the world during the 50s and 60s. Raised in Florida, she trained as a lyric soprano at the Juilliard School of Music in New York, supplementing her income by singing in night-clubs. At one of them, she was spotted by the French impresario, Bernard Hilda, who offered her a contract to sing in Paris. Within weeks of arriving in France she became a major attraction and, during the next few years became established throughout Europe. On her return to the USA, she was billed as 'The American Girl From Paris', and appeared successfully on television and in night-clubs. Signed for Kapp Records, she had a minor hit in 1956 with 'Two Different Worlds', one of the several tracks she recorded with pianist Roger Williams.

In the following year she had a million seller with 'Fascination', an old French number, 'Valtse Tzigane', with an English lyric by Dick Manning, which was the theme for the Cary Grant-Audrey Hepburn movie, *Love In The Afternoon*. Despite the rock 'n' roll revolution, she continued to be successful, especially in Europe, and in 1958, she had a UK number 1 with Gilbert Becaud and Carl Sigman's 'The Day The Rains Came'. Her French version of the song was on the b-side. She had several more hits in the early 60s including 'If Only I Could Live My Life Again', 'With Open Arms' and 'Romantica'. In 1957 her album, *Fascination*, made the US Top 20, and her other releases, through the 60s, included *All The Way, Something Old, Something New, Great Songs From Great Shows Of The Century* (two volumes), *Jane In Spain, Ballads Of Lady Jane, At The Coconut Grove, Jane Morgan Time, Love Makes The World Go 'Round, In My Style, In Gold, Kiss Tomorrow, Fresh Flavour* and more, including several 'Greatest Hits' compilations. Subsequently, Morgan married Jerry Weintraub, who was instrumental in Elvis Presley's re-emergence in the early 70s, and managed several top US singers such as John Denver.

Morley, Angela

In the 50s, 60s and into the 70s, Wally Stott was a highly respected conductor, arranger and composer on the UK music scene. In the early 70s he underwent a sex-change operation, and was subsequently know professionally as Angela Morley. Stott was born in 1924 in Sheffield, England. He attended the same Mexboro school as Tony Mercer, who went on to become one of the principal singers with the *Black And White Minstrel Show*. Mercer sang and played the piano accordion, while Stott concentrated on the saxophone. On leaving school, they each spent some time with Archie's Juveniles and Oscar Rabin's Band. Stott's route to Rabin was via the bands of Billy Merrin and Bram Martin. By 1944, after some years with the Rabin Band, Stott was leading the saxophone section on alto, and had become the band's sole arranger: a great future was already being forecast for him. Stott's next move was to Geraldo, with whom he stayed for about four years, leaving in late 1948 to 'pursue arranging and film music work, which he is to make his future career'. He still managed to find the time to play the saxophone for outfits such as Jack Nathan's Coconut Grove Orchestra. In the early 50s Stott joined Philips Records, and soon became one of their key arrangers, along with Peter Knight and Ivor Raymonde. During the next 20 years he arranged and conducted for some of the UK's most popular artists, such as Frankie Vaughan ('Green Door', 'The Garden Of Eden' and 'The Heart Of A Man'), Anne Shelton ('Lay Down Your Arms' and *My Heart Sings*), Harry Secombe ('This Is My Song'), the Beverley Sisters ('Somebody Bad Stole De Wedding Bell' and 'Happy Wanderer'), Roy Castle (*Newcomer*), Ronnie Carroll ('Say Wonderful Things' and Carroll Calling), the Kaye Sisters ('Paper Roses'), Shirley Bassey ('Banana Boat Song' and 'As I Love You'), Muriel Smith ('Hold Me, Thrill Me, Kiss Me'), the Polka Dots (*Nice Work & You Can Buy It*) and many more, plus a few 'foreigners', too, as on *Mel Tormé Meets The British* (1959). Stott also made several of his own instrumental albums, sometimes augmented by a vocal chorus. He began writing music early in his career, and his first significant piece came to light in November 1954, when *Hancock's Half Hour* began. It proved to be one of BBC Radio's most popular programmes, later moving to television, and it's opening theme, played on a tuba over Tony Hancock's stuttering introduction, was composed by Stott. He also wrote and arranged the show's instrumental links, and conducted the orchestra for many other radio programmes, including *The Last Goon Show Of All*. In the late

60s and early 70s, Stott wrote the music for several films, including *The Looking Glass War*, *Captain Nemo And The Underwater City* and *When Eight Bells Toll*, and for television productions such as *Hugh And I*, and the *The Maladjusted Busker*. Around that time, credits began to be given in the name of Angela Morley, and these include two Academy Award nominations, for her arrangements of Alan Jay Lerner and Frederick Loewe's score for *The Little Prince* (1974), and the Richard M. and Robert B. Sherman's score for *The Slipper And The Rose* (1977). Morley also composed for the animated feature, *Watership Down*, the Italian production, *La Colina Dei Comali*, and for televison films such as *Friendships*, *Secrets And Lies*, *Madame X*, *Summer Girl*, *Two Marriages* and *Threesome* (1984). Most of this work has been completed in the USA, where Morley is reported to have been living for most of last 20 years.

Selected albums: *Wally Stott Tribute To George Gershwin* (1955), *Tribute To Irving Berlin* (1956), *Tribute To Jerome Kern* (1957), *London Pride* (1959), *Chorale In Concert* (1967), *Christmas By The Fireside* (1969).

Mudlarks

Soprano Mary Mudd, baritone Fred Mudd and tenor Jeff Mudd were the Mudlarks: a clean-cut family pop trio from Bedford, Bedfordshire, England. They started singing in public as the Mudd Trio in 1951 when they were just 12, 14 and 16 years old. Discovered by disc jockey David Jacobs and produced on Columbia Records by Norrie Paramor, they had a hit in 1958 with their second single, 'Lollipop', a cover of the Chordettes' US hit. Their follow-up 'Book Of Love', originally by the Monotones, also made the UK Top 10. They were often seen on the pioneering UK television series, *6.5 Special*, and won the *New Musical Express* poll award as Top British Vocal Group for both 1958 and 1959. Jeff was called up by the army in early 1959 and David Lane replaced him until his return two years later. One of the few UK pop groups in the 50s, they recorded several more covers of US hits without further chart success.

Murray, Ruby

b. 29 March 1935, Belfast, Northern Ireland. One of the most popular singers in the UK during the 50s, Murray toured Ulster as a child singer in various variety shows and, after being spotted by producer Richard Afton, made her television debut at the age of 12. Stringent Irish laws regarding child performers held her back for two years, and she returned to school in Belfast until she was 14. In 1954, she travelled to London in comedian Tommy Morgan's touring revue, *Mrs. Mulligan's Hotel*, and was again seen by Afton, at the famous Metropolitan Theatre, Edgware Road. He offered her the part of resident singer on BBC television's *Quite Contrary*, replacing Joan Regan, who was about to leave. Signed to UK Columbia by recording manager and musical director, Ray Martin, Murray's first release, 'Heartbeat', made the UK Top 5 in 1954, and was followed by 'Softly, Softly'. The latter reached number 1 in 1955, and became an ideal theme song, reflecting her shy, indigenous image. In the early part of 1955, Murray had five singles in the Top 20 at the same time, an extraordinary feat that lasted until the emergence of Madonna in the 80s. Murray's hits included 'Happy Days And Lonely Nights', 'Let Me Go Lover', 'If Anyone Finds This, I Love You' (with Anne Warren), 'Evermore', 'I'll Come When You Call', 'Real Love', 'Goodbye Jimmy, Goodbye' and 'You Are My First Love'. The last number was featured in the film musical, *It's Great To Be Young* in which Murray dubbed the vocal for actress Dorothy Bromiley. Murray's own film appearances included the comedy, *A Touch Of The Sun*, with Frankie Howerd and Dennis Price. During a hectic period in the mid-50s, she had her own television show, starred at the London Palladium in *Painting The Town* with Norman Wisdom, appeared in a Royal Command Performance, and toured the USA, Malta and North Africa. In 1957, while appearing in a summer season at Blackpool, she met Bernie Burgess, a member of the vocal group, the Jones Boys. They married, in secret, 10 days later. Burgess became her personal manager and, during the early 60s, they toured as a double act. In 1970, Murray had some success with 'Change Your Mind', and released an album with the same title, which included contemporary songs such as 'Raindrops Keep Falling On My Head', and re-vamped some of her hits. *Ruby Murray's EMI Years* included other songs regularly featured in her act such as 'Mr. Wonderful', 'Scarlet Ribbons' and 'It's The Irish In Me'. In the 90s, based in Torquay, Devon with her second husband, impresario Ray Lamar, she was still performing in cabaret and nostalgia shows with other stars of the 50s.

Selected albums: *Irish And Proud Of It* (1962), with various artists *St. Patrick's Day* (1964). Compilation: *Ruby Murray's EMI Years* (1989).

Ruby Murray

Music Man

This stage musical came to Broadway on 19 December 1957 after a difficult pre-opening history. With book, music and lyrics by Meredith Willson, the show had undergone several rewrites but the author's persistence paid off and on opening night the audience was caught up in the revivalist enthusiasm of the show's characters. Telling the story of Harold Hill, an itinerant con-man who persuades the citizens of River City that he can teach their children to play musical instruments even though the instruments, which he sells them, are nowhere in sight, *The Music Man* was filled with engaging old-fashioned charm. The songs ranged from the soulful 'Goodnight, My Someone' and 'Till There Was You' to the rousing 'Seventy-Six Trombones', by way of 'Marian The Librarian', 'The Sadder-But-Wiser Girl', 'Pickalittle', 'Gary, Indiana', 'Wells Fargo Wagon', 'Piano Lesson' and 'Lida Rose'. In casting film actor Robert Preston, who had never before danced or sung, in the central role of Harold Hill, the producers took a big chance because many of Willson's songs were far more complex than they appeared on the surface. As it turned out, it was inspired casting, with Preston ably charming his way through a minefield of counter melodies, rhythmic dialogue and strutting dance routines to earn rapturous applause and critical praise. Co-starring with Preston was Barbara Cook as Marian Paroo; other cast members included David Burns, Iggie Wolfington, Helen Raymond and Pert Kelton. The show enjoyed success with several touring companies and was staged in Europe including a London production in 1961. The show was revived on Broadway in 1965 and 1980. The 1962 film version starred Shirley Jones as Marian and, thankfully, Robert Preston, thus allowing millions to appreciate the exuberance of his magnificent, larger-than-life performance as Professor Harold Hill.

My Fair Lady

One of the most successful shows in the history of American musical theatre, *My Fair Lady* opened to rave reviews on 15 March 1956. Based upon George Bernard Shaw's play *Pygmalion*, the story follows attempts by Professor Henry Higgins to transform a Cockney flower girl, Eliza Doolittle, into a society lady simply through teaching her the correct way to speak. In the course of the story Higgins and Eliza fall in love and all ends happily, if a little differently from the way Shaw ended his play. With book, music and lyrics by Alan J. Lerner

and Frederick Loewe, the show was awash with marvellous tunes and the superb staging and excellent performances from a large cast led critics into an explosion of hyperbole. Words like 'legendary' and 'genius' became commonplace in their attempts to describe the show to their readers. The show starred Rex Harrison and Julie Andrews as Higgins and Eliza, with a strong supporting cast including Stanley Holloway, John Michael King, Robert Coote and Cathleen Nesbitt. The songs from the show, many of which became minor and in some cases major hits, included 'Wouldn't It Be Loverly?', 'The Rain In Spain', 'I Could Have Danced All Night', 'On The Street Where You Live', 'Get Me To The Church On Time', 'With A Little Bit Of Luck', 'Show Me', 'I'm An Ordinary Man', 'Hymn To Him', 'Why Can't The English?' and 'I've Grown Accustomed to Her Face'. *My Fair Lady* ran on Broadway for six-and-a-half years, notching up 2,717 performances. Numerous touring companies took the show across the USA and productions were staged in more than 20 other countries. The London production, which starred Harrison, Andrews, Holloway and Coote, was also massively successful and played for five years. At the time of its Broadway opening, *My Fair Lady* had swept the board of Tony Awards, and the 1964 film version did the same with the Oscars, taking eight, including Best Film and, for Harrison, Best Actor. Holloway also appeared in the film but the role of Eliza went to Audrey Hepburn whose songs were dubbed by Marni Nixon. The original cast recording and the film soundtrack became best-sellers. The American musical historian David Ewen suggests that in one way or another *My Fair Lady* has generated approximately $800 million.

N

Nelson, Ricky

b. Eric Hilliard Nelson, 8 May 1940, Teaneck, New Jersey, USA, d. 31 December 1985, De Kalb, Texas, USA. Nelson came from a showbusiness family and his parents had sung in bands during the 30s and 40s. They had their own US radio show,

The Adventures Of Ozzie And Harriet, soon transferred to television, in which Ricky and his brother David appeared. By 1957 Nelson embarked on a recording career, with the million selling, double-sided 'I'm Walkin''/'A Teenager's Romance'. A third hit soon followed with 'You're My One And Only Love'. A switch from the label Verve to Imperial saw Nelson enjoy further success with the rockabilly 'Be-Bop Baby'. In 1958 Nelson formed a full-time group for live work and recordings, which included James Burton (guitar), James Kirkland (later replaced by Joe Osborn) (bass), Gene Garf (piano) and Richie Frost (drums). Early that year Nelson enjoyed his first transatlantic hit with 'Stood Up' and registered his first US chart topper with 'Poor Little Fool'. His early broadcasting experience was put to useful effect when he starred in the Howard Hawks movie western, *Rio Bravo* (1959), alongside John Wayne and Dean Martin. Nelson's singles continued to chart regularly and it says much for the quality of his work that the b-sides were often as well known as the a-sides. Songs such as 'Believe What You Say', 'Never Be Anyone Else But You', 'It's Late', 'Sweeter Than You', 'Just A Little Too Much' and 'I Wanna Be Loved' showed that Nelson was equally adept at singing ballads and uptempo material. One of his greatest moments as a pop singer occurred in the spring of 1961 when he issued the million-selling 'Travelin' Man' backed with the exuberant Gene Pitney composition 'Hello Mary Lou'. Shortly after the single topped the US charts, Nelson celebrated his 21st birthday and announced that he was changing his performing name from Ricky to Rick.

Several more pop hits followed, most notably 'Young World', 'Teenage Idol', 'It's Up To You', 'String Along' (his first for his new label, Decca), 'Fools Rush In' and 'For You'. With the emergence of the beat boom, Nelson's clean-cut pop was less in demand and in 1966 he switched to country music. His early albums in this vein featured compositions from such artists as Willie Nelson, Glen Campbell, Tim Hardin, Harry Nilsson and Randy Newman.

In 1969 Nelson formed a new outfit the Stone Canyon Band featuring former Poco member Randy Meisner (bass), Allen Kemp (guitar), Tom Brumley (steel guitar) and Pat Shanahan (drums). A version of Bob Dylan's 'She Belongs To Me' brought Nelson back into the US charts and a series of strong, often underrated albums followed. A performance at Madison Square Garden in late 1971 underlined Nelson's difficulties at the time.

Although he had recently issued the accomplished *Rick Sings Nelson*, on which he wrote every track, the audience were clearly more interested in hearing his early 60s hits. Nelson responded by composing the sarcastic 'Garden Party', which reaffirmed his determination to go his own way. The single, ironically, went on to sell a million and was his last hit record. After parting with the Stone Canyon Band in 1974, Nelson's recorded output declined, but he continued to tour extensively. On 31 December 1985, a chartered plane carrying him to a concert date in Dallas caught fire and crashed near De Kalb, Texas. Nelson's work deserves a place in rock history as he was one of the few 'good looking kids' from the early 60s who had a strong voice which, coupled with exemplary material, remains durable.

Albums: *Teen Time* (1957), *Ricky* (1957), *Ricky Nelson* (1958), *Ricky Sings Again* (1959), *Songs By Ricky* (1959), *More Songs By Ricky* (1960), *Rick Is 21* (1961), *Album Seven By Rick* (1962), *A Long Vacation* (1963), *For Your Sweet Love* (1963), *Ricky Sings For You* (1964), *The Very Thought Of You* (1964), *Spotlight On Rick* (1965), *Best Always* (1965), *Love And Kisses* (1966), *Bright Lights And Country Music* (1966), *Country Fever* (1967), *On The Flip-Side* (1967, film soundtrack), *Another Side Of Rick* (1969), *In Concert* (1970), *Rick Sings Nelson* (1970), *Rudy The Fifth* (1971), *Garden Party* (1972), *Windfall* (1974), *Intakes* (1977), *Playing To Win* (1981). Compilations: *It's Up To You* (1963), *Million Sellers* (1964), *The Very Best Of Rick Nelson* (1970), *Legendary Masters* (1972), *The Singles Album 1963-1976* (1977), *The Singles Album 1957-63* (1979), *Rockin' With Ricky* (1984), *String Along With Rick* (1984), *The Best Of Ricky Nelson* (1985), *All The Best* (1986).

Further reading: *Ricky Nelson*, Joel Selvin.

Newley, Anthony

b. 24 September 1931, London, England. After attending the Italia Conti Stage School Newley worked as a child actor in several films, including *The Little Ballerina*, *Vice Versa*, and in 1948 played the Artful Dodger in David Lean's successful version of *Oliver Twist*. He made his London theatrical debut in John Cranko's revue, *Cranks*, in 1955, and had character parts in well over 20 films before he was cast as rock 'n' roll star Jeep Jackson in *Idle On Parade* in 1959. Newley's four-track vocal EP, and his version of the film's hit ballad, Jerry Lordan's 'I've Waited So Long', started a three-year UK chart run which included 'Personality', 'If She Should Come To You', 'And

Anthony Newley

The Heavens Cried', the novelty numbers 'Pop Goes The Weasel' and 'Strawberry Fair' and two UK number 1 hits, 'Why' and Lionel Bart's, 'Do You Mind'. Newley also made the album charts in 1960 with his set of old standards, *Love Is A Now And Then Thing*. He made later appearances in the charts with *Tony* (1961), and the comedy album *Fool Britannia* (1963), on which he was joined by his wife, Joan Collins and Peter Sellers. In 1961 Newley collaborated with Leslie Bricusse (b. 29 January 1931, London, England) on the off-beat stage musical, *Stop The World - I Want To Get Off*. Newley also directed, and played Littlechap, the small man who fights the system. The show, which stayed in the West End for 16 months, ran for over 500 performances on Broadway, and was filmed in 1966. It produced several hit songs, including 'What Kind Of Fool Am I', 'Once In A Lifetime' and 'Gonna Build A Mountain'.

In 1964 Bricusse and Newley wrote the lyric to John Barry's music for Shirley Bassey to sing over the titles of the James Bond movie, *Goldfinger*. The team's next musical show in 1965, *The Roar Of The Greasepaint - The Smell Of The Crowd*, with comedian Norman Wisdom in the lead, toured the north of England but did not make the West End. When it went to Broadway Newley took over (co-starring with Cyril Ritchard), but was not able to match the success of *Stop The World*, despite a score containing such numbers as 'Who Can I Turn To?', 'A Wonderful Day Like Today', 'The Joker', 'Look At That Face' and 'This Dream'. In 1967 Newley appeared with Rex Harrison and Richard Attenborough in the film musical *Doctor Dolittle*, with script and songs by Bricusse. Despite winning an Oscar for 'Talk To The Animals', the film was considered an expensive flop, as was Newley's own movie project in 1969, a pseudo-autobiographical sex-fantasy entitled *Can Heironymus Merkin Ever Forget Mercy Humppe And Find True Happiness?* Far more successful, in 1971, was *Willy Wonka And The Chocolate Factory*, a Roald Dahl story with music and lyrics by Bricusse and Newley. Sammy Davis Jnr. had a million-selling record with one of the songs, 'The Candy Man'. They also wrote several songs for the 1971 NBC television musical adaptation of *Peter Pan*, starring Mia Farrow and Danny Kaye. Bricusse and Newley's last authentic stage musical, *The Good Old Bad Old Days*, opened in London in 1972 and had a decent run of 309 performances. Newley sang some of the songs, including 'The People Tree', on his own *Ain't It Funny*. In his cabaret act he continually bemoans the fact that he has not had a hit with one of his own songs. A major 1989 London revival of *Stop The World - I Want To Get Off*, directed by Newley, and in which he also appeared, closed after five weeks, and, in the same year, he was inducted into the Songwriters' Hall Of Fame, along with Leslie Bricusse. In 1991, Newley appeared on UK television with his ex-wife, Joan Collins, in Noel Coward's *Private Lives*, which included the famous 'Red Peppers' segment. In the following year, having lived in California for some years, Newley announced that he was returning to Britain, and bought a house there to share with his 90-year-old mother. In the same year, he also appeared in England, at the Alexandra Theatre, Birmingham, in a successful limited run of the musical, *Scrooge*, which Bricusse adapted for the stage from the 1970 film.

Albums: *Love Is A Now And Then Thing* (1960), *Tony* (1961), *Stop The World - I Want To Get Off* (1962, London Cast), with Peter Sellers, Joan Collins *Fool Britannia* (1963), *The Roar Of The Greasepaint - The Smell Of The Crowd* (1965, Broadway Cast). Compilations: *The Romantic World Of Anthony Newley* (1970), *The Lonely World Of Anthony Newley* (1972), *The Singer And His Songs* (1978), *Anthony Newley: Mr. Personality* (1985), *Greatest Hits* (1991).

O'Day, Anita

b. Anita Colton, 18 October 1919, Kansas City, Missouri, USA. As Anita Colton, in her early teens she scraped a living as a professional Walkathon contestant (marathon dancer). During this period she changed her surname to O'Day. Along with other contestants she was encouraged to sing and during one Walkathon was accompanied by Erskine Tate's orchestra, an event which made her think that singing might be a better route to showbiz fame than dancing. By her late teens she had switched to singing and was told by Gene Krupa, who heard her at a Chicago club, that if he ever had a slot for her he would call. In the meantime she failed an audition with Benny

Anita O'Day

Goodman, who complained that she did not stick to the melody, and upset Raymond Scott, who disliked her scatting (vocalese) - actually, she had momentarily forgotten the words of the song. Eventually Krupa called and O'Day joined the band early in 1941, just a few weeks before Roy Eldridge was also hired. The combination of Krupa, Eldridge and O'Day was potent and the band, already popular, quickly became one of the best of the later swing era. O'Day helped to give the band some of its hit records, notably 'Let Me Off Uptown', (also a feature for Eldridge), 'Alreet', 'Kick It' and 'Bolero At The Savoy'. After Krupa folded in 1943, O'Day went with Stan Kenton, recording hits with 'And Her Tears Flowed Like Wine' and 'The Lady In Red'. In 1945 she was back with the reformed Krupa band for more hit records including, 'Opus No. 1'. In 1946 she went solo and thereafter remained a headliner. She made a number of fine albums in the 50s, including a set with Ralph Burns in 1952, and made a memorable appearance at the 1958 Newport Jazz Festival. This performance, at which she sang 'Tea For Two' and 'Sweet Georgia Brown', resplendent in cartwheel hat, gloves and stoned out of her mind, was captured on film in *Jazz On A Summer's Day* (1958). Drug addiction severely damaged O'Day's life for many years, although she continued to turn out excellent albums, including *Cool Heat* with Jimmy Giuffre, *Trav'lin' Light* with Johnny Mandel and Barney Kessel and *Time For Two* with Cal Tjader. Extensive touring, high living and a punishing life style (not to mention a dozen years of heroin addiction) eventually brought collapse, and she almost died in 1966. Eventually clear of drugs, O'Day continued to tour, playing clubs, concerts and festivals around the world. She recorded less frequently, but thanks to forming her own record company, Emily, in the early 70s many of the albums that she did make were entirely under her control. In 1985 she played Carnegie Hall in celebration of 50 years in the business, and towards the end of the decade appeared in the UK at Ronnie Scott's club and at the Leeds Castle Jazz Festival in Kent. O'Day's singing voice is throaty and she sings with great rhythmic drive. Her scat singing and the liberties she takes on songs, especially when singing up-tempo, result in some remarkable vocal creations. In her hey-days her diction was exceptional and even at the fastest tempos she articulated clearly and precisely. On ballads she is assured and distinctive, and although very much her own woman, her phrasing suggests the influence of Billie Holiday. On stage she displays enormous rapport with musicians and audience, factors which make some of her studio recordings rather less rewarding than those made in concert. Late in her career some of her performances were marred by problems of pitch but, live at least, she compensated through sheer force of personality. Her autobiography makes compulsive reading.

Albums: *Specials* (1951), *Singing And Swinging* (1953), *Collate* (1953), *Anita O'Day* (1954), *Anita O'Day Sings Jazz* (1955), *An Evening With Anita O'Day* (1956), *Anita* (1956), *Pick Yourself Up* (1956), *The Lady Is A Tramp* (1956), *Anita Sings The Most* (1957), *Anita Sings The Winners* (1958), *Anita O'Day At Mr Kelly's* (1958), *Cool Heat* (1959), *Anita O'Day Swings Cole Porter With Billy May* (1959), *Waiter, Make Mine Blues* (1960), *Incomparable!* (1960), *Anita O'Day And Billy May Swing Rodgers And Hart* (1960), *Trav'lin' Light* (1961), *All The Sad Young Men* (1961), *Time For Two* (1962), *Anita O'Day And The Three Sounds* (1962), *Anita O'Day In Tokyo 1963* (1963), *Once Upon A Summertime* (c.1969), *Live At The Berlin Jazz Festival* (1970), *Anita '75* (1975), *My Ship* (1975), *Live In Tokyo* (1975), *Live At Mingo's* (1976), *Skylark* (1978), *Angel Eyes* (1978), *Mello' Day* (1979), *Live At The City, Vols 1 & 2* (1979), *Misty* (1981), *A Song For You* (c.1984), *Wave* (1986), *In A Mellow Tone* (1989). Compilations: *Anita O'Day Sings With Gene Krupa* (1941-42 recordings), *Singin' And Swingin' With Anita O'Day* (1947 recordings), *Hi Ho Trailus Boot Whip* (1947 recordings), *Anita O'Day 1949-1950* (1949-50 recordings), *Tea For Two* (1958-66 recordings), *The Big Band Sessions* (1959-61 recordings).

Further reading: *High Times, Hard Times*, Anita O'Day with George Eells.

Otis, Johnny

b. 28 December 1921, Vallejo, California, USA. Born into a family of Greek immigrants, was raised in a largely black neighbourhood where he thoroughly absorbed the prevailing culture and lifestyle. He began playing drums in his mid-teens and worked for a while with some of the locally-based jazz bands, including, in 1941, Lloyd Hunter's orchestra. In 1943 he gained his first name-band experience when he joined Harlan Leonard for a short spell. Some sources suggest that, during the difficult days when the draft was pulling musicians out of bands all across the USA, Otis then replaced another ex-Leonard drummer Jesse Price in the Stan Kenton band. In the mid-40s Otis also recorded with several jazz groups including, Illinois Jacquet's all-star band and a septet led by Lester Young, which also featured Howard McGhee and Willie Smith. In 1945 Otis formed his own big band in Los Angeles. In an early edition assembled for a recording session, he leaned strongly towards a blues-based jazz repertoire and hired such musicians as Eli Robinson, Paul Quinichette, Teddy Buckner, Bill Doggett, Curtis Counce and singer Jimmy Rushing. This particular date produced a major success in 'Harlem Nocturne'. He also led a small band, including McGhee and Teddy Edwards, on a record date backing Wynonie Harris. However, Otis was aware of audience interest in R&B and began to angle his repertoire accordingly. He quickly became one of the leading figures in the R&B boom of the late 40s and early 50s. Otis also enjoyed credit for writing several songs, although, in some cases, this was an area fraught with confusion and litigation. Amongst his songs was 'Every Beat Of My Heart', which was recorded by Jackie Wilson in 1951 and became a minor hit followed, a decade later, by a massive hit version from Gladys Knight. Otis was instrumental in the discovery of Etta James and Willie Mae 'Big Mama' Thornton. A highly complex case of song co-authorship came to light with 'Hound Dog', which was recorded by Thornton. Otis, who had set up the date, was listed first as composer, then as co-composer with its originators, Leiber And Stoller. After the song was turned into a multi-million dollar hit by Elvis Presley other names appeared on the credits and the lawyers stepped in. Otis had a hit record in the UK with an updated version of 'Ma, He's Making Eyes At Me' in 1957. During the 50s Otis broadcast daily in the USA as a radio disc jockey, and had a weekly television show with his band and also formed several recording companies; all of which helped to make him a widely recognized force in west coast R&B. During the 60s and 70s, Otis continued to appear on radio and television, touring with his well-packaged R&B-based show. His son, Johnny 'Shuggie' Otis Jnr., appeared with the show and at the age of 13 had a hit with 'Country Girl'. In addition to his busy musical career, Johnny also found time to write a book, *Listen To The Lambs*, written in the aftermath of the Watts riots of the late 60s.

Albums: *Mel Williams And Johnny Otis* (1955), *Rock 'N' Roll Parade, Volume 1* (1957), *The Johnny Otis Show* (1958), *Cold Shot* (1968), *Cuttin' Up* (1970), *Live At Monterey* (1971), *The New Johnny Otis Show* (1982), *Spirit Of The Black Territory Bands* (1993).

Page, Patti

b. Clara Ann Fowler, 8 November 1927, Tulsa, Oklahoma, USA. A popular singer, who allegedly sold more records during the 50s than any other female artist; her total sales (singles and albums), are claimed to be in excess of 60 million. One of eight girls, in a family of 11, Fowler started her career singing country songs on radio station KTUL in Tulsa, and played weekend gigs with Art Klauser And His Oklahomans. She successfully auditioned for KTUL's *Meet Patti Page* show, sponsored by the Page Milk Company, and took the name with her when she left. Jack Rael, who was road manager and played baritone saxophone for the Jimmy Joy band, heard her on the radio and engaged her to sing with them; he later became her manager for over 40 years. In 1948, Page appeared on the top rated *Breakfast Club* on Chicago radio, and sang with the Benny Goodman Septet. In the same year she had her first hit record, 'Confess', on which, in the cause of economy, she overdubbed her own voice to create the effect of a vocal group.

In 1949, she used that revolutionary technique again on her first million-seller, 'With My Eyes Wide Open I'm Dreaming'. The song was re-released 10 years later with a more modern orchestral backing. Throughout the 50s, the hits continued to flow: 'I Don't Care If The Sun Don't Shine', 'All My Love' (US number 1), 'The Tennessee Waltz' (said to be the first real 'cross-over' hit from country music to pop, and one of the biggest record hits of all time), 'Would I Love You (Love You, Love You)', 'Mockin' Bird Hill' (a cover version of the record made by Les Paul and Mary Ford, who took multi-tracking to the extreme in the 50s), 'Mister And Mississippi', 'Detour' (recorded for her first country music album), 'I Went To Your Wedding', 'Once In Awhile', 'You Belong To Me', 'Why Don't You Believe Me', '(How Much Is) That Doggie In The Window', written by novelty song specialist, Bob Merrill, and recorded by Page for a children's album; 'Changing Partners', 'Cross Over The Bridge', 'Steam Heat', 'Let Me Go, Lover', 'Go On With The Wedding', 'Allegheny Moon', 'Old Cape Cod', 'Mama From The Train' (sang in a Pennsylvanian Dutch dialect), 'Left Right Out Of Your Heart', and many more. Her records

Patti Page

continued to sell well into the 60s, and she had her last US Top 10 entry in 1965 with the title song from the Bette Davis-Olivia De Havilland movie, *Hush, Hush, Sweet Charlotte*. Page also appeared extensively on US television during the 50s, on shows such as the *Scott Music Hall*, the *Big Record* variety show, and her own shows for NBC and CBS. She also appeared in films, including *Elmer Gantry* (1960), *Dondi* (1961, a comedy-drama, in which she co-starred with David Janssen) and *Boys Night Out* (1962). In the 70s, she recorded mainly country material, and in the 80s, after many successful years with Mercury and Columbia Records, signed for the Nashville-based company Plantation Records, a move which reunited her with top record producer Shelby Singleton. In 1988, Page gained excellent reviews when she played the Ballroom in New York, her first appearance in that city for nearly 20 years.

Albums: *Let's Get Away From It All* (1955), *I've Heard That Song Before* (1955), *Patti Page On Camera* (1955), *Three Little Words* (1955), *The Waltz Queen* (1955), *Indiscretion* (1955), *Romance On The Range* (1955), *I'll Remember April* (1956), *Page I* (1956), *Page II* (1956), *Page III* (1956), *You Go To My Head* (1956), *In The Land Of Hi Fi* (1956), *Music For Two In Love* (1956), *The Voices Of Patti Page* (1956), *Page IV* (1956), *My Song* (1956), *The East Side* (1956), *Manhattan Tower* (1956), *Just A Closer Walk With Thee* (1957), *Sings And Stars In 'Elmer Gantry'* (1960), *Country And Western Golden Hits* (1961), *Go On Home* (1962), *Golden Hit Of The Boys* (1962), *Patti Page On Stage* (1963), *Say Wonderful Things* (1963), *Blue Dream Street* (1964), *The Nearness Of You* (1964), *Hush, Hush, Sweet Charlotte* (1965), *Gentle On My Mind* (1968), *Patti Page With Lou Stein's Music, 1949* (1988). Compilations: *Patti Page's Greatest Hits* (1961), *Patti Page's Golden Hits, Volume 2* (1963), *The Best Of Patti Page* (1984).

Paint Your Wagon

Despite the qualities of its writers, the stage musical *Paint Your Wagon* had only modest success. Opening on Broadway on 12 November 1951, the show ran for less than 300 performances. Well-staged and with excellent choreography by Agnes de Mille, *Paint Your Wagon* was set in California during the 1850s gold rush. The songs, by Alan Jay Lerner and Frederick Loewe, were sung by a cast portraying hard-bitten prospectors and their equally tough girlfriends. Cast members included Tony Bavaar, Olga San Juan, Rufus Smith and James Barton. Amongst the songs from the show were

'They Call The Wind Maria', 'I Still See Elisa', 'Wand'rin' Star' and 'I Talk To The Trees'. The 1969 film version, which starred Clint Eastwood, Jean Seberg and Lee Marvin, was an all-round disaster although Marvin's singing (well, gruff whispering, really) of 'Wand'rin' Star' became a UK number 1 hit in 1970, perhaps more for curiosity value than any real musical merit.

Pajama Game

An adaptation of a novel by Richard Bissell, the stage musical *Pajama Game* opened on 13 May 1954 with only limited expectations. For one thing, the show's writers, Richard Adler and Jerry Ross, were relatively unknown to Broadway audiences, as was choreographer Bob Fosse; and for another, mid-May is late in the season for a show to have a chance to take off. However, take off it did and ran for more than 1,000 performances, won a Tony amongst other awards, and presented recording artists with hit parade material. Amongst the show's songs were 'Hernando's Hideaway', 'Steam Heat', 'I'll Never Be Jealous Again', 'Once A Year Day' and 'Hey, There'. Set against the unlikely backdrop of a factory manufacturing pajamas and with an industrial dispute as its central dramatic device, the show had strong central performances from Janis Paige, John Raitt and Carol Haney. The 1957 film version achieved the impossible and actually improved upon the original with dazzling performances from Doris Day, Raitt and Haney.

Paramor, Norrie

b. 1913, London, England, d. 9 September 1979. The most prolific producer of UK pop chart-toppers was a mild, bespectacled gentleman who had studied piano, and worked as an accompanist, prior to playing and arranging with a number of London dance bands, among them Maurice Winnick's Orchestra. During his time in the RAF during World War II, Paramor entertained servicemen in the company of artists such as Sydney Torch and Max Wall, served as a musical director for Ralph Reader's Gang Shows, and scored music Noel Coward, Mantovani and Jack Buchanan. After the war he was the featured pianist with Harry Gold And His Pieces Of Eight, and toured with the lively dixieland unit for five years. In 1950 he cut some sides for the Oriole label with Australian singer, Marie Benson, and, two years later, joined Columbia Records, an EMI subsidiary, as arranger and A&R manager. In 1954, he produced the first of two UK number 1 hits for

Eddie Calvert, and another for Ruby Murray the following year. Although quoted as believing that rock 'n' roll was 'an American phenomenon - and they do it best', he still provided Columbia with such an act in Tony Crombie's Rockets but had better luck with the mainstream efforts of Michael Holliday and the Mudlarks - both backed by the Ken Jones Orchestra. Then, in 1958, a demo tape by Cliff Richard And The Drifters arrived on his desk. With no rock 'n' roller currently on his books, he contracted Cliff intending to play it safe with a US cover with the Jones band until persuaded to stick with the Drifters (soon renamed the Shadows) and push a group original ('Move It') as the a-side. Partly through newspaper publicity engineered by Paramor, 'Move It' was a smash, and a consequent policy was instigated of Richard recording singles of untried numbers - among them, at Paramor's insistence, Lionel Bart's 'Living Doll'. Columbia was successful too with the Shadows - even if Paramor wished initially to issue 'Apache' - their first smash - as a b-side. Later, he offended Shadows purists by augmenting the quartet on disc with horn sections and his trademark lush string arrangements.

Other Paramor signings were not allowed to develop to the same idiosyncratic extent as Richard and his associates. Ricky Valance scored his sole chart-topper with a cover of Ray Peterson's US hit, 'Tell Laura I Love Her', while Helen Shapiro was visualized as a vague 'answer' to Brenda Lee; Paramor even booking and supervising some Shapiro sessions in Nashville in 1963. His greatest success during this period, however, was with Frank Ifield, who dominated the early 60s UK pop scene with three formidable number 1 hits. Even as late as 1968, Paramor racked up another number 1 with Scaffold's 'Lily The Pink'. Throughout his career, Paramor wrote, and co-wrote, many hit songs, several of them for films, such as *Expresso Bongo* ('A Voice In The Wilderness', Cliff Richard), *The Young Ones* ('The Savage') and *The Frightened City* (title song), both performed by the Shadows; *Play It Cool* ('Once Upon A Dream', Billy Fury), *It's Trad, Dad!* ('Let's Talk About Love', Helen Shapiro) and *Band Of Thieves* ('Lonely', Acker Bilk). He also composed several complete movie scores, and some light orchestral works such as 'The Zodiac' and 'Emotions', which he recorded with his Concert Orchestra, and released several 'mood' albums in the USA, including *London After Dark*, *Amore, Amore!*, *Autumn*, and *In London, In Love*, which made the US Top 20. In complete contrast, the Big Ben

Banjo, and Big Ben Hawaiian Bands, along with similar 'happy-go-lucky' 'trad jazz' line-up, were originally formed in 1955 purely as recording units, utilising the cream of UK session musicians. Paramor was in charge of them all, and their popularity was such, that 'live' performances had to be organized. The Big Ben Banjo Band appeared in the Royal Variety Performance in 1958, and was resident on BBC Radio's *Everybody Step* programme, as well as having its own Radio Luxembourg series. Two of the band's 'Let's Get Together' singles, and *More Minstrel Melodies*, reached the UK Top 20. One of the highlights of Paramor's career came in 1960 when he arranged and conducted for Judy Garland's British recording sessions, and was her musical director at the London Palladium and subsequent dates in Europe. In the same year, with his Orchestra, he made the UK singles chart with 'Theme From A Summer Place' and in 1962, registered again with 'Theme From Z Cars'. From 1972-78 Paramor was the Director of the BBC Midland Radio Orchestra, but he continued to dabble in independent production for such as the Excaliburs, and his publishing company was still finding material for Cliff in the 70s. Paramor remains one of the most underrated figures in the history of UK pop and a posthumous reappraisal of his work is overdue.

Selected albums: *In London, In Love ...* (1956), *The Zodiac* (1957), *New York Impressions* (1957), *Emotions* (1958), *Dreams And Desires* (1958), *The Wonderful Waltz* (1958), *My Fair Lady* (1959), *Paramor In Paris* (1959), *Jet Flight* (1959), *Lovers In Latin* (1959), *Staged For Stereo* (1961), *Autumn* (1961), *The Golden Waltz* (1961), *Lovers In London* (1964), with Patricia Clark *Lovers In Tokio* (1964), *Warm And Willing* (1965), *Shadows In Latin* (1966), *Norrie Paramor Plays The Hits Of Cliff Richard* (1967), *Soul Coaxing* (1968), *BBC Top Tunes* (1974), *Radio 2 Top Tunes, Volume 1* (1974), *Radio 2 Top Tunes, Volume 2 and 3* (both 1975), *Love* (1975), *My Personal Choice* (1976), *Silver Serenade* (1977), *Norrie Paramor Remembers ... 40 Years Of TV Themes* (1976), *Temptation* (1978), *Rags And Tatters* aka *Ragtime* (1978), *Classical Rhythm* (1979). Compilations: *Paramagic Pianos* (1977), *The Best Of Norrie Paramor* (1984), *Ragtime* (1985).

Parker, Fess

b. 16 August 1925, Fort Worth, Texas, USA. An actor and singer, Parker did some stage work before making his film debut in the western, *Untamed Frontier*, which starred Joseph Cotton and Shelley Winters. In 1954, he appeared as the famous Indian scout-legislator-Alamo defender, Davy Crockett, in three episodes of the television series *Disneyland*. The shows were extremely popular, and the theme, 'The Ballad Of Davy Crockett', written by scriptwriter, Tom Blackburn, and George Bruns, became a US number 1 hit for Bill Hayes, well known on television himself for *Show Of Shows*. Subsequently, Parker's own version of the song made the US Top 10. When the big screen version, *Davy Crockett, King Of The Wild Frontier!*, was made in 1955, coonskin caps abounded, nationwide and beyond; the inevitable sequel, *Davy Crockett And The River Pirates*, was released in 1956. In the same year, Parker starred in Disney's, *Westward Ho, The Wagons!*, which contained five new songs, including 'Wringle Wrangle', Parker's second, and last, chart success. His other movies, through to the 60s, included *The Great Locomotive Chase* (1956), *Old Yeller* (1957) – the first of the many Disney films about a boy and his dog, *The Hangman* (1959) and *Hell Is For Heroes* (1962), an exciting World War II drama, with Steve McQueen and Bobby Darin. Parker was also prominent on US television; in 1962 he co-starred with country singer Red Foley in a series based on Lewis R. Foster's classic, *Mr. Smith Goes To Washington*. Two years later, he returned to the backwoods and portrayed yet another legendary American pioneer, in *Daniel Boone*, which ran until 1968, and in 1972, played the tough sheriff in the US television movie, *Climb An Angry Mountain*. After he retired from show business, Parker moved to Santa Barbara, California, and concentrated on a career in real estate.

Selected albums: *The Adventures Of Davy Crockett* (1955), *Yarns And Songs* (50s/60s), *Cowboy And Indian Songs* (50s/60s), *Fess Parker Sings* (1964).

Parlophone Records

The label's roots go back to March 1911 when Carl Gesellschaft Lindstrom (b. 1867, d. 1932) launched the Parlophon (sic) label in Europe. In March 1920 it was taken over by the Transoceanic Trading Co of Holland who formed the Parlophone Co. Ltd in London on 8 August 1923. Taken under UK Columbia's wing in 1925, it subsequently became part of EMI when that organization was formed by the merger of Columbia and several other labels in April 1931. The label started to come into its own during the 50s when it was run by Oscar Preuss and his assistant George Martin, whom he had rescued from the BBC Gramphone Library. They released largely lightweight dance music and Scottish reels

until 1955 when Preuss retired and Martin took over. Looking for a new angle he saw that comedy records were few and far between and began to make recordings of such people as Flanders And Swan, Peter Sellers and Mike and Bernie Winters. He moved into more contemporary music by releasing American rock 'n' roll records by Mac Curtis, Boyd Bennett, Charlie Gracie and others, as well as putting out home-grown talent like the Vipers, Jim Dale, Rory Blackwell and Vince Eager. As the 60s arrived, so did the bigger selling artists such as Adam Faith, Mike Sarne, Shane Fenton and the Temperance Seven, but it was in 1962 that George Martin ensured his place in pop history. Although not over impressed with the Beatles at first, he did think them a worthwhile signing! The Beatles, Cilla Black, Billy J. Kramer, Cliff Bennett, the Hollies and Adam Faith were all Parlophone recording acts that dominated the charts in the 60s. There were also less well-known names such as Byron Lee And The Dragonaires (Lee was a top Jamaican producer), Kippington Lodge (including Nick Lowe), Davy Jones (later known as David Bowie), the Herd (featuring Peter Frampton) and a very young Marc Bolan. Aside from the pop music Parlophone continued to release comedy material - most notably spin-offs from television satire programmes like *That Was The Week That Was*. They even continued with the odd Scottish reel: Jimmy Shand would come down to London once a year, record several dozen tunes, return home and watch while they were slowly released as singles over a 12-month period. George Martin left in 1965 to form his own independent production company, AIR, and the Beatles set up their own Apple label - though their records were still released in Parlophone's sequence but with the Apple logo. By the early 70s only the solo Beatles releases were coming out in the Parlophone series. In 1979, however, the label underwent something of a revival and in 1982 on the anniversary of the release of 'Love Me Do' they issued '101 Damnations' by Beatles soundalikes Scarlet Party. Since then the label has been the home for releases by Dexy's Midnight Runners, the Pet Shop Boys, Queen, EMF and, boosting the label's credibility, signing UK 'indie' stars the Sundays in the early part of 1992.

Parnes, Larry

b. Laurence Maurice Parnes, 1930, Willesden, London, England, d. 4 August 1989. Parnes was the most famous British pop manager and impresario of the 50s, and one of the greatest of all

Larry Parnes (left) with Billy Fury

time. After briefly working in the family clothing business, he took over a bar in London's West End called La Caverne. The establishment was frequented by many theatrical agents and producers and, before long, Parnes was inveigled into investing in a play titled *Women Of The Streets*. One night at a coffee bar he met publicist John Kennedy, who was then overseeing the affairs of singer Tommy Hicks. After seeing the boy perform at Lionel Bart's suggestion Parnes was impressed and went into partnership with Kennedy. Hicks was rechristened Tommy Steele and became Britain's first rock 'n' roll celebrity. He later emerged as an all round entertainer and star of several musicals. Parnes specialized in discovering young boys, who would be systematically groomed, launched on the rock 'n' roll circuit, and finally assimilated into traditional showbusiness areas. The technique was habitual. Parnes played the part of the svengali, carefully renaming his acts with some exotically powerful surname that suggested power, virility or glamour. His second discovery proved another winner. Reg Smith was quickly snapped up by the starmaker, rechristened Marty Wilde and soon enjoyed a string of UK hits, before 'retiring' from rock 'n' roll at the close of the 50s.

By this time, Parnes had a network of contacts, including A&R managers like Hugh Mendl, Dick Rowe and Jack Baverstock, who would always take notice of a Parnes act. The bombastic television producer Jack Good also realized that supporting Parnes ensured a steady flow of teenage talent. Finally, there were the songwriters like Lionel Bart, who could provide original material, although cover versions of US hits were always popular. Parnes' third great discovery of the 50s was Billy Fury, one of the most important figures to emerge from British rock 'n' roll. Significantly, Parnes remained with the star for a considerable time and was still handling his business affairs during the late 60s. The irrepressible Joe Brown was another major find for Parnes, though their association was often stormy. Brown was an exceptional guitarist and was frequently used to back other Parnes acts. For every star he unearthed, however, there were a series of lesser talents or unlucky singers who failed to find chart success. Among the famous Parnes' 'stable of stars' were Dickie Pride, Duffy Power, Johnny Gentle, Sally Kelly, Terry Dene, Nelson Keene and Peter Wynne. Larry was also briefly associated with Georgie Fame and the Tornados. Beyond his management interests, Parnes was a great provider of package shows with grandiloquent titles such as 'The Big New Rock 'n' Roll Trad Show' and the 'Star Spangled Nights'. Parnes' influence effectively ended during the early to mid-60s when new managers and entrepreneurs such as Brian Epstein and Andrew Oldham took centre stage. Ironically, Parnes had two chances to sign the Beatles but passed up the opportunity. Like his stars, he seemed intent on abdicating his position in rock 'n' roll and increasingly moved into more conservative areas of British showbusiness and theatre. During the 60s, he was involved in such musicals as *Charlie Girl* and *Chicago*. During the 70s, he returned to management in a different sphere, administering the business affairs of ice-skater John Currie. He subsequently fell ill with meningitis and effectively retired. His public image remained contradictory and subject to caricature. As the prototype British pop svengali, he was used as the inspiration for the vapid, camp starmaker in the movie *Absolute Beginners*. Ever self-protective and litigious, his wrath descended upon the BBC, among others, when he won a substantial out-of-court settlement for an alleged libel by Paul McCartney on, a most unlikely programme, *Desert Island Discs*. Parnes died in London on 4 August 1989.

Further reading: *Starmakers & Svengalis: The History Of British Pop Management*, Johnny Rogan.

Paul, Les

b. 9 June 1915, Wankesha, Wisconsin, USA. Paul began playing guitar and other instruments while still a child. In the early 30s he broadcast on the radio and in 1936 was leading his own trio. In the late 30s and early 40s he worked in New York, where he was featured on Fred Waring's radio show. He made records accompanying singers such as Bing Crosby and the Andrews Sisters. Although his work was in the popular vein, with a strong country leaning, Paul was highly adaptable and frequently sat in with jazz musicians. One of his favourites was Nat 'King' Cole, whom he knew in Los Angeles, and the two men appeared together in a Jazz At The Philharmonic concert in 1944, on which Paul played some especially fine blues. Dissatisfied with the sound of the guitars he played, Paul developed his own design for a solid-bodied instrument, which he had made at his own expense. Indeed, the company, Gibson, were so cool towards the concept that they insisted that their name should not appear on the instruments they made for him. In later years, when it seemed that half the guitarists in the world were playing Les Paul-style Gibson guitars, the company's

attitude was understandably a little different. Paul's dissatisfaction with existing techniques extended beyond the instrument and into the recording studios. Eager to experiment with a multi-tracking concept, he built a primitive studio in his own home. He produced a succession of superb recordings on which he played multi-track guitar, amongst them 'Lover', 'Nola', 'Brazil' and 'Whispering'. During the 50s Paul continued his experimentation with other, similar recordings, while his wife, Mary Ford (b. 7 July 1928, d. 30 September 1977), sang multiple vocal lines. Other major record successes were 'The World Is Waiting For The Sunrise', 'How High The Moon', which reached number 1, and 'Vaya Con Dios', another US number 1 hit. By the early 60s Paul had tired of the recording business and retired. He and Ford were divorced in 1963 and he spent his time inventing and helping to promote Gibson guitars. In the late 70s he returned to the studios for two successful albums of duets with Chet Atkins, but towards the end of the decade had retired again. A television documentary in 1980, *The Wizard Of Wankesha*, charted his life and revived interest in his career. In 1984 he made a comeback to performing and continued to make sporadic appearances throughout the rest of the decade. He was performing at the guitar festival in Seville, Spain in 1992. A remarkably gifted and far-sighted guitarist, Paul's contribution to popular music must inevitably centre upon his pioneering work on multi-tracking and his creation of the solid-bodied guitar. It would be sad, however, if his efforts in these directions wholly concealed his considerable abilities as a performer.
Selected albums: with Mary Ford *New Sound, Volume 1 & 2* (mid-50s), with Ford *Les And Mary* (1955), *Bye, Bye Blues* (mid-50s), with Ford *The Hitmakers* (mid-50s), with Ford *Les And Mary* (late 50s), with Ford *Time To Dream* (late 50s), with Ford *Lover's Luau* (1959), with Ford *Warm And Wonderful* (1962), with Ford *Bouquet Of Roses* (1962), with Ford *Swingin' South* (1963), *Les Paul Now* (1968), with Chet Atkins *Chester And Lester* (1977), with Atkins *Guitar Masters* (1978). Compilations: with Mary Ford *The Hits Of Les And Mary* (1960), *The Very Best Of Les Paul And Mary Ford* (1974), *The Capitol Years* (1989).

Peers, Donald

b. Donald Rhys Hubert Peers, 1909, Ammanford, Dyfed, Wales, d. 9 August 1973. Peers was an extremely popular singer during the late 40s and early 50s in the UK, especially with female audiences who swooned and screamed in a most un-British manner. Peers' father, a Welsh colliery worker, was a prominent member of the Plymouth Brethren, and would never go inside a theatre to see and hear his son at work. Peers was to have been a schoolteacher, but ran away and became a house painter, a steward on a British tanker vessel, and a singer with a seaside concert party. He made his first broadcast in 1927 with the popular comedy duo, Clapham And Dwyer, and continued to have success in the medium. In 1940 he enlisted in the Armed Forces, and was invalided out on D-Day, 1944. In the same year he recorded 'In A Shady Nook (By A Babbling Brook)', written by E.G. Nelson and Harry Pease in 1927; it became his life-long theme. Other 40s recordings included 'I Can't Begin To Tell You', 'Bow Bells', 'Far Away Places', 'On The 5.45' (a vocal version of 'Twelfth Street Rag', with a lyric by Andy Razaf), 'Powder Your Face With Sunshine' (one of his biggest successes), 'Lavender Blue', 'A Strawberry Moon (In A Blueberry Sky)', 'Everywhere You Go', 'Clancy Lowered The Boom', 'It Happened In Adano', 'A Rose In A Garden Of Weeds', 'I'll String Along With You' and 'Down In The Glen'. He toured the UK Variety circuit and spent lucrative summer seasons at top locations such as Blackpool, and in 1949 presented his one-man show at the Royal Albert Hall and the London Palladium. He also had his own radio show *Cavalier Of Song*, a television series *Donald Peers*, and he made several films including *Sing Along With Me*. His record success was sustained through the early 50s with songs such as 'The Last Mile Home', 'Dear Hearts And Gentle People', 'Out Of A Clear Blue Sky', 'Music! Music! Music!', 'If I Knew You Were Comin', I'd've Baked A Cake', 'Enjoy Yourself (It's Later Than You Think')', 'Dearie', 'I Remember The Cornfields', 'Beloved, Be Faithful', 'Me And My Imagination', 'Mistakes', 'In A Golden Coach' (a celebratory number for the Coronation of Queen Elizabeth II), 'Is It Any Wonder' and 'Changing Partners'. In the late 50s he worked often in South Africa, Australia and India, and on his return to the UK, had to rebuild his career via the northern club circuit which had taken over from the music halls. He had a Top 10 chart entry in 1968 with 'Please Don't Go', written by comedian Jackie Rae and Les Reed. In 1972 Peers returned to the stage after overcoming a severe back injury sustained in Australia, and had his last chart entry with the aptly titled, 'Give Me One More Chance'.
Album: *The Last Broadcast* (1974). Compilations:

Penguins

The World Of Donald Peers (1970), The World Of Donald Peers, Volume Two (1973), The Donald Peers Collection (1978), The Golden Age Of Donald Peers (1987).

Penguins

Formed in 1954 in Fremont High School, Los Angeles, California, USA, the Penguins were one of the most important R&B vocal groups from the west coast in the early 50s. Their hit ballad 'Earth Angel' remains one of the most fondly recalled 'doo-wop' recordings to date. The group consisted of lead vocalist Cleveland 'Cleve' Duncan (b. 23 July 1935, Los Angeles, California, USA), Bruce Tate (baritone), Curtis Williams (first tenor) and Dexter Tisby (second tenor). Williams learned 'Earth Angel' from LA R&B singer Jesse Belvin, and passed it along to his group. Some sources give co-writing credit to Williams, Belvin and Gaynel Hodge, a member of vocal group the Turks. Hodge won a 1956 lawsuit recognizing his role in the writing of the song. However, most reissues of 'Earth Angel' still list only either Belvin, Williams or both. The Penguins, who took their name from a penguin on a cigarette pack, signed with the local DooTone Records, owned by Dootsie Williams. Their recording date was as a backing group for a blues singer, Willie Headon. They next recorded 'Hey Sinorita', an uptempo number. 'Earth Angel' was chosen as their first single's b-side but when both sides were played on LA radio station KGJF, listeners called in to request the 'Earth Angel' side be played again. It ultimately reached number 1 in the US Billboard R&B chart. It also reached the pop Top 10, but was eclipsed by a cover version by the white group the Crew-Cuts. The song has also charted by Gloria Mann (1955), Johnny Tillotson (1960), the Vogues (1969) and New Edition (1986). The Penguins continued to record other singles for DooTone (plus one album for the related Dooto label) and then Mercury Records before disbanding in 1959. Members Williams and Tate have since died, Tisby retired from music, and Duncan later formed new bands under the name Penguins and was still performing under that name in the early 90s.
Album: The Cool, Cool Penguins (1959).

Perkins, Carl

b. Carl Lee Perkins, 9 April 1932, Ridgely, Tennessee, USA (his birth certificate misspelled the last name as Perkings). Carl Perkins was one of the most renowned rockabilly artists recording for Sun Records in the 50s and the author of the classic song 'Blue Suede Shoes'. As a guitarist, he influenced many of the next generation of rock 'n' rollers, most prominently George Harrison and Dave Edmunds. His parents, Fonie 'Buck' and Louise Brantley Perkins, were share-croppers during the 30s Depression and the family was thus very poor. As a child Perkins listened to the Grand Ole Opry on the radio, exposing him to C&W (or hillbilly) music, and he listened to the blues being sung by a black sharecropper named John Westbrook across the field from where he worked. After World War II the Perkins family relocated to Bemis, Tennessee, where he and his brothers picked cotton; by that time his father was unable to work due to a lung illness. Having taught himself rudimentary guitar from listening to such players as Butterball Page and Arthur Smith, Perkins bought an electric guitar and learned to play it more competently. In 1953 Carl, his brothers Jay (rhythm guitar) and Clayton (upright bass), and drummer W.S. 'Fluke' Holland formed a band that worked up a repertoire of hillbilly songs performing at local honky-tonks, primarily in the Jackson, Tennessee area, where Carl moved with his recent wife Valda Crider in 1954.

Borrowing some of his technique from the black musicians he had studied set Carl Perkins apart from the many other country guitarists in that region at that time; his style of playing lead guitar fills around his own vocals was similar to that used in the blues. Encouraged by his wife, and by hearing a record by Elvis Presley on the radio, Perkins decided in 1954 to pursue a musical career. That October the Perkins brothers travelled to Memphis to audition for Sam Phillips at Sun Records. Phillips was not overly impressed, but agreed the group had potential. In February 1955 he issued two songs from that first Perkins session, 'Movie Magg' and 'Turn Around', on his new Flip label. Pure country in nature, these did not make a dent in the market. Perkins' next single was issued in August, this time on Sun itself. One track, 'Let The Jukebox Keep On Playing', was again country, but the other song, 'Gone! Gone! Gone!' was pure rockabilly. Again, it was not a hit. That November, after Phillips sold Presley's Sun contract to RCA Records, Phillips decided to push the next Perkins single, an original called 'Blue Suede Shoes'. The song had its origins when Johnny Cash, another Sun artist, suggested to Perkins that he write a song based on the phrase 'Don't step on my blue suede shoes'. It was recorded at Sun on 19 December 1955, along with three other songs, among them the b-side 'Honey

Carl Perkins (left) with Sam Phillips

Don't', later to be covered by the Beatles. 'Blue Suede Shoes' entered the US *Billboard* chart on 3 March 1956 (the same day Presley's first single entered the chart), by which time several cover versions had been recorded, by a range of artists from Presley to Lawrence Welk. Perkins' version quickly became a huge hit and was also the first country record to appear on both the R&B chart and the pop chart, in addition to the country chart. Just as Perkins was beginning to enjoy the fruits of his labour, the car in which he and his band were driving to New York was involved in a severe accident near Dover, Delaware, when their manager, Stuart Pinkham, fell asleep at the wheel. Perkins and his brother Clayton suffered broken bones; brother Jay suffered a fractured neck; and the driver of the truck they hit, Thomas Phillips, was killed. 'Blue Suede Shoes' ultimately reached number 2 on the pop chart, a number 1 country hit and an R&B number 2. Owing to the accident, Perkins was unable to promote the record, the momentum was lost, and none of his four future chart singles would climb nearly as high. In the UK, 'Blue Suede Shoes' became Perkins' only chart single, and was upstaged commercially by the Presley cover. Perkins continued to record for Sun until mid-1958, but the label's newcomers, Johnny Cash and Jerry Lee Lewis, occupied most of Sam Phillips' attention. Perkins' follow-up to 'Blue Suede Shoes', 'Boppin' The Blues', only reached

number 70, and 'Your True Love' number 67. While still at Sun, Perkins did record numerous tracks that would later be revered by rockabilly fans, among them 'Everybody's Trying To Be My Baby' and 'Matchbox', both of which were also covered by the Beatles. On 4 December 1956, Perkins was joined by Lewis and a visiting Presley at Sun in an impromptu jam session which was recorded and released two decades later under the title 'The Million Dollar Quartet'. (Johnny Cash, despite having his photograph taken with Presley, Lewis and Carl, did not take part in the 'million dollar session' - he went shopping instead.) One of Perkins' last acts while at Sun was to appear in the film *Jamboree*, singing a song called 'Glad All Over'. In January 1958, Perkins signed with Columbia Records, where Cash would soon follow. Although some of the songs he recorded for that label were very good, only two, 'Pink Pedal Pushers' and 'Pointed Toe Shoes', both obvious attempts to recapture the success of his first footwear-oriented hit, had a minor impression on the charts. Later that year Jay Perkins died of a brain tumour, causing Carl to turn alcoholic, an affliction from which he would not recover until the late 60s.

In 1963 Perkins signed with Decca Records, for which there would be no successful releases. He also toured outside of the USA in 1963-64; while in Britain he met the Beatles, and watched as they recorded his songs. Perkins, who, ironically, was becoming something of a legend in Europe (as were many early rockers), returned to England for a second tour in October 1964. By 1966 he had left Decca for the small Dollie Records, a country label. In 1967 he joined Johnny Cash's band as guitarist and was allotted a guest singing spot during each of Cash's concerts and television shows. In 1969, Cash recorded Perkins' song 'Daddy Sang Bass', a minor hit in the USA. By 1970, Perkins was back on Columbia, this time recording an album together with new rock revival group NRBQ. In 1974 he signed with Mercury Records. Late that year his brother Clayton committed suicide and their father died. Perkins left Cash in 1976 and went on the road with a band consisting of Perkins' two sons, with whom he was still performing in the 90s. A tribute single to the late Presley, 'The EP Express', came in 1977 and a new album, now for the Jet label, was released in 1978. By the 80s Perkins' reputation as one of rock's pioneers had grown. He recorded an album with Cash and Lewis, *The Survivors* (another similar project, with Cash, Lewis and Roy Orbison, *The Class Of '55*, followed in 1986). Perkins spent much of the 80s touring and working with younger musicians who were influenced by him, among them Paul McCartney and the Stray Cats. In 1985 he starred in a television special to mark the 30th anniversary of 'Blue Suede Shoes'. It co-starred Harrison, Ringo Starr, Dave Edmunds, two members of the Stray Cats, Rosanne Cash and Eric Clapton. In 1987 Perkins was elected to the Rock And Roll Hall of Fame. He signed to the Universal label in 1989 and released *Born To Rock*. His early work has been anthologized many times in several countries.

Selected albums: *The Dance Album Of Carl Perkins* (1957), *Whole Lotta Shakin'* (1958), *Teen Beat/The Best Of Carl Perkins* (1961), *Country Boy Dreams* (1968), *Greatest Hits* (1969), *Blue Suede Shoes* (1969), *On Top* (1969), with the NRBQ *Boppin' The Blues* (1970), *My Kind Of Country* (1974), *Carl Perkins Show* (1976), *From Jackson, Tennessee* (1977), *Ol' Blue Suede's Back* (1978), with Jerry Lee Lewis and Johnny Cash *The Survivors* (1982), *The Sun Years* (1982), *The Class Of '55* (1986), *Up Through The Years, 1954-1957* (1986), *Original Sun Greatest Hits* (1986), *The Heart And Soul Of Carl Perkins* (1987), *Honky Tonk Gal: Rare And Unissued Sun Masters* (1989), *The Classic Carl Perkins* (1990, box-set), *Born To Rock* (1990), *Friends, Family & Legends* (1992), *Restless* (1993).

Phillips, Sam

b. 1923, Florence, Alabama, USA. Although harbouring ambitions as a criminal lawyer, Phillips was obliged to drop out of high school to support his family. In 1942 he took up a post as disc jockey at station WLAY in Muscle Shoals, before moving to WREC in Memphis as an announcer four years later. In 1950 he opened Sam's Memphis Recording Studio at 706 Union Avenue and although initial work largely consisted of chronicling weddings and social gatherings, Phillips' main ambition was to record local blues acts and license the resultant masters. Howlin' Wolf, Bobby 'Blue' Bland, Ike Turner, B.B. King and Roscoe Gordon were among the many acts Phillips produced for independent outlets Chess, Duke and RPM. Their success inspired the founding of Sun Records in February 1952, a venture which flourished the following year when Rufus Thomas scored a notable R&B hit with 'Bear Cat'. Success was maintained by 'Little' Junior Parker and Billy 'The Kid' Emerson, while Phillips looked to expand the label's horizons by recording country acts. His wish to find a white singer comfortable with R&B was answered in 1954 with the arrival of Elvis Presley. The singer's five singles recorded with Phillips rank among pop's greatest achievements, and although criticized for allowing his protege to sign for RCA Records, the producer used the settlement fee to further the careers of Carl Perkins, Johnny Cash and, later, Jerry Lee Lewis. Phillips' simple recording technique - single track, rhythmic string bass and judicious echo - defined classic rockabilly and for a brief period the label was in the ascendant. The style, however, proved too inflexible and by the beginning of the 60s new Memphis-based studios, Stax and Hi Records, challenged Sun's pre-eminent position. Phillips also became increasingly distracted by other ventures, including mining concerns, radio stations and, more crucially, his share of the giant Holiday Inn hotel chain. In 1969 he sold the entire Sun empire to country entrepreneur Shelby Singleton, thus effectively ending an era. Sam Phillips is nonetheless still revered as one of the leading catalysts in post-war American music and, if nothing else, for launching the career of Elvis Presley.

Piaf, Edith

b. Edith Giovanna Gassion, 19 December 1915, Paris, France, d. 11 October 1963. Born into desperate poverty, Piaf survived desertion by her

Edith Piaf

mother and temporary childhood blindness, to eke a living singing on the streets of Paris. After a brief period living in the country she sang in the streets with her father, an impoverished entertainer. The owner of Cerny's cabaret, Louis Leplée, heard the little girl and not only encouraged her but, struck by her diminutive stature, nicknamed her 'piaf', Parisian argot for 'little sparrow'. Piaf's dramatic singing style and her anguished voice appealed to French audiences and by the outbreak of World War II she had become a star. She proved her capacity for survival when she maintained her popularity despite being held as a material witness to Leplée's murder and in the face of accusations of collaboration with the German occupying forces. After the war Piaf's reputation spread internationally and she appeared in New York, singing at Carnegie Hall. In her private life Piaf was as tormented as the heroines of her songs and she had many relationships, most causing her severe emotional damage. She collapsed in 1959 but came back to sing with renewed vigour even if her physical condition was visibly deteriorating. Among her many hits were several songs which she made her own, 'Les Tres Cloche's', 'Milord', 'La Vie En Rose' and, above all others if only because the sentiment expressed in title and lyric so eloquently expressed her attitude to life, 'Non, Je Ne Regrette Rien'.

Selected albums: *Sincerely* (1960), *Piaf At The Paris Olympia* (1961), *C'est La Piaf* (1962), *La Reine De La Chanson* (1963), *I Regret Nothing* (1971), *Her Legendary Live Recordings* (1979), *De L'Accordeoniste A Milord* (1983), *Edith Piaf, Volumes 1-4* (1986), *The Best Of Edith Piaf* (1936-43), *Volumes 1 & 2* (1986), *Heart And Soul* (1987), *25th Anniversary Album* (1988).

Further reading: *The Piaf Legend*, David Bret.

Platters

One of the leading R&B vocal groups of the 50s, they were the first black group to be accepted as a major chart act and, for a short time, were the most successful vocal group in the world. The Platters were formed in Los Angeles in 1953 by entrepreneur/songwriter Buck Ram (b. 1908, Chicago, Illinois, USA). By means of owning the Platters' name, Ram was able to control the group throughout their career, but his talent for composing and arranging enabled the Platters to make a lasting impression upon popular music. Their original line-up, Tony Williams (b. 5 April 1928, Elizabeth, New Jersey, USA; lead tenor), David Lynch (b. 1929, St. Louis, Missouri, USA,

d. 2 January 1981; tenor), Alex Hodge (baritone) and Herb Reed (b. 1931, Kansas City, Missouri, USA; bass), recorded unsuccessfully the following year, precipitating the arrival of two new members, Paul Robi (b. 1931, New Orleans, Louisiana, USA), who replaced Hodge, and Zola Taylor (b. 1934; contralto). Signed to the Mercury label, the Platters secured their first hit in 1955 with 'Only You' reaching the US Top 5, an effortlessly light performance which set the pattern for subsequent releases including 'The Great Pretender', 'My Prayer' and 'Twilight Time', each of which reached number 1 in the US charts. 'Smoke Gets In Your Eyes' (previously a hit for Paul Whiteman in 1934), was an international number 1 hit single in 1958-59, highlighted their smooth delivery and arguably remains the group's best-loved release. Lead singer Williams left for a solo career in 1961, taking with him much of the Platters' distinctive style. His departure led to further changes, with Sandra Dawn and Nate Nelson replacing Taylor and Robi. With Sonny Turner as the featured voice, the group began embracing a more contemporary direction, seen in such occasional pop hits as 'I Love You 1000 Times' (1966) and 'With This Ring' (1967). During the late 60s, and for a long time afterwards, personnel changes brought much confusion as to who were the legitimate Platters. Sonny Turner and Herb Reed formed their own version, while Tony Williams did like-wise. The Platters' legacy has since been undermined by the myriad of line-ups performing under their name, some of which bore no tangible link to the actual group. This should not detract from those seminal recordings which bridged the gap between the harmonies of the Mills Brothers and the Ink Spots and the sweet soul of the ensuing decade.

Selected albums: *The Platters* (1955, released on Federal, King and Mercury labels), *The Platters, Volume 2* (1956), *The Flying Platters* (1957), *The Platters On Parade* (1959), *Flying Platters Around The World* (1959), *Remember When* (1959), *Reflections* (1960), *Encore Of Golden Hits* (1960), *More Encore Of Golden Hits* (1960), *The Platters* (1960), *Life Is Just A Bowl Of Cherries* (1961), *The Platters Sing For The Lonely* (1962), *Encore Of The Golden Hits Of The Groups* (1962), *Moonlight Memories* (1963), *Platters Sing All The Movie Hits* (1963), *Platters Sing Latino* (1963), *Christmas With The Platters* (1963), *New Soul Campus Style Of The Platters* (1965), *I Love You 1000 Times* (1966), *Going Back To Detroit* (1967), *I Get The Sweetest Feeling* (1968), *Sweet Sweet Lovin'* (1968), *Encore Of Broadway Golden Hits*

Poni-Tails

(1972), *Live* (1974), *The Original Platters - 20 Classic Hits* (1978), *Platterama* (1982), *Platters Collection* (1986), *Magic Touch: An Anthology* (1992), *Greatest Hits* (1993).

Poni-Tails

A US female trio known for the 1958 Top 10 hit 'Born Too Late', the Poni-Tails - who, naturally, sported that hairstyle - were lead vocalist Toni Cistone, Patti McCabe (low harmony - replacing original member Karen Topinka) and LaVerne Novak (high harmony). The group met at their high school in Lyndhurst, Ohio, USA, in 1957. They first recorded for Point Records, an RKO Pictures division, but their two singles for that label were not successful. The members were then signed to ABC-Paramount Records, and their first single for that company fared badly. The next one, 'Born Too Late', an innocent ballad about being passed over by an older boy, catapulted to number 7 in the US chart the following year. Two further singles for ABC reached the charts but came nowhere near hit status and the group disbanded, each member retiring from the music business. McCabe died in 1989.

Prado, Perez

b. Damaso Perez Prado, 11 December 1916, Mantanzas, Cuba, d. 14 September 1989, Mexico City, Mexico. Prado played organ and piano in cinemas and clubs before becoming an arranger for the mambo-style local bands in 1942. He formed his own unit in 1948 in Mexico when the mambo beat was becoming very popular. Prado was 'King of the Mambo' in Latin America with his scorching brass and persuasive percussion, exemplified in his 1950 recording of 'Mambo Jambo'. He had minor success in the USA in 1953-54 with the title theme from the Italian movie *Anne*, and a South African song 'Skokiaan'. Strong indications that the mambo craze was catching on in the USA in 1954 were the successes of chart entries by Perry Como with 'Papa Loves Mambo' and 'Mambo Italiano' by Rosemary Clooney. Prado's world-wide breakthrough came in 1955 when RCA Records released 'Cherry Pink And Apple Blossom White', with an exciting trumpet solo by Billy Regis. It stayed at number 1 in the US charts for 10 weeks and was featured in the Jane Russell/Richard Egan film, *Underwater!* (1955). In Britain, Eddie Calvert and the Ted Heath orchestra had their own best-selling versions. Prado's follow-up in 1958 was another instrumental, his own composition 'Patricia'. Another chart topper, it contained more

than a hint of the current burgeoning pop sounds with its heavy bass and rocking organ rhythms, along with the cha-cha-cha beat.
Selected albums: *'Prez'* (1959), *A Cat In Latin* (1964). Compilations: *Perez Prado* (1979), *Perez Prado And Orchestra* (1988), *Guantanamera* (1989), *Go Go Mambo* (1993).

Presley, Elvis

b. Elvis Aaron Presley, 8 January 1935, Tupelo, Mississippi, USA, d. 16 August 1977, Memphis, Tennessee. The most celebrated popular music phenomenon of his era and, for many, the purest embodiment of rock 'n' roll, Elvis's life and career have become part of rock legend. The elder of twins, his younger brother, Jesse Garon, was stillborn, a tragedy which partly contributed to the maternal solicitude that affected his childhood and teenage years. Presley's first significant step towards a musical career took place at the age of eight when he won $5.00 in a local song contest performing the lachrymose Red Foley ballad, 'Old Shep'. His earliest musical influence came from attending the Pentecostal Church and listening to the psalms and gospel songs. He also had a strong grounding in country and blues and it was the combination of these different styles that was to provide his unique musical identity.
By the age of 13, Presley had moved with his family to Memphis and during his later school years began cultivating an outsider image with long hair, spidery sideburns and ostentatious clothes. After leaving school he took a job as a truck driver, a role in keeping with his unconventional appearance. In spite of his rebel posturing, Elvis remained studiously polite to his elders and was devoted to his mother. Indeed, it was his filial affection that first prompted him to visit Sun Records, whose studios offered the sophisticated equivalent of a fairground recording booth service. As a birthday present to his mother, Gladys, Elvis cut a version of the Ink Spots' 'My Happiness', backed with the Raskin/Brown/Fisher standard 'That's When Your Heartaches Begin'. The studio manager, Marion Keisker, noted Presley's unusual but distinctive vocal style and informed Sun's owner/producer Sam Phillips of his potential. Phillips nurtured the boy for almost a year before putting him together with country guitarist Scotty Moore and bassist Bill Black. Their early sessions showed considerable promise, especially when Presley began alternating his unorthodox low-key delivery with a high-pitched whine. The amplified guitars of Moore and Black contributed strongly to

the effect and convinced Phillips that the singer was startlingly original. In Presley, Sam saw something that he had long dreamed of discovering: a white boy who sang like a negro.

Presley's debut disc on Sun was the extraordinary 'That's All Right (Mama)', a showcase for his rich, multi-textured vocal dexterity, with sharp, solid backing from his compatriots. The b-side, 'Blue Moon Of Kentucky', was a country song but the arrangement showed that Presley was threatening to slip into an entirely different genre, closer to R&B. Local response to these strange-sounding performances was encouraging and Phillips eventually shifted 20,000 copies of the disc. For his second single, Presley cut Roy Brown's 'Good Rockin' Tonight' backed by the zingy 'I Don't Care If The Sun Don't Shine'. The more roots-influenced 'Milkcow Blues Boogie' followed, while the b-side 'You're A Heartbreaker' had some strong tempo changes which neatly complemented Presley's quirky vocal. 'Baby Let's Play House'/'I'm Left, You're Right, She's Gone' continued the momentum and led to Presley performing on the *Grand Old Opry* and *Louisiana Hayride* radio programmes. A series of live dates commenced in 1955 with drummer D.J. Fontana added to the ranks. Presley toured clubs in Arkansas, Louisiana and Texas billed as 'The King Of Western Bop' and 'The Hillbilly Cat'. Audience reaction verged on the fanatical, which was hardly surprising given Presley's semi-erotic performances. His hip-swivelling routine, in which he cascaded across the stage and plunged to his knees at dramatic moments in a song, was remarkable for the period and prompted near-riotous fan mania. The final Sun single, a cover of Junior Parker's 'Mystery Train', was later acclaimed by many as the definitive rock 'n' roll single with its chugging rhythm, soaring vocal and enticing lead guitar breaks. It established Presley as an artist worthy of national attention and ushered in the next phase of his career, which was dominated by the imposing figure of Colonel Tom Parker.

The Colonel was a former fairground huckster who managed several country artists including Hank Snow and Eddy Arnold. After relieving disc jockey Bob Neal of Presley's managership, Parker persuaded Sam Phillips that his financial interests would be better served by releasing the boy to a major label. RCA Records had already noted the commercial potential of the phenomenon under offer and agreed to pay Sun Records a release fee of $35,000, an incredible sum for the period. The sheer diversity of Presley's musical heritage and his

remarkable ability as a vocalist and interpreter of material enabled him to escape the cultural parochialism of his R&B-influenced predecessors. The attendant rock 'n' roll explosion, in which Presley was both a creator and participant, ensured that he could reach a mass audience, many of them newly-affluent teenagers.

It was on 10 January 1956, a mere two days after his 21st birthday, that Elvis entered RCA's studios in Nashville to record his first tracks for a major label. His debut session produced the epochal 'Heartbreak Hotel', one of the most striking pop records ever released. Co-composed by Hoyt Axton's mother Mae, the song evoked nothing less than a vision of absolute funereal despair. There was nothing in the pop charts of the period that even hinted at the degree of desolation described in the song. Presley's reading was extraordinarily mature and moving, with a determined avoidance of any histrionics in favour of a pained and resigned acceptance of loneliness as death. The economical yet acutely emphatic piano work of Floyd Cramer enhanced the stark mood of the piece, which was frozen in a suitably minimalist production. The startling originality and intensity of 'Heartbreak Hotel' entranced the American public and pushed the single to number 1 for an astonishing eight weeks. Whatever else he achieved, Presley was already assured a place in pop history for one of the greatest major label debut records ever released. During the same month that 'Heartbreak Hotel' was recorded, Presley made his national television debut displaying his sexually-enticing gyrations before a bewildered adult audience whose alleged outrage subsequently persuaded producers to film the star exclusively from the waist upwards. Having outsold his former Sun colleague Carl Perkins with 'Blue Suede Shoes', Presley released a debut album which contained several of the songs he had previously cut with Sam Phillips, including Little Richard's 'Tutti Fruitti', the R&B classic 'I Got A Woman' and an eerie, wailing version of Richard Rodgers/Lorenz Hart's 'Blue Moon', which emphasized his remarkable vocal range.

Since hitting number 2 in the UK lists with 'Heartbreak Hotel', Presley had been virtually guaranteed European success and his profile was increased via a regular series of releases as RCA took full advantage of their bulging back catalogue. Although there was a danger of overkill, Presley's talent, reputation and immensely strong fan base vindicated the intense release schedule and the quality of the material ensured that the public was not disappointed. After hitting number 1 for the second time with the slight ballad 'I Want You, I Need You, I Love You', Presley released what was to become the most commercially successful double-sided single in pop history, 'Hound Dog'/'Don't Be Cruel'. The former was composed by the immortal rock 'n' roll songwriting team of Leiber And Stoller, and presented Presley at his upbeat best with a novel lyric, complete with a striking guitar solo and spirited handclapping from his backing group the Jordanaires. Otis Blackwell's 'Don't Be Cruel' was equally effective with a striking melody line and some clever and amusing vocal gymnastics from the hiccupping King of Western Bop, who also received a co-writing credit. The single remained at number 1 in the USA for a staggering 11 weeks and both sides of the record were massive hits in the UK.

Celluloid fame for Presley next beckoned with *Love Me Tender*, produced by David Weisbert, who had previously worked on James Dean's *Rebel Without A Cause*. Elvis's movie debut received mixed reviews but was a box office smash, while the smouldering, perfectly-enunciated title track topped the US charts for five weeks. The spate of Presley singles continued in earnest through 1957 and one of the biggest was another Otis Blackwell composition, 'All Shook Up' which the singer used as a cheekily oblique comment on his by now legendary dance movements. By late 1956 it was rumoured that Presley would be drafted into the US Army and, as if to compensate for that irksome eventuality, RCA, Twentieth Century Fox and the Colonel stepped up the work-rate and release schedules. Incredibly, three major films were completed in the next two-and-a-half years. *Loving You* boasted a quasi-autobiographical script with Presley playing a truck driver who becomes a pop star. The title track became the b-side of '(Let Me Be Your) Teddy Bear' which reigned at number 1 for seven weeks. The third movie, *Jailhouse Rock*, was Elvis's most successful to date with an excellent soundtrack and some inspired choreography. The Leiber and Stoller title track was an instant classic which again topped the US charts for seven weeks and made pop history by entering the UK listings at number 1. The fourth celluloid outing, *King Creole* (adapted from the Harold Robbins' novel, *A Stone For Danny Fisher*) is regarded by many as Presley's finest film of all and a firm indicator of his sadly unfulfilled potential as a serious actor. Once more the soundtrack album featured some surprisingly strong material such as the haunting 'Crawfish' and the vibrant 'Dixieland Rock'.

By the time *King Creole* was released in 1958, Elvis had already been inducted into the US Forces. A publicity photograph of the singer having his hair shorn symbolically commented on his approaching musical emasculation. Although rock 'n' roll purists mourned the passing of the old Elvis, it seemed inevitable in the context of the 50s that he would move towards a broader base appeal and tone down his rebellious image. From 1958-60, Presley served in the US Armed Forces, spending much of his time in Germany where he was regarded as a model soldier. It was during this period that he first met 14-year-old Priscilla Beaulieu, whom he would later marry in 1967. Back in America, the Colonel kept his absent star's reputation intact via a series of films, record releases and extensive merchandising. Hits such as 'Wear My Ring Around Your Neck', 'Hard Headed Woman', 'One Night', 'I Got Stung', 'A Fool Such As I' and 'A Big Hunk O' Love' filled the long two-year gap and by the time Elvis reappeared, he was ready to assume the mantle of an all-round entertainer. The change was immediately evident in the series of number 1 hits that he enjoyed in the early 60s. The enormously successful 'It's Now Or Never', based on the Italian melody 'O Sole Mio', revealed the King as an operatic crooner, far removed from his earlier raucous recordings. 'Are You Lonesome Tonight?', originally recorded by Al Jolson as early as 1927, allowed Presley to quote some Shakespeare in the spoken-word middle section as well as showing his ham-acting ability with an overwrought vocal. The new clean-cut Presley was presented on celluloid in *GI Blues*. The movie played upon his recent Army exploits and saw him serenading a puppet on the charming chart-topper 'Wooden Heart', which also allowed Elvis to show off his knowledge of German. The grandiose 'Surrender' completed this phase of big ballads in the old-fashioned style. For the next few years Presley concentrated on an undemanding spree of films including *Flaming Star*, *Wild In The Country*, *Blue Hawaii*, *Kid Galahad*, *Girls! Girls! Girls!*, *Follow That Dream*, *Fun In Acapulco*, *It Happened At The World's Fair*, *Kissin' Cousins*, *Viva Las Vegas*, *Roustabout*, *Girl Happy*, *Tickle Me*, *Harem Scarem*, *Frankie And Johnny*, *Paradise Hawaiian Style* and *Spinout*. Not surprisingly, most of his album recordings were hastily completed soundtracks with unadventurous commissioned songs. For his singles he relied increasingly on the formidable Doc Pomus/Mort Shuman team who composed such hits as 'Mess Of Blues', 'Little Sister' and 'His Latest Flame'. More and more, however, the hits were adapted from films and their chart positions suffered accordingly. After the 1963 number 1 'Devil In Disguise', a bleak period followed in which such minor songs as 'Bossa Nova Baby', 'Kiss Me Quick', 'Ain't That Lovin' You Baby' and 'Blue Christmas' became the rule rather than the exception. Significantly, his biggest success of the mid-60s, 'Crying In The Chapel', had been recorded five years before, and part of its appeal came from the realization that it represented something ineffably lost.

In the wake of the Beatles' rise to fame and the beat boom explosion Presley seemed a figure out of time. Yet, in spite of the dated nature of many of his recordings, he could still invest power and emotion into classic songs. The sassy 'Frankie And Johnny' was expertly sung by Elvis as was his moving reading of Ketty Lester's 'Love Letters'. His other significant 1966 release, 'If Everyday Was Like Christmas', was a beautiful festive song unlike anything else in the charts of the period. By 1967, however, it was clear to critics and even a large proportion of his devoted following that Presley had seriously lost his way. He continued to grind out pointless movies such as *Double Trouble*, *Speedway*, *Clambake* and *Live A Little, Love A Little*, even though the box office returns were increasingly poor. His capacity to register instant hits, irrespective of the material was also wearing thin as such lowly-placed singles as 'You Gotta Stop' and 'Long Legged Woman' demonstrated all too alarmingly. However, just as Elvis's career had reached its all-time nadir he seemed to wake up, take stock, and break free from the artistic malaise in which he found himself.

Two songs written by country guitarist Jerry Reed, 'Guitar Man' and 'US Male', proved a spectacular return to form for Elvis in 1968, such was Presley's conviction that the compositions almost seemed to be written specifically for him. During the same year Colonel Tom Parker had approached NBC-TV about the possibility of recording a Presley Christmas special in which the singer would perform a selection of religious songs similar in feel to his early 60s album *His Hand In Mine*. However, the executive producers of the show vetoed that concept in favour of a one-hour spectacular designed to capture Elvis at his rock 'n' rollin' best. It was a remarkable challenge for the singer, seemingly in the autumn of his career, and he responded to the idea with unexpected enthusiasm. The *Elvis TV Special* was broadcast in America on 3 December 1968 and has since gone down as one of the most celebrated moments in pop broadcasting history. The show was not merely good but an absolute revelation, with the King emerging as if he had been frozen in time for 10 years. His determination to recapture past glories oozed from every movement and was discernible in every aside. With his leather jacket and acoustic guitar strung casually round his neck, he resembled nothing less than the consummate pop idol of the 50s who had entranced a generation. To add authenticity to the proceedings he was accompanied by his old sidekicks Scotty Moore and D.J. Fontana. There was no sense of self-parody in the show as Presley joked about his famous surly curled-lip movement and even heaped passing ridicule on his endless stream of bad movies. The music concentrated heavily on his 50s classics but, significantly, there was a startling finale courtesy of the passionate 'If I Can Dream' in which he seemed to sum up the frustration of a decade in a few short lines.

The critical plaudits heaped upon Elvis in the wake of his television special prompted the singer to undertake his most significant recordings in years. With producer Chips Moman overseeing the sessions in January 1969, Presley recorded enough material to cover two highly-praised albums, *From Elvis In Memphis* and *From Memphis To Vegas/From Vegas To Memphis*. The former was particularly strong with such distinctive tracks as the eerie 'Long Black Limousine' and the engagingly melodic 'Any Day Now'. On the singles front, Presley was back in top form and finally coming to terms with contemporary issues, most notably on the socially aware 'In The Ghetto' which hit number 2 in the UK and number 3 in the USA. The glorious 'Suspicious Minds', a wonderful song of marital jealousy with cascading tempo changes and an exceptional vocal arrangement, gave him his first US chart-topper since 'Good Luck Charm' back in 1962. Subsequent hits such as the maudlin 'Don't Cry Daddy', which dealt with the death of a marriage, ably demonstrated Elvis's ability to read a song. Even his final few films seemed less disastrous than expected. In 1969's *Charro*, he grew a beard for the first time in his portrayal of a moody cowboy, while *A Change Of Habit* dealt with more serious matter than usual. More importantly, Presley returned as a live performer at Las Vegas with a strong backing group including guitarist James Burton and pianist Glen D. Hardin. In common with John Lennon, who also returned to the stage that same year with the Plastic Ono Band, Presley opened his set with Carl Perkins' 'Blue Suede Shoes'. His comeback was well-received and one of the live songs, 'The Wonder

Of You', stayed at number 1 in Britain for six weeks during the summer of 1970. There was also a revealing documentary film of the tour Elvis - *That's The Way It Is* and a companion album which included contemporary cover songs such as Tony Joe White's 'Polk Salad Annie', Creedence Clearwater Revival's 'Proud Mary' and Neil Diamond's 'Sweet Caroline'.

During the early 70s Presley continued his live performances, but soon fell victim to the same artistic atrophy that had bedevilled his celluloid career. Rather than re-entering the studio to record fresh material he relied on a slew of patchy live albums which saturated the marketplace. What had been innovative and exciting in 1969 swiftly became a tedious routine and an exercise in misdirected potential. The backdrop to Presley's final years was a sordid slump into drug dependency, reinforced by the pervasive unreality of a pampered lifestyle in his fantasy home, Gracelands. The dissolution of his marriage in 1973 coincided with a further decline and an alarming tendency to put on weight. Remarkably, he continued to undertake live appearances, covering up his bloated frame with brightly coloured jump suits and an enormous, ostentatiously-jewelled belt. He collapsed onstage on a couple of occasions and finally on 16 August 1977 his tired, burnt-out body expired. The official cause of death was a heart attack, no doubt brought on by barbiturate usage over a long period. In the weeks following his demise, his record sales predictably rocketed and 'Way Down' proved a fittingly final UK number 1. The importance of Presley in the history of rock 'n' roll and popular music remains incalculable. In spite of his iconographic status, the Elvis image was never captured in a single moment of time like that of Bill Haley, Buddy Holly or even Chuck Berry. Presley, in spite of his apparent creative inertia, was not a one-dimensional artist clinging to history but a multi-faceted performer whose career spanned several decades and phases. For purists and rockabilly enthusiasts it is the early Elvis who remains of greatest importance and there is no doubting that his personal fusion of black and white musical influences, incorporating R&B and country, produced some of the finest and most durable recordings of the century. Beyond Elvis 'The Hillbilly Cat', however, there was the face that launched a thousand imitators, that black-haired, smiling or smouldering presence who stared from the front covers of numerous EPs, albums and film posters of the late 50s and early 60s. It was that well-groomed, immaculate pop star who inspired a generation of performers and second-rate imitators in the 60s. There was also Elvis the Las Vegas performer, vibrant and vulgar, yet still distant and increasingly appealing to a later generation brought up on the excesses of 70s rock and glam ephemera. Finally, there was the bloated Presley who bestrode the stage in the last months of his career. For many, he has come to symbolize the decadence and loss of dignity that is all too often heir to pop idolatry. It is no wonder that Presley's remarkable career so sharply divides those who testify to his ultimate greatness and those who bemoan the gifts that he seemingly squandered along the way. In a sense, the contrasting images of Elvis have come to represent everything positive and everything destructive about the music industry.

Albums: *Rock 'N' Roll* (1956), *Rock 'N' Roll No. 2* (1957), *Loving You* (1957), *Elvis' Christmas Album* (1957), *King Creole* (1958), *Elvis' Golden Records, Volume 1* (1958), *Elvis* (1959), *A Date With Elvis* (1959), *Elvis' Golden Records, Volume 2* (1960), *Elvis Is Back!* (1960), *G.I. Blues* (1960), *His Hand In Mine* (1961), *Something For Everybody* (1961), *Blue Hawaii* (1961), *Pot Luck* (1962), *Girls! Girls! Girls!* (1963), *It Happened At The World's Fair* (1963), *Fun In Acapulco* (1963), *Elvis' Golden Records, Volume 3* (1964), *Kissin' Cousins* (1964), *Roustabout* (1964), *Girl Happy* (1965), *Flaming Star And Summer Kisses* (1965), *Elvis For Everyone* (1965), *Harem Holiday* (1965), *Frankie And Johnny* (1966), *Paradise, Hawaiian Style* (1966), *California Holiday* (1966), *How Great Thou Art* (1967), *Double Trouble* (1967), *Clambake* (1968), *Elvis' Golden Records, Volume 4* (1968), *Speedway* (1968), *Elvis - TV Special* (1968), *From Elvis In Memphis* (1970), *On Stage February 1970* (1970), *That's The Way It Is* (1971), *I'm 10,000 Years Old - Elvis Country* (1971), *Love Letters From Elvis* (1971), *Elvis Sings The Wonderful World Of Christmas* (1971), *Elvis Now* (1972), *He Touched Me* (1972), *Elvis As Recorded At Madison Square Garden* (1972), *Aloha From Hawaii Via Satellite* (1973), *Elvis* (1973), *Raised On Rock* (1973), *A Legendary Performer, Volume 1* (1974), *Good Times* (1974), *Elvis Recorded On Stage In Memphis* (1974), *Hits Of The 70s* (1974), *Promised Land* (1975), *Having Fun With Elvis On Stage* (1975), *Today* (1975), *The Elvis Presley Sun Collection* (1975), *From Elvis Presley Boulevard, Memphis, Tennessee* (1976), *Welcome To My World* (1977), *A Legendary Performer* (1977), *He Walks Beside Me* (1978), *The '56 Sessions, Vol. 1* (1978), *Elvis's 40 Greatest* (1978), *Elvis - A Legendary Performer, Volume 3* (1979), *Our Memories Of Elvis* (1979), *The '56 Sessions, Vol. 2* (1979), *Elvis Presley*

Sings Leiber And Stoller (1980), *Elvis Aaron Presley* (1979), *Elvis Sings The Wonderful World Of Christmas* (1979), *The First Year* (1979), *The King ... Elvis* (1980), *This Is Elvis* (1981), *Guitar Man* (1981), *Elvis Answers Back* (1981), *The Ultimate Performance* (1981), *Personally Elvis* (1982), *The Sound Of Your Cry* (1982), *Jailhouse Rock/Love In Las Vegas* (1983), *The First Live Recordings* (1984), *A Golden Celebration* (1984), *Rare Elvis* (1985), *Essential Elvis* (1986).

Further reading: *Elvis: A Biography*, Jerry Hopkins. *Elvis: The Final Years*, Jerry Hopkins. *Elvis '56: In The Beginning*, Alfred Wertheimer And Gregory Martinelli. *Elvis*, Albert Goldman. *Up And Down With Elvis Presley*, Marge Crumbaker. *Elvis*, Dave Marsh. *Elvis: The Complete Illustrated Record*, Roy Carr And Mick Farren. *Elvis And Gladys: The Genesis Of The King*, Elaine Dundy.

Previn, André

b. 6 April 1929, Berlin, Germany. After studying music in Berlin and Paris, Previn came to the USA in 1938 when his family emigrated. Resident in Los Angeles, he continued his studies and while still at school worked as a jazz pianist and as an arranger in the film studios. From the mid-40s he made records with some measure of success, but it was in the middle of the following decade that he achieved his greatest renown. The breakthrough came with a series of jazz albums with Shelly Manne, the first of which featured music from the popular show *My Fair Lady*. Previn recorded with lyricist Dory Langdon, who he later married. The marriage broke-up in 1965 and was controversially chronicled in Dory Previn's later solo recordings. In the 60s Previn continued to divide his time between jazz and studio work but gradually his interest in classical music overtook these other fields. By the 70s he was established as one of the world's leading classical conductors. His term as conductor for the London Symphony Orchestra saw him emerge as a popular personality, which involved him television advertising and making celebrated cameo appearances for such light-entertainers as Morecambe And Wise. He became conductor of the Pittsburg Symphony Orchestra in 1976 and later the London Philharmonic, the Los Angeles Philharmonica. He continues to involve himself in many facets of music throughout the 80s and into the 90s - his most recent project, in 1992, was a jazz album with opera singer Dame Kiri Te Kanawa and jazz bass player Ray Brown.

Selected albums: *Previn At Sunset* (1945), *André Previn All-Stars* (1946), *André Previn Plays Fats Waller* (1953), *Let's Get Away From It All* (1955), *But Beautiful* (1956), with Shelly Manne *My Fair Lady* i (1956), *André Previn And His Friends: Li'l Abner* (1957), *André And Dory Previn* (1957), *Double Play* (1957), *Pal Joey* (1957), *Gigi* (1958), *Sessions, Live* (1958), *André Previn Plays Songs By Vernon Duke* (1958), *King Size* (1958), *André Previn Plays Songs By Jerome Kern* (1959), *West Side Story* (1959), with the David Rose Orchestra *Secret Songs For Young Lovers* (1959), *The Previn Scene* (c.1959), *Composer, Arranger, Conductor, Pianist* (60s), *The Magic Moods Of André Previn* (60s), *Like Love* (1960), *André Previn Plays Harold Arlen* (1961), *André Previn* (1960), *Give My Regards To Broadway* (1960), *Thinking Of You* (1960), *Music From Camelot* (1960), *A Touch Of Elegance* (1961), *André Previn And J.J. Johnson Play Mack The Knife And Bilbao Song* (1961), *André Previn And J.J. Johnson* (c.1962), *Two For The See-saw* (c.1962), *Sittin' On A Rainbow* (1962), *The Light Fantastic: A Tribute To Fred Astaire* (c.1963), *4 To Go!* (1963), *André Previn In Hollywood* (1963), *Soft And Swinging* (1964), *Sound Stage* (1964), *My Fair Lady* ii (1964), *Previn At Sunset* (1975), with Itzhak Perlman *A Different Kind Of Blues* (1981), with Perlman *It's A Breeze* (c.1981).

Further reading: *André Previn*, Michael Freedland.

Price, Lloyd

b. 9 March 1933, Kenner, Louisiana, USA. Price, who launched his career in the early 50s performing rocking R&B, New Orleans-style, was - like his Crescent City compatriot, Fats Domino - made for the rock 'n' roll era. He did not have to modify his approach one iota to become a rock 'n' roll hit-maker in the late 50s. Price formed his own band in New Orleans in 1949 and in 1952 was signed with the Los Angeles-based Specialty Records, which made a practice of recording New Orleans artists. His first hit, 'Lawdy Miss Clawdy' (US R&B number 1, 1952) established his career in the R&B field and he followed with four more Top 10 hits. Military service intervened and took Price out of action from 1954-56. On returning to civilian life he settled in Washington, D.C. and set up a record company with Harold Logan. Price regained his place on the chart in 1957 with 'Just Because' (US R&B number 3 and pop Top 30). Signed to ABC-Paramount, the company transformed their R&B veteran into a rock 'n' roll hitmaker for the new teen market. He and Logan revamped an old blues, 'Stack-O-Lee', that had been a hit for Ma Rainey in the 20s and made it one of his biggest successes (US R&B and pop

Louis Prima

number 1, 1959). In the UK, it entered the Top 10. Price's chart career peaked in 1959, with such hits as 'Where Were You (On Our Wedding Day)' (US R&B number 4 and pop Top 30), 'Personality' (US R&B number 1 and pop number 2), 'I'm Gonna Get Married' (US R&B number 1 and pop number 3). In the UK, he found success in the pop charts with 'Where Were You' (number 15), 'Personality' (number 9), 'I'm Gonna Get Married' (number 23). The hits continued, to a lesser extent, the following year with 'Lady Luck' (US R&B number 3 and pop Top 20) and 'Question' (US R&B number 5 and number 19 pop). Three years later Price re-surfaced on the Double-L label (owned by Price and Logan), briefly making an impact on the emerging soul market with his reworking of jazz standards 'Misty' (US R&B number 11 and pop Top 30) and 'Bill Bailey' (US R&B Top 40 and pop Top 100 as 'Billy Baby'). Price's last chart record was in 1976 on the LPG label, a label he formed in partnership with the notorious boxing promoter Don King.
Albums: *Lloyd Price* (1959), *The Exciting Lloyd Price* (1959), *Mr. Personality* (1959), *Mr. Personality Sings The Blues* (1960), *The Fantastic Lloyd Price* (1960), *Lloyd Price Sings The Million Sellers* (1961), *Cookin' With Lloyd Price* (1961), *The Lloyd Price Orchestra* (1963), *Misty* (1963), *Lloyd Swings For Sammy* (1965), *Lloyd Price Now* (1969), *To The Roots And Back* (1972), *The Nominee* (1978). Compilations: *Mr. Personality's Big 15* (1960), *The Best Of Lloyd Price* (1970), *Lloyd Price's 16 Greatest Hits* (1972), *Original Hits* (1972), *The ABC Collection* (1976), *Misty* (1977), *Mr. Personality Revisited* (1983), *Lawdy!* (1991).

Pride, Dickie

b. Richard Knellar, Thornton Heath, England. Pride, a former Royal College of Church Music chorister and trainee stonemason, was 'discovered' in 1958 singing rock 'n' roll in a London pub by Russ Conway who recommended him to both EMI producer Norrie Paramor and pop svengali Larry Parnes. Groomed and given a *nom de théâtre*, the diminutive youth's voice rather than his face was his fortune - though his onstage convulsions earned him the nickname 'The Sheik Of Shake'. The first that Britain at large saw of him was on ITV's *Oh Boy!*, plugging his 1959 cover of Little Richard's 'Slippin' And Slidin'.' While his third single, 'Primrose Lane', touched the Top 30, the failure of later singles contradicted a notion some had that Pride was a potential rival to Cliff Richard. Nevertheless, he was still impressing

audiences in 1960 when he recorded a creditable album of Tin Pan Alley chestnuts with Ted Heath's orchestra. This ploy might have set him on the road of the 'all round entertainer' had not his dabbling with amphetamines alienated him from Parnes and precipitated a fall from grace that found him delivering coal and nursing debilities related to the drug abuse that brought him to an early grave.
Album: *Pride Without Prejudice* (1960).

Prima, Louis

b. 7 December 1911, New Orleans, Louisiana, USA, d. 24 August 1978. A self-taught trumpet player, Prima was working professionally in his home town from the mid-20s. He attracted a good local following and it was 1935 before he was lured away for more than a brief trip. In Chicago and Los Angeles he held long residencies, made films and records and for the rest of the 30s and throughout the 40s and 50s was rarely out of work, making a number of successful records with his then wife Keely Smith (whom he divorced in 1961). Although his later career was devised to suit nightclub and casino audiences from New York to Las Vegas, Prima could still turn in good jazz solos which recalled his 30s and 40s recordings. His hoarse singing voice was used to good effect on such records as 'That Old Black Magic' and 'Buena Sera' and on the soundtrack of the 1966 Walt Disney film *Jungle Book* (he was 'King Louis' the orang-utan). He died in August 1978, having long been in a coma following an operation for a brain tumour.
Selected albums: *A Nite On 52nd Street* (1939), *One Night Stand With Louis Prima* i (1944), *Louis Prima At Frank Dailey's Terrace Room* (1944), *One Night Stand With Louis Prima* ii (1947), *Louis Prima Swings* (1955), *The Wildest Show At Tahoe* (1955), *The Wildest* (1957), *Jump, Jive And Wail* (1958), with Keely Smith *Hey Boy! Hey Girl!* (1958), with Smith *Las Vegas Prima Style* (1958), *Call Of The Wildest* (1958), with Smith *Senior Prom* (1959), with Smith *Louis And Keely!* (1959), *Louis Prima* (1959), *Strictly Prima* (1959), with Smith *Together* (1960), *Wonderland By Night* (1960), *Doin' The Twist* (1961), *The Wildest Comes Home* (1962), *Plays Pretty For The People* (1964). Compilations: *The Hits Of Louis And Keely* (1961), *Jimmie Lunceford And Louis Prima, 1945* (1979), *Jump, Jive An' Wail* (1986), *Live From Las Vegas* (1988), *Just A Gigolo 1945-50* (1988).

R

Rainwater, Marvin

b. Marvin Karlton Percy, 2 July 1925, Wichita, Kansas, USA. A big-voiced, rockabilly singer-songwriter, who is a quarter Cherokee Indian (using his mother's maiden name on stage). He became a regular on Red Foley's *Ozark Mountain Jubilee* in the early 50s and after being spotted on Arthur Godfrey's Talent Scouts television show in the mid-50s was signed to Coral. The first of his two singles for them 'I Gotta Go Get My Baby' became a hit for the label when their top act Teresa Brewer covered his record. Rainwater then joined MGM and his second release, the self composed 'Gonna Find Me A Bluebird', in 1957 gave him his only US Top 40 hit. Later that year a duet with Connie Francis (before her string of hits), 'Majesty Of Love', graced the US Top 100. In 1958 another of his songs 'Whole Lotta Woman', which only reached number 60 in his homeland, topped the UK chart and his UK recorded follow-up 'I Dig You Baby' also entered the British Top 20. He later recorded without success for Warwick, Warner Brothers, United Artists, Wesco, his own label Brave, as well as UK labels Philips, Sonet and Westwood. In subsequent years, the man who performed in full American Indian regalia, has played the rockabilly and country circuit on both sides of the Atlantic.
Albums: *Marvin Rainwater Sings* (1958), *Marvin Rainwater* (1962). Compilation: *Classic Recordings* (1992).

Ray, Johnnie

b. 10 January 1927, Dallas, Oregon, USA, d. 24 February 1990, Los Angeles, California, USA. Ray was known at various times in his career as the Prince of Wails, The Nabob of Sob, and The Howling Success because of his highly emotional singing and apparent ability to cry at will. Ray is rated an important influence in the development of 50s and early 60s popular music. Of North American Indian origin, he became deaf in his right ear at the age of 12, which caused him to wear a hearing-aid throughout his career. He was heavily influenced by gospel and R&B music and performed in bars and clubs around Detroit in the late 40s, singing to his own piano accompaniment. Signed by Columbia Records in 1951, his first two releases were on their small OKeh label, usually reserved for black artists. His first record, 'Whiskey And Gin', was followed by 'Cry'. Unsophisticated, full of anguish, despair and a good deal of sobbing, it shocked a pop world accustomed to male singers crooning in front of big bands, and streaked to the top of the US charts, complete with Ray's own composition, 'The Little White Cloud That Cried', on the b-side. 'Cry' became his 'identity' song, and a multi-million-seller.

Ray was then transferred to the Columbia label, and during the next couple of years, had several massive US hits including 'Please Mr Sun', 'Here Am I - Broken Hearted', 'Walkin' My Baby Back Home' and 'Somebody Stole My Gal'. His stage performances, with their overt sexuality and hysterical audience reaction, made him *persona non grata* to parents of teenagers, worldwide. For a few years during the 50s, he enjoyed phenomenal success, revolutionizing popular music and symbolizing teenagers' frustrations and desires. Always acknowledging his gospel roots, Ray recorded several tracks associated with black artists, including the Drifters' R&B hit, 'Such a Night' (1954), which was banned on several USA radio stations, and 'Just Walkin' In the Rain' (1956), which climbed to number 2 in the US charts, and was originally recorded by the Prisonaires. By contrast, in 1954, he played a young singer who decides to be a priest in Irving Berlin's musical film, *There's No Business Like Show Business*. Ray sang the gospel-styled 'If You Believe' and 'Alexander's Ragtime Band'. During the late 50s in the USA, rumours were rife concerning his possible homosexuality and of drug-taking, and as a result he became more popular abroad than at home. In the UK, in-person and on-record, he had been a favourite since 1952. Three of his US hits reached UK number 1, including 'Yes Tonight Josephine' (1957). Other UK successes included 'Faith Can Move Mountains', 'Hey There' and 'Look Homeward Angel'. Ray also duetted with Doris Day ('Ma Says Pa Says, 'Full Time Job', 'Let's Walk That-Away') and Frankie Laine ('Good Evening Friends'). In the early 60s, suffering from financial problems and alcoholism, and left behind as the musical climate rapidly changed, he turned to cabaret in the USA. During the 70s he began to recreate his career, leaning heavily on his old material for its nostalgic appeal. Always in demand in the UK, he was headlining there until the late 80s. His last performance is reported to have been in his hometown in October 1990. He died of liver failure in 1990 in Los Angeles. As to his

Johnnie Ray (second left'

influence and effect, one writer concluded: 'Ray was the link between Frank Sinatra and Elvis Presley, re-creating the bobby-sox mayhem that elevated "The Voice" while anticipating the sexual chaos that accompanied Presley'.

Selected albums: *Johnnie Ray Sings The Big Beat* (1957), *Johnnie Ray At The Desert Inn In Las Vegas* (1959), *A Sinner Am I* (1959), *'Til Morning* (1959), *Johnnie Ray On The Trail* (1959), *I Cry For You* (1960), *Johnnie Ray* (1962), *Yesterday, Today And Tomorrow* (1980). Compilations: *Johnnie Ray's Greatest Hits* (1959), *An American Legend* (1979), *Portrait Of A Song Stylist* (1989).

Regan, Joan

b. 19 January 1928, Romford, Essex, England. Regan was a popular singer in the UK during the 50s and early 60s, with a particularly glamorous image. It was after working at various jobs, which included a photographer's re-toucher, that Regan first made an impression on the music scene in 1953. Her private recordings of 'Too Young' and 'I'll Walk Alone' gained her a contract with Decca Records, partly because it was thought she had a 'Vera Lynn sound'. Her first releases, 'Till I Waltz Again With You' and 'I'll Always Be Thinking Of You', were followed by 'Ricochet', on which she was backed by Ronnie Aldrich's Squadronaires. It made the UK Top 10, and led to the nationwide fame she achieved when she became the resident singer on producer Richard Afton's television series, *Quite Contrary*, followed later by four series of her own *Be My Guest* programmes. After being knocked out by a descending safety curtain during her first appearance in variety, she developed her act to include effective impressions of artists such as Gracie Fields, Judy Garland, and actress, Anna Neagle, to whom Regan bore a remarkable facial resemblance. During the late 50s and early 60s, Regan appeared in several shows at the London Palladium, including *We're Having A Ball*, with Max Bygraves; *Stars In Your Eyes*, with Russ Conway, Cliff Richard, Edmund Hockridge and Billy Dainty; in pantomime with Frankie Vaughan and Jimmy Edwards; and several Royal Command Performances. Her other record hits, through to 1961, included 'Someone Else's Roses', 'If I Give My Heart To You', 'Prize Of Gold', 'Open Up Your Heart', 'May You Always', 'Happy Anniversary', 'Papa Loves Mama', 'One Of The Lucky Ones', 'Must Be Santa', 'Wait For Me' (with the Johnston Brothers). She also recorded several duets, including 'Seven And A Half Cents'/'Good Evening Friends', with Max Bygraves; 'Cleo And Me-O', with Dickie Valentine; and 'Open Up Your Heart', with her son, Rusty. She also released *Just Joan, The Girl Next Door, Don't Talk To Me About Love* and *Joan And Ted* (with Edmund Hockridge). In July 1957, Regan married Harry Claff, the joint general manager and box office manager of the London Palladium. In November, the *Daily Herald* reported that she was to have a baby in February of the following year - seven months after the wedding. After receiving 'abusive and wounding letters from people who were personally unknown to her', Regan successfully sued the newspaper for libel, and her daughter was born in April. In 1963, she was involved in a far more serious court case, when her husband was sentenced to five years' imprisonment for 'frauds on his employers involving £62,000'. Regan, who had known nothing about the deceptions, suffered a nervous breakdown, and divorced him later on the grounds of adultery. She resumed work later and, in 1968, married a doctor, Martin Cowan, and eventually, settled in Florida, USA. In 1984, she slipped in the shower, hit her head on the tiles, and suffered a brain haemorrhage. After an emergency operation she was left paralysed and speechless. Her recovery, which entailed much physical and speech therapy, was aided by her miming to her old records. In 1987, some of those tracks, together with others by various 'Stars Of The Fifties', Dickie Valentine, Lita Roza and Jimmy Young, were issued on the double album, *Unchained Melodies*. In the same year, while on holiday in the UK, Regan was invited to sing on stage again, by her old accompanist, Russ Conway, and continued to travel from her Florida base to appear in UK summer shows, into the 90s.

Compilation: *The World Of Joan Regan* (1976).

Reynolds, Debbie

b. Mary Francis Reynolds, 1 April 1932, El Paso, Texas, USA. After moving to California in 1940 she became a majorette and played French horn with the Burbank Youth Orchestra. It was here she was spotted by talent scouts at a Miss Burbank competition in 1948. She quickly became a leading light in film musicals throughout the 50s, most notably *Singing In The Rain* (1952), *Susan Slept Here* (1954), *Tammy And The Batchelor* (1957). She recorded her first million selling single Honeymoon in 1951 via a duet with Carleton Carpenter 'Ada Daba Honeymoon' from the film *Two Weeks With Love*. She also went to the top of the US charts in 1957 with 'Million Selling

Joan Regan

'Tammy' (from *Tammy And The Batchelor*). She married the singer and actor Eddie Fisher in September 1955, and their daughter Carrie is now an established actor and writer. They divorced in 1959 when Fisher married Elizabeth Taylor. In 1966 Reynolds returned to play *The Singing Nun* (a fictionalized story about Soeur Sourire) on film, before appearing in her own television series *Debbie* in 1969. She later became a successful comedienne and produced her own keep fit videos.

Albums: *The Singing Nun* (1966), *Debbie* (1985).

Richard, Cliff

b. Harry Roger Webb, 14 October 1940, Lucklow, India. One of the most popular and enduring talents in the history of UK showbusiness, Richard began his career as a rock 'n' roll performer in 1957. His fascination for Elvis Presley encouraged him to join a skiffle group and several months later he teamed up with drummer Terry Smart and guitarist Ken Payne to form the Drifters. They played at various clubs in the Cheshunt/Hoddesdon area of Hertfordshire before descending on the famous 2Is coffee bar in London's Old Compton Street. There they were approached by lead guitarist Ian Samwell and developed their act as a quartet. In 1958, they secured their big break in the unlikely setting of a Saturday morning talent show at the Gaumont cinema in Shepherd's Bush. It was there that the senatorial theatrical agent George Ganyou recognized Cliff's sexual appeal and singing abilities and duly financed the recording of a demonstration tape of 'Breathless' and 'Lawdy Miss Clawdy'. A copy reached the hands of EMI producer Norrie Paramor who was impressed enough to grant the ensemble an audition. Initially, he intended to record Richard as a solo artist backed by an orchestra, but the persuasive performer insisted upon retaining his own backing group. With the assistance of a couple of session musicians, the unit recorded the American teen ballad 'Schoolboy Crush' as a projected first single. An acetate of the recording was paraded around Tin Pan Alley and came to the attention of the influential television producer Jack Good. It was not the juvenile 'Schoolboy Crush' which captured his attention, however, but the Ian Samwell b-side 'Move It'. Good reacted with characteristically manic enthusiasm when he heard the disc, rightly recognizing that it sounded like nothing else in the history of UK pop. The distinctive riff and unaffected vocal seemed authentically American, completely at odds with the mannered material that

usually emanated from British recording studios. With Good's ceaseless promotion, which included a full-page review in the music paper *Disc*, Cliff's debut was eagerly anticipated and swiftly rose to number 2 in the UK charts. Meanwhile, the star made his debut on Good's television showcase *Oh Boy!*, and rapidly replaced Marty Wilde as Britain's premier rock 'n' roll talent. The low-key role offered to the Drifters persuaded Samwell to leave the group to become a professional songwriter, and by the end of 1958 a new line-up emerged featuring Hank B. Marvin and Bruce Welch. Before long, they changed their name to the Shadows, in order to avoid confusion with the black American R&B group, the Drifters.

Meanwhile, Richard consolidated his position in the rock 'n' roll pantheon, even outraging critics in true Elvis Presley fashion. The *New Musical Express* denounced his 'violent, hip-swinging' and 'crude exhibitionism' and pontificated: 'Tommy Steele became Britain's teenage idol without resorting to this form of indecent, short-sighted vulgarity'. Critical mortification had little effect on the screaming female fans who responded to the singer's boyish sexuality with increasing intensity.

1959 was a decisive year for Richard and a firm indicator of his longevity as a performer. With management shake-ups, shifts in national musical taste and some distinctly average singles his career could easily have been curtailed, but instead he matured and transcended his Presley-like beginnings. A recording of Lionel Bart's 'Living Doll' provided him with a massive UK number 1 and three months later he returned to the top with the plaintive 'Travellin' Light'. He also starred in two films, within 12 months. *Serious Charge*, a non-musical drama, was banned in some areas as it dealt with the controversial subject of homosexual blackmail. The Wolf Mankowitz directed *Expresso Bongo*, in which Richard played the delightfully named Bongo Herbert, was a cinematic pop landmark, brilliantly evoking the rapacious world of Tin Pan Alley. It remains one of the most revealing and humorous films ever made on the music business and proved an interesting vehicle for Richard's varied talents.

From 1960 onwards Richard's career progressed along more traditional lines leading to acceptance as a middle-of-the-road entertainer. Varied hits such as the breezy, chart-topping 'Please Don't Tease', the rock 'n' rolling 'Nine Times Out Of Ten' and reflective 'Theme For A Dream' demonstrated his range, and in 1962 he hit a new peak with 'The Young Ones'. A glorious pop

Cliff Richard with musical comedy star Adele Leigh

anthem to youth, with some striking guitar work from Hank Marvin, the song proved one of his most memorable number 1 hits. The film of the same name was a charming period piece, with a strong cast and fine score. It broke box office records and spawned a series of similar movies from its star, who was clearly following Elvis Presley's cinematic excursions as a means of extending his audience. Unlike the King, however, Richard supplemented his frequent movie commitments with tours, summer seasons, regular television slots and even pantomime appearances. The run of UK Top 10 hits continued uninterrupted until as late as mid-1965. Although the showbiz glitz had brought a certain aural homogeneity to the material, the catchiness of songs like 'Bachelor Boy', 'Summer Holiday', 'On The Beach' and 'I Could Easily Fall' was undeniable. These were neatly, if predictably, complemented by ballad releases such as 'Constantly', 'The Twelfth Of Never' and 'The Minute You're Gone'.

The formula looked likely to be rendered redundant by the British beat boom, but Richard expertly rode that wave, even improving his selection of material along the way. He bravely, though relatively unsuccessfully, covered a Rolling Stones song, 'Blue Turns To Grey', before again hitting top form with the beautifully melodic 'Visions'. During 1966, he had almost retired after converting to fundamentalist Christianity, but elected to use his singing career as a positive expression of his faith. The sparkling 'In The Country' and gorgeously evocative 'The Day I Met Marie' displayed the old strengths to the full, but in the swiftly changing cultural climate of the late 60s, Richard's hold on the pop charts could no longer be guaranteed. The 1968 Eurovision Song Contest offered him a chance of further glory, but the jury placed him a close second with the 'oom-pah-pah'-sounding 'Congratulations'. The song was nevertheless a consummate Eurovision performance and proved one of the biggest UK number 1s of the year. Immediately thereafter, Cliff's chart progress declined and his choice of material proved at best desultory. Although there were a couple of solid entries, Raymond Froggatt's 'Big Ship' and a superb duet with Hank Marvin 'Throw Down A Line', Richard seemed a likely contender for Variety as the decade closed.

The first half of the 70s saw him in a musical rut. The chirpy but insubstantial 'Goodbye Sam, Hello Samantha' was a Top 10 hit in 1970 and heralded a notable decline. A second shot at the Eurovision Song Contest with 'Power To All Our Friends' brought his only other Top 10 success of the period and it was widely assumed that his chart career was spent. However, in 1976 there was a surprise resurgence in his career when Bruce Welch of the Shadows was assigned to produce his colleague. The sessions resulted in the best-selling album *I'm Nearly Famous*, which included two major hits 'Miss You Nights' and 'Devil Woman'. The latter was notable for its decidedly un-Christian imagery and the fact that it gave Richard a rare US chart success. Although Welch remained at the controls for two more albums, time again looked as though it would kill off Richard's perennial chart success. A string of meagre singles culminated in the dull 'Green Light' which stalled at number 57, his lowest chart placing since he started singing. Coincidentally, his backing musicians, Terry Britten and Alan Tarney, had moved into songwriting and production at this point and encouraged him to adopt a more contemporary sound on the album *Rock 'N' Roll Juvenile*. The most startling breakthrough however was the attendant single 'We Don't Talk Anymore', written by Tarney and produced by Welch. An exceptional pop record, which gave the singer his first UK number 1 hit in over a decade and also reached the Top 10 in the US. The 'new' Richard sound, so refreshing after some of his staid offerings in the late 70s, brought further well arranged hits, such as 'Carrie' and 'Wired For Sound', and ensured that he was a chart regular throughout the 80s.

Although he resisted the temptation to try anything radical, there were subtle changes in his musical approach. One feature of his talent that emerged during the 80s was a remarkable facility as a duettist. Collaborations with Olivia Newton-John, Phil Everly, Sarah Brightman, Sheila Walsh, Elton John and Van Morrison added a completely new dimension to his career. It was something of a belated shock to realize that Richard may be one of the finest harmony singers working in the field of popular music. His perfectly enunciated vocals and the smooth texture of his voice have the power to complement work that he might not usually tackle alone.

The possibility of his collaborating with an artist even further from his sphere than Van Morrison remains a tantalizing challenge. Throughout his three decades in the pop charts, Cliff has displayed a valiant longevity. He parodied one of his earliest hits with comedy quartet the Young Ones and registered yet another number 1; he appeared in the stage musical *Time*; he sang religious songs on gospel tours; he sued the *New Musical Express* for an appallingly libellous review far more vicious than their acerbic comments back in 1958; he was decorated by the Queen; and he celebrated his 50th birthday with a move into social commentary with the anti-war hit 'From A Distance'. And so he goes on. Richard has outlasted every musical trend of the past four decades with a sincerity and commitment that may well be unmatched in his field. He is British pop's most celebrated survivor.

Selected albums: *Cliff* (1959), *Cliff Sings* (1959), *Me And My Shadows* (1960), *Listen To Cliff* (1961), *21 Today* (1961), *The Young Ones* (1961), *32 Minutes And 17 Seconds With Cliff Richard* (1962), *Summer Holiday* (1963), *Cliff's Hit Album* (1963), *When In Spain* (1963), *Wonderful Life* (1964), *Aladdin And His Wonderful Lamp* (1964), *Cliff Richard* (1965), *More Hits By Cliff* (1965), *When In Rome* (1965), *Love Is Forever* (1965), *Kinda Latin* (1966), *Finders Keepers* (1966), *Cinderella* (1967), *Don't Stop Me Now* (1967), *Good News* (1967), *Cliff In Japan* (1968), *Two A Penny* (1968), *Established 1958* (1968), *The Best Of Cliff* (1969), *Sincerely Cliff* (1969), *It'll Be Me* (1969), *Cliff 'Live' At The Talk Of The Town* (1970), *All My Love* (1970), *About That Man* (1970), *Tracks 'N' Grooves* (1970), *His Land* (1970), *Cliff's Hit Album* (1971), *The Cliff Richard Story* (1972), *The Best Of Cliff Volume 2* (1972), *Take Me High* (1973), *Help It Along* (1974), *The 31st Of February Street* (1974), *Everybody Needs Somebody* (1975), *I'm Nearly Famous* (1976), *Cliff Live* (1976), *Every Face Tells A Story* (1977), *Small Corners* (1977), *Green Light* (1978), *Thank You Very Much* (1979), *Rock 'N' Roll Juvenile* (1979), *40 Golden Greats* (1979), *Rock On With Cliff* (1980), *The Cliff Richard Songbook* (1980), *Listen To Cliff* (1980), *I'm No Hero* (1980), *Love Songs* (1981), *Wired For Sound* (1981), *Now You See Me, Now You Don't* (1982), *Dressed For The Occasion* (1983), *Silver* (1983), *Cliff In The 60s* (1984), *Cliff And The Shadows* (1984), *Walking In The Light* (1984), *The Rock Connection* (1984), *Time* (1986), *Hymns And Inspirational Songs* (1986), *Always Guaranteed* (1987), *Private Collection* (1988), *The Album* (1993).

Riddle, Nelson

b. Nelson Smock Riddle, 1 June 1921, Oradell, New Jersey, USA, d. 6 October 1985. After studying piano, Riddle took up the trombone when in his early teens and in the late 30s played in a number of big bands, including those led by Jerry Wald, Charlie Spivak, Tommy Dorsey and Bob Crosby. After a stint in the army, he settled in California and studied arranging with Mario Castelnuovo-Tedesco and conducting with Victor Bay. In the late 40s Riddle joined NBC, but was lured to Capitol Records and registered immediately with a driving arrangement of 'Blacksmith Blues' for Ella Mae Morse. He confirmed his outstanding ability when he began work on records by Nat 'King' Cole, and Frank Sinatra. Among these were some of Cole's most engaging and memorable sides, such as 'Unforgettable', 'Somewhere Along The Way' and 'Ballerina', along with a good many of his best-selling albums. In addition, Riddle usually conducted the orchestra, and his backings can be heard on Sinatra's important early Capitol albums, such as *Songs For Young Lovers*, *Swing Easy*, *Songs For Swingin' Lovers*, *In The Wee Small Hours*, and many other later ones. He also served as musical director on most of the singer's popular television specials. To a considerable extent, Riddle's easy swinging charts, with their echoes of the big band music of an earlier era, and the distinctive solos of George Roberts (trombone) and Harry Edison (trumpet), were of considerable importance in re-establishing Sinatra as a major star of popular music. Riddle also worked extensively with Ella Fitzgerald on albums such as *Ella Swings Brightly With Nelson*, and the highly acclaimed *Songbook* series. Other artists to benefit from the distinctive Riddle touch were Judy Garland (*Judy*), Rosemary Clooney (*Rosie Solves The Swinging Riddle*), Sammy Davis Jnr., (*That's Entertainment*), Eddie Fisher (*Games That Lovers Play*), Jack Jones (*There's Love*), Peggy Lee (*Jump For Joy*), Dean Martin (*This Time I'm Swinging*), Johnny Mathis (*I'll Buy You A Star*), Antonio Carlos Jobim (*The Brazilian Mood*), Shirley Bassey (*Let's Face The Music*), Dinah Shore (*Yes Indeed*), and many more. In 1954, Riddle had some success with 'Brother John', adapted from the French song, 'Frere Jacques', and, in the following year his instrumental version of 'Lisbon Antigua' topped the US chart. He also made some fine, non vocal albums, which contrasted the lush ballads of *The Tender Touch* and *The Joy Of Living* with the up-tempo exuberance of *Hey...Let Yourself Go* and *C'mon...Get Happy*. Although under contract to Capitol at the time, he is usually credited with conducting and arranging another label's *Phil Silvers Swings Bugle Calls For Big Band*, which contained Riddle compositions (with US Army/Sgt. Bilko connotations) such as 'Chow, A Can Of Cow And Thou' and 'The Eagle Screams'. Another unusual record item was *Sing A Song With Riddle*, a set of genuine Riddle arrangements, complete with sheet music and an invitation to the listener to become

Edmundo Ros

the featured vocalist. From the mid-50s Riddle was also active in television and feature films; he wrote the theme for the long-running series *Route 66*, and received Oscar nominations for his background scores for movies such as *Li'l Abner, Can-Can, Robin And The Seven Hoods*, and *Paint Your Wagon*, and won an Academy Award in 1974 for his music for *The Great Gatsby*. Some of his other film credits included *The Pajama Game, St. Louis Blues, Merry Andrew* and several Sinatra movies such as *The Joker Is Wild* and *Pal Joey*. After attempting retirement, Riddle made an unexpected and hugely successful comeback in the early 80s, when he recorded three albums with Linda Ronstadt: *What's New, Lush Life*, and *For Sentimental Reasons*. A gentle, self-effacing man, he was in poor heath in his later years, and died in October 1985.

Selected albums: *Oklahoma!* (1955), *Moonglow* (1955), *Lisbon Antigua* (1956), *Hey...Let Yourself Go!* (1957), *The Tender Touch* (1957), *C'mon...Get Happy!* (1958), *Sea Of Dreams* (1958), *Sing A Song With Riddle* (1959), *The Joy Of Living* (1959), *Love Tide* (1961), *Tenderloin* (1961), *Magic Moments* (1962), *Route 66 And Other Great TV Themes* (1962), *Love Is Just A Game Of Poker* (1962), *British Columbia Suite* (1963), *Bright And The Beautiful* (1967), *Music For Wives & Lovers* (1967), *Riddle Of Today* (1968), *The Today Sound Of Nelson Riddle* (1969), *Nat - An Orchestral Portait* (1969), *Nelson Riddle Conducts The 101 Strings* (1970), *Vivé Legrand!* (1973), *The Look Of Love* (1982), *Romance Fire And Fancy* (1983). Selected compilations: *The Silver Collection* (1985), *The Capitol Years* (1993).

Rivieras

This R&B vocal group hailed from Englewood, New Jersey, USA. The members were, Homer Dunn (lead), Charles Allen (bass), Ronald Cook (tenor) and Andrew Jones (baritone). The group specialized in singing doo-wop versions of old big band hits, especially those of Glenn Miller. Homer Dunn formed his first group, the Bob-O-Links, in 1952 in Hackensack, New Jersey. Moving to Englewood, Dunn formed the Rivieras in 1955, and they managed to stay together for three years playing local gigs before being eventually signed to the Coed label. The Rivieras' principal hits were 'Count Every Star' (1958), which was previously a hit for Ray Anthony, and 'Moonlight Seranade' (1959) a Miller hit in 1939. Other outstanding releases put out before the group disbanded in 1961 were 'Our Love' (1959) and 'Moonlight Cocktail' (1960), previously hits for Tommy Dorsey and, Miller respectively.

Albums: with the Duprees *Jerry Blavat Presents Drive-In Sounds* (late 50s), *The Rivieras Sing* (late 50s). Compilation: *Moonlight Cocktails* (1992).

Rodgers, Jimmie

b. James Frederick Rodgers, 18 September 1933, Camus, Washington, USA. After being taught by his mother, the young Rodgers successfully auditioned for the Arthur Godfrey talent show and impressed Luigi Creatore and Hugo Peretti who signed him to their recently formed Roulette Records. Rodgers' creamy, effortless voice and blend of folk-tinged pop appealed to a post-war middle America, and over the next decade he made the *Billboard* singles chart 25 times. He never however, topped his debut, 'Honeycomb', which stayed at number 1 for four weeks in 1957 (number 30 in the UK). His early successes included 'Kisses Sweeter Than Wine' a Top 3 hit in 1957 which vied with Frankie Vaughan in the UK for the best position, (Rodgers number 7, Vaughan number 8). One of Rodgers' most memorable songs was the innocent but catchy 'English Country Garden', which although it became his biggest UK hit (reaching the Top 5) it did not appear to warrant an American release, possibly because of its title. Rodgers suffered a serious mugging in 1967 which left him with a fractured skull. Although he eventually returned to performing full-time, his career had lost its momentum. He was still singing professionally in the late 80s.

Selected albums: *Jimmie Rodgers* (1957), *Its Over* (1966), *Child Of Clay* (1968), *Windmills Of Your Mind* (1969), *This Is Jimmie Rodgers* (1987). Compilation: *Best Of Jimmie Rodgers* (1988), *Kisses Sweeter Than Wine* (1988).

Ros, Edmundo

b. 7 December 1910, Port Of Spain, Trinidad. While spending his early life in Venezuela, Ros attended the Military Academy at Caracas, where, via the Academy's band, he became interested in music and learned to play the euphonium or 'bombardin'. Despite harbouring ambitions to become a criminal lawyer, he travelled to the UK in 1937 and studied composition and harmony at the Royal Academy of Music. Although he recorded with jazzman Fats Waller in 1938, Ros mainly sang and served as percussionist, with various Latin-styled bands, including one led by pianist Don Marino Barretto. He formed his own five piece unit, Rumba With Ros, in 1940, and, for the next 35 years, played and recorded with

Lita Roza

groups such as Ros's Rumba Romeos, his Rumba Band, and Edmundo Ros And His Orchestra. After making his London debut at the New Cosmos Club and St. Regis Hotel, he played all the smartest nightspots, including the Bagatelle, before opening his own Edmundo Ros Club, on the site of the Coconut Grove, in 1949. By then, with his gently rhythmic style and engaging vocals, he was enormously popular with the public generally, and a favourite of London's high society and some members of the Royal Family. Earlier in his career, he had decided that the best way to introduce complex Latin rhythms to his audiences would be to apply them to popular and familiar songs, and throughout the 40s and 50s, on radio and records, he had great success with numbers such as 'Enjoy Yourself', 'Melodie D'Amour', 'Tico, Tico', 'I Got The Sun In The Morning', 'South America, Take It Away', ' I'm Crazy For You', 'Her Bathing Suit Never Got Wet', 'The Coffee Song', 'No Can Do', 'The Maharajah Of Magador', his theme, 'The Cuban Love Song', and especially 'The Wedding Samba', which was also a hit in the US in 1949, although he wasn't allowed to perform there because of Musicians' Union regulations. His music was popular in many other parts of the world too, particularly in Japan. In the early 60s, he collaborated on an album with Ted Heath which exploited the relatively new stereo system. The shift in musical tastes during the decade affected Ros's standing but he played on into the 70s, until, disillusioned with the business, he disbanded in 1975, and destroyed most of the bands' arrangements, keeping just one set in case he received an offer he could not refuse. He retired to Spain, emerging occasionally for events such as his 80th birthday celebrations in 1990, and to introduce a series of record programmes for BBC Radio in 1992. Often the butt of the musical elite he was gently satirized by the Bonzo Dog Doo-Dah Band in 'Look Out There's A Monster Coming'.

Selected albums: *Calypsos* (1956), *Mambos* (1956), *Rhythms Of The South* (1957), *Calypso Man* (1958), *Perfect For Dancing* (1958), *Ros On Broadway* (1959), *Hollywood Cha Cha Cha* (1959), *Dance Again* (1963), *Sing And Dance With Edmundo Ros* (1963) *Heath Versus Ros* (1964), *Ros Remembers* (1974), *Edmundo Ros Today* (1978), *Latin Favourites* (1979), *Latin Song And Dance Men* (1980), *Music For The Millions* (1983), *Strings Latino* (1985), *Cuban Love Song* (1985), *Latin Magic* (1987), *Edmundo Ros & His Rumba Band, 1939-1941* (1992).

Roza, Lita

b. 1926, Liverpool, England. A popular singer, particularly during the 50s, whose name is forever associated with the renowned Ted Heath Orchestra. At the age of 12, she appeared in a Christmas pantomime in Norwich, and, at 15, took part in the revue, *Black Velvet*, which starred top UK comedian, Ted Ray. After working outside showbusiness for a while, she became the resident vocalist at the New York restaurant in the northern seaside resort of Southport. By the time she was 17, she had joined Harry Roy's Band for a tour of the Middle East, and then sang with Art Thompson's group at London's Embassy Club, and later toured with Edmundo Ros, before moving to the USA, where she stayed until 1950. On her return to the UK, Roza successfully auditioned for Ted Heath by singing on one of his popular London Palladium Swing Concerts, and was allocated the middle stool, between Dickie Valentine and Dennis Lotis. During her stay of over four years with Heath, she recorded with his band, and in her own right. In 1951 she had a big hit with Irving Gordon's 'Allentown Jail', followed by other successful sides, such as 'High Noon', 'Half As Much', 'Walkin' to Missouri', 'I Went To Your Wedding', 'Why Don't You Believe Me' and 'Hi-Lili, Hi-Lo'. In 1953 she topped the UK chart with Bob Merrill's novelty, '(How Much Is) That Doggie In The Window', a cover of Patti Page's enormous US hit. Her other chart entries included 'Hey There', the big ballad from *The Pajama Game*, which was also successful in the UK for Rosemary Clooney, Sammy Davis Jnr. and Johnnie Ray; and, finally, 'Jimmy Unknown'. She also sang 'A Tear Fell', on *All Star Hit Parade*, a single record which also featured songs by Joan Regan, David Whitfield, Dennis Lotis, Winifred Atwell and Dave King. When Roza left Heath, she toured the UK Variety circuit and appeared extensively on radio and television, in shows such as *Off The Record*, *The Jack Jackson Show*, *Saturday Spectacular*, *Music Shop* and the top pop music programmes, *6.5 Special* and *Oh Boy*; she also featured in the ITV series, *The Ted Heath Story*. She continued to record into the 60s, releasing several albums, including *Between The Devil And The Deep Blue Sea* and *Drinka Lita Roza Day* (presumably a play on the television advertising slogan: 'Drinka Pinta Milka Day'); but eventually became yet another victim of the rapidly changing musical climate. In later years she made television and concert appearances with her contemporaries, celebrating the good times of years gone by. In the 80s, still affectionately

Marion Ryan

remembered, she sang standards on the re-issued *Love Songs For Night People* and *You're Driving Me Crazy* (with Billy Munn's All-Stars); and was one of the 'Four Stars Of The 50s', along with Jimmy Young, Dickie Valentine and Joan Regan, on the double album, *Unchained Melodies*.

Selected albums: *Me On A Carousel* (1958), *Between The Devil And The Deep Blue Sea* (c.60s), *Drinka Lita Roza Day* (c.60s), *Love Songs For Night People* (1983), *You're Driving Me Crazy* (1983). Compilation: includes performances with Dennis Lotis and the Ted Heath Orchestra *Lita Roza* (1977).

Ryan, Marion

b. Middlesbrough, England. This popular singer, with a vivacious style, was successful in the UK in the 50s and early 60s. In one sense Marion Ryan's contribution to the UK charts began in 1948, when she gave birth to twins, Paul And Barry Ryan, who had hits of their own in the late 60s. Barry's 'Eloise' went to number 2, which was three places higher than his mother's best effort. Marion Ryan first appeared on the UK music scene in 1953 after a spell singing with Edmundo Ros, and became a favourite on UK television with programmes such as *Off The Record*, *Music Shop*, *Festival Of British Song*, *Jack Jackson's Record Roundup*, *Gerry's Inn*, *Sunday Night At Blackpool*, *6.5 Special*, *Oh Boy* and *Two's Company*. She also starred in four series of *Spot The Tune* with Canadian vocalist-comedian, Jackie Rae. She sang regularly with the Ray Ellington Quartet, including an appearance in the 1956 movie, *Eric Winstone's Stagecoach*. In the late 50s, Ryan covered several big hits, including Perry Como's 'Hot Diggity', Peggy Lee's 'Mr Wonderful' and Rosemary Clooney's 'Mangos'. In 1958, Ryan had chart success with 'Love Me Forever', which beat the Eydie Gorme version and rose to number 5. Her other releases included *A Lady Loves*, a collection of standards, and some EPs and four-track mini-albums including *That Ryan Gal* and *Hit Parade*. In 1963 she featured in the Tommy Steele movie, *It's All Happening*, with Russ Conway, Danny Williams, John Barry and Shane Fenton. Shortly afterwards, she retired from singing. Her husband, is impresario Harold Davison.

S

Salad Days

Hastily assembled to fill a three-week gap in the schedule of the Bristol Old Vic in 1954, the stage musical *Salad Days* was swiftly transferred to London where it opened on 5 August that same year. Composed by Julian Slade with book and lyrics by Slade and Dorothy Reynolds, the show told a slight story about three eccentric university dons who discover a magic piano which makes all who hear it dance. Amongst the songs were 'We Said We'd Never Look Back', 'I Sit In The Sun', 'Oh! Look At Me!' and 'The Time Of My Life'. The show starred Eleanor Drew and John Warner and ran for 2,283 performances. Curiously British, the show ran on Broadway for only 80 performances at the end of 1958. Londoners, however, were more appreciative and it was revived in 1961, 1964 and again in 1973. In 1983 a television version was screened in the UK.

Sands, Tommy

b. 27 August 1937, Chicago, Illinois, USA. The son of a professional pianist, Benny, and singer, Grace Lou Dixon. He sang in a local folk music television series *Lady Of The Montain* when he was only five years old. His first recording was 'Love Pains' on Freedom in 1949, when aged only 12. In 1952 with help from his new manager, Colonel Tom Parker, he joined RCA Records as a country artist. In the early and mid-50s Sands played many country shows including ones with Hank Williams, Elvis Presley and Johnny Cash. His big break came when he got the part of a rock 'n' roll star in NBC's *The Singing Idol*, a role that was originally offered to Elvis. The show was a smash and the main song from it, 'Teen-Age Crush', totalled over a half-a-million advance orders and shot to number 2 in the US charts. The television show was snapped up by Hollywood and became his first film *Sing, Boy, Sing* (1958). The first of his five albums on Capitol Records, *Steady Date With Tommy Sands* and *Sing Boy Sing* both made the US Top 20 and he was tipped by some as likely to replace Elvis. However, of his other eight charting singles only 'Goin' Steady' in 1957 made the US Top 40. That same year in the UK he was the subject of BBC television's *This Is Your Life*. He made a string of films including *Mardi Gras* with Pat Boone, *Love*

Tommy Sands

In A Goldfish Bowl with Fabian, *Babes In Toyland* with Annette, the star-studded *The Longest Day* and *None But The Brave* with his father-in-law Frank Sinatra (he was married to Nancy Sinatra from 1960-65). Together with his group the Raiders (aka the Sharks), which included the future number one session drummer Hal Blaine, he later recorded on ABC, Paramount, Imperial and Liberty without further chart success. In the late 60s he moved to Hawaii and opened a club. He tried for his first comeback between 1974 and 1979 and his second one in 1987 playing his first UK dates in 1990.

Albums: *Steady Date With Tommy Sands* (1957), *Sing, Boy, Sing* (1958, film soundtrack), *Sands Storm* (1959), *Teenage Rock* (1959), *This Thing Called Love* (1959), *When I'm Thinking Of You* (1960), *Sands At The Sands* (1960), *Dream Of Me* (1961), *The Parent Trap* (1961, film soundtrack), *Babes In Toyland* (1961, film soundtrack), *Blue Ribbon Baby* (1987), *Down By Bendy's Lane* (1988), *Beyond The Shadows* (1992).

Scott, Jack

b. Jack Scafone Jnr., 24 January 1936, Windsor, Ontario, Canada. This distinctive deep voiced rock 'n' roll and ballad singer/songwriter moved to Michigan at the age of 10 and fronted the Southern Drifters from 1954. He signed to ABC in 1957 and his first release was the rocker 'Baby She's Gone'. Scott joined Carlton in 1958 and had a transatlantic Top 10 hit with his double-sided debut for the label 'My True Love'/'Leroy'. Always backed on records by session vocal group, the Chantones, he had a further seven US Top 40 successes over the next two years, including the Top 10 hits 'Goodbye Baby' in 1958, 'What In The World's Come Over You' (a UK Top 20 hit) and 'Burning Bridges' both in 1960 (the latter two released on Top Rank). He achieved a couple of minor hits on Capitol in 1961 and later recorded on various labels including Groove, Guaranteed, RCA, Jubilee, GRT, Dot (where he notched up a country hit in 1974) and Ponie. He remains a top drawing act on the rock 'n' roll club circuit around the world.

Albums: *Jack Scott* (1958), *What Am I Living For* (1958), *I Remember Hank Williams* (1960), *What In The World's Come Over You?* (1960), *The Spirit Moves Me* (1961), *Burning Bridges* (1964), *Scott On Groove* (1980), *Greaseball* (1985). Compilation: *Grizzily Bear* (1986).

Scott, Ronnie

b. 28 January 1927, London, England. Scott began playing on the soprano saxophone but switched to tenor in his early teens. After playing informally in clubs he joined the Johnny Claes band in 1944, before spells with Ted Heath, Bert Ambrose and other popular British dance bands. Scott also played on transatlantic liners in order to visit the USA and hear bebop at first hand. By the late 40s he was a key figure in the London bop scene, playing at the Club Eleven, of which he was a co-founder. During the 50s he led his own band and was also co-leader with Tubby Hayes of the Jazz Couriers. In 1959, he opened his own club in Gerrard Street, London, later transferring to Frith Street. During the 60s he divided his time between leading his own small group and running the club, but also found time to play with the Clarke-Boland Big Band. In the 70s and 80s he continued to lead small bands, usually a quartet, occasionally touring but most often playing as the interval band between sessions by the modern American jazz musicians he brought to the club. As a player, Scott comfortably straddles the mainstream and modern aspects of jazz. His big tone lends itself to a slightly aggressive approach, although in his ballad playing he displays the warmth which characterized the work of Zoot Sims and late-period Stan Getz, musicians he admires, but does not imitate. Although a gifted player, Scott's greatest contribution to jazz lies in his tireless promotion of fine British musicians and in his establishment of his club, a venue which has become renowned throughout the world for the excellence of its setting and the artists on display. In 1981, Scott was awarded an OBE in recognition of his services to music.

Albums: *Battle Royal* (1951), *The Ronnie Scott Jazz Group* i (1952), *Live At The Jazz Club* (1953), *The Ronnie Scott Jazz Group* ii (1954), *The Jazz Couriers In Concert* (1958), *The Last Word* (1959), *The Night Is Scott And You're So Swingable* (1965), *Live At Ronnie's* (1968), *Scott At Ronnie's* (1973), *Serious Gold* (1977), *Great Scott* (1979), with various artists *Ronnie Scott's 20th Anniversary Album* (1979), *Never Pat A Burning Dog* (1990).

Further reading: *Let's Join Hands And Contact The Living*, John Fordham.

Secombe, Harry

b. Harold Donald Secombe, 8 September 1921, Swansea, West Glamorgan, Wales. Harry Secombe's development as an all-round entertainer began as a product of the post-war 'fair play' policy of London's West End Windmill Theatre. This ensured that men recently, or soon-to-be demobbed from the armed forces, were given the chance to prove themselves to an audience and get noticed by agents. Secombe worked at the theatre before becoming a regular on the variety circuit in the late 40s. In 1949 he teamed up with Peter Sellers, Spike Milligan and Michael Bentine to form the highly-influential British radio comedy team, the Goons, taking on characters, created by Spike Milligan, such as the popular Neddy Seagoon. With his large build, gentle humour and resonant Welsh baritone, which he put to good effect on light operatic arias as well as popular tunes, Secombe became a regular fixture at the London Palladium, including Royal Command performances from the 50s through to the 80s. His screen appearances included both comedy and 'straight' roles including *Helter Skelter* (1949, his debut), *Fake's Progress* (1950), *Down Among The Z Men* (1952), *Davy* (1957), *Oliver!* (1968), *The Bedsitting Room* (1968), *Song Of Norway* (1969), *Rhubarb* (1969) and *The Magnificent Seven Deadly Sins* (1971). He appeared regularly on UK television screens, in variety shows and his own series in the 60s and 70s. He scored his first solo UK chart hit with 'On With The Motley' in 1955, which reached number 16. It was not until 1963 that Secombe recorded the song that was to become one of the singer's theme tunes, the Leslie Bricusse and Cyril Ornadel- penned 'If I Ruled The World', reaching the UK Top 20. After another hiatus, he achieved his biggest hit to date in 1967 with Charlie Chaplin's 'This Is My Song', reaching number 2 and prevented from reaching the number 1 slot by Petula Clark's version of the very same song.

During his career this multi-faceted performer has also managed to appear in the London stage musicals *Pickwick* (1963), *The Four Musketeers* (1967) and *The Plumber's Progress* (1975). Following a massive reduction in his weight(for medical reasons) a trimmed-down Secombe has in recent years carved out a career since 1983 as the presenter of Independent Television's religious programme, *Highway* which required Secombe to master another skill, that of the interview technique. He has over the years been actively involved in charity organizations and fund-raising and after being awarded the CBE in 1963, Harry Secombe was knighted in 1981. In 1993 he announced his intention to star in a revival of *Pickwick*.

Albums (excluding Goons and other comedy albums): *At Your Request* (late 50s), *Operatic Arias* (late 50s), *Richard Tauber Favourites* (late 50s), *Secombe Sings* (1959), *Harry Secombe Showcase* (1960), *Sacred Songs* (1961), *Vienna, City Of My Dreams* (early 60s), *Show Souvenirs* (early 60s), *Sacred Songs* (early 60s), *Immortal Hymns* (early 60s), *Secombe's Personal Choice* (1967), *If I Ruled The World* (1971), *Songs For Sunday* (1972), *This Is Harry Secombe, Volume Four* (1974), *A Man And His Dreams* (1976), *Far Away Places* (1977), *Twenty Songs Of Joy* (1978), *Bless This House* (1979), *Songs Of My Homeland* (1979), *These Are My Songs* (1980), with Moira Anderson *Golden Memories* (1981, reissued as *This Is My Lovely Day* on CD), *A Song And A Prayer* aka *How Great Thou Art* (1981), *The Musical World Of Harry Secombe* (1983), *Highway Of Life* (1986), *The Highway Companion* (1987), *Onward Christian Soldiers* (1987), *Yours Sincerely* (1991). Compilations: *Spotlight On Harry Secombe* (1975), *The Harry Secombe Collection* (1976), *Portrait* (1978).

Further reading: *Arias And Raspberries*, Sir Harry Secombe.

Seeger, Pete

b. 3 May 1919, New York City, New York, USA. Educated at Harvard University, he is the brother of Peggy Seeger and half brother of Mike Seeger. Pete Seeger's mother was a violin teacher, and his father a renowned musicologist. While still young Pete Seeger learned to play banjo and ukulele, and shortly afterwards he developed his interest in American folk music. Seeger took his banjo round the country, playing and learning songs from the workers and farmers. He served in the US Army during World War II. In addition to being a member of the Weavers from 1949-58, he had earlier been in a group called the Almanac Singers. The group included Woody Guthrie, Lee Hays and Millard Lampell. The Almanac Singers had frequently given free performances to union meetings and strikers' demonstrations. Despite such apparent diversions, Seeger maintained a successfully high profile in his own solo career. The era of McCarthyism put a blight on many live performances, owing to the right-wing political paranoia that existed at the time. It was in 1948 that Seeger was blacklisted and had to appear before the House of Un-American Activities Committee for his alleged communist sympathies. This did not stop Seeger from performing sell-out concerts abroad and speaking out on a wide range of civil rights and environmental issues. He became known for popularizing songs such as 'Little Boxes', 'Where Have All The Flowers Gone', and 'We Shall Overcome'. In more recent times Seeger also performed and recorded with Arlo Guthrie. Seeger was also involved with the Clearwater Sloop project on the Hudson River, attempting to publicize the threat of pollution. He has always worked and campaigned for civil rights, peace and equality, and has never compromised his ideals. By the mid-70s, Seeger had released in excess of 50 albums, several of which were instructional records for banjo playing. In addition to these albums Seeger has appeared on the work of many other artists providing either vocal or instrumental back-up. Seeger is one of the most important figures ever in the development of free speech and humanitarian causes through folk music.

Albums: *We Sing Vol.1* (1950), *Darling Corey* (1950), *Pete Seeger Concert* (1953), *Pete Seeger Sampler* (1954), *Goofing-Off Suite* (1954), *How To Play The Five String Banjo* (1954), *Frontier Ballads, Vol. 1* (1954), *Frontier Ballads, Vol. 2* (1954), *Birds, Beasts, Bugs And Little Fishes* (1954), *Birds, Beasts, Bugs And Bigger Fishes* (1955), *The Folksinger's Guitar Guide* (1955), *Bantu Choral Folk Songs* (1955), *Folksongs Of Our Continents* (1955), *With Voices Together We Sing* (1956), *American Industrial Ballads* (1956), *Love Songs For Friends And Foes* (1956), *American Ballads* (1957), *American Favorite Ballads* (1957), *Gazette With Pete Seeger, Vol. 1* (1958), *Sleep Time* (1958), *Pete Seeger And Sonny Terry* (1958), *We Shall Overcome* (1958), *Song And Play Time With Pete Seeger* (1958), *American Favorite Ballads, Vol. 2* (1959), *Hootenanny Tonight* (1959), *Folk Songs For Young People* (1959), *Folk Festival At Newport, Vol. 1* (1959), with Frank Hamilton *Nonesuch* (1959), *American Favorite Ballads, Vol. 3* (1960), *Songs Of The Civil War* (1960), *Champlain Valley Songs* (1960), *At Village Gate, Vol. 1* (1960), *The Rainbow Quest* (1960), *Sing Out With Pete* (1961), *American Favorite Ballads, Vol. 4* (1961), *Gazette, Vol. 2* (1961), *Pete Seeger: Story Songs* (1961), *At Village Gate, Vol. 2* (1962), *American Favorite Ballads, Vol. 5* (1962), *In Person At The Bitter End* (1962), *American Game And Activity Songs For Children* (1962), *The Bitter And The Sweet* (1963), *Pete Seeger, Children's Concert At Town Hall* (1963), *We Shall Overcome* (1963), *Broadside Ballads, Vol. 2* (1963), *Little Boxes And Other Broadsides* (1963), *The Nativity* (1963), *In Concert, Vol. 2 (St. Pancras Town Hall)* (1964, rec. 1959), *Broadsides Songs And Ballads* (1964), *Broadsides 2* (1964), *Freight Train* (1964), *Little Boxes* (1964), *Pete Seeger And Big Bill Broonzy In Concert* (1964), *Strangers And Cousins* (1965), *The Pete Seeger Box* (1965), *Songs Of Struggle And Protest* (1965), *I Can See A New Day* (1965), *God Bless The Grass* (1966),

Dangerous Songs!? (1966), *Pete Seeger Sings Woody Guthrie* (1967), *Waist Deep In The Big Muddy* (1967), *Traditional Christmas Carols* (1967), *Pete Seeger Sings Leadbelly* (1968), *American Folksongs For Children* (1968), *Pete Seeger Sings And Answers Questions At The Ford Hall Forum In Boston* (1968), *Where Have All The Flowers Gone* (1969), *Leadbelly* (1969), *Pete Seeger Now* (1969), *Pete Seeger Young Vs. Old* (1971), *Rainbow Race* (1973), *Banks Of Marble* (1974), *Pete Seeger And Brother Kirk Visit Sesame Street* (1974), *Pete Seeger And Arlo Guthrie Together In Concert* (1975), with Ed Renehan *Fifty Sail On Newburgh Bay* (1976), *Tribute To Leadbelly* (1977), *Circles And Seasons* (1979), *American Industrial Ballads* (1979), *Singalong-Sanders Theater 1980* (1980). Compilations: *The World Of Pete Seeger* (1974), *The Essential Pete Seeger* (1978), *Live At The Royal Festival Hall* (1986), *Can't You See This System's Rotten Through And Through* (1986). Further reading: *How Can I Keep From Singing*, David King Dunaway. *Everybody Says Freedom*, Bob Reiser.

Sensations

This Philadelphia R&B ensemble featured the warm chirpy lead of Yvonne Mills Baker (b. Philadelphia, Pennsylvania, USA). The group was formed in 1954, and in 1956 they scored with two minor ballad hits, a remake of the old standard, 'Yes Sir That's My Baby' (US R&B number 15) and 'Please Mr. Disc Jockey' (US R&B number 13) for the Atlantic subsidiary label Atco. The group included lead Yvonne Mills, alternate lead Tommy Wicks and bass Alphonso Howell. The Sensations failed to register further hits and disbanded. In 1961 Howell persuaded Baker to reform the group and they added Richard Curtain (tenor) and Sam Armstrong (baritone). Through their mentor and producer, Philadelphia disc jockey Kae Williams, the Sensations won a contract with the Chess subsidiary label, Argo. Singing with greater robustness and at a faster clip the group hit first with a remake of the Teresa Brewer oldie, 'Music Music Music' (US R&B number 12 in 1961). The following year they struck gold with 'Let Me In' (US R&B number 2 and pop number 4). The last chart record for the Sensations was a remake of the Frankie Laine hit, 'That's My Desire' (US pop Top 75 in 1962). The group disbanded around 1964 and Baker continued making records for a few more years in the soul idiom.

Album: *Let Me In* (1963).

Seville, David

b. Ross Bagdasarian, 27 January 1919, Fresno, California, USA, d. 16 January 1972. This singer/songwriter/conductor and actor is best remembered as the creator of the Chipmunks. He first appeared on Broadway in the late 30s and was drafted to Britain during the war. His first musical success came in 1951 when a song he had co-written a decade earlier, 'Come On-A My House' topped the chart by Rosemary Clooney. He recorded on Coral in 1951 and joined Mercury two years later. Seville first charted in 1956 under the name Alfi & Harry with 'The Trouble With Harry' (inspired by the film of the same name, which he appeared in) which made the UK Top 20. He had a hit again later that year with 'Armen's Theme' (inspired not by his Armenian descent but by his wife, singer Kay Armen). His biggest 'solo' hit came in 1958 with the transatlantic novelty smash 'Witch Doctor', which topped the US chart. He extended the idea of a speeded-up voice (as used on that hit) to produce a trio which he called the Chipmunks. They sold millions of records and had a top-rated cartoon television show before he retired them in 1967. After his death on 16 January 1972, his son Ross Jnr. brought the Chipmunks back and they have since enjoyed more success on both sides of the Atlantic.

Album: *The Music Of David Seville* (1958).

Shearing, George

b. 13 August 1919, London, England. Shearing was born blind but started to learn piano at the age of three. After limited training and extensive listening to recorded jazz, he began playing at hotels, clubs and pubs in the London area, sometimes as a single, occasionally with dance bands. In 1940 he joined Harry Parry's popular band and also played with Stephane Grappelli. Shortly after visiting the USA in 1946, Shearing decided to settle there. Although at this time in his career he was influenced by bop pianists, notably Bud Powell, it was a complete break with this style that launched his career as a major star. Developing the locked-hands technique of playing block-chords, and accompanied by a discreet rhythm section of guitar, bass, drums and vibraphone, he had a succession of hugely popular records including 'September In The Rain' and his own composition, 'Lullaby Of Birdland'. His most successful collaboration was with Nat 'King' Cole, which featured one of the most famous piano introductions of all time on the glorious 'Let There Be Love' (UK number 11). With shifting personnel, which over the years included Cal Tjader, Margie Hyams, Denzil Best, Israel Crosby, Joe Pass and Gary Burton, the Shearing quintet remained popular until 1967. Later, Shearing played with a trio, as a solo and increasingly in duo. Amongst his collaborations have been sets with the Montgomery Brothers, Marian McPartland, Brian Torff, Jim Hall, Hank Jones and Kenny Davern (on a rather polite Dixieland selection). Over the years he has worked fruitfully with singers, including Peggy Lee, Ernestine Anderson, Carmen McRae, and, especially, Mel Tormé, with whom he performed frequently in the late 80s and early 90s at festivals, on radio and record dates. Shearing's interest in classical music resulted in some performances with concert orchestras in the 50s and 60s, and his solos frequently touch upon the musical patterns of Claude Debussy and, particularly, Erik Satie. Indeed, Shearing's delicate touch and whimsical nature should make him an ideal interpreter of Satie's work. As a jazz player Shearing has sometimes been the victim of critical indifference and even hostility. Mostly reactions such as these centre upon the long period when he led his quintet. It might well be that the quality of the music; was often rather lightweight but a second factor was the inability of some commentators on the jazz scene to accept an artist who had achieved wide public acceptance and financial success. That critical disregard should follow Shearing into his post-quintet years is inexplicable and unforgivable. Many of his late performances, especially his solo albums and those with Torff, bassist Neil Swainson, and Tormé, are superb examples of a pianist at the height of his powers. Inventive and melodic, his improvisations are unblushingly romantic but there is usually a hint of whimsy which happily reflects the warmth and offbeat humour of the man himself.

Albums: *Latin Escapade* (1956), *Velvet Carpet* (1956), *Black Satin* (1957), *Burnished Brass* (1958), with Peggy Lee *Americana Hotel* (1959), *Shearing On Stage* (1959-63), *White Satin* (1960), *San Francisco Scene* (1960), *The Shearing Touch* (1960), with the Montgomery Brothers *Love Walked In* (1961), *Satin Affair* (1961), *Nat 'King Cole' Sings/George Shearing Plays* (1962), *Jazz Concert* (1963), *My Ship* (1974), *Light, Airy And Swinging* (1974), *The Way We Are* (1974), *Continental Experience* (1975), with Stephane Grappelli *The Reunion* (1976), *The Many Facets Of George Shearing* (1976), *500 Miles High* (1977), *Windows* (1977), *On Target* (1979), with Brian Torff *Blues Alley & Jazz* (1979), *Getting In The Swing Of Things* (1979), *On*

A Clear Day (1980), with Carmen McRae *Two For The Road* (1980), with Marian McPartland *Alone Together* (1981), with Jim Hall *First Edition* (1981), *An Evening With Mel Tormé And George Shearing* (1982), with Mel Tormé *Top Drawer* (1983), *Bright Dimensions* (1984), *Live At The Cafe Carlyle* (1984), *Grand Piano* (1985), with Tormé *An Elegant Evening* (1985), *George Shearing And Barry Treadwell Play The Music Of Cole Porter* (1986), *More Grand Piano* (1986), *Breakin' Out* (1987), *Dexterity* (1987), *A Vintage Year* (1987), with Ernestine Anderson *A Perfect Match* (1988), with Hank Jones *The Spirit Of 176* (1988), *Piano* (1989), *George Shearing In Dixieland* (1989), with Tormé *Mel And George 'Do' World War II* (1990). Compilations: *The Young George Shearing (1939-44)* (1983), *The Best Of George Shearing* (1983).

Shelton, Anne

b. Patricia Sibley, 10 November 1924, Dulwich, London, England. Shelton was one of the most important and popular of UK pop singers. She came to prominence during World War II and remained a fondly-regarded figure thereafter. Shelton made her first BBC radio broadcast on 30 May 1940, in *Monday Night At Eight*, in which she sang 'Let The Curtain Come Down'. Her performance was heard by top UK bandleader, Bert Ambrose, who signed her to sing with his band, and with whom she appeared on radio in *School Uniform*. Her own radio show, *Introducing Anne*, aimed mainly at British troops in the North African Desert, ran for four years, and she co-hosted *Calling Malta* with comedy actor Ronald Shiner; the programme was the only link with British troops on the Island during the air bombardment and siege during the early months of 1942. In that same year, Shelton started her recording career, and in 1944 had an enormous hit with her signature tune, 'Lili Marlene', a German song which was equally popular with the armed forces of 'both sides', and to which UK songwriter Tommy Connor added an English lyric. Also in 1944, she was one of the UK 'guest' vocalists who sang in concerts and on broadcasts with the American Band of the Supreme Allied Command and the American Band of the Allied Expeditionary Force, directed by Glenn Miller. Shelton also worked on radio with Bing Crosby. She appeared in several films, a mixture of musicals and comedies, including *Miss London*, *Bees In Paradise*, and *King Arthur Was A Gentleman* (each starring diminutive comedian Arthur Askey) and *Come Dance With Me* (with comedians Derek Roy and

Max Wall). After the war, she toured the UK Variety circuit, and in 1949 updated her wartime hit by recording 'The Wedding Of Lilli Marlene'. In the same year she had two US hits with 'Be Mine' and 'Galway Bay', and in 1951, became the first British artist to tour the USA coast to coast, staying there for almost a year. In the UK she appeared extensively on radio and television during the 50s, and had several successful records, including 'I Remember The Cornfields', 'My Yiddishe Momma', 'Once In A While', ' I'm Praying To St. Christopher', 'Arrivederci Darling', 'Seven Days', 'Lay Down Your Arms', (a Swedish song with an English lyric by Paddy Roberts, which spent several weeks at the top of the UK chart), and 'Village Of Bernadette'. Her last chart entry, in 1961, was 'Sailor', a song of Austrian origin, which was a UK number 1 for Petula Clark. Albums around this time included *Favourites Volume I and II*, *Songs From Her Heart* and *The Shelton Sound* (which contained impressive readings of standards such as 'Happiness Is Just A Thing Called Joe', 'Tangerine' and 'I'll Never Smile Again'). Throughout her career she worked with the cream of musical directors, including Percy Faith, Stanley Black, George Melachrino, Frank Cordell, Ken Mackintosh, Robert Farnon, Reg Owen, David Rose, Jerry Gray and many more. In later years Shelton continued to appear on television and tour extensively including the UK, Europe, USA and Hong Kong. In 1978 she appeared in cabaret when 1,200 US veterans revisited the the D-Day Normandy beaches, and in the following year, performed one of her most popular 40s songs, 'I'll Be Seeing You', in John Schlesinger's film, *Yanks*, starring Richard Gere. In 1980 she sang 'You'll Never Know' for the Queen Mother on the occasion of her 80th birthday, and during the rest of the decade took part in charity and reunion affairs in aid of the British Legion and British Services organizations. These included occasions such as the 40th anniversary of D-Day, when she sang on UK television with a contemporary 'Glenn Miller' Band, and the 50th anniversary of the start of World War I. She was also the Entertainments Officer for the Not Forgotten Association, which looked after disabled ex-servicemen and women from as far back as World War I. She released several records during the 80s, including 'Crazy', *Anne Shelton's Sentimental Journey*, *I'll Be Seeing You*, *The Magic Of Anne Shelton*, *Sing It Again, Anne*, and *Anne Shelton Sings With Ambrose & His Orchestra*. In 1990 she was awarded the OBE for services to the Not

Dinah Shore

Forgotten Association, but the occasion was marred by the death of her husband, Lieutenant Commander David Reid, whom she had met when she was only 17 years of age.

Selected albums: *Anne Shelton Showcase* (1960), *The World Of Anne Shelton* (1971), *I'll Be Seeing You* (1977), *The Anne Shelton Collection* (1979), *Anne Shelton's Sentimental Journey* (1982), *Sing It Again, Anne* (1983), *Anne Shelton Sings With Ambrose And His Orchestra* (1984), *The Magic Of Anne Shelton* (1984).

Shore, Dinah

b. Frances Rose Shore, 1 March 1917, Winchester, Tennessee, USA. While still at school Shore sang on the radio in Nashville. Further broadcasting and theatre engagements in New York soon followed, and she recorded with Xaviar Cugat and Ben Bernie; she sang on some of Cugat's early 40s hits, such as 'The Breeze And I', 'Whatever Happened To You?', 'The Rhumba-Cardi', and 'Quierme Mucho (Yours)'. Shore was one of the first vocalists to break free from the big bands and become a star in her own right. She became extremely popular on both radio and disc, making her solo recording debut in 1939. Her smoky, low-pitched voice was especially attractive on slow ballads, and from 1940-57, she had a string of 80 US chart hits, including 'Yes, My Darling Daughter', 'Jim', 'Blues In The Night', 'Skylark', 'You'd Be So Nice To Come Home To', 'Murder, He Says', 'Candy', 'Laughing On The Outside (Crying On The Inside)', 'All That Glitters Is Not Gold', 'Doin' What Comes Natur'lly ', 'You Keep Coming Back Like A Song', 'I Wish I Didn't Love You So', 'You Do', 'Baby, It's Cold Outside' (with Buddy Clark), 'Dear Hearts And Gentle People', 'My Heart Cries For You', 'A Penny A Kiss', 'Sweet Violets'; and number 1's, 'I'll Walk Alone', 'The Gypsy', 'Anniversary Song', and 'Buttons And Bows'. She made a number of film appearances, including *Thank Your Lucky Stars* (1943), *Up In Arms* (1944), *Follow The Boys* (1944), *Belle Of The Yukon* (1945), *Till The Clouds Roll By* (1946), *Aaron Slick From Punkin Crick* (1952), and *Oh God* (1977). In 1951 Shore began appearing regularly on television, making several spectaculars. Later, it was her continuing success on television that brought about a career change when she became host of a highly popular daytime talk show, a role she maintained into the 80s. In 1986, in concert at Latham, New York, her programme consisted of a series of medleys, including one of country songs ('all about

dyin' - lyin' - cryin"), and 'The Story Of My Life', 'Come Out And Play With Me', and 'He Needed Me'.

Selected albums: *Blues In The Night* (1952), with Buddy Clark *'SWonderful* (c.50s), *Holding Hands At Midnight* (1955), *Moments Like These* (c.50s), *Buttons And Bows* (1959), *Dinah, Yes Indeed!* (1959), with André Previn *Dinah Sings, Previn Plays* (1960), *Lavender Blue* (1960), with the Red Norvo Quintet *Some Blues With Red* (1962), *Dinah, Down Home!* (1962), *Lower Basin St. Revisited* (1965), *Make The World Go Away* (1987), *Oh Lonesome Me* (c.80s).

Selected compilations: *Fabulous Hits* (1965), *The Best Of* (1984).

Sinatra, Frank

b. Francis Albert Sinatra, 12 December 1915, Hoboken, New Jersey, USA. After working for a while in the office of a local newspaper, *The Jersey Observer*, Sinatra decided to pursue a career as a singer. Already an admirer of Bing Crosby, Sinatra was impelled to pursue this course after attending a 1933 Crosby concert. Sinatra sang whenever and wherever he could, working locally in clubs and bars. Then, in 1935 he entered a popular US radio talent show, *Major Bowes Amateur Hour*. Also on the show was a singing trio and the four young men found themselves teamed together by the no-nonsense promoter. The ad-hoc teaming worked and the group, renamed 'The Hoboken Four', won first prize. Resulting from this came a succession of concert dates with the Major Bowes travelling show along with club and occasional radio dates. By 1938 Sinatra was singing on several shows on each of a half-dozen radio stations, sometimes for expenses often for nothing. The experience and especially the exposure were vital if he was to be recognised. Among the bands with which he performed was one led by songwriter Harold Arlen but in 1939, shortly after he married his childhood sweetheart, Nancy Barbato, he was heard and hired by Harry James who had only recently formed his own big band. James recognised Sinatra's talent from the start and also identified the source of his determination to succeed, his massive self-confidence and powerful ego. During their brief association, James remarked to an interviewer, 'His name is Sinatra, and he considers himself the greatest vocalist in the business. Get that! No one's even heard of him! He's never had a hit record, and he looks like a wet rag, but he says he's the greatest.' In 1939 and early 1940 Sinatra made a number of records with James and began to develop a small following. His

Frank Sinatra

records with James included 'My Buddy' and 'All Or Nothing At All'.

In 1940 Sinatra was approached with an offer by Tommy Dorsey, then leading one of the most popular swing era bands. Only some six months had expired on Sinatra's two-year contract with James,who must have realised he was parting with a potential goldmine but he was a generous-spirited man and let the singer go. Sinatra had many successful records with Dorsey including 'Polka Dots And Moonbeams', 'Imagination', 'Fools Rush In', 'I'll Never Smile Again', 'The One I Love', 'Violets For Your Furs', 'How About You?' and 'In The Blue Of The Evening', some of which became fixtures in his repertoire. One record from this period became a major hit a few years later when the USA entered World War II. This song, recorded at Sinatra's second session with Dorsey in February 1940, was 'I'll Be Seeing You' and its lyric gained a special significance for servicemen and the women they had left behind. Sinatra's popularity with those females, achieved despite or perhaps because of his gangling unheroic and rather vulnerable appearance, prompted him to leave Dorsey and begin a solo career. Despite a tough line taken by Dorsey over the remaining half of his five-year contract (Dorsey allegedly settled for 43% of the singer's gross over the next 10 years), Sinatra quit.

Within months his decision was proved to be right. He had become the idol of hordes of teenage girls, his public appearances were sell-outs and his records jostled with one another for hit status. In the early 40s he had appeared in a handful of films as Dorsey's vocalist but by the middle of the decade was appearing in feature films as actor-singer. These included lightweight if enjoyable fare such as *Higher And Higher* (1944), *Anchors Aweigh* (1945), *It Happened In Brooklyn* (1947), *The Kissing Bandit* (1948) and *Double Dynamite* (1951). By the 50s, however, Sinatra's career was in trouble ; both as singer and actor he appeared to have reached the end of the road. His acting career had suffered in part from the quality of material he was offered, and accepted. Nevertheless, it was his film career that was the first to revive when he landed the role of Angelo Maggio in *From Here To Eternity* (1953) for which he won an Academy Award as Best Supporting Actor. Thereafter, he was taken seriously as an actor even if he rarely was given the same standard of role or achieved the same quality of performance.

He continued to make films, usually in straight acting roles but occasionally in musicals. Among the former were *The Man With The Golden Arm* (1955), one of the roles which matched his breakthrough performance as Maggio, *Johnny Concho* (1956), *Kings Go Forth* (1958), *A Hole In The Head* (1959), *The Manchurian Candidate* (1962), *Robin And The 7 Hoods* (1964), *Von Ryan's Express* (1965), *Assault On A Queen* (1966), *Tony Rome* (1967) and *The Detective* (1968). His musicals included *Guys And Dolls* (1955), *High Society* (1956) and *Can Can* (1960). Later, he appeared in an above average television movie, *Contract On Cherry Street* (1977) and *The First Deadly Sin* (1980).

Soon after his Oscar-winning appearance in *From Here To Eternity*, Sinatra made a comeback as a recording artist. He had been recording for Columbia where he fell out of step when changes were made to the company's musical policy and in 1953 he was signed by Capitol Records. Sinatra's first session at Capitol was arranged and conducted by Axel Stordahl whom Sinatra had known on the Dorsey band. For the next session, however, he was teamed with Nelson Riddle. Sinatra had heard the results of earlier recording sessions made by Nat 'King' Cole at Capitol on which Riddle had collaborated. Sinatra was deeply impressed by the results and some sources suggest that on joining Capitol he had asked for Riddle. The results of this partnership set Sinatra's singing career firmly in the spotlight. Over the next few years classic albums such as *Songs For Young Lovers*, *This Is Sinatra*, *A Swingin' Affair*, *Come Fly With Me*, *Swing Easy*, *In The Wee Small Hours* and the exceptional *Songs For Swingin' Lovers* set standards for popular singers which have been rarely equalled and almost never surpassed. The two men were intensely aware of one another's talents and although critics were unanimous in their praise of Riddle, the arranger was unassumingly diffident, declaring that it was the singer's 'great talent that put him back on top.' For all Riddle's diffidence, there can be little doubt that the arranger encouraged Sinatra's latent feeling for jazz which helped create the relaxed yet superbly swinging atmosphere which epitomised their work together. On his albums for Capitol, his own label Reprise, and other labels, sometimes with Riddle, other times with Robert Farnon, Neal Hefti, Gordon Jenkins, Quincy Jones, Billy May or Stordahl, Sinatra built upon his penchant for the best in American popular song, displaying a deep understanding of the wishes of composer and lyricist.

Fans old and new bought his albums in their tens of thousands and several reached the top in the

Billboard charts. The 1955 album, *In The Wee Small Hours*, was in for 29 weeks reaching number 2; the following year's *Songs For Swingin' Lovers* charted for 66 weeks, also reaching the second spot. *Come Fly With Me*, from 1958, spent 71 weeks in the charts reaching number 1 and other top positions were attained by 1958's *Only The Lonely*, 120 weeks, 1960's *Nice 'N' Easy*, 86 weeks, and in 1966, *Strangers In The Night*, 73 weeks. The title song from this last album also made number 1 in *Billboard*'s singles charts as did the following year's 'Something Stupid' on which he duetted with his daughter, Nancy Sinatra. At a time in popular music's history when ballads were not the most appealing form, and singers were usually in groups and getting younger by the minute, these were no mean achievements for a middle-aged solo singer making a comeback. The secret of this late success lay in Sinatra's superior technical ability, his wealth of experience, his abiding love for the material with which he worked and the invariably high standards of professionalism he brought to his recordings and public performances. During his stint with Dorsey, the singer had taken a marked professional interest in the band leader's trombone playing. He consciously learned breath control, in particular circular breathing, and the use of dynamics from Dorsey. Additionally, he employed Dorsey's legato style which aided the smooth phrasing of his best ballad work. Complementing this, Sinatra's enjoyment of jazz and the company of jazz musicians prompted him to adopt jazz phrasing which greatly enhanced his rhythmic style. More than any other popular singer of his or previous generations, Sinatra learned the value of delayed phrasing and singing behind the beat, and he and his arrangers invariably found exactly the right tempo. His relaxed rhythmic style contrasted strikingly with the stiffer-sounding singers who preceded him. Even Crosby, whose popularity Sinatra eventually surpassed, later accommodated some of Sinatra's stylistic devices. (Crosby's habitual lazy-sounding style was of a different order from Sinatra's and until late in his career he never fully shook off his 2/4 style while Sinatra, almost from the start, was completely at home with the 4/4 beat of swing.)

Sinatra's revived career brought him more attention even than in his heyday as the bobby-soxers' idol. Much of the interest was intrusive and led to frequently acrimonious and sometimes violent clashes with reporters. With much of what is written about him stemming from a decidedly ambivalent view, the picture of the man behind the voice is often confused. Undoubtedly, his private persona is multi-faceted. He has been described by acquaintances as quick-tempered, pugnacious, sometimes vicious and capable of extreme verbal cruelty and he has often displayed serious misjudgement in the company he keeps. In marked contrast, others have categorically declared him to be enormously generous to friends in need and to individuals and organizations he believes can benefit from his personal or financial support. His political stance has changed dramatically over the years and here again his judgement seems to be flawed. At first a Democrat, he supported Roosevelt and later Kennedy with enormous enthusiasm. His ties with the Kennedy clan were close, and not always for the best of reasons. Sinatra was unceremoniously dropped by the Kennedys following revelations that he had introduced to John Kennedy a woman who became simultaneously the mistress of the President of the United States and a leading figure in the Mafia. Sinatra then became a Republican and lent his support as fund-raiser and campaigner to Richard Nixon and Ronald Reagan, apparently oblivious to their serious flaws.

An immensely rich man, with interests in industry, real estate, recording companies, film and television production, Sinatra has chosen to continue working, making frequent comebacks and presenting a never-ending succession of 'farewell' concerts which, as time passed, became less like concerts and more like major events in contemporary popular culture. He continued to attract adoring audiences and in the late 80s and early 90s, despite being in his mid- to late seventies, could command staggering fees for personal appearances. Ultimately, however, when an assessment has to be made of his life, it is not the money or the worship of his fans that matters; neither is it the mixed quality of his film career and the uncertainties surrounding his personal characteristics and shortcomings. What really matters is that in his treatment of the classics from the Great American Songbook, Sinatra has made a unique contribution to 20th-century popular music. Despite an occasional lapse, when he replaces carefully-crafted lyrics with his own inimitable (yet all-too-often badly imitated) phrases, over several decades he fashioned countless timeless performances. There are some songs which, however many singers may have recorded them before or since Sinatra, or will record them in the future, have become inextricably linked with his name: 'I'll Walk Alone', 'It Could Happen To

You', 'I'll Never Smile Again', 'Violets For Your Furs', 'How About You?', 'Jeepers Creepers', 'All Of Me', 'Taking A Chance On Love', 'Just One Of Those Things', 'My Funny Valentine', 'They Can't Take That Away From Me', 'I Get A Kick Out Of You', 'You Make Me Feel So Young', 'Old Devil Moon', 'The Girl Next Door', 'My One And Only Love', 'Three Coins In The Fountain', 'Love And Marriage', 'Swingin' Down The Lane', 'Come Fly With Me', 'Fly Me To The Moon', 'The Tender Trap', 'Chicago', 'New York, New York', 'Let Me Try Again', 'Night And Day', 'Here's That Rainy Day', 'You Make Me Feel So Young', 'Strangers In The Night', 'I Thought About You', 'Lady Is A Tramp', 'Anything Goes', 'Night And Day', 'All The Way', 'One For My Baby', 'I've Got You Under My Skin'.

Not all these songs are major examples of the songwriters' art yet even on lesser material, of which 'My Way' is a notable example, he provides a patina of quality the songs and their writers may not deserve and which no one else could have supplied. Since the 70s Sinatra's voice has shown serious signs of decay. The pleasing baritone had given way to a worn and slightly rusting replica of what it once had been. Nevertheless, he sang on, adjusting to the changes in his voice and as often as not still creating exemplary performances of many of his favourite songs. In these twilight years he was especially effective in the easy swinging mid-tempo he had always preferred and which concealed the inevitable vocal deterioration wrought by time. He made records into the 80s, *LA Is My Lady* being the last although with so many farewell concerts and television spectaculars who can say if the last record has yet been released. In assessing Sinatra's place in popular music it is very easy to slip into hyperbole. After all, through dedication to his craft and his indisputable love for the songs he sang, Sinatra became the greatest exponent of a form of music which he helped turn into an art form. In so doing he became an icon of popular culture which is no mean achievement for a skinny kid from Hoboken. Writing in the *Observer*, when Sinatra's retirement was thought, mistakenly, to be imminent, music critic Benny Green observed: 'What few people, apart from musicians, have never seemed to grasp is that he is not simply the best popular singer of his generation . . . but the culminating point in an evolutionary process which has refined the art of interpreting words set to music. Nor is there even the remotest possibility that he will have a successor. Sinatra was

the result of a fusing of a set of historical circumstances which can never be repeated.' Sinatra himself has never publicly spoken of his work in such glowing terms, choosing instead to describe himself simply as a 'saloon singer'. Deep in his heart, however, Sinatra must know that Green's judgement is the more accurate and it is one which will long be echoed by countless millions of fans all around the world. Musically at least, it is a world better for the care which Frank Sinatra has lavished upon its popular songs. In 1992, a two-part television biography, *Sinatra*, was transmitted in the USA, produced by Tina Sinatra, and starring Philip Casnoff in the leading role. Almost inevitably, it topped the weekly ratings.

Selected albums: *Sing And Dance With Frank Sinatra* (1950), *Songs For Young Lovers* (1955), *Swing Easy* (1955), *In The Wee Small Hours* (1955), *Songs For Swingin' Lovers* (1956), *High Society* (1956, film soundtrack), *Close To You* (1957), *A Swingin' Affair!* (1957), *Where Are You?* (1957), *Pal Joey* (1957, film soundtrack), *A Jolly Christmas From Frank Sinatra* (1957), *Come Fly With Me* (1958), *Frank Sinatra Sings For Only The Lonely* (1958), *Come Dance With Me!* (1959), *No One Cares* (1959), *Can-Can* (1960, film soundtrack), *Nice 'N' Easy* (1960), *Sinatra's Swinging Session!!!* (1961), *Ring-A-Ding Ding!* (1961), *Sinatra Swings* (1961), *Come Swing With Me!* (1961), *I Remember Tommy...*(1961), *Sinatra And Strings* (1961), *Point Of No Return* (1961), *Sinatra And Swingin' Brass* (1962), *All Alone* (1962), with Count Basie *Sinatra-Basie* (1962), *The Concert Sinatra* (1963), *The Select Johnny Mercer* (1963), *Sinatra's Sinatra* (1963), *Come Blow Your Horn* (1963, film soundtrack), *Days Of Wine And Roses, Moon River, And Other Academy Award Winners* (1964), with Bing Crosby, Fred Waring *America I Hear You Singing* (1964), with Basie *It Might As Well Be Swing* (1964), *Softly As I Leave You* (1964), *Sinatra '65* (1965), *September Of My Years* (1965), *My Kind Of Broadway* (1965), *Moonlight Sinatra* (1965), *A Man And His Music* (1965), *Strangers In The Night* (1966), *Sinatra At The Sands* (1966), *That's Life* (1966), *Francis Albert Sinatra And Antonio Carlos Jobim* (1967), *Frank Sinatra (The World We Knew)* (1967), with Nancy Sinatra *Frank And Nancy* (1967), with Duke Ellington *Francis A. And Edward K.* (1968), *Cycles* (1968), *The Sinatra Family Wish You A Merry Christmas* (1968), *My Way* (1969), *A Man Alone And Other Songs By Rod McKuen* (1969), *Watertown* (1970), with Antonio Carlos Jobim *Sinatra And Company* (1971), *Ol' Blue Eyes Is Back* (1973), *Some Nice Things I've Missed* (1974), *Sinatra - The Main Event Live* (1974), *Trilogy: Past, Present,*

Future (1980), *She Shot Me Down* (1981), *LA Is My Lady* (1984). Compilations: *This Is Sinatra!* (1956), *That Old Feeling* (1956) *Frankie* (1957), *Adventures Of The Heart* (1957), *This Is Sinatra, Volume 2* (1958), *The Frank Sinatra Story* (1958), *Look To Your Heart* (1959), *All The Way* (1961), *Sinatra Sings...Of Love And Things* (1962), *Tell Her You Love Her* (1963), *Sinatra: A Man And His Music (1960-65)* (1965), *The Movie Songs (1954-60)* (1967), *Frank Sinatra's Greatest Hits!* (1968), *Frank Sinatra's Greatest Hits, Vol. 2* (1972), *Round # 1* (1974), *Portrait Of Sinatra* (1977), *Radio Years* (1987), *Rare Recordings 1935-70* (1989), *Gold Collection* (1993).

Further reading: *Sinatra*, Robin Douglas Home. *Sinatra: A Biography*, Arnold Shaw. *The Frank Sinatra Scrapbook*, Richard Peters. *Sinatra: The Man And His Music - The Recording Artistry Of Francis Albert Sinatra 1939-1992*, Ed O'Brien and Scott P. Sayers. *His Way: The Unauthorized Biography Of Frank Sinatra*, Kitty Kelly. *Frank Sinatra: My Father*, Nancy Sinatra.

Smith, Keely

b. 9 March 1932, Norfolk, Virginia USA, Smith was a jazzy singer who worked with her husband, bandleader Louis Prima. She made her professional debut in 1950, joining Prima three years later. As well as her solo spots with the big band, she frequently duetted with Prima on stylized versions of well-known songs. In 1958 one of these, Johnny Mercer and Harold Arlen's 'That Old Black Magic' became a surprise US Top 20 hit. The duo followed up with the minor successes 'I've Got You Under My Skin' and 'Bei Mir Bist Du Schoen', a revival of the 1937 Andrews Sisters hit. Smith appeared with Prima in the movie *Hey Boy, Hey Girl* (1959), singing 'Fever' and she also sang on the soundtrack of *Thunder Road* (1958). In the early 60s, Smith separated from Prima and signed to Reprise, where her musical director was Nelson Riddle. In 1965, she had Top 20 hits in the UK with an album of Beatles' compositions and a version of 'You're Breaking My Heart'.

Selected albums: *I Wish You Love* (1957), *Politely* (1958), *Swinging Pretty* (1959), *Because You're Mine* (1959), *Be My Love* (1959), *Twist With Keely Smith* (1962), *Little Girl Blue, Little Girl New* (1963), *Lennon-McCartney Songbook* (1964).

Sound Of Music, The

Even before its Broadway opening on 16 November 1959, *The Sound Of Music* was set to become a financial success. Advance sales exceeded three million dollars and with numerous touring versions, best-selling albums and a blockbuster film, it made a fortune for its composers, Richard Rodgers and Oscar Hammerstein II. The show had a strong narrative book, by Howard Lindsey and Russel Crouse, which was based upon the real-life story of Maria Rainer, her marriage to George von Trapp and her relationship with his family of singing youngsters. The family's evasion of capture by the Nazis during World War II gave the story a tense dramatic core and the fact that the family became professional singers meant that music and song blended well into the narrative, even if, at times, there seemed to be rather more sentiment than reality would have allowed. Starring Mary Martin as Maria, Theodore Bikel and Patricia Neway, the show was filled with songs which became very popular, amongst them the title song, 'Do Re Mi', 'My Favorite Things', 'Edelweiss', 'So Long, Farewell', 'You Are Sixteen', 'How Can Love Survive?', 'The Lonely Goatherd' and 'Climb Ev'ry Mountain'. Sentimental or not, it is hard to imagine that at the time he was working on this show, Hammerstein was a sick man and less than a year after the Broadway opening he was dead. *The Sound Of Music* played for over 1,400 performances, enjoyed a London production in 1961, a New York revival in 1967. The 1965 film version, which starred Julie Andrews, won three Oscars including Best Picture and became a huge money-spinner in its own right. The soundtrack album broke numerous longevity records and towered like a collosus in the charts during the second half of the 60s (227 weeks USA and 382 in the UK including 70 weeks at number 1).

Southern, Jeri

b. Genevieve Hering, 5 August 1926, Royal, Nebraska, USA, d. 4 August 1991, Los Angeles, California, USA. A warm, 'smokey' voiced jazz-influenced singer/pianist, Southern studied at the Notre Dame Academy, Omaha, and later played piano at the local Blackstone Hotel. After touring with a US Navy recruiting show, where she began singing, she worked at several venues in Chicago in the late 40s, including the Hi Note Club, where she supported stars such as Anita O'Day. After obtaining a nightly spot on television, she was signed to Decca Records, and had a US Top 30 hits with 'You Better Go Now' (1951), and 'Joey' (1954). Her wistful version of 'When I Fall In Love' established her as a favourite in the UK where she also had a Top 30 hit with 'Fire Down Below' (1957). She then switched to the Capitol label making a highly-acclaimed *Jeri Southern Sings Cole Porter*, featuring a set of humourous arrangements by Billy May, including a 20s setting of 'Don't Look At Me That Way'. Of her many album releases, *When I Fall In Love*, released by MCA Records in 1984, contained several numbers closely identified with Southern, including 'An Occasional Man' She retired from performing in the mid-60s to become a vocal and piano coach for professional artists. She subsequently moved to Hollywood, and worked on arrangements with the film music writer, Hugo Friedhofer, and later, cared for him. She also published a book, *Interpreting Popular Music At The Keyboard*. Her last public performance was early in 1991 at the Vine Street Bar and Grill, where she was persuaded to emerge from the audience by Anita O'Day, and played a medley of Jerome Kern songs at the piano. She died of pneumonia in August 1991.

Albums: *You Better Go Now* (50s), *When Your Hearts On Fire* (50s), *Warm* (1955) *Jeri Gently Jumps* (1958), *Prelude To A Kiss* (1958), *Southern Hospitality* (1959), *Jeri Southern Meets Cole Porter* (1959), *At The Crescendo* (1960), *Southern Breeze* (1959), *Coffee, Cigarettes And Memories* (1959), *Jeri Southern Meets Johnny Smith* (1959), *You Better Go Now* (1989). Compilation: *When I Fall In Love* (1984).

Spaniels

This vocal ensemble was formed in 1952 in Gary, Indiana, USA. The Spaniels were universally recognized as one of the great R&B vocal harmony groups of the 50s, whose magnificent body of work was not truly reflected in their moderate chart success. The group originally consisted of Roosevelt High students James 'Pookie' Hudson (lead), Ernest Warren (first tenor), Opal Courtney (baritone), Willis C. Jackson (baritone), and Gerald Gregory (bass). In 1953 the quintet enjoyed an R&B Top 10 hit with 'Baby, It's You', but the following year achieved their biggest success when 'Goodnite Sweetheart, Goodnite' reached the US pop Top 30 despite competition from an opportunistic pop-style version by the McGuire Sisters. The Spaniels' delicate doo-wop harmonies turned this ballad into one of the era's best-loved performances with an emotional pull outweighing its intrinsic simplicity. The Spaniels in 1955 followed with two fine regional hits, 'Let's Make Up' and 'You Painted Pictures'. The Spaniels reorganized in 1956, and Hudson and Gregory were now augmented by James Cochran (baritone), Carl Rainge (tenor), and Don Porter

(second tenor). Top recordings of this group included the 'You Gave Me Peace Of Mind' (1956) and 'Everyone's Laughing' (number 13 R&B 1957), and 'I Lost You' (1958). Another reorganization i 1960 in which Hudson and Gregory brough. in Andy McGruder, Billy Cary, and Ernest Warren, yielded the group's last hit featuring the classic Spaniels sound, 'I Know' (US R&B number 23 in 1960). Hudson went solo in 1961, but formed a soul-styled Spaniels group in 1969 that brought 'Fairy Tales' to the charts in 1970.

Albums: *Goodnite, It's Time To Go* (1958), *The Spaniels* (1960), *Spaniels* (1968). Compilations: *Hits Of The Spaniels* (1971), *Great Googley Moo!* (1981), *16 Soulful Serenades* (1984), *Stormy Weather* (1986), *Play It Cool* (1990).

Specialty Records

Formed in 1946 in Los Angeles, California, USA by Art Rupe, originally from Pittsburgh, Pennsylvania. Specialty Records gave rise to some of the most powerful early R&B and rock 'n' roll performers, particularly Little Richard. Rupe had briefly run the small-time label Juke Box Records and with money earned there launched Specialty. Among the label's first signing were blues singers Percy Mayfield and Joe Liggins. He also signed gospel artists including the Soul Stirrers. In 1952 Rupe expanded his artist roster beyond the west coast and signed New Orleans R&B singer Lloyd Price, who was the label's greatest success to that time with his number 1 R&B hit 'Lawdy Miss Clawdy'. Other New Orleans acts on Specialty included Art Neville and Ernie K-Doe. In 1955, Rupe signed Little Richard (Penniman), who became the label's greatest success and one of the pioneers of early rock 'n' roll. All of Little Richard's hits, including 'Tutti Frutti', 'Good Golly Miss Molly' and 'Lucille', were on the Specialty label. Other Specialty rock 'n' roll/R&B artists included Larry Williams and Don And Dewey. The label was wound down during the 60s, but later revived in the 80s by Beverly Rupe, daughter of Art (who had died), who launched a reissue campaign making much of the classic Specialty material available again.

Album: *The Specialty Story Volume One* (1985).

Squires, Dorothy

b. Edna May Squires, 25 March 1918, Llanelli, Dyfed, Wales. A dynamic, dramatic and highly emotional singer, who retained an army of fans throughout a career spanning over 50 years. At her 'live' performances, especially during the 70s, the audience came, not just to be entertained, but to pay homage. At the age of 18, she moved to London to become a singer, and worked at the Burlington Club, where she was discovered by American pianist and bandleader, Charlie Kunz. She joined his band at the Casani Club, and made her first radio broadcast from there. In 1938, she joined songwriter Billy Reid And His Orchestra, beginning a partnership which lasted until 1951, when she left to concentrate on a solo career. In between, she recorded many of Reid's songs, such as 'The Gypsy', 'It's A Pity To Say Goodnight', 'A Tree In A Meadow' and 'When China Boy Meets China Girl'. During the 40s, Reid and Squires teamed up to become one of the most successful double acts on the UK Variety circuit, and she made frequent appearances on BBC Radio's *Melody Lane, Band Parade, Variety Fanfare* and *Henry Hall's Guest Night*. In 1953, she had a UK chart hit with one of Reid's biggest hit songs, 'I'm Walking Behind You' and, in the same year, married the young actor Roger Moore. They settled in California for most of the 50s, sometimes playing cabaret engagements. After the couple's acrimonious split in 1961, Squires made the UK Top 30 in collaboration with personality pianist, Russ Conway, with her own composition, 'Say It With Flowers'. She also became the first British artist to play London's Talk Of The Town. In 1968, after several unfruitful years, she financed her own album, *Say It With Flowers*, for President Records. This was followed by a version of the Stevie Wonder hit, 'For Once In My Life', 'Till' and 'My Way' (an anthem which fitted her as perfectly as it did Frank Sinatra). During 1970, her version spent nearly six months in the UK chart, and inspired her to hire the London Palladium for a sell-out comeback concert, which she played to an ecstatic reception; a double album was released on Decca.

In the 70s, Squires was headlining again throughout the UK, in concerts and cabaret, and also returned to the USA to play New York's Carnegie Hall. She hired the Palladium again, in 1974, for a concert in memory of Billy Reid, and in 1979, released another double album, *With All My Heart*. During the 80s she became semi-retired, giving a few concerts, one of which became *We Clowns - Live At The Dominion* (1984), on her own Esban label; she also released *Three Beautiful Words Of Love* on Conifer. Squire's career was bathed in controversy and she became one of the most notoriously prolific libel litigants in show-business

history. In 1989, she was evicted from her 17-bedroom Thames-side mansion that once belonged to the celebrated actress, Lily Langtry. During the early 90s, Squires was still performing occasionally and, in 1991, released *The Best Of The EMI Years*, a 20-track compilation of her work with Billy Reid, some of her own compositions, and several of the other recordings she made for Columbia during the early 60s.

Album: *Dorothy Squires Sings Billy Reid* (1958), *Say It With Flowers* (1968), *With All My Heart* (1979), *We Clowns - Live At The Dominion* (1984), *Three Beautiful Words Of Love* (1988). Compilation: *The Best Of The EMI Years* (1991).

Squires, Rosemary

b. Joan Rosemary Yarrow, 7 December 1928, Bristol, Avon, England. This civil servant's daughter underwent vocal, piano and guitar lessons before and during study at Salisbury's St. Edmund's Girls School. In 1940, a broadcast on the BBC Home Service's *Children's Hour* created demand for her in local venues that embraced US army bases. With an endearing West Country burr, she sang in various combos formed within these camps as well as the Polish Military Band while employed in an antique bookshop and then an office. After becoming a professional performer, she was employed by big band conductors such as Ted Heath, Geraldo and Cyril Stapleton, and also smaller jazz bands led by Max Harris, Kenny Baker and Alan Clare - with whose trio she appeared at a BBC Festival of Jazz at the Royal Albert Hall. She has long been known to Britain at large, having been omnipresent since the late 40s on BBC radio light entertainment programmes - including *Melody Time, Workers' Playtime* and many of her own series. In 1962, she hovered just outside the UK chart with a version of 'The Gypsy Rover'. Now living again in Salisbury, she remains an active musician with Tibetan culture among her extra-mural interests. She was secretary of Britain's Tibet Society from 1972-75. In 1991, she surprised her friends (and herself) by marrying for the first time, although it is far from being the first occasion on which she has changed her name: she recorded one of her most successful titles, 'Frankfurter Sandwiches', as Joanne And The Streamliners, and in the USA and for *Readers Digest* her psuedenym was Roberta Starr. In the 90s, she still continues with her 'second career', singing for television jingles, and plays the role of DJ, on her Sunday afternoon record programme on Radio Wiltshire. Selected album: *A Time For Rosemary* (c.90s).

Jo Stafford

Stafford, Jo

b. 12 November 1920, Coalinga, near Fresno, California, USA. The Stafford family moved to Long Beach when Jo was just four and while at high school she studied for two years towards an operatic career. She joined her two older sisters in their country music act, but later left to freelance on radio with the seven-man vocal group, the Pied Pipers. In 1939, after appearing on radio with Tommy Dorsey, they reduced the group to a quartet and joined Dorsey permanently. A large part of their appeal was Stafford's pure, almost academic tone, her distinctive vocal timbre and the complete lack of vibrato which provided a rock-steady lead. While with Dorsey she had solo success with 'Little Man With A Candy Cigar', 'Manhattan Serenade' and a 12-inch disc of 'For You'. She also duetted with Dorsey arranger Sy Oliver on his own composition, 'Yes Indeed'. When the Pipers left Dorsey in 1942 and started recording for Capitol Records, Jo was soon out on her own as one of the top stars of the 40s. She stayed with the label until 1950, having hits such as 'Candy' (with Johnny Mercer), 'That's For Me', 'Serenade Of The Bells', 'Some Enchanted Evening' and 'Tennessee Waltz'. There were also several duets with Gordon MacRae, including 'My Darling, My Darling' from the Broadway musical *Where's Charley*, and 'Whispering Hope' an old religious song also recorded by Pat Boone. In 1950 she switched to Columbia, immediately having further success with 'Make Love To Me', 'Shrimp Boats', 'Keep It A Secret', 'Jambalaya' and her biggest seller 'You Belong To Me'. Just as important as the singles were a series of high-class albums of standards scored by her husband, ex-Dorsey arranger Paul Weston, who had become her musical alter-ego. Her reputation in some quarters as being a purely academic singer was given the lie on two notable occasions. The first was when she recorded pseudonymously as the lunatic Cinderella G. Stump on Red Ingle And The Natural Seven's 1947 comedy hit 'Temptation'; and the second a decade later when, with her husband, she made a series of albums as 'Jonathan And Darlene Edwards', in which they wickedly sent up amateur pianists and singers. In 1959 Stafford retired from public performing, but recorded until the mid-60s, sometimes for Frank Sinatra's Reprise label. Dissatisfied with their former recording companies' neglect of their output, Stafford and Weston acquired the rights themselves and released them on their own Corinthian label.

Albums: with Gordon MacRae *Sunday Evening Songs* (1953), with Gordon MacRae *Memory Songs* (mid-50s), with Frankie Laine *Musical Portrait Of New Orleans* (mid-50s), *Happy Holiday* (mid-50s), *Ski Trails* (1956), *Once Over Lightly* (mid-50s), *Swingin' Down Broadway* (1958), *I'll Be Seeing You* (1959), *Ballad Of The Blues* (1959), *Jo + Jazz* (1960), *Jo + Blues* (early 60s, reissued 1980), *Jo + Broadway* (early 60s, reissued 1979), with Gordon MacRae *Old Rugged Cross* (early 60s), *Songs Of Faith Hope And Love* (early 60s, reissued 1978), *American Folk Songs* (1962, reissued 1978), with Gordon MacRae *Whispering Hope* (1962), with Gordon MacRae *Peace In The Valley* (1963), *Sweet Hour Of Prayer* (1964), *Joyful Season* (1964), *Getting Sentimental Over Tommy Dorsey* (mid-60s), *Do I Hear A Waltz?* (1966), *This Is Jo Stafford* (1966), *G.I. Joe - Songs Of World War II* (1979), *Broadway Revisited - Romantic Ballads From The Theater* (1983), *Fan Favourites Through The Years* (1984), *International Hits* (1988). Compilations: *Jo Stafford's Greatest Hits* (1959), *Jo Stafford Showcase* (1960), *The Hits Of Jo Stafford* (1963), *Jo Stafford's Greatest Hits - Best On Columbia* (1977), *Hits Of Jo Stafford* (1984), *Stars Of The 50s* (1984), *Introducing Jo Stafford* (1987), *Broadway Revisited* (1988). As Jonathan And Darlene Edwards *Sing Along With Jonathan And Darlene Edwards - Only The Chorus Is For Real* (50s/60s), *Jonathan And Darlene's Original Masterpiece* (50s/60s), *In Paris - Grammy Award Winning Album* (1960). Compilation: *Jonathan And Darlene's Greatest Hits* (80s).

Stapleton, Cyril

b. 31 December 1914, Nottingham, England, d. 25 February, 1974. Stapleton played the violin at the age of 11, and served in pit orchestras for silent movies before joining Henry Hall as a violinist in the early 30s. In 1939, at the outbreak of World War II he had moved on to working under Billy Ternent, via Jack Payne, and had married impressionist, Beryl Orde. He joined the Royal Air Force, initially as an air-gunner, later conducting the RAF Symphony Orchestra at the Potsdam Summit Conference. At the end of the war he formed a band to play at Fisher's Restaurant in London's New Bond Street. In the late 40s, the band, plus strings, was featured on BBC radio programmes such as *Hit Parade* and *Golden Slipper*. In the 50s he became known as the UK's 'Mr. Music' when he took over the all-star BBC Show Band from Stanley Black in 1952, playing on radio three nights a week. He led the band for five years, playing host to star US artists such as Frank Sinatra, and Nat 'King' Cole, along with residents Janie Marlow and the Stargazers vocal group. With his own band he had a string of UK chart hits for Decca, from 1955-57 including 'Elephant Tango', 'Blue Star' (theme from the US television series, *The Medics*), 'The Italian Theme', 'The Happy Whistler' and 'Forgotten Dreams'. In the USA Stapleton made the Top 30 with 'The Children's Marching Song' (from the movie, *The Inn Of The Sixth Happiness*) which, along with 'Blue Star', sold a million copies. In 1966 the Stapleton band moved to Pye Records, and later, he became A&R controller and an independent producer, masterminding the million-selling *Singalong* series of albums by Max Bygraves. In the last few years of his life Stapleton began to tour with a big band, attempting to re-create the old sounds. He died in February 1974.

Albums: *Songs You Won't Forget* (1962), *My Fair Lady/King And I* (1969). Compilations: *The Big Band's Back* (1974), *Golden Hour Of Strict Tempo* (1974).

Stargazers

Formed in 1949, they developed into Britain's most popular vocal group in the early 50s. The original line-up consisted of Dick James, Cliff Adams, Marie Benson, Bob Brown, Fred Datchler and Ronnie Milne. They first attracted attention on radio programmes such as *The Derek Roy Show* and *The Family Hour*, later moving to *Top Score*, the *Goon Show* and *Take it From Here*. The Stargazers began recording towards the end of 1949, working for a variety of labels, including Decca, HMV, Columbia and Polygon, backing artist such as Dick James, Steve Conway and Benny Lee, and later, Dennis Lotis and Jimmy Young. Their own releases included 'Me And My Imagination', 'Red Silken Stockings' 'A-Round The Corner' and 'Sugarbush'. In April 1953, they became the first British act to get to number 1 in the infant *New Musical Express* chart, with 'Broken Wings'. Amost a year later, they hit the top spot again, with Meredith Wilson's 'I See The Moon'. They continued to record into the late 50s, and made the UK chart with 'Happy Wanderer', 'Somebody', 'Crazy Otto Rag', 'Close The Door', 'Twenty Tiny Fingers' and 'Hot Diggity' (1956). They also worked constantly in radio, and their own series, *The Stagazers' Music Shop*, opened for business on Radio Luxembourg in 1952, crossing to the BBC nearly five years later. The group also had a regular slot on the *BBC Show Band Show* with Cyril Stapleton, and toured the UK variety circuit. Their

first permanent personnel change came in 1953, when David Carey replaced Ronnie Milne. Milne emigrated to Canada and took up a post in the Canadian Army, training young musicians. Two years later, the group appeared in the Royal Variety Performance, and, in the same year, Eula Parker took over from her fellow Australian, Marie Benson, who embarked on a solo career, armed with a two year contract with Philips Records. Parker herself was later succeeded by June Marlow. After being replaced by Bob Brown, Dick James, the Stargazers' original leader, had solo hits with 'Robin Hood' and 'Garden Of Eden' before becoming a successful music publisher and the proprietor of DJM Records. Cliff Adams, went on to devise the radio programme, *Sing Something Simple*, in 1959, and he and his Singers, have remained with the show ever since. Fred Datchley became a member of the Polka Dots, a vocal group bearing some resemblance to the Hi-Lo's. Datchley's son, Clark, was a founder member of the 80s vocal/instrumental band, Johnny Hates Jazz.

Selected albums: *Make It Soon* (1955), *South Of The Border* (1960).

Starr, Kay

b. Katherine LaVerne Starks, 21 July 1922, Dougherty, Oklahoma, USA. While she was still a child Starr's family moved to Dallas, Texas, where she made her professional debut on local radio before she had left school. In 1939 she was hired briefly by Glenn Miller when his regular singer, Marion Hutton, was sick. Starr made records with Miller, but was soon on the move. She spent brief spells with the bands of Bob Crosby and Joe Venuti, and attracted most attention during her mid-40s stint with Charlie Barnet. Among the records she made with Barnet was 'Share Croppin' Blues', which was a minor hit. The record sold well enough to interest Capitol Records, and, from 1948-54, she had string of hits with the label, including 'So Tired', 'Hoop-Dee-Doo', 'Bonaparte's Retreat', 'I'll Never Be Free', 'Oh, Babe!', 'Come On-A My House', 'Wheel Of Fortune' (US number 1 1952), Comes A-Long A-Love (UK number 1 1952), 'Side By Side', 'Half A Photograph', 'Allez-Vous-En', 'Changing Partners', 'The Man Upstairs', 'If You Love Me (Really Love Me)' and 'Am I A Toy Or A Treasure?'. In 1955 she switched to RCA, and went straight to the top of the charts in the US and UK with 'Rock And Roll Waltz'. Her last singles hit was 'My Heart Reminds Me' (1957). Starr sang

Dakota Staton

with controlled power and a strong emotional undertow, which made her an appealing in-person performer. In the 60s she became a regular attraction at venues such as Harrah's, Reno, and, as recently as the late 80s, she returned there, and played New York clubs as a solo attraction and as part of nostalgia packages such as '3 Girls 3' (with Helen O'Connell and Margaret Whiting), and '4 Girls 4' (add Kaye Ballard). In the spring of 1993, she joined another popular 50s singer, Pat Boone, on The April Love Tour of the UK.

Selcted albums: *In A Blue Mood* (1955), *Blue Starr* (1955), *Movin'* (1959), *Rockin' With Kay* (c.1959), *I Hear The Word* (1959), *Just Plain Country* (1959, reissued 1987), *Movin' On Broadway* (1960), *Kay Starr* (1960), *Losers Weepers* (1960), *One More Time* (1960), *Jazz Singer* (1961), *Cry By Night* (1962), *Tears And Heartaches* (1966), *Kay Starr And Count Basie* (1968). Compilations: *Pure Gold* (1981), with Bob Crosby *Suddenly It's 1939* (1985), *1947; Kay Starr* (1986), *Wheel Of Fortune* (1989).

Staton, Dakota

b. 3 June 1932, Pittsburgh, Pennsylvania, USA. After singing in clubs in a style modelled on that of such diverse artists as Dinah Washington and Sarah Vaughan, Staton began to attract wider attention in the mid-50s. She extended her repertoire to include popular songs, R&B, soul and gospel and made a number of successful record albums. In the mid-60s she took up residence in the UK and Europe, but was back in the USA early in the following decade. She is at her best with mainstream jazz accompaniment, whether a big band, such as Manny Albam's or Kurt Edelhagen's, or a small group, such as those led by George Shearing and Jonah Jones. Staton's R&B material is less attractive, often performed at feverish tempos and with a deliberate coarsening of her powerful voice.

Albums: *The Late, Late Show* (1957), *Dakota Staton i* (1958), *Dakota Staton ii* (1959), *Dakota Staton iii* (1960), *Dakota Staton iv* (1960), *Dakota Staton v* (1960), *Dakota Staton At Storyville* (1961), *Dakota Staton vi* (1963), *Dakota Staton At Newport* (1963), *Dakota Staton vii* (c.1964), *Dakota Staton viii* (1967), with Richard 'Groove' Holmes *Let Me Off Uptown* (c.1972), *Dakota Staton With The Manny Albam Big Band* (1973), *Please Save Your Love* (1992).

Steele, Tommy

b. Thomas Hicks, 17 December 1936, Bermondsey, London, England. After serving as a merchant seaman Hicks formed the skiffle trio, the Cavemen with Lionel Bart and Mike Pratt, before being discovered by entrepreneur John Kennedy in the 2 I's coffee bar in Soho, London. A name change to Tommy Steele followed and after an appearance at London's Condor Club the boy was introduced to manager Larry Parnes. From thereon, his rise to stardom was meteoric. Using the old 'working-class boy makes good' angle, Kennedy launched the chirpy cockney in the unlikely setting of a debutante's ball. Class conscious Fleet Street lapped up the idea of Tommy as the 'Deb's delight' and took him to their hearts. His debut single, 'Rock With The Caveman' was an immediate Top 20 hit and although the follow-up 'Doomsday Rock'/'Elevator Rock' failed to chart, the management was unfazed. Their confidence was rewarded when Steele hit number 1 in the UK charts with a cover of Guy Mitchell's 'Singing The Blues' in January 1957. By this point, he was Britain's first and premier rock 'n' roll singer and, without resorting to sexual suggestiveness, provoked mass teenage hysteria unseen since the days of Johnnie Ray. At one stage, he had four songs in the Top 30, although he never restricted himself to pure rock 'n' roll. A bit-part in the film *Kill Me Tomorrow* led to an autobiographical musical *The Tommy Steele Story*, which also spawned a book of the same title. For a time Steele performed the twin role of rock 'n' roller and family entertainer but his original persona faded towards the end of the 50s. Further movie success in *The Duke Wore Jeans* (1958) and *Tommy The Toreador* (1959) effectively redefined his image. His rocking days closed with covers of Ritchie Valens' 'Come On Let's Go' and Freddy Cannon's 'Tallahassee Lassie'. The decade ended with the novelty 'Little White Bull', after which it was goodbye to rock 'n' roll.

After appearing on several variety bills during the late 50s, Steele sampled the 'legit' side of show business in 1960 when he played Tony Lumpkin in *She Stoops To Conquer* at the Old Vic, and he was back in the straight theatre again in 1969, in the role of Truffaldino in *The Servant Of Two Masters* at the Queen's Theatre. In years between those two plays, he experienced some of the highlights of his career. In 1963, he starred as Arthur Kipps in the stage musical, *Half A Sixpence*, which ran for 18 months in the West End before transferring to Broadway in 1965; Steele re-created the role in the film version in 1967. A year later, he appeared in another major musical movie, *Finan's Rainbow*,

Tommy Steele and the Dallas Boys

with Fred Astaire and Petula Clark. His other films included *Touch It Light, It's All Happening, The Happiest Millionaire* and *Where's Jack?* In 1974, Steele made one of his rare television appearances, in the autobiographical, *My Life, My Song*, and, in the same year, appeared at the London Palladium in *Hans Anderson*, the first of three stage adaptations of famous Hollywood films. He also starred in the revival three years later. In 1979-80 his one-man musical show was resident at London's Prince of Wales Theatre for a record 60 weeks - the Variety Club Of Great Britain made him their Entertainer Of The Year. He was also awarded the OBE. Steele was back at the Palladium again in 1983 and 1989, in the highly popular *Singin' In The Rain*, which he also directed. In the latter capacity he tried, too late as it transpired, to save impresario Harold Fielding's *Ziegfeld* (1988) from becoming a spectacular flop. Fielding had originally cast Steele in *Half A Sixpence* some 25 years earlier. Off-stage in the 80s, Steele published his first novel, a thriller, *The Final Run*; had one of his paintings exhibited at the Royal Academy; was commisioned by Liverpool City Council to fashion a bronze statue of 'Eleanor Rigby' as a tribute to the Beatles; and composed 'A Portrait Of Pablo' and 'Rock Suite - An Elderly Person's Guide To Rock'. The third, and least successful of Steele's movie-to-stage transfers was *Some Like It Hot* (1992). A hybrid of Billy Wilder's classic film, and the Broadway stage musical *Sugar* (1972), it received derisory reviews ('The show's hero is Mr Steele's dentist'), and staggered along for three months in the West End on the strength of its star's previous box-office appeal. In 1993, Steele was presented with the Hans Andersen Award at the Danish Embassy in London.

Albums: *The Tommy Steele Stage Show* (1957), *The Tommy Steele Story* (1957), *Stars Of 6.05* (late 50s), *The Duke Wore Jeans* (1958, film soundtrack), *Tommy The Toreador* (1959, film soundtrack), *So This Is Broadway* (1964), *Light Up The Sky* (1959), *Cinderella* (1959, stage cast), *Get Happy With Tommy* (1960), *It's All Happening* (1962), *Half A Sixpence* (1963, stage recording), *Everything's Coming Up Broadway* (1967), *The Happiest Millionire* (1967), *My Life My Song* (1974), *Hans Andersen* (1978, London stage cast), with Sally Ann Howes *Henry Fielding's Hans Anderson* (1985). Compilations: *The Happy World Of Tommy Steele* (1969), *The World Of Tommy Steele, Volume 2* (1971), *Focus On Tommy Steele* (1977), *The Family Album* (1979), *20 Greatest Hits* (1983), *Tommy Steele And The Steelmen - The Rock 'N' Roll Years* (1988).

Further reading: *Quincy's Quest*, Tommy Steele,

based on the children's television programme he scripted. *Tommy Steele*, John Kennedy.

Stone, Kirby, Four

This vocal quartet comprised Kirby Stone (b. 27 April 1918, New York, USA), Eddie Hall, Larry Foster and Mike Gardner. They had a hip brand of humour and a distinctive, upbeat, swinging style. Originally an instrumental quintet, the group became a vocal foursome before making a name for themselves in nightclubs and local television shows. They came to prominence in 1958 with an appearance on the *Ed Sullivan Show*, which led to a contract with Columbia Records, and the release of *Man, I Flipped...When I Heard The Kirby Stone Four*. It was a mixture of standards, such as 'S'Wonderful' and 'It Could Happen To You'; and special material written by Stone and Gardner. Their material included 'Juke Box Dream', a vehicle for Foster's uncanny vocal impressions. In the same year they also had a Top 30 single with their extremely original conception of 'Baubles, Bangles And Beads', from Alexander Borodin's buoyant *Kismet*. The accompanying album reached the US Top 20. Amongst their other album releases, 1962's *Guys And Dolls (Like Today)* included a 'liberetto-ture' (a combination of libretto and overture) by Kirby Stone and the group's frequent arranger and conductor, Dick Hyman, as an attempt to present the Abe Burrows/Jo Swerling/Frank Loesser masterpiece as a 'show for the ear alone'. Stone added some extra lyrics for his 'guys', who were augmented by the 'dolls', a female vocal chorus; plus a 25 piece orchestra, which included such luminaries as Alvino Rey, Shelly Mann and Al Klink. Subsequently, the Kirby Stone Four continued to flourish, and 'went forward, armed with this common credo - A pox on all harmonica players, nightclub owners named Rocky and juveniles who win contests by playing 'Lady Of Spain' on white accordions'.
Albums: *Man, I Flipped...When I Heard The Kirby Stone Four* (1958), *Baubles, Bangles And Beads* (1958), *The Kirby Stone Touch* (1960), *Guys And Dolls (Like Today)* (1962).

Storm, Gale

b. Josephine Cottle, 5 April 1922, Bloomington, Texas, USA. A dynamic singer who came to fame mainly through covering the hits of others, Storm arrived in Hollywood in 1939 after winning a 'Gateway To Hollywood' contest in her home state. She was soon working for the Universal and RKO studios, though she ultimately achieved popularity playing Margie Albright in *My Little Margie* (1952-54), a television series, credited as being the first of its kind to be screened five days a week. By 1955, she was recording for Randy Wood's Dot label, getting into the US Top 5 with her cover of Smiley Lewis's 'I Hear You Knocking', followed by 'Teen Age Prayer', Memories Are Made Of This' (both 1955), 'Why Do Fools Fall In Love?', 'Ivory Tower' (both 1956) and 'Dark Moon' (1957). During 1956-59, she had her own 125-segment television series which is considered a precursor for *Love Boat*. By the late 70s, Storm was living in the San Fernando Valley, but still working with local theatre companies.
Albums: *Gale Storm* (1956), *Sentimental Me* (1956), *Soft And Tenderly* (1959), *Gale Storm Sings* (1959). Compilation: *Gale Storm Hits* (1958).

Stott, Wally (see Morley, Angela)

Sullivan, Ed

b. 28 September 1902, New York City, New York, USA, d. 13 October 1974. Sullivan hosted the most popular variety programme on US television during the 50s and 60s. He presented hundreds of the most important musical acts of the era to a wide audience; it was on *The Ed Sullivan Show* that most of America first saw Elvis Presley and the Beatles. Guest musical acts nearly always performed live, some backed by Sullivan's orchestra, led by Ray Bloch. Sullivan was one of seven children, and grew up in New York's Harlem section until the age of five, when his family moved to the suburb of Port Chester, New York, north of the city. He had no particular desire to be an entertainer and took a job as a sportswriter with a Port Chester newspaper as a teenager. In the early 20s he was hired by the *New York Evening Graphic* newspaper in the city, and then by the larger *New York Daily News* in 1932.
While at that paper he began hosting vaudeville shows, which led, in 1947, to an offer by CBS Television to host a new programme (at that time *all* television programmes were new, the medium having opened up at the close of World War II) called *Toast of The Town*. It debuted on 20 June 1948; he held on to his newspaper column as well. On 25 September 1955 the programme's name was changed to *The Ed Sullivan Show*. On his show, Sullivan featured any kind of entertainment he thought would grab a portion of the viewing audience, from opera singers to jugglers, dancing

chimps to pop groups. The programme became one of the highest-rated on American television, and was a Sunday night ritual for millions of Americans. Sullivan became a celebrity himself while his mannerisms and way of speaking became fodder for many comedians and impressionists. Among the hundreds of musical artists to have appeared on the show, in addition to Presley and the Beatles, were Louis Armstrong, Judy Garland, Liberace, the Rolling Stones, the Doors and Ella Fitzgerald. (In 1990, the audio and video rights to some of those performances were leased, and compilation albums featuring music from *The Ed Sullivan Show* began to appear in the USA.) The programme was broadcast for the last time on 6 June 1971.

Sumac, Yma

b. Emperatriz Chavarri, 10 September 1927, Ichocan, Peru. A flamboyant singer, of striking appearance, who was the subject of a series of publicity campaigns designed to shroud her origins in mystery: was she an Inca princess, one of the chosen 'Golden Virgins'? Or a Brooklyn housewife named Amy Camus (Yma Sumac spelt backwards)? Whatever the doubts as to her heritage, what is abundantly clear is her four octave range, ascending from 'female baritone, through lyric soprano, to high coloratura'. The rest of the story goes like this: she was the sixth child of a full-blooded Indian mother and a mixed Indian and Spanish father, and was raised a Quechuan. After performing in local Indian festivals, she moved with her family to Lima, and joined the Compania Peruana de Arte, a group of 46 Indian dancers, singers and musicians. In 1942, Sumac married the Compania's leader, musician and composer, Moises Vivanco, and, four years later, travelled to New York with him, and her cousin, Cholita Rivero, as the Inca Taqui Trio. In the late 40s the Trio played nightclubs such as New York's Blue Angel, and appeared on radio programmes and Arthur Godfrey's television show. Other work included an eight week tour of the Borscht Circuit in the Catskill mountains. Signed for Capitol Records, her first album, *Voice Of Xtabay*, was released in 1950. It featured Sumac 'imitating birds and kettledrums, and singing a selection of strangely compelling songs, such as 'Chant Of The Chosen Maidens' and 'Virgin Of The Sun God', which were written for her by Moises Vivanco, and based on ancient Peruvian folk music'. With only the advantage of minimum publicity (at first), and the notorious 'phony biography', the 10-inch album

sold half a million copies 'overnight'. It was followed by several more in the same vein, and led to an enormously successful concert appearance at the Hollywood Bowl. In 1951, Sumac made her Broadway debut in the short-lived musical, *Flahooley*, singing three songs written for her by Vivanco 'with no lyrics and no real relevance to the story'. During the 50s she continued to be 'hot', playing Carnegie Hall, the Roxy Theatre with Danny Kaye, Las Vegas nightclubs and concert tours of South America and Europe. She also appeared in the movie, *Secret Of The Incas* (1954), with Charlton Heston and Robert Young. By the end of the decade she was beginning to be regarded by some as 'passe', and, eventually, as a 'nostalgic camp icon'. She retired in the early 60s, but is reported to have performed in 1975 at the Chateau Madrid club in Manhattan. In 1987 she hit the comeback trail with a three week engagement at New York's Ballroom, and, a year later, gained favourable reviews in Los Angeles for 'charming and frequently breathtaking performance'. In her set she featured well-know Latin songs such as 'La Molina' as well as the ethereal material 'that I recorded for Capitol 2,000 years ago!'. In 1992, a German documentary film, *Yma Sumac: Hollywood's Inca Princess*, mapped out her exotic career, and attempted to examine her remarkable range with the aid of computer technology. The lady herself declined to co-operate with the venture, thereby leaving the mystery, and the legend, intact.
Selected albums: *Voice Of The Xtabay* (1950), *Legend Of The Sun Virgin* (1951), *Mambo* (1953), *Inca Taqui* (1955), *Legend Of The Jivaro* (1957), *Feugo Del Ande* (1959), *Live In Concert* (1961).

Sun Records

The Sun Record Company was founded in Memphis, Tennessee in February 1952. It evolved out of the Memphis Recording Service, a small studio installed two years earlier by Sam Phillips, a former disc jockey on stations WMSL and WREC. Although early work often comprised of social occasions, Phillips' ambitions focused on an untapped local blues market. Completed masters were leased to a variety of independent outlets, including Chess, Duke and RPM, in the process launching the careers of B.B. King, Howlin' Wolf and Bobby 'Blue' Bland. The Sun label was the natural extension of this success and its early reputation for superior R&B was established with hits by Rufus Thomas ('Bear Cat') and 'Little' Junior Parker ('Feelin' Good'). In 1954 Phillips

312

began recording country music, and the confluence of these two styles resulted in rockabilly. Its most vocal proponent was Elvis Presley, signed by Phillips that year, who completed five exceptional singles for the label before joining RCA Victor. Presley's recordings, which included 'That's Alright Mama', 'Good Rockin' Tonight' and 'Mystery Train', featured Scotty Moore on guitar and Bill Black on bass, whose sparse, economical support enhanced the singer's unfettered delivery. The crisp production defined Sun rockabilly, a sound the singer was unable to recapture following his move to a major label. Although many commentators questioned Phillips' decision, he retorted that he could now develop the careers of Carl Perkins and Johnny Cash. The former's exemplary releases included 'Blue Suede Shoes', (Sun's first national pop hit), 'Matchbox' and 'Boppin' The Blues', but a near-fatal car crash undermined his progress. His mantle was taken up by other rockabilly singers - Warren Smith, Sonny Burgess and Billy Lee Riley - but these lesser acts failed to establish a consistent career. Roy Orbison and Charlie Rich enjoyed limited success on Sun, but found greater acclaim elsewhere. The aforementioned Cash then became Sun's most commercial property and he enjoyed several hits, including 'I Walk The Line' (1957), 'Ballad Of A Teenage Queen' and 'Guess Things Happen That Way' (both 1958), thus emphasizing the label's country heritage. Four million-sellers - 'Whole Lotta Shakin' Goin' On', 'Great Balls Of Fire', 'Breathless' and 'High School Confidential' - by the exuberant Jerry Lee Lewis, closed a highly-productive decade, but the same singer's rapid fall from grace, coupled with the loss of Cash and Perkins, proved hard to surmount.

Sun's simple, rhythmic sound - the only device used to enhance a performance was echo - now proved anachronistic, yet a move to new, larger premises in 1960 paradoxically meant it was lost forever. The label was never Phillips' sole business investment; radio stations, mining and the Holiday Inn Hotel chain vied for his attention, while new record companies, Hi and Stax, seemed better able to capture the now-changing Memphis music scene. Paradoxically, this allowed Sun's achievements to remain untarnished and thus its legend is still undiminished. On July 1 1969, Sam Phillips sold the entire company to country music entrepreneur Shelby Singleton who, with the able assistance of British licensees Charly Records, have completed a series of judicious repackages.
Compilations: *The Roots Of Rock Volumes 1-13* (1977), *Sun Golden Hits* (1981), *The Sun Box* (1982), *Sun: The Blues* (1985), *Sun Country Box* (1986), *Sun Records - The Rocking Years* (1987), *The Sound Of Sun* (1988), *The Sun Story Vols 1 & 2* (1991), *The Very Best Of Sun Rock 'N' Roll* (1991). Further reading: *Sun Records*, Colin Escott and Martin Hawkins.

T

Tarriers
Formed c.1954, the Tarriers are remembered for two primary reasons: their 1957 US Top 5 recording of 'The Banana Boat Song' and the fact that one of its members was Alan Arkin, who went on to become a highly successful actor. The folk group was put together by Erik Darling (b. 25 September 1933, Baltimore, Maryland, USA), who was influenced by the folk revivalists of the day. After performing briefly with a large troupe of vocalists, Darling hooked up with Arkin (b. 26 March 1934, Brooklyn, New York) and Bob Carey as the Tunetellers. The group changed its name to the Tarriers and wrote and recorded 'The Banana Boat Song' to capitalize on the calypso music craze then sweeping the USA. Simultaneously they recorded a similar song called 'Cindy, Oh Cindy' with singer Vince Martin. Both singles were released on Glory Records, 'Cindy' reaching number 9 and 'The Banana Boat Song' number 4. The Tarriers never again made the charts, however, and the original trio dissolved two years later. Darling joined the Weavers and later went on to form the Rooftop Singers, Arkin began his acting career and Carey kept a Tarriers group alive until 1964.
Albums: *The Tarriers* (1957), *Hard Travelin'* (1959), *Tell The World About This* (1960), *The Tarriers* (1962), *Gather 'Round* (1963), *The Original Tarriers* (1963).

Taylor, Vince
One of the first, and most authentic British rock 'n' rollers, Taylor was virtually ignored by his native Britons but managed to make a decent living in France where he spent most of his life. He started

out in 1958 backed by his Playboys, who comprised Tony Harvey (guitar), Tony Sheridan (guitar/vocals), Brian 'Licorice' Locking (bass) and Brian Bennett (drums). They appeared regularly on the pioneering UK television rock show *Oh Boy!* and released a cover of a Charlie Rich song, 'Right Behind You Baby', on Parlophone. A second single in 1959, 'Brand New Cadillac', penned by Taylor, ranks alongside Ian Samwell's 'Move It' as one of *the* authentic British rock records. The Clash would later contribute a version which restored it to the British rock tradition. The band split in early 1959 (Locking and Bennett moved to various bands including the Shadows, Sheridan to Hamburg where he worked with the fledgling Beatles) and Taylor assembled a new backing band with Harvey plus Alan LeClaire on piano, Johnny Vance on bass, and Bobby Woodman on drums. This line-up of the Playboys also backed Screaming Lord Sutch in 1960. Taylor toured with Sutch, Keith Kelly and Lance Fortune on a '2 I's (coffee bar)' package tour. Around the Summer of 1961 Harvey joined Nero And The Gladiators, the rest of the Playboys went to France to back Johnny Hallyday, and Taylor followed their trail, becoming a minor celebrity in the process. He continued to record throughout the 60s, 70s and 80s, mostly doing covers of rock 'n' roll classics. He died in 1991.

Albums: *Le Rock C'est Ça!* (1961), *Vince* (1965), *Alive, Well & Rocking In Paris* (1972), *Cadillac* (1975), *Live 1977* (1979), *Luv* (1980), *Bien Compris* (1987), *Black Leather Rebel* (1993).

Teddy Bears

Were it not for the fact that Phil Spector began as a member of the Teddy Bears, this one-hit-wonder trio would likely be a minor footnote in the history of rock. Spector moved to the USA with his family at the age of nine following the suicide of his father, whose tombstone bore the legend 'To know him is to love him'. While in high school in Los Angeles, Spector sang at talent shows and assembled a group called the Sleepwalkers. He formed the Teddy Bears with singers Marshall Leib, Annette Kleinbard and Harvey Goldstein (who left the group shortly after its formation), after graduating from high school in June 1958. The group recorded a demo of Spector's composition, 'Don't You Worry, My Little Pet', which Dore Records released. For the b-side, Spector's 'To Know Him Is To Love Him' was recorded and it was that side which caught the ear of the public, rising to number 1 in the US charts

in late 1958. Following that success, the group signed with the larger Imperial Records and recorded an album (which is very rare and valuable today) as well as further singles. No more were hits and the group disbanded after Kleinbard was seriously injured in a 1960 car accident. The striking 'To Know Him Is To Love Him' became a standard, and was later successfully revived by Peter And Gordon in 1965. The later career of Spector has been well-documented. Kleinbard, after her recovery, changed her name to Carol Connors and became a successful songwriter ('Hey Little Cobra' for the Rip Chords, Vicki Lawrence's 'The Night The Lights Went Out In Georgia', and music for numerous films including two of the *Rocky* series). Marshall Leib joined the group the Hollywood Argyles, played guitar on some Duane Eddy records and produced records by the Everly Brothers and others.

Album: *The Teddy Bears Sing!* (1959).

Temperance 7

Formed in 1955 to play 20s style jazz, the Temperance 7 consisted at various times of Whispering Paul McDowell (vocals), Captain Cephas Howard (trumpet/euphonium and various instruments), Joe Clark (clarinet), Alan Swainston-Cooper (pedal clarinet/swanee whistle), Philip 'Finger' Harrison (banjo/alto and baritone sax), Canon Colin Bowles (piano/harmonica), Clifford Beban (tuba), Brian Innes (drums), Dr. John Grieves-Watson (banjo), Sheik Haroun el John R.T. Davies (trombone/alto sax) and Frank Paverty (sousaphone). Their first single, 'You're Driving Me Crazy' was producer George Martin's first number 1 and it was followed by three more 1961 hits and a string of misses. In 1963 they appeared in the play *The Bed Sitting Room* written by John Antrobus and Spike Milligan. They split in the mid 60s but their spirit resurfaced in groups like the Bonzo Dog Doo-Dah Band and the New Vaudeville Band. The Temperance 7 were reformed in the 70s by Ted Wood, brother of Ron.

Albums: *Temperance 7* (1961), *Temperance 7 Plus One* (1961), *Hot Temperance 7* (1987), *Tea For Eight* (1990), *33 Not Out* (1990).

Tormé, Mel

b. 13 September 1925, Chicago, Illinois, USA. A child prodigy, Tormé first sang on radio as a toddler and while still in his teens was performing as singer, pianist, drummer and dancer. He was also composing songs and wrote arrangements for the

Mel Tormé

band led by Chico Marx. He acted on radio and in films and in addition to singing solo led his own vocal group, the Mel-Tones. In this last capacity he recorded with Artie Shaw, enjoying a hit with 'Sunny Side Of The Street'. By the 50s he was established as one of the leading song stylists, performing the great standards and often working with a jazz backing, notably with the Marty Paich Dek-tette on albums such as *Lulu's Back In Town*. He headlined concert packages across the USA and in Europe, appeared on television, often producing his own shows, and always delivering performances of impeccable professionalism. He continued in such vein throughout the 60s and 70s, making many fine albums of superior popular music, several on which he was accompanied by jazzmen. Amongst these were Shorty Rogers, (*'Round Midnight*), Al Porcino, (*Live At The Maisonette*), Buddy Rich, (*Together Again - For The First Time*), Gerry Mulligan, (*Mel Tormé And Friends*) and Rob McConnell (*Mel Tormé With Rob McConnell And The Boss Brass*). Of all his musical collaborations, however, the best and most satisfying has been a long series of concerts and radio and television shows, many of which were issued on record, with George Shearing. Amongst these albums are *An Evening At Charlie's*, *An Elegant Evening*, *A Vintage Year* and *Mel And George "Do" World War II*. In the early 90s Tormé was still drawing rave reviews for record albums and personal appearances, with Shearing, at festivals in California and the Channel Islands, and with Bill Berry's big band at the Hollywood Bowl. As a songwriter Tormé has several hundred compositions to his credit, of which the best known by far is 'A Christmas Song', first recorded by Nat 'King' Cole. As a performer Tormé often features himself on drums - for many years he used a drum kit formerly the property of Gene Krupa - and he plays with unforced swing. As a singer, Tormé's work is touched with elegant charm. His voice, with the characteristic huskiness which earned him the sobriquet 'The Velvet Fog', has deepened over the years and by the early 90s still retained all the qualities of his youth, not least the remarkable pitch and vocal control. In his choice of material he has never shown anything other than perfect taste and his repertoire is an object lesson in musical quality. The fact that he also writes almost all the arrangements of the songs he sings adds to his status as a major figure in the story of American popular song.

Albums: *California Suite* (1949), *Musical Sounds Are The Best Songs* (1954), *It's A Blue World* (1955), *Mel Tormé And The Mart Paich Dek-tette* (1956), *Lulu's Back In Town* (1957), *Mel Tormé Sings Astaire* (1956), *'Round Midnight* i (1957), *Live At The Crescendo* (1957), *Tormé* (1958), *Olé Tormé* (1959), *Back In Town* (1959), *Mel Tormé Swings Shubert Alley* (1960), *Swingin' On The Moon* (1960), with Margaret Whiting *Broadway Right Now!* (1960), *I Dig The Duke, I Dig The Count* (1961), *'Round Midnight* ii (c.1961), *Mel Tormé At The Red Hill* (1962), *Sunday In New York* (1963), *Live At The Maisonette* (1974), *Together Again - For The First Time* (1978), *Mel Tormé And Friends* (c.1981), *Encore At Marty's, New York* (1982), *An Evening At Charlie's* (1983), *An Elegant Evening* (1985), *Mel Tormé With Rob McConnell And The Boss Brass* (1986), *A Vintage Year* (1987), *Reunion* (1988), *Night At The Concord Pavilion* (1990), *Mel And George 'Do' World War II* (1990), *In Hollywood* (1992, rec 1954), *Live At Fujitsu - Concord Jazz Festival 1992* (1992). Compilations: *A Foggy Day* (late 1940s recordings), *Walkman Jazz* (1958-61 recordings).

Further reading: *The Other Side Of The Rainbow: With Judy Garland On The Dawn Patrol*, Mel Tormé. *It Wasn't All Velvet: An Autobiography*, Mel Tormé.

Troup, Bobby

b. 18 October 1918, Harrisburg, Pennsylvania, USA. After studying extensively, including taking a degree in economics, Troup turned to songwriting and singing to his own piano accompaniment. In 1941 he was hired by Tommy Dorsey, but was drafted the same year. After five years in the US Navy, where he wrote scores for several shows, he settled in Los Angeles. He played night clubs, married Julie London and formed a jazz trio. He began making films, gaining small acting roles and sometimes playing piano and singing. Among these films were *The Duchess Of Idaho* (1950), *The Five Pennies* (1959) and *The Gene Krupa Story* (1960). Troup wrote scores for several films, including *The Girl Can't Help It* (1956), for which he also wrote the title song, and *Man Of The West* (1958). Among his other songs are 'Daddy', '(Get Your Kicks On) Route 66', 'Baby, Baby, All The Time', both of which were recorded by Nat 'King' Cole, and 'The Meaning Of The Blues'; he also wrote the lyrics for 'Free And Easy' and 'Girl Talk'. By the early 60s Troup's acting career was in good shape; he had leading roles in several films and also appeared on television in *Acapulco*, for which he wrote the background music. Also in the 60s and on through the 70s he took leading roles in such television movies as *Dragnet* (1966) and *Benny And Barney: Las Vegas Undercover* (1976). He also acted in *Emergency!* (1971) and its spin-off series, in which Julie London appeared. His 80s film roles included *M*A*S*H* (1981). Not surprisingly, given the number of acting roles he has been offered over the years, this area of Troup's work has tended to overshadow his music. In some respects this might be thought a pity because although an eclectic piano player, Troup sings with an engaging simplicity and a dedication to the intentions of the lyricist seldom displayed by many more famous performers.

Albums: *The Distinctive Style Of Bobby Troup* (1955), *Bobby Troup With Bob Enevoldson And His Orchestra* (1955), *Bobby Troup Sings Johnny Mercer* (1955), *In A Class Beyond Compare* (1957), *Stars Of Jazz* (1958).

Twitty, Conway

b. Harold Lloyd Jenkins, 1 September 1933, Friars Point, Mississippi, USA, d. 5 June 1993, Springfield, Missouri, USA. His father, a riverboat pilot, named him after a silent film comedian and gave him a guitar when he was five years old. The boat travelled between Mississippi and Arkansas, and the family moved to Helena, Arkansas. Twitty's schoolboy friends - Jack Nance, Joe E. Lewis and John Hughey - have played in his professional bands. In 1946, he recorded a demo, 'Cry Baby Heart', at a local radio station, although he was convinced that his real calling was to be a preacher. He was drafted into the US army in 1954 and worked the Far East service bases with a country band, the Cimarrons. He hoped for a baseball career, but when he returned to the USA in 1956 and heard Elvis Presley's 'Mystery Train', he opted for a career in music. Like Presley, he was signed by Sam Phillips to Sun Records, although his only significant contribution was writing 'Rockhouse', a minor US hit for Roy Orbison. His various Sun demos are included, along with later recordings for Mercury and MGM, in the eight-album, Bear Family set, *Conway Twitty - The Rock 'n' Roll Years*.

In 1957, whilst touring with a rockabilly package, he and his manager stuck pins in a map and the combination of a town in Arkansas with another in Texas led to Conway Twitty, a name as memorable as Elvis Presley. Twitty then moved to Mercury where 'I Need Your Lovin'' made number 93 in the USA pop charts. He had written 'It's Only Make Believe' with his drummer Jack Nance in-between sets at the Flamingo Lounge,

Toronto, and he recorded it for MGM with the Jordanaires, a croaky vocal and a huge crescendo. The record became a transatlantic number 1, and subsequent UK Top 10 versions of 'It's Only Make Believe' are by Billy Fury (1964), Glen Campbell (1970) and Child (1978). Twitty's record sounded like an Elvis Presley parody so it was ironic that Peter Sellers should lampoon him as Twit Conway and that he became the model for Conrad Birdie in the musical, *Bye Bye Birdie*. Twitty, unwisely but understandably, followed 'It's Only Make Believe' with more of the same in 'The Story Of My Love', while the b-side, the harsh and sexy 'Make Me Know You're Mine', remains one of the 'great unknowns'. His debut, *Conway Twitty Sings*, includes a beat treatment of 'You'll Never Walk Alone', which was undoubtedly heard by Gerry And The Pacemakers.

Twitty came to the UK for ITV television's pioneering *Oh Boy!* and his presence eased his rock 'n' roll version of Nat 'King' Cole's 'Mona Lisa' into the Top 10. His US Top 10 recording of a song, 'Lonely Blue Boy', which had been left out of Elvis Presley's film *King Creole*, led to him naming his band the Lonely Blue Boys, although they subsequently became the Twitty Birds. Another US hit, 'Danny Boy' could not be released in the UK because the lyric was still in copyright, this did not apply to its melody, 'The Londonderry Air', so Twitty recorded a revised version, 'Rosaleena'. Whilst at MGM, he appeared in such unremarkable movies as *Platinum High School* and *Sex Kittens Go To College*, which also featured Brigitte Bardot's sister. Twitty continued croaking his way through 'What Am I Living For?' and 'Is A Bluebird Blue?', but was also recording such country favourites as 'Faded Love' and 'You Win Again'. After being dropped by MGM and a brief spell with ABC-Paramount, Twitty concentrated on placing his country songs with other artists including 'Walk Me To The Door' for Ray Price. He began recording his own country records for producer Owen Bradley and USA Decca Records in Nashville, saying, 'After nine years in rock 'n' roll, I had been cheated and hurt enough to sing country and mean it.' In March 1966 Twitty appeared in the US country charts for the first time with 'Guess My Eyes Were Bigger Than My Heart'. His first US country number 1 was with 'Next In Line' in 1968 and this was followed by 'I Love You More Today' and 'To See An Angel Cry'.

He became the most consistent country chartmaker of all-time, although, strangely enough, none of his

Conway Twitty

country records made the UK charts. His most successful country record on the US pop charts is 'You've Never Been This Far Before', which made number 22 in 1973. 'Hello Darlin'' was heard around the world when he recorded a Russian version for the astronauts on a USA-USSR space venture in 1975. His records, often middle-of-the-road ballads, include 'I See The Want To In Your Eyes', 'I'll Never Make It Home Tonight', 'I Can't Believe She Gives It All To Me', 'I'd Love To Lay You Down' and 'You Were Named Co-Respondent'. He has recorded several successful duet albums with Loretta Lynn, and also recorded with Dean Martin and his own daughter, Joni Lee ('Don't Cry, Joni'). His son, who began recording as Conway Twitty Jnr., changed to Mike Twitty, while another daughter, Kathy Twitty, had minor country hits both as herself ('Green Eyes') and as Jesseca James ('Johnny One Time'). Through the 70s, Twitty expanded into property, banking and fast food, although his Twittyburgers came to a greasy end. His wife Mickey, whom he married and divorced twice, published *What's Cooking At Twitty City?*, in 1985. His tacky museum and theme park, Twitty City, is up for sale. By the end of 1988, Twitty's total of number 1 country hits totalled 40. Despite his new successes, the focal point of his stage act was still 'It's Only Make Believe' right up until his death in 1993.

Albums: *Conway Twitty Sings* (1958), *Saturday Night With Conway Twitty* (1959), *Lonely Blue Boy* (1960), *The Rock 'N' Roll Story* (1961), *The Conway Twitty Touch* (1961), *'Portrait Of A Fool' And Others* (1962), *R&B '63* (1963), *Hit The Road* (1964), *Look Into My Teardrops* (1966), *Country* (1967), *Here's Conway Twitty* (1968), *Next In Line* (1968), *I Love You More Today* (1969), *You Can't Take The Country Out Of Conway* (1969), *Darling, You Know I Wouldn't Lie* (1969), *Hello Darling* (1970), *Fifteen Years Ago* (1970), *To See My Angel Cry* (1970), *How Much More Can She Stand?* (1971), *Conway Twitty* (1972), *I Wonder What She'll Think About Me Leaving* (1971), *Conway Twitty Sings The Blues* (1972), *Shake It Up* (1972), *I Can't Stop Loving You* (1973), *You've Never Been This Far Before* (1973), *I Can't See Me Without You* (1972), *She Needs Someone To Hold Her* (1973), *Clinging To A Saving Hand* (1973), *Honky Tonk Angel* (1974), *I'm Not Through Loving You Yet* (1974), *Linda On My Mind* (1975), *The High Priest Of Country Music* (1975), *Twitty* (1975), *Now And Then* (1976), *Play Guitar Play* (1977), *I've Already Loved You In My Mind* (1977), *Georgia Keeps Pulling On My Ring* (1978), *Conway* (1978), *Cross Winds* (1979), *Country-Rock*

(1979), *Boogie Grass Band* (1979), *Rest Your Love* (1980), *Heart And Soul* (1980), *Rest Your Love On Me* (1980), *Mr. T.* (1981), *Southern Comfort* (1982), *Dream Maker* (1982), *Merry Twismas* (1983), *Lost In The Feeling* (1983), *By Heart* (1984), *Chasing Rainbows* (1985), *Live At Castaway Lounge* (1987), *Borderline* (1987), *House On The Old Lonesome Road* (1989), *Crazy In Love* (1990), *Even Now* (1991); with Loretta Lynn *We Only Make Believe* (1971), *Lead Me On* (1971), *Louisiana Woman, Mississippi Man* (1973), *Feelin's* (1975), *United Talent* (1976), *Dynamic Duo* (1977), *Country Partners* (1974), *Honky Tonk Heroes* (1978), *Diamond Duets* (1979), *Two's A Party* (1981), *Making Believe* (1988).

Further reading: *The Conway Twitty Story - An Authorised Biography*, Wilbur Cross and Michael Kosser.

V

Vale, Jerry

b. Genaro Louis Vitaliano, 8 July 1932, Bronx, New York, USA. A popular singer, especially of ballads *Italiano*, with several chart hits to his credit during the 50s and 60s. Vale studied piano and worked as a shoeshine boy while still at school. Later, he was employed in an electrical component factory, and sang in his spare time. After winning a talent contest at the Club del Rio, he stayed there for over a year, and then, while performing at the Enchanted Room in New York, he was spotted by Guy Mitchell, who recommended him to Columbia Records' A&R manager, Mitch Miller. His first chart entry for the label, 'You Can Never Give Me Back My Heart' (1953), on which he was accompanied by Percy Faith And His Orchestra, was followed by 'Two Purple Shadows', 'I Live Each Day', 'Innamorata' and 'You Don't Know Me' (1956). Despite the 60s beat boom, Vale registered in the best-sellers lists with singles such as 'Have You Looked Into Your Heart?' (1964), and entered the US Top 40 album chart six times between 1963 and 1966. He continued to be popular in clubs and on television during the 70s and 80s, and, in 1988, was the recipient of a Friars

Ritchie Valens

Club dinner, given to honour his long and successful career. Vale wound up the proceedings by singing a few favourites, including his signature, 'Al Di La', the winner of the San Remo Song Festival in 1961.

Selected albums: *I Remember Buddy* (1958), *I Remember Russ* (1958), *Same Old Moon* (1959), *I Have But One Heart* (1962), *Arrivederci Roma* (1963), *Language Of Love* (1963), *Till The End Of Time* (1964), *Be My Love* (1964), *Moonlight Becomes You* (1965), *Have You Looked?* (1965), *Standing Ovations* (1965), *There Goes My Heart* (1965), *Everybody Loves Somebody* (1966), *Great Moments* (1966), *It's Magic* (1966), *Impossible Dream* (1967), *Time Alone* (1967). Compilations: *Greatest Hits* (1960), *More Greatest Hits* (1967).

Valens, Ritchie

b. Richard Steve Valenzuela, 13 May 1941, Los Angeles, California, USA, d. 3 February 1959, Iowa, USA. Valens was the first major Hispanic-American rock star, the artist who popularized the classic 50s hit 'La Bamba'. He grew up in the city of Pacoima, California, and was raised in poverty. His parents separated when he was a child and Valens lived with his father until the latter's death in 1951. Afterwards he lived with his mother and brothers and sisters. Occasionally they stayed with other relatives, who introduced him to traditional Mexican music. He also enjoyed cowboy songs by Roy Rogers and Gene Autry and began playing in junior high school. While attending Pacoima Junior High School Valens was exposed to R&B music and rock 'n' roll. In 1956 Valens joined the Silhouettes (not the group which recorded 'Get A Job'), which performed at record hops in the San Fernando Valley area. Valens also performed solo and was heard by Bob Keane of Del-Fi Records, who took him into Gold Star Studios to record several songs. (Keane also shortened the singer's name from Valenzuela to Valens and added the 't' to Richie.) A session band including Earl Palmer (drums), Carol Kaye (electric bass), Red Collendar (stand-up bass), Ernie Freeman (piano) and Rene Hall (guitar) played behind Valens (who also played guitar). One of the songs they recorded for that first album was 'La Bamba', a traditional Mexican folk song. Their first single release 'Come On, Let's Go', which Valens wrote, reached number 42 in the USA. Valens went on an 11-city US tour after its release. In October 1958 the single 'Donna'/'La Bamba' was issued. It was actually the ballad 'Donna', written by Valens about his high school friend Donna Ludwig, that was, contrary to popular belief, the side of the record which was the bigger hit, reaching number 2. 'La Bamba', the b-side, only reached number 22 in the USA but is the more fondly-remembered song.

'La Bamba' was a traditional huapango song from the Vera Cruz region of eastern Mexico, performed as early as World War II, and sung at weddings. (A huapango is a Mexican song consisting of nonsense verses, the meaning of the lyrics often known only to the composer.) Valens was reportedly reluctant to record the song, fearing its Spanish lyrics would not catch on with American record buyers. Following the record's release, Valens again went on tour, performing in California, Hawaii and on the *American Bandstand* show in Philadelphia.

It was during the winter part of the tour that Valens and his fellow performers met their fate, choosing to charter a small aeroplane rather than ride to the next concert site in a bus whose heater had broken. It was on 3 February 1959 when he, Buddy Holly and the Big Bopper were killed in an aeroplane crash following a concert in Clear Lake, Iowa. In the wake of Valen's death, several further singles were issued, only two of which – 'That's My Little Suzie' and 'Little Girl' – were minor chart hits. Three albums – *Ritchie Valens*, *Ritchie* and *Ritchie Valens In Concert At Pacoima Junior High* – were released from sessions recorded for Del-Fi and at a performance for Valens' classmates. Valens' status grew in the years following his death, culminating in the 1987 film *La Bamba*, a dramatized version of Valens' brief life and stardom. His songs have been covered by several artists, including the Hispanic-American group Los Lobos, who supervised the film's music and recorded 'La Bamba'. Their version, ironically, went to number 1 in 1987, outperforming Valens' original chart position.

Albums: *Ritchie Valens* (1959), *Ritchie* (1959), *Ritchie Valens In Concert At Pacoima Jnr High* (1960). Compilations: *A History Of Ritchie Valens* (1985), *Greatest Hits* (1987).

Valente, Caterina

b. 14 January 1931, Paris, France. From an Italian circus family – her mother was a clown and her father an accordion virtuoso – Valente made her circus debut as a child. Her career as a multi-lingual vocalist began in 1953 when she joined the Kurt Edelhagen Band in Germany. Valente made her recording debut for Polydor the same year, enjoying international success with two songs by Cuban composer Ernesto Lecuona, 'Malaguena'

Caterina Valente

and 'Andalucia'. In its English translation, 'The Breeze And I', the latter was a big hit in the UK and USA in 1955. Valente's cabaret act and her frequent recordings included material in six languages (French, German, Italian, English, Spanish and Swedish). During the early 60s, she recorded for Decca, and scored numerous European hits with such items as 'Itsy Bitsy Teenie Weenie, Honolulu Strand Bikini', 'Pepe' and 'Quando, Quando, Quando'. Her version of 'La Golondrina' appeared in 1963 on *All Star Festival*. It was one of the first charity albums, issued to raise money to aid refugees. Valente continued recording into the 70s, usually spicing up her collections of standards with recent hits. *Caterina 86* was recorded with the Count Basie Orchestra.

Selected albums: *Great Continental Hits* (1959), *Superfonics* (1960), *Classics With A Chaser* (1962), *Valente In Swingtime* (1963), *Around the World* (1965), *This Is Me* (1975), *In A Swinging Mood* (1987), *Caterina 86* (1988). Compilations: *Greatest Hits* (1966), the *Edition* series: volumes 1-13 cover the years 1954-58 (1986-87).

Valentine, Dickie

b. Richard Brice, 4 November 1929, London, England, d. 6 May 1971. At the age of three, Valentine appeared in the Jack Hulbert/Cicely Courtneidge comedy film *Jack's The Boy*. As a back-stage assistant at Her Majesty's Theatre he became the protege of Canadian stage star Bill O'Connor, who sent him for singing tuition. After playing the club circuit as singer/impressionist he made his debut with the successful Ted Heath band at an Aeolian Hall broadcast. Initially Heath featured him as a straight ballad vocalist, but later allowed him to display his range of impressions, including those of Mario Lanza, Nat 'King' Cole, Billy Daniels and an accurate parody of Johnnie Ray. Good-looking, with dark, curly hair and a rich melodic voice, Valentine became Britain's number one band singer, a heart-throb who set the teenagers screaming. In 1952 he recorded 'Never', from the Mitzi Gaynor movie *Golden Girl* and 'Lorelei' for Melodisc Records. The following year he signed for Decca, and throughout the 50s produced a string of Top 20 hits, including 'Broken Wings', 'Endless', 'Mr Sandman', 'A Blossom Fell', 'I Wonder', 'Old Pianna Rag', 'Christmas Island', 'Venus' and two number 1 hits, 'Finger Of Suspicion' and 'Christmas Alphabet'. In 1959 he again made the Top 20 with 'One More Sunrise (Morgen)' for Pye, but groups rather than solo singers were soon to dominate the charts and

Valentine described his own 'Rock 'N' Roll Party' as 'the biggest clanger I have dropped'. At the height of his career he performed on American television's *Ed Sullivan Show*, and headlined at theatres where he had once been employed. He remained a firm favourite on the British club circuit. While returning from one such engagement in Wales, he died in a car crash in 1971.

Selected compilations: *The World Of Dickie Valentine* (1981), *The Best Of Dickie Valentine* (1984), *My Favourite Songs* (1993).

Vanguard Records

Formed in 1950 in New York City, Vanguard Records became one of the most important US folk and blues labels of the 50s and 60s. Brothers Maynard and Seymour Solomon founded the company and signed primarily classical and international/ethnic artists until 1954, when they began signing jazz acts. Among the jazz artists who recorded for the label were Louis Armstrong, Larry Coryell, Count Basie, Stephane Grappelli, Ruby Braff, Buck Clayton, Sadao Watanabe and Stomu Yamash'ta. In 1957 they recruited the Weavers, the most important folk group of its era. In 1959 they signed folk singer Joan Baez, who became their biggest selling artist. During the early 60s Vanguard hit its peak with a roster that included blues performers Mississippi John Hurt, Buddy Guy, Big Mama Thornton, Junior Wells, James Cotton, Skip James, Jimmy Rushing, Otis Spann, Pee Wee Crayton, Otis Rush, John Hammond, Johnny Shines and J.B. Hutto. In addition to Baez, the company's folk artists included Ian And Sylvia, Buffy Sainte-Marie, Eric Andersen, Mimi and Richard Farina, Odetta, Doc and Merle Watson, Paul Robeson and Tom Paxton. Vanguard also released country and bluegrass records, including performers Jerry Jeff Walker, the Clancy Brothers, Kinky Friedman and the Country Gentlemen.

Their catalogue also featured instrumentalists whose meditative music prefigured new age, such as John Fahey, Sandy Bull and Oregon. In the mid-60s Vanguard signed political protest-rockers Country Joe And The Fish, who became one of the label's most popular acts. Their 60s roster also included the Siegel-Schwall Blues Band and the Jim Kweskin Jug Band. In the early 70s the label ceased signing new acts, and briefly shifted direction at the end of that decade. During the 80s dance artists such as Alisha, who had a strong regional disco hit in the New York clubs with her 'Baby Talk', joined the organization. In 1986, the

Frankie Vaughan

Solomon brothers sold Vanguard to the Welk Group, a company run by the son of bandleader Lawrence Welk, who did not take an active part in the running of the company. Vanguard has since reissued most of its original album catalogue on compact disc and began signing new artists again in 1990.

Compilations: *The Best Of The Chicago Blues Volume One* (1988), *Greatest Folksingers Of The Sixties* (1988).

Vaughan, Frankie

b. Frank Abelson, 3 February 1928, Liverpool, England. While studying at Leeds College of Art, Vaughan's vocal performance at a college revue earned him a week's trial at the music hall, Kingston Empire. Warmly received, he went on to play the UK variety circuit, developing a stylish act with trademarks which included a top hat and cane, a particularly athletic side kick, and his theme song 'Give Me The Moonlight'. From 'That Old Piano Roll Blues' in 1950 through to the late 60s,with 'There Must Be A Way' in 1967, he was consistently high in the UK charts with songs such as 'Green Door', 'Garden Of Eden', 'Kisses Sweeter Than Wine', 'Kewpie Doll', 'The Heart Of A Man', 'Tower Of Strength' and 'Loop-De-Loop'.

His film debut in 1956 as Elmer in the Arthur Askey comedy *Ramsbottom Rides Again*, was followed by a straight role in *These Dangerous Years*, and a musical frolic with the normally staid Anna Neagle in *The Lady Is A Square*. In 1961, following his role in *Let's Make Love* with Marilyn Monroe and Yves Montand, his disaffection for Hollywood ensured that a US film career was not pursued. At home, however, he had become an extremely well-established performer, headlining at the London Palladium and enjoying lucrative summer season work, appealing consistently to mainly family audiences. In 1985 he was an unexpected choice to replace James Laurenson as the belligerent Broadway producer Julian Marsh in the West End hit musical *42nd Street*. A one-year run in the show ended with ill-health and some acrimony. His career-long efforts for the benefit of young people, mainly through the assignment of record royalties to bodies such as the National Association of Boys' Clubs, was recognized by an OBE in 1965.

Selected albums: *Frankie Vaughan Showcase* (1958), *Frankie Vaughan At The London Palladium* (1959), *Frankie Vaughan Songbook* (1967), *There Must Be A Way* (1967), *Double Exposure* (1971), *Frankie* (1973), *Frankie Vaughan's Sing Song* (1973), *Sincerely Yours, Frankie Vaughan* (1975), *Sings* (1975), *Seasons For Lovers* (1977), *Time After Time* (1986). Compilations: *Spotlight On Frankie Vaughan* (1975), *100 Golden Greats* (1977), *Golden Hour Presents Frankie Vaughan* (1978), *Greatest Hits* (1983), *Love Hits And High Kicks* (1985), *Music Maestro Please* (1986).

Vaughan, Malcolm

b. Abercynon, Mid Glamorgan, Wales. A popular ballad singer with a strong tenor voice, Vaughan first made an impression in the early 50s as the 'singing straight man' in a double act with comedian Kenny Earle. They were touring the UK Variety circuit when Vaughan was spotted by EMI Records' recording manager, Wally Ridley. In 1955 Vaughan had his first Top 10 hit, on the HMV label, with 'Every Day Of My Life', which stayed in the chart for four months. Several other hits followed, through to 1959, including 'With Your Love', 'St. Therese Of The Roses', 'The World Is Mine', 'Chapel Of The Roses', 'My Special Angel', 'To Be Loved', 'More Than Ever (Come Prima)' and 'Wait For Me'. His UK television appearances included *Sunday Night At The London Palladium*, *Startime*, *Saturday Spectacular*, *Music Shop*, *Melody Dances* and *The Jack Jackson Show*. After surviving the initial onslaught of rock 'n' roll, Vaughan's recording career suffered, along with so many others of his style, in the face of the 60s beat boom. In the early part of the decade he still retained an association with Earle, although with variety on the wane, clubs and cabaret were the main showplaces. In 1990 *Malcolm Vaughan's EMI Years* proved a reminder that he was still a popular night club attraction in the north of England.

Selected albums: *The Best Of Malcolm Vaughan* (1974), *The Very Best Of Malcom Vaughan - 16 Favourites Of The 50s* (1984), *Malcolm Vaughan's EMI Years* (1990).

Vaughan, Sarah

b. Sarah Lois Vaughan, 27 March 1924, Newark, New Jersey, USA, d. 3 April 1990. Although she was not born into an especially musical home environment (her father was a carpenter and her mother worked in a laundry), the young Sarah Vaughan had plenty of contact with music-making. As well as taking piano lessons for nearly 10 years, she sang in her church choir and became the organist at the age of 12. Her obvious talent for singing won her an amateur contest at Harlem's

Malcolm Vaughan (right) with Kenny Earle

Sarah Vaughan

Apollo Theater in 1942, and opportunities for a musical career quickly appeared. Spotted by Billy Eckstine, who was at the time singing in Earl Hines' big band, she was invited to join Hines' band as a female vocalist and second pianist in 1943. Eckstine had been sufficiently impressed by Vaughan to give her a place in his own band, formed a year later. It was here that she met fellow band members and pioneers of modern jazz Charlie Parker and Dizzy Gillespie. Recording with Eckstine's band in 1945, full as it was of modern stylists, gave her a fundamental understanding of the new music that characterized her entire career. After leaving Eckstine, she spent a very short time with John Kirby's band, and then decided it was time to perform under her own name. In 1947 she married trumpeter George Treadwell, whom she had met at the Cafe Society. Recognizing his wife's huge potential, Treadwell became her manager, as she began a decade of prolific recording and worldwide tours. She began by recording with Miles Davis in 1950, and then produced a torrent of albums in either a popular vein for Mercury Records, or more jazz-oriented material for their subsidiary label EmArcy. On the EmArcy recordings she appeared with Clifford Brown, Cannonball Adderley and members of the Count Basie band; these remain some of her most satisfying work. By the 60s, as Vaughan rose to stardom, her activity decreased slightly, and the emphasis remained on commercial, orchestra-backed recordings. It was not until the 70s that she began to perform and record with jazz musicians again on a regular basis. Vaughan performed at the 1974 Monterey Jazz Festival and made an album in 1978 with a quartet consisting of Oscar Peterson, Joe Pass, Ray Brown, and Louie Bellson. The following year she recorded her *Duke Ellington Song Book One*, on which a large number of top swing players appeared, including Zoot Sims, Frank Foster, Frank Wess, J.J. Johnson, and Joe Pass. This quicker pace increased in the following decade.

In 1980 she appeared in a much-heralded concert at Carnegie Hall, and returned to the place where her career had began to sing with Billy who had encouraged her at that early stage. They worked the Apollo Theater in a show recorded and broadcast by NBC-TV. She recorded an album of latin tunes in 1987, and around this time appeared in another televised concert, billed as *Sass And Brass*. With a rhythm section featuring Herbie Hancock, Ron Carter, and Billy Higgins, as well as a collection of trumpeters including Dizzy

Gillespie, Don Cherry, Maynard Ferguson, and Chuck Mangione, she proved herself a musical force to still be reckoned with. Sarah Vaughan won the *Esquire* New Star poll in 1945, the *Downbeat* poll (1947-52) and the *Metronome* poll (1948-52). She also sang at the White House as early as 1965; Vaughan's name has been synonymous with jazz singing for two generations. Gifted with an extraordinary range and perfect intonation, she would also subtly control the quality of her voice to aid the interpretation of a song, juxtaposing phrases sung in a soft and warm tone with others in a harsh, nasal vibrato or throaty growl. Her knowledge of bebop, gained during her time with Billy Eckstine's band, enabled her to incorporate modern passing tones into her sung lines, advancing the harmonic side of her work beyond that of her contemporaries. Her recordings will continue to influence vocalists for many years to come.

Selected albums: *Sarah Vaughan* (1954), *Lullaby Of Birdland* (1954), *Sarah Vaughan With Clifford Brown* (1954), *My Kinda Love* (1955), *Sarah Vaughan In The Land Of Hi Fi* (1955), *After Hours With Sarah Vaughan* (1955), *In The Land Of Hi-Fi* (1955), *Vaughan And Violins* (1955), *Great Songs From Hit Shows* (1955), *Sarah Vaughan Sings George Gershwin* (1955), *Great Songs From Hit Shows, Volume 2* (1956), *Sarah Vaughan At The Blue Note* (1956), *The Magic Of Sarah Vaughan* (1956), *Sarah Vaughan In Hi Fi* (1956), *Linger Awhile* (1956), *Sassy* (1956), *Swinging Easy* (1957), *Wonderful Sarah* (1957), *In A Romantic Mood* (1957), *Close To You* (1957), *Sarah Vaughan And Billy Eckstine Sing The Best Of Irving Berlin* (1957), *Sarah Vaughan At Mr. Kelly's* (1958), *After Hours At The London House* (1958), *No Count Sarah* (1958), *Songs Of Broadway* (1959), *Dreamy* (1960), *Divine One* (1960), *Count Basie/Sarah Vaughan* (1960), *After Hours* (1961), *My Heart Sings* (1961), *You're Mine, You* (1962), *Snowbound* (1962), *The Explosive Side Of Sarah* (1962), *Star Eyes* (1963), *Sassy Swings The Tivoli* (1963), *Vaughan With Voices* (1964), *Viva Vaughan* (1964), with Dinah Washington and Joe Williams *We Three* (1964), *The Lonely Hours* (1964), *The World Of Sarah Vaughan* (1964), *Sweet 'N' Sassy* (1964), *Sarah Sings Soulfully* (1965), *Sarah Plus Two* (1965), *Mancini Songbook* (1965), *The Pop Artistry Of Sarah Vaughan* (1966), *New Scene* (1966), *Sassy Swings Again* (1967), *I'm Through With Love* (1970), *Sarah Vaughan/Michel Legrand* (1972), *Live In Japan* (1973), *Feelin' Good* (1973), *The Summer Knows* (1973), *A Time In My Life* (1974), *Sarah Vaughan And The Jimmy Rowles Quintet* (1975), with Oscar

Peterson, Joe Pass, Ray Brown, Louie Bellson *How Long Has This Been Going On?* (1978), *Live At Ronnie Scott's* (1978), with Barney Kessel, Joe Comfort *The Two Sounds Of Sarah* (1981), *Send In The Clowns* (1978), *Duke Ellington Songbook One* (1979), *I Love Brazil* (1979), *Songs Of The Beatles* (1981), *Copacabana* (1981), *Crazy And Mixed Up* (1982), *O, Some Brasileiro De* (1984). Compilations: with Billy Eckstine *Passing Strangers* (1981, coupled with a Dinah Washington and Brook Benton collection), *Spotlight On Sarah Vaughan* (1984), *The Sarah Vaughan Collection* (1985), *The Rodgers And Hart Songbook* (1985), *The Best Of Sarah Vaughan - Walkman Series* (1987), *16 Greatest Hits* (1993).
Further reading: *Sassy - The Life Of Sarah Vaughan*, Leslie Gourse.

Vaughn, Billy

b. Richard Vaughn, 12 April 1931, Glasgow, Kentucky, USA. Vaughn was an extremely successful orchestra leader, arranger and musical director during the 50s and early 60s. In 1952, singing baritone and playing piano, he formed a vocal quartet, the Hilltoppers, with Jimmy Sacca, Seymour Speigelman and Don McGuire. They had a string of US hits up to 1957 commencing in August 1952 with Vaughn's composition, 'Trying' and in the following year with the million-selling 'P.S I Love You'. When Vaughn left the group in 1955 to become musical director for Dot Records, the other three members continued together until the early 60s, when they too accepted jobs with Dot. Throughout the 50s, Vaughn contributed significantly to the label's chart success, particularly with his arrangements for the somewhat antiseptic 'cover-versions' of rock 'n' roll and R&B hits, especially those by black artists, who were unacceptable to some sections of the US audience. Most of the Fontane Sisters' hits, which were backed by Vaughn's Orchestra, were covers, including their million-seller, 'Hearts Of Stone', which was first released by the R&B group, Otis Williams And The Charms. Others included Gale Storm's cover version of Smiley Lewis's 'I Hear You Knocking', written by Dave Bartholomew and Pearl King; and several Pat Boone hits, including another Bartholomew number, 'Ain't That A Shame', originally released by the co-writer of the song, Fats Domino. Several of Vaughn's own instrumental hits were in the same vein: His first, 'Melody Of Love' (1954), was also successful for Frank Sinatra and Ray Anthony, the Four Aces and David Carroll. 'The Shifting Whispering Sands' (with narration by Ken Nordine), was a hit

for country singer Rusty Draper; and the classic 'Raunchy' was a million-seller for Sun Records' musical director, Bill Justis.
Vaughn's other US Top 20 chart entries included 'When The Lilacs Bloom Again', 'Look For A Star' and German-born orchestra leader, Bert Kaempfert's 'A Swingin' Safari'. Vaughn was very popular in Germany, his versions of 'Wheels', 'La Paloma', and a revival of the 1937 song, 'Sail Along Silv'ry Moon', reputedly sold a million copies in that country alone. From 1958-70, Vaughn was ever-present in the US album charts with 36 titles entering the Top 200, including the 1960 number 1, *Theme From A Summer Place*. Having been one of the most successful orchestra leaders during the rock 'n' roll era, Vaughn perhaps found the 60s beat scene a little too alien to his tastes. Ironically, his last single of any significance, in 1966, was a cover version of the Beatles' 'Michelle'.
Albums: *Sail Along Silv'ry Moon* (1958), *Billy Vaughn Plays The Million Sellers* (1958), *Christmas Carols* (1958), *Billy Vaughn Plays* (1959), *Blue Hawaii* (1959), *Golden Saxophones* (1959), *Theme From A Summer Place* (1960), *Look For A Star* (1960), *Theme From The Sundowners* (1960), *Orange Blossom Special And Wheels* (1961), *Golden Waltzes* (1961), *Berlin Melody* (1961), *Greatest String Band Hits* (1962), *Chapel By The Sea* (1962), *A Swingin' Safari* (1962), *1962's Greatest Hits* (1963), *Sukiyaki And 11 Hawaiian Hits* (1963), *Number 1 Hits, Volume 1* (1963), *Blue Velvet And 1963's Great Hits* (1963), *Forever* (1964), *Another Hit Album!* (1964), *Pearly Shells* (1964), *Mexican Pearls* (1965), *Moon Over Naples* (1965), *Michelle* (1966), *Great Country Hits* (1966), *Alfie* (1966), *Sweet Maria* (1967), *That's Life And Pineapple Market* (1967), *Josephine* (1967), *I Love You* (1967), *Ode To Billy Joe* (1967), *A Current Set Of Standards* (1968), *As Requested* (1968), *Quietly Wild* (1969), *The Windmills Of Your Mind* (1969), *True Grit* (1970), *Winter World Of Love* (1970). Compilations: *Golden Hits/The Best Of Billy Vaughn* (1967), *The Best Of Billy Vaughn* (1974), *Moonlight Serenade* (1979).

VeeJay Records

Founded in 1953 by Vivian 'Vee' Carter and James 'Jay' C. Bracken, this US independent record label rose from regional obscurity to a position as one of black music's leading outlets. Their initial signings included the Spaniels, who provided the company's first major success when their haunting doo-wop ballad, 'Goodnite Sweetheart, Goodnite', was a hit in the R&B and pop chart. The couple, now married, established their offices in Chicago's East 47th Street. Vivian's brother, Calvin Carter, also joined the company; this intuitive individual was responsible for attracting several important acts, including vocal groups the El Dorados and the Dells, as well as gospel artists the Staple Singers and the Swan Silvertones. VeeJay's staff was considerably bolstered by the addition of Ewart Abner, whose business acumen did much to facilitate the label's meteoric rise. By the early 60s the VeeJay roster included the Jerry Butler, Dee Clark and Gene Chandler, each of whom enjoyed popular success, while influential blues performers Jimmy Reed and John Lee Hooker recorded their best-known material for the outlet. However, by 1963 the label was encountering financial difficulties. VeeJay had diversified into white pop by securing the Four Seasons, and had won the rights to the Beatles' early releases when Capitol Records declined their option. When the former act scored several hits, the label was unable to meet royalty payments and a protracted law suit ensued. Capitol then rescinded their Beatles' agreement; although VeeJay latterly retained material already licensed, the rights to future recordings were lost. This controversial period also saw Abner's departure, while the label moved its operations to Los Angeles. However, by 1965 VeeJay was back in Chicago, with Abner reinstated to his former position. Such upheavals proved fatal. Unsettled artists moved to other outlets, and when interim manager Randy Wood sued for breach of contract, VeeJay filed for bankruptcy. In May 1966, the company closed its offices and released its remaining employees. Arguably capable of rivalling Tamla/Motown had they overcome their internal problems, VeeJay nonetheless holds an important place in the development of black music. Abner eventually rose to become president of Motown, while James Bracken died in 1972 owning a record shop. Calvin Carter died in 1986, while Vivian Carter ran a radio station in her hometown of Gary, Indiana. She later died in 1989.

Vincent, Gene

b. Eugene Vincent Craddock, 11 February 1935, Norfolk, Virginia, USA, d. 12 October 1971. One of the original bad boys of rock 'n' roll, the self-destructive Vincent was involved in a motorcycle crash in 1955 and his left leg was permanently damaged. Discharged from the US Navy, he began appearing on country music radio and came under the wing of disc jockey 'Sheriff' Tex Davis, who supervised his recording of a demo of 'Be-Bop A-Lula'. In May 1956, the track was re-recorded at Capitol Records's Nashville studio, with backing by the Blue Caps. The original line-up comprised: Cliff Gallup (lead guitar), Jack Neal (upright bass), Willie Williams (acoustic guitar) and Dickie Harrell (drums). Weeks later, 'Be-Bop-A-Lula' stormed the charts, temporarily providing Capitol with their own version of Elvis Presley. The strength of the single lay in Vincent's engaging vocal and the loping guitar runs of the influential Cliff Gallup. Vincent's image was brooding, inarticulate and menacing and with such rock 'n' roll authenticity he was not easily marketable in the USA. His second single, 'Race With The Devil', failed to chart in his homeland, but proved successful in the UK, where he attracted a devoted following. Dogged by bad advice and often unsuitable material, Vincent rapidly lost the impetus that had thrust him to the centre stage as a rock 'n' roll icon. Even an appearance in the movie *The Girl Can't Help It* failed to arrest his commercial decline. A respite was offered by the million-selling 'Lotta Love', but line-up changes in the Blue Caps and a plethora of personal problems were conspiring against him. His damaged leg was perpetually threatening to end his singing career and renewed injuries resulted in the limb being supported by a metal brace. Vincent's alcoholism and buccaneering road life made him a liability to promoters and by the late 50s, his career seemed in ruins. He relocated to England, where Jack Good exacerbated his rebel image by dressing him in black leather and encouraging the star to accentuate his limp.

Although he failed to retrieve past glories on record, he toured frequently and survived the car crash which killed Eddie Cochran. Thereafter, he appeared regularly in the UK and France, having come under the wing of the notoriously proprietorial manager Don Arden. Increasingly redundant during the beat group era, his lifestyle grew more erratic and uncontrollable and alcoholism made him a bloated and pathetic figure. A comeback album of sorts, *I'm Back And I'm Proud*, lacked sufficient punch to revitalize his career and he continued playing with pick-up groups, churning out his old repertoire. He often railed against old friends and grew increasingly disillusioned about the state of his career. Still regarded as a legend of rock 'n' roll and a true original, he seemed frustratingly stuck in a time warp and lacked any sense of a career pattern. The often intolerable pain he suffered due to his festering leg merely exacerbated his alcoholism,

Gene Vincent

which in turn devastated his health. On 12 October 1971, his abused body finally succumbed to a fatal seizure and rock 'n' roll lost one of its genuinely great rebellious spirits.

Albums: *Blue Jean Bop!* (1956), *Gene Vincent And The Blue Caps* (1957), *Gene Vincent Rocks And The Bluecaps Roll* (1958), *A Gene Vincent Record Date* (1958), *Sounds Like Gene Vincent* (1959), *Crazy Times* (1960), *Crazy Beat Of Gene Vincent* (1963), *Shakin' Up A Storm* (1964), *Bird Doggin''* (1967), *I'm Back And I'm Proud* (1970), *If Only You Would See Me Today* (1971), *The Day The World Turned Blue* (1971). Archive compilations: *The Bop They Couldn't Stop* (1981), *Dressed In Black* (1982), *From LA To 'Frisco* (1983), *For Collectors Only* (1984), *Forever Gene Vincent* (1984), *Ain't That Too Much* (1984), *Born To Be A Rolling Stone* (1985). Compilations: *The Best Of Gene Vincent* (1967), *The Bop That Just Won't Stop* (1974), *The Gene Vincent Singles Album* (1982), *Gene Vincent's Greatest Hits* (1982), *Gene Vincent: The Capitol Years* (1988). Further reading: *Gene Vincent And The Blue Caps*, Rob Finnis and Bob Dunham. *The Day The World Turned Blue*, Britt Hagarty.

Vipers Skiffle Group

Formed in 1956, the group consisted of various members, including Wally Whyton, Tommy Steele, Hank Marvin, Jet Harris and Bruce Welch. It grew out of the 'frothy coffee' scene, centred at the 2I's coffee bar, in London's Soho district in the late 50s. Whyton was the musical brains, and with Bill Varley, wrote the group's first hit, 'Don't You Rock Me Daddy-O', which was even more successful for the 'King Of Skiffle', Lonnie Donegan. After having their 'cleaned up' version of 'Maggie May' banned by the BBC, the Vipers had two other UK chart entries in 1957: 'Cumberland Gap' and 'Streamline Train'. However, the whole skiffle craze was short-lived. Before long, Steele had become an 'all-round entertainer'. Marvin, Harris and Welch had formed the Shadows, via the Drifters; and Whyton had carved out a career as a singer and broadcaster on radio programmes such as *Country Meets Folk* and *Country Club*; and previously as a host of childrens' television shows, notably with the irritating glove-puppet, Pussy Cat Willum. In 1960 the Vipers sang 11 songs in the musical play, *Mr. Burke M.P.* at London's Mermaid Theatre. Whyton also played the part of 'The Commentator'.

Compilation: *Coffee Bar Sessions* (1986).

Viscounts

When three disgruntled members of the Morton Fraser Harmonica Gang decided to leave Variety and join the English rock 'n' roll live circuit, the Viscounts were born. Gordon Mills (b. 1935, Madras, India, d. 29 July 1986), Don Paul and Ronnie Wells were not only harmonica champions but excellent harmony singers, whose tireless professionalism was in great demand on the debilitating package tours put together by UK promoters such as Larry Parnes. The Viscounts specialized in all-purpose backing vocals, comedy routines and parodic impressions of other acts. They released several singles before charting with the standard 'Short'nin' Bread' in 1960. They registered in the chart again the following year with the number 21 hit cover version of Barry Mann's 'Who Put The Bomp?'. Mills, however, was looking beyond the the group and after writing hits for Johnny Kidd And The Pirates and Cliff Richard became a full-time composer and later, manager. He was briefly replaced by former Parnes discovery Johnny Gentle but by 1964 the Viscounts decided to split up. Wells remained on the periphery of the pop scene and recorded for Mills' MAM label under the name Darren Wells. Don Paul later teamed up with Tony Stratton-Smith as co-manager of Paddy, Klaus And Gibson.

W

Wakely, Jimmy

b. Clarence Wakely, 16 February 1914, near Mineola, Arkansas, USA, d. 25 September 1982, Mission Hills, California, USA. Wakely's family relocated to Oklahoma when he was child, moving several times as they struggled to make a living usually by sharecropping. He gave himself the name of Jimmy, attended High School at Cowden, Oklahoma, learned to play the guitar and piano and worked on various projects, until after winning a local radio talent contest, he became a musician. In 1937, he married and moved to Oklahoma City, where he first worked as the pianist with a local band and appeared in a medicine show, before he was given a spot on WKY with Jack Cheney and Scotty Harrel as the Bell Boys. (Cheney was soon replaced by Johnny Bond). In 1940, as the Jimmy Wakely Trio, they were hired by Gene Autry to appear on his CBS *Melody Ranch* radio show in Hollywood. He worked with Autry for two years, at one time being known as the Melody Kid, before leaving to form his own band, which at times included Merle Travis, Cliffie Stone and Spade Cooley. Wakely made his film debut in 1939, in the Roy Rogers b-movie western *Saga Of Death Valley* and went on to appear in support roles (sometimes with his trio) in many films and with many other cowboy stars. In 1944, he starred in *Song Of The Range* and between then and 1949, when he made *Lawless Code*, he starred in almost 30 Monogram films. He became so popular as a cowboy actor that, in 1948, he was voted the number 4 cowboy star after Rogers, Autry and Charles Starrett. He made his first appearance in the US country charts in 1944 with his Decca recording of 'I'm Sending You Red Roses'. In 1948, recording for Capitol, he charted two country number 1 hits - 'One Has My Name, The Other Has My Heart' (which held the top spot for 11 weeks and remained in the country charts for 32, as well as being a national US Top 10 hit) and 'I Love You So Much It Hurts'.

In 1949, he had even more success with solo hits including 'I Wish I Had A Nickel' and 'Someday You'll Call My Name', plus several duet hits with Margaret Whiting, including their million-selling recording of Floyd Tillman's song 'Slipping Around', which was a country and pop number 1. At this time, Wakely's popularity was such that, in *Billboard*'s nationwide poll, he was voted America's third most popular singer behind Perry Como and Frankie Laine - edging Bing Crosby into fourth place. Wakely and Whiting followed it with several more Top 10 country and pop hits including 'I'll Never Slip Around Again' and 'A Bushel And A Peck'. Strangely, after his 1951 solo Top 10 hits 'My Heart Cries For You' (a UK pop hit for Guy Mitchell), 'Beautiful Brown Eyes' and a further duet with Margaret Whiting, entitled 'I Don't Want To Be Free', Wakely never made the country charts again. During the late 40s and the 50s, he toured extensively throughout the USA, the Pacific, the Far East, Korea and Alaska, sometimes appearing with Bob Hope. Musical tastes changed with the coming of Hank Williams and other country singers and the cowboy song and image lost much of its appeal. Wakely, however, hosted his own network radio show from

1952-58 and in 1961 he co-hosted a network television series with another silver screen cowboy Tex Ritter. During the 60s and throughout much of the 70s, he was still a popular entertainer, mainly performing on the west coast (he made his home in Los Angeles) or playing the club circuits of Las Vegas and Reno with his family show, which featured his children Johnny and Linda. He had formed his own Shasta label in the late 50s and in the 70s, he subsequently recorded a great deal of material on that label. In 1971, he was elected to the Nashville Songwriters Association International Hall Of Fame. Jimmy Wakely died, after a prolonged illness, in 1982.

Albums: *Christmas On The Range* (1954), *Songs Of The West* (1954), *Santa Fe Trail* (1956), *Enter And Rest And Pray* (1957), *Country Million Sellers* (1959), *Merry Christmas* (1959), *Sings* (1960), *Christmas With Jimmy Wakely* (1966), *Slipping Around* (1966), with Margaret Whiting *I'll Never Slip Around Again* (1967), *Show Me The Way* (1968), *Heartaches* (1969), *Here's Jimmy Wakely* (1969), *Lonesome Guitar Man* (60s), *Now And Then* (1970), *Big Country Songs* (1970), *Jimmy Wakely Country* (1971), *Blue Shadows* (1973), *Family Show* (1973), *The Wakely Way With Country Hits* (1974), *Jimmy Wakely* (1974), *On Stage Volume 1* (1974), *Western Swing And Pretty Things* (1975), *The Gentle Touch* (1975), *The Jimmy Wakely CBS Radio Show* (1975), *Jimmy Wakely Country* (1975), *Singing Cowboy* (1975), *An Old Fashioned Christmas* (1976), *A Tribute To Bob Wills* (1976), *Precious Memories* (1976), *Moments To Remember* (1977), *Reflections* (1977).

Ward, Billy, And The Dominoes

This group was sometimes billed as the Dominoes, or Billy Ward And His Dominoes. Ward (b. 19 September 1921, Los Angeles, California, USA), was a songwriter, arranger, singer and pianist. As a child, he studied music in Los Angeles and at the age of 14 won a nationwide contest with his composition, 'Dejection'. During a spell in the US Army in the early 40s he took up boxing, and continued with the sport when he was released. After working as a sports columnist for the *Transradio Express*, and spending some time with a New York advertising agency, Ward became a vocal coach in his own studio at Carnegie Hall, and founded the Dominoes in 1950. The vocal quintet originally consisted of Clyde McPhatter, Charlie White (b. 1930, Washington, DC, USA; second tenor), Joe Lamont (baritone), Bill Brown (bass) and Ward on piano. Ward rarely sang, but, over the years, was the only constant member of the group. Important changes in personnel came in 1952 when White was replaced by James Van Loan, and Bill Brown by David McNeil; and in 1953, when Jackie Wilson took over from McPhatter who went on to found his own group, the Drifters. Ward originally formed the group as a gospel unit and, as such they appeared on the *Arthur Godfrey Talent Show*. However, they began singing more blues numbers and, in the early 50s, made the R&B charts with 'Do Something For Me', 'Sixty Minute Man' (written by Ward and regarded by many as the proto-type rock 'n' roll record and featured a scorching lead vocal from McPhatter), 'I Am With You', 'Have Mercy Baby', 'I'd Be Satisfied', 'One Mint Julep', 'That's What You're Doing To Me', 'The Bells', 'Rags To Riches' and 'These Foolish Things'. By 1956, when *Billy Ward And The Dominoes* was released, the group's personnel consisted of Gene Mumford, Milton Merle, Milton Grayson, Cliff Owens and Ward. In the late 50s they had US Top 20 hits with 'St. Therese Of The Roses', 'Deep Purple' and 'Stardust', which sold over a million copies. After those, the record hits dried up, but the Dominoes, regarded as one of the important, pioneer R&B vocal groups of the 50s, continued to be a popular US concert draw throughout the 60s.

Albums: *Billy Ward And His Dominoes* (1956), *Clyde McPhatter With Billy Ward* (1957), *Sea Of Glass* (1959), *Yours Forever* (1959), *Pagan Love Song* (1959). Compilations: *Billy Ward And His Dominoes With Clyde McPhatter* (1958), *Billy Ward & His Dominoes Featuring Clyde McPhatter And Jackie Wilson* (1961), *The Dominoes Featuring Jackie Wilson* (1977), *Have Mercy Baby* (1985), *14 Original Hits* (1988), *21 Original Greatest Hits* (1988), *Feat* (1988), *Sixty Minute Man* (1991).

Washington, Dinah

b. Ruth Jones, 29 August 1924, Tuscaloosa, Alabama, USA, d. 14 December 1963. Raised in Chicago, Dinah Washington first sang in church choirs for which she also played piano. She then worked in local clubs, where she was heard by Lionel Hampton, who promptly hired her. She was with Hampton from 1943-46, recording hits with 'Evil Gal Blues', written by Leonard Feather, and 'Salty Papa Blues'. After leaving Hampton she sang R&B, again achieving record success, this time with 'Blow Top Blues' and 'I Told You Yes I Do'. In the following years Washington continued to sing R&B, but also sang jazz, blues, popular songs

of the day, standards, and was a major voice of the burgeoning, but as yet untitled, soul movement. However, her erratic lifestyle caught up with her and she died suddenly at the age of 39. Almost from the start of her career, Washington successfully blended the sacred music of her childhood with the sometimes earthily salacious secularity of the blues. This combination was a potent brew and audiences idolized her, thus helping her towards riches rarely achieved by black artists of her generation. She thoroughly enjoyed her success, spending money indiscriminately on jewellery, cars, furs, drink, drugs and men. She married many times and had countless liaisons. Physically, she appeared to thrive on her excesses, as can be seen from her performance in the film of the 1958 Newport Jazz Festival, *Jazz On A Summer's Day*. She was settling down happily with her seventh husband when she took a lethal combination of pills, probably by accident after having too much to drink. Washington's voice was rich and she filled everything she sang with heartfelt emotion. Even when the material was not of the highest quality, she could make the tritest of lyrics appear deeply moving. Amongst her popular successes were 'What A Diff'rence A Day Makes', her biggest hit, which reached number 8 in the USA in 1959, and 'September In The Rain', which made number 35 in the UK in 1961. Washington usually sang alone but in the late 50s she recorded some duets with her then husband, Eddie Chamblee. These records enjoyed a measure of success and were followed in 1960 with songs with Brook Benton, notably 'Baby (You Got What It Takes)' and 'A Rockin' Good Way (To Mess Around And Fall In Love)', which proved to be enormously popular, achieving numbers 5 and 7 respectively in the US charts. Washington left a wealth of recorded material, ranging from *The Jazz Sides*, which feature Clark Terry, Jimmy Cleveland, Blue Mitchell and others, to albums of songs by or associated with Fats Waller and Bessie Smith. On these albums, as on almost everything she recorded, Washington lays claim to being one of the major jazz voices and probably the most versatile of all the singers to have worked in jazz.

Albums: *Dinah Washington Sings* (1950), *Dynamic Dinah* (1951), *Blazing Ballads* (1951), *Music For Late Hours* (early 50s), *Dinah Washington Sings Fats Waller* (early 50s), *After Hours With Miss D* (1954), *Dinah Jams* (1954), *For Those In Love* (1955), *Dinah* (1956), *In The Land Of Hi Fi* (1956), *The Swingin' Miss D* (1956), *Dinah Washington Sings Bessie Smith* (1958), *What A Difference A Day Makes!* (1960),

Dinah Washington

Unforgettable (1961), *I Concentrate On You* (1961), *For Lonely Lovers* (1961), *September In The Rain* (1961), *Tears And Laughter* (1962), with the Quincy Jones Orchestra *I Wanna Be Loved* (1962), *The Good Old Days* (1963), with Sarah Williams, Joe Williams *We Three* (1964), *Dinah '62* (1962), *In Love* (1962), *Drinking Again* (1962), *Back To The Blues* (1963), *Dinah '63* (1963), *A Stranger On Earth* (1964). Compilations: *This Is My Story, Volume One* (1963), *This Is My Story, Volume Two* (1963), *In Tribute* (1963), *The Best Of Dinah Washington* (1965), with Brook Benton *The Two Of Us* (1978, coupled with a Sarah Vaughan and Billy Eckstine collection), *Spotlight On Dinah Washington* (1980), *The Best Of Dinah Washington* (1987), *The Complete Dinah Washington Vols. 1-14 (1943-55)* (1990).
Further reading: *Queen Of The Blues: A Biography Of Dinah Washington*, James Haskins.

Weavers

This US folk group was formed in 1949, from artists with a background of traditional music and comprised Lee Hays (b. 1914, Little Rock, Arkansas, USA, d. 26 August 1981; vocals/guitar), Fred Hellerman (b. 13 May 1927, New York, USA; vocals/guitar), Ronnie Gilbert (b. vocals) and Pete Seeger (b. 3 May 1919, New York City, New York, USA; vocals/guitar/banjo). Previously Seeger and Hays had been members of the Almanac Singers with Woody Guthrie. Unlike many similar groups of the time, the Weavers were able to attain commercial acceptance and success, without having to compromise their folk heritage. Virtually all their record releases charted, a precedent for a folk group. They have at times been credited with creating the climate for the post-war folk revival. Many songs became 'standards' as a result of the popularity achieved by the group, in particular 'Goodnight Irene', which sold one million copies in 1950. Other successful songs were, 'Kisses Sweeter Than Wine' and 'On Top Of Old Smokey', the latter remaining at number 1 for three months. Despite Seeger being blacklisted in 1952, and brought before the House of Un-American Activities Committee, the group still sold over four million records during that period. The Weavers disbanded the same year because of personal reasons as well as the pressures brought about by the McCarthy era. The group had lost bookings after being added to the blacklist of left-wing, or even suspected left-wing sympathizers at the time.
In 1955, their manager Harold Leventhal, persuaded them to reunite for a Christmas concert at Carnegie Hall. Such was the success of the event that they continued to tour internationally for a few more years, while still recording for the Vanguard Records label. Despite the acclaim, Seeger was still able to combine a successful solo career but, by 1958, he had left the group. He was replaced in fairly quick succession by Erik Darling, then Frank Hamilton and finally Bernie Krause. The Weavers disbanded at the end of 1963, after 15 years together, and capped the event with an anniversary concert at Carnegie Hall. Travelling and personal ambitions were given as the reasons for the split. After the group left the music scene, there were many who tried to fill their space but none had the combination of enthusiasm and commitment that had made the Weavers such a popular act. Lee Hays, in his latter years confined to a wheelchair, died after many years of poor health in 1981. In compliance with Hay's wishes, his ashes were mixed with his garden compost pile! Nine months earlier, the original line-up had joined together to film the documentary *Wasn't That A Time?* recalling the group's earlier successes. Albums: *Folk Songs From Around The World* (c.50s), *Travelling On With The Weavers* (c.50s), *The Weavers At Home* (c.50s), *Almanac* (50s), *The Weavers At Carnegie Hall* (1956), *The Weavers At Carnegie Hall, Volume Two* (1960), *The Weavers Reunion At Carnegie Hall Volumes 1 & 2* (1963), *Songbook* (1965), *We Shall Overcome - Songs Of The Freedom Riders And The Sit-Ins* (c.60s), *Weavers On Tour* (1970), *Together Again* (1984). Compilations: *The Best Of The Weavers* (c.50s), *Greatest Hits* (1957), *Weavers Greatest Hits* (1970), *Best Of The Weavers* (1984).

Weber, Joan

b. 1936, Paulsboro, New Jersey, USA, d. 13 May 1981. Joan Weber had a number 1 hit in the USA in January 1955 but was unable to follow up that success. The record was 'Let Me Go Lover', released on Columbia Records. Weber was 18 when she met manager Eddie Joy, who brought her to Charles Randolph Green (a 'one-hit wonder' himself in the late 60s), who worked in A&R at the famed Brill Building in New York. Green gave Weber's demo tape of a song called 'Marionette' to Mitch Miller at Columbia, who signed her to the label. Miller took a song titled 'Let Me Go, Devil' and had it rewritten as 'Let Me Go Lover', which Weber recorded. Performed on the television program *Studio One*, the song became an immediate success, selling half-a-million copies and reaching the top of the chart in the

USA and peaking at number 16 in the UK. Weber had given birth around the time her record was most successful and was unable to devote herself to promoting her career. Subsequently, she was dropped from Columbia's roster and never had another hit. She later died in 1981.

Weedon, Bert

b. 10 May 1920, London, England. Weedon may be one of the most omnipotent of British electric guitarists, given that fretboard heroes including Jeff Beck and George Harrison, began by positioning as yet uncalloused fingers on taut strings while poring over exercises prescribed in Weedon's best-selling *Play In A Day* and *Play Every Day* manuals. This self-taught guitarist started learning flamenco guitar at the age of 12 before playing in London dance bands. During World War II, he strummed chords in the touring groups of Django Reinhardt and Stéphane Grappelli. With such prestigious experience, he became the featured soloist with Mantovani, Ted Heath and, by the early 50s, Cyril Stapleton's BBC Show Band.

By 1956, he was leading his own quartet and had released a debut single, 'Stranger Than Fiction', but only his theme to television's *$64,000 Question* sold even moderately before 1959. That year his cover of the Virtues' 'Guitar Boogie Shuffle' made the UK Top 10. Subsequent hit parade entries, however, proved less lucrative than countless record dates for bigger stars. Although he accompanied visiting Americans such as Frank Sinatra, Rosemary Clooney and Nat 'King' Cole - later, the subject of a Weedon tribute album - his bread-and-butter was sessions for domestic artists from Dickie Valentine and Alma Cogan to the new breed of Elvis Presley-inspired teen idols - Tommy Steele, Cliff Richard, Billy Fury *et al*. Steele would win music press popularity polls as Best Guitarist but the accolade belonged morally to his middle-aged hireling.

In the early 60s Weedon's singles hovered round the lower middle of the Top 40. The most notable of these was 1960's 'Apache' which was eclipsed by the Shadows' version. Although the group was dismissive of his 'Apache', they acknowledged an artistic debt to Weedon by penning 'Mr. Guitar', his singles chart farewell. Nevertheless, he remained in the public eye through a residency on ITV children's series *Five O' Clock Club* - as well as a remarkable 1964 spot on *Sunday Night At The London Palladium* on which he showed that he could rock out on his Hofner 'cutaway' as well as anyone. Indeed, it was as a rock 'n' roller that

Weedon succeeded seven years later - with *Rockin' At The Roundhouse*, a budget-price album much at odds with the easy-listening efforts that sustained him during the 70s. A renewal of interest in guitar instrumentals suddenly placed him at the top of the album chart in 1976 with *22 Golden Guitar Greats*. Nothing since has been as successful - and 1977's *Blue Echoes* was criticized severely in the journal *Guitar*, but - hit or miss - Bert Weedon, ever the professional, continued to record production-line albums throughout his sixth decade.

Albums: *King Size Guitar* (1960), *Honky Tonk Guitar* (1961), *The Romantic Guitar Of Bert Weedon* (1970), *Rockin At The Roundhouse* (1971), *Sweet Sounds* (1971), *Bert Weedon Remembers Jim Reeves* (1973), *The Gentle Guitar Of Bert Weedon* (1975), *Bert Weedon Remembers Nat 'King' Cole* (1975), *22 Golden Guitar Greats* (1976), *Let The Good Times Roll* (1977), *Blue Echoes* (1977), *Honky Tonk Guitar Party* (1977), *16 Country Guitar Greats* (1978), *40 Guitar Greats* (1979), *Heart Strings* (1980), *Dancing Guitars* (1982), *Guitar Favourites* (1983), *Love Letters* (1983), *Mr Guitar* (1984), *An Hour Of Bert Weedon* (1987), *Once More With Feeling* (1988). Compilation: *Guitar Gold - 20 Greatest Hits* (1978).

Welk, Lawrence

b. 11 March 1903, Strasburg, North Dakota, USA. After achieving a measure of competence on the piano-accordion Welk decided to form a dance band. This was around 1925 and he swiftly rose to enormous popularity with engagements at leading hotels and endless one-night stands on the country's dancehall circuit. The band was widely criticized in the musical press for its lack of imagination and simplistic arrangements, coupled with occasionally elementary playing. Nevertheless, Welk's star continued to rise and his became one of the most successful broadcasting bands in the history of American popular music. Welk called his style 'champagne music' and he made no concessions to changing tastes, firmly believing that he knew exactly what middle-Americans wanted to hear. He must have been right because he retained his popularity throughout the 30s and 40s and in 1951 his regular radio shows transferred smoothly to television. For the next four years he had a weekly show from the Aragon Ballroom at Pacific Ocean Park and in 1955 switched to ABC and even greater success. In 1961 two of his albums spent the entire year in the charts, *Calcutta* was lodged at number 1 for 11 weeks. During his unprecedented chart run between 1956 and 1972 no less than 42 albums made the lists. During the

Lawrence Welk

early' 60s there was always a Welk album in the bestsellers. Also in 1961 he signed a lifetime contract with the Hollywood Palladium and a decade later was still on television, by now syndicated across the North American continent. The band's musical policy, which stood it in such good stead for so many years, had a central core of European music, including waltzes, seasoned with numerous ballads. Although the band's book occasionally hinted that Welk was aware of other forms of music, even jazz, the bland arrangements he used so watered down the original that it sounded barely any different from the wallpaper music he usually played. The astonishing longevity of the band's popular appeal suggests that, however cynical musicians and critics might have been about him, Welk clearly had his finger much closer to the silent majority's pulse than almost any other bandleader in history.

Albums: *Lawrence Walk And His Sparkling Strings* (1955), *TV Favourites* (1956), *Shamrocks And Champagne* (1956), *Bubbles In The Wine* (1956), *Say It With Music* (1956), *Champagne Pops Parade* (1956), *Moments To Remember* (1956), *Merry Christmas* (1956), *Pick-A-Polka!* (1957), *Waltz With Lawrence Welk* (1957), *Lawrence Welk Plays Dixieland* (1957), *Jingle Bells* (1957), *Last Date* (1960), *Calcutta!* (1961), *Yellow Bird* (1961), *Moon River* (1961), *Silent Night And 13 Other Best Loved Christmas Songs* (1961), *Young World* (1962), *Baby Elephant Walk And Theme From The Brothers Grimm* (1962), *Waltz Time* (1963), *1963's Early Hits* (1963), *Scarlett O'Hara* (1963), *Wonderful! Wonderful!* (1963), *Early Hits Of 1964* (1964), *A Tribute To The All-Time Greats* (1964), *The Lawrence Welk Television Show 10th Anniversary* (1964), *The Golden Millions* (1964), *My First Of 1965* (1965), *Apples And Bananas* (1965), *Today's Great Hits* (1966), *Champagne On Broadway* (1966), *Winchester Cathedral* (1966), *Lawrence Welk's 'Hits Of Our Time'* (1967), *Love Is Blue* (1968), *Memories* (1969), *Galveston* (1969), *Lawrence Welk Plays 'I Love You Truly' And Other Songs Of Love* (1969), *Jean* (1969), *Candida* (1970). Compilations: *Golden Hits/The Best Of Lawrence Welk* (1967), *Reminiscing* (1972), *22 All-Time Big Band Favourites* (1989), *22 All-Time Favourite Waltzes* (1989), *22 Great Songs For Dancing* (1989), *22 Of The Greatest Waltzes* (1989), *Dance To The Big Band Sounds* (1989), *The Best Of Lawrence Welk* (1989).

Further reading: *Wunnerful, Wunnerful*, Lawrence Welk.

Welsh, Alex

b. 9 July 1929, Edinburgh, Scotland, d. 25 June 1982. Welsh began his musical career in Scotland playing cornet, then later trumpet, in trad jazz bands. In the early 50s he moved to London and formed a band which quickly became one of the most proficient of its kind. With every chair filled by musicians of great skill and enthusiasm, the Welsh band was a major force in the British trad jazz movement. Eschewing the fancy dress eccentricities and pop music escapades of many of his rivals (although 'Tansy' did reach the UK Top 50 in 1961), Welsh concentrated on creating exciting music that echoed the vitality of the best of Chicago-style dixieland jazz. Amongst Welsh's sidemen over the years were Archie Semple, Fred Hunt, Roy Crimmins, Roy Williams, John Barnes, Lennie Hastings and Al Gay. During the 60s and early 70s Welsh toured the UK and Europe, building up a rapturous following, and also made occasional successful sorties to the USA. In common with Chris Barber, Welsh saw the need to maintain a wide repertoire, drawing (as jazz always has), from the best of popular music and thus creating a band which effectively swam in the mainstream. By the mid-70s Welsh's health was poor, but he continued to play for as long as he could. Throughout his career Welsh blew with great exuberance, sometimes sang too and always encouraged his sidemen by his example. Not only popular with audiences, he was also respected and admired by his fellow musicians.

Selected albums: *Music Of The Mauve Decade* (1957), *The Melrose Folio* (1958), *Alex Welsh In Concert* (1961), *Echoes Of Chicago* (1962), *Strike One* (1966), *At Home With Alex Welsh* (1967), *Vintage '69* (1969), *Classic Concert* (1971), *If I Had A Talking Picture Of You* (1975), *In A Party Mood* (1977), *Live At The Royal Festival Hall (1954-55)* (1988), *Doggin' Around* (1993).

West Side Story

Opening on Broadway on 26 September 1957, the stage musical *West Side Story* shook audiences with its powerful, even aggressive score, dancing and storyline. Transposing the *Romeo And Juliet* story to contemporary New York, the plot traced the doomed love affair between a member of one of the incoming Puerto Rican families and a native-born American. Maria, the Puerto Rican girl, and Tony, her lover, are denied happiness through the conflict between the two sides in the urban gang war. In a fight, Tony kills Maria's brother, Bernardo. Later, Tony, believing that Maria has been killed by Bernardo's friend, Chino, is himself killed. This death stuns the rival gangs, the Puerto Rican 'Sharks' and the American 'Jets'. Composed by Leonard Bernstein, with the book by Arthur Laurents, lyrics by Stephen Sondheim and choreography by Jerome Robbins (who had also conceived the idea for the show), *West Side Story* blasted many preconceptions about form and content of American musical comedy. The first song, 'America', cynically contrasted the difference between the expectations of immigrants and the reality they found in their new homeland (although some later recordings managed to turn it into a paean of praise for the USA). 'Gee, Officer Krupke' was wickedly funny and realistically disrespectful of authority. Amongst the songs that had a lighter mood than those which dominated much of the show were 'I Feel Pretty', sung by Carol Lawrence as Maria, 'Maria' sung by Larry Kert as Tony, and 'Tonight', a duet by Maria and Tony. Amongst other songs were 'Something's Coming', 'One Hand, One Heart', 'Cool', 'Somewhere', and 'A Boy Like That' which was sung by Chita Rivera as Anita. Rivera also led the ensemble in 'America'. Press reviews of the show were good, and word of mouth reports were ecstatic. The show ran for 732 performances. *West Side Story* was staged in London in 1958 and was revived in 1973 and again in the mid-80s. The 1961 screen version starred Natalie Wood as Maria (dubbed by Marni Nixon), Richard Beymer as Tony (dubbed by Jimmy Bryant), Rita Moreno as Anita, Russ Tamblyn and George Chakiris. The film picked up a shelf of Oscars including Best Film, and individual awards for Robbins's choreography and Moreno as Best Supporting Actress. In 1985, Bernstein conducted the original full-length score for the first time in a studio session with opera stars, Kiri Te Kanawa and José Carreras. The event, which was filmed and televised to much acclaim, assisted the album to achieve top-selling status. The musical has also spawned many hits in radically different interpretations from artists as diverse as P.J. Proby ('Somewhere' and 'Maria') and the Nice ('America').

Whitfield, David

b. 2 February 1925, Hull, Yorkshire, England, d. 15 January 1980, Sydney, Australia. Whitfield was a popular ballad singer in the UK during the 50s, with a tenor voice which proved suitable for light opera. After working as a labourer, and singing in local clubs, he spent some time in the merchant

David Whitfield (left) with Joan Regan and Terry Thomas

navy before signing to Decca Records in 1953. He had his first big hit that year with 'Bridge Of Sighs', followed by 'Answer Me', which went to number 1 in the UK. He toured the variety circuit and appeared in a Royal Command Performance. Throughout the 50s, he defied the onslaught of rock 'n' roll, and was frequently in the UK chart with numbers such as 'Rags To Riches' and 'The Book'. The extraordinary 'Cara Mia', accompanied by Mantovani And His Orchestra, dominated the UK number 1 position for a staggering 10 weeks and sold over three-and-a-half million copies. The song also reached the US Top 10, a rare feat for a British singer at the time.

Other Whitfield releases included, 'Santo Natale', 'Beyond The Stars', 'Mama', 'Everywhere', 'When You Lose The One You Love', 'My September Love' (UK number 3), 'Adoration Waltz' (UK Top 10), 'I'll Find You' and 'On The Street Where You Live'. He also had some success in the USA with 'Smile', originally written for the Charles Chaplin movie, *Modern Times* (1936). By the turn of the 60s, singers of Whitfield's style had begun to go out of fashion, and in 1961, he indicated his future direction by releasing *My Heart And I*, a selection of operetta favourites, such as 'I Kiss Your Hand Madame' and 'You Are My Heart's Delight'. Subsequently, he toured abroad, and had recently sung aboard a Chinese passenger liner on a cruise in the South Pacific Islands, and just concluded his tenth tour of Australia, when he died in Sydney. His ashes were later scattered at sea off Hull, near to where he was born.

Albums: *Whitfield Favourites* (late 50s), *From David With Love* (late 50s), *Alone* (1961), *My Heart And I* (1961), *Great Songs For Young Lovers* (1966), *Hey There, It's David Whitfield* (1975). Compilations: *The World Of David Whitfield* (1969), *World Of David Whitfied Volumes 1 & 2* (1975), *Focus On David Whitfield* (1978), *Greatest Hits* (1983), *The Magic Of David Whitfield* (1986).

Whiting, Margaret

b. 22 July 1924, Detroit, Michigan, USA, Margaret Whiting was a popular vocalist of the 40s and 50s, recording dozens of hits for Capitol Records. She was the daughter of Richard Whiting, himself a successful songwriter, author of, amongst others, 'On The Good Ship Lollipop', 'The Japanese Sandman' and 'Ain't We Got Fun?'. Margaret began singing as a small child and by the age of seven she was working with Johnny Mercer, the popular songwriter and founder of Capitol Records, for whom her father worked. When

Mercer and two partners launched Capitol, Margaret Whiting was one of their first signings. Whiting started recording for the label in 1942, her first major hit being the Mercer-Harold Arlen composition 'That Old Black Magic', as featured singer with Freddie Slack And His Orchestra. That was followed in 1943 by 'Moonlight In Vermont', with Whiting singing as a member of Billy Butterfield's Orchestra, and 'It Might As Well Be Spring', with Paul Weston And His Orchestra, from the film *State Fair*. Whiting first recorded under her own name in late 1945, singing the Jerome Kern-Oscar Hammerstein II composition 'All Through The Day', which became a best-seller in the spring of 1946, and 'In Love In Vain', both of which were featured in the film *Centennial Summer*. Whiting also had hits with songs from the Broadway musicals *St. Louis Woman* and *Call Me Mister* in 1946. Those first recordings under her name were recorded in New York. In late 1946 Whiting returned to California and began recording there, with Jerry Gray And His Orchestra; 'Guilty' and 'Oh, But I Do' were the best-selling fruits of that session. Whiting's hit streak continued in 1948-49. Due to a musician's strike in the USA, orchestral tracks were recorded outside of the country and vocals added in US studios. Whiting supplied vocals to tracks cut by Frank DeVol And His Orchestra, including 'A Tree In The Meadow', a number 1 hit in the summer of 1948, recorded in London. Her next number 1 occurred in 1949 with 'Slippin' Around', one of a series of duet recordings made with country film star Jimmy Wakely. Also during that year, Whiting recorded a duet with Mercer, 'Baby, It's Cold Outside'. In 1950, she had a hit with 'Blind Date', a novelty record she made with Bob Hope and the Billy May Orchestra. Whiting continued recording hits for Capitol into the mid-50s, until her run of hits dried up. She left Capitol in 1958 for Dot Records but scored only one hit with that label. She switched to Verve Records in 1960 and recorded a number of albums, including one with jazz vocalist Mel Tormé. A brief return to Capitol was followed by a hiatus, after which Whiting signed to London Records in 1966, for which she recorded her last two charting pop singles. Her recordings continued to appear on the easy listening charts into the 70s. Whiting was still recording in the early 90s, and performing in cabarets and music halls.

Selected albums: *Margaret Whiting Sings Rodgers And Hart* (c.50s), *Love Songs By Margaret Whiting* (c.50s, reissued 1985), *Margaret Whiting Sings For The*

Starry-Eyed (c.50s), *The Jerome Kern Songbook* (50s, reissued 1987), *Goin' Places* (1957), *Margaret* (1958), *Top Ten Hits* (1960), *Just A Dream* (1960), *Past Midnight* (1962), *Wheel Of Hurt* (1967), *Maggie Isn't Margaret Anymore* (1967), *Pop Country* (1968), *The Lady's In Love With You* (1986), *Come A Little Closer* (1988), *Too Marvelous For Words* (1988). Compilation: *Greatest Hits* (1959).

Whitman, Slim

b. Otis Dewey Whitman Jnr., 20 January 1924, Tampa, Florida, USA. Whitman was unhappy because his stutter was ridiculed by other children and consequently he left school as soon as he could. Even though his stutter is now cured, he has never cared for public speaking and says little during his stage act. Several members of his family were musical and he became interested in Jimmie Rodgers' recordings when he discovered that he too could also yodel. After leaving school, he worked in a meat-packing plant where he lost part of a finger, which, several years later led to him turning a guitar tutor upside down and learning to play left-handed. He later remarked, 'Paul McCartney saw me in Liverpool and realized that he too could play the guitar left-handed.' Whitman sang at his family's local church, the Church of the Brethren, and it was here, in 1938, that he met the new minister's daughter, Geraldine Crisp. After borrowing $10 from his mother for the license, he married her in 1941. Whitman regards his long-standing marriage as a major ingredient in his success, and he wrote and dedicated a song to her, 'Jerry'. During World War II, he worked as a fitter in a shipyard and then saw action in the US Navy. Whilst on board, he realized his talents for entertaining his fellow crew but in his first concert, he foolishly chose to sing 'When I'm Gone You'll Soon Forget Me'! No matter, his singing became so popular that the captain blocked his transfer to another ship - fortunately for Whitman, as the other ship was sunk with all hands lost.

After his discharge, he had some success in baseball, but he preferred singing, choosing the name Slim Whitman as a tribute to Wilf Carter (Montana Slim), and often working on radio. He first recorded for RCA-Victor, at the suggestion of Tom Parker, in 1949. After moderate successes with 'I'm Casting My Lasso Towards The Sky' and 'Birmingham Jail', he moved to Shreveport, Louisiana so that he could appear each week on the radio show, *Louisiana Hayride*. His wife embroidered black shirts for Whitman and the band which has led him to claim he was the original 'Man In Black'. His steel player, Hoot Rains, developed an identifiable sound, but it came about by accident: when Rains overshot a note on 'Love Song Of The Waterfall', Whitman decided to retain it as a trademark. Whitman maintained a level-headed attitude towards his career and was working as a postman whilst his first single for Imperial Records, 'Love Song Of The Waterfall', was selling half-a-million copies. 'You don't quit on one record,' he says, 'Then I had 'Indian Love Call' and I decided to go. I was told that if I ever wanted my job back, I could have it'. 'Indian Love Call' came from Rudolf Friml's operetta, *Rose Marie*, and, in 1955, its title song gave Slim Whitman 11 consecutive weeks at the top of the UK charts, an achievement which was only beaten in 1992 by Bryan Adams' 'Everything I Do'. 'All I did was throw in a few yodels for good measure,' says Slim, 'and the folks seemed to go for it.' The b-side of 'Indian Love Call', 'China Doll', was a UK hit in its own right, and his other chart records include 'Cattle Call', 'Tumbling Tumbleweeds', 'Serenade' and 'I'll Take You Home Again, Kathleen', although, astonishingly, he has never topped the US country charts. He says, 'A lot of people think of me as a cowboy because I've sung 'Cattle Call' and one or two others. The truth is, I've never been on a horse in my life.' In 1955, Whitman moved back to Florida, which restricted his appearances on the *Grand Ole Opry* because he found the trips too time-consuming. In 1956 Whitman became the first country star to top a bill at the London Palladium. Despite being a light-voiced country balladeer, he was featured in the 1957 rock 'n' roll film, *Disc Jockey Jamboree*. He has always taken a moral stance on what he records, perhaps because he is married to a preacher's daughter, refusing, for example, to record 'Almost Persuaded'. He says, 'I'm not a saint. It's just that I've no interest in singing songs about cheating or the boozer'. His popularity in Britain was such that his *25th Anniversary Concert* album was recorded at the Empire Theatre, Liverpool in March 1973. He had a UK hit in 1974 with 'Happy Anniversary', but United Artists executive, Alan Warner, decided that his US country albums were wrong for the UK market and that he should record albums of pop standards which could be marketed on television. His 1976 album, *The Very Best Of Slim Whitman*, entered the UK album charts at number 1, and was followed by *Red River Valley* (number 1) and *Home On The Range* (number 2). Whitman then repeated his role as a purveyor of love songs for the middle-aged in the US. Since 1977,

Slim Whitman

Whitman has toured with his son, Byron (b. 1957), whom he says is matching him 'yodel for yodel', and they have pioneered the double yodel. Of his continued success, constantly playing to full houses, he says, 'I don't know the secret. I guess it's the songs I sing and my friendly attitude. When I say hello, I mean it'.

Albums: *Slim Whitman Sings And Yodels* (1954), *America's Favorite Folk Artist* (1954), *Slim Whitman Favorites* (1956), *Slim Whitman Sings* (1957), *Slim Whitman Sings* (1958), *Slim Whitman* (1958), *Slim Whitman Sings* (1959), *I'll Walk With God* (1960), *Slim Whitman Sings Annie Laurie* (1961), *Just Call Me Lonesome* (1961), *Once In A Lifetime* (1961), *Slim Whitman Sings* (1961), *Heart Songs And Love Songs* (1963), *Irish Songs - The Slim Whitman Way* (1963), *I'm A Lonely Wanderer* (1963), *Yodeling* (1963), *Love Song Of The Waterfall* (1964), *Reminiscing* (1964), *More Than Yesterday* (1965), *Forever* (1966), *God's Hand In Mine* (1966), *A Time For Love* (1966), *A Travellin' Man* (1966), *A Lonesome Heart* (1967), *Country Memories* (1967), *In Love, The Whitman Way* (1968), *Unchain Your Heart* (1968), *Happy Street* (1969), *Slim!* (1969), *Slim Whitman* (1969), *The Slim Whitman Christmas Album* (1969), *Ramblin' Rose* (1970), *Tomorrow Never Comes* (1970), *It's A Sin To Tell A Lie* (1971), *Guess Who* aka *Snowbird* (1971), *I'll See You When* (1973), *25th Anniversary Concert* (1973), *Happy Anniversary* (1974), *Everything Leads Back To You* (1975), *Home On The Range* (1977), *Red River Valley* (1977), *Ghost Riders In The Sky* (1978), *Just For You* (1980), *Songs I Love To Sing* (1980), *Christmas With Slim Whitman* (1980), *Mr. Songman* (1981), *Till We Meet Again* (1981), *I'll Be Home For Christmas* (1981), *Country Songs, City Hits* (1982), *Angeline* (1984), *A Dream Come True - The Rarities Album* (1987), with Byron Whitman *Magic Moments* (1990). Compilations: *All Time Favourites* (1964), *Fifteenth Anniversary* (1967), *The Very Best Of Slim Whitman* (1976), *All My Best* (1979), *Slim Whitman's 20 Greatest Love Songs* (1979), *20 Golden Greats* (1992), *EMI Country Masters: 50 Orginal Tracks* (1993, 2 CD set).

Further reading: *Mr. Songman - The Slim Whitman Story*, Kenneth L. Gibble.

Wilde, Marty

b. Reginald Leonard Smith, 15 April 1936, London, England. After playing briefly in a skiffle group, this UK rock 'n' roll singer secured a residency at London's Condor Club under the name Reg Patterson. He was spotted by songwriter Lionel Bart, who subsequently informed entrepreneur Larry Parnes. The starmaker was keen to sign the singer and rapidly took over his career. Reg Smith henceforth became Marty Wilde. The Christian name was coined from the sentimental film *Marty* while the surname was meant to emphasize the wilder side of Smiths' nature. Parnes next arranged a record deal with Philips Records, but Wilde's initial singles, including a reading of Jimmie Rodgers' 'Honeycomb', failed to chart. Nevertheless, Wilde was promoted vigorously and appeared frequently on BBC Television's music programme, *6.5 Special*. Extensive media coverage culminated with a hit recording of Jody Reynolds' alluringly morbid 'Endless Sleep' in 1957. Soon after, Parnes persuaded the influential producer Jack Good to make Wilde the resident star of his new television programme *Oh Boy!* The arrangement worked well for Wilde until Good objected to his single 'Misery's Child' and vetoed the song. Worse followed when Good effectively replaced Marty with a new singing star Cliff Richard. Before long, Cliff had taken Marty's mantle as the UK's premier teen idol and was enjoying consistent hits. Wilde, meanwhile, was gradually changing his image. After considerable success with such songs as 'Donna', 'Teenager In Love', 'Sea Of Love' and his own composition 'Bad Boy', he veered away from rock 'n' roll. His marriage to Joyce Baker of the Vernon Girls was considered a bad career move at the time and partly contributed to Wilde's announcement that he would henceforth be specializing in classy, Frank Sinatra-style ballads. For several months he hosted a new pop show *Boy Meets Girls* and later starred in the London West End production of *Bye Bye Birdie*. Although Parnes was intent on promoting Wilde as an actor, the star was resistant to such a move. His last major success was with a lacklustre version of Bobby Vee's 'Rubber Ball' in 1961. Later in the decade he recorded for several labels, including a stint as the Wilde Three with his wife Joyce, and future Moody Blues' vocalist Justin Hayward. Wilde enjoyed considerable radio play and was unfortunate not to enjoy a belated hit with the catchy 'Abergavenny' in 1969. He also scored some success as the writer of hits like Status Quo's 'Ice In The Sun'. By the 70s, Wilde was managing his son Ricky who was briefly promoted as Britain's answer to Little Jimmy Osmond. Ricky later achieved success as a songwriter for his sister, Kim Wilde, who would go on to achieve far greater chart fame in the UK and USA than her father.

Albums: *Bad Boy* (1960), *Wilde About Marty* (1959),

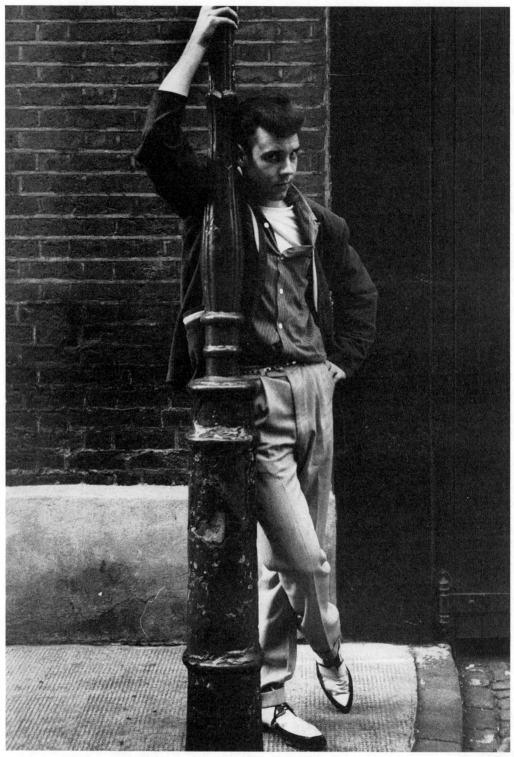

Marty Wilde

Showcase (1960), *The Versatile Mr. Wilde* (1960), *Diversions* (1969), *Rock 'N' Roll* (1970), *Good Rocking - Then And Now* (1974). Compilations: *Wild Cat Rocker* (1981), *The Hits Of Marty Wilde* (1984).

Williams, Andy

b. Howard Andrew Williams, 3 December 1928, Wall Lake, Iowa, USA. Williams began his singing career in the local church choir with his three brothers. The quartet became popular on their own radio shows from Cincinnati, Des Moines and Chicago. They backed Bing Crosby on his Oscar winning song, 'Swinging On A Star', from the 1944 movie, *Going My Way* and in the same year appeared in the minor musical film, *Kansas City Kitty*. In the following year, Andy Williams dubbed Lauren Bacall's singing voice in her first film with Humphrey Bogart, *To Have And Have Not*. From 1947-48 the Williams Brothers worked with top pianist/singer Kay Thompson in nightclubs and on television. Andy Williams went solo in 1952, and featured regularly on Steve Allen's *Tonight Show* for over two years. Signed to the Cadence label, Williams had his first success in 1956 with 'Canadian Sunset', followed by a string of Top 20 entries including, 'Butterfly' (number 1), 'I Like Your Kind Of Love' (a duet with Peggy Powers), 'Lips Of Wine', 'Are You Sincere', 'Promise Me, Love', 'The Hawaiian Wedding Song', 'Lonely Street' and 'The Village Of St. Bernadette'. In 1961, Williams moved to Columbia Records. His first big hit for the label was the Doc Pomus/Mort Shuman composition, 'Can't Get Used To Losing You', which went to number 2 in the US charts in 1963. From then, until 1971, when the singles hits dried up, he was in the US Top 20 with 'Hopeless', 'A Fool Never Learns' and '(Where Do I Begin) Love Story'. Williams reached number 4 in the UK charts in 1973, with Neil Sedaka's song, 'Solitaire'. It was in the album charts however, that Williams found greater success.

By the early 70s it was estimated that he had received 13 worldwide gold disc awards for chart albums such as *Moon River & Other Great Movie Themes*, *Days Of Wine And Roses* (a US number 1), *The Wonderful World Of Andy Williams*, *Dear Heart*, *Born Free*, *Love Andy* (a UK number 1), *Honey*, *Happy Heart*, *Home Loving Man* (another UK number 1) and *Love Story*. The enormous sales were no doubt assisted by his extremely successful weekly variety show which ran from 1962-71, and won an Emmy for 'Best Variety Show'. It also gave

the Osmond Brothers consistent nationwide exposure. In 1964, Williams made his film debut in *I'd Rather Be Rich*, starring Maurice Chevalier, Robert Goulet, Sandra Dee, and Hermione Gingold. It was a remake of the 1941 comedy, *It Started With Eve*, and Williams sang the Jerry Keller/Gloria Shayne number, 'Almost There', which reached number 2 in the UK chart during 1965. Despite the lack of consistent television exposure in the late 70s, Williams still sold a remarkable number of albums, particularly in the UK where his *Solitaire*, *The Way We Were*, and *Reflections*, all made the Top 10. In 1984, the album, *Greatest Love Classics* featured Williams singing contemporary lyrics to classical themes, accompanied by the Royal Philharmonic Orchestra. He remains one of America's most popular singers, renowned for his smooth vocal texture and relaxed approach. As a stylist, he is the equal of any popular singer from his era.

Albums: *Lonely Street* (1959), *'Danny Boy' And Other Songs I Like To Sing* (1962), *Moon River & Other Great Movie Themes* (1962), *Warm And Willing* (1962), *Days Of Wine And Roses* (1963), *The Andy Williams Christmas Album* (1963), *The Wonderful World Of Andy Williams* (1964), *The Academy Award Winning 'Call Me Irresponsible'* (1964), *The Great Songs From 'My Fair Lady' And Other Broadway Hits* (1964), *Dear Heart* (1965), *Almost There* (1965), *Can't Get Used To Losing You* (1965), *Hawaiian Wedding Song* (1965), *Canadian Sunset* (1965), *Merry Christmas* (1965), *The Shadow Of Your Smile* (1966), *May Each Day* (1966), *In The Arms Of Love* (1967), *Born Free* (1967), *Love, Andy* (1967), *Honey* (1968), *Happy Heart* (1969), with the Osmonds *Get Together With Andy Williams* (1969), *Can't Help Falling In Love* (1970), *Raindrops Keep Falling On My Head* (1970), *The Andy Williams' Show* (1970), *Home Loving Man* (1971), *Love Story* (1971), *You've Got A Friend* (1971), *The Impossible Dream* (1972), *Love Theme From 'The Godfather'* (1972), *A Song For You* (1972), *Alone Again (Naturally)* (1972), *The First Time Ever I Saw Your Face* (1973), *Solitaire* (1973), *You Lay Easy On My Mind* (1974), *The Way We Were* (1974), *An Evening With Andy Williams, Live In Japan* (1975), *The Other Side Of Me* (1975), *Showstoppers* (1977), *Let's Love While We Can* (1980), with the Royal Philharmonic Orchestra *Greatest Love Classics* (1984), *Close Enough For Love* (1986). Compilations: *Andy Williams' Best* (1962), *Andy Williams' Newest Hits* (1966), *The Andy Williams Sound Of Music* (1969), *Andy Williams' Greatest Hits* (1970), *Andy Williams' Greatest Hits, Volume Two*

Andy Williams

(1973), *Reflections* (1978), *Great Songs Of The Seventies* (1979), *Great Songs Of The Sixties* (1980), *Portrait Of A Song Stylist* (1989), *16 Most Requested Songs* (1993).

Williams, Billy

b. 28 December 1910, Waco, Texas, USA, d. 1972. Williams formed the very successful gospel group the Charioteers in the early 30s while studying theology at Wilberforce College, Ohio. The group had regular radio spots in Cincinnati and New York and worked with Bing Crosby on the west coast. In the 40s they had seven hits of their own and also charted with Frank Sinatra. In 1949 Williams left and formed the Billy Williams Quartet with Eugene Dixon (bass), Claude Riddick (baritone) and John Ball (tenor). The group were often seen on television including over 160 appearances on Sid Caesar's *Your Show Of Shows*. They recorded with little impact for Mercury and MGM Records before joining Coral in 1954 and after a few unsuccessful covers of R&B hits the group collected nine US chart entries. The biggest of these was a revival of Fats Waller's 'I'm Gonna Sit Right Down And Right Myself A Letter': a US Top 3 and UK Top 30 hit in 1957. The jazzy R&B artist sadly lost his voice, due to diabetes, in the early 60s. He moved to Chicago where he became a social worker, employed on a model cities project and helping alcoholics until his death in 1972.

Williams, Larry

b. 10 May 1935, New Orleans, Louisiana, USA, d. 2 January 1980, Los Angeles, California, USA. Williams recorded a handful of raucous rock 'n' roll songs for Specialty Records which, among others, later influenced John Lennon. Williams learned to play the piano while in New Orleans, and moved to Oakland, California with his family while in his teens. There he joined a group called the Lemon Drops. In 1954, while visiting his old home town of New Orleans, he met and was hired as pianist by Lloyd Price, who recorded for Specialty. Price introduced Williams to producer Robert 'Bumps' Blackwell. At that time Speciality head Art Rupe signed Williams. His first record was a cover of Price's 'Just Because', which reached number 11 on the R&B chart for Williams and number 3 for Price. Backed by fellow Specialty artist Little Richard's band, Williams recorded his own 'Short Fat Fannie', which reached number 1 in the R&B chart and number 5 in the pop chart during 1957. To follow up his song about the fat girl, Williams next recorded one about a skinny girl, 'Bony Moronie', which was almost as big a hit. Williams had one final chart single for Specialty the following year, 'Dizzy, Miss Lizzy', which reached number 69. (It was later covered by the Beatles, with Lennon singing. They also covered 'Slow Down' and 'Bad Boy', while Lennon later recorded 'Bony Moronie' and 'Just Because' as a solo, providing Williams with steady royalties income until his death.) A number of singles and an album were issued by Specialty up until 1959 none of which were hits.

That year he was arrested for selling drugs and sentenced to prison, causing Specialty to drop him and his career to fade. He recorded later on for Chess Records, Mercury Records and for Island Records and Decca Records in the mid-60s, by which time he was working with Johnny 'Guitar' Watson. In 1966 Williams became a producer for OKeh Records and recorded an album with Watson for that label. He was virtually inactive between 1967 and 1979 at which point he recorded a funk album for Fantasy Records. In January 1980, Williams was found in his Los Angeles home with a gunshot wound in the head, ruled to be self-inflicted, although it was rumoured that Williams was murdered owing to his involvement with drugs and, reportedly, prostitution.

Albums: *Here's Larry Williams* (1959), *Live* (1965), *The Larry Williams Show* (1965), with Johnny 'Guitar' Watson *Two For The Price Of One* (1967), *That Larry Williams* (1979) *Unreleased* (1986), *Hocus Pocus* (1986), *Alacazam* (1987), *Slow Down* (1987), *Bad Boy* (1989). Compilations: *Greatest Hits* (1967), *The Best Of Larry Williams* (1988).

Wilson, Jackie

b. 9 June 1934, Detroit, Michigan, USA, d. 21 January 1984, New Jersey, USA. When parental pressure thwarted his boxing ambitions, Wilson took to singing in small, local clubs. He sang with the Thrillers (a predecessor group to the Royals) and recorded some solo tracks for Dizzy Gillespie's Dee Gee label as Sonny Wilson, before replacing Clyde McPhatter in Billy Ward And The Dominoes. Jackie joined this notable group in 1953, but embarked on a solo career four years later with Brunswick Records. His first single for that label, was the exuberant 'Reet Petite', a comparative failure in the USA where it crept to a lowly pop position and missed the R&B lists altogether. In the UK, however, it soared to number 6 thereby establishing Wilson in the minds of the British pop purchasing audience. 'Reet Petite' had been written by Berry Gordy and Tyran Carlo (Roquel 'Billy' Davis), who went on to compose several of Wilson's subsequent releases which included the hits 'Lonely Teardrops' (1958), 'That's Why (I Love You So)' (1959) and 'I'll Be Satisfied' (1959).

In 1960, Jackie enjoyed two R&B number 1 hits with 'Doggin' Around' and 'A Woman, A Lover, A Friend'. His musical direction then grew increasingly erratic, veering from mainstream to pseudo-opera. There were still obvious highlights such as 'Baby Workout' (1963), 'Squeeze Her Please Her' (1964), 'No Pity (In The Naked City)' (1965), but all too often his wonderfully fluid voice was wasted on cursory, quickly-dated material. The artist's live appearances, however, remained both exciting and dramatic, capable of inspiring the ecstasy his sometimes facile recordings belied. Wilson's career was rejuvenated in 1966. Abandoning his New York recording base, he moved to Chicago where he worked with producer Carl Davis. Here, at last, was a more consistent empathy and 'Whispers (Gettin' Louder)' (1966), '(Your Love Keeps Lifting Me) Higher And Higher' (1967) and the sublime 'I Get The Sweetest Feeling' (1968), stand amongst his finest recordings. It was not to last. 'This Love Is Real (I Can Feel Those Vibrations)' (1970) proved to be Wilson's last Top 10 R&B entry, by which time his work was influenced by trends rather than setting them. In September 1975, while touring with the Dick Clark revue, Wilson suffered a near fatal heart attack onstage at New Jersey's Latin Casino. He struck his head on falling and the resulting brain damage left him comatose. He remained hospitalized until his death on 21 January 1984.

Wilson's career remains a puzzle; he never did join Berry Gordy's Motown empire, despite their early collaboration and friendship. Instead the singer's legacy was flawed; dazzling in places, disappointing in others. Immortalized in the Van Morrison song, 'Jackie Wilson Said', which was also a UK Top 5 hit for Dexy's Midnight Runners in 1982, his name has remained in the public's eye. Fate left its final twist for in 1987, when an imaginative video (which some claimed belittled the singer's memory) using plasticine animation, propelled 'Reet Petite' to number 1 in the UK charts.

Albums: He's So Fine (1958), Lonely Teardrops (1959), Doggin' Around (1959), So Much (1960), Night (1960), Jackie Wilson Sings The Blues (1960), A Woman A Lover A Friend (1961), Try A Little Tenderness (1961), You Ain't Heard Nothing Yet (1961), By Special Request (1961), Body And Soul (1962), Jackie Wilson At The Copa (1962), Jackie Wilson Sings The World's Greatest Melodies (1962), Baby Workout (1963), Merry Christmas (1963), with Linda Hopkins Shake A Hand (1963), Somethin' Else (1964), Soul Time (1965), Spotlight On Jackie Wilson (1965), Soul Galore (1966), Whispers (1967), Higher And Higher (1967), with Count Basie Manufacturers Of Soul (1968), with Basie Too Much (1968), I Get The Sweetest Feeling (1968), Do Your Thing (1970), This Love Is Real (1970), You Got Me Walking (1971), Beautiful Day (1973), Nowstalgia (1974), Nobody But You (1976). Compilations: My Golden Favourites (1960), My Golden Favourites - Volume 2 (1964), Jackie Wilson's Greatest Hits (1969), It's All Part Of Love (1969), Classic Jackie Wilson (1984), Reet Petite (1985), The Soul Years (1985), The Soul Years Volume 2 (1986), Higher And Higher (1986), The Very Best Of Jackie Wilson (1987), Original Hits (1993).

Wisdom, Norman

b. 4 February 1918, Paddington, London, England. A slapstick comedian, singer and straight actor, Wisdom has been a much-loved entertainer for four decades in the UK, not to mention such unlikely places as Russia and China. He broke into films in 1953 with Trouble In Store, and in the 50s had a string of box office smashes with One Good Turn, Man Of The Moment, Up In The World, Just My Luck, The Square Peg and Follow A Star. Dressed in his famous tight-fitting Gump suit, he was usually accompanied by straight man Jerry Desmonde, and, more often than not, portrayed the little man battling against the odds, to win justice and his sweetheart. He nearly always sang in his films and his theme song 'Don't Laugh At Me', which he co-wrote, was a number 3 hit in 1954 on EMI/Columbia. He also made the Top 20 in 1957 with a version of the Five Keys' 'Wisdom Of A Fool'. In 1958, Wisdom appeared in the West End musical, Where's Charley?, based on Brandon Thomas's classic farce, Charley's Aunt. Frank Loesser's score included 'Once In Love With Amy' and 'My Darling, My Darling', and the show ran for 18 months. In 1965, Wisdom played the lead in Bricusse and Newley's musical The Roar Of The Greasepaint - The Smell Of The Crowd, which toured UK provincial theatres. He was not considered sufficiently well-known in the US to play the part on Broadway, but did make his New York debut the following year when he starred in Walking Happy, a musical version of Hobson's

Choice with a score by Cahn and Van Heusen. He also appeared on US television in the role of Androcles, with Noel Coward as Julius Caesar, in Richard Rodgers' musical adaptation of Bernard Shaw's *Androcles And The Lion*. His feature films during the 60s included *On the Beat*, *A Stitch In Time* and *The Night They Raided Minsky's* with Jason Robards and Britt Ekland. Thanks to television re-runs of his films he is regarded with warm affection by many sections of the British public, and can still pack theatres, although, like many show business veterans, he is not called on to appear much on television. In his heyday, he made two celebrated 'live', one-hour appearances on *Sunday Night At The London Palladium*, in the company of Bruce Forsyth, that are considered to be classics of their kind. In 1992, with the UK rapidly running out of traditional funny men (Benny Hill and Frankie Howerd both died in that year), Wisdom experienced something of a renaissance when he played the role of a gangster in the movie *Double X*, starred in a radio series, *Robbing Hood*, released an album, *A World Of Wisdom*, completed a sell-out tour of the UK, and published his autobiography.

Selected albums: *I Would Like To Put On Record* (1956), *Where's Charley?* (1958, London Cast), *Walking Happy* (1966, Broadway Cast), *Androcles And The Lion* (1967, television soundtrack), *A World Of Wisdom* (1992).

Further reading: *Trouble In Store*, Richard Dacre. *Don't Laugh At Me*, Norman Wisdom.

Yana

b. Pamela Guard, 16 February 1932, Romford, Essex, England, d. 21 November 1989, London, England. A popular singer in the UK during the 50s and 60s, Yana became a model while still in her teens, before being 'discovered' when singing at a private party at London's Astor club. This led to engagements at several top nightspots and a contract with Columbia Records. In the 50s her singles releases included sultry renderings of 'Small Talk', 'Something Happened To My Heart', 'Climb Up The Wall', 'If You Don't Love Me', 'I Miss You, Mama', 'I Need You Now' and 'Mr Wonderful'. Her glamorous image made her a natural for television, and she was given her own BBC series in 1956. Later, following the advent of ITV, she appeared regularly on *Sunday Night At The London Palladium*. In 1958 Yana starred in Richard Rodgers and Oscar Hammerstein's *Cinderella* at the London Coliseum: her solo numbers in the show and on the Original Cast album, were 'In My Own Little Corner' and 'A Lovely Night', and she duetted with Tommy Steele ('When You're Driving Through The Moonlight'), Betty Marsden ('Impossible') and Bruce Trent ('Do I Love You?' and 'Ten Minutes Ago'). Two years later she was back in the West End, with Norman Wisdom in the London Palladium's longest running pantomime, *Turn Again Whittington*. She was becoming a pantomime 'specialist', and, throughout the 60s and into the 70s, was one of Britain's leading principal boys. It is probably not a coincidence that the second of her three marriages was to the actor, Alan Curtis, who is a renowned as a player of the 'Demon King' and other 'nasty' pantomime characters, although he is probably better known in the 90s for his PA work at important cricket matches. In her heyday Yana toured abroad, including the Middle East, and she appeared on several US variety shows, hosted by Bob Hope and Ed Sullivan. She also played small roles in the British films, *Zarak*, with Victor Mature and Michael Wilding, and *Cockleshell Heroes*, an early Anthony Newley feature. Her last performance is said to have been as the 'Good Fairy' in *The Wizard Of Oz* at an English provincial theatre in 1983. She died of throat cancer six years later.

Young, Jimmy

b. 21 September 1923, Cinderford, Gloucestershire, England. A popular ballad singer in the UK during the 50s, Young was fortunate enough to branch out into other areas of broadcasting when the record hits ceased. The son of a miner, he was an excellent boxer and rugby player, but turned down an offer of a professional career with top rugby union club, Wigan. Always keen on music, he was taught to play the piano by his mother, and received professional voice training. He worked as a baker and an electrician before joining the Royal Air Force in 1939. After demobilization he intended training as a teacher, but was spotted, singing at a sports club, by BBC

Yana (left) with Vera Lynn

producer George Innes, and made his first broadcast two weeks later, subsequently touring the UK variety circuit. From 1951 he had several successful records on the small Polygon label including 'My Love And Devotion', 'Because Of You' and 'Too Young'. In January 1953, two months after the first UK singles chart appeared in the music newspaper, the *New Musical Express*, Young had a hit with 'Faith Can Move Mountains' for his new label, Decca, and followed that with 'Eternally (Terry's Theme)', from the Charlie Chaplin film, *Limelight*.

In 1955 Young became the first UK artist to top the *NME* chart with successive releases. The first, 'Unchained Melody', made the top spot in spite of intense competition from Al Hibbler, Les Baxter, and Liberace. The second, the title song from the movie, *The Man From Laramie*, and another 1955 hit, 'Someone On My Mind', clinched Young's position as the UK's second biggest selling artist of the year - after Ruby Murray. Following further 50s hits, including 'Chain Gang', 'The Wayward Wind', 'Rich Man Poor Man', 'More' and 'Round And Round', Young switched to EMI's Columbia label in the early 60s, and had some success with a recording of Charles and Henry Tobias's 1929 song, 'Miss You', and a re-recording of his 1955 hit, 'Unchained Melody'. In 1960 he introduced BBC radio's popular record request programme, *Housewives' Choice*, for two weeks. It was the start of a new career which has lasted more than 30 years, initially as a conventional disc jockey and compere, and then, from 1967, as host of his own daily BBC morning radio show, mixing records with consumer information, discussions on current affairs, and interviews with figures in the public eye, including Prime Ministers. For his work on that programme, he was awarded the OBE, and later, the CBE.

Albums: *T.T.T.J.Y.S.* (1974), *Too Young* (1981), *The Ballymena Cowboy* (1987). Compilations: *The World Of Jimmy Young* (1969), *This Is Jimmy Young* (1980).

Further reading: *JY*, Jimmy Young.

Proposed Titles for Inclusion in the

Guinness Who's Who of Popular Music Series

The Guinness Who's Who of 50s Music★
The Guinness Who's Who of 60s Music★
The Guinness Who's Who of 70s Music★
The Guinness Who's Who of 80s Music
The Guinness Who's Who of Indie and New Wave Music★
The Guinness Who's Who of Blues★
The Guinness Who's Who of Folk Music★
The Guinness Who's Who of R&B Music
The Guinness Who's Who of Soul Music★
The Guinness Who's Who of Country Music★
The Guinness Who's Who of Jazz★
The Guinness Who's Who of Heavy Metal Music★
The Guinness Who's Who of Gospel Music
The Guinness Who's Who of UK Rock and Pop
The Guinness Who's Who of USA Rock and Pop
The Guinness Who's Who of Danceband Music
The Guinness Who's Who of World Music
The Guinness Who's Who of Stage Musicals
The Guinness Who's Who of Reggae

★ Already published

For further information on any of these titles please write to:
Section D
The Marketing Department
Guinness Publishing
33 London Road, Enfield, Middlesex, EN2 6DJ, England